Andrew Mellon

Secretary of the Treasury Annual Report

1872

Andrew Mellon

Secretary of the Treasury Annual Report
1872

ISBN/EAN: 9783741135743

Manufactured in Europe, USA, Canada, Australia, Japa

Cover: Foto ©Thomas Meinert / pixelio.de

Manufactured and distributed by brebook publishing software
(www.brebook.com)

Andrew Mellon

Secretary of the Treasury Annual Report

ANNUAL REPORT

OF THE

SECRETARY OF THE TREASURY

ON THE

STATE OF THE FINANCES

FOR

THE YEAR 1872.

WASHINGTON:
GOVERNMENT PRINTING OFFICE.
1872.

TABLE OF CONTENTS.

[Index by subjects will be found on page 553.]

REPORT

OF

THE SECRETARY OF THE TREASURY.

TREASURY DEPARTMENT,
December 2, 1872.

SIR: Whatever degree of success has attended the administration of the Treasury Department during the year is due largely to the ability and fidelity of the officers and clerks of the several bureaus and divisions. There have been some exceptions to the general good conduct of the working force, but the number of these will not be thought large when it is known that more than three thousand persons are employed in Washington, of whom nearly fourteen hundred are constantly engaged in handling coin, notes, and money securities of the Government.

Many of these persons are paid fair wages for the services rendered; but others, who fill places of great responsibility, are not by any means adequately compensated. Officers and clerks of known ability and established reputation are frequently drawn away by offers of better pay elsewhere. This competition will leave the business of the Department finally in the hands of the less valuable part of its officers.

A sense of justice leads me to recommend an increase of salaries in many cases, including the salaries of the Assistant Secretaries of the Treasury.

Since my last annual report the business of negotiating two hundred million of five per cent. bonds, and the redemption of two hundred million of six per cent. five-twenty bonds, has been completed, and the accounts have been settled by the accounting officers of the Treasury.

Further negotiations of five per cent. bonds can now be made upon the basis of the former negotiation.

I think it expedient, as a means of giving additional value to the bonds authorized by the Funding Act of July 14, 1870, and additional security to the owners, that registered bonds of every issue should be made convertible into coupon bonds at the will of the holder. When this privilege is granted the desire to reconvert them will cease.

The moneys received and covered into the Treasury during the fiscal year ended June 30, 1872, were:

From customs	$216, 370, 286 77
Sales of public lands	2, 575, 714 19
Internal revenue	130, 642, 177 72
Tax on national bank circulation, &c	6, 523, 396 39
Repayment of interest by Pacific Railway companies	749, 861 87
Customs fines, &c	1, 136, 442 34
Fees—consular, patent, land, &c	2, 284, 095 92
Miscellaneous sources	4, 412, 254 71
Total ordinary receipts	364, 694, 229 91
Premium on sales of coin	9, 412, 637 65
Total net receipts	374, 106, 867 56
Balance in Treasury June 30, 1871, (including $18,228 35 received from "unavailable"	109, 935, 705 59
Total available cash	484, 042, 573 15

The net expenditures by warrants, during the same period, were:

For civil expenses		$16, 187, 059 20
Foreign intercourse		1, 839, 369 14
Indians		7, 061, 728 82
Pensions		28, 533, 402 76
Military establishment, including fortifications, river and harbor improvements, and arsenals		35, 372, 157 20
Naval establishment, including vessels and machinery and improvements at navy yards		21, 249, 809 99
Miscellaneous civil, including public buildings, light-houses, and collecting the revenue		42, 958, 329 08
Interest on the public debt		117, 357, 839 72
Total, exclusive of principal and premium on the public debt		270, 559, 695 91
Premium on bonds purchased	$6, 958, 266 76	
Redemption of the public debt	99, 960, 253 54	
		106, 918, 520 30
Total net disbursements		377, 478, 216 21
Balance in Treasury June 30, 1872		106, 564, 356 94
Total		484, 042, 573 15

From the foregoing statement it appears that the net reduction of the principal of the debt during the fiscal year ended June 30, 1872, was $99, 960, 253 54.

The sources of this reduction are as follows:

Net ordinary receipts during the year	$364, 694, 229 91
Net ordinary expenditures, including interest on the public debt	270, 559, 695 91
Leaving a surplus revenue of	94, 134, 534 00
Add amount received from premium on sales of gold, in excess of the premium paid on bonds purchased	2, 454, 370 89
Add the amount of the reduction of the cash balance at the close of the year, as compared with same at commencement of year	3, 371, 348 65
	99, 960, 253 54

This statement treats solely of the principal of the public debt.

By the monthly statement of the public debt, which includes the principal, interest due and unpaid, and interest accrued to date not due, and deducts the cash in the Treasury as ascertained on the day of publication, the reduction was $100, 544, 491 28.

The source of this reduction is as follows:

Reduction in principal account	$99, 960, 003 54
Reduction in unpaid-interest account	3, 330, 952 96
	103, 290, 956 50
Reduction in cash on hand	2, 746, 465 22
	100, 544, 491 28

A comparison of the reduction in the principal account as shown by the above tables discloses a difference of $250, occasioned by an error, recently discovered, and which is fully explained in a note on page 6 of the appendix to this report.

On the basis of the last table the statements show a reduction of the public debt from March 1, 1869, to the present time, as follows:

From March 1, 1869, to March 1, 1870	$87, 134, 782 84
March 1, 1870, to March 1, 1871	117, 619, 630 25
March 1, 1871, to March 1, 1872	94, 895, 348 94
March 1, 1872, to November 1, 1872, (8 months)	64, 047, 237 84
Total	363, 696, 999 87

And a reduction in the annual interest of $24,187,851.

The receipts during the first quarter of the current fiscal year were—

From Customs	$57, 729, 540 27
Sales of public lands	797, 324 57
Internal revenue	34, 169, 047 22
Tax on circulation, &c., of national banks	3, 307, 238 69
Repayment of interest by Pacific railways	119, 093 73
Customs fines, &c	103, 787 30
Consular, patent, and other fees	479, 306 03
Proceeds of Government property	336, 801 88
Miscellaneous sources	1, 346, 257 47
Net ordinary receipts	98, 388, 397 16
Premium on sales of coin	2, 426, 736 91
Total receipts	100, 815, 134 07
Balance in Treasury June 30, 1872, including $1,014 48 received from "unavailable"	106, 565, 371 42
Total available	207, 380, 505 49

The expenditures during the same period were as follows:

For civil and miscellaneous expenses, including public buildings, light-houses, and collecting the revenues		$18, 299, 891 28
Indians		3, 037, 343 83
Pensions		9, 135, 389 71
Military establishment, including fortifications, river and harbor improvements, and arsenals		12, 876, 982 41
Naval establishment, including vessels and machinery and improvements at navy yards		7, 305, 146 48
Interest on the public debt, including Pacific Railway bonds		36, 196, 894 83
Total, exclusive of the principal and premium, on public debt		86, 851, 648 54
For premium on purchased bonds	$1, 702, 568 53	
For net redemption of the public debt	16, 932, 138 72	
		18, 634, 707 25
Total net expenditures		105, 486, 355 79
Balance in the Treasury September 30, 1872		101, 894, 149 70
		207, 380, 505 49

For the remaining three-quarters of the current fiscal year it is estimated that the receipts will be:

From customs	$135,000,000 00
Sales of public lands	1,500,000 00
Internal revenue	74,000,000 00
Tax on national banks	3,000,000 00
Pacific railways	500,000 00
Customs fines, &c	800,000 00
Consular, patent, and other fees	1,700,000 00
Sales of public property	600,000 00
Miscellaneous sources	1,400,000 00
Total	218,500,000 00

For the same period it is estimated that the expenditures will be:

For civil expenses	$13,000,000 00
Foreign intercourse	900,000 00
Indians	4,000,000 00
Pensions	20,000,000 00
Military establishment	23,000,000 00
Naval establishment	13,500,000 00
Miscellaneous civil	27,800,000 00
Interest on the public debt	71,500,000 00
Total	173,700,000 00

This will leave $44,800,000 surplus revenue applicable to the purchase or redemption of the public debt.

The amount required for this purpose, under the sinking-fund law, for the year, will be about $29,200,000.

It is estimated that the receipts for the fiscal year ending June 30, 1874, will be:

From customs	$200,000,000 00
Sales of public lands	3,000,000 00
Internal revenue	103,000,000 00
Tax on national banks	6,300,000 00
Pacific railways	900,000 00
Customs fines, &c	1,100,000 00
Consular, patent, and other fees	2,300,000 00
Sales of public property	1,500,000 00
Miscellaneous sources	2,200,000 00
Total	320,300,000 00

The foregoing estimates are based upon the amount of revenue collected since the acts of May and June, 1872, went into operation; but the imports have been large, and considerable sums have been obtained by internal revenue officers on account of old taxes and claims; hence it will be wise to leave the sources of revenue undisturbed for the present session.

It is estimated that the expenditures for the same period will be:

For civil expenses	$18,000,000 00
Foreign intercourse	1,325,000 00
Indians	5,700,000 00
Pensions	30,500,000 00
Military establishment, including fortifications, river and harbor improvements, and arsenals	36,000,000 00
Naval establishment, including vessels and machinery and improvements at navy yards	22,500,000 00
Miscellaneous civil, including public buildings, light-houses, and collecting the revenues	41,500,000 00
Interest on the public debt	98,000,000 00
Interest on Pacific Railway bonds	3,875,000 00
Sinking fund	29,200,000 00
Total	286,600,000 00
Leaving the estimated surplus revenue	$33,700,000 00

The estimates received from the several Executive Departments show that the following amounts will be required for the same period:

Legislative	$2,973,274 40
Executive	17,129,261 90
Judicial	3,587,050 00
Foreign intercourse	1,326,754 00
Military	32,894,854 84
Naval	20,154,220 15
Indians	5,700,975 28
Pensions	30,500,000 00
Public works	29,687,345 69
Postal deficiency	6,310,602 00
Postal subsidies	1,100,000 00
Miscellaneous	9,596,974 52
Permanent	16,293,163 49
Interest on public debt	98,000,000 00
Interest on Pacific Railway stocks	3,877,410 72
Sinking fund	29,191,369 28
Total	308,323,256 27

The reduction in taxation since the close of the war is estimated to have been—

IN INTERNAL REVENUE:

By the act of July 13, 1866	$65,000,000
By the act of March 2, 1867	40,000,000
By the act of February 3, 1868	23,000,000
By the acts of March 31, 1868, and July 20, 1868	45,000,000
By the act of July 14, 1870	55,000,000
By the act of June 6, 1872	20,651,000
Total of internal revenue	248,651,000

IN CUSTOMS:

By the act of July 14, 1870	$29,526,410
By the acts of May 1, 1872, and June 6, 1872	31,172,761
Total of customs	60,699,171
A total reduction of	309,350,171

Since the institution of the sinking fund, in May, 1869, and in accordance with the act of February 25, 1862, there has been purchased on this account, up to and including June 30, 1872, $99,397,600 in bonds of the various issues known as five-twenties, at a net cost in currency of $110,997,185 89, or an estimated cost, in gold, of $94,097,243 82.

In addition to the purchases for the sinking fund, bonds have been purchased to the amount of $173,237,950, at a net cost, in currency, of $195,008,288 53, or an estimated cost, in gold, of $163,376,054 35.

The cost of these bonds, estimated in gold, has varied from $82 21 per $100 to $99 99 per $100—the most recent purchase being at the rate of $98 66 per $100.

The average cost, in gold, of the whole amount of the purchases, up to and including the last day of September, was $94 64 per $100.

In this connection I would call attention to the various tables accompanying this report, which furnish elaborate details of the money operations and accounts of the Government.

The condition of our carrying trade with foreign countries is always a subject of interest, and at the present moment it is one of solicitude. The imports and exports of the United States, excluding gold and silver, amounted to $1,070,641,163, for the fiscal year ending June 30, 1872, and of this vast trade only 28½ per cent. was in American vessels. In the year 1860 nearly 71 per cent. of our foreign commerce was in American ships; but in 1864 it had fallen to 46 per cent., in 1868 to 44 per cent., and in 1871 to less than 38 per cent. The earnings of vessels engaged in the foreign carrying trade probably exceed one hundred million dollars a year, of which less than one-third is earned under our own flag. The act of Congress allowing a drawback on foreign articles used in the construction of American vessels has given encouragement to ship-building; but I am of opinion that this measure is entirely inadequate. When we consider that nearly three-fourths of the foreign commerce of the country is under foreign flags, it is plain that there can be no considerable and speedy change unless the Government shall act at once and in a liberal and comprehensive spirit.

The rise in the price of iron and the advance in the wages of labor in England during the past year favor the Government and people of the United States; but this advantage, due to natural causes, should not lead us to trust the future to the force of those causes, but should induce us rather to act at once and with vigor. It may happen that we cannot regain the control of the direct trade between Europe and the United States, but there is an immense field to be occupied upon the Pacific Ocean and in the South Atlantic. England controls the markets of the world by controlling the channels of communication, and I am convinced that a wonderful impetus will be given to the agricultural and manufacturing interests of the country by the increase of our commercial marine. Merchants in distant countries must purchase goods at points with which they have frequent and regular communication, and when such communication exists with one country only, the cost of merchandise becomes unimportant, as there are no means of comparison; nor is there opportunity for the advantages of competition. Hence a great producing country can afford to establish and maintain lines of steamships upon the ocean, as the indirect benefits will much exceed the cost.

The details of our trade with foreign countries, as represented by the returns made to the Statistical Bureau, are also unsatisfactory. From these returns it appears that the imports of merchandise for the fiscal year ending June 30, 1872, were $626,595,077, and the exports estimated in gold, were $444,046,086, showing a balance against the country of $182,548,991. This balance is in some degree apparent rather than real. On the 30th of June, 1871, the value of goods remaining in warehouse was $68,324,659, while on the 30th of June, 1872, it was $122,211,266, showing an excess at the close of the last fiscal year of $53,886,607. Deducting this excess, we have a balance based upon the actual consumption of the country of $128,662,384. From this a further reduction should be made of $66,133,845, being the excess of exports over the imports of gold. After these deductions there still remains an adverse balance of $62,528,539. This adverse balance has been met probably by freight on merchandise carried in American vessels, profits on exports made on account of American merchants and shippers, the sale of bonds abroad, and investments in the United States by inhabitants of other countries.

The exports of merchandise for the year 1872 were $13,298,933 less than for the year 1871. The exports of wheat, wheat flour, raw cotton, cotton manufactures, gold and silver, fire-arms, manufactures of leather, illuminating oil, and beef, fell off $82,066,325, while there was a gain of $68,767,392 in the exports of corn, furs, hides, skins, bacon, hams, lard, leaf tobacco, manufactures of iron, wood, leather, and many minor articles. There was an increase of exports in every branch of manufactures, except cotton, leather, and fire-arms.

The decrease of our exports in wheat and wheat flour was twelve million dollars; raw cotton, thirty-seven million dollars; manufactured cotton, one million two hundred and fifty thousand dollars; gold and silver, eleven million six hundred thousand dollars; fire-arms, twelve million dollars; manufactures of leather, six hundred thousand dollars; illuminating oils, three million five hundred thousand dollars; and beef, two million dollars.

The statistics of imports show an increase of seven million in coffee, eighteen million in sugar, nearly six million in tea, nearly three million in tin plates, more than seventeen million in raw wool, two million in pig iron, ten million in manufactures of iron, five million in manufactures of cotton, four million in manufactures of silk, and about seven million in manufactures of wool.

These statistics are not presented as affording a basis for legislation, but rather because they are exceptional in character, and not likely to be repeated.

During the last year thorough examinations have been made of the Mint at Philadelphia, and of the branch mints at San Francisco and Carson City, and exhaustive reports upon the condition of each, and also upon several questions of a general character connected with the mint service, made by Doctor Linderman and Professor Rogers, are to be printed for the use of the Department and Congress. From these reports it appears that the service is in a satisfactory condition. In the last ten years the commercial value of silver has depreciated about three per cent. as compared with gold, and its use as currency has been discontinued by Germany and some other countries. The financial condition of the United States has prevented the use of silver as currency for more than ten years, and I am of opinion that upon grounds of public policy no attempt should be made to introduce it, but that the coinage should be limited to commercial purposes, and designed exclusively for commercial uses with other nations.

The intrinsic value of a metallic currency should correspond to its commercial value, or metal should be used only for the coinage of tokens redeemable by the Government at their nominal value. As the depreciation of silver is likely to continue it is impossible to issue coin redeemable in gold without ultimate loss to the Government; for when the difference becomes considerable holders will present the silver for redemption, and leave it in the hands of the Government to be disposed of subsequently at a loss.

If the policy should be adopted of issuing silver coin irredeemable, but whose intrinsic and nominal value should correspond to gold, the time must come when the country would suffer from the presence of a depreciated silver currency, not redeemable by the Government nor current in the channels of trade.

Tokens of base coin, except for small denominations, are less convenient than paper, and are subject to many other serious objections. The provision made by the Treasury Department for the redemption of mutilated paper money is much more ample than formerly, and I think it practicable, through the Post Office Department, to make an arrangement by which the whole country shall be supplied with fresh issues of fractional currency.

Therefore, in renewing the recommendations heretofore made for the passage of the Mint bill, I suggest such alterations as will prohibit the coinage of silver for circulation in this country, but that authority be given for the coinage of a silver dollar that shall be as valuable as the Mexican dollar, and to be furnished at its actual cost. The Mexican dollar is used generally in trade with China and is now sold at a premium of about eight per cent. over the actual expense of coining. As the production of silver is rapidly increasing, such a coinage will at once furnish a market for the raw material and facilitate commerce between the United States and China.

It is no exaggeration to say that a necessity exists for a new issue of national bank notes. The reasons for such issue were given in my last annual report.

I take this occasion to call the attention of Congress to a communication made by me to the House of Representatives on the 22d day of March, 1872, (Ex. Doc. 283, 42d Cong., 2d Sess.,) in which I recommended the enactment of a law for the relief of the Treasurer from responsibility on account of the dishonesty of Seth Johnson and Frederick A. Marden, formerly clerks in his office; and also for the correction of certain discrepancies in the public accounts, amounting to $406 35, that the books of the Department may be made to conform to the facts.

An examination of the affairs of the Office of the Assistant Treasurer at New York, made in September and October last, disclosed a defalcation in the stamp division, in charge of James I. Johnson, of $185,131 72. The report of the committee explains the course of proceeding by which Johnson was able to embezzle this amount of money.

The report further represents that Mr. Hillhouse, the Assistant Treasurer, cannot be charged properly with any neglect of duty, and in this opinion I concur.

The business of keeping and selling stamps was imposed upon the several Assistant Treasurers by virtue of the authority conferred upon the Secretary of the Treasury in the 6th section of the act of August 6, 1846; but by the terms of that act it was not competent for the Treasury Department to allow the Assistant Treasurer at New York compensation for the labor and responsibility of the stamp division, although the commissions which would have been payable to him at the rate allowed to private parties by the 161st section of the act of 1864, amount to more than five hundred thousand dollars.

The circumstances of this case are such as to justify me in recommending the passage of a law by which Mr. Hillhouse shall be relieved from responsibility in the matter of the defalcation of Johnson.

The report of the Supervising Architect of the Treasury furnishes a concise statement of the cost and condition of the public buildings in charge of this Department. Large sums of money will be needed for the buildings already begun or authorized, and I respectfully advise that, beyond the erection of pavilion hospitals, and a building for the accommodation of the Bureau of Engraving and Printing and the storage of the books and papers of this Department, no new works be authorized at the present session of Congress.

The business of the office of the Supervising Architect of the Treasury is fully equal to the force employed, and the necessary appropriations are so large as to justify Congress in refusing all applications during the present session.

The destruction of the buildings on the easterly side of the new post office in the city of Boston furnishes an opportunity that ought not to be lost for the purchase of the remainder of the square.

An act approved June 8, 1872, authorized and directed the Secretary of the Treasury to purchase a lot of ground in Philadelphia for the accommodation of the post office and United States courts, and to erect a building thereon, the cost of the whole not to exceed the sum of one million five hundred thousand dollars. Under this act, and following the usage of the Department, I appointed a commission of citizens of Philadelphia, who were authorized to receive proposals for the sale to the Government of a suitable lot of land. The report of the commission has been submitted to the Department, from which it appears that the lot thought to be most desirable, situated on the corner of Chestnut and Ninth streets, can be purchased at a cost of $925,333 33. It also appears that the cost of a sufficient quantity of land to make the site of the present post office available would exceed half a million dollars.

Accepting the conclusions of the commission as final in reference to the cost of a suitable site, I have declined to proceed further without additional authority from Congress; it being clear that it is impossible to procure land and erect a building for the sum specified in the act.

Similar circumstances have prevented the purchase of land for a public building at Cincinnati.

The increase of books and papers, not in daily or frequent use, is so great as to seriously interfere with the business of the Department. The annual accumulation requires 7,688 cubic feet of space for storage. All the available rooms in the building, including some that might be used for clerks' desks, and portions of the public halls, have been given up for the deposit of such books and papers, and the time has come when other provision should be made. I, therefore, recommend the erection of a brick fire-proof building upon the public grounds south of the Treasury sufficient for storage and for the accommodation of the Bureau of Engraving and Printing. The relief which these changes would afford is essential for the proper transaction of the business of the Treasury Department.

The operations of the Coast Survey, as well as those of the Light-house Board, appear to have been economically and efficiently managed.

The Revenue Marine consists of twenty-seven steam and six sailing vessels, carrying sixty-five guns, and manned by one hundred and ninety-eight officers and eight hundred and sixty men. This service has constantly improved in efficiency and in the economy of its management since the summer of 1869. At that time a commission was appointed for the general and professional examination of all the officers employed, and upon their report thirty-nine were discharged, and those who were approved were assigned to duty and given rank, according to their merits. From that time to the present all vacancies in the service have been filled after an examination, and by those found to be best qualified. At the same time a commission was appointed for the entire revision of the service. Their report was submitted to Congress on the 26th of May, 1870. (Ex. Doc 93, 41st Cong., 2d Sess.) The vessels then employed were rated at 9,208 tons. A reduction has already been effected of 657 tons, and the vessels now building and authorized will work a further reduction of 1,232 tons, making an aggregate reduction of 1,889 tons.

The cost of maintaining the Revenue Marine has been reduced from $1,293,661 67, in 1868, to $930,249 81 for the year ending June 30, 1872.

Statistical tables prepared from the returns show that, in the essential particulars of assistance rendered to vessels, seizures made, number of vessels examined, and number of lives saved upon the ocean and the lakes, the work performed during the last fiscal year is nearly twice as great as the average for the ten preceding years.

Under existing laws the officers and seamen of the Revenue Marine are entitled to a pension only when they have been wounded or disabled in the line of duty, and whilst coöperating with the Navy during war, and then at the rate established by the act of 1814. When it is considered that this service is constant, and that from the first of November to the first of April in each year the vessels are required to cruise along the coast, and as near the land as possible, within their respective districts, and not to make a port except for supplies or under the pressure of positive necessity, it is clear that their services are not less hazardous than those in which the Navy is engaged in time of peace. I, therefore, recommend that the Navy pension laws be made applicable to the officers and seamen of the Revenue Marine.

The number of commissioned officers is limited by law, and each year adds to those who are disqualified by sickness or unfitted by age for active duty. The hardship resulting from the dismissal of officers under such circumstances is so great that I have declined to exercise a power which may, perhaps, in contemplation of law, be a duty; but in view of the fact that their compensation is small, and the nature of the service such as to bring disease and the infirmities of age upon them prematurely, I think it a plain duty for the Government to provide a retired list so that the active service may be supplied constantly with able and efficient men.

From the appropriation of $200,000, made April 20, 1871, "for more effectually securing life and property on the coasts of New Jersey and Long Island," seven of the old life-saving station-houses have been repaired and enlarged, and sixty-one new ones have been built, and new apparatus sufficient for ordinary use has been procured for the larger number of them.

A station-house has been erected and furnished at Narragansett pier.

From the appropriation of $50,000, "for the establishment of life-saving stations on the coasts of Cape Cod and Block Island, R. I., nine houses have been erected on Cape Cod and one on Block Island, and they will be supplied with apparatus and ready for use by the first of January next. An appropriation is required for the support of keepers and crews.

The Block Island station and the station at Narragansett pier should be annexed to the Long Island district.

Twenty-two vessels have been wrecked on the coasts of Long Island and New Jersey since July 1, 1871, valued, with their cargoes, at over $500,000, on which the loss was about $200,000. The officers and crews numbered two hundred and six persons, all of whom were saved, and mainly, it is believed, through the agency of the life-saving stations.

I respectfully recommend the extension of the system to the coast in the vicinity of Cape Hatteras.

From the report of the Supervising Surgeon of Marine Hospitals it appears that that branch of the public service is in a satisfactory condition.

During the last fiscal year 13,156 patients were treated in the several hospitals of the country at an average cost of about 97 cents each per day, or a total expenditure of $396,263 11, against a total expenditure for the preceding year of $453,082 42, or an average cost per patient of $1 04 per day.

The increased receipts and diminished expenses for the last fiscal year, as compared with the year next preceding, show a net gain to the Government of $56,819 31.

During the same period the number of districts in which relief was furnished was greater than ever before, and the salaries of medical officers at several of the principal ports were increased.

The financial improvement shown is due largely to a more careful scrutiny of the applicants for relief, to the rejection of those who were not entitled under the law, and also to greater vigilance in collecting the hospital dues.

The law limits the charge for relief to seamen belonging to foreign vessels to seventy-five cents a day, while the actual cost is nearly one dollar. Authority should be given to the Secretary of the Treasury to fix the charge within certain limits, according to the expenses incurred at the hospitals where relief is furnished.

I renew the recommendation heretofore made for the erection of pavilion hospitals at New York, San Francisco, and Pittsburg. The increase of railway and general business in the vicinity of the hospital at Pittsburg has rendered it unfit for further use.

The Supervising Surgeon recommends the erection in future of pavilion hospitals of wood, with the understanding that after ten or fifteen years' use they are to be destroyed and new ones built in their stead. This recommendation appears to be wise, being at once economical for the Government and advantageous to the patients.

The act of February 28, 1871, to provide for the better security of life on board vessels propelled in whole or in part by steam, has not been in operation a sufficient time to test its value in all respects; but the result in the main is satisfactory. The Supervising Inspector

General, in his annual report, recommends several alterations in the law not affecting its character materially. A bill will be prepared providing for such alterations as, upon further consideration, shall seem expedient.

On the 16th day of May, 1872, I transmitted to Congress a bill entitled "A bill to amend and consolidate the navigation and customs collection laws of the United States," together with a communication explaining the character and purpose of the measure. (Ex. Doc. 290, 42d Cong., 2d Sess.) I respectfully ask the attention of Congress to the bill and the reasons for its passage.

The time has come when the attention of the public is turned naturally to the future financial policy of the country. That policy must rest upon the past and the present.

The war caused three great changes in business and financial affairs that have received the careful consideration of the American people.

I. The country was compelled to impose heavy customs duties upon merchandise, and thus, without general observation and without argument upon the principles involved, the nation entered upon a broad system of protection.

II. The Government issued Treasury notes for general circulation as currency, and prohibited banks of issue by State authority.

III. A system of national banks was established, and their circulation protected by the national credit.

The wisdom of these measures, speaking generally, has been established; and, subject to such changes as the changing condition and opinions of the country and people may demand, they will remain a part of our public policy until the financial consequences of the war disappear. The weight of the national debt has been so great that for more than ten years there has been no opportunity for the practical discussion of the doctrines of protection and free trade, and in that long period of an unchanged protective policy incident to the burdens of the war the nation has advanced rapidly and safely in the development of its natural resources.

Anticipating a condition of peace, we may also anticipate a general reduction in the percentage of customs duties. This reduction, however, should not be measured solely by the wants of the Treasury; but regard should be had also to the condition of the various branches of industry in which the people are engaged. In presence of the fact that the leading pursuits of the country are stronger than ever before in the possession of adequate capital and a supply of intelligent laborers, there may be a moderate reduction from time to time in the rate of duties, as the diminishing expenses of the Government shall permit, without either alarming capital or injuring labor.

For the purposes of government, the principles of political economy are national, and not cosmopolitan. A nation that can produce a given article at less cost than it can be produced elsewhere may wisely accept free trade in it; but a nation having natural advantages for its production, yet destitute of skill in the incident art or trade, must wait for the opportunity that sometimes comes from the calamity of war, or secure a more economical and a more constant support in the policy of its Government. If average natural facilities exist, the period of necessary protection is a short one compared with the lifetime of a nation; while the advantages gained can never be wholly lost. But if reasonable natural facilities do not exist, then a system of duties for protection is a present and future burden without adequate compensation. So varied and rich, however, are the natural resources of the United States, that we either are or may soon be in successful competition with the older and more experienced countries of the world in the production of the chief articles of personal necessity, comfort, and luxury, and of the machinery by which these articles are produced or obtained.

Herein is a sufficient justification for the existing protective system, and for its continuance during the transition period.

Nor is the prospect of ultimate successful competition with other countries disturbed by the circumstance that the wages of labor are higher in this country than in those. If, ten years since, it was the thought of any that the only way to a successful contest with Europe was in the reduction of the wages of labor to the European standard, that thought has disappeared, probably, in presence of the fact that high wages on this side of the Atlantic have stimulated emigration, until there is a near approach to equality in the cost of labor, and of the coëxisting fact that the addition thus made to the number of laborers has only aided in the development of our resources, without yielding in any quarter an excess of products, or retarding in any degree the prosperity of the laboring population.

This prosperity on their part is associated with a higher and constantly improving intellectual and social culture and condition. It being given that an intelligent person has all the special knowledge of an art or trade possessed by the most experienced and best-trained operative, who, outside of this special training and experience, is an ignorant person, and equal advantages of capital and machinery being given also, the intelligent person proceeds to improve and simplify methods of production to such an extent that an addition to his wages of even a hundred per cent. represents but a small part of the advantage gained.

Yet the special training and knowledge of the ignorant man is the basis of the improvements made. This truth, considered first with reference to a single American laborer and then multiplied many hundred thousand times, represents the advantage of America over Europe and Asia in the contest for final peaceful supremacy in the affairs of the world. Thus is America solving the industrial problem of the ages by extorting cheap production from expensive labor.

The reason for these remarks may be found in the opinion I entertain, that the tariff system of the country has contributed largely to the general prosperity; and that such general and continued prosperity is the only basis on which even a wise financial policy can rest.

In discussing the other changes caused by the war, the issues of United States notes and of notes by the national banks should be considered together; indeed they are necessary parts of our financial system, and neither can be substituted for the other without general disturbance and permanent injury. The national banking system is so far superior to the State bank system, and to any system of private banks, as to render argument in its behalf, in these respects, unnecessary; while the substitution of an equal amount of United States notes as currency would be productive of serious evils and losses.

First. The national banks hold nearly four hundred million United States bonds, which otherwise would be thrown upon the market, absorbing domestic capital, or, if purchased abroad, adding, by the amount of the interest, to the annual balances against us in our account current with other countries.

Secondly. One office of a bank is to aggregate the capital of small possessors, and thereby to furnish means in aid of important commercial and financial undertakings, not only at the centres, but in the remote and newly-settled parts of the country.

Thirdly. The national banks are used as aids to the Government, which otherwise would require a large increase in the number of designated depositaries, and a proportionate increase of the public expenses without the least appreciable advantage.

Fourthly. They facilitate exchanges between different sections of the country, thus diminishing the cost of commercial transactions.

Fifthly. They are generally less disposed than private parties, controlling equal capital, to demand exorbitant rates of interest.

But it does not follow from these views, nor would it follow from those of a similar character which might be presented, that the system is perfect; nor does it follow that the issue of notes directly by the Government should be surrendered and the business of furnishing a currency yielded to the national banks.

The circulation of each bank is fixed arbitrarily by a rule of law. The aggregate circulation is therefore a fixed sum, and consequently there is practically no reserve to meet the increased demand for money due occasionally to extraordinary events at home or abroad, and arising periodically with the incoming of the harvest. The old State bank system is sometimes commended for the quality termed elasticity; but that quality as found in that system was the principal source of financial disaster. Under that system, in the absence of a present demand for coin, there was practically no limit to the issue of paper currency.

The increase of the circulation was attended and followed by an advance in prices, excessive importations, a consequent demand for coin drawn from the banks to meet balances abroad, a simultaneous reduction of the paper currency, and the consequent distress of merchants and bankers.

As the circulation of a bank is a source of profit, and as the managers are usually disposed to oblige their patrons by loans and accommodations, it can never be wise to allow banks or parties who have pecuniary interests at stake to increase or diminish the volume of currency in the country at their pleasure. Nor do I find in the condition of things a law or rule on which we can safely rely. Upon these views I form the conclusion that the circulation of the banks should be fixed and limited, and that the power to change the volume of paper in circulation, within limits established by law, should remain in the Treasury Department.

A degree of flexibility in the volume of currency is essential for two reasons:

First. The business of the Department cannot be transacted properly if a limit is fixed, and the power to raise the circulation above or reduce it below that limit is denied.

A rule of this nature would compel the Secretary to accumulate a large currency balance and to hold it; as, otherwise, the credit of the Government, in meeting the ordinary daily claims upon it, would be at the mercy of every serious business and political revulsion in the United States or Europe.

Especially would this be true now that our ordinary currency expenditures are greatly in excess of our currency revenue.

Secondly. There is a necessity every autumn for moving the crops without delay from the South and West to the seaboard that they may be in hand for export and consumption as wanted. This work should be done in the main before the lakes, rivers, and canals are closed, and yet it cannot be done without the use of large amounts of currency.

In the summer months funds accumulate at the centres, but the renewal of business in August and September gives employment for large sums, and leaves little or nothing for forwarding the crops in October and November.

Nor would this difficulty be obviated by a permanent increase or a permanent reduction of the volume of currency. The difficulty is due to the natural order of things, and increases with the prosperity of the country as shown in the abundance of its harvests.

The crops cannot be moved generally by the aid of bank balances, checks, and letters of credit, but only by bank notes and United States notes paid at once to the producers. This money finds its way speedily into the channels of trade and to the commercial centres; but if it be allowed to remain for general use, after the reason for its issue has ceased, the volume of currency would be increased permanently and the year following the same process would be repeated with the same results, and thus would the country depart more and more widely from the policy of resumption.

The problem is to find a way of increasing the currency for moving the crops and diminishing it at once when that work is done. This is a necessary work, and, inasmuch as it cannot be confided to the banks, where, but in the Treasury Department, can the power be reposed?

While the currency revenue was in excess of the currency expenses it was practicable to accumulate large balances in the Treasury during the summer, to be used, if necessary, in the purchase of bonds in the autumn, thereby meeting the usual demand for currency at that season of the year.

Hereafter such accumulations must be made by the sale of gold, and the sale of gold in large quantities during the summer, when business is the least active, may not always be consistent with the best interests of the country. Reliance cannot, therefore, be placed upon the ability of the Treasury to accumulate a currency balance each year for the purpose indicated.

The argument in favor of a paper currency, composed in part of United States notes and in part of national bank notes, is strengthened by the aid which may thus be furnished in resuming and maintaining specie payments. In the view I am now to take, I exclude the idea that the Government will ever abandon the issue of national bank notes, and undertake the issue of United States notes in their place. The result of such a policy may be foreseen. The people, deprived of the facilities for business afforded by banks, would seek relief through State institutions, and without much delay Congress would concede to them the right to issue notes for circulation. This concession would be followed by a surrender by the General Government of all control over the paper circulation of the country.

The true policy will be found in continuing the national banking system, without, however, yielding to the claim for a material increase of its issues in proportion to the volume of paper in circulation.

There are two effectual and certain ways of placing the country in a condition when specie and paper will possess the same commercial value. By diminishing the amount of paper in circulation, the difference between the commercial value of paper and coin will diminish, and by pursuing this policy the difference will disappear altogether.

All legislation limited in its operation to the paper issues of the banks and of the Government, whether bearing interest or not, and which in its effects shall tend to diminish the market value of coin, will be found, upon analysis, to contain a plan for contracting the volume of paper currency; and all legislation, so limited, which does not contain such a plan, will prove ineffectual.

Accepting this proposition, and believing that the country is not prepared to sustain the policy of contraction, it only remains for me to consider the means by which the value of our currency may be improved.

The basis of a policy of improvement must be found in a sturdy refusal to add to the paper in circulation, until it is of the same value, substantially, as coin.

This being accepted as the settled purpose of the country, there can be no permanent increase of the difference between paper and coin, and an opportunity will be given for the influence of natural causes, tending, upon the whole, to a better financial condition.

We may count, first, among these, the increase of population and its distribution over new fields of business and labor. Secondly, in the South especially, the number of persons having property and using and holding money will increase. Next, we may anticipate a more general use of paper in Texas and the Pacific States, by which, practically, for the rest of the country, the volume of paper will be diminished and the quantity of coin increased—two facts tending to produce an equality of value.

The influence of these natural causes will be counteracted in some degree by the increasing facility for the transfer of money from one point to another, and by the greater use of bank checks and certificates of deposit. The rapid transit of merchandise, in bringing the period of its consumption nearer to the time of its production, is an agency of a similar sort. Giving to these views their full weight, I am prepared to say that the experience of the last three years coincides with the best judgment I can form, and warrants the opinion that under the influence of existing natural causes our financial condition will gradually improve. During the last fiscal year there were several circumstances of an unusual character tending to counteract the natural course of affairs. Our exports of cotton fell off thirty-seven million dollars, and there were excessive imports of wool, tea, coffee, and sugar.

The stock of wool in warehouse on the 30th of June was sufficient for six months' consumption, of sugar for four and a half months, of coffee for five months, and of tea for twelve months. In the ordinary course of trade, the importation of these articles will be small during the current year, with a consequent favorable effect upon the balance between this and other countries.

This anticipation of the wants of the country, in connection with the decrease of our exports, augmented the balance of trade, created an active demand for coin, and advanced the price.

Notwithstanding these adverse influences, gold has averaged substantially the same premium from January 1 to November 1 of the present year as for the corresponding period of 1871. Not doubting that natural causes will in time produce the result sought, it is yet advisable to bring the power of the Government in aid of the movement as far as practicable.

The revival of our foreign commerce is one instrumentality, and perhaps the most efficient one of all. If the annual earnings of American vessels were eighty million instead of thirty the difference in the amount of exchange available abroad would meet a large part of the adverse balance in ordinary years. The experience of Europe tends to show that the ability of a country to maintain specie payments is due largely to the condition of its foreign trade. Next, every measure which increases or improves the channels of transportation between the seaboard and the cotton and grain-growing regions of the country, or lessens the cost of freight, adds something to our capacity to compete successfully in the markets of the world.

Finally, those measures which encourage American manufactures, especially of iron, wool, and cotton, and discourage the importation of like products, affect favorably the balance of trade and help us towards the end we seek.

This statement, in three parts, is a general statement of a policy that in my opinion will aid the country in reaching a condition when it will be practicable to resume and maintain specie payments.

Anticipating that day, I anticipate also that the burden of resumption will rest upon the Government. There are now more than nineteen hundred banks in the country, and I cannot imagine a condition of things so favorable for a period of years as to enable them at all times to redeem their notes in specie only. Without proceeding to the discussion of the subject in detail, I think that all will have been gained that is of value when the Treasury shall be prepared to pay the demand notes of the Government in coin, and the banks shall be prepared to pay their notes either in coin or in legal-tender notes; and then our good fortune will clearly appear in this, that our paper currency is not exclusively of national bank notes nor exclusively of United States notes.

GEO. S. BOUTWELL,
Secretary of the Treasury.

Hon. JAMES G. BLAINE,
Speaker of the House of Representatives.

TABLES ACCOMPANYING THE REPORT.

TABLE A.—*Statement of the net receipts (by warrants) during the fiscal year ended June 30, 1872.*

CUSTOMS.		
Quarter ended September 30, 1871	$62, 289, 329 37	
Quarter ended December 31, 1871	45, 822, 613 17	
Quarter ended March 31, 1872	58, 635, 524 14	
Quarter ended June 30, 1872	49, 622, 820 09	
		$216, 370, 286 77
SALES OF PUBLIC LANDS.		
Quarter ended September 30, 1871	602, 680 61	
Quarter ended December 31, 1871	616, 056 44	
Quarter ended March 31, 1872	692, 391 06	
Quarter ended June 30, 1872	664, 586 08	
		2, 575, 714 19
INTERNAL REVENUE.		
Quarter ended September 30, 1871	35, 553, 175 01	
Quarter ended December 31, 1871	29, 479, 321 28	
Quarter ended March 31, 1872	30, 409, 569 90	
Quarter ended June 30, 1872	35, 200, 111 44	
		130, 642, 177 72
TAX ON CIRCULATION, DEPOSITS, ETC., OF NATIONAL BANKS.		
Quarter ended September 30, 1871	3, 175, 946 38	
Quarter ended December 31, 1871	11, 879 17	
Quarter ended March 31, 1872	3, 311, 110 50	
Quarter ended June 30, 1872	24, 460 34	
		6, 523, 396 39
REPAYMENT OF INTEREST BY PACIFIC RAILWAY COMPANIES.		
Quarter ended September 30, 1871	223, 013 69	
Quarter ended December 31, 1871	152, 178 16	
Quarter ended March 31, 1872	186, 823 21	
Quarter ended June 30, 1872	187, 846 81	
		749, 861 87
CUSTOMS FINES, PENALTIES, AND FEES.		
Quarter ended September 30, 1871	318, 216 85	
Quarter ended December 31, 1871	301, 751 76	
Quarter ended March 31, 1872	201, 061 48	
Quarter ended June 30, 1872	315, 412 25	
		1, 136, 442 34
FEES—CONSULAR, LETTERS-PATENT, STEAMBOAT, AND LAND.		
Quarter ended September 30, 1871	482, 052 40	
Quarter ended December 31, 1871	509, 679 44	
Quarter ended March 31, 1872	599, 932 01	
Quarter ended June 30, 1872	692, 431 98	
		2, 284, 095 92
MISCELLANEOUS SOURCES.		
Quarter ended September 30, 1871	940, 112 73	
Quarter ended December 31, 1871	896, 077 25	
Quarter ended March 31, 1872	976, 025 50	
Quarter ended June 30, 1872	1, 600, 039 23	
		4, 412, 254 71
Total receipts, exclusive of loans and premium on coin		364, 694, 229 91
PREMIUM ON SALES OF COIN.		
Quarter ended September 30, 1871	3, 613, 847 47	
Quarter ended December 31, 1871	2, 331, 318 95	
Quarter ended March 31, 1872	563, 803 43	
Quarter ended June 30, 1872	2, 903, 667 80	
		9, 412, 637 65
Total net receipts		374, 106, 867 56
Balance in Treasury June 30, 1871, (including $18,228.35 received from "unavailable")		109, 935, 705 59
Total		484, 042, 573 15

TABLE B.—*Statement of the net disbursements (by warrants) during the fiscal year ended June 30, 1872.*

CIVIL.		
Congress	$4, 672, 587 66	
Executive	6, 239, 141 65	
Judiciary	3, 594, 077 52	
Government of Territories	313, 773 42	
Sub-treasuries	430, 835 82	
Public land-offices	557, 359 95	
Inspection of steam-vessels	218, 684 33	
Mints and assay-offices	110, 598 85	
Total civil list		$16, 187, 059 20
FOREIGN INTERCOURSE.		
Diplomatic salaries	345, 453 26	
Consular salaries	431, 315 41	
Contingencies of consulates	86, 778 41	
Rescuing American citizens from shipwreck	5, 075 00	
Relief and protection of American seamen	209, 275 53	
Hudson's Bay and Puget Sound Agricultural Company commission	314, 869 03	
American and Mexican claims commission	28, 436 70	
American and Spanish claims commission	12, 647 35	
American and British claims commission	56, 493 13	
Tribunal of arbitration at Geneva	117, 566 59	
Expenses of the Japanese embassy	25, 000 00	
Capitalization of Scheldt dues	61, 584 00	
Return of consular receipts	9, 087 39	
War expenses in Madrid, Paris, Berlin, and London	40, 826 96	
Contingent and miscellaneous	94, 900 38	
Total foreign intercourse		1, 839, 369 14
MISCELLANEOUS.		
Mint establishment	784, 099 97	
Coast survey	729, 000 00	
Light-House Establishment	1, 627, 504 59	
Building and repairs of light-houses	1, 543, 371 33	
Refunding excess of deposits for unascertained duties	2, 420, 555 13	
Revenue-cutter service	930, 249 81	
Building revenue-cutters	148, 262 27	
Custom-houses, court-houses, post-offices, &c	3, 344, 642 72	
Furniture, fuel, &c., for public-buildings under Treasury Department	401, 757 96	
Repairs and preservation of public buildings under Treasury Department	236, 329 29	
Collecting customs-revenue	6, 950, 189 81	
Debenture and drawbacks under customs laws	625, 188 23	
Refunding duties erroneously or illegally collected	137, 215 70	
Marine hospital establishment	421, 897 03	
Marine hospital, Chicago, Illinois	153, 245 93	
Distributive shares of fines, penalties, and forfeitures	353, 427 42	
Assessing and collecting internal revenue	5, 097, 288 34	
Punishing violation internal revenue laws	35, 199 61	
Internal revenue stamps	425, 584 71	
Refunding duties erroneously or illegally collected	604, 297 70	
Internal revenue allowances and drawbacks	650, 414 80	
Carrying free mail-matter	700, 000 00	
Mail steamship service	906, 250 00	
Deficiencies in revenue of Post-Office Department	3, 568, 750 00	
Telegraphic communication between the Atlantic and Pacific	23, 432 05	
Refunding proceeds of captured and abandoned property	1, 312, 943 78	
Expenses national loan	2, 490, 912 26	
Expenses refunding national debt	644, 169 12	
Expenses national currency	231, 532 83	
Suppressing counterfeiting and frauds	125, 028 70	
Contingent expenses, independent treasury	59, 860 60	
Public-buildings and grounds in Washington	673, 789 57	
Capitol extension and dome	101, 500 00	
State, War, and Navy Department building	700, 000 00	
Columbian Institute for Deaf and Dumb	15, 500 00	
Government Hospital for the Insane	64, 482 00	
Charitable institutions in Washington	186, 311 78	
Metropolitan police	205, 969 36	
Support of sixty transient paupers	12, 000 00	
Surveys of public lands	836, 514 96	
Refunding excess of deposits for surveying public lands	40, 168 26	
Repayment for lands erroneously sold	22, 084 83	
Proceeds of swamp-lands to States	8, 364 97	
Five per cent. fund, &c., to States	115, 164 74	
Expenses of eighth and ninth census	1, 356, 179 61	
Penitentiaries in the Territories	8, 259 83	
Payments under relief acts	237, 095 96	
Preserving life and property from shipwrecked vessels	51, 246 17	
Unenumerated items	39, 075 35	
Total miscellaneous		2, 958, 329 08

INTERIOR DEPARTMENT.

Indians		$7,061,728 82	
Pensions		28,533,402 76	
Total Interior Department			$35,595,131 58

MILITARY ESTABLISHMENT.

Pay Department		10,408,246 90	
Commissary Department		1,418,676 43	
Quartermaster's Department		10,663,169 74	
Ordnance Department		94,299 15	
Medical Department		486,539 83	
Military Academy		85,865 00	
Expenses of recruiting		107,760 53	
Contingencies		273,934 87	
Signal-service		108,501 00	
Refugees, freedmen, and abandoned lands		173,882 15	
Bounties to soldiers		4,442,627 81	
Re-imbursing States for raising volunteers		296,145 61	
Military organizations in Kansas		308,475 28	
Claims of loyal citizens for supplies		191,707 07	
Payments under relief acts		102,605 49	
Forts and fortifications		1,540,747 65	
Improvements of rivers and harbors		5,401,493 62	
		36,254,678 13	
Deduct excess of repayments on appropriations, where the repayments exceed the expenditures, viz:			
Collecting, &c., volunteers	$855,824 65		
Draft and substitute fund	26,696 28		
		882,520 93	
Total military establishment			35,372,157 20

NAVAL ESTABLISHMENT.

Pay and contingent of the Navy		7,632,636 43	
Marine Corps		821,166 79	
Navigation		256,200 92	
Ordnance		932,708 69	
Provisions and Clothing		2,018,994 68	
Medicine and Surgery		297,905 99	
Equipment and Recruiting		1,566,809 34	
Construction and Repairs		4,426,797 26	
Steam-Engineering		1,062,584 48	
Yards and Docks		2,143,221 28	
Payments under relief acts		90,784 13	
Total naval establishment			21,249,809 99
INTEREST ON THE PUBLIC DEBT			117,357,839 72
Total net disbursements, exclusive of premium and principal of public debt			270,559,695 91
Premiums on bonds purchased		6,958,266 76	
Redemption of the public debt		99,960,253 54	
			106,918,520 30
Total net disbursements			377,478,216 21
Balance in Treasury June 30, 1872			106,564,356 94
Total			484,042,573 15

TABLE C.—*Statement of the redemption and issue of loans and Treasury notes (by warrants) for the fiscal year ended June 30, 1872.*

Character of loans.	Redemptions.	Issues.	Excess of redemptions.	Excess of issues.
Temporary loan, acts of February 25, 1862, March 17, 1862, July 11, 1862, and June 30, 1864	$2,000 00		*$2,000 00	
Coin certificates, act of March 3, 1863, section 5	51,029,500 00	$63,229,500 00		$12,200,000 00
Three per cent. certificates, acts of March 2, 1867, and July 25, 1868	19,730,000 00	†65,000 00	19,665,000 00	
Treasury notes prior to 1846, acts of October 12, 1847, May 21, 1838, March 31, 1840, and March 3, 1843	100 00		100 00	
Treasury notes of 1861, act of March 2, 1861	50 00		50 00	
Seven-thirties of 1861, act of July 17, 1861	3,100 00		3,100 00	
Old demand notes, acts of July 17, 1861, August 5, 1861, and February 12, 1862	8,209 25		8,209 25	
Legal-tender notes, acts of February 25, 1862, July 11, 1862, January 17, 1863, and March 3, 1863	68,099,804 00	69,599,804 00		1,500,000 00
Fractional currency, acts of July 17, 1862, March 3, 1863, and June 30, 1864	31,543,939 29	31,816,900 00		272,960 71
One-year notes of 1863, act of March 3, 1863	21,250 00		21,250 00	
Two-year notes of 1863, act of March 3, 1863	9,800 00		9,800 00	
Compound-interest notes, acts of March 3, 1863, and June 30, 1864	174,980 00		174,980 00	
Seven-thirties of 1864 and 1865, acts of June 30, 1864, and March 3, 1865	120,650 00		120,650 00	
Loan of 1842, acts of July 21, 1841, and April 15, 1842	6,000 00		6,000 00	
Loan of 1847, act of January 28, 1847	500 00		500 00	
Bounty-land scrip, act of February 11, 1847	75 00		75 00	
Loan of 1848, act of March 31, 1848	19,400 00		19,400 00	
Texan indemnity stock, act of September 9, 1850	7,000 00		7,000 00	
Loan of 1860, act of June 22, 1860	39,000 00		39,000 00	
Loan of July and August, 1861, acts of July 17, 1861, and August 5, 1861		‡3,100 00		3,100 00
Five-twenties of 1862, act of February 25, 1862	184,234,750 00		184,234,750 00	
Five-twenties of March, 1864, act of March 3, 1864	270,100 00		270,100 00	
Five-twenties of June, 1864, act of June 30, 1864	13,120,100 00		13,120,100 00	
Five-twenties of 1865, act of March 3, 1865	8,151,150 00		8,151,150 00	
Consols of 1865, act of March 3, 1865	20,305,850 00		20,305,850 00	
Consols of 1867, act of March 3, 1865	7,949,500 00	§1,900 00	7,947,600 00	
Consols of 1868, act of March 3, 1865	160,500 00		160,500 00	
Funded loan of 1881, acts of July 14, 1870, and January 20, 1871		¶140,330,850 00		140,330,850 00
Totals	405,007,307 54	305,047,054 00		
Excess of redemptions			254,267,164 25	154,306,910 71
Excess of issues			154,306,910 71	
Net excess of redemptions charged in receipts and expenditures			99,960,253 54	

* A comparison of the statements of the public debt for July, 1871, and July, 1872, makes the amount of this loan redeemed $250 less than the amount here given. This error arose from the fact that a certificate for this amount was redeemed and deducted from the debt statement in December, 1869. In January, 1870, an advance was made to the Treasurer for the same certificate, and the amount was again deducted from the debt statement. This made the amount outstanding by the debt statement $250 less than it should be. The discovery and correction of this error in October, 1871, occasions the discrepancy in the two accounts.

† Issued in conversion of compound-interest notes.

‡ Issued in conversion of seven-thirties of 1861, (old caveat cases.)

§ Issues in conversion of seven-thirties of 1864 and 1865, (old caveat cases.)

¶ Issued in lieu of five-twenties and consols converted and called for redemption.

D.—*Statement of the net receipts (by warrants) for the quarter ended September* 30, 1872.

RECEIPTS.

Customs	$57, 729, 540 27
Sales of public lands	797, 324 57
Internal revenue	34, 169, 047 22
Premium on sales of coin	2, 426, 736 91
Tax on circulation, deposits, &c., of national banks	3, 307, 238 69
Repayment of interest by Pacific Railway Companies	119, 093 73
Customs fines, penalties, and fees	103, 787 30
Consular, letters-patent, homestead, and land fees	479, 306 03
Proceeds of sales of Government property	336, 801 88
Miscellaneous	1, 346, 257 47
Total receipts, exclusive of loans	100, 815, 134 07
Balance in Treasury June 30, 1872, including $1, 014. 48 received from "unavailable"	106, 565, 371 42
Total	207, 380, 505 49

E.—*Statement of the net disbursements (by warrants) for the quarter ended September* 30, 1872.

CIVIL AND MISCELLANEOUS.

Customs		$6, 284, 813 91
Internal revenue		1, 711, 741 54
Diplomatic service		431, 704 96
Judiciary		931, 442 39
Interior, (civil)		1, 581, 635 27
War, (civil)		7, 844 87
Treasury proper		7, 227, 426 86
Quarterly salaries		123, 281 48
Total civil and miscellaneous		18, 299, 891 28
Indians	$3, 037, 343 83	
Pensions	9, 135, 389 71	
Military establishment	12, 876, 982 41	
Naval establishment	7, 305, 146 48	
Interest on public debt	36, 196, 894 83	
		68, 551, 757 26
Total net ordinary expenditures		86, 851, 648 54
Premiums on purchase of bonds	1, 702, 568 53	
Excess of net redemptions of loans over receipts	16, 932, 138 72	
		18, 634, 707 25
Total net expenditures		105, 486, 355, 79
Balance in Treasury, September 30, 1872		101, 894, 149 70
Total		207, 380, 505 49

TABLE F.—*Statement of outstanding principal of the public debt of the United States on the 1st of January of each year from* 1791 *to* 1843, *inclusive, and on the* 1st *of July of each year from* 1844 *to* 1872, *inclusive.*

Year.	Amount.
1791	$75,463,476 52
1792	77,227,924 66
1793	80,352,634 04
1794	78,427,404 77
1795	80,747,587 39
1796	83,762,172 07
1797	82,064,479 33
1798	79,228,529 12
1799	78,408,660 77
1800	82,796,294 35
1801	83,038,050 80
1802	80,712,632 25
1803	77,054,686 30
1804	86,427,120 88
1805	82,312,150 50
1806	75,723,270 66
1807	69,218,398 64
1808	65,196,317 97
1809	57,023,192 09
1810	53,173,217 52
1811	48,005,587 76
1812	45,209,737 90
1813	55,962,827 57
1814	81,487,846 24
1815	99,833,660 15
1816	127,334,933 74
1817	123,491,965 16
1818	103,466,633 83
1819	95,529,648 28
1820	91,015,566 15
1821	89,987,427 66
1822	93,546,676 98
1823	90,875,877 28
1824	90,269,777 77
1825	83,788,432 71
1826	81,054,059 99
1827	73,987,357 20
1828	67,475,043 87
1829	58,421,413 67
1830	48,565,406 50
1831	39,123,191 68
1832	24,322,235 18
1833	7,001,698 83
1834	4,760,082 08
1835	37,513 05
1836	336,957 83
1837	3,308,124 07
1838	10,434,221 14
1839	3,573,343 82
1840	5,250,875 54
1841	13,594,480 73
1842	20,601,226 28
1843	32,742,922 00
1844	23,461,652 50
1845	15,925,303 01
1846	15,550,202 97
1847	38,826,534 77
1848	47,044,862 23
1849	63,061,858 69
1850	63,452,773 55
1851	68,304,796 02
1852	66,199,341 71
1853	59,803,117 70
1854	42,242,222 42
1855	35,586,956 56
1856	31,972,537 90
1857	28,699,831 85
1858	44,911,881 03
1859	58,496,837 88
1860	64,842,287 88
1861	90,580,873 72
1862	524,176,412 13
1863	1,119,772,138 63
1864	1,815,784,370 57
1865	2,680,647,869 74
1866	2,773,236,173 69

TABLE F.—*Statement of outstanding principal of the public debt, &c.*—Continued.

Year.	Amount.
1867	$2,678,126,103 87
1868	2,611,687,851 19
1869	2,588,452,213 94
1870	2,480,672,427 81
1871	2,353,211,332 11
1872	2,253,251,328 78

TABLE G.—*Statement of the receipts of the United States from March 4, 1789, to June*

Year.	Balance in the Treasury at commencement of year.	Customs.	Internal revenue.	Direct tax.	Public lands.	Miscellaneous.
1791	....	$4,399,473 09	....	....	....	$10,478 10
1792	$973,905 75	3,443,070 85	$208,942 81	....	....	9,918 65
1793	783,444 51	4,255,306 56	337,705 70	....	....	21,410 88
1794	753,661 69	4,801,065 28	274,089 62	....	....	53,277 97
1795	1,151,924 17	5,588,461 26	337,755 36	....	....	28,317 97
1796	516,442 61	6,567,987 94	475,289 60	....	$4,836 13	1,169,415 98
1797	888,995 42	7,549,649 65	575,491 45	....	83,540 60	399,139 29
1798	1,021,899 04	7,106,061 93	644,357 95	....	11,963 11	58,192 81
1799	617,451 43	6,610,449 31	779,136 44		....	86,187 56
1800	2,161,867 77	9,080,932 73	809,396 55	$734,223 97	443 75	152,712 10
1801	2,623,311 99	10,750,778 93	1,048,033 43	534,343 38	167,726 06	345,649 15
1802	3,295,391 00	12,438,235 74	621,898 89	206,565 44	188,628 02	1,500,505 86
1803	5,020,697 64	10,479,417 61	215,179 69	71,879 20	165,675 69	131,945 44
1804	4,825,811 60	11,098,565 33	50,941 29	50,198 44	487,526 79	139,075 53
1805	4,037,005 26	12,936,487 04	21,747 15	21,882 91	540,193 80	40,382 30
1806	3,999,388 99	14,667,698 17	20,101 45	55,763 86	765,245 73	51,121 86
1807	4,538,123 80	15,845,521 61	13,051 40	34,732 56	466,163 27	38,550 42
1808	9,643,850 07	16,363,550 58	8,190 23	19,159 21	647,939 06	21,822 85
1809	9,941,809 96	7,257,506 62	4,034 29	7,517 31	442,252 33	62,162 57
1810	3,848,056 78	8,583,309 31	7,430 63	12,448 68	696,548 82	84,476 84
1811	2,672,276 57	13,313,222 73	2,295 95	7,666 66	1,040,237 53	59,211 22
1812	3,502,305 80	8,958,777 53	4,903 06	859 22	710,427 78	126,165 17
1813	3,862,217 41	13,224,623 25	4,755 04	3,805 52	835,655 14	271,571 00
1814	5,196,542 00	5,998,772 08	1,662,984 82	2,219,497 36	1,135,971 09	164,399 81
1815	1,727,848 63	7,282,942 22	4,678,059 07	2,162,673 41	1,287,959 28	285,282 84
1816	13,106,592 88	36,306,874 88	5,124,708 31	4,253,635 09	1,717,985 03	273,782 35
1817	22,033,519 19	26,283,348 49	2,678,100 77	1,834,187 04	1,991,226 06	109,761 08
1818	14,989,465 48	17,176,385 00	955,270 20	264,333 36	2,606,564 77	57,617 71
1819	1,478,526 74	20,283,608 76	229,593 63	83,650 78	3,274,422 78	57,098 42
1820	2,079,992 38	15,005,612 15	106,260 53	31,586 82	1,635,871 61	61,338 44
1821	1,198,461 21	13,004,447 15	69,027 63	29,349 05	1,212,966 46	152,589 43
1822	1,681,592 24	17,589,761 94	67,665 71	20,961 56	1,803,581 54	452,957 19
1823	4,237,427 55	19,088,433 44	34,242 17	10,337 71	916,523 10	141,129 84
1824	9,463,922 81	17,878,325 71	34,663 37	6,201 96	984,418 15	127,603 60
1825	1,946,597 13	20,098,713 45	25,771 35	2,330 85	1,216,090 56	130,451 81
1826	5,201,650 43	23,341,331 77	21,589 93	6,638 76	1,393,785 09	94,588 66
1827	6,358,686 18	19,712,283 29	19,885 68	2,626 90	1,495,845 26	1,315,722 83
1828	6,668,286 10	23,205,523 64	17,451 54	2,218 81	1,018,308 75	65,126 49
1829	5,972,435 81	22,681,965 91	14,502 74	11,335 05	1,517,175 13	112,648 55
1830	5,755,704 79	21,922,391 39	12,160 62	16,980 59	2,329,356 14	73,227 77
1831	6,014,539 75	24,224,441 77	6,933 51	10,506 01	3,210,815 48	584,124 05
1832	4,502,914 45	28,465,237 24	11,630 65	6,791 13	2,623,381 03	270,410 61
1833	2,011,777 55	29,032,508 91	2,759 00	394 12	3,967,682 55	470,096 67
1834	11,702,905 31	16,214,957 15	4,196 09	19 80	4,857,600 69	480,812 32
1835	8,892,858 42	19,391,310 59	10,459 48	4,263 33	14,757,600 75	759,972 13
1836	26,749,803 96	23,409,940 53	370 00	728 79	24,877,179 86	2,245,902 23
1837	46,708,436 00	11,169,290 39	5,493 84	1,687 70	6,776,236 52	7,001,444 59
1838	37,327,252 69	16,158,800 36	2,467 27	....	3,730,945 66	6,410,348 45
1839	36,891,196 94	23,137,924 81	2,553 32	755, 22	7,361,576 40	979,939 86
1840	33,157,503 68	13,499,502 17	1,682 25	....	3,411,818 63	2,567,112 28
1841	29,963,163 46	14,487,216 74	3,261 36	....	1,365,627 42	1,004,054 75
1842	28,685,111 08	18,187,908 76	495 00	....	1,335,797 52	451,995 97
1843*	30,521,979 44	7,046,843 91	103 25	....	898,158 18	285,895 92
1844	39,186,284 74	26,183,570 94	1,777 34	....	2,059,939 80	1,075,419 70
1845	36,742,829 62	27,528,112 70	3,517 12	....	2,077,022 30	361,453 68
1846	36,194,274 81	26,712,667 87	2,897 26	....	2,694,452 48	289,950 13
1847	38,261,959 65	23,747,864 66	375 00	....	2,498,355 20	220,808 30
1848	33,079,276 43	31,757,070 96	375 00	....	3,328,642 56	612,610 69
1849	29,416,612 45	28,346,738 82	....	....	1,688,959 55	685,379 13
1850	32,827,082 69	39,668,686 42	....	....	1,859,894 25	2,064,308 21
1851	35,871,753 31	49,017,567 92	....	....	2,352,305 30	1,185,166 11
1852	40,158,353 25	47,339,326 62	....	....	2,043,239 58	464,249 40
1853	43,338,860 02	58,931,865 52	....	....	1,667,084 99	988,081 17
1854	50,261,901 09	64,224,190 27	....	....	8,470,798 39	1,105,352 74
1855	48,591,073 41	53,025,794 21	....	....	11,497,049 07	827,731 40
1856	47,777,672 13	64,022,863 50	....	....	8,917,644 93	1,116,190 81
1857	49,108,229 80	63,875,905 05	....	....	3,829,486 64	1,259,920 88
1858	46,802,855 00	41,789,620 96	....	....	3,513,715 87	1,352,029 13
1859	35,113,334 22	49,565,824 38	....	....	1,756,687 30	1,454,596 24
1860	33,193,248 60	53,187,511 87	....	....	1,778,557 71	1,088,530 25
1861	32,979,530 78	39,582,125 64	....	....	870,658 54	1,023,515 31
1862	30,963,857 83	49,056,397 62	....	1,795,331 73	152,203 77	915,327 97
1863	46,965,304 87	69,059,642 40	37,640,787 95	1,485,103 61	167,617 17	3,741,794 38
1864	36,523,046 13	102,316,152 99	109,741,134 10	475,648 96	588,333 29	30,291,701 86
1865	134,433,738 44	84,928,260 60	209,464,215 25	1,200,573 03	996,553 31	25,441,556 00

* For the half year from Jan

30, 1872, *by calendar years to* 1843 *and by fiscal years* (*ended June* 30) *from that time.*

Year	Dividends.	Net ordinary receipts.	Interest.	Premiums.	Receipts from loans and Treasury notes.	Gross receipts.	Unavailable.
1791		$4,409,951 19			$361,391 34	$4,771,342 53	
1792	$8,028 00	3,669,960 31			5,102,498 45	8,772,458 76	
1793	38,500 00	4,652,923 14			1,797,272 01	6,450,195 15	
1794	303,472 00	5,431,904 87			4,007,950 78	9,439,855 65	
1795	160,000 00	6,114,534 59	$4,800 00		3,396,424 00	9,515,758 59	
1796	160,000 00	8,377,529 65	42,800 00		320,000 00	8,740,329 65	
1797	80,960 00	8,688,780 99			70,000 00	8,758,780 99	
1798	79,920 00	7,900,495 80	78,675 00		200,000 00	8,179,170 80	
1799	71,040 00	7,546,813 31			5,000,000 00	12,546,813 31	
1800	71,040 00	10,848,749 10			1,565,229 24	12,413,978 34	
1801	88,800 00	12,935,330 95	10,125 00			12,945,455 95	
1802	39,960 00	14,995,793 95				14,995,793 95	
1803		11,064,097 63				11,064,097 63	
1804		11,826,307 38				11,826,307 38	
1805		13,560,693 20				13,560,693 20	
1806		15,559,931 07				15,559,931 07	
1807		16,398,019 26				16,398,019 26	
1808		17,060,661 93				17,060,661 93	
1809		7,773,473 12				7,773,473 12	
1810		9,384,214 28			2,750,000 00	12,134,214 28	
1811		14,422,634 09				14,422,634 09	
1812		9,801,132 76			12,837,900 00	22,639,032 76	
1813		14,340,409 95	300 00		26,184,135 00	40,524,844 95	
1814		11,181,625 16	85 79		23,377,826 00	34,559,536 95	
1815		15,696,916 82	11,541 74	$32,107 64	35,220,671 40	50,961,237 60	
1816		47,676,985 66	68,665 16	686 09	9,425,084 91	57,171,421 82	
1817	202,426 30	33,099,049 74	267,819 14		466,723 45	33,833,592 33	
1818	525,000 00	21,585,171 04	412 62		8,353 00	21,593,936 66	
1819	675,000 00	24,603,374 37			2,291 00	24,605,665 37	
1820	1,000,000 00	17,840,669 55		40,000 00	3,000,824 13	20,881,493 68	
1821	105,000 00	14,573,379 72			5,000,324 00	19,573,703 72	
1822	297,500 00	20,232,427 94				20,232,427 94	
1823	350,000 00	20,540,666 26				20,540,666 26	
1824	350,000 00	19,381,212 79			5,000,000 00	24,381,212 79	
1825	367,500 00	21,840,858 02			5,000,000 00	26,840,858 02	
1826	402,500 00	25,260,434 21				25,260,434 21	
1827	420,000 00	22,966,363 96				22,966,363 96	
1828	455,000 00	24,763,629 23				24,763,629 23	
1829	490,000 00	24,827,627 38				24,827,627 38	
1830	490,000 00	24,844,116 51				24,844,116 51	
1831	490,000 00	28,526,820 82				28,526,820 82	
1832	490,000 00	31,867,450 66				31,867,450 66	$1,889 50
1833	474,985 00	33,948,426 25				33,948,426 25	
1834	234,349 50	21,791,935 55				21,791,935 55	
1835	506,480 82	35,430,087 10				35,430,087 10	
1836	292,674 67	50,826,796 08				50,826,796 08	
1837		24,954,153 04			2,992,989 15	27,947,142 19	63,288 35
1838		26,302,561 74			12,716,820 86	39,019,382 60	
1839		31,482,749 61			3,857,276 21	35,340,025 82	1,458,782 93
1840		19,480,115 33			5,589,547 51	25,069,662 84	37,469 25
1841		16,860,160 27			13,659,317 38	30,519,477 65	
1842		19,976,197 25			14,808,735 64	34,784,932 89	11,188 00
1843		8,231,001 26		71,700 83	12,479,708 36	20,782,410 45	
1844		29,320,707 78		666 00	1,877,181 35	31,198,555 73	
1845		29,970,105 80				29,970,105 80	28,251 90
1846		29,699,967 74				29,699,967 74	
1847		26,467,403 16		28,365 91	28,872,399 45	55,368,168 52	30,000 00
1848		35,698,699 21		37,080 00	21,256,700 00	56,992,479 21	
1849		30,721,077 50		487,065 48	28,588,750 00	59,796,892 98	
1850		43,592,888 88		10,550 00	4,045,950 00	47,649,388 88	
1851		52,555,039 33		4,264 92	203,400 00	52,762,704 25	
1852		49,846,815 60			46,300 00	49,893,115 60	
1853		61,587,031 68		22 50	16,350 00	61,603,404 18	103,301 37
1854		73,800,341 40			2,001 67	73,802,343 07	
1855		65,350,574 68			800 00	65,351,374 68	
1856		74,056,699 24			200 00	74,056,899 24	
1857		68,965,312 57			3,900 00	68,969,212 57	
1858		46,655,365 96			23,717,300 00	70,372,665 96	
1859		52,777,107 92		709,357 72	28,287,500 00	81,773,965 64	15,408 34
1860		56,054,599 83		10,008 00	20,776,800 00	76,841,407 83	
1861		41,476,299 49		33,630 90	41,861,709 74	83,371,640 13	
1862		51,919,261 09		68,400 00	529,692,460 50	581,680,121 59	11,110 81
1863		112,094,945 51		602,345 44	776,682,361 57	889,379,652 52	6,000 01
1864		243,412,971 20		21,174,101 01	1,128,873,945 36	1,393,461,017 57	9,210 40
1865		322,031,158 19		11,683,446 89	1,472,224,740 85	1,805,939,345 93	6,095 11

uary 1, 1843, to June 30, 1843.

TABLE G.—*Statement of the receipts of the United States*

Year.	Balance in the Treasury at commencement of year.	Customs.	Internal revenue.	Direct tax.	Public lands.	Miscellaneous.
1866	$33,933,657 89	$179,046,651 58	$309,226,813 42	$1,974,754 12	$665,031 03	$29,036,314 23
1867	160,817,099 73	176,417,810 88	266,027,537 43	4,200,233 70	1,163,575 76	15,037,522 15
1868	198,076,537 09	164,464,599 56	191,087,589 41	1,788,145 85	1,348,715 41	17,745,403 59
1869	158,936,082 87	180,048,426 63	158,356,460 86	765,685 61	4,020,344 34	13,997,338 65
1870	183,781,985 76	194,538,374 44	184,899,756 49	229,102 88	3,350,481 76	12,942,118 30
1871	177,604,116 51	206,270,408 05	143,098,153 63	580,355 37	2,388,646 08	22,093,541 21
1872	138,019,122 15	216,370,286 77	130,642,177 72	....	2,575,714 19	15,106,051 23
	....	3,197,031,077 48	1,762,462,639 05	27,239,672 42	194,289,186 27	235,573,091 02

from March 4, 1789, to June 30, 1872, &c.—Continued.

Year.	Dividends.	Net ordinary receipts.	Interest.	Premiums.	Receipts from loans and Treasury notes.	Gross receipts.	Unavailable.
1866	....	$519,949,564 38	....	$38,083,055 68	$712,851,553 05	$1,270,884,173 11	$172,094 29
1867	....	462,846,679 92	....	27,787,330 35	640,426,910 29	1,131,060,920 56	721,827 93
							2,675,918 19
1868	....	376,434,453 82	....	29,203,629 50	625,111,433 20	1,030,749,516 52	....
1869	....	357,188,256 09	....	13,755,491 12	238,678,081 06	609,621,828 27	*2,070 73
1870	....	395,959,833 87	....	15,295,643 76	285,474,496 00	696,729,973 63	....
1871	....	374,431,104 94	....	8,892,839 95	268,768,523 47	652,092,468 36	*3,396 18
1872	....	364,694,229 91	....	9,412,637 65	305,047,054 00	679,153,921 56	*18,228 35
	9,720,136 29	5,426,915,802 53	485,224 45	177,424,427 94	7,399,588,005 38	13,004,413,550 30	2,652,222 93

* Amounts heretofore credited to the Treasurer as unavailable, and since recovered and charged to his account.

TABLE H.—*Statement of the expenditures of the United States from March 4, 1789, to June*

Year.	War.	Navy.	Indians.	Pensions.	Miscellaneous.
1791	$632, 804 03	....	$27, 000 00	$175, 813 88	$1, 083, 971 61
1792	1, 100, 702 09	....	13, 648 85	109, 243 15	4, 672, 664 38
1793	1, 130, 249 08	....	27, 282 83	80, 087 81	511, 451 01
1794	2, 639, 097 59	$61, 408 97	13, 042 46	81, 399 24	750, 350 74
1795	2, 480, 910 13	410, 562 03	23, 475 68	68, 673 22	1, 378, 920 66
1796	1, 260, 263 84	274, 784 04	113, 563 98	100, 843 71	801, 847 58
1797	1, 039, 402 46	382, 631 89	62, 396 58	92, 256 97	1, 259, 422 62
1798	2, 009, 522 30	1, 381, 347 76	16, 470 09	104, 845 33	1, 139, 524 94
1799	2, 466, 946 98	2, 858, 081 84	20, 302 19	95, 444 03	1, 039, 391 68
1800	2, 560, 878 77	3, 448, 716 03	31 22	64, 130 73	1, 337, 613 22
1801	1, 672, 944 08	2, 111, 424 00	9, 000 00	73, 533 37	1, 114, 768 45
1802	1, 179, 148 25	915, 561 87	94, 000 00	85, 440 39	1, 462, 929 40
1803	822, 055 85	1, 215, 230 53	60, 000 00	62, 902 10	1, 842, 635 76
1804	875, 423 93	1, 189, 832 75	116, 500 00	80, 092 80	2, 191, 009 43
1805	712, 781 28	1, 597, 500 00	196, 500 00	81, 854 59	3, 768, 598 75
1806	1, 224, 355 38	1, 649, 641 44	234, 200 00	81, 875 53	2, 890, 137 01
1807	1, 288, 685 91	1, 722, 064 47	205, 425 00	70, 500 00	1, 697, 897 51
1808	2, 900, 834 40	1, 884, 067 80	213, 575 00	82, 576 04	1, 423, 285 61
1809	3, 345, 772 17	2, 427, 758 80	337, 503 84	87, 833 54	1, 215, 803 79
1810	2, 294, 323 94	1, 654, 244 20	177, 625 00	83, 744 16	1, 101, 144 98
1811	2, 032, 828 19	1, 965, 566 39	151, 875 00	75, 043 88	1, 367, 291 40
1812	11, 817, 798 24	3, 959, 365 15	277, 845 00	91, 402 10	1, 683, 088 21
1813	19, 652, 013 02	6, 446, 600 10	167, 358 28	86, 989 91	1, 729, 435 61
1814	20, 350, 806 86	7, 311, 290 60	167, 394 86	90, 164 36	2, 208, 029 70
1815	14, 794, 294 22	8, 660, 000 25	530, 750 00	69, 656 06	2, 898, 870 47
1816	16, 012, 096 80	3, 908, 278 30	274, 512 16	188, 804 15	2, 989, 741 17
1817	8, 004, 236 53	3, 314, 598 49	319, 463 71	297, 374 43	3, 518, 936 76
1818	5, 622, 715 10	2, 953, 695 00	505, 704 27	890, 719 90	3, 835, 839 51
1819	6, 506, 300 37	3, 847, 640 42	463, 181 39	2, 415, 939 85	3, 067, 211 41
1820	2, 630, 392 31	4, 387, 990 00	315, 750 01	3, 208, 376 31	2, 592, 021 94
1821	4, 461, 291 78	3, 319, 243 06	477, 005 44	242, 817 25	2, 223, 121 54
1822	3, 111, 981 48	2, 224, 458 98	575, 007 41	1, 948, 199 40	1, 967, 996 24
1823	3, 096, 924 43	2, 503, 765 83	380, 781 82	1, 780, 588 52	2, 022, 093 99
1824	3, 340, 939 85	2, 904, 581 56	429, 987 90	1, 499, 326 59	7, 155, 308 81
1825	3, 659, 914 18	3, 049, 083 86	724, 106 44	1, 308, 810 57	2, 748, 544 89
1826	3, 943, 194 37	4, 218, 902 45	743, 447 83	1, 556, 593 83	2, 600, 177 79
1827	3, 948, 977 88	4, 263, 877 45	750, 624 88	976, 138 86	2, 713, 476 58
1828	4, 145, 544 56	3, 918, 786 44	705, 084 24	850, 573 57	3, 676, 052 64
1829	4, 724, 291 07	3, 308, 745 47	576, 344 74	949, 594 47	3, 082, 234 65
1830	4, 767, 128 88	3, 239, 428 63	622, 262 47	1, 363, 297 31	3, 237, 416 04
1831	4, 841, 835 55	3, 856, 183 07	930, 738 04	1, 170, 665 14	3, 064, 646 10
1832	5, 446, 034 88	3, 956, 370 29	1, 352, 419 75	1, 184, 422 40	4, 577, 141 45
1833	6, 704, 019 10	3, 901, 356 75	1, 802, 980 93	4, 589, 152 40	5, 716, 245 93
1834	5, 696, 189 38	3, 956, 260 42	1, 003, 953 20	3, 364, 285 30	4, 404, 728 95
1835	5, 759, 156 89	3, 864, 939 06	1, 706, 444 48	1, 954, 711 32	4, 229, 698 53
1836	11, 747, 345 25	5, 807, 718 23	5, 037, 022 88	2, 882, 797 96	5, 393, 279 72
1837	13, 682, 730 80	6, 646, 914 53	4, 348, 036 19	2, 672, 162 45	9, 893, 370 27
1838	12, 897, 224 16	6, 131, 580 53	5, 504, 191 34	2, 156, 057 29	7, 160, 664 76
1839	8, 916, 995 80	6, 182, 294 25	2, 528, 917 28	3, 142, 750 51	5, 725, 990 89
1840	7, 095, 267 23	6, 113, 896 89	2, 331, 794 86	2, 603, 562 17	5, 995, 398 96
1841	8, 801, 610 24	6, 001, 076 07	2, 514, 837 12	2, 388, 434 51	6, 490, 881 45
1842	6, 610, 438 02	8, 397, 242 95	1, 199, 099 68	1, 378, 931 33	6, 775, 624 61
1843*	2, 908, 671 95	3, 727, 711 53	578, 371 00	839, 041 12	3, 202, 713 00
1844	5, 218, 183 66	6, 498, 199 11	1, 256, 532 39	2, 032, 008 99	5, 645, 183 86
1845	5, 746, 291 28	6, 297, 177 89	1, 539, 351 35	2, 400, 788 11	5, 911, 760 98
1846	10, 413, 370 58	6, 455, 013 92	1, 027, 693 64	1, 811, 097 56	6, 711, 283 89
1847	35, 840, 030 33	7, 900, 635 76	1, 430, 411 30	1, 744, 883 63	6, 885, 608 35
1848	27, 688, 334 21	9, 408, 476 02	1, 252, 296 81	1, 227, 496 48	5, 650, 851 25
1849	14, 558, 473 26	9, 786, 705 92	1, 374, 161 55	1, 328, 867 64	12, 885, 334 24
1850	9, 687, 024 58	7, 904, 724 66	1, 663, 591 47	1, 866, 886 02	16, 043, 763 36
1851	12, 161, 965 11	8, 880, 581 38	2, 829, 801 77	2, 293, 377 22	17, 888, 992 18
1852	8, 521, 506 19	8, 918, 842 10	3, 043, 576 04	2, 401, 858 78	17, 504, 171 45
1853	9, 910, 498 49	11, 067, 789 53	3, 880, 494 12	1, 756, 306 20	17, 463, 068 01
1854	11, 722, 282 87	10, 790, 096 32	1, 550, 339 55	1, 232, 665 00	26, 672, 144 68
1855	14, 648, 074 07	13, 327, 095 11	2, 772, 990 78	1, 477, 612 33	24, 090, 425 43
1856	16, 963, 160 51	14, 074, 834 64	2, 644, 263 97	1, 296, 229 65	31, 794, 038 87
1857	19, 159, 150 87	12, 651, 694 61	4, 354, 418 87	1, 310, 380 58	28, 565, 498 77
1858	25, 679, 121 63	14, 053, 264 64	4, 978, 266 18	1, 219, 768 30	26, 400, 016 42
1859	23, 154, 720 53	14, 690, 927 90	3, 490, 534 53	1, 222, 222 71	23, 797, 544 40
1860	16, 472, 202 72	11, 514, 649 83	2, 991, 121 54	1, 100, 802 32	27, 977, 978 30
1861	23, 001, 530 67	12, 387, 156 52	2, 865, 481 17	1, 034, 599 73	23, 327, 287 69
1862	389, 173, 562 29	42, 640, 353 09	2, 327, 948 37	852, 170 47	21, 385, 862 59
1863	603, 314, 411 82	63, 261, 235 31	3, 152, 032 70	1, 078, 513 36	23, 198, 382 37
1864	690, 391, 048 66	85, 704, 963 74	2, 629, 975 97	4, 985, 473 90	27, 572, 216 87

* For the half year from Janu

30, 1872, *by calendar years, to 1843, and by fiscal years (ending June 30) from that time.*

Year.	Net ordinary expenditures.	Premiums.	Interest.	Public debt.	Gross expenditures.	Balance in Treasury at the end of the year.
1791	$1, 919, 589 52		$1, 177, 863 03	$699, 984 23	$3, 797, 436 78	$973, 905 75
1792	5, 896, 258 47		2, 373, 611 28	693, 050 25	8, 962, 920 00	783, 444 51
1793	1, 749, 070 73		2, 097, 859 17	2, 633, 048 07	6, 479, 977 97	753, 661 69
1794	3, 545, 299 00		2, 752, 523 04	2, 743, 771 13	9, 041, 593 17	1, 151, 924 17
1795	4, 362, 541 72		2, 947, 059 06	2, 841, 639 37	10, 151, 240 15	516, 442 61
1796	2, 551, 303 15		3, 239, 347 68	2, 577, 126 01	8, 367, 776 84	888, 995 42
1797	2, 836, 110 52		3, 172, 516 73	2, 617, 250 12	8, 625, 877 37	1, 021, 899 04
1798	4, 651, 710 42		2, 955, 875 90	976, 032 09	8, 583, 618 41	617, 451 43
1799	6, 480, 166 72		2, 815, 651 41	1, 706, 578 84	11, 002, 396 97	2, 161, 867 77
1800	7, 411, 369 97		3, 402, 601 04	1, 138, 563 11	11, 952, 534 12	2, 623, 311 99
1801	4, 981, 669 90		4, 411, 830 06	2, 879, 876 98	12, 273, 376 94	3, 295, 391 00
1802	3, 737, 079 91		4, 239, 172 16	5, 294, 235 24	13, 270, 487 31	5, 020, 697 64
1803	4, 002, 824 24		3, 949, 462 36	3, 306, 697 07	11, 258, 983 67	4, 825, 811 60
1804	4, 452, 858 91		4, 185, 048 74	3, 977, 206 07	12, 615, 113 72	4, 037, 005 26
1805	6, 357, 234 62		2, 657, 114 22	4, 583, 960 63	13, 598, 309 47	3, 999, 388 99
1806	6, 080, 209 36		3, 368, 968 26	5, 572, 018 64	15, 021, 196 26	4, 538, 123 80
1807	4, 984, 572 89		3, 369, 578 48	2, 938, 141 62	11, 292, 292 99	9, 643, 850 07
1808	6, 504, 338 85		2, 557, 074 23	7, 701, 288 96	16, 762, 702 04	9, 941, 809 96
1809	7, 414, 672 14		2, 866, 074 90	3, 586, 479 26	13, 867, 226 30	3, 848, 056 78
1810	5, 311, 082 28		3, 163, 671 09	4, 835, 241 12	13, 309, 994 49	2, 672, 276 57
1811	5, 592, 604 86		2, 585, 435 57	5, 414, 564 43	13, 592, 604 86	3, 502, 305 80
1812	17, 829, 498 70		2, 451, 272 57	1, 998, 349 88	22, 279, 121 15	3, 862, 217 41
1813	28, 082, 396 92		3, 599, 455 22	7, 508, 668 22	39, 190, 520 36	5, 196, 542 00
1814	30, 127, 686 38		4, 593, 239 04	3, 307, 304 90	38, 028, 230 32	1, 727, 848 63
1815	26, 953, 571 00		5, 990, 090 24	6, 638, 832 11	39, 582, 493 35	13, 106, 592 88
1816	23, 373, 432 58		7, 822, 923 34	17, 048, 139 59	48, 244, 495 51	22, 033, 519 19
1817	15, 454, 609 92		4, 536, 282 55	20, 886, 753 57	40, 877, 646 04	14, 989, 465 48
1818	13, 808, 673 78		6, 209, 954 03	15, 086, 247 59	35, 104, 875 40	1, 478, 526 74
1819	16, 300, 273 44		5, 211, 730 56	2, 492, 195 73	24, 004, 199 73	2, 079, 992 38
1820	13, 134, 530 57		5, 151, 004 32	3, 477, 489 96	21, 763, 024 85	1, 198, 461 21
1821	10, 723, 479 07		5, 126, 073 79	3, 241, 019 83	19, 090, 572 69	1, 681, 592 24
1822	9, 827, 643 51		5, 172, 788 79	2, 676, 160 33	17, 676, 592 63	4, 237, 427 55
1823	9, 784, 154 59		4, 922, 475 40	607, 541 01	15, 314, 171 00	9, 463, 922 81
1824	15, 330, 144 71		4, 943, 557 93	11, 624, 835 83	31, 898, 538 47	1, 946, 597 13
1825	11, 490, 459 94		4, 366, 757 40	7, 728, 587 38	23, 585, 804 72	5, 201, 650 43
1826	13, 062, 316 27		3, 975, 542 95	7, 065, 539 24	24, 103, 398 46	6, 358, 686 18
1827	12, 653, 095 65		3, 486, 071 51	6, 517, 596 88	22, 656, 764 04	6, 668, 286 10
1828	13, 296, 041 45		3, 098, 800 60	9, 064, 637 47	25, 459, 479 52	5, 972, 435 81
1829	12, 641, 210 40		2, 542, 843 23	9, 860, 304 77	25, 044, 358 40	5, 755, 704 79
1830	13, 229, 533 33		1, 912, 574 93	9, 443, 173 29	24, 585, 281 55	6, 014, 539 75
1831	13, 864, 067 90		1, 373, 748 74	14, 800, 629 48	30, 038, 446 12	4, 502, 914 45
1832	16, 516, 388 77		772, 561 50	17, 067, 747 79	34, 356, 698 06	2, 011, 777 55
1833	22, 713, 755 11		303, 796 87	1, 239, 746 51	24, 257, 298 49	11, 702, 905 31
1834	18, 425, 417 25		202, 152 98	5, 974, 412 21	24, 601, 982 44	8, 892, 858 42
1835	17, 514, 950 28		57, 863 08	328 20	17, 573, 141 56	26, 749, 803 96
1836	30, 868, 164 04				30, 868, 164 04	46, 708, 436 00
1837	37, 243, 214 24			21, 822 91	37, 265, 037 15	37, 327, 252 69
1838	33, 849, 718 08		14, 996 48	5, 590, 723 79	39, 455, 438 35	36, 891, 196 94
1839	26, 496, 948 73		399, 833 89	10, 718, 153 53	37, 614, 936 15	33, 157, 503 68
1840	24, 139, 920 11		174, 598 08	3, 912, 015 62	28, 226, 533 81	29, 963, 163 46
1841	26, 196, 840 29		284, 977 55	5, 315, 712 19	31, 797, 530 03	28, 685, 111 08
1842	24, 361, 336 59		773, 549 85	7, 801, 990 09	32, 936, 876 53	30, 521, 979 44
1843	11, 256, 508 60		523, 583 91	338, 012 64	12, 118, 105 15	39, 186, 284 74
1844	20, 650, 108 01		1, 833, 452 13	11, 158, 450 71	33, 642, 010 85	36, 742, 829 62
1845	21, 895, 369 61	$18, 231 43	1, 040, 458 18	7, 536, 349 49	30, 490, 408 71	36, 194, 274 81
1846	26, 418, 459 59		842, 723 27	371, 100 04	27, 632, 282 90	38, 261, 959 65
1847	53, 801, 569 37		1, 119, 214 72	5, 600, 067 65	60, 520, 851 74	33, 079, 276 43
1848	45, 227, 454 77		2, 390, 765 88	13, 036, 922 54	60, 655, 143 19	29, 416, 612 45
1849	39, 933, 542 61	82, 865 81	3, 565, 535 78	12, 804, 478 54	56, 386, 422 74	32, 827, 082 69
1850	37, 165, 990 09		3, 782, 393 03	3, 656, 335 14	44, 604, 718 26	35, 871, 753 31
1851	44, 054, 717 66	69, 713 19	3, 696, 760 75	654, 912 71	48, 476, 104 31	40, 158, 353 25
1852	40, 389, 954 56	170, 063 42	4, 000, 297 80	2, 152, 293 05	46, 712, 608 83	43, 338, 860 02
1853	44, 078, 156 35	420, 498 64	3, 665, 832 74	6, 412, 574 01	54, 577, 061 74	50, 261, 901 09
1854	51, 967, 528 42	2, 877, 818 69	3, 070, 926 69	17, 556, 896 95	75, 473, 170 75	48, 591, 073 41
1855	56, 316, 197 72	872, 047 39	2, 314, 464 99	6, 662, 065 86	66, 164, 775 96	47, 777, 672 13
1856	66, 772, 527 64	385, 372 90	1, 953, 822 37	3, 614, 618 66	72, 726, 341 57	49, 108, 229 80
1857	66, 041, 143 70	363, 572 39	1, 593, 265 23	3, 276, 606 05	71, 274, 587 37	46, 802, 855 00
1858	72, 330, 437 17	574, 443 08	1, 652, 055 67	7, 505, 250 82	82, 062, 186 74	35, 113, 334 22
1859	66, 355, 950 07		2, 637, 649 70	14, 685, 043 15	83, 678, 642 92	33, 193, 248 60
1860	60, 056, 754 71		3, 144, 120 94	13, 854, 250 00	77, 055, 125 65	32, 979, 530 78
1861	62, 616, 055 78		4, 034, 157 30	18, 737, 100 00	85, 387, 313 08	30, 963, 857 83
1862	456, 379, 896 81		13, 190, 344 84	96, 097, 322 09	565, 667, 563 74	46, 965, 304 87
1863	694, 004, 575 56		24, 729, 700 62	181, 081, 635 07	899, 815, 911 25	36, 523, 046 13
1864	811, 283, 679 14		53, 685, 421 69	430, 572, 014 03	1, 295, 541, 114 86	134, 433, 738 44

ary 1, 1843, to June 30, 1843.

TABLE H.—*Statement of the expenditures of the United*

Year.	War.	Navy.	Indians.	Pensions.	Miscellaneous.
1865	$1,030,690,400 06	$122,617,434 07	$5,059,360 71	$16,347,621 34	$42,989,383 10
1866	263,154,676 06	43,285,662 00	3,295,729 32	15,605,549 88	40,613,114 17
	3,568,638,312 28	717,551,816 39	103,369,211 42	119,607,656 01	643,604,554 33
	*3,621,780 07	*77,992 17	*53,286 61	*9,737 87	*718,769 52
	3,572,260,092 35	717,629,808 56	103,422,498 03	119,617,393 88	644,323,323 85
1867	95,224,415 63	31,034,011 04	4,642,531 77	20,936,551 71	51,110,223 72
1868	123,246,648 62	25,775,502 72	4,100,682 32	23,782,386 78	53,009,867 67
1869	78,501,990 61	20,000,757 97	7,042,923 06	28,476,621 78	56,474,061 53
1870	57,655,675 40	21,780,229 87	3,407,938 15	28,340,202 17	53,237,461 56
1871	35,799,991 82	19,431,027 21	7,426,997 44	34,443,894 88	60,481,916 23
1872	35,372,157 20	21,249,809 99	7,061,728 82	28,533,402 76	60,984,757 42
	3,998,060,971 63	856,901,147 36	137,105,209 59	284,130,453 96	979,621,611 98

* Outstanding

NOTE.—This statement is made from warrants *paid* by the Treasurer up to June 30, 1866. The balance in the Treasury June 30 1872, by this statement, is $134,666,001. 85, from which should be 30, 1872, $106,564,356. 94.

States from March 4, 1789, to June 30, 1872—Continued.

Year.	Net ordinary expenditures.	Premiums.	Interest.	Public debt.	Gross expenditures.	Balance in Treasury at the end of the year.
1865	$1,217,704,199 28	$1,717,900 11	$77,395,090 30	$609,616,141 68	$1,906,433,331 37	$33,933,657 89
1866	385,954,731 43	58,476 51	133,067,624 91	620,263,249 10	1,139,344,081 95	165,301,654 76
	5,152,771,550 43	7,611,003 56	502,689,519 27	2,374,677,103 12	8,037,749,176 38	
	*4,481,566 24	....	*2,888 48	*100 31	*4,484,555 03	*4,484,555 03
	5,157,253,116 67	7,611,003 56	502,692,407 75	2,374,677,203 43	8,042,233,731 41	160,817,099 73
1867	202,947,733 87	10,813,349 38	143,781,591 91	735,536,980 11	1,093,079,655 27	198,076,537 09
1868	229,915,088 11	7,001,151 04	140,424,045 71	692,549,685 88	1,069,889,970 74	158,936,082 87
1869	190,496,354 95	1,674,680 05	130,694,242 80	261,912,718 31	584,777,996 11	183,781,985 76
1870	164,421,507 15	15,996,555 60	129,235,498 00	393,254,282 13	702,907,842 88	177,604,116 51
1871	157,583,827 58	9,016,794 74	125,576,565 93	399,503,670 65	691,680,858 90	138,019,122 15
1872	153,201,856 19	6,958,266 76	117,357,839 72	405,007,307 54	682,525,270 21	134,666,001 85
	6,255,819,484 52	59,071,801 13	1,289,762,191 82	5,262,441,848 05	12,867,095,325 52	....

warrants.

outstanding warrants are then added, and the statement is by warrants *issued* from that date. The deducted the amount deposited with the States, $28,101,644.91, leaving the net available balance, June

TABLE I.—*Statement of the differences between the several accounts showing the outstanding principal of the public debt, with an explanation thereof, so far as the examination of the accounts has progressed.*

The statement of receipts (Table G) shows the amount which has been covered into the Treasury, as derived from loans and Treasury notes, from the organization of the Government to and including June 30, 1872, to have been	$7,399,588,095 38
The statement of expenditures (Table H) shows the payments from the Treasury for the redemption and purchase of loans and Treasury notes for the same period to have been	5,262,441,848 05
Showing the principal outstanding by these tables, June 30, 1872	2,137,146,247 33
The *actual* outstanding principal, at that date, as shown by Tables F and O, and by the debt statement of July 1, 1872, was	2,253,251,328 78
Showing	116,105,081 45

more outstanding and unpaid principal by the debt statement, and by Tables F and O, than by the receipts and expenditures, Tables G and H. (This amount differs from the amount as given in the finance report of last year (1871) by $250, which is explained in a note on page 6, *ante*.)

This difference of $116,105,081.45 is thus explained: The following stocks were issued in payment of various debts and claims, but in the transaction no money ever came into the Treasury. When the stock matured it was paid out of the general funds then in the Treasury. This showed an expenditure where there had been no corresponding receipt, and, of course, a statement of the debt made from the receipts and expenditures on account of loans and Treasury notes would not be correct unless these items were added to the receipt side of the account. This cannot be done until legislation has been had authorizing it:

French farmers-general loan	$153,688 89
French loan of eighteen million livres	3,267,000 00
Spanish loan of 1781	174,017 13
French loan of ten million livres	1,815,000 00
French loan of six million livres	1,089,000 00
Balance of supplies due France	24,332 86
Dutch loan of 1782	2,000,000 00
Dutch loan of 1784	800,000 00
Debt due foreign officers	186,988 78
Dutch loan of 1787	400,000 00
Dutch loan of 1788	400,000 00
Interest due on the foreign debt	1,771,496 00
Domestic debt of the Revolution, *estimated*	63,918,475 44
The above are the details (so far as the progress of the examination has developed them) of the item in the finance report of 1871, (page 20,) "Revolutionary debt, *estimated*, $76,000,000."	
Mississippi-purchase stock	4,282,151 12
Louisiana-purchase stock	11,250,000 00
Washington and Georgetown debt assumed by the United States	1,500,000 00
United States Bank subscription stock	7,000,000 00
Six per cent. Navy stock	711,700 00
Texas-purchase stock	5,000,000 00
Mexican indemnity stock	303,573 92
Bounty-land scrip	233,075 00
Tompkins fraud in loan of 1798	1,000 00
The following amounts represent the discounts suffered in placing the loans named; only the money actually received was covered into the Treasury. The difference between this and the face value of the stock issued was the discount. To make the receipts and expenditures on the loan accounts correct, these discounts should be credited to the loans as receipts and charged to a discount account. This also requires legislation to enable it to be done:	
Loan of 1796	10,000 00
Loan of February, 1813	2,109,377 43
Loan of August, 1813	998,581 95
Ten-million loan of 1814	1,983,895 25
Six-million loan of 1814	1,076,826 97
Undesignated stock of 1814	93,868 95
Loan of March, 1815	588,820 93
Loan of February, 1861	2,019,776 10
The foregoing are the details of the difference of $116,105,081.45, so far as the examination of the public-debt accounts has progressed. There still remains to be explained	942,433 83
Which is the resultant error arising out of differences yet to be discovered and reconciled. The full details of this item can only be given after the accounts have all been examined and corrected, and the amount of it may be increased or diminished when the examination of the domestic debt of the Revolution shall have shown what *its* true amount is.	
Total	116,105,081 45

TABLE K.—*Statement showing the condition of the sinking-fund, from its institution in May, 1869, to and including June 30, 1872.*

R. THE SECRETARY OF THE TREASURY IN ACCOUNT WITH SINKING-FUND. CR.

uly 1, 1868..	To ½ of 1 per cent. on the principal of the public debt, being for the three months from April 1 to June 30, 1868	$6,529,219 63	June 30, 1869.	By amount of principal purchased, $8,691,000, including $1,000 donation, estimated in gold	$7,261,437 30
une 30, 1869.	To interest on $8,691,000, being amount of principal of public debt purchased during fiscal year 1869 on this account	196,590 00		By accrued interest on the amount of purchases in 1869	136,392 56
	Balance to new account	672,020 23			
		7,397,829 86			7,397,829 86
uly 1, 1869..	To 1 per cent. on the principal of the public debt on June 30, 1869, $2,588,452,213.94	25,884,522 14	July 1, 1869..	By balance from last year	672,020 23
uno 30, 1870.	To interest on $8,691,000, amount of redemption in 1869.	521,460 00	June 30, 1870.	By amount of principal purchased, $28,151,900, estimated in gold	25,893,143 57
	To interest on $28,151,900, amount of principal of public debt purchased during fiscal year 1870 on this account	1,254,897 00		By accrued interest on account of purchases in 1870	351,003 54
				By balance to new account	744,711 80
		27,660,879 14			27,660,879 14
uly 1, 1870..	To balance from last year	744,711 80	June 30, 1871.	By amount of principal purchased, $29,936,250, estimated in gold	28,694,017 73
	To 1 per cent. on the principal of the public debt on June 30, 1870, $2,480,672,427.81	24,806,724 28		By accrued interest on account of purchases in 1871	367,782 53
une 30, 1871.	To interest on redemption of 1869, $8,691,000	521,460 00		By balance to new account	257,474 32
	To interest on redemption of 1870, $28,151,900	1,689,114 00			
	To interest on $29,936,250, amount of principal of public debt purchased during fiscal year 1871 on this account	1,557,264 50			
		29,319,274 58			29,319,274 56
uly 1, 1871..	To balance from last year	257,474 32	June 30, 1872.	By amount of principal purchased, $32,618,450, estimated in gold	32,248,645 22
	To 1 per cent. on the principal of the public debt on June 30, 1871, $2,353,211,332.32	23,532,113 32		By accrued interest on account of purchases in 1872	430,908 38
une 30, 1872.	To interest on redemption of 1869, $8,691,000	521,460 00			
	To interest on redemption of 1870, $28,151,900	1,689,114 00			
	To interest on redemption of 1871, $29,936,250	1,796,175 00			
	To interest on redemption of $32,618,450, amount of principal of public debt purchased during fiscal year 1872 on this account	2,059,325 50			
	To balance to new account	2,823,891 46			
		32,679,553 00			32,679,553 60

TABLE L.—*Statement showing the purchases of bonds on account of the sinking-fund during each fiscal year from its institution in May, 1869, to and including June 30, 1872.*

Year ended—	Principal redeemed.	Premium paid.	Net cost in currency.	Net cost estimated in gold.	Interest due at close of fiscal year.	Accrued interest paid in coin.	Balance of interest due at close of fiscal year.
JUNE 30, 1869.							
Five-twenties of 1862	$1,621,000 00	$253,822 84	$1,874,822 84	$1,349,970 02	$16,210 00	$7,384 60	$8,825 40
Five-twenties of March, 1864	70,000 00	11,725 00	81,725 00	57,552 82	700 00	218 63	481 37
Five-twenties of June, 1864	1,051,000 00	161,946 45	1,212,946 45	873,205 61	10,510 00	1,470 42	9,039 58
Five-twenties of 1865	465,000 00	74,969 00	539,969 00	387,566 28	4,650 00	2,683 54	1,966 46
Consols, 1865	461,000 00	73,736 80	534,736 80	387,903 26	13,830 00	429 04	13,400 96
Consols, 1867	4,718,000 00	749,208 08	5,467,208 08	3,948,586 11	141,540 00	116,032 35	25,507 65
Consols, 1868	305,000 00	49,442 50	354,442 50	256,653 20	9,150 00	8,173 98	976 02
Total	8,691,000 00	1,374,850 67	10,065,850 67	7,261,437 30	196,590 00	136,392 56	60,197 44
JUNE 30, 1870.							
Five-twenties of 1862	3,542,050 00	493,479 42	4,035,529 42	3,263,099 51	160,919 50	45,994 49	114,925 01
Five-twenties of March, 1864	85,000 00	15,742 87	100,742 87	75,658 54	5,350 00	1,080 99	4,269 01
Five-twenties of June, 1864	3,971,400 00	506,189 91	4,477,589 91	3,647,628 29	165,834 00	49,946 00	115,888 00
Five-twenties of 1865	2,790,250 00	361,735 43	3,151,985 43	2,606,636 20	105,257 50	37,113 53	68,143 97
Consols, 1865	11,532,150 00	1,454,778 37	12,986,928 37	10,681,736 97	495,421 50	145,518 29	349,903 21
Consols, 1867	5,882,550 00	861,763 73	6,744,313 73	5,309,810 90	302,734 50	66,111 51	236,622 99
Consols, 1868	348,500 00	53,363 95	401,863 95	308,573 16	19,380 00	5,238 73	14,141 27
Total	28,151,900 00	3,747,053 68	31,898,953 68	25,893,143 57	1,254,897 00	351,003 54	903,893 46
JUNE 30, 1871.							
Five-twenties of 1862	2,702,950 00	227,607 56	3,020,557 56	2,680,209 05	145,975 00	36,657 80	109,317 20
Five-twenties of March, 1864	29,500 00	2,277 20	31,777 20	28,590 88	1,240 00	388 35	851 65
Five-twenties of June, 1864	3,967,350 00	340,529 63	4,307,879 63	3,847,182 42	201,375 00	51,703 46	149,671 54
Five-twenties of 1865	6,768,600 00	574,923 00	7,343,523 00	6,525,231 42	331,933 50	92,259 58	239,673 92
Consols, 1865	10,222,200 00	850,949 79	11,073,149 79	9,762,387 78	522,117 00	109,455 28	412,661 72
Consols, 1867	6,103,050 00	541,559 41	6,644,609 41	5,800,618 37	351,528 00	76,745 93	274,782 07
Consols, 1868	52,600 00	4,784 61	57,384 61	49,797 81	3,096 00	572 13	2,523 87
Total	29,836,250 00	2,542,631 20	32,478,881 20	28,694,017 73	1,557,264 50	367,782 53	1,189,481 97

JUNE 30, 1872.							
Five-twenties of 1862	6, 417, 850 00	764, 055 21	7, 181, 905 21	6, 345, 391 98	427, 849 00	75, 179 43	352, 669 57
Five-twenties of March, 1864	127, 100 00	14, 959 03	142, 059 03	126, 123 46	8, 894 00	1, 338 70	7, 555 30
Five-twenties of June, 1864	3, 604, 650 00	438, 656 16	4, 043, 306 16	3, 573, 223 63	246, 001 50	57, 449 80	188, 551 70
Five-twenties of 1865	3, 635, 200 00	436, 838 70	4, 072, 038 70	3, 594, 747 85	246, 562 00	37, 817 37	208, 744 63
Consols, 1865	11, 788, 900 00	1, 436, 989 46	13, 225, 889 46	11, 660, 785 89	707, 334 00	149, 248 21	558, 085 79
Consols, 1867	6, 958, 900 00	833, 600 15	7, 792, 500 15	6, 863, 777 39	417, 534 00	108, 487 92	300, 046 08
Consols, 1868	85, 850 00	9, 951 63	95, 801 63	84, 595 02	5, 151 00	1, 386 95	3, 764 05
Total	32, 618, 450 00	3, 935, 050 34	36, 553, 500 34	32, 248, 645 22	2, 059, 325 50	430, 908 38	1, 628, 417 12
Grand total	99, 397, 600 00	11, 599, 585 89	110, 997, 185 89	94, 097, 243 82	5, 068, 077 00	1, 286, 087 01	3, 781, 989 99

TABLE M.—*Statement showing the purchases of bonds in excess of the amount required for the sinking-fund during each fiscal year from the commencement of the purchases in May, 1869, to and including June 30, 1872.*

Year end—	Principal redeemed.	Premium paid.	Net cost in currency.	Net cost estimated in gold.	Interest due at close of fiscal year.	Accrued interest paid in coin.	Balance of interest due at close of fiscal year.
JUNE 30, 1870.							
Five-twenties of 1862	$9,975,250 00	$1,438,465 74	$11,413,715 74	$9,026,361 36	$502,456 55	$110,968 99	$391,487 56
Five-twenties of March, 1864	597,400 00	116,951 00	714,351 00	532,078 21	40,948 00	9,621 13	31,326 87
Five-twenties of June, 1864	11,742,700 00	1,767,653 37	13,510,353 37	10,680,518 21	589,697 55	146,031 16	443,666 39
Five-twenties, 1865	7,620,350 00	1,102,967 36	8,723,317 36	7,051,018 61	328,437 85	94,005 47	234,432 38
Consols, 1865	36,118,200 00	5,242,087 61	41,360,287 61	32,775,094 65	1,861,918 50	483,633 72	1,378,284 78
Consols, 1867	18,426,800 00	2,922,445 22	21,349,245 22	16,374,250 02	1,037,727 00	206,748 21	830,978 79
Consols, 1868	2,105,500 00	364,879 14	2,470,379 14	1,869,116 40	123,495 00	23,141 27	100,353 73
Total	86,586,200 00	12,955,449 44	99,541,649 44	78,308,437 46	4,484,680 45	1,074,149 95	3,410,530 50
JUNE 30, 1871.							
Five-twenties of 1862	7,695,250 00	725,443 91	8,420,693 91	7,517,031 86	315,865 00	88,115 14	227,749 86
Five-twenties of March, 1864	100,500 00	10,862 25	111,362 25	100,135 51	1,335 00	196 94	1,138 06
Five-twenties of June, 1864	7,145,950 00	657,670 36	7,803,620 36	6,968,994 28	280,772 50	88,675 02	192,097 48
Five-twenties, 1865	9,117,750 00	877,459 15	9,995,209 15	8,875,458 67	362,211 00	90,147 01	272,063 99
Consols, 1865	24,476,800 00	2,348,715 50	26,825,515 50	23,917,450 48	988,482 00	355,280 04	633,201 96
Consols, 1867	10,741,550 00	1,011,485 32	11,753,035 32	10,430,837 44	478,047 00	153,991 14	324,055 86
Consols, 1868	163,600 00	16,802 01	180,402 01	159,625 18	6,813 00	2,780 76	4,032 24
Total	59,441,400 00	5,648,438 50	65,089,838 50	57,969,533 42	2,433,525 50	779,186 05	1,654,339 45
JUNE 30, 1872.							
Five-twenties of 1862	12,364,000 00	1,359,618 69	13,723,618 69	12,317,868 38	354,487 00	132,389 84	222,097 16
Five-twenties of March, 1864	54,000 00	6,549 90	60,549 90	53,884 81	1,020 00	389 92	630 08
Five-twenties of June, 1864	4,299,550 00	495,186 15	4,794,736 15	4,279,233 48	104,153 50	46,626 09	57,527 41
Five-twenties, 1865	1,868,400 00	209,232 93	2,077,632 93	1,858,868 91	49,536 00	16,649 96	32,886 04
Consols, 1865	7,909,700 00	999,620 72	8,909,320 72	7,875,863 64	237,501 00	155,887 37	81,613 63
Consols, 1867	705,750 00	95,071 84	800,821 84	703,446 24	21,285 00	13,956 70	7,328 30
Consols, 1868	8,950 00	1,170 36	10,120 36	8,918 01	283 50	186 94	96 56
Total	27,210,350 00	3,166,450 59	30,376,800 59	27,098,083 47	768,266 00	366,086 82	402,179 18
Grand total	173,237,950 00	21,770,338 53	195,008,288 53	163,376,054 35	7,686,471 95	2,219,422 82	5,467,049 13

TABLE N.—*Statement showing the purchases of bonds from May, 1869, to September 30, 1872.*

Date of purchase.		Opening price of gold.	Principal.	Amount paid.	Currency value of interest accrued on bonds bought "flat."	Net cost.	Net cost estimated in gold.	Average rate of premium on each purchase.	Average cost in gold of each purchase.	Average rate of premium on total purchases to date.	Average cost in gold of total purchases to date.
1869.											
May	12	138½	$1,000,000 00	$1,155,070 00	$2,504 36	$1,152,565 64	$832,177 36	15.26	83.22		
	19	142	70,000 00	81,718 00		81,718 00	57,548 45	16.74	82.21		
	19	142	1,000,000 00	1,168,512 10		1,168,512 10	822,395 85	16.85	82.29		
	27	139½	1,000,000 00	1,153,581 50		1,153,581 50	826,940 14	15.36	82.69	15.84	82.72
June	3	138¼	1,000,000 00	1,164,058 90	711 78	1,164,770 68	842,510 43	16.48	84.25		
	10	138⅝	1,000,000 00	1,161,967 00		1,161,967 00	838,208 84	16.20	83.82		
	16	138	1,000 00	1,155 00		1,155 00	835 44	15.50	83.54		
	17	138¼	1,000,000 00	1,152,950 00		1,152,950 00	833,960 21	15.30	83.40		
	23	137⅛	1,620,000 00	1,870,402 50		1,870,402 50	1,364,012 76	15.46	84.20		
	26	137½	1,000,000 00	1,158,228 25		1,158,228 25	842,347 82	15.82	84.23	15.82	83.55
July	1	137½	1,000,000 00	1,158,098 75		1,158,098 75	842,253 63	15.81	84.22		
	3	137	3,000,000 00	3,496,474 00		3,496,474 00	2,552,170 80	16.54	85.07		
	9	136	3,000,000 00	3,518,044 00		3,518,044 00	2,586,797 06	17.27	86.23		
	14	137⅜	3,000,000 00	3,607,622 90		3,607,622 90	2,626,113 12	20.25	87.54		
	15	137	1,000,000 00	1,201,850 00		1,201,850 00	877,262 77	20.18	87.73		
	21	135⅛	3,000,000 00	3,600,028 80		3,600,028 80	2,664,221 12	20.00	88.81		
	28	136½	3,000,000 00	3,604,859 00		3,604,859 00	2,640,922 34	20.16	88.03		
	29	135¾	1,000,000 00	1,201,570 55		1,201,570 55	885,134 84	20.16	88.51	17.85	85.93
August	4	136	2,000,000 00	2,431,136 80		2,431,136 80	1,787,600 59	21.56	89.38		
	11	135½	2,000,000 00	2,422,038 27		2,422,038 27	1,787,482 12	21.10	89.37		
	12	135⅛	1,000,000 00	1,198,931 70		1,198,931 70	887,276 00	19.89	88.73		
	18	133	2,000,000 00	2,378,781 81		2,378,781 81	1,788,557 75	18.94	89.43		
	25	133¼	2,000,000 00	2,389,539 01		2,389,539 01	1,793,275 07	19.48	89.66		
	26	133⅞	1,000,000 00	1,196,247 80		1,196,247 80	893,555 78	19.63	89.36	18.46	86.87
September	1	133⅜	2,000,000 00	2,401,991 00		2,401,991 00	1,800,930 46	20.10	90.05		
	8	136	2,000,000 00	2,356,000 00		2,356,000 00	1,732,352 94	17.80	86.62		
	9	135⅞	1,000,000 00	1,183,972 53		1,183,972 53	871,368 92	18.40	87.14		
	15	136⅛	2,000,000 00	2,369,039 55		2,369,039 55	1,740,782 04	18.48	87.04		
	22	137¾	2,000,000 00	2,337,657 62		2,337,657 62	1,697,029 12	16.88	84.85		
	23	141⅞	1,000,000 00	1,165,548 50		1,165,548 50	822,082 17	16.55	82.30		
	25	133⅝	3,000,000 00	3,537,158 16		3,537,158 16	2,647,078 14	17.91	88.24		
	29	133⅝	3,000,000 00	3,473,533 12		3,473,533 12	2,599,463 51	15.78	86.65	18.38	86.91
October	6	130	2,000,000 00	2,319,139 18		2,319,139 18	1,783,953 22	15.96	89.20		
	7	131⅛	1,000,000 00	1,159,945 10		1,159,945 10	884,610 18	15.99	88.46		
	7	131⅛	*153,500 00	178,187 69		178,187 69	135,891 47	16.08	88.53		
	13	130⅛	2,000,000 00	2,318,883 53		2,318,883 53	1,782,043 06	15.94	89.10		
	20	130	2,000,000 00	2,314,079 00		2,314,079 00	1,780,060 77	15.70	89.00		

TABLE N.—*Statement showing the purchases of bonds from May, 1869, to September 30, 1872*—Continued.

Date of purchase.		Opening price of gold.	Principal.	Amount paid.	Currency value of interest accrued on bonds bought "flat."	Net cost.	Net cost estimated in gold.	Average rate of premium on each purchase.	Average cost in gold of each purchase.	Average rate of premium on total purchases to date.	Average cost in gold of total purchases to date.
1869.											
October	21	130⅛	$1,000,000 00	$1,152,000 00	....	$1,152,000 00	$885,302 59	15.20	88.53	....	....
	27	130⅛	2,000,000 00	2,292,600 00	....	2,292,600 00	1,761,844 38	14.63	88.09	17.80	87.20
November	3	127⅝	2,000,000 00	2,257,255 21	....	2,257,255 21	1,768,662 26	12.86	88.43	....	....
	4	126⅝	1,000,000 00	1,126,843 74	....	1,126,843 74	889,906 21	12.68	88.99	....	....
	4	126⅝	1,000,000 00	1,129,090 29	....	1,129,090 29	891,680 39	12.91	89.17	....	....
	5	126½	*201,300 00	227,580 43	$167 43	227,413 00	179,773 12	12.97	89.31	....	....
	5	126½	*433,000 00	492,158 94	2,917 87	489,241 07	386,751 83	12.99	89.32	....	....
	10	126⅞	2,000,000 00	2,259,000 00	....	2,259,000 00	1,780,492 61	12.95	89.02	....	....
	17	127⅛	2,000,000 00	2,256,513 69	....	2,256,513 69	1,775,035 35	12.83	88.75	....	....
	17	127⅛	1,000,000 00	1,129,039 02	....	1,129,039 02	888,132 95	12.00	88.81	....	....
	24	126⅝	3,000,000 00	3,382,483 67	....	3,382,483 67	2,671,260 54	12.75	89.04	16.97	87.48
December	1	122⅛	2,000,000 00	2,206,992 21	....	2,206,992 21	1,807,158 41	10.35	90.36	....	....
	2	122¼	1,000,000 00	1,102,659 61	....	1,102,659 61	901,971 06	10.27	90.20	....	....
	8	123⅝	2,000,000 00	2,248,236 56	....	2,248,236 56	1,818,593 78	12.41	90.93	....	....
	15	121¾	2,000,000 00	2,239,710 90	....	2,239,710 90	1,839,598 27	11.98	91.98	....	....
	16	121⅝	1,000,000 00	1,118,412 34	....	1,118,412 34	919,557 94	11.84	91.96	....	....
	22	120⅛	2,000,000 00	2,215,985 83	....	2,215,985 83	1,844,733 26	10.80	92.24	....	....
	29	119⅞	2,000,000 00	2,220,427 12	....	2,220,427 12	1,852,285 40	11.02	92.61	....	....
	30	119⅞	1,000,000 00	1,110,507 80	....	1,110,507 80	926,388 15	11.05	92.64	16.13	88.20
1870.											
January	5	119¾	2,000,000 00	2,246,595 03	....	2,246,595 03	1,876,071 01	12.33	93.80	....	....
	11	122½	*451,700 00	517,400 49	....	517,400 49	422,367 75	14.54	93.51	....	....
	11	122½	*1,342,550 00	1,539,826 93	32 58	1,539,794 35	1,256,974 98	14.09	93.63	....	....
	13	121⅝	1,000,000 00	1,141,010 09	....	1,141,010 09	938,137 79	14.10	93.81	....	....
	19	121½	2,000,000 00	2,281,555 49	....	2,281,555 49	1,877,823 45	14.08	93.89	....	....
	27	122	1,000,000 00	1,142,872 27	....	1,142,872 27	936,780 55	14.29	93.68	15.94	88.55
February	10	120¾	1,000,000 00	1,126,500 00	....	1,126,500 00	932,919 25	12.65	93.30	....	....
	11	120⅛	50,000 00	56,325 00	....	56,325 00	46,888 66	12.65	93.78	....	....
	24	117⅝	1,000,000 00	1,115,764 80	....	1,115,764 80	948,577 94	11.57	94.86	....	....
	24	117⅝	1,000,000 00	1,117,488 85	....	1,117,488 85	950,043 66	11.75	95.04	15.79	88.73
March	2	116⅜	1,000,000 00	1,107,377 50	....	1,107,377 50	951,559 61	10.74	95.16	....	....
	10	111	1,000,000 00	1,067,347 35	....	1,067,347 35	961,574 19	6.73	96.16	....	....
	17	112	1,000,000 00	1,067,480 27	....	1,067,480 27	953,107 39	6.75	95.31	....	....
	24	112½	1,000,000 00	1,060,440 34	....	1,060,440 34	942,613 63	6.04	94.26	....	....
	30	111⅞	1,000,000 00	1,069,985 26	....	1,069,985 26	956,411 41	7.00	95.64	15.42	89.04

21	113⅝	1,000,000 00	1,078,778 18	....	1,078,778 18	951,513 28	7.88	95.15	....	....
27	113⅞	1,000,000 00	1,100,490 79	....	1,100,490 79	966,402 45	10.05	96.64	....	....
30	114⅞	*345,400 00	390,847 25	7,826 85	383,020 40	333,423 63	10.89	96.53	....	....
30	114⅞	*758,800 00	859,029 25	18,099 70	840,929 55	732,038 78	10.82	96.47	15.10	89.36
May 5	114⅝	2,000,000 00	2,215,447 70	....	2,215,447 70	1,932,778 60	10.77	96.64	....	....
12	115⅝	*1,850 00	2,074 31	3 85	2,070 46	1,794 55	11.92	97.00	....	....
12	115⅝	1,000,000 00	1,118,370 86	....	1,118,370 86	969,335 52	11.84	96.93	....	....
19	114⅜	2,000,000 00	2,230,611 87	....	2,230,611 87	1,943,888 34	11.53	97.19	....	....
26	114¼	1,000,000 00	1,108,910 71	....	1,108,010 71	970,600 18	10.89	97.06	14.90	89.76
June 2	114½	2,000,000 00	2,223,786 41	....	2,223,786 41	1,942,171 53	11.19	97.11	....	....
9	113½	1,000,000 00	1,109,976 64	....	1,109,976 64	977,952 99	11.00	97.79	....	....
16	113¼	2,000,000 00	2,217,755 94	....	2,217,755 94	1,960,447 24	10.89	98.02	....	....
23	111⅝	1,000,000 00	1,104,612 10	....	1,104,612 10	989,574 11	10.46	98.96	....	....
30	111⅞	2,000,000 00	2,218,005 71	....	2,218,005 71	1,987,015 19	10.90	99.35	14.65	90.31
July 7	112⅛	1,000,000 00	1,107,000 00	....	1,107,000 00	987,290 97	10.70	98.73	....	....
11	115½	*690,400 00	758,749 60	....	758,749 60	659,065 88	9.90	95.46	....	....
11	115⅛	*1,683,150 00	1,648,423 98	....	1,848,423 98	1,605,580 00	9.82	95.39	....	....
14	112⅞	2,000,000 00	2,182,332 89	....	2,182,332 89	1,933,406 77	9.12	96.67	....	....
21	121¼	1,000,000 00	1,070,136 00	....	1,070,136 00	878,961 81	7.01	87.90	....	....
28	121½	2,000,000 00	2,162,085 83	....	2,162,085 83	1,777,665 64	8.10	88.88	14.29	90.52
August 4	121⅛	1,000,000 00	1,085,712 21	....	1,085,712 21	891,755 41	8.57	89.17	....	....
11	116½	2,000,000 00	2,191,414 93	....	2,191,414 93	1,885,088 11	9.57	94.25	....	....
18	116¾	1,000,000 00	1,097,329 29	....	1,097,329 29	939,896 61	9.73	93.99	....	....
25	117¼	2,000,000 00	2,181,093 02	....	2,181,093 02	1,850,344 02	9.05	92.52	14.07	90.62
September 1	116¾	1,000,000 00	1,091,038 65	....	1,091,038 65	937,519 78	9 10	93.75	....	....
8	114	3,000,000 00	3,272,957 77	....	3,272,957 77	2,871,015 58	9.10	95.70	....	....
15	114⅜	2,000,000 00	2,183,503 11	....	2,183,503 11	1,909,073 76	9.18	95.45	....	....
22	113⅞	3,000,000 00	3,281,789 74	....	3,281,789 74	2,881,922 93	9.39	96.06	....	....
29	113⅞	2,000,000 00	2,177,057 86	....	2,177,057 86	1,911,796 14	8.85	95.59	13.71	90.98
October 6	113	2,000,000 00	2,174,300 26	....	2,174,300 26	1,924,159 52	8.72	96.21	....	....
13	113¼	2,000,000 00	2,170,465 37	....	2,170,465 37	1,906,006 91	8.52	95.30	....	....
20	112⅜	2,000,000 00	2,170,236 48	....	2,170,236 48	1,922,690 12	8.51	96.13	....	....
27	112	2,000,000 00	2,165,529 30	....	2,165,529 30	1,933,508 30	8.28	96.68	13.44	91.24
November 3	110⅜	1,000,000 00	1,077,698 19	....	1,077,698 19	973,090 92	7.77	97.31	....	....
3	110¾	*245,850 00	265,173 81	....	265,173 81	239,434 59	7.86	97.39	....	....
3	110½	*542,250 00	584,808 61	8 06	584,800 55	528,036 61	7.85	97.39	....	....
10	110⅜	1,000,000 00	1,072,263 90	....	1,072,263 90	971,473 52	7.23	97.15	....	....
17	113	1,000,000 00	1,064,972 36	....	1,064,972 36	942,453 42	6.50	94.25	....	....
25	112	1,000,000 00	1,065,650 15	....	1,065,650 15	951,473 35	6.56	95.15	13.25	91.39
December 1	110¼	1,000,000 00	1,064,917 08	....	1,064,917 08	962,636 91	6.49	96.26	....	....
8	110⅝	1,000,000 00	1,063,854 32	....	1,063,854 32	961,676 22	6.38	96.17	....	....
15	111½	1,000,000 00	1,065,972 75	....	1,065,972 75	958,177 75	6.60	95.82	....	....
22	110⅜	1,000,000 00	1,064,459 26	....	1,064,459 26	962,223 06	6.45	96.22	....	....
29	110¾	1,000,000 00	1,064,473 95	....	1,064,473 95	961,150 29	6.45	96.11	13.05	91.53
1871.										
January 4	110¼	2,000,000 00	2,147,345 03	....	2,147,345 03	1,938,911 99	7.37	96.96	....	....
11	111	1,000,000 00	1,074,257 50	....	1,074,257 50	967,709 55	7.43	96.78	....	....
18	110⅝	2,000,000 00	2,144,457 32	....	2,144,457 32	1,938,492 49	7.22	96.92	....	....
25	110⅝	1,000,000 00	1,074,651 96	....	1,074,651 96	971,436 80	7.46	97.14	12.85	91.72
February 1	111¼	2,000,000 00	2,173,985 90	....	2,173,985 90	1,943,227 62	8.70	97.16	....	....
8	111½	2,000,000 00	2,175,643 46	....	2,175,643 46	1,946,884 53	8.78	97.34	....	....

TABLE N.—*Statement showing the purchases of bonds from May, 1869, to September 30, 1872*—Continued.

Date of purchase.		Opening price of gold.	Principal.	Amount paid.	Currency value of interest accrued on bonds bought "flat."	Net cost.	Net cost estimated in gold.	Average rate of premium on each purchase.	Average cost in gold of each purchase.
1871.									
February	15	111¼	$2,000,000 00	$2,184,170 19	....	$2,184,170 19	$1,963,299 05	9.21	98.16
	21	111⅛	2,000,000 00	2,191,633 24	....	2,191,633 24	1,970,007 41	9.58	98.50
March	1	110⅞	2,000,000 00	2,199,585 00	....	2,199,585 00	1,983,842 16	9.98	99.19
	8	111⅛	2,000,000 00	2,199,570 48	....	2,199,570 48	1,977,142 00	9.98	98.85
	15	111⅜	2,000,000 00	2,191,702 96	....	2,191,702 96	1,967,859 00	9.58	98.39
	22	110⅝	2,000,000 00	2,188,826 83	....	2,188,826 83	1,974,139 19	9.94	98.71
	29	110⅞	2,000,000 00	2,183,254 76	....	2,183,254 76	1,980,276 42	9.16	99.01
April	3	110½	216,000 00	235,807 20	....	235,807 20	213,884 08	9.17	99.02
	5	110⅜	3,000,000 00	3,295,500 00	....	3,295,500 00	2,985,730 46	9.85	99.52
	12	110⅝	2,000,000 00	2,197,018 24	....	2,197,018 24	1,995,022 24	9.85	99.75
	19	111⅛	3,000,000 00	3,317,193 80	....	3,317,193 80	2,971,730 17	10.57	99.06
	26	110⅞	2,000,000 00	2,215,181 72	....	2,215,181 72	1,997,909 10	10.76	99.90
May	3	111⅛	2,000,000 00	2,221,571 71	....	2,221,571 71	1,999,164 04	11.08	99.96
	10	111¼	2,000,000 00	2,223,162 54	....	2,223,162 54	1,998,348 35	11.16	99.92
	17	111⅝	2,000,000 00	2,228,989 07	....	2,228,989 07	1,992,392 46	11.45	99.62
	24	111⅜	2,000,000 00	2,224,133 69	....	2,224,133 69	1,992,504 98	11.21	99.63
	31	111⅝	2,000,000 00	2,225,697 70	....	2,225,697 70	1,989,450 54	11.28	99.47
June	7	112¼	1,000,000 00	1,115,811 40	....	1,115,811 40	994,041 33	11.58	99.40
	14	112⅜	1,000,000 00	1,114,175 30	....	1,114,175 30	991,479 69	11.42	99.15
	21	112⅞	1,000,000 00	1,116,587 05	....	1,116,587 05	993,625 85	11.66	99.36
	28	113⅛	1,000,000 00	1,118,691 60	....	1,118,691 60	988,898 65	11.87	98.89
July	5	113¼	1,000,000 00	1,132,384 49	....	1,132,384 49	997,095 59	13.24	99.77
	12	112⅞	1,000,000 00	1,122,692 96	....	1,122,692 96	999,059 35	12.27	99.91
	19	112⅛	385,600 00	433,278 38	....	433,278 38	385,136 33	12.36	99.88
	26	112⅜	1,000,000 00	1,122,086 99	....	1,122,086 99	999,632 06	12.21	99.96
August	2	112⅛	162,750 00	182,407 63	....	182,407 63	162,682 30	12.08	99.96
	9	112	20,100 00	22,509 99	....	22,509 99	20,098 20	11.99	99.99
	16	112¼	1,000,000 00	1,122,127 56	....	1,122,127 56	999,668 21	12.21	99.97
	23	112⅜	1,000,000 00	1,121,011 54	....	1,121,011 54	998,673 98	12.10	99.87
	30	113⅜	1,000,000 00	1,125,650 82	....	1,125,650 82	993,952 16	12.56	99.39
September	6	113⅝	1,000,000 00	1,128,864 31	....	1,128,864 31	991,318 82	12.89	99.13
	13	113⅛	1,000,000 00	1,125,800 00	....	1,125,800 00	988,627 83	12.58	98.86
	20	114⅛	3,000,000 00	3,375,135 99	....	3,375,135 99	2,957,402 84	12.50	98.58
	25	115	3,000,000 00	3,397,836 15	....	3,397,836 15	2,954,640 13	13.26	98.49
	27	114½	2,000,000 00	2,262,400 68	....	2,262,400 68	1,975,895 78	13.12	98.79

October 18	112½	4,000,000 00	4,414,343 08		4,414,343 08	3,915,160 16	10.36	97.88		
18	112¾	50,000 00	55,100 00		55,100 00	48,922 39	10.32	97.84		
25	111⅝	2,000,000 00	2,217,901 51		2,217,901 51	1,986,921 84	10.89	99.35	12.31	93.82
November 1	112	1,000,000 00	1,113,421 29		1,113,421 29	994,126 15	11.34	99.41		
8	111⅝	1,000,000 00	1,114,150 87		1,114,150 87	998,119 48	11.41	99.81		
15	111½	21,100 00	23,452 74		23,452 74	21,081 11	11.11	99.88		
21	110¾	1,000,000 00	1,107,389 47		1,107,389 47	999,900 20	10.74	99.09	12.30	93.90
December 6	109⅞	517,450 00	568,325 56		568,325 56	517,247 38	9.83	99.96		
13	109½	43,700 00	47,734 84		47,734 84	43,693 21	9.24	99.99		
20	108¾	81,000 00	88,083 15		88,083 15	80,996 00	8.74	99.99		
27	108½	240,550 00	260,908 91		260,908 91	240,469 04	8.46	99.97	12.28	93.91
1872.										
January 4	109⅛	566,200 00	617,775 00		617,775 00	566,116 84	9.11	99.99		
18	109	899,750 00	978,713 38		978,713 38	897,902 18	8.78	99.80	12.27	93.95
February 1	109¾	1,000,000 00	1,091,919 01		1,091,919 01	994,914 81	9.19	99.49		
15	110¼	1,000,000 00	1,092,584 13		1,092,584 13	991,006 01	9.26	99.10		
29	110½	1,000,000 00	1,091,388 34		1,091,388 34	984,341 23	9.14	98.43	12.23	94.02
March 14	110⅜	1,000,000 00	1,092,821 91		1,092,821 91	992,346 80	9.28	99.23		
28	110⅝	1,000,000 00	1,095,961 25		1,095,961 25	992,943 37	9.60	99.29	12.21	94.05
April 3	109⅞	1,000,000 00	1,097,435 25		1,097,435 25	998,803 41	9.74	99.88		
10	110¼	1,000,000 00	1,100,721 08		1,100,721 08	998,386 46	10.07	99.84		
17	110⅞	2,000,000 00	2,213,295 42		2,213,295 42	1,996,207 82	10.66	99.81		
24	111⅞	263,850 00	294,794 93		294,794 93	263,503 85	11.73	99.87	12.18	94.15
May 1	112¼	691,650 00	776,203 34		776,203 34	691,495 18	12.22	99.98		
8	113⅛	5,000 00	5,640 00		5,640 00	4,963 70	12.80	99.27		
8	113⅛	4,000,000 00	4,519,795 84		4,519,795 84	3,977,818 12	12.99	99.44		
15	114	3,000,000 00	3,395,826 68		3,395,826 68	2,978,795 34	13.19	99.29		
22	113¼	2,000,000 00	2,267,116 41		2,267,116 41	1,993,069 37	13.36	99.65		
29	113½	2,000,000 00	2,274,174 07		2,274,174 67	1,997,079 84	13.71	99.85	12.22	94.38
June 5	114⅛	825,950 00	945,245 28		945,245 28	824,641 46	14.44	99.84		
12	114	47,850 00	54,486 79		54,468 79	47,795 42	13.87	99.88		
19	113½	921,900 00	1,047,373 04		1,047,373 04	919,756 79	13.61	99.77		
26	113⅜	1,084,400 00	1,227,634 17		1,227,634 17	1,082,808 53	13.22	99.85	12.24	94.44
July 2	113¾	300,850 00	342,155 19		342,155 19	300,795 77	13.73	99.98		
10	113½	511,750 00	581,975 72		581,975 72	511,627 01	13.72	99.98		
17	114⅛	1,000,000 00	1,144,063 85		1,144,063 85	999,182 40	14.41	99.92		
24	114¼	47,200 00	53,956 89		53,956 89	47,123 92	14.32	99.84		
31	115¼	1,000,000 00	1,146,489 17		1,146,489 17	995,864 64	14.65	99.59	12.26	94.49
August 7	115¼	2,000,000 00	2,296,663 19		2,296,663 19	1,992,766 31	14.83	99.64		
7	115⅛	7,000 00	8,038 80		8,038 80	6,975 10	14.84	99.64		
14	114¾	1,000,000 00	1,145,208 63		1,145,208 63	998,003 16	14.52	99.80		
21	114¾	34,300 00	38,996 39		38,996 39	34,132 50	13.60	99.51		
22	114¼	5,000 00	5,683 00		5,683 00	4,974 18	13.66	99.48		
28	113	1,000,000 00	1,123,616 18		1,123,616 18	994,350 60	12.36	99.44	12.29	94.57
September 4	113¼	1,000,000 00	1,123,204 81		1,123,204 81	992,888 23	12.32	99.29		
11	113	1,000,000 00	1,112,251 60		1,112,251 60	984,293 45	11.23	98.43		
18	114½	3,000,000 00	3,343,130 94		3,343,130 94	2,926,154 00	11.44	97.54		
25	113⅝	1,000,000 00	1,120,903 75		1,120,993 75	986,573 14	12.10	98.66	12.27	94.64
Total		285,541,650 00	320,622,751 45	30,848 92	320,591,902 53	270,249,002 58			12.27	94.64

TABLE N.—*Statement showing the purchases of bonds from May*, 1869, *to September* 30, 1872—Continued.

Date of purchase.	Opening price of gold.	Principal.	Amount paid.	Currency value of interest accrued on bonds bought "flat."	Net cost.	Net cost estimated in gold.	Average rate of premium on each purchase.	Average cost in gold of each purchase.	Average rate of premium on total purchases to date.	Average cost in gold of total purchases to date.
RECAPITULATION BY LOANS.										
Five-twenties of 1862	....	$48, 082, 950 00	$53, 836, 461 40	$938 14	$53, 835, 523 26	46, 147, 342 90	....	....	12.00	95.97
Five-twenties of March, 1864	....	1, 113, 500 00	1, 299, 952 23	12 48	1, 299, 939 75	1, 023, 805 14	....	....	16.74	91.94
Five-twenties of June, 1864	....	37, 054, 900 00	41, 594, 692 75	*4, 024 32	41, 590, 668 43	35, 131, 299 28	....	....	12.24	94.81
Five-twenties of 1865	....	33, 168, 150 00	36, 924, 906 60	53 48	36, 924, 853 12	31, 793, 383 60	....	....	11.33	95.85
Consols of 1865	....	108, 293, 250 00	121, 469, 614 93	24, 983 68	121, 444, 631 25	102, 776, 621 81	....	....	12.14	94.90
Consols of 1867	....	54, 572, 350 00	61, 713, 355 64	744 92	61, 712, 610 72	50, 453, 792 34	....	....	13.09	92.45
Consols of 1868	....	3, 250, 550 00	3, 783, 767 90	91 90	3, 783, 676 00	2, 922, 757 51	....	....	16.18	89.75
Total	....	285, 541, 650 00	320, 622, 751 45	30, 848 92	320, 591, 902 53	270, 249, 002 58	....	....	12.27	94.64

NOTE.—The bonded debt of the United States has been reduced by the amount of these bonds, which have ceased to bear interest and have been canceled and destroyed. This statement does not include the six-per-cent. bonds converted into fives, nor the redemption of past due and called securities, which have also ceased to bear interest and have been canceled and destroyed. Those items marked (*) are the bonds bought with the proceeds of the interest collected on the bonds previously purchased. These "interest-purchases" were discontinued after the passage of the act of July 14, 1870, (16 Statutes, 272,) authorizing the refunding of the national debt and directing the cancellation and destruction of the bonds purchased. All bonds, whether purchased, redeemed, or received in exchange for other bonds bearing a lower rate of interest, either before or since the date of that act, have ceased to bear interest, and the annual interest-charge has been reduced by the amount of interest that would have been payable on the first two classes, and the difference in rate on the last class, but for such redemption, purchase, or exchange.

TABLE O.—*Statement of the outstanding principal of the public debt of the United States, June* 30, 1872.

	Length of loan.	When redeemable.	Rate of interest.	Price at which sold.	Amount authorized.	Amount issued.	Amount outstanding.
OLD DEBT.							
Unclaimed dividends upon debt created prior to 1800, and the principal and interest of the outstanding debt created during the war of 1812, and up to 1837.	....	On demand ...	5 and 6 per cent.	....	....	....	$57,665 00
TREASURY NOTES PRIOR TO 1846.							
The acts of October 12, 1837, (5 Statutes, 201;) May 21, 1838, (5 Statutes, 228;) March 31, 1840, (5 Statutes, 370;) February 15, 1841, (5 Statutes, 411;) January 31, 1842, (5 Statutes, 469;) August 31, 1842, (5 Statutes, 581;) and March 3, 1843, (5 Statutes, 614;) authorized the issue of Treasury notes in various amounts, and with interest at rates named therein from 1 mill to 6 per centum per annum.	1 and 2 years	1 and 2 years from date.	1 mill to 6 per cent.	Par	....	....	82,575 35
TREASURY NOTES OF 1846.							
The act of July 22, 1846, (9 Statutes, 39,) authorized the issue of Treasury notes in such sums as the exigencies of the Government might require; the amount outstanding at any one time not to exceed $10,000,000, to bear interest at not exceeding 6 per centum per annum, redeemable one year from date. These notes were receivable in payment of all debts due the United States, including customs duties.	1 year	1 year from date.	6 per cent ...	Par	$10,000,000 00	....	6,000 00
MEXICAN INDEMNITY.							
A proviso in the civil and diplomatic appropriation act of August 10, 1846, (9 Statutes, 94,) authorized the payment of the principal and interest of the fourth and fifth instalments of the Mexican indemnities due April and July, 1844, by the issue of stock, with interest at 5 per centum, payable in five years.	5 years	April and July, 1849.	5 per cent ...	Par	350,000 00	$303,573 92	1,104 91
TREASURY NOTES OF 1847.							
The act of January 28, 1847, (9 Statutes, 118,) authorized the issue of $23,000,000 Treasury notes, with interest at not exceeding 6 per centum per annum, or the issue of stock for any portion of the amount, with interest at 6 per centum per annum. The Treasury notes under this act were redeemable at the expiration of one or two years; and the interest was to cease at the expiration of sixty days' notice. These notes were receivable in payment of all debts due the United States, including customs duties.	1 and 2 years	After 60 days' notice.	6 per cent ...	Par	23,000,000 00	....	950 00

TABLE O.—*Statement of the outstanding principal of the public debt, &c.*—Continued.

	Length of loan.	When redeemable.	Rate of interest.	Price at which sold.	Amount authorized.	Amount issued.	Amount outstanding.
LOAN OF 1847.							
The act of January 28, 1847, (9 Statutes, 118,) authorized the issue of $23,000,000 Treasury notes, with interest at not exceeding 6 per centum per annum, or the issue of stock for any portion of the amount, with interest at 6 per centum per annum, re-imbursable after December 31, 1867. Section 14 authorized the conversion of Treasury notes under this or any preceding act into like stock, which accounts for the apparent over-issue.	20 years.....	January 1, 1868	6 per cent...	Par.....	$23,000,000 00	$28,207,000 00	$1,650 00
BOUNTY-LAND SCRIP.							
The 9th section of February 11, 1847, (9 Statutes, 125,) authorized the issue of land-warrants to soldiers of the Mexican war, or scrip, at the option of the soldiers, to bear 6 per centum interest per annum, redeemable at the pleasure of the Government, by notice from the Treasury Department. Interest ceases July 1, 1849.	Indefinite...	July 1, 1849 ...	6 per cent...	Par.....	Indefinite.....	....	3,900 00
TEXAN INDEMNITY STOCK.							
The act of September 9, 1850, (9 Statutes, 447,) authorized the issue of $10,000,000 stock, with interest at 5 per centum per annum, to the State of Texas, in satisfaction of all claims against the United States arising out of the annexation of the said State. This stock was to be redeemable at the end of fourteen years.	14 years.....	January 1, 1865.	5 per cent...	Par.....	10,000,000 00	5,000,000 00	174,000 00
LOAN OF 1848.							
The act of March 31, 1848, (9 Statutes, 217,) authorized a loan of $16,000,000, with interest at not exceeding 6 per centum per annum, reimbursable after July 1, 1868. The Secretary of the Treasury was authorized to purchase this stock at any time.	20 years.....	July 1, 1868 ...	6 per cent...	Par.....	16,000,000 00	16,000,000 00	5,500 00
TREASURY NOTES OF 1857.							
The act of December 23, 1857, (11 Statutes, 257,) authorized the issue of $20,000,000 in Treasury notes, $6,000,000 with interest at not exceeding 6 per centum per annum, and the remainder with interest at the lowest rates offered by bidders, but not exceeding 6 per centum per annum. These notes were redeemable at the expiration of one year, and interest was to cease at the expiration of sixty days' notice after maturity. They were receivable in payment of all debts due the United States, including customs duties.	1 year	60 days' notice.	5 and 5½ per cent.	Par.....	20,000,000 00	20,000,000 00	2,000 00

LOAN OF 1858.							
The act of June 14, 1858, (11 Statutes, 365,) authorized a loan of $20,000,000, with interest at not exceeding 5 per centum per annum, and redeemable any time after January 1, 1874.	15 years	Jan. 1, 1874	5 per cent	Par	20,000,000 00	20,000,000 00	20,000,000 00
LOAN OF 1860.							
The act of June 22, 1860, (12 Statutes, 79,) authorized a loan of $21,000,000, (to be used in redemption of Treasury notes,) with interest at not exceeding 6 per centum per annum, redeemable in not less than ten nor more than twenty years.	10 years	Jan. 1, 1871	5 per cent	Par	21,000,000 00	7,022,000 00	10,000 00
LOAN OF FEBRUARY, 1861, (1881's.)							
The act of February 8, 1861, (12 Statutes, 129,) authorized a loan of $25,000,000, with interest at not exceeding 6 per centum per annum, reimbursable in not less than ten nor more than twenty years from the date of the act.	10 or 20 yrs.	Jan. 1, 1881	6 per cent	Par	25,000,000 00	18,415,000 00	18,415,000 00
TREASURY NOTES OF 1861.							
The act of March 2, 1861, (12 Statutes, 178,) authorized a loan of $10,000,000, with interest at not exceeding 6 per centum per annum, redeemable on three months' notice after July 1, 1871, and payable July 1, 1881. If proposals for the loan were not satisfactory, authority was given to issue the whole amount in Treasury notes, with interest at not exceeding 6 per centum per annum. The same act gave authority to substitute Treasury notes for the whole or any part of loans authorized at the time of the passage of this act. These notes were to be received in payment of all debts due the United States, including customs duties, and were redeemable at any time within two years from the date of the act.	2 years 60 days	2 years after date. 60 days after date.	6 per cent	Par	22,468,100 00 12,896,350 00	35,364,450 00	3,150 00
OREGON WAR DEBT.							
The act of March 2, 1861, (12 Statutes, 198,) appropriated $2,800,000 for the payment of expenses incurred by the Territories of Washington and Oregon, in the suppression of Indian hostilities in the years 1855 and 1856. Section 4 of the act authorized the payment of these claims in bonds redeemable in twenty years, with interest at 6 per centum per annum.	20 years	July 1, 1881	6 per cent	Par	2,800,000 00	1,090,850 00	945,000 00
LOAN OF JULY AND AUGUST 1861, (1881's.)							
The act of July 17, 1861, (12 Statutes, 259,) authorized the issue of $250,000,000 bonds, with interest at not exceeding 7 per centum per annum, redeemable after twenty years. The act of August 5, 1861, (12 Statutes, 313,) authorized the issue of bonds, with interest at 6 per centum per annum, payable after twenty years from date, in exchange for 7-30 notes issued under the act of July 17, 1861. None of such bonds were to be issued for a sum less than $500, and the whole amount of them was not to exceed the whole amount of 7-30 notes issued under the above act of July 17. The amount issued in exchange for 7-30's was $139,321,200.	20 years	July 1, 1881	6 per cent	Par	250,000,000 00	50,000,000 00 139,321,200 00	189,321,200 00

TABLE O.—*Statement of the outstanding principal of the public debt, &c.*—Continued.

	Length of loan.	When redeemable.	Rate of interest.	Price at which sold.	Amount authorized.	Amount issued.	Amount outstanding.
OLD DEMAND NOTES.							
The act of July 17, 1861, (12 Statutes, 259,) authorized the issue of $50,000,000 Treasury notes, not bearing interest, of a less denomination than fifty dollars and not less than ten dollars, and payable on demand by the Assistant Treasurers at Philadelphia, New York, or Boston. The act of August 5, 1861, (12 Statutes, 313,) authorized the issue of these notes in denominations of five dollars; it also added the Assistant Treasurer at Saint Louis and the designated depositary at Cincinnati to the places where these notes were made payable. The act of February 12, 1862, (12 Statutes, 338,) increased the amount of demand notes authorized $10,000,000.	....	On demand....	None	Par.....	$60,000,000 00	$60,030,000 00	$88,296 25
SEVEN-THIRTIES OF 1861.							
The act of July 17, 1861, (12 Statutes, 259,) authorized a loan of $250,000,000, part of which was to be in Treasury notes, with interest at 7 3-10 per centum per annum, payable three years after date.	3 years......	August 19 and October 1, 1864.	7 3-10 per ct.	Par.....	140,094,750 00	140,094,750 00	20,000 00
FIVE-TWENTIES OF 1862.							
The act of February 25, 1862, (12 Statutes, 345,) authorized a loan of $500,000,000, for the purpose of funding the Treasury notes and floating debt of the United States, and the issue of bonds therefor, with interest at 6 per centum per annum. These bonds were redeemable after five and payable twenty years from date. The act of March 3, 1864, (13 Statutes, 13,) authorized an additional issue of $11,000,000 of bonds to persons who subscribed for the loan on or before January 21, 1864. The act of January 28, 1865, (13 Statutes, 425,) authorized an additional issue of $4,000,000 of these bonds, and their sale in the United States or Europe.	5 or 20 years.	May 1, 1867...	6 per cent...	Par.....	515,000,000 00	514,771,600 00	279,498,750 00
LEGAL-TENDER NOTES.							
The act of February 25, 1862, (12 Statutes, 345,) authorized the issue of $150,000,000 United States notes, not bearing interest, payable to bearer at the Treasury of the United States, and of such denominations, not less than five dollars, as the Secretary of the Treasury might deem expedient, $50,000,000 to be in lieu of demand notes authorized by the act of July 17, 1861; these notes to be a legal tender. The act of July 11, 1862, (12 Statutes, 532,) authorized an additional issue of $150,000,000 United States Treasury notes, of such denominations as the Secretary of the Treasury might deem expedi-	....	On demand ...	None	Par.....	450,000,000 00	915,420,031 00	357,500,000 00

not more than $35,000,000 of a lower denomination than five dollars; these notes to be a legal tender. The act of March 3, 1863, (12 Statutes, 710,) authorized an additional issue of $150,000,000 United States notes, payable to bearer, of such denominations, not less than one dollar, as the Secretary of the Treasury might prescribe; which notes were made a legal tender. The same act limited the time at which Treasury notes might be exchanged for United States bonds to July 1, 1863. The amount of notes authorized by this act were to be in lieu of $100,000,000 authorized by the resolution of January 17, 1863, (12 Statutes, 822.)							
TEMPORARY LOAN.							
The act of February 25, 1862, (12 Statutes, 346,) authorized temporary loan deposits of $25,000,000, for not less than thirty days, with interest at 5 per centum per annum, payable after ten days' notice. The act of March 17, 1862, (12 Statutes, 370,) authorized the increase of temporary loan deposits to $50,000,000. The act of July 11, 1862, (12 Statutes, 532,) authorized a further increase of temporary loan deposits to $100,000,000. The act of June 30, 1864, (13 Statutes, 218,) authorized a further increase of temporary loan deposits to not exceeding $150,000,000, and an increase of the rate of interest to not exceeding 6 per centum per annum, or a decrease of the rate of interest on ten days' notice, as the public interest might require.	Not less than 30 days.	After 10 days' notice.	4, 5, and 6 per cent.	Par	150,000,000 00	....	78,560 00
CERTIFICATES OF INDEBTEDNESS.							
The act of March 1, 1862, (12 Statutes, 352,) authorized the issue of certificates of indebtedness to public creditors who might elect to receive them, to bear interest at the rate of 6 per centum per annum, and payable one year from date, or earlier, at the option of the Government. The act of May 17, 1862, (12 Statutes, 370,) authorized the issue of these certificates in payment of disbursing officers' checks. The act of March 3, 1863, (12 Statutes, 710,) made the interest payable in lawful money.	1 year	1 year after date.	6 per cent ...	Par	No limit	561,753,241 65	5,000 00
FRACTIONAL CURRENCY.							
The act of July 17, 1862, (12 Statutes, 592,) authorized the use of postal and other stamps as currency, and made them receivable in payment of all dues to the United States less than five dollars. The fourth section of the act of March 3, 1863, (12 Statutes, 711,) authorized the issue of fractional notes in lieu of postal and other stamps and postal currency; made them exchangeable in sums not less than three dollars for United States notes, and receivable for postage and revenue stamps, and in payment of dues to the United States, except duties on imports, less than five dollars; and limited the amount to $50,000,000. The fifth section of the act of June 30, 1864, (13 Statutes, 220,) authorized an issue of $50,000,000 in fractional currency, and provided that the whole amount of these notes, outstanding at any one time, should not exceed this sum.	....	On presentation.	None	Par	50,000,000 00	223,625,663 45	40,855,835 27

TABLE O.—*Statement of the outstanding principal of the public debt, &c.*—Continued.

	Length of loan.	When redeemable.	Rate of interest.	Price at which sold.	Amount authorized.	Amount issued.	Amount outstanding.
LOAN OF 1863.							
The act of March 3, 1863, (12 Statutes, 709,) authorized a loan of $900,000,000, and the issue of bonds, with interest at not exceeding six per centum per annum, and redeemable in not less than ten nor more than forty years, principal and interest payable in coin. The act of June 30, 1864, (13 Statutes, 219,) repeals so much of the preceding act as limits the authority thereunder to the current fiscal year, and also repeals the authority altogether except as relates to $75,000,000 of bonds already advertised for.	17 years.....	July 1, 1881....	6 per cent ...	Average premium of 4.13.	$75,000,000 00	$75,000,000 00	$75,000,000 00
ONE-YEAR NOTES OF 1863.							
The act of March 3, 1863, (12 Statutes, 710,) authorized the issue of $400,000,000 Treasury notes, with interest at not exceeding six per centum per annum, redeemable in not more than three years, principal and interest payable in lawful money, to be a legal tender for their face value.	1 year	1 year after date.	5 per cent ...	Par	400,000,000 00	44,520,000 00	101,817 00
TWO-YEAR NOTES OF 1863.							
The act of March 3, 1863, (12 Statutes, 710,) authorized the issue of $400,000,000 Treasury notes, with interest at not exceeding six per centum per annum, redeemable in not more than three years, principal and interest payable in lawful money, to be a legal tender for their face value.	2 years......	2 years after date.	5 per cent ...	Par	400,000,000 00	166,480,000 00	65,705 00
COIN-CERTIFICATES.							
The fifth section of the act of March 3, 1863, (12 Statutes, 711,) authorized the deposit of gold coin and bullion with the Treasurer or any Assistant Treasurer, in sums not less than $20, and the issue of certificates therefor in denominations the same as United States notes; also authorized the issue of these certificates in payment of interest on the public debt. It limits the amount of them to not more than 20 per centum of the amount of coin and bullion in the Treasury, and directs their receipt in payment for duties on imports.	....	On demand....	None........	Par	Indefinite.....	562,776,400 00	32,086,300 00
COMPOUND-INTEREST NOTES.							

act of June 30, 1864, (13 Statutes, 218,) authorized the issue of $200,000,000 Treasury notes, of any denomination not less than $10, payable not more than three years from date, or redeemable at any time after three years, with interest at not exceeding seven and three-tenths per centum, payable in lawful money at maturity, and made them a legal tender for their face to the same extent as United States notes; $177,045,770 of the amount issued was in redemption of 5 per cent. notes.							
TEN-FORTIES OF 1864.							
The act of March 3, 1864, (13 Statutes, 13,) authorized the issue of $200,000,000 bonds, at not exceeding six per centum per annum, redeemable after five and payable not more than forty years from date, in coin.	10 or 40 years	March 1, 1874..	5 per cent ...	Par to 7 per c't. prem.	200, 000, 000 00	$196, 117, 300 00	194, 567, 300 00
FIVE-TWENTIES OF MARCH, 1864.							
The act of March 3, 1864, (13 Statutes, 13,) authorized the issue of $200,000,000 bonds, at not exceeding six per centum per annum, redeemable after five and payable not more thau forty years from date, in coin.	5 or 20 years.	Nov. 1, 1869 ...	6 per cent ...	Par	....	3, 882, 500 00	2, 349, 500 00
FIVE-TWENTIES OF JUNE, 1864.							
The act of June 30, 1864, (13 Statutes, 218,) authorized a loan of $400,000,000, and the issue therefor of bonds redeemable not less than five nor more than thirty (or forty, if deemed expedient) years from date, with interest at not exceeding 6 per centum per annum, payable semi-annually, in coin.	5 or 20 years.	Nov. 1, 1869 ...	6 per cent...	Par.....	400, 000, 000 00	125, 561, 300 00	72, 846, 150 00
SEVEN-THIRTIES OF 1864 AND 1865.							
The act of June 30, 1864, (13 Statutes, 218,) authorized the issue of $200,000,000 Treasury notes, of not less than $10 each, payable at not more than three years from date, or redeemable at any time after three years, with interest at not exceeding 7 3-10 per centum per annum. The act of March 3, 1865, (13 Statutes, 468,) authorized a loan of $600,000,000, and the issue therefor of bonds or Treasury notes. The notes to be of denominations not less than $50, with interest in lawful money at not more than 7 3-10 per centum per annum.	3 years....	Aug. 15, 1867 June 15, 1868 July 15, 1868	7 3-10 per ct.	Par.....	800, 000, 000 00	829, 992, 500 00	332, 150 00
NAVY PENSION FUND.							
The act of July 1, 1864, (13 Statutes, 414,) authorized the Secretary of the Navy to invest in registered securities of the United States so much of the Navy pension fund in the Treasury January 1 and July 1 in each year as would not be required for the payment of naval pensions. Section 2 of the act of July 23, 1868, (15 Statutes, 170,) makes the interest on this fund 3 per centum per annum in lawful money, and confines its use to the payment of naval pensions exclusively.	Indefinite...	....	3 per cent...	Par.....	Indefinite.....	14, 000, 000 00	14, 000, 000 00

TABLE O.—*Statement of the outstanding principal of the public debt, &c.*—Continued.

	Length of loan.	When redeemable.	Rate of interest.	Price at which sold.	Amount authorized.	Amount issued.	Amount outstanding.
FIVE-TWENTIES OF 1865.							
The act of March 3, 1865, (13 Statutes, 468,) authorized the issue of $600,000,000 of bonds or Treasury notes in addition to amounts previously authorized; the bonds to be for not less than $50, payable not more than forty years from date of issue, or after any period not less than five years; interest payable semi-annually at not exceeding 6 per centum per annum when in coin, or 7 3-10 per centum per annum when in currency. In addition to the amount of bonds authorized by this act, authority was also given to convert Treasury notes or other interest-bearing obligations into bonds authorized by it. The act of April 12, 1866, (14 Statutes, 31,) construed the above act to authorize the Secretary of the Treasury to receive any obligations of the United States, whether bearing interest or not, in exchange for any bonds authorized by it, or to sell any of such bonds, provided the public debt is not increased thereby.	5 or 20 years.	Nov. 1, 1870 ...	6 per cent...	Par.....	$203, 327, 250 00	$203, 327, 250 00	$159, 499, 650 00
CONSOLS OF 1865.							
The act of March 3, 1865, (13 Statutes, 468,) authorized the issue of $600,000,000 of bonds or Treasury notes in addition to amounts previously authorized; the bonds to be for not less than $50, payable not more than forty years from date of issue, or after any period not less than five years, interest payable semi-annually, at not exceeding 6 per centum per annum when in coin, or 7 3-10 per centum per annum when in currency. In addition to the amount of bonds authorized by this act, authority was also given to convert Treasury notes or other interest-bearing obligations into bonds authorized by it. The act of April 12, 1866, (14 Statutes, 31,) construed the above act to authorize the Secretary of the Treasury to receive any obligations of the United States, whether bearing interest or not, in exchange for any bonds authorized by it, or to sell any of such bonds, provided the public debt is not increased thereby.	5 or 20 years.	July 1, 1870 ...	6 per cent...	Par.....	332, 998, 950 00	332, 998, 950 00	222, 277, 300 00
CONSOLS OF 1867.							
The act of March 3, 1865, (13 Statutes, 468,) authorized the issue of $600,000,000 of bonds or Treasury notes in addition to amounts previously authorized; the bonds to be for not less than $50, payable not more than forty years from date of issue, or after any period not less than five years; interest payable semi-annually, at not exceeding 6 per centum per annum when in coin, or 7 3-10 per centum per annum when in currency. In addition to the amount of bonds	5 or 20 years.	July 1, 1872 ...	6 per cent...	Par.....	379, 602, 350 00	379, 616, 050 00	320, 299, 350 00

notes or other interest-bearing obligations into bonds authorized by it. The act of April 12, 1866, (14 Statutes, 31,) construed the above act to authorize the Secretary of the Treasury to receive any obligation of the United States, whether bearing interest or not, in exchange for any bonds authorized by it, or to sell any of such bonds, provided the public debt is not increased thereby.							
CONSOLS OF 1868.							
The act of March 3, 1865, (13 Statutes, 468,) authorized the issue of $600,000,000 of bonds or Treasury notes in addition to amounts previously authorized; the bonds to be for not less than $50, payable not more than forty years from the date of issue, or after any period not less than five years; interest payable semi-annually, at not exceeding 6 per centum per annum, when in coin, or 7 3-10 per centum per annum, when in currency. In addition to the amount of bonds authorized by this act, authority was also given to convert Treasury notes or other interest-bearing obligations into bonds authorized by it. The act of April 12, 1866, (14 Statutes, 31,) construed the above act to authorize the Secretary of the Treasury to receive any obligation of the United States, whether bearing interest or not, in exchange for any bonds authorized by it, or to sell any of such bonds, provided the public debt is not increased thereby.	5 or 20 years.	July 1, 1873 ...	6 per cent...	Par	42, 539, 350 00	42, 539, 350 00	39, 258, 450 00
THREE PER CENT. CERTIFICATES.							
The act of March 3, 1867, (14 Statutes, 558,) authorized the issue of $50,000,000 in temporary loan certificates of deposit, with interest at 3 per centum per annum, payable in lawful money on demand, to be used in redemption of compound-interest notes. The act of July 25, 1868, (15 Statutes, 183) authorized $25,000,000 additional of these certificates for the sole purpose of redeeming compound-interest notes.	Indefinite...	On demand ...	3 per cent...	Par	75, 000, 000 00	85, 150, 000 00	12, 220, 000 00
CERTIFICATES OF INDEBTEDNESS OF 1870.							
The act of July 8, 1870, (16 Statutes, 197,) authorized the issue of certificates of indebtedness, payable five years after date, with interest at 4 per centum per annum, payable semi-annually, principal and interest, in lawful money, to be hereafter appropriated and provided for by Congress. These certificates were issued, one-third to the State of Maine, and two-thirds to the State of Massachusetts, both for the use and benefit of the European and North American Railway Company, and were in full adjustment and payment of any and all claims of said States or railway company for moneys expended (or interest thereon) by the State of Massachusetts on account of the war of 1812-'15.	5 years	Sept. 1, 1875...	4 per cent...	Par	678, 362 41	678, 362 41	678, 000 00

TABLE O.—*Statement of the outstanding principal of the public debt, &c.*—Continued.

	Length of loan.	When redeemable.	Rate of interest.	Price at which sold.	Amount authorized.	Amount issued.	Amount outstanding.
FUNDED LOAN OF 1881.							
The act of July 14, 1870, (16 Statutes, 272,) authorizes the issue of $200,000,000 at 5 per centum, $300,000,000 at 4½ per centum, and $1,000,000,000 at 4 per centum, principal and interest payable in coin of the present standard value, at the pleasure of the United States Government, after ten years, for the 5 per cents; after fifteen years, for the 4½ per cents; and after thirty years, for the 4 per cents; these bonds to be exempt from the payment of all taxes or duties of the United States, as well as from taxation in any form, by or under State, municipal, or local authority. Bonds and coupons payable at the Treasury of the United States. This act not to authorize an increase of the bonded debt of the United States. Bonds to be sold at not less than par in coin, and the proceeds to be applied to the redemption of outstanding 5-20's, or to be exchanged for said 5-20's, par for par. Payment of these bonds, when due, to be made in order of dates and numbers, beginning with each class last dated and numbered. Interest to cease at the end of three months from notice of intention to redeem. The act of January 20, 1871, (16 Statutes, 399,) increases the amount of 5 per cents to $500,000,000, provided the total amount of bonds issued shall not exceed the amount originally authorized, and authorizes the interest on any of these bonds to be paid quarterly.	10 years....	May 1, 1881....	5 per cent...	Par.....	$500,000,000 00	$200,000,000 00	$200,000,000 00
	....	....	....	....	....	....	$2,253,251,328 78

TABLE. P.—*Statement of 30-year 6 per cent. bonds (interest payable January and July) issued to the several Pacific Railway companies, under the acts of July 1, 1862, (12 Statutes, 492,) and July 2, 1864, (13 Statutes, 359.)*

Railway companies.	Amount of bonds outstanding.	Amount of interest accrued and paid to date, as per preceding statement.	Amount of interest due, as per Register's schedule.	Total interest paid by the United States.	Repayment of interest by transportation of mails, troops, &c.	Balance due the United States on interest account, deducting repayments.	Balance of accrued interest due the United States on interest account.	Total amount of interest due the United States from Pacific Railway companies.
On July 1, 1865:								
Central Pacific	$1,258,000 00		$37,740 00	$37,740 00				$37,740 00
Kansas Pacific								
Union Pacific								
Central Branch Union Pacific								
Western Pacific								
Sioux City and Pacific								
	1,258,000 00		37,740 00	37,740 00				37,740 00
On January 1, 1866:								
Central Pacific	2,362,000 00	$37,740 00	55,056 83	92,796 83				92,796 83
Kansas Pacific	640,000 00		6,417 53	6,417 53				6,417 53
Union Pacific								
Central Branch Union Pacific								
Western Pacific								
Sioux City and Pacific								
	3,002,000 00	37,740 00	61,474 36	99,214 36				99,214 36
On July 1, 1866:								
Central Pacific	3,002,000 00	92,796 83	83,169 03	175,965 86				175,965 86
Kansas Pacific	1,360,000 00	6,417 53	33,026 56	39,444 09				39,444 09
Union Pacific	1,680,000 00		19,917 09	19,917 09				19,917 09
Central Branch Union Pacific								
Western Pacific								
Sioux City and Pacific								
	6,042,000 00	99,214 36	136,112 68	235,327 04				235,327 04
On January 1, 1867:								
Central Pacific	3,962,000 00	175,965 86	111,837 51	287,803 37				287,803 37
Kansas Pacific	2,080,000 00	39,444 09	55,186 84	94,630 93				94,630 93
Union Pacific	4,320,000 00	19,917 09	97,755 65	117,672 74				117,672 74
Central Branch Union Pacific	640,000 00		10,099 74	10,099 74				10,099 74

TABLE P.—*Statement of 30-year 6 per cent. bonds (interest payable January and July) issued to the several Pacific Railway companies, &c.*—Continued.

Railway companies.	Amount of bonds outstanding.	Amount of interest accrued and paid to date as per preceding statement.	Amount of interest due, as per Register's schedule.	Total interest paid by the United States.	Repayment of interest by transportation of mails, troops, &c.	Balance due the United States on interest account, deducting repayments.	Balance of accrued interest due the United States on interest account.	Total amount of interest due the United States from Pacific Railway companies.
On January 1, 1867.—Continued.								
Western Pacific								
Sioux City and Pacific								
	$11, 002, 000 00	$235, 327 04	$274, 879 74	$510, 206 78				$510, 206 78
On July 1, 1867:								
Central Pacific	4, 602, 000 00	287, 803 37	136, 534 50	424, 337 87	22, 849 07	401, 488 80		401, 488 80
Kansas Pacific	3, 360, 000 00	94, 630 93	78, 654 29	173, 285 22	27, 444 40	145, 840 82		145, 840 82
Union Pacific	5, 520, 000 00	117, 672 74	147, 826 87	265, 499 61		265, 499 61		265, 499 61
Central Branch Union Pacific	960, 000 00	10, 099 74	22, 408 75	32, 508 49		32, 508 49		32, 508 49
Western Pacific	320, 000 00		8, 206 03	8, 206 03		8, 206 03		8, 206 03
Sioux City and Pacific								
	14, 762, 000 00	510, 206 78	393, 630 44	903, 837 22	50, 293 47	853, 543 75		853, 543 75
On January 1, 1868:								
Central Pacific	6, 074, 000 00	424, 337 87	145, 613 83	509, 951 70	29, 899 07	540, 052 63		540, 052 63
Kansas Pacific	4, 880, 000 00	173, 285 22	122, 580 26	295, 865 48	148, 935 26	146, 930 22		146, 930 22
Union Pacific	8, 160, 000 00	265, 499 61	210, 562 28	476, 061 89	249, 191 98	226, 869 91		226, 869 91
Central Branch Union Pacific	1, 280, 000 00	32, 508 49	30, 325 50	62, 833 99		62, 833 99		62, 833 99
Western Pacific	320, 000 00	8, 206 03	9, 600 00	17, 806 03		17, 806 03		17, 806 03
Sioux City and Pacific								
	20, 714, 000 00	903, 837 22	518 681 87	1, 422, 519 09	428, 026 31	994, 492 78		994, 492 78
On July 1, 1868:								
Central Pacific	7, 920, 000 00	569, 951 70	185, 641 16	755, 592 86	36, 949 07	718, 643 79		718, 643 79
Kansas Pacific	6, 080, 000 00	295, 865 48	165, 258 16	461, 123 64	266, 367 71	194, 755 93		194, 755 93
Union Pacific	12, 957, 000 00	476, 061 89	288, 593 86	764, 655 75	524, 853 03	243, 802 72		243, 802 72
Central Branch Union Pacific	1, 600, 000 00	62, 833 99	46, 974 27	109, 808 26		109, 808 26		109, 808 26
Western Pacific	320, 000 00	17, 806 03	9, 600 00	27, 406 03		27, 406 03		27, 406 03
Sioux City and Pacific	1, 112, 000 00		19, 603 76	19, 603 76		19, 603 76		19, 603 76
	29, 089, 000 00	1, 422, 519 09	715, 671 21	2, 138, 190 30	828, 169 81	1, 314, 020 49		1, 314, 020 49

On January 1, 1869:								
Central Pacific	16,624,000 00	755,592 86	347,193 73	1,102,786 59	46,158 10	1,056,628 49	....	1,056,628 49
Kansas Pacific	6,303,000 00	461,123 64	184,599 45	645,723 09	368,406 97	277,316 12	....	277,316 12
Union Pacific	24,078,000 00	764,655 75	549,109 77	1,313,765 52	719,214 87	594,550 65	....	594,550 65
Central Branch Union Pacific	1,600,000 00	109,808 26	48,000 00	157,808 26	....	157,808 26	....	157,808 26
Western Pacific	320,000 00	27,406 03	9,600 00	37,006 03	....	37,006 03	....	37,006 03
Sioux City and Pacific	1,112,000 00	19,603 76	33,360 00	52,963 76	16 27	52,947 49	....	52,947 49
	50,097,000 00	2,138,190 30	1,171,862 95	3,310,053 25	1,133,796 21	2,176,257 04	....	2,176,257 04
On July 1, 1869:								
Central Pacific	22,789,000 00	1,102,786 59	616,429 59	1,719,216 18	72,666 99	1,646,549 19	....	1,646,549 19
Kansas Pacific	6,303,000 00	645,723 09	189,090 00	834,813 09	546,569 10	288,243 99	....	288,243 99
Union Pacific	25,996,000 00	1,313,765 52	768,104 37	2,081,869 89	906,446 11	1,175,423 78	....	1,175,423 78
Central Branch Union Pacific	1,600,000 00	157,808 26	48,000 00	205,808 26	3,490 79	202,317 47	....	202,317 47
Western Pacific	320,000 00	37,006 03	9,600 00	46,606 03	....	46,606 03	....	46,606 03
Sioux City and Pacific	1,628,320 00	52,963 76	43,544 93	96,508 69	16 27	96,492 42	....	96,492 42
	58,638,320 00	3,310,053 25	1,674,768 89	4,984,822 14	1,529,189 26	3,455,632 88	....	3,455,632 88
On January 1, 1870:								
Central Pacific	25,881,000 00	1,719,216 18	772,528 08	2,491,744 26	116,765 86	2,374,978 40	....	2,374,978 40
Kansas Pacific	6,303,000 00	834,813 09	189,090 00	1,023,903 09	631,224 99	392,678 10	....	392,678 10
Union Pacific	27,075,000 00	2,081,869 89	809,859 96	2,891,729 85	1,107,427 54	1,784,302 31	....	1,784,302 31
Central Branch Union Pacific	1,600,000 00	205,808 26	48,000 00	253,808 26	5,301 92	248,506 34	....	248,506 34
Western Pacific	1,648,000 00	46,606 03	26,682 73	73,288 76	....	73,288 76	....	73,288 76
Sioux City and Pacific	1,628,320 00	96,508 69	48,849 60	145,358 29	369 40	144,988 89	....	144,988 89
	64,135,320 00	4,984,822 14	1,895,010 37	6,879,832 51	1,861,089 71	5,018,742 80	....	5,018,742 80
On July 1, 1870:								
Central Pacific	25,881,000 00	2,491,744 26	770,023 58	3,261,767 84	164,054 17	3,097,713 67	$155,730 40	3,253,444 07
Kansas Pacific	6,303,000 00	1,023,903 09	189,090 00	1,212,993 09	684,359 12	528,633 97	28,717 58	557,351 55
Union Pacific	27,075,000 00	2,891,729 85	821,641 20	3,713,371 05	1,289,576 87	2,423,794 18	67,767 69	2,491,561 87
Central Branch Union Pacific	1,600,000 00	253,808 26	48,000 00	301,808 26	7,401 92	294,406 34	17,857 43	312,263 77
Western Pacific	1,970,000 00	73,288 76	57,908 60	131,197 36	....	131,197 36	4,274 71	135,472 07
Sioux City and Pacific	1,628,320 00	145,358 29	48,849 60	194,207 89	396 08	193,811 81	5,154 20	198,966 01
	64,457,320 00	6,879,832 51	1,935,512 98	8,815,345 49	2,145,788 16	6,669,557 33	279,502 01	6,949,059 34
On January 1, 1871:								
Central Pacific	25,881,000 00	3,261,767 84	776,430 00	4,038,197 84	241,638 70	3,796,559 14	326,995 81	4,123,554 95
Kansas Pacific	6,303,000 00	1,212,993 09	189,090 00	1,402,083 09	768,148 66	633,934 43	56,879 25	690,813 68
Union Pacific	27,236,512 00	3,713,371 05	817,095 36	4,530,466 41	1,434,952 33	3,095,514 08	194,389 56	3,289,903 64
Central Branch Union Pacific	1,600,000 00	301,808 26	48,000 00	349,808 26	7,401 92	342,406 34	35,410 83	377,817 17
Western Pacific	1,970,000 00	131,197 36	59,100 00	190,297 36	8,281 25	182,016 11	10,598 09	192,614 20
Sioux City and Pacific	1,628,320 00	194,207 89	48,849 60	243,057 49	396 08	242,664 41	15,762 43	258,423 84
	64,618,832 00	8,815,345 49	1,938,564 96	10,753,910 45	2,460,818 94	8,293,091 51	640,035 97	8,933,127 48

TABLE P.—*Statement of 30-year 6 per cent. bonds (interest payable January and July) issued to the several Pacific Railway companies, &c.*—Continued.

Railway companies.	Amount of bonds outstanding.	Amount of interest accrued and paid to date, as per preceding statement.	Amount of interest due, as per Register's schedule.	Total interest paid by the United States.	Repayment of interest by transportation of mails, troops, &c.	Balance due the United States on interest account, deducting repayments.	Balance of accrued interest due the United States on interest account.	Total amount of interest due the United States from Pacific Railway companies.
On July 1, 1871.								
Central Pacific	$25, 881, 000 00	$4, 038, 197 84	$776, 430 00	$4, 814, 627 84	$343, 266 90	$4, 471, 360 94	$449, 753 57	$4, 921, 114 51
Kansas Pacific	6, 303, 000 00	1, 402, 083 09	189, 090 00	1, 591, 173 09	857, 330 93	733, 842 16	76, 932 82	810, 774 98
Union Pacific	27, 236, 512 00	4, 530, 466 41	817, 095 36	5, 347, 561 77	1, 755, 303 15	3, 592, 258 62	289, 874 27	3, 882, 132 89
Central Branch Union Pacific	1, 600, 000 00	349, 808 26	48, 000 00	397, 808 26	9, 276 92	388, 531 34	46, 725 32	435, 256 66
Western Pacific	1, 970, 000 00	190, 297 36	59, 100 00	249, 397 36	8, 281 25	241, 116 11	16, 376 52	257, 492 63
Sioux City and Pacific	1, 628, 320 00	243, 057 49	48, 849 60	291, 907 09	401 88	291, 505 21	23, 515 13	315, 020 34
	64, 618, 832 00	10, 753, 910 45	1, 938, 564 96	12, 692, 475 41	2, 973, 861 03	9, 718, 614 38	903, 177 63	10, 621, 792 01
On January 1, 1872.								
Central Pacific	25, 881, 000 00	4, 814, 627 84	776, 430 00	5, 591, 057 84	422, 556 33	5, 168, 501 51	595, 968 12	5, 764, 469 63
Kansas Pacific	6, 303, 000 00	1, 591, 173 09	189, 090 00	1, 780, 263 09	927, 829 30	852, 433 79	100, 272 17	952, 705 96
Union Pacific	27, 236, 512 00	5, 347, 561 77	817, 095 36	6, 164, 657 13	1, 964, 850 08	4, 199, 807 05	402, 429 22	4, 602, 236 27
Central Branch Union Pacific	1, 600, 000 00	397, 808 26	48, 000 00	445, 808 26	9, 276 92	436, 531 34	59, 783 02	496, 314 36
Western Pacific	1, 970, 000 00	249, 397 36	59, 100 00	308, 497 36	9, 350 25	299, 147 11	24, 078 92	323, 226 03
Sioux City and Pacific	1, 628, 320 00	291, 907 09	48, 849 60	340, 756 69	401 88	340, 354 81	32, 965 74	373, 320 55
	64, 618, 832 00	12, 692, 475 41	1, 938, 564 96	14, 631, 040 37	3, 334, 264 76	11, 296, 775 61	1, 215, 497 19	12, 512, 272 80
On July 1, 1872:								
Central Pacific	25, 885, 120 00	*5, 591, 057 84	*777, 318 23	6, 368, 376 07	†527, 025 39	5, 841, 350 68	766, 898 68	6, 608, 249 36
Kansas Pacific	6, 303, 000 00	1, 780, 263 09	189, 090 00	1, 969, 353 09	973, 904 69	995, 448 40	128, 262 25	1, 123, 710 65
Union Pacific	27, 236, 512 00	6, 164, 657 13	817, 095 36	6, 981, 752 49	2, 181, 989 43	4, 799, 763 06	537, 973 22	5, 337, 736 28
Central Branch Union Pacific	1, 600, 000 00	445, 808 26	48, 000 00	493, 808 26	†15, 839 42	477, 968 84	74, 538 53	552, 507 37
Western Pacific	1, 970, 560 00	*308, 497 36	*59, 181 98	367, 679 34	9, 350 25	358, 329 09	33, 775 70	392, 104 79
Sioux City and Pacific	1, 628, 320 00	340, 756 69	48, 849 60	389, 606 29	825 60	386, 780 69	44, 165 12	432, 945 81
	64, 623, 512 00	14, 631, 040 37	1, 939, 535 17	16, 570, 575 54	3, 708, 934 78	12, 861, 640 76	1, 585, 613 50	14, 447, 254 26

* These figures will be found to vary from those in the statement of the public debt for July 1, 1872. The differences are: In the Central Pacific account this statement is $764.63 and in the Western Pacific account $65.18 less than is shown by the debt statement for the same items in the first column, and the same amounts more in the second column. This difference arises out of the issue of $4,120 in bonds to the first-named road and $560 in bonds to the last named, in final settlement of their account. The interest on these bonds was paid on special schedules and the amount was included in the debt statement as paid, without being shown in the "Interest due and not yet paid" column. The subsequent statements of the debt will be found to agree with this statement.

† In the debt statement for July 1, 1872, these items differ from this statement by $4,687.50, arising from this amount, earned by the Central Branch Union Pacific, having been credited in the stock-ledger to the Central Pacific. The error was not discovered until the accounts of the several roads were settled in October, 1872, and after that date the error is corrected in the debt statement.

TABLE Q.—*Statement showing the reduction of the principal and interest of the public debt of the United States, from March 1, 1869, to November 1, 1872.*

	Debt and interest less cash in Treasury.	Decrease of debt during preceding month.	Total decrease from March 1, 1869, to date.	Monthly interest charge.	Decrease in monthly interest charge.	Decrease in annual interest charge.
1869.						
Mar. 1	$2, 525, 463, 260 01	....	....	$10, 532, 462 50	....	....
April 1	2, 525, 196, 461 74	$266, 798 27	....	10, 526, 238 00	$6, 224 50	$74, 694 00
May 1	2, 518, 797, 391 09	6, 399, 070 65	$6, 665, 868 92	10, 522, 835 75	9, 626 75	115, 521 00
June 1	2, 505, 412, 613 12	13, 384, 777 97	20, 050, 646 89	10, 507, 090 25	25, 372 25	304, 467 00
July 1	2, 489, 002, 480 58	16, 410, 132 54	36, 460, 779 43	10, 476, 840 25	55, 622 25	667, 467 00
Aug. 1	2, 481, 566, 736 29	7, 435, 744 29	43, 896, 523 72	10, 383, 568 75	148, 893 75	1, 786, 725 00
Sept. 1	2, 475, 962, 501 50	5, 604, 234 79	49, 500, 758 51	10, 333, 518 75	198, 943 75	2, 387, 325 00
Oct. 1	2, 468, 495, 072 11	7, 467, 429 39	56, 968, 187 90	10, 252, 933 75	279, 528 75	3, 354, 345 00
Nov. 1	2, 461, 131, 189 36	7, 363, 882 75	64, 332, 070 65	10, 194, 903 75	337, 558 75	4, 050, 705 00
Dec. 1	2, 453, 559, 735 23	7, 571, 454 13	71, 903, 524 78	10, 130, 625 75	401, 836 75	4, 822, 041 00
1870.						
Jan. 1	2, 448, 746, 953 31	4, 812, 781 92	76, 716, 306 70	10, 061, 506 25	470, 956 25	5, 651, 475 00
Feb. 1	2, 444, 813, 288 92	3, 933, 664 39	80, 649, 971 09	10, 022, 498 00	509, 964 50	6, 119, 574 00
Mar. 1	2, 438, 328, 477 17	6, 484, 811 75	87, 134, 782 84	10, 007, 312 75	525, 149 75	6, 301, 797 00
April 1	2, 432, 562, 127 74	5, 766, 349 43	92, 901, 132 27	9, 982, 350 00	550, 112 50	6, 601, 350 00
May 1	2, 420, 864, 334 35	11, 697, 793 39	104, 598, 925 66	9, 956, 759 50	575, 703 00	6, 908, 436 00
June 1	2, 406, 562, 371 78	14, 301, 962 57	118, 900, 888 23	9, 926, 762 75	605, 699 75	7, 268, 397 00
July 1	2, 386, 358, 599 74	20, 203, 772 04	139, 104, 660 27	9, 886, 812 75	645, 649 75	7, 747, 797 00
Aug. 1	2, 369, 324, 476 00	17, 034, 123 74	156, 138, 784 01	9, 854, 633 00	677, 829 50	8, 133, 954 00
Sept. 1	2, 355, 921, 150 41	13, 403, 325 59	169, 542, 109 60	9, 814, 590 00	717, 872 50	8, 614, 470 00
Oct. 1	2, 346, 913, 652 28	9, 007, 498 13	178, 549, 607 73	9, 768, 940 00	763, 522 50	9, 162, 270 00
Nov. 1	2, 341, 784, 355 55	5, 129, 296 73	183, 678, 904 46	9, 718, 436 58	814, 025 92	9, 768, 311 04
Dec. 1	2, 334, 308, 494 65	7, 475, 860 90	191, 154, 765 36	9, 686, 164 42	846, 298 08	10, 155, 576 96
1871.						
Jan. 1	2, 332, 067, 793 75	2, 240, 700 90	193, 395, 466 26	9, 644, 043 63	888, 418 87	10, 661, 026 44
Feb. 1	2, 328, 026, 807 00	4, 040, 986 75	197, 436, 453 01	9, 610, 386 13	922, 076 37	11, 064, 916 44
Mar. 1	2, 320, 708, 846 92	7, 317, 960 08	204, 754, 413 09	9, 571, 007 41	961, 455 09	11, 537, 461 08
April 1	2, 309, 697, 596 27	11, 011, 250 65	215, 765, 663 74	9, 527, 212 67	1, 005, 249 83	12, 062, 997 96
May 1	2, 303, 572, 543 14	6, 124, 053 13	221, 889, 716 87	9, 459, 959 17	1, 072, 503 33	12, 870, 039 96
June 1	2, 299, 134, 184 81	4, 439, 358 33	226, 329, 075 20	9, 408, 362 33	1, 124, 100 17	13, 489, 202 04
July 1	2, 292, 308, 034 90	7, 103, 349 91	233, 432, 425 11	9, 329, 110 87	1, 203, 351 63	14, 440, 219 56
Aug. 1	2, 283, 328, 857 98	8, 701, 976 92	242, 134, 402 03	9, 302, 345 50	1, 230, 117 00	14, 761, 404 00
Sept. 1	2, 274, 122, 560 38	9, 206, 297 60	251, 340, 699 63	9, 286, 615 46	1, 245, 847 04	14, 950, 164 48
Oct. 1	2, 260, 663, 939 87	13, 458, 620 51	264, 799, 320 14	9, 248, 001 83	1, 284, 460 67	15, 413, 528 04
Nov. 1	2, 251, 713, 448 03	8, 950, 491 84	273, 749, 811 98	9, 168, 453 42	1, 364, 009 08	16, 368, 108 96
Dec. 1	2, 248, 251, 367 85	3, 462, 080 18	277, 211, 892 16	9, 137, 342 83	1, 395, 119 67	16, 741, 436 04
1872.						
Jan. 1	2, 243, 838, 411 14	4, 412, 956 71	281, 624, 848 87	9, 101, 968 54	1, 430, 493 96	17, 065, 927 52
Feb. 1	2, 238, 204, 949 50	5, 633, 461 64	287, 258, 310 51	9, 065, 892 96	1, 466, 569 54	17, 598, 834 48
Mar. 1	2, 225, 813, 497 98	12, 391, 451 52	299, 649, 762 03	9, 015, 469 58	1, 516, 992 92	18, 203, 915 04
April 1	2, 210, 331, 529 34	15, 481, 968 64	315, 131, 730 67	8, 825, 416 50	1, 707, 046 00	20, 484, 552 00
May 1	2, 197, 743, 440 72	12, 588, 088 62	327, 719, 819 29	8, 743, 121 75	1, 789, 340 75	21, 472, 089 00
June 1	2, 193, 517, 378 94	4, 226, 061 78	331, 945, 881 07	8, 698, 919 25	1, 833, 543 25	22, 002, 519 00
July 1	2, 191, 486, 343 62	2, 031, 035 32	333, 976, 916 39	8, 665, 705 25	1, 866, 757 25	22, 401, 087 00
Aug. 1	2, 188, 058, 656 44	3, 427, 687 18	337, 404, 603 57	8, 648, 257 75	1, 884, 204 75	22, 610, 457 00
Sept. 1	2, 177, 322, 020 55	10, 736, 635 89	348, 141, 239 46	8, 599, 848 75	1, 932, 613 75	23, 191, 365 00
Oct. 1	2, 166, 994, 677 46	10, 327, 343 09	358, 468, 582 55	8, 566, 151 25	1, 966, 311 25	23, 595, 735 00
Nov. 1	2, 161, 766, 260 14	5, 228, 417 32	363, 696, 999 87	8, 516, 808 25	2, 015, 654 25	24, 187, 851 00

TABLE R.—*Returns, by award of the United States Court of Claims, of proceeds of property seized as captured or abandoned under the act of March* 12, 1863, *paid from July*, 1, 1871, *to June* 30, 1872.

Date.	To whom paid.	Amount.
July 6, 1871	Lewis Fried	$5,192 63
July 6, 1871	William Duggan	165 57
July 6, 1871	Thomasine B. Hoyt and James M. Latta	7,987 79
July 12, 1871	Henry Wurzburg and Simon Witkowski	56,790 51
July 12, 1871	Michael Gordon	993 42
July 18, 1871	Francis J. Rnekh	692 40
July 18, 1871	Jacob Cohen	2,649 12
July 27, 1871	William T. Porter	3,955 46
July 29, 1871	Patrick Kennedy	465 13
July 29, 1871	Charles and Margaret Schubert	624 70
Aug. 2, 1871	Joanna Moulton	2,803 30
Aug. 2, 1871	Terence Nugent, jr	2,166 72
Aug. 2, 1871	Charlotte M. E. Gallie	19,206 12
Aug. 2, 1871	James A. Seddon	43,022 50
Aug. 8, 1871	Lewis Ross	1,178 59
Aug. 8, 1871	Michael Boley	1,158 99
Aug. 14, 1871	Samuel Worthington's administratrix	157,342 13
Aug. 16, 1871	Philip Dzialynski, and Davis Greenfield	34,207 59
Aug. 25, 1871	Elias and Morris Brown	723 32
Aug. 25, 1871	Simon Gerstman	1,321 45
Aug. 25, 1871	Helen Aubert	698 90
Aug. 25, 1871	Finley Y. Clark	496 51
Aug. 25, 1871	Jacob Mayer	695 50
Aug. 25, 1871	Max S. Mayer	645 36
Aug. 25, 1871	Randolph Mott	8,992 81
Aug. 26, 1871	Louis de Bebian	15,653 75
Aug. 26, 1871	William J. Myers, Son & Co	50,002 14
Aug. 29, 1871	John W. Carmalt	218 79
Aug. 29, 1871	Patrick J. Coogan	420 50
Aug. 29, 1871	Margaret Bond	73 83
Aug. 29, 1871	George D. Cunningham	312 85
Aug. 29, 1871	John Deighen	74 00
Aug. 29, 1871	Joseph Mertens	94 19
Aug. 29, 1871	Patrick Moran	265 75
Aug. 29, 1871	Celestine Eslava	693 98
Aug. 29, 1871	Joseph Purcell	467 59
Aug. 29, 1871	Samuel G. Courtney	94 19
Aug. 29, 1871	Daniel Hans	11,413 80
Aug. 30, 1871	Mary Ann Cherrill	1,014 56
Aug. 30, 1871	James S. Rhodes, administrator	5,371 53
Sept. 1, 1871	James Mix	5,318 27
Sept. 1, 1871	Alexander and Hugh C. Lecky	2,233 00
Sept. 12, 1871	Francis T. Willis	22,186 38
Sept. 15, 1871	Andrew M. Ross, administrator	9,021 20
Sept. 20, 1871	William J. Minor's executrix	20,481 71
Sept. 27, 1871	Richard Kelly, administrator	760 92
Oct. 3, 1871	Maximilian A. Dauphin	15,665 75
Oct. 3, 1871	Louis F. Koester	15,103 60
Oct. 3, 1871	Frederick Chastanet	2,843 31
Oct. 23, 1871	Henry Schaben	7,450 65
Nov. 6, 1871	Max Levy	4,863 63
Nov. 6, 1871	Benjamin Mantoue	9,496 46
Nov. 14, 1871	Azariah Mims	719 88
Nov. 24, 1871	David and Thomas Harrison	51,161 13
Nov. 24, 1871	George Taylor and William Tipper	8,278 50
Nov. 24, 1871	Stephen Watson	69,539 40
Dec. 5, 1871	Shelden W. Wight	6,622 80
Feb. 2, 1872	Edward Laplante	112,659 25
Feb. 14, 1872	Victor F. Wilson's administrator	125,300 00
Mar. 11, 1872	Ralph Meldrim	7,233 99
Apr. 4, 1872	Thomas G. W. Crussell	26,275 62
Apr. 4, 1872	John Silvoy	27,715 38
Apr. 24, 1872	Jean Sauvestre	1,127 65
Apr. 26, 1872	Dolway B. Walkington	16,160 20
May 6, 1872	Catharine Peterson, administratrix	366 21
May 16, 1872	Oliver H. Long, guardian of Lida Moore	6,640 50
May 21, 1872	Ramon Molina	3,973 68
May 23, 1872	David Bush's executrix	11,203 20
May 23, 1872	John V. Sevier	5,181 48
May 27, 1872	Gustave A. Wirth	3,957 60
June 13, 1872	Joseph Block	22,848 00
June 14, 1872	John F. Hamilton	15,426 63
June 14, 1872	Harry Haym	69,077 46
June 14, 1872	James Foley	1,324 56
June 14, 1872	Edmund H. Martin	7,358 40
June 18, 1872	William Hunt	4,638 66
June 18, 1872	Wolfe Barnett	4,242 14
June 18, 1872	James Wilde, jr	862 82
June 18, 1872	James H. Johnson	19,472 13
June 20, 1872	George W. Carroll's executrix	93,353 65

TABLE S.—*Awards of the United States Court of Claims of proceeds of property seized as captured or abandoned under act of March 12, 1863, decreed but not paid during the fiscal year ending June 30, 1872.*

Date of decree.	Name of claimant.	Amount awarded.
Apr. 1, 1872	Eido F. Torck	$81, 340 23
Apr. 1, 1872	William W. Worthington	45, 177 00
Apr. 1, 1872	Asher Ayres	36, 643 97
Apr. 1, 1872	Melvin B. Wilbur	1, 173 07
Apr. 1, 1872	Simon Queyrouze's administrator	14, 592 00
Apr. 1, 1872	William and Robert McIntyre	5, 072 67
Apr. 1, 1872	Dominick O'Grady's executors	72, 450 00
Apr. 1, 1872	Daniel F. Lerguson	15, 343 88
Apr. 2, 1872	William H. Greene	10, 885 67
Apr. 8, 1872	James J. Waring	2, 629 95
Apr. 8, 1872	James K. Reilly	10, 519 80
Apr. 8, 1872	Albert Johnson's executrix, use of Tally	421 96
Apr. 8, 1872	Henry Lightfoot and David Flanders	14, 201 73
Apr. 8, 1872	George W. Anderson	6, 026 54
Apr. 8, 1872	William Hunter	3, 506 60
Apr. 8, 1872	Daniel H. Baldwin	12, 974 42
Apr. 8, 1872	James Cantwell	10, 817 39
Apr. 8, 1872	Theodore B. Marshall and George S. Marshall	14, 727 72
Apr. 8, 1872	Levi De Witt and Richard Morgan	11, 880 79
Apr. 8, 1872	Alexander Abrams	1, 577 97
Apr. 15, 1872	Esadore Cohn	6, 044 50
Apr. 15, 1872	Edward Padelford's executors	3, 476 85
Apr. 15, 1872	Edward Padelford's executors	9, 467 82
Apr. 15, 1872	Chandler H. Smith	26, 650 16
Apr. 15, 1872	Erastus Henry	5, 687 78
Apr. 15, 1872	John C. Schreiner and Sons	7, 519 19
Apr. 15, 1872	Samuel F. O'Neil	3, 155 94
Apr. 15, 1872	James W. and Harvey W. Lathrop	9, 039 61
Apr. 15, 1872	John Stevenson	1, 928 63
Apr. 15, 1872	John A. Simpson's administrators	12, 630 42
Apr. 15, 1872	Ezekiel E. Simpson	28, 380 13
Apr. 15, 1872	Eli Coté, use of J. C. Martin *et al*	10, 483 71
Apr. 16, 1872	Desiré Godet	5, 760 00
Apr. 17, 1872	Henry C. Freeman's administrator	58, 384 89
Apr. 22, 1872	Andrew Low	474, 685 89
Apr. 22, 1872	Adolph B. Woslow	5, 785 89
Apr. 22, 1872	Lawrence De Give	2, 317 90
Apr. 22, 1872	Herman Parker's administratrix	5, 600 00
Apr. 29, 1872	Edward Padelford's executors	18, 058 79
Apr. 29, 1872	Edwin Parsons	5, 417 61
Apr. 29, 1872	George Parsons	3, 611 78
Apr. 29, 1872	Edwin Parsons	10, 940 60
Apr. 29, 1872	George Parsons	7, 293 72
Apr. 29, 1872	Henry A. Richmond's administrator, and Samuel Wilmot	19, 006 78
Apr. 29, 1872	Anthony Fernandez	20, 668 94
Apr. 29, 1872	Michel Castille	18, 240 00
May 6, 1872	Ralph Meldrim	2, 717 61
May 6, 1872	Julius Witkowski	92, 547 00
May 6, 1872	Henry and Isaac Meinhard	10, 430 55
May 8, 1872	Alfred Austell	12, 325 88
May 8, 1872	Hibernia Armstrong	23, 097 72
May 8, 1872	William B. Adams	22, 430 20
May 8, 1872	Abraham Backer	44, 610 91
May 8, 1872	Luke Christie	4, 733 91
May 8, 1872	William Lattimore	701 32
May 8, 1872	Edward Lovell	6, 736 80
May 8, 1872	Edward and Nathaniel Lovell and William Lattimore	5, 557 05
May 8, 1872	Herman Bulwinkle	8, 541 31
May 8, 1872	Alexander Oldham	7, 000 00
May 8, 1872	Aaron Wilbur's executor	17, 883 66
May 8, 1872	John R. Wilder	15, 969 84
May 8, 1872	Edwin M. Price	68, 712 93
May 8, 1872	Simon Witkowski	20, 688 94
May 8, 1872	John K. Elgee's executrix	137, 882 62
May 8, 1872	Cornelius V. Woodruff and Adolph Bouchard	155, 922 26
May 8, 1872	Woodruff and Bouchard, use of Charles S. Lobdell	72, 365 95
May 13, 1872	William Lindon	1, 803 81
	Total	1, 804, 970 36

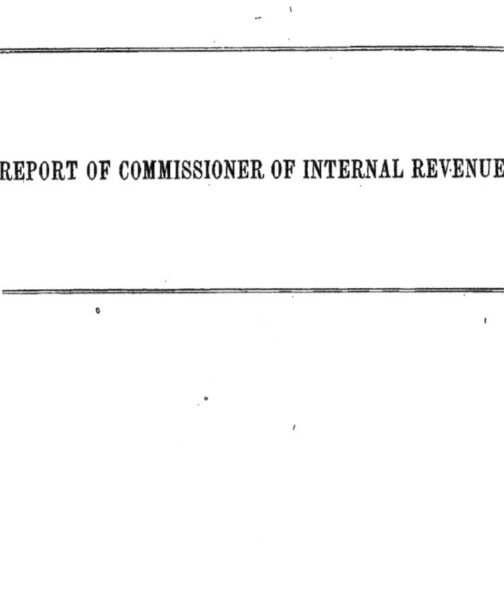

REPORT OF COMMISSIONER OF INTERNAL REVENUE.

REPORT

OF

THE COMMISSIONER OF INTERNAL REVENUE.

TREASURY DEPARTMENT, OFFICE OF INTERNAL REVENUE,
Washington, November 30, 1872.

SIR: I have the honor to transmit herewith the tabular statements made up from the accounts of this Office, which the Secretary of the Treasury is required to lay before Congress, as follows:

Table A, showing the receipts from each specific source of revenue, and the amounts refunded in each collection district, State, and Territory of the United States for the fiscal year ended June 30, 1872.

Table B, showing the number and value of internal revenue stamps ordered monthly by the Commissioner, the receipts from the sale of stamps, and the commissions allowed on the same; also the number and value of stamps for tobacco, cigars, snuff, distilled spirits, and fermented liquors, issued monthly to collectors during the fiscal year ended June 30, 1872.

Table C, showing the territorial distribution of internal revenue from various sources in the United States for the fiscal years ended June 30, 1864, 1865, 1866, 1867, 1868, 1869, 1870, 1871, and 1872.

Table D, showing the aggregate receipts from each collection district, State, and Territory for the fiscal years ended June 30, 1863, 1864, 1865, 1866, 1867, 1868, 1869, 1870, 1871, and 1872.

Table E, showing the total collections from each specific source of revenue for the fiscal years ended June 30, 1863, 1864, 1865, 1866, 1867, 1868, 1869, 1870, 1871, and 1872.

Table F, showing the ratio of receipts from specific sources to the aggregate of all collections for the fiscal years ended June 30, 1864, 1865, 1866, 1867, 1868, 1869, 1870, 1871, and 1872.

Table G, an abstract of reports of district attorneys, concerning suits and prosecutions under the internal revenue laws during the fiscal year ended June 30, 1872.

Table H, an abstract of seizures of property for violation of internal revenue laws during the fiscal year ended June 30, 1872.

Table I, showing the number of proof gallons of spirits in each collection district, State, and Territory in the United States, exclusive of the quantity in internal revenue warehouses, May 1, 1872.

The aggregate receipts from all sources, exclusive of the duty upon the capital, circulation, and deposits of national banks, were for the fiscal years ended June 30—

1870	$185,235,867 97
1871	144,011,176 24
1872	131,770,946 73

These amounts include sums refunded and allowed on drawbacks.

The decrease in the aggregate receipts for the last two years is due to legislation approved July 14, 1870, which reduced the revenue to the estimated amount of $55,000,000 per annum, but which did not go into full operation before the close of the fiscal year 1871.

The amount of drawbacks and sums refunded for taxes illegally assessed and collected for the last three years, were as follows:

	Drawback.	Sums refunded.
1870	$5,838 55	$196,809 81
1871	22,887 97	617,581 07
1872	13,704 67	587,609 19

The total amount of drawback allowed by this Office prior to June 30, 1872, was $6,526,514 67, and of sums refunded, $4,719,806 56. During the fiscal year ended June 30, 1872, drawbacks were allowed only on general merchandise under section 171, act of June 30, 1864, limited by act of March 31, 1868.

TOTAL AMOUNT OF TAXES RETURNED FROM SEVERAL SPECIFIC AND ALL GENERAL SOURCES PRIOR TO JUNE 30, 1872.

The following table exhibits the aggregate amount of taxes returned from the several general sources of revenue from the organization of this Office to the close of the last fiscal year.

Sources.		Total collections from September 1, 1862, to June 30, 1872.
1st. *Articles and occupations now taxable, including penalties:*		
Spirits	$336,138,546	
Tobacco	200,213,837	
Fermented liquors	52,954,800	
Banks and bankers	28,644,495	
Adhesive stamps	131,673,669	
Penalties	7,384,218	
		$757,009,565
2d. *Articles and occupations now exempt from tax:*		
Manufactures and productions	401,391,295	
Gross receipts	55,924,677	
Sales	37,558,907	
Special taxes not relating to spirits, tobacco, and fermented liquors	85,437,647	
Income	341,706,036	
Special income tax of 1864	29,381,862	
Gas	17,912,330	
Legacies and successions	14,805,648	
Articles in Schedule A	8,964,869	
Miscellaneous	8,250,993	
		1,001,334,264
Aggregate receipts		1,758,343,829

SPIRITS.

The revenue derived from leading sources under spirits was as follows:

Gallon tax	$257,862,240
Per diem tax on distilleries	7,360,008
Distillers' special and barrel tax	23,374,443
Retail liquor dealers' special tax	28,618,900
Wholesale liquor dealers' special tax, including tax on sales	11,840,602

TOBACCO.

The tax paid on snuff and the higher grades of manufactured tobacco was $131,185,501; on smoking-tobacco, $23,633,146; and on cigars, $39,753,395. The number of pounds of manufactured tobacco and snuff returned for tax was 602,302,045. The number of cigars on which the tax was paid amounted to 7,758,820,609.

TOTAL RECEIPTS FROM SPECIFIC SOURCES UNDER MANUFACTURES AND PRODUCTS, GROSS RECEIPTS, SALES, SPECIAL TAXES, AND ARTICLES IN SCHEDULE A:

MANUFACTURES AND PRODUCTS.	
Boots and shoes	$14,687,824
Bullion	1,632,796
Candles	1,549,928
Clocks, clock-movements, &c	457,270
Cloth and other fabrics of cotton	38,606,287
Cloth and other fabrics of wool	29,922,434
Clothing, not including boots and shoes	25,422,745
Coal	2,966,961
Confectionery	3,541,773
Cotton, raw	68,072,389
Gunpowder	1,045,395
India rubber	2,169,077
Iron and steel and their manufactures	35,306,728
Leather of all descriptions	14,350,793
Oil distilled from coal and crude petroleum	20,456,552
Paper, including pasteboard, binders' board, &c	4,336,177
Petroleum, crude	2,415,697
Piano-fortes and other musical instruments	1,452,023
Pins	161,426
Salt	1,462,246
Wood-screws	687,296
Silk	1,211,577
Soap	3,971,253
Steam-engines	3,179,781
Sugar, brown and refined	11,818,343
Thread and twine	2,014,243
Turpentine, spirits of	1,097,247
GROSS RECEIPTS.	
Express companies	3,882,983
Insurance companies	8,683,902
Railroad companies	32,654,008
Steamboat companies	2,142,845
Telegraph companies	1,549,236
SALES.	
Auction	1,931,024
Brokers, commercial	2,932,956
Brokers, sales of stocks, bonds, gold and silver, &c	6,591,375
Dealers' sales	15,741,483
Manufacturers' sales	9,435,986
SPECIAL TAXES.	
Apothecaries	413,547
Auctioneers	690,685
Banks and bankers	8,081,818
Brokers of all descriptions	4,518,606
Butchers	1,495,983
Claim agents	396,995
Dealers, wholesale	20,844,383
Dealers, retail	15,092,874
Dentists	399,525
Hotels	4,385,256
Insurance agents	842,976
Lawyers	2,352,505

Manufacturers	$8,533,656
Peddlers	4,762,640
Photographers	515,704
Physicians and surgeons	3,598,520

ARTICLES IN SCHEDULE A.

Carriages kept for use	2,377,170
Plate of gold and silver	1,606,917
Watches, gold or gilt	2,814,895
Piano-fortes, &c	1,455,230

INCOME.

Of the $341,706,036 returned on income prior to June 30, 1872, exclusive of the special income tax of 1864, the sum of $260,700,986 was paid by individuals; $29,048,443 were withheld from dividends and additions to surplus of banks; $5,680,392 from the dividends of insurance companies; $20,655,808 from dividends of railroad companies; $9,852,202 from the interest on bonds of railroad companies, and $13,772,062 from salaries of United States officers and employés.

The following statement shows the number of persons in the United States who paid the income tax from 1867 to 1870, in each of the five classes below named. These returns were made under act of March 2, 1867, which provides that the amount of exemption shall be $1,000, and the rate of tax 5 per cent:

Classes.	Number of persons assessed for income in—			
	1867.	1868.	1869.	1870.
First class, tax $20 or less	101,219	100,558	107,997	112,874
Second class, tax over $20 and not over $50	68,680	55,949	69,184	68,900
Third class, tax over $50 and not over $100	40,899	38,957	41,196	40,839
Fourth class, tax over $100 and not over $500	46,055	51,188	45,002	44,732
Fifth class, tax over $500	9,282	7,965	9,464	9,316
Total	266,135	254,617	272,843	276,661

The following is a similar statement of returns made for the years 1871 and 1872, under act of July 14, 1870, the exemption being $2,000 and the rate of tax 2½ per cent:

Classes.	Number of persons assessed for income in—	
	1871.	1872.
First class, tax $20 or less	25,479	22,610
Second class, tax over $20 and not over $50	19,795	18,887
Third class, tax over $50 and not over $100	12,917	13,335
Fourth class, tax over $100 and not over $250	10,742	11,355
Fifth class, tax over $250 and not over $500	3,707	4,264
Sixth class, tax over $500	2,135	2,480
Total	74 77	72,949

No returns for 1872 have been received at the date of this report from the following districts, viz: 1st and 2d Arkansas, 6th Illinois, 7th Indiana, 1st Mississippi, 2d Missouri, Montana, Nebraska, 19th and 28th New York, 7th North Carolina, 1st Ohio, 19th Pennsylvania, 3d Tennessee, and Wyoming.

SPIRITS.

The following is a comparative statement showing the receipts from the several sources under "spirits" during the fiscal years ended, June 30, 1871 and 1872, with the increase and decrease from each source:

Sources.	1871.	1872.	Increase.	Decrease.
Spirits distilled from apples, peaches, or grapes	$1, 236, 005 67	$544, 848 83		$691, 156 84
Spirits distilled from materials other than apples, peaches, or grapes	29, 921, 308 48	32, 572, 940 16	$2, 651, 631 68	
Distilleries, per diem tax on	1, 901, 602 98	2, 010, 986 53	109, 383 55	
Distillers' special and barrel tax	5, 683, 077 31	6, 489, 786 01	806, 708 70	
Wine made in imitation of champagne		20 00	20 00	
Rectifiers	959, 800 18	955, 704 91		4, 095 27
Dealers, retail liquor	3, 651, 484 73	4, 028, 604 93	377, 120 20	
Dealers, wholesale liquor	2, 151, 281 06	2, 065, 563 63		85, 717 43
Manufacturers of stills	1, 927 49	1, 391 66		535 83
Stills or worms manufactured	3, 240 00	4, 260 00	1, 020 00	
Stamps, distillery warehouse	249, 699 00	290, 264 00	40, 565 00	
Stamp, rectifiers'	374, 723 00	367, 424 00		7, 299 00
Stamps, wholesale liquor dealers'	134, 005 00	139, 602 75	5, 597 75	
Excess of gaugers' fees	13, 693 20	4, 118 95		9, 574 25
Total	46, 281, 848 10	49, 473, 516 36	3, 992, 046 88	798, 378 62

Aggregate increase, $3,193.668, or 6.9 per cent.

The number of distilleries (other than fruit) registered during the last fiscal year was	511
The number of fruit distilleries registered was	3, 138
Total	3, 649

Of the distilleries, (other than fruit,) 456 were operated during the year, and of the fruit distilleries, 2,676.

The returns to this Office for the last fiscal year show a total production, in taxable gallons, from materials other than fruit, of	68, 275, 745
From fruit	757, 788
Total yearly production	69, 033,533

The following tabular statement shows the distribution of distilleries in the various States and Territories:

Statement showing the number of distilleries registered and operated during the fiscal year ended June 30, 1872.

States and Territories.	Grain.		Molasses.		Fruit.		Total number registered.	Total number operated.
	No. registered.	No. operated.	No. registered.	No. operated.	No. registered.	No. operated.		
Alabama	4				86	68	90	68
Arkansas	1	1			25	21	26	22
California	6	6			294	256	300	262
Connecticut	5	5			79	50	84	55
Delaware					13	13	13	13
Georgia	1	1			690	645	691	646
Idaho	2	1					2	1
Illinois	56	56			42	42	98	98
Indiana	27	27			94	94	121	121
Iowa	2	2			16	16	18	18
Kansas	5				4	2	9	2
Kentucky	126	126			114	111	240	237
Louisiana	4	3					4	3
Maine			1	1			1	1

Statement showing the number of distilleries registered, &c.—Continued.

States and Territories.	Grain.		Molasses.		Fruit.		Total number registered.	Total number operated.
	No. registered.	No. operated.	No. registered.	No. operated.	No. registered.	No. operated.		
Maryland	8	8			20	20	28	28
Massachusetts	2	2	7	7	23	19	32	28
Michigan	1	1					1	1
Minnesota								
Mississippi					48	43	48	43
Missouri	17	13			88	78	105	91
Montana								
Nebraska	1						1	
Nevada	1						1	
New Hampshire			1	1	2	2	3	3
New Jersey	2	2			121	114	123	116
New Mexico					5	2	5	2
New York	18	18			76	74	94	92
North Carolina	6	6			210	160	216	166
Ohio	81	50			129	51	210	110
Oregon					6	6	6	6
Pennsylvania	73	69	1	1	17	16	91	86
Rhode Island			1	1			1	1
South Carolina					103	102	103	102
Tennessee	29	22			343	224	372	246
Texas					29	29	29	29
Utah								
Vermont					7	5	7	5
Virginia	10	6			376	336	386	342
Washington								
West Virginia	1	1			78	77	79	78
Wisconsin	11	10					11	10
Total	500	445	11	11	3,138	2,676	3,649	3,132

The following statement shows the number of grain and molasses distilleries in operation at the beginning of each month during the last fiscal year:

Months.	Number of distilleries.		Capacity of grain distilleries.		Capacity of molasses distilleries.		Total spirit-producing capacity.
	Grain.	Molasses.	Bushels.	Gallons.	Gallons.	Spirits.	
July	192	7	49,107	172,849	9,401	7,990	180,839
August	168	9	41,387	145,020	11,919	10,131	155,151
September	170	9	45,519	162,820	9,451	8,032	170,852
October	177	9	49,977	174,505	11,139	9,467	183,972
November	205	10	66,188	230,108	12,946	11,004	241,112
December	236	9	62,877	217,555	12,223	10,389	227,944
January	278	11	69,255	247,150	13,176	11,199	258,349
February	313	11	69,585	232,185	13,331	11,318	243,503
March	350	10	74,138	258,150	13,021	11,054	269,204
April	357	10	73,869	254,281	12,340	10,475	264,756
May	345	11	71,145	246,287	10,016	8,498	254,785
June	226	9	57,674	200,375	9,896	8,411	208,786
Total	3,017	115	730,741	2,541,285	138,859	117,968	2,659,253

	Taxable gallons.
The quantity of spirits in bond July 1, 1871, was	6,742,118
The quantity entered in bond during the year ended June 30, 1872, was	68,275,745
The quantity withdrawn from bond during the same period was	64,914,471
The quantity remaining in bond June 30, 1872, was	10,103,392
The quantity remaining in bond July 1, 1871, as per present report, less than the quantity stated in the report for 1871, as shown by corrected reports of collectors received subsequent to the publication of the report for 1871, was	2,242

The total quantity of spirits in the United States not in internal revenue warehouses on the 1st of May, 1872, was 39,672,197 proof-gallons.

I would recommend that section 54 of the act of July 20, 1868, as amended by the act of June 6, 1872, be further amended so as to authorize you, in a more explicit manner than at present provided, to require export bonds of persons applying to export distilled spirits for the benefit of drawback. It is desirable that the language on this point should be perfectly clear and unquestionable, inasmuch as the exportation of spirits on which the tax has not been paid will be affected thereby as well as that provided for in section 54.

By the act of June 6, 1872, the fees of gaugers and the *per diem* compensation of storekeepers were made payable by the United States without re-imbursement by distillers, except by the increased rate of tax on distilled spirits, this increased rate having been determined partly by taking into account the amount heretofore paid for the services of such officers. But experience has already demonstrated that the amount to be paid will be not only greater (notwithstanding my most strenuous efforts to the contrary) than ever before, but also greater in proportion to the quantity of spirits produced.

It is apparent that the retention of spirits in the warehouse after the distiller has ceased operations, extends the time for payment of the tax due, and is therefore for his benefit only. In view of this, and the foregoing statement, I would recommend that when a distiller has ceased operations, the pay of the storekeeper for subsequent services at his distillery warehouse, in consequence of spirits remaining therein, shall be re-imbursed to the United States by the distiller.

FERMENTED LIQUORS.

By the act of June 6, 1872, the act of July 13, 1866, so far as it relates to fermented liquors, was re-enacted with some amendments, made at the solicitation of the principal brewers of the United States, designed to afford brewers better facilities than heretofore for the conduct of their business under internal revenue laws.

These concessions do not appear to have been of a character to endanger the public interests, as the following statement will show:

The tax received on fermented liquors at $1 per barrel during the first quarter of the fiscal year ended June 30, 1872, was $2,217,291 93, while the receipts from the same source during the first three months of the present fiscal year amount to $2,684,241, an increase of $466,949 07.

The average increase of about a million dollars annually during the last three fiscal years, as contrasted with the stationary character of the receipts during the four years next preceding, is certainly gratifying, but the increase during the first three months of the present fiscal year, as above stated, far exceeds that of any corresponding period in any other year since the organization of this Office.

The tax received on fermented liquors, at $1 per barrel, was, for the years—

1867	$5,819,345 49	1870	$6,081,520 54
1868	5,685,663 70	1871	7,159,740 20
1869	5,866,400 98	1872	8,009,969 72

The number of persons engaged in the manufacture of fermented liquors during the fiscal year ended June 30, 1872, was 3,421, distributed as follows: Alabama, 5; Arizona, 10; Arkansas, 1; California, 226; Colorado, 36; Connecticut, 25; Dakota, 6; Delaware, 2; District of Columbia, 15; Florida, 2; Georgia, 4; Idaho, 12; Illinois, 216; Indiana, 169; Iowa, 171; Kansas, 46; Kentucky, 46; Louisiana, 16; Maine, 1; Maryland, 72; Massachusetts, 56; Michigan, 189; Minnesota, 114; Mississippi, 2; Missouri, 124; Montana, 36; Nebraska, 23; Nevada, 41; New Hampshire, 5; New Jersey, 83; New Mexico, 8; New York, 479; North Carolina, 1; Ohio, 288; Oregon, 31; Pennsylvania, 443; Rhode Island, 4; South Carolina, 2; Tennessee, 11; Texas, 44; Utah, 16; Vermont, 4; Virginia, 13; Washington, 14; West Virginia, 17; Wisconsin, 292.

I would recommend that sections 18 and 22 be so amended as to provide for packages known as "thirds." The act of March 2, 1867, authorized their use to accommodate brewers west of the Rocky Mountains, who are compelled to send their products from their breweries to the consumer or retailer on the backs of mules; this sized package being specially adapted to such a mode of conveyance. "Thirds" appear to have been omitted in the act of June 6, 1872, through inadvertence, and they should be restored.

The amendments made by the act of June 6, 1872, to section 59 of the act of July 20, 1868, as amended April 10, 1869, relating to the special taxes for selling spirituous and malt liquors and wines, were, it has appeared to me, intended simply to provide that, in addition to the former classes of liquor dealers, there should be two classes at a lower special tax authorized to sell malt liquors only, leaving to the former classes of liquor dealers the privilege of selling malt liquors which they previously possessed; also leaving unchanged the exemption from special tax as wholesale dealers extended to brewers who sold fermented liquors of their own production at the brewery in the original packages. Nevertheless that intention is not so clearly expressed by the language of the section as amended as is desirable in so important a provision of law.

To prevent the injustice which might be done by acting upon a more technical construction of the language used as to the several classes of liquor dealers and malt liquor dealers, I issued on the 30th of September last instructions to assessors and collectors to make assessments and collections in accordance with the above expressed view of the intentions of Congress, until I could bring the question to the attention of that body; and I also suspended the collection of all assessments which had been made contrary to that construction.

In view of this, I would respectfully recommend that the language of the section be made more explicit. I would also recommend that retail dealers in malt liquors be limited in their sales to quantities less than five gallons, and that those selling in quantities of five gallons and upwards be required to pay the wholesale dealer's tax.

TOBACCO.

The total receipts from tobacco for the fiscal year ended June 30, 1872, were $33,736,170 52. Compared with the total receipts for the fiscal year ended June 30, 1871, the following results are shown:

Year ended June 30, 1872, tobacco—chewing, &c., and snuff	$18,674,569 26
Year ended June 30, 1871, tobacco—chewing, &c., and snuff	20,677,717 84
Showing a decrease in class 32 cents of	2,003,148 58
Year ended June 30, 1872, tobacco—smoking, scraps, shorts, &c	$5,896,206 33
Year ended June 30, 1871, tobacco—smoking, scraps, shorts, &c	4,882,821 83
Showing an increase in class 16 cents of	1,013,384 50

Year ended June 30, 1872, cigars, cheroots, &c.	$7,566,156 86
Year ended June 30, 1871, cigars, cheroots, &c.	6,598,173 24
Showing an increase on cigars, &c., of	967,983 62
Year ended June 30, 1872, received from sale of export stamps	$53,576 25
Year ended June 30, 1871, received from sale of export stamps	66,147 00
Decrease from sale of export stamps	12,570 75
Year ended June 30, 1872, received from dealers in leaf tobacco	$260,487 62
Year ended June 30, 1871, received from dealers in leaf tobacco	221,661 98
Increased collection from dealers in leaf tobacco	38,825 64
Year ended June 30, 1872, received from dealers in manufactured tobacco	$1,102,357 89
Year ended June 30, 1871, received from dealers in manufactured tobacco	970,017 96
Increased collection from dealers in manufactured tobacco	132,339 93
Year ended June 30, 1872, from special taxes of tobacco and cigar manufacturers	$182,816 31
Year ended June 30, 1871, from special taxes of tobacco and cigar manufacturers	162,367 33
Increased collection from special taxes of tobacco and cigar manufacturers	20,448 98

Showing an increase in the total receipts from the manufacture and sale of tobacco in all its forms, over the receipts from the same sources for the preceding fiscal year, of $157,263 34.

ANNUAL PRODUCTION.

The quantity of manufactured tobacco represented by the collection of taxes from this source for the fiscal year ended June 30, 1872, is as follows:

	Pounds.
Of chewing tobacco, snuff, &c., class 32 cents	58,358,029
Of smoking tobacco, scraps, shorts, &c., class 16 cents	36,851,290
Exported to foreign countries	9,565,981
Excess in warehouses June 30, 1872, over June 30, 1871	2,485,555
Total product for the year	107,260,855

The number of cigars, cheroots, &c., on which taxes were collected during the last fiscal year, was 1,527,705,972.

From the above statement it will be seen that the entire product of manufactured tobacco reported for the fiscal year ended June 30, 1872, exceeds the total product of the preceding fiscal year by 1,431,892 pounds, while the aggregate quantity which reached taxation for the last fiscal year was only 73,815 pounds in excess of the quantity which reached taxation the preceding year.

During the last fiscal year the quantity of class 16 cents, or smoking tobacco, was increased by 6,333,654 pounds, while the quantity of class 32 cents, or chewing tobacco, was diminished by 6,259,839 pounds, as compared with the preceding year. This change in the relative proportions of the two classes of tobacco was owing, no doubt, in a great measure, to the agitation of the question of taxation during several months prior to the passage of the act of June 6, 1872, which provides for a uniform rate of 20 cents per pound on all descriptions of manufactured tobacco, in lieu of a graded tax. The anticipated increase of tax on class 16 cents smoking tobacco greatly stimulated the production and sale of this grade of tobacco during the last months of the year, while the prospect of a decrease of tax on class 32 cents, or chewing tobacco, operated largely to diminish the sale or removal, except in bond, of this grade of tobacco. Since July 1, the time when the new rate of taxation took effect, the sale and removal of plug and other kinds of tobacco on which the tax was diminished has been unprecedently large, and the collections for the first quarter of the present fiscal year from tobacco are greatly in excess of those made from the same source during the same quarter for any previous fiscal year.

UNIFORM RATE OF TAX.

So far as I am able to judge, the law providing for a uniform rate of tax on all manufactured tobacco, whether chewing or smoking, is operating very satisfactorily. There is now no reason why revenue officers should examine into the modes of manufacturing tobacco employed by any one, or for opening or examining any package to ascertain the character of its contents. If the package is a legal one, and has upon it a proper revenue stamp denoting the payment of the tax, with such additional marks, brands, and labels as the law prescribes, no officer is authorized to examine it further. Owing to the disturbing causes already referred to which have affected the trade for some months past it is now too early to predict with entire certainty what will be the actual result of the present uniform tax on the amount of revenue to be collected. I have, however, reason to believe that, with the additional safe guards provided by the new law against the sale of manufactured tobacco in fraud of the revenue, and with the taxes imposed upon the sale at retail of raw or leaf tobacco for consumption without its being subjected to any process of manufacture, the collections from tobacco under the uniform rate of 20 cents a pound, which is a reduction of more than six cents a pound from the average rate for the last two fiscal years, will reach nearly if not quite the sums realized for either of the same years. In making this estimate I am relying upon making collections on from eight to ten millions of pounds more of manufactured tobacco in consequence of the restrictions which the act of June 6, 1872, has placed upon the sale, for consumption, of raw or leaf tobacco.

EXPORT BONDED WAREHOUSES AND MANUFACTURED TOBACCO IN BOND.

	Pounds.
There were remaining in store in the several export bonded warehouses on the 1st day of July, 1871	5,650,597
Placed in bond during the fiscal year ended June 30, 1872	21,194,662
Making a total of	26,845,259
There were withdrawn for export during the fiscal year ended June 30, 1872	9,565,981
Withdrawn on payment of tax during the fiscal year ended June 30, 1872.	9,143,126
Making a total withdrawn during the fiscal year ended June 30, 1872	18,709,107
And leaving a balance in the warehouses July 1, 1872, of	8,136,152

By the act of June 6, 1872, the system of export bonded warehouses authorized by the act of July 20, 1868, was abolished, and the several warehouses established under said act are to be discontinued after the expiration of six months from the passage of the first named act. As the average quantity of tobacco withdrawn for export and consumption for the fiscal years ended June 30, 1871, and June 30, 1872, respectively, exceeded twenty millions of pounds, it was thought at the time of the passage of the law that six months would be ample time for the holders of tobacco then in bond, which was considerably less than eight millions of pounds, but increased after the passage of the act to the quantity given above as the balance on the 1st day of July, either to withdraw the same for export, or for sale and consumption, upon the payment of the tax. The reports received from month to month from the collectors in charge of bonded warehouses show that this quantity has been constantly diminishing, so that no great hardship will be imposed upon the owners of this tobacco by requiring them to affix stamps and withdraw the comparatively small quantity remaining in the warehouses at the expiration of the six months which the law allows for closing them out. This view of the case is especially apparent when the fact is taken into consideration that the owners of this tobacco have already had six months' credit for the taxes due on all of it, and on a considerable portion, a much longer time; and also the further fact, that these tobaccos, after having been stamped, can at any time be exported, and the owners obtain a drawback for the amount of tax which shall be shown to have been paid on them. In Baltimore the two warehouses have already been closed out by the action of the warehouse men, and I have given instructions to the different collectors under whose control the other warehouses are, to take the proper steps to close them all out immediately upon the expiration of the time fixed by law, by advertising for sale by the Government all tobacco which shall not then have been withdrawn by the owners.

The act of June 6, 1872, provides two modes for the exportation of manufactured tobacco to foreign countries. First, directly from the manufactory without the payment of any tax; and secondly, from the store or warehouse of the jobber, dealer, or commission merchant, after the tax has been paid, with an allowance of drawback on the presentation of proper evidence that the tobacco has been exported and landed in a foreign country or lost at sea. The few months that have intervened since the adoption of the new system have by no means afforded sufficient opportunity to test its practicability. Thus far, the two systems have both been in operation at the same time, the tobacco stored in warehouses being exported under the regulations in force at the time when the late act was passed, while direct exportations from the manufactories have been made under the new regulations. The two systems operating concurrently have not tended to harmony. I have seen nothing, however, as yet, which leads me to distrust the practicability and complete success of the provisions made by the act of June 6, 1872, for facilitating the exportation of tobacco to foreign countries. Any radical change in the law and regulations touching a business so varied and extensive as is the tobacco trade, requires time for persons engaged in it to accustom themselves to the alteration. For this reason such changes should be as infrequent as possible, and only made upon urgent necessity. That such a necessity existed for abolishing the old system of bonded warehouses at ports of entry, which allowed tobacco to be stored therein for home consumption as well as for export, and to be withdrawn therefrom at any time upon the payment of the tax, few persons except those who enjoyed the privileges of such warehouses have expressed a doubt. Under the present law the credit system is entirely dispensed with, and no special privileges are given for making a monopoly of the trade in manufactured tobacco. All tobacco is required to have proper stamps affixed, indicating the payment of the tax, before it is removed from the place where it is made, except that which is intended for and actually bonded for export to a foreign country before it leaves the manufactory. This system, it is believed, will greatly widen the field for exportation, since it provides for direct shipments from any district in the country, the manufacturer filing his bonds and completing his shipping papers in his own district. It provides, also, for the shipment of tax-paid tobacco by any person who desires to export, giving him an allowance of drawback for the taxes paid; a privilege which was not allowed under the previous law. Persons having in their possession tax-paid tobacco, however badly damaged and unsalable, even to such a degree as to render it worthless for sale or consumption, can, by exporting the same, always realize therefrom an amount equal to the tax.

NEW DIES FOR CANCELLATION OF STAMPS.

Since the passage of the act of June 6, 1872, which authorizes the Commissioner of Internal Revenue to prescribe such instruments for cancelling stamps for tobacco, &c., as he and the Secretary of the Treasury may approve, a steel die for the cancellation of registered tobacco stamps has been prepared and furnished to every manufacturer of plug and fine-cut chewing tobacco in the country at the expense of the Government. This die is so constructed as to drive several portions of every stamp into the wooden package and lodge them there, so that if the stamp should be taken from the package it would be quite impossible to supply the portions thus driven into the wood to be re-used on any other package; and without the presence of the portions required to be driven into the wood, the fraud would immediately be apparent.

The use of this die is made imperative by regulations, and its operation is very generally satisfactory. With an entire re-issue of tobacco stamps, which has been made within the last year, printed on paper which the Government has made for this special use, and printed with different colored impressions, so as to preclude the possibility of counterfeiting by photography, with a more perfect cancellation effected with the new die, I am not aware that any new or additional device or contrivance of a mechanical nature is required to perfect the machinery which the Government is employing to collect the taxes on tobacco. Some additional device may be required to prevent the re-use of cigar-boxes from which the stamps have not been removed or destroyed. Should any such device hereafter be found which commends itself to the Government, there is authority given in the amended law for its adoption.

The present law relating to tobacco, though not claimed to be perfect, undoubtedly contains in its various provisions the practical results obtained from ten years of experience in internal revenue enactments. Under this law the tobacco business is believed to be safe and prosperous, while equal and ample protection is given to all. For these reasons I advise that there be no additional legislation on this subject at present.

Abstract of cases compromised.

The whole number of cases compromised, as provided under section 102, act of July 20, 1868, during the fiscal year ended June 30, 1872, was 479.

Amount of tax accepted	$104,612 86
Assessed penalty fixed by law	2,947 99
Specific penalty in lieu of fines, penalties, and forfeitures	129,158 62
Total amount received by compromises	236,719 47

Abstracts of reports of district attorneys for the fiscal year 1872.

SUITS COMMENCED.

Number of criminal actions	4,070
Number of civil actions *in personam*	1,542
Number of actions *in rem*	729
Whole number commenced	6,341

SUITS DECIDED IN FAVOR OF UNITED STATES.

Number of criminal actions	1,297
Number of civil actions *in personam*	1,024
Number of actions *in rem*	636
Total number of suits decided in favor of United States	2,957

SUITS DECIDED AGAINST THE UNITED STATES.

Number of criminal actions	523
Number of civil actions *in personam*	196
Number of actions *in rem*	64
Total number of suits decided against the United States	783

SUITS SETTLED OR DISMISSED.

Number of criminal actions	1,873
Number of civil actions *in personam*	390
Number of actions *in rem*	145
Total number of suits settled or dismissed	2,408

SUITS PENDING JULY 1, 1872.

Number of criminal actions	3,668
Number of civil actions *in personam*	2,009
Number of actions *in rem*	568
Total number of suits pending July 1, 1872	6,245

Amount of judgments recovered by United States in suits in criminal actions	$333,930 53
Amount of judgments recovered by United States in suits in civil actions *in personam*	1,337,361 09
Amount collected on judgments and paid into court in suits in criminal actions	109,939 10
Amount collected on judgments and paid into court in suits in civil actions *in personam*	443,431 93
Amount collected on judgments and paid into court in actions *in rem* or proceeds of forfeiture	185,452 08

ABSTRACT OF SEIZURES.

Seizures of property for violation of internal revenue law during the fiscal year ended June 30, 1872, were as follows:

187,619 gallons of distilled spirits, valued at	$211,544 71
9,633 barrels of fermented liquors, valued at	47,847 00
102 pounds of snuff, valued at	65 65
254,836 pounds of tobacco, valued at	72,113 76
1,181,099 cigars, valued at	18,274 87
Miscellaneous property, valued at	296,417 08
Total value of seizures	646,263 27

The following table exhibits a comparison of the receipts from all sources taxable during the last two fiscal years, not already presented in this report:

	Receipts, fiscal year 1871.	Receipts, fiscal year 1872.	Increase.	Decrease.
BANKS AND BANKERS.				
Bank deposits	$2,702,196 84	$3,643,272 19	$941,075 35	
Bank capital	919,262 77	976,092 13	56,829 36	
Bank circulation	22,781 92	8,864 82		$13,917 10
Total	3,644,241 53	4,628,229 14	997,904 71	13,917 10
INCOME.				
Income from individuals, including salaries	15,222,211 94	8,711,250 52		6,510,961 42
Bank dividends and undistributed profits	1,542,667 75	2,162,564 31	619,896 56	
Railroad companies' dividends and undistributed profits	1,121,439 59	1,851,296 30	729,856 71	
Railroad companies' interest on bonds	974,345 35	1,291,026 68	316,681 33	
Insurance companies' dividends and undistributed profits	243,205 21	270,531 14	27,325 93	
All other collections from income	58,780 91	150,192 83	91,411 92	
Total	19,162,650 75	14,436,861 78	1,785,172 45	6,510,961 42
Gas	2,573,122 92	2,831,718 56	258,595 64	
Adhesive stamps	15,342,739 46	16,177,320 60	834,581 14	

The increase on banks and bankers is $983,988; on gas, $258,596; and on adhesive stamps, $834,581. The decrease in the receipts of income from individuals was $6,510,961. $1,785,172 were, however, offset by the increase in the returns from corporations, so that the balance shows a total decrease of only $4,725,789. The large apparent falling off in the receipts of income from individuals is chiefly owing to a difference in the rate of tax. Of the $14,434,950, exclusive of the salary-tax returned in 1871, $10,680,967, or nearly 75 per cent. were collected at 5 per cent. under act of March 2, 1867, while the balance for that year and the whole amount for 1872 were returned under act of July 14, 1870, at 2½ per cent. Estimating 2½ per cent. on the taxable income of the two years, there is a difference of only $677,781 in favor of 1871. The collections on the annual and monthly lists of 1871 amounted to $7,625,409. The receipts to date on the lists of 1872 are slightly in excess of eight millions of dollars.

I present herewith a statement of the receipts for the first quarter of the present fiscal year, in connection with those of like character for the corresponding period of the year preceding. Returns from the following districts not having been received at the date of this report are not included in the receipts for the first quarter of the current year, viz: Nebraska for July, August, and September; 7th Tennessee for September; 4th Texas for July, August, and September, and Utah for September.

Comparative statement showing the collections of internal revenue for the first three months of the fiscal years ending June 30, 1872 and 1873; also the increase and decrease from each source.

Sources of revenue.	Receipts from July 1, 1871, to Sept. 30, 1871.	Receipts from July 1, 1872, to Sept. 30, 1872.	Increase.	Decrease.
SPIRITS.				
Spirits distilled from apples, peaches, or grapes	$103, 072 37	$288, 976 55	$185, 304 18	....
Spirits distilled from materials other than apples, peaches, or grapes	7, 263, 209 00	8, 729, 472 36	1, 466, 263 36	....
Wine made in imitation of champagne, &c	....	22 40	22 40	....
Rectifiers	103, 023 56	174, 689 31	71, 665 75	....
Dealers, retail liquor	1, 500, 382 99	1, 393, 527 45	....	$106, 855 54
Dealers, wholesale liquor	232, 409 41	356, 552 33	124, 142 92	....
Manufacturers of stills, and stills and worms manufactured	2, 944 17	2, 011 61	....	932 56
Stamps, distillery warehouse, for rectified spirits, &c	169, 074 00	146, 060 80	....	23, 013 20
Stamps for distilled spirits intended for export	....	518 75	518 75	....
Distilleries, per diem tax on, distillers' special and barrel tax, excess of gaugers' fees, &c	2, 084, 600 46	1, 646, 757 89	....	437, 842 57
Total	11, 459, 915 96	12, 739, 189 45	1, 847, 917 36	568, 643 87
TOBACCO.				
Cigars, cheroots, and cigarettes	1, 863, 989 87	2, 199, 537 97	335, 548 10	....
Manufacturers of cigars	32, 800 96	34, 698 32	1, 897 36	....
Snuff	110, 217 03	258, 352 71	148, 135 68	....
Tobacco, manufactured, of all descriptions	7, 089, 994 17	7, 071, 847 12	....	18, 147 05
Stamps for tobacco or snuff intended for export	19, 104 00	1, 342 80	....	17, 761 20
Dealers in leaf tobacco	30, 254 51	29, 243 16	....	1, 011 35
Dealers in manufactured tobacco	322, 273 72	391, 553 31	69, 279 59	....
Manufacturers of tobacco	5, 093 86	2, 133 95	....	2, 959 91
Peddlers of tobacco	....	17, 194 77	17, 194 77	....
Sales of cigars, leaf tobacco, manufactured tobacco, &c	91, 653 96	40, 733 56	....	50, 920 40
Total	9, 565, 382 08	10, 046, 637 67	572, 055 50	90, 799 91
FERMENTED LIQUORS.				
Fermented liquors, tax of $1 per barrel on	2, 217, 291 93	2, 684, 241 00	466, 949 07	....
Brewers' special tax	78, 264 09	73, 606 17	....	4, 657 92
Dealers in malt liquors	....	6, 039 50	6, 039 50	....
Total	2, 295, 556 02	2, 763, 886 67	472, 988 57	4, 657 92
BANKS AND BANKERS.				
Bank deposits	1, 181, 188 50	1, 148, 215 16	....	32, 973 34
Bank capital	239, 909 92	188, 182 63	....	51, 727 29
Bank circulation	3, 002 70	17, 462 79	14, 460 09	....
Total	1, 424, 101 12	1, 353, 860 58	14, 460 09	84, 700 63
INCOME.				
Income from individuals, including salaries	3, 518, 466 95	3, 318, 542 65	....	199, 924 30
Bank dividends and undistributed profits	955, 880 03	60, 967 36	....	894, 912 67
Railroad companies' dividends and undistributed profits	889, 800 38	70, 055 29	....	819, 745 09
Railroad companies' interest on bonds	480, 509 39	39 61J 11	....	440, 899 28
Insurance companies' dividends and undistributed profits	141, 612 69	1, 636 11	....	139, 976 58
All other collections from income	36, 952 89	23, 608 10	....	13, 344 79
Total	6, 023, 282 33	3, 514 479 62	....	2, 508, 802 71
Adhesive stamps	3, 527, 479 70	2, 664, 801 21	....	862, 678 49
Penalties	117, 310 36	155, 099 30	37, 788 94	....
Articles and occupations formerly taxed but now exempt	1, 262, 467 90	674, 666 90	....	587, 801 00

The increase on spirits for the above period is $1,279,273; on tobacco, $481,256; on fermented liquors, $468,331; on penalties, 37,789. Total increase, $2,266,649. The falling off in receipts from banks and bankers is due to provisions in the act of June 6, 1872, one of which raises the exemption of all sums deposited in savings banks, &c., in the name of one person from $500 to $2,000, and the other exempts certain borrowed capital.

The decrease in the receipts from income is owing to the expiration of the tax by limitation with the assessment on incomes for the calendar year 1871. The receipts from stamps for the first quarter of the present fiscal year were doubtless diminished in anticipation of the repeal, October 1, ultimo, of all general stamps except those on bank checks, drafts, or orders. The receipts from sources formerly taxed, but now exempt, being collections on old lists, are of course constantly decreasing.

The receipts for the last fiscal year exceeded my estimate by $6,770,946 73.

Important changes having been made in the law by act of June 6, 1872, touching spirits and tobacco, it is impossible to state with certainty at this early day how much the receipts for the current fiscal year will be affected by the modified provisions of the law. From the best information now obtainable, I estimate that they will not fall short under the present law of $110,000,000.

CONSOLIDATION OF DISTRICTS.

The act of June 6, 1872, required the reduction of the internal revenue districts in the United States to not exceeding eighty in number, by uniting two or more districts into one; and also the reduction of the minor officers in the service to as small a number as would be consistent with their limited duties. Immediately upon the passage of this act general inquiry for information was made with a view to a prompt compliance with the law. This inquiry early developed the opinion of the leading officers in the service, whose positions rendered them impartial in the matter, that to consolidate at once would largely interfere, to the loss of the Government, with the collection of taxes from assessments under repealed laws then in the hands of collectors. These collections could only be made with dispatch and certainty by those acquainted with the special localities and circumstances of tax-payers. To avoid a much greater loss by this untimely disturbance than could possibly be compensated by the consequent reduced expenditure, temporary delay was universally advised and finally determined upon. The interim was used in pushing to a rapid close the collection of these balances. The result has justified the propriety of the delay. It was estimated that by the act of June, 1872, the whole amount of internal revenue, exclusive of the balances under repealed laws, would be about $110,000,000 per annum; while the actual receipts for the first quarter of the current fiscal year were at the rate of $135,400,000, showing several millions of dollars in excess of the estimated receipts, and this very considerably from taxes due under the repealed laws. To have violently taken the lists containing these evidences of taxation out of the hands of almost every two of three collectors and committed them to the care of the remaining one would have introduced dangerous delay in the receipts and would probably have caused large loss at last. The collections have been large, and reflect great credit upon the officers.

The act of June 6 reduced the duties of assessors and assistant assessors so as to leave but *three things*, which could not be done with equal propriety by the collectors and their deputies, two classes of officers remaining, both numerous and expensive, for a work that one class could as well do. The three duties referred to are the assessment of the *deficiency taxes on distillers*, an exceptional tax, only occasionally due, and the *data* for assessing which are always at hand from daily reports in this office. The majority of such assessments being reviewed and re-adjusted under the present system, all of them could as readily be certified from this Office to the collectors in the first instance. This would insure uniformity of adjustment, a thing almost impossible where two or three hundred unassociated minds are reading and interpreting law and regulations. Second, the *special* or license taxes, which are collected as a general rule but once (May) each year. The special tax certificates can be issued in books, as are the spirit and tobacco stamps, and charged to the collectors at their face value, crediting them (collectors) only with cash or the unused certificates returned to this Office. This system works admirably in the matter of spirits and tobacco, and can be very easily adapted to this other source of revenue. The *third*, and only remaining duty with which the collectors might not be entirely intrusted, is the tax on banks and bankers. This tax is payable but twice during each year, and is the sole remaining tax on corporations. The tax upon corporations was at one period all collected directly by this Office, at a time when it extended to railroad, insurance, canal and turnpike companies, in addition to banks and bankers. The history of this class of taxation shows that when so collected it was well collected, and the whole work done by less than fifteen clerks, at an average salary not exceeding $1,400 per annum each. If fifteen men could collect this tax when it reached $13,000,000 per annum and embraced five species under the class, all of them requiring monthly returns, it is not seen why a comparatively smaller number may not now manage one-fifth of the class, and only yielding, as estimated for the current fiscal year, $800,000 in all. It further appeared that the exceptional labor could be done in this Office without increasing its force materially, and thus enable the discharge of the entire body of assessing officers. Inasmuch as the plan of reduction under the act of June 6 only provided *absolutely* for the reduction of some two-thirds of the principal officers, (460 in all,) and left the reduction of the assistants (over 1,300) *discretionary*, it seemed to be the better plan to ask Congress to make the larger reduction and make that absolute. It is not an easy matter to put out of commission a thousand or more officers. Experience has demonstrated that nothing short of unequivocal, inexorable law can surely do it. Discretion admits of doubt and suggests delay.

In view of the great confusion and loss of revenue anticipated by a general disturbance of the collecting offices; the simplicity and security of a system which shall have but one class of officers and those all under bonds; the fact that nothing is left for the assessing class to do that cannot be done either by the collectors or this Office; and that a saving of from one to two millions per annum of expense in salaries, &c., greater than would be effected under the act of June last, can safely be anticipated, I have had prepared the outlines of a law which will give effect to the above idea. This will be presented to the proper committees of the House of Representatives and the Senate immediately upon their assemblage in December proximo. If it is the judgment of Congress that this plan is preferable to that contemplated by the act of June, I ask their early adoption of its provisions, that it may be put into operation completely by the 30th of June, 1873.

In preparing the proposed plan I have consulted freely with the leading officers now in the service, as well as with many of those who heretofore have been prominent in it. Without an exception it has met their hearty concurrence. They have commended it with a view to its simplicity, concentration of responsibility, economy, and the just expectation of the nation that no more officers shall be retained than are clearly necessary for the due enforcement of the law. In this recommendation I have not forgotten that the plan, if accepted by Congress, will bring personal inconvenience to many of the ablest and best citizens of the country, now and for years in the service; and while I express the tribute of this Office to their intelligent, faithful, and efficient discharge of important duties, I cannot but suppose that their individual loss will be largely compensated in the consciousness of a great public gain.

Respectfully,

J. W. DOUGLASS,
Commissioner.

Hon. GEORGE S. BOUTWELL,
Secretary of the Treasury.

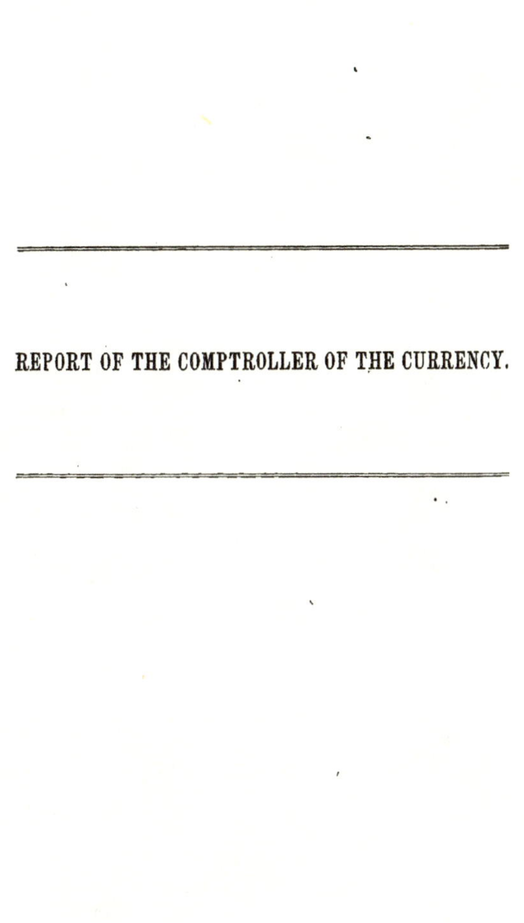

REPORT OF THE COMPTROLLER OF THE CURRENCY.

REPORT

OF THE

COMPTROLLER OF THE CURRENCY.

TREASURY DEPARTMENT,
OFFICE OF THE COMPTROLLER OF THE CURRENCY,
Washington, November 20, 1872.

SIR: I have the honor to submit for the consideration of Congress the following report:

The national currency act provides that it shall be the duty of the Comptroller of the Currency to report annually to Congress a summary of the state and condition of all the national banks, exhibiting their resources and liabilities, as returned in different reports during the preceding year; that he shall suggest amendments to the act by which the system may be improved, and present such other information with reference to the affairs of the national banks as may, in his judgment, be useful. The act also provides that the circulation shall be apportioned to associations in the States and Territories upon the basis of population, resources, business, and bank capital, and that a new apportionment of circulation not issued shall be made as soon as practicable, based upon the census of 1870.

The national currency act became a law on the 25th of February, 1863, and nearly ten years have therefore elapsed since the organization of the system. During this period the agricultural products, the manufactures, and the internal commerce of the country have increased beyond any former precedent; and notwithstanding the enormous waste of a protracted war, the reduction of nearly two thousand millions of dollars in the valuation of property by the abolition of slavery, (more than compensated, it is true, by the conversion of slaves to freemen,) and the collection of five thousand millions of dollars of taxes* imposed by the National and State Governments, the census returns of 1870 show an increase of population for the ten years previous of more than seven millions of persons, and an increase in the total wealth of the Union, of nearly fourteen thousand millions of dollars.

Since the organization of the national banking system, two thousand and sixty-one national banks have been organized; twenty-one of these have failed, and ninety-six gone into voluntary liquidation, by a vote of two-thirds of the shareholders, under section 42 of the act, leaving nineteen hundred and forty-four banks in existence on November 1, 1872.

---

*The amount of national taxation, from 1863 to 1872, inclusive, is shown by the official returns to be as follows: From customs, $1,573,460,608; from internal revenue, $1,740,184,621; direct taxes, $12,699,598.

The taxation not national, for the year 1870, is stated in the census returns at $281,180,312. Assuming that the taxation "not national" was the same amount annually for the decade, the total taxation collected would be $6,138,147,947.

The following table* will exhibit the progress of the system from October, 1863, to October, 1872:

RESOURCES.	October, 1863.	October, 1864.	October, 1865.	October, 1866.	October, 1867.
	66 banks.	508 banks.	1513 banks.	1644 banks.	1642 banks.
Loans and discounts	$5, 466, 088	$93, 238, 657	$487, 170, 136	$603, 247, 503	$609, 675, 214
United States bonds	5, 662, 600	108, 064, 496	427, 731, 300	426, 657, 350	418, 963, 050
Due from banks and bankers	2, 625, 597	34, 017, 116	107, 372, 212	119, 734, 408	103, 618, 336
Bills of national banks	764, 725	4, 687, 727	16, 247, 241	17, 437, 699	11, 841, 104
†Specie	....	....	18, 072, 012	9, 220, 483	12, 798, 044
Lawful money	1, 446, 607	44, 801, 497	189, 988, 496	205, 770, 641	157, 439, 099
LIABILITIES.					
Capital stock	7, 188, 393	86, 782, 802	393, 157, 206	415, 278, 969	420, 073, 415
Surplus	....	2, 010, 286	38, 713, 380	53, 359, 277	66, 695, 587
National bank-notes outstand'g	....	45, 260, 504	171, 321, 903	280, 129, 558	293, 237, 941
Deposits	8, 497, 681	122, 166, 536	549, 081, 254	597, 960, 993	568, 212, 337
Due to banks and bankers	981, 178	34, 862, 384	174, 199, 998	137, 483, 456	112, 756, 181

RESOURCES.	October, 1868.	October, 1869.	October, 1870.	October, 1871.	October, 1872.
	1644 banks.	1617 banks.	1615 banks.	1767 banks.	1919 banks.
Loans and discounts	$657, 668, 847	$682, 883, 106	$715, 928, 080	$831, 552, 210	$872, 520, 104
United States bonds	414, 664, 800	384, 088, 050	378, 562, 750	410, 316, 950	409, 668, 700
Due from banks and bankers	110, 127, 370	100, 853, 544	109, 426, 971	143, 176, 640	128, 180, 542
Bills of national banks	11, 842, 974	10, 776, 023	12, 512, 927	14, 197, 653	15, 734, 098
Specie	11, 749, 442	23, 002, 406	18, 460, 011	13, 252 998	10, 229, 756
Lawful money	156, 047, 205	129, 564, 295	122, 669, 577	134, 469, 735	118, 971, 104
LIABILITIES.					
Capital stock	420, 634, 511	426, 399, 151	430, 399, 301	458, 255, 696	479, 629, 144
Surplus	77, 995, 761	86, 165, 334	94, 061, 439	101, 112, 671	110, 257, 516
‡National bank-notes outstand'g	295, 769, 489	293, 593, 645	291, 798, 640	315, 519, 117	333, 495, 027
Deposits	603, 084, 550	523, 029, 491	512, 765, 708	626, 774, 021	625, 708, 307
Due to banks and bankers	123, 135, 226	118, 917, 204	130, 042, 203	171, 942, 684	143, 836, 431

* The tables of which these values are an abstract are found in full on pages 2-9 of the appendix to this report.

† During the years 1863 and 1864 the items of specie and other lawful money were not separated in the bank reports.

‡ The whole amount of circulation issued and unredeemed on November 1, 1872, including circulation of banks which have ceased to do business, was $342,593,470.

DISTRIBUTION OF THE CURRENCY.

The act of June 3, 1864, limited the issue of notes of circulation to three hundred millions of dollars. The act of March 3, 1865, provided that one-half of this amount shall be apportioned according to "the representative population," and the remainder among associations formed in the different States, District of Columbia, and Territories, "having due regard to the existing banking capital resources and business of each State, District, and Territory." The three hundred millions of circulation authorized were not, however, distributed in accordance with the act of March 3, 1865, already quoted. At the date of the passage of that act, only about ninety-nine millions of dollars had been issued, but contemporary with its passage, an amendment to the internal-revenue law (act of June 30, 1864) was passed, providing "that every national banking association, State bank, or State banking association, shall pay a tax of ten per centum on the amount of notes of any State bank or State banking association, paid out by them after the 1st day of July, 1866." But a subsequent section also provided that State banks already organized, applying for authority to become national banks before the 1st day of July following, should receive such authority in preference to new associations applying for the same. Under this provision the State associations, whose circulation had been taxed out of existence, generally applied for authority to re-organize as national banks, and the result was that the banks in the Eastern and Middle States obtained a large excess of the amount to which they were entitled in the apportionment.

To remedy this inequality, the act of July 12, 1870, was passed, providing for an additional issue of circulating notes, amounting to fifty-four millions of dollars, to be distributed among those States having less than their proportion, and requiring the cancellation monthly of three per cent. certificates,* not less than the amount of circulation issued, and a new apportionment of the increased circulation as soon as practicable, based upon the census of 1870.

This additional circulation has been distributed to associations already organized, or in process of organization, in the following States and Territories:

States and Territories.	Circulation already issued.	Amount due to banks organized.	Amount due to banks in process of organization.	Total circulation issued and authorized.
District of Columbia	$544, 500	$29, 700	....	$574, 200
Virginia	1, 607, 520	90, 000	$270, 000	1, 967, 520
West Virginia	443, 790	19, 800	....	463, 590
North Carolina	1, 019, 500	189, 000	....	1, 208, 500
South Carolina	1, 544, 760	459, 300	27, 000	2, 031, 060
Georgia	970, 500	18, 000	135, 000	1, 123, 500
Alabama	793, 180	431, 100	297, 000	1, 521, 280
Louisiana	2, 584, 000	575, 000	180, 000	3, 339, 000
Texas	239, 975	90, 000	157, 500	487, 475
Arkansas	27, 500	22, 500	45, 000	95, 000
Kentucky	4, 357, 450	284, 500	720, 000	5, 361, 950
Tennessee	1, 620, 950	116, 400	180, 000	1, 917, 350
Missouri	2, 065, 250	614, 400	135, 000	2, 814, 650
Ohio	4, 268, 780	860, 000	410, 600	5, 539, 380
Indiana	3, 309, 890	234, 000	459, 000	4, 002, 890
Illinois	6, 251, 740	1, 493, 800	683, 500	8, 429, 040
Michigan	2, 753, 425	949, 350	135, 000	3, 837, 775
Wisconsin	766, 900	38, 650	247, 500	1, 053, 050
Iowa	2, 146, 550	311, 400	405, 000	2, 862, 950
Minnesota	1, 161, 320	284, 000	435, 000	1, 880, 320
Kansas	1, 027, 000	63, 000	450, 000	1, 540, 000
Nebraska	558, 500	....	45, 000	603, 500
Oregon	136, 500	....	....	136, 500
Colorado	223, 000	....	....	223, 000
Utah	179, 990	180, 000	....	359, 990
Idaho	26, 500	....	....	26, 500
Montana	157, 500	18, 000	....	175, 500
Dakota	....	....	45, 000	45, 000
Wyoming	27, 000	....	....	27, 000
New Mexico	180, 000	90, 000	....	270, 000
	40, 993, 470	7, 461, 900	5, 462, 100	53, 917, 470

The census of 1870 does not furnish the banking capital of the country or sufficient data upon which an estimate can be made of the business of each State or Territory. If the statistics of the agriculture, the manufactures, and the commerce of every State of the Union were at hand, it would be necessary to estimate the proportion to which each branch of

*The amount of three per cent. certificates outstanding on July 1, 1870, was $45,545,000.

industry would be entitled. No satisfactory basis for this purpose can be obtained, and, after consultation with the Secretary of the Treasury, it was decided that the distribution of the circulation, one-half upon population and one-half upon the resources or wealth* of the country, would comply with both the letter and the spirit of the act more nearly than any estimate not derived from official data.

---

* The following table contains an estimate of the ratio of circulation to population and wealth in the United States in 1860 and 1870; and a similar estimate for Great Britain and France in 1868:

UNITED STATES, 1860.	
Population, (census of 1860)	31, 443, 321
Wealth, (census of 1860)	$16, 159, 616, 068
Specie, 1862	$200, 000, 000
Bank circulation, 1862	238, 671, 218
	438, 671, 218
Ratio of circulation to wealth	2. 71 per cent.
Circulation *per capita*	13. 95 +

UNITED STATES, 1870.	
Population, (census of 1870)	38, 558, 371
Wealth, (census of 1870)	$30, 068, 918, 507
Legal-tenders authorized	$350, 000, 000
National bank notes authorized	354, 000, 000
Fractional currency	40, 000, 000
Specie in circulation	40, 000, 000
	790, 000, 000
Ratio of circulation to wealth	2. 62 per cent.
Circulation *per capita*	20. 48 +

[1]UNITED KINGDOM—ENGLAND, SCOTLAND, AND IRELAND.	
Population. (estimated, 1868)	31, 000, 000
Wealth (1868)	$40, 000, 000, 000
Specie (August, 1868)	$400, 000, 000
[2]Bank-notes, 1868	196, 000, 000
	596, 000, 000
Ratio of circulation to wealth	1. 49 per cent.
Circulation *per capita*	19. 48 +

FRANCE.	
Population (1868)	38, 000, 000
Wealth (1865)	$40, 000, 000, 000
Specie (October 1, 1868)	$700, 000, 000
Bank-notes, 1868	252, 000, 000
	952, 000, 000
Ratio of circulation to wealth	2. 38 per cent.
Circulation *per capita*	25. 05 +

---

[1] Leone Levi, in his volume "On Taxation," page 5, estimates the wealth of Great Britain, in 1858, at six thousand millions of pounds. Paul Boiteau, in his work, "The Wealth and Finances of France," estimates the wealth of France, in 1865, at two thousand milliards of francs, or, say, four thousand millions of dollars. The estimates of the wealth and circulation of Great Britain and of the population and circulation of France, in 1868, are obtained from H. of R. Ex. Doc. No. 16, Fortieth Congress, third session, pp. 92-3-6.

[2]*Bank circulation of Great Britain and Ireland, October* 1872.

Bank of England, average for four weeks, ending October 30	£26, 437, 664
Private banks, average for four weeks, ending October 26	2, 853, 723
Joint stock banks, average for four weeks, ending October 26	2, 500, 815
Total	31, 792, 202
Scotch banks, average for month of October	5, 472, 734
Irish banks, average for month of October	7, 593, 784
Total for United Kingdom	£44, 858, 720

The circulation of the Bank of France for week ending October 31, was 2, 618, 663, 911 francs.

[*London Economist*, *November* 9, 1872, *pp*. 1372 and 1378.]

The following table will exhibit the amount of circulation outstanding and authorized to be issued to each State, and the amount to which each State is entitled upon the basis of population and wealth.

States and Territories.	Apportionment on population.	Apportionment on wealth.	Aggregate apportionment.	Outstanding and authorized circulation.
Maine	$2, 877, 818	$2, 053, 200	$4, 931, 018	$7, 612, 792
New Hampshire	1, 461, 138	1, 486, 800	2, 947, 938	4, 550, 875
Vermont	1, 517, 376	1, 380, 600	2, 897, 976	6, 642, 170
Massachusetts	6, 689, 889	12, 549, 300	19, 239, 189	58, 506, 686
Rhode Island	997, 747	1, 752, 300	2, 750, 047	13, 379, 900
Connecticut	2, 467, 152	4, 566, 600	7, 033, 752	17, 955, 858
New York	20, 118, 813	38, 267, 400	58, 386, 213	61, 719, 254
New Jersey	4, 159, 382	5, 540, 100	9, 699, 482	10, 863, 320
Pennsylvania	16, 167, 317	22, 425, 900	38, 593, 217	41, 479, 049
Delaware	573, 873	566, 400	1, 140, 273	1, 299, 005
Maryland	3, 584, 651	3, 787, 800	7, 372, 451	9, 233, 097
District of Columbia	604, 560	743, 400	1, 347, 960	1, 577, 996
Virginia	5, 624, 042	2, 407, 200	8, 031, 242	3, 908, 946
West Virginia	2, 029, 041	1, 115, 100	3, 144, 141	2, 393, 907
North Carolina	4, 918, 022	1, 539, 900	6, 457, 922	1, 733, 420
South Carolina	3, 239, 045	1, 221, 300	4, 460, 345	2, 315, 580
Georgia	5, 435, 587	1, 575, 300	7, 010, 887	2, 282, 301
Florida	861, 846	265, 500	1, 127, 346	....
Alabama	4, 576, 646	1, 185, 900	5, 762, 546	1, 806, 983
Mississippi	3, 800, 529	1, 239, 000	5, 039, 529	8, 876
Louisiana	3, 336, 863	1, 893, 900	5, 230, 763	4, 409, 624
Texas	3, 757, 640	938, 100	4, 695, 740	849, 220
Arkansas	2, 223, 936	920, 400	3, 144, 336	304, 750
Kentucky	6, 064, 027	3, 557, 700	9, 621, 727	7, 574, 333
Tennessee	5, 777, 118	2, 938, 200	8, 715, 318	3, 094, 851
Ohio	12, 234, 726	13, 151, 100	25, 385, 826	24, 063, 947
Indiana	7, 714, 871	7, 469, 400	15, 184, 271	14, 988, 369
Illinois	11, 659, 230	12, 496, 200	24, 155, 430	18, 175, 352
Michigan	5, 435, 357	4, 230, 300	9, 665, 657	7, 582, 943
Wisconsin	4, 841, 403	4, 141, 800	8, 983, 203	3, 283, 793
Iowa	5, 481, 081	4, 230, 300	9, 711, 381	5, 796, 307
Minnesota	2, 018, 445	1, 345, 200	3, 363, 645	3, 407, 470
Missouri	7, 901, 509	7, 557, 900	15, 459, 409	6, 835, 926
Kansas	1, 672, 754	1, 115, 100	2, 787, 854	1, 879, 700
Nebraska	564, 592	407, 100	971, 692	796, 400
Nevada	195, 052	177, 000	372, 052	34, 363
Oregon	417, 377	300, 900	718, 277	225, 000
California	2, 571, 783	3, 752, 400	6, 324, 183	....
Colorado	182, 993	123, 900	306, 893	475, 500
Utah	398, 396	88, 500	486, 896	433, 339
Idaho	68, 852	35, 400	104, 252	81, 000
Montana	94, 540	88, 500	183, 040	210, 500
Wyoming	41, 855	35, 400	77, 255	27, 500
New Mexico	421, 742	194, 700	616, 442	270, 000
Arizona	44, 334	17, 700	62, 034	....
Dakota	65, 096	35, 400	100, 496	45, 000
Washington Territory	109, 964	88, 500	198, 464	....
Fractional redemptions added	....	....	....	8
	177, 000 000	177, 000, 000	354, 000, 000	353, 917, 470

The final distribution of the fifty-four millions will still leave a deficiency of forty millions in different States of the Union, which will require to be filled before the proportion among the several States will be equalized upon the basis of wealth and population. This deficiency arises from the fact that while fifty-four millions of new circulation were authorized, there was, at the time of the passage of the act, a deficiency existing of ninety-four millions of dollars.

Section 6 of the act of July 12, 1870, provides that, after the whole fifty-four millions of circulation shall have been distributed, twenty-five millions additional shall be withdrawn from banking associations organized in States having an excess, and distributed among States having less than their proportion, first, by reducing, in such States, the circulation of all banks having more than one million of dollars, to that amount; and, secondly, by withdrawing from other banks having a circulation exceeding $300,000 their circulation *pro rata* in excess of that amount. Under this act it will be the duty of the Comptroller, as soon as the amount of circulation authorized shall have been issued, to make requisition upon the banks indicated as prescribed. The twenty-five millions of circulation would be withdrawn from the following cities and States: From four banks in the city of New York, $5,018,000; from thirty-six banks in the city of Boston, $11,403,000; from fifty-three country banks of Massachusetts, $2,894,000; from fifteen banks in Connecticut, $2,997,000; from sixteen banks in the city of Providence, $2,688,000. This would reduce the circulation of all the banks of Massachusetts, of Rhode Island, and of Connecticut to $300,000, without reference to the business of each. If the banks do not respond to these requisitions—and, as their notes are scattered throughout the whole country, it will be impracticable for them to do so—the Comptroller is required at the end of one year to sell a sufficient amount of bonds and redeem their notes as they come into the Treasury, until the whole amount required shall have been returned. The notes will not come to the Treasury for redemption unless first assorted by the brokers and resold by them to new national banks about to be organized. This will encourage the objectionable practice of authorizing new national banks with circulation upon the condition that currency shall be purchased of brokers in the market at from four to six per cent. premium—a practice which should not be encouraged or authorized by law. The Comptroller therefore recommends the repeal of this section, and the authorization of the issue of five millions of dollars of additional circulation annually for the next five years, to be distributed among the States which are deficient.

This, with the fifty-four millions of circulation recently authorized, will probably furnish all the additional currency required during the next five years for the establishment of new national banks in the States which are deficient, and virtually inaugurate a free banking system.

The Comptroller also recommends that the law be so amended that national banks may be organized in accordance with its provisions, without circulation, upon the deposit of ten thousand dollars of United States bonds with the Treasurer, instead of the deposit of one-third of the capital paid up, as now required.

Three national gold-banks have been organized in California, under the act of July 12, 1870, with an aggregate capital of $2,800,000, and circulation $1,480,000, based upon United States bonds at the rate of 80 cents on the dollar. This currency is redeemable in coin, is more convenient than the coin itself in the transaction of business, and circulates freely at par upon the Pacific coast. Other applications have been received for the organization of similar institutions, and it is probable that this kind of circulation will be considerably increased during the coming year.

The following table will exhibit the number of banks organized, the number closed and closing, and the number in operation, with their capital, amount of bonds on deposit, and circulation, in each State and Territory, on the 1st day of November, 1872:

States and Territories.	Banks organized.	Closed and closing.	In operation.	Capital paid in.	Bonds on deposit.	Circulation issued.	In actual circulation.
Maine	63	2	61	$9,225,000 00	$8,499,250 00	$9,201,296 00	$7,612,792 25
New Hampshire	43	1	42	5,148,370 60	5,113,000 00	5,442,555 00	4,550,875 00
Vermont	42	1	41	8,010,012 50	7,413,500 00	7,930,900 00	6,642,170 00
Massachusetts	214	3	211	89,147,000 00	66,305,750 00	75,731,725 00	58,506,686 50
Rhode Island	62	....	62	20,464,800 00	14,972,400 00	16,545,930 00	13,379,900 00
Connecticut	83	3	80	25,291,820 00	20,256,800 00	22,440,240 00	17,955,858 50
New York	320	34	286	111,104,141 00	69,945,050 00	90,831,645 00	61,719,254 50
New Jersey	61	1	60	13,340,350 00	12,060,650 00	13,035,175 00	10,663,320 00
Pennsylvania	212	10	202	52,960,240 00	46,890,250 00	51,969,540 00	41,479,049 50
Delaware	11	....	11	1,528,185 00	1,453,200 00	1,612,345 00	1,299,005 00
Maryland	34	1	33	13,540,202 50	10,391,250 00	11,738,070 00	9,233,097 25
District of Columbia	8	3	5	1,752,000 00	1,701,000 00	2,082,500 00	1,548,296 60
Virginia	25	4	24	3,835,000 00	3,876,000 00	4,069,450 00	3,548,946 75
West Virginia	19	2	17	2,596,000 00	2,552,750 00	2,928,000 00	2,374,107 00
North Carolina	10	....	10	1,952,500 00	1,740,100 00	1,605,500 00	1,544,420 00
South Carolina	10	....	10	3,036,000 00	2,063,000 00	1,846,180 00	1,829,260 00
Georgia	13	2	11	2,620,000 00	2,356,400 00	2,340,050 00	2,129,301 75
Alabama	10	1	9	1,296,000 00	1,183,000 00	1,225,400 00	1,078,883 25
Mississippi	2	2	......	....	....	66,000 00	8,876 25
Louisiana	9	1	8	4,850,000 00	4,074,000 00	4,014,320 00	3,654,824 50
Texas	5	....	5	725,000 00	725,000 00	792,270 00	601,720 00
Arkansas	3	1	2	205,000 00	180,000 00	281,750 00	237,250 00
Kentucky	34	1	33	7,676,000 00	7,127,150 00	7,260,020 00	6,569,833 00
Tennessee	24	1	23	3,246,300 00	3,133,650 00	3,152,450 00	2,798,451 25
Ohio	176	10	166	27,312,645 00	25,262,850 00	26,462,970 00	22,793,347 60
Indiana	91	3	88	16,662,900 00	15,926,300 00	17,148,995 00	14,295,369 25
Illinois	139	4	135	19,843,371 97	17,702,500 00	18,782,405 00	15,998,052 70
Michigan	76	3	73	8,848,800 00	7,386,550 00	7,602,780 00	6,498,593 00
Wisconsin	48	6	42	3,300,000 00	3,221,050 00	3,886,310 00	2,997,643 60
Iowa	81	8	73	5,752,000 00	5,568,000 00	6,347,825 00	5,081,967 40
Minnesota	31	2	29	3,162,600 00	3,008,150 00	3,147,190 00	2,688,470 00
Missouri	41	4	37	9,475,300 00	6,724,350 00	7,372,350 00	6,086,526 00
Kansas	24	....	24	1,625,000 00	1,590,000 00	1,506,400 00	1,366,700 00
Nebraska	10	1	9	850,000 00	850,000 00	796,800 00	751,400 00
Nevada	1	1	......	....	....	146,200 00	34,363 50
Oregon	1	....	1	250,000 00	250,000 00	231,500 00	225,000 00
Colorado	6	....	6	575,000 00	530,000 00	519,140 00	475,500 00
Utah	4	1	3	350,000 00	350,000 00	356,610 00	253,339 00
Idaho	1	....	1	100,000 00	100,000 00	99,200 00	81,000 00
Montana	4	....	4	300,000 00	236,000 00	197,800 00	192,500 00
Wyoming	1	....	1	75,000 00	30,000 00	27,500 00	27,500 00
New Mexico	2	....	2	300,000 00	200,000 00	185,500 00	180,000 00
Total	2,057	117	1,940	482,432,538 57	382,968,900 00	434,960,786 00	340,993,470 30
GOLD-BANKS.							
Massachusetts	1	....	1	300,000 00	150,000 00	120,000 00	120,000 00
California	3	....	3	2,800,000 00	1,850,000 00	1,481,100 00	1,480,000 00
Total	4	....	4	3,100,000 00	2,000,000 00	1,601,100 00	1,600,000 00

The following comparative tables will exhibit the amount of circulation issued under State laws, previous to the establishment of the national banking system, and the amount authorized by Congress; the ratio of bank circulation issued in 1862 and now issued, to capital and to deposits; the per capita of circulation in 1862; and the per capita of circulation authorized by Congress:

COMPARATIVE TABLE NO. 1.—*Exhibiting, by States, the *bank circulation, the per capita, the ratio of circulation to wealth, to capital, and to deposits, previous to the organization (in 1862) of the national banking system.*

	Bank circulation, 1862.	Population, 1860.	Circulation per capita.	Wealth, 1860.	Ratio of circulation to wealth.	Ratio of circulation to capital	Ratio of circulation to deposits.
					Pr. ct.	*Pr. ct.*	*Pr. ct.*
Maine	$6, 488, 478	628, 279	$10 33	$190, 211, 600	3. 4	81. 3	128
New Hampshire	4, 192, 034	326, 073	12 86	156, 310, 860	2. 6	85. 3	243
Vermont	5, 621, 851	315, 098	17 84	122, 477, 170	4. 6	143. 7	607
Massachusetts	28, 957, 630	1, 231, 066	23 52	815, 237, 433	3. 5	42. 8	65
Rhode Island	6, 413, 404	174, 620	36 73	135, 337, 588	4. 7	30. 7	119
Connecticut	13, 842, 758	460, 147	30 08	444, 274, 114	3. 1	63. 5	156
Total Eastern States	65, 516, 155	3, 135, 283	20 90	1, 863, 848, 765	3. 5	51. 7	98
New York	39, 182, 819	3, 880, 735	10 10	1, 843, 338, 517	2. 1	36. 0	19
New Jersey	8. 172, 398	672, 035	12 16	467, 918, 324	1. 7	99. 8	85
Pennsylvania	27, 689, 504	2, 906, 215	9 53	1, 416, 501, 818	1. 9	100. 8	64
Delaware	678, 340	112, 216	6 04	46, 242, 181	1. 5	176. 2	133
Maryland	6, 649, 030	687, 049	9 68	376, 919, 944	1. 8	54. 9	48
Total Middle States	82, 372, 091	8, 258, 250	9 97	4, 150, 920, 784	2. 0	53. 1	31
District of Columbia	....	75, 080	......	41, 084, 945	....	......	....
Virginia	19, 817, 148	1, 596, 318	12 41	793, 249, 681	2. 5	120. 2	277
West Virginia	....	....	......	....	....	......	....
North Carolina	5, 218, 598	992, 622	5 26	358, 739, 399	1. 4	66. 3	250
South Carolina	6, 089, 036	703, 708	8 65	548, 138, 754	1. 1	40. 7	183
Georgia	8, 311, 728	1, 057, 286	7 86	645, 895, 237	1. 3	50. 2	216
Florida	116, 250	140, 424	83	73, 101, 500	. 1	27. 3	107
Alabama	5, 055, 222	964, 201	5 24	495, 237, 078	1. 0	101. 5	147
Mississippi	....	791, 305	......	607, 324, 911	....	......	....
Louisiana	8, 876, 519	708, 002	12 54	602, 118, 568	1. 5	51. 0	153
Texas	....	604, 215	......	365, 200, 614	....	......	....
Arkansas	....	435, 450	......	219, 256, 473	....	......	....
Kentucky	9, 035, 724	1, 155, 684	7 82	666, 043, 112	1. 3	65. 5	118
Tennessee	4, 540, 906	1, 109, 801	4 09	493, 903, 892	. 9	127. 4	403
Missouri	4, 037, 277	1, 182, 012	3 42	501, 214, 398	. 8	35. 9	117
Total Southern and Southwestern States	71, 098, 408	11, 516, 108	6 17	6, 410, 508, 562	1. 1	66. 3	187
Ohio	9, 057, 837	2, 339, 511	3 87	1, 193, 898, 422	. 7	159. 6	77
Indiana	6, 782, 890	1, 350, 428	5 02	528, 835, 371	1. 3	150. 9	225
Illinois	619, 286	1, 711, 951	36	871, 860, 282	. 1	31. 4	155
Michigan	131, 087	749, 113	17	257, 163, 983	. 0	......	9
Wisconsin	1, 643, 200	775, 881	2 12	273, 671, 668	. 6	53. 8	49
Iowa	1, 249, 000	674, 913	1 85	247, 338, 265	. 5	150. 5	97
Minnesota	198, 494	172, 023	1 15	52, 294, 413	. 4	62. 4	213
Kansas	2, 770	107, 206	03	31, 327, 895	. 0	5. 3	46
Nebraska	....	28, 841	......	9, 131, 056	....	......	....
Total Western States	19, 684, 564	7, 909, 867	2 49	3, 465, 521, 355	. 6	125. 4	93
Nevada	....	6, 857	......	....	....	......	....
Oregon	....	52, 465	......	28, 930, 637	....	......	....
California	....	379, 994	......	207, 874, 613	....	......	....
Colorado	....	34, 277	......	....	....	......	....
Utah	....	40, 273	......	5, 596, 118	....	......	....
Idaho	....	....	......	....	....	......	....
Montana	....	....	......	....	....	......	....
Wyoming	....	....	......	....	....	......	....
New Mexico	....	93, 516	......	20, 813, 768	....	......	....
Arizona	....	....	......	....	....	......	....
Dakota	....	4, 837	......	....	....	......	....
Washington Territory	....	11, 594	......	5, 601, 466	....	......	....
Total Pacific States and Territories	....	623, 813	......	268, 816, 602	....	......	....
Grand total of States and Territories	238, 671, 218	31, 443, 321	7 59	16, 159, 616, 068	1. 5	58. 9	61

* The circulation of the State banks in the year 1862 has been obtained from page 210 of the report of the Secretary of the Treasury on the condition of the banks at the commencement of the year 1863. The returns from Delaware, Maryland, Louisiana, Tennessee, and Kentucky were not complete. The aggregate amount of State bank circulation reported at that time was much greater than at any previous period.

COMPARATIVE TABLE No. 2.—*Exhibiting, by States, the amount of authorized circulation, (aggregate, $354,000,000,) together with the population and wealth in 1870, the authorized circulation per capita, the ratio of authorized circulation to wealth, and the ratio of circulation issued (aggregate $340,993,470) to capital and to deposits.*

	Outstanding and authorized circulation.	Population, 1870.	Authorized circulation per capita.	Wealth, 1870.	Ratio of authorized circulation to wealth.	Ratio of circulation outstanding. To capital.	Ratio of circulation outstanding. To deposits.
					Pr. ct.	Pr. ct.	Pr. ct.
Maine	$7,612,792	626,915	$12 14	$348,155,671	2.2	83	139
New Hampshire	4,550,875	318,300	14 30	252,624,112	1.8	68	167
Vermont	6,642,170	330,551	20 09	235,349,553	2.8	83	190
Massachusetts	58,506,686	1,457,351	40 15	2,132,148,741	2.7	61	89
Rhode Island	13,379,900	217,353	61 56	296,965,646	4.5	65	192
Connecticut	17,955,856	537,454	33 41	774,631,524	2.3	71	125
Total Eastern States	108,048,281	3,487,924	31 15	4,039,875,247	2.7	69	110
New York	61,719,254	4,382,759	14 08	6,500,841,264	.9	56	25
New Jersey	10,663,320	906,096	11 77	940,976,064	1.1	80	61
Pennsylvania	41,479,049	3,521,951	11 78	3,808,340,112	1.1	78	51
Delaware	1,290,005	125,015	10 39	97,180,833	1.3	85	75
Maryland	9,233,097	780,894	11 82	643,748,976	1.4	68	61
Total Middle States	124,393,725	9,716,715	12 80	11,991,087,249	1.0	65	35
District of Columbia	1,577,996	131,700	11 98	126,873,618	1.2	88	54
Virginia	3,908,946	1,225,163	3 19	409,588,133	1.0	93	55
West Virginia	2,393,907	442,014	5 41	190,651,491	1.3	91	89
North Carolina	1,733,420	1,071,361	1 62	260,757,244	.7	79	63
South Carolina	2,315,580	705,606	3 28	208,146,989	1.1	60	108
Georgia	2,282,301	1,184,109	1 93	268,169,207	.9	81	110
Florida	....	187,748	....	44,163,655	......	....	......
Alabama	1,806,983	996,992	1 81	201,855,841	.9	83	108
Mississippi	8,876	827,922	01	209,197,345	.0	....	......
Louisiana	4,409,824	726,915	6 07	323,125,666	1.4	75	57
Texas	849,220	818,579	1 04	159,052,542	.5	63	74
Arkansas	304,750	484,471	63	156,394,691	.2	116	206
Kentucky	7,574,333	1,321,011	5 73	604,318,552	1.3	86	208
Tennessee	3,094,851	1,258,520	2 46	498,237,724	.6	86	71
Missouri	6,835,926	1,721,295	3 97	1,284,922,897	.5	64	96
Total Southern and Southwestern States	39,096,913	13,103,406	2 98	4,945,455,595	.8	79	85
Ohio	24,063,947	2,665,260	9 03	2,235,430,300	1.1	83	76
Indiana	14,988,369	1,680,637	8 92	1,268,180,543	1.2	86	113
Illinois	18,175,352	2,539,891	7 16	2,121,680,579	.9	81	49
Michigan	7,582,943	1,184,059	6 40	719,208,118	1.1	73	58
Wisconsin	3,283,793	1,054,670	3 11	702,307,329	.5	91	47
Iowa	5,798,367	1,194,020	4 86	717,644,750	.8	88	65
Minnesota	3,407,470	439,706	7 75	228,909,590	1.5	85	54
Kansas	1,879,700	364,399	5 10	188,892,014	1.0	84	56
Nebraska	796,400	122,993	6 48	69,277,483	1.1	88	35
Total Western States	79,976,341	11,245,635	7 11	8,251,530,706	1.0	83	66
Nevada	34,363	42,491	81	31,134,012	.1	....	......
Oregon	225,000	90,923	2 47	51,558,932	.4	90	40
California	....	560,247	....	638,767,017	......	....	......
Colorado	475,500	39,864	11 93	20,243,303	2.3	83	24
Utah	433,339	86,786	4 90	16,159,995	2.7	70	52
Idaho	81,000	14,999	5 40	6,552,681	1.2	81	85
Montana	210,500	20,595	10 22	15,184,522	1.4	64	43
Wyoming	27,500	9,118	3 02	7,016,748	.4	36	34
New Mexico	270,000	91,874	2 94	31,349,793	.9	60	198
Arizona	....	9,658	....	3,440,791	......	....	......
Dakota	45,000	14,181	....	5,999,752	......	....	......
Washington Territory	....	23,955	....	13,562,164	......	....	......
Total Pacific States and Territories	1,802,202	1,004,691	1 75	840,969,710	.2	75	212
Fractional redemptions added	8	....	....	....	......	....	......
Grand total of States and Territories	353,917,470	38,558,371	9 18	30,068,918,507	1.2	71	56

TAXATION, EARNINGS, AND DIVIDENDS.

The national banks pay the following taxes to the Treasurer of the United States: One per cent. annually on circulation outstanding; one-half of one per cent. annually upon deposits; and one-half of one per cent. annually on capital not invested in United States bonds. These taxes are payable semi-annually. The amount of taxes collected by the Treasurer from January 1, 1864, to January 1, 1872, was as follows:

On circulation	$19,177,734 54
On deposits	18,611,945 72
On capital	2,453,025 17
Total	40,242,705 43

The national banks, prior to May 1, 1871, also paid to the Commissioner of Internal Revenue a license or special tax of $2 on each $1,000 of capital, and an income-tax on net earnings to December 1, 1871. The special or license tax from May 1, 1864, to May 1, 1871, amounted to $5,322,688.43; the income-tax from March 1, 1869, to September 1, 1871, amounted to $5,539,289.17. The following table will exhibit the amount of taxes collected from these sources during the years 1870-'71:

Duty on circulation, deposits, and capital.		License-tax on capital.		Taxation of earnings.		Total taxation.
Year ended-	Amount.	Year ending-	Amount.	Year ending-	Amount.	
Dec. 31, 1870	$6,017,460 34	April 30, 1870	$866,238 54	Aug. 31, 1870	$2,696,035 27	$9,579,734 15
Dec. 31, 1871	6,505,812 11	April 30, 1871	884,016 49	Aug. 31, 1871	1,371,105 31	8,760,933 91
Totals...	12,523,272 45	....	1,750,255 03	....	4,067,140 58	18,340,668 06

The Comptroller, in his report for the year 1867, made careful statements of the taxes on national banks for the year 1866, from which it appears that the banks, during that year, paid over sixteen millions of United States and State taxes, as follows:

To the United States Government	$8,069,938
To the States	7,949,451

The amount of taxes paid to the several States was derived from specific returns of about fourteen hundred banks, the minimum rate in each State being calculated for those banks which made no returns. A similar statement for the year ending December 31, 1867, exhibits the following results:

Amount of taxes paid to the United States	$9,525,607 31
Amount of taxes paid to the State authorities	8,813,126 92
Aggregate taxes paid	18,338,734 23

Or $4\frac{1}{3}$ per cent. upon a capital of $422,804,666.

The aggregate State tax was believed to be considerably below the actual amount paid. Assuming the amount of State taxes paid by the national banks to be the same as that paid to the United States Government, (which is a moderate estimate,) we shall have the total taxes paid by the national banks during these four years:

1866	$16,019,389 00
1867	18,338,734 23
1870	19,159,468 30
1871	17,529,867 82

The act of March 3, 1869, required specific returns to be made of the dividends and net earnings of the national banks after the declaration of each dividend. From these returns the following table has been prepared, exhibiting the aggregate capital and surplus; total dividends and total earnings of the national banks, with the ratio of dividends to capital; dividends to capital and surplus; and earnings to capital and surplus, for each half-year, commencing March 1, 1869, and ended September 1, 1872.

Period of six months ending—	Number of banks.	Capital.	Average surplus.	Total dividends.	Total net earnings.	Ratios.		
						Dividends to capital.	Dividends to capital and surplus.	Earnings to capital and surplus.
						Per. ct.	Per. ct.	Per. ct.
Aug. 31, 1869.	1,481	$401,650,802	$82,105,848	$21,767,831	$29,221,184	5.42	4.50	6.04
Feb. 28, 1870.	1,571	416,366,991	86,118,210	21,479,095	28,996,934	5.16	4.27	5.77
Aug. 31, 1870.	1,601	425,317,104	91,630,620	21,080,343	26,813,885	4.96	4.08	5.19
Feb. 28, 1871.	1,605	428,699,165	94,672,401	22,205,150	27,243,162	5.18	4.24	5.21
Aug. 31, 1871.	1,693	445,999,264	98,286,591	22,125,279	27,315,311	4.96	4.07	5.02
Feb. 28, 1872.	1,750	450,693,706	99,431,243	22,859,826	27,502,539	5.07	4.16	5.
Aug. 31, 1872.	1,852	465,676,023	105,181,942	23,827,289	30,572,891	5.12	4.17	5.36

The following table will exhibit, in a concise form, the ratios of dividends to capital; dividends to capital and surplus; and earnings to capital and surplus, of the national banks in every State of the Union, and in the redemption cities, semi-annually, from March 1, 1869, to September 1, 1872:

Table exhibiting by States and redemption cities the ratios of dividends to

	States, Territories, and cities.	Ratios of dividends to capital for six months ending—						
		Aug. 31, 1869.	Feb. 28, 1870.	Aug. 31, 1870.	Feb. 28, 1871.	Aug. 31, 1871.	Feb. 28, 1872.	Aug. 31, 1872.
		Per ct.	*Per ct.*	*Per ct.*	*Per ct.*	*Per ct.*	*Per ct.*	*Per ct.*
1	Maine	5. 19	5. 14	5. 23	5. 18	5. 13	5. 07	5. 23
2	New Hampshire	4. 88	4. 96	4. 82	4. 82	4. 68	4. 80	4. 64
3	Vermont	4. 87	4. 99	5. 28	4. 66	4. 76	4. 84	4. 64
4	Massachusetts	5. 41	5. 30	4. 99	5. 42	5. 29	5. 45	5. 40
5	Boston	5. 49	4. 95	4. 92	4. 94	4. 81	4. 73	4. 55
6	Rhode Island	4. 44	4. 51	4. 45	4. 43	4. 31	4. 39	4. 39
7	Connecticut	4. 99	5. 33	5. 16	5. 30	5. 20	5. 25	5. 29
8	New York	4. 90	4. 36	4. 44	4. 84	4. 44	4. 70	4. 37
9	New York City	5. 16	4. 90	4. 59	4. 71	4. 66	4. 69	4. 67
10	Albany	5. 32	5. 13	5. 32	5. 32	4. 94	4. 15	5. 74
11	New Jersey	5. 70	5. 84	5. 39	5. 62	5. 12	5. 74	5. 40
12	Pennsylvania	5. 55	5. 57	5. 58	5. 35	5. 23	5. 36	5. 21
13	Philadelphia	6. 09	5. 96	5. 79	4. 90	5. 70	5. 74	5. 76
14	Pittsburgh	5. 51	5. 14	5. 16	5. 15	5. 36	5. 41	5. 32
15	Delaware	5. 70	5. 38	5. 53	5. 13	5. 12	5. 12	5. 06
16	Maryland	5. 61	5. 75	5. 23	5. 57	5. 20	5. 16	5. 26
17	Baltimore	5. 40	5. 49	4. 98	4. 79	4. 70	5. 09	5. 27
18	District of Columbia	....	....	....	....	....	....	4.
19	Washington	5.	5.	5.	5.	5.	2. 62	4. 58
20	Virginia	5. 11	5. 50	4. 90	4. 75	4. 34	4. 61	4. 66
21	West Virginia	5. 20	5. 04	5. 05	5. 29	4. 18	5. 44	5. 31
22	North Carolina	7. 31	5. 65	4. 15	4. 27	4. 44	6.	5. 05
23	South Carolina	5. 81	13. 59	5. 53	6.	5. 48	5. 40	5. 10
24	Georgia	6. 40	5. 73	5. 63	9. 34	5. 33	4. 88	5. 34
25	Alabama	....	....	....	4. 75	5. 60	3. 41	6. 44
26	New Orleans	5.	6. 15	6. 15	6. 15	5. 21	5. 64	5. 53
27	Texas	6. 67	4. 33	13. 81	1. 90	5. 92	4. 38	7. 68
28	Arkansas	....	....	....	....	....	....	....
29	Kentucky	5. 24	5. 16	4. 99	5. 03	4. 63	4. 19	4. 84
30	Louisville	5. 32	5. 60	5. 32	5. 05	11.	5. 37	5.
31	Tennessee	7. 86	10. 32	5. 92	8. 65	5. 62	5. 82	6.
32	Ohio	5. 83	5. 13	4. 79	5. 75	5. 63	5. 82	5. 99
33	Cincinnati	6. 41	5. 69	5. 71	4. 86	5. 43	4. 95	5. 45
34	Cleveland	5. 72	5. 65	3. 82	2. 97	3. 88	4. 19	5. 09
35	Indiana	5. 58	5. 41	5. 21	6. 06	5. 58	5. 37	5. 88
36	Illinois	6. 96	6. 26	6. 59	6. 29	6. 07	5. 71	5. 49
37	Chicago	6. 33	3. 21	2. 75	4. 80	5. 05	....	6. 21
38	Michigan	7. 40	6. 10	5. 68	6. 13	5. 08	6. 47	6. 12
39	Detroit	4. 57	5.	5.	5.	5.	5. 29	5.
40	Wisconsin	6. 50	6. 19	5. 94	9. 83	4. 12	4. 94	4. 92
41	Milwaukee	5. 69	4. 35	4. 60	5. 31	4. 60	4. 87	19.
42	Iowa	7. 96	6. 43	5. 38	5. 80	5. 12	4. 76	14. 13
43	Minnesota	6. 89	7. 02	5. 49	8. 11	6. 91	5. 25	5. 90
44	Missouri	6. 22	5. 25	6. 28	17. 27	5. 33	5. 24	4. 73
45	Saint Louis	5. 11	4. 27	3. 71	3. 14	3. 29	3. 20	3. 19
46	Kansas	5. 41	6. 45	7. 59	6. 16	5. 63	4. 65	5. 49
47	Leavenworth	10.	10.	22. 40	8.	5.	10.	....
48	Nebraska	7. 50	7. 14	4.	6. 25	6. 25	7. 08	6. 61
49	Oregon	15.	15.	....	....	4.	6.	6.
50	San Francisco	....	....	....	....	....	0. 83	5.
51	New Mexico	....	....	....	....	4.	7.	7.
52	Colorado	....	5. 71	2. 86	....	8. 57	2. 50	3. 26
53	Utah	....	....	....	....	....	50.	....
54	Wyoming	....	....	....	....	....	....	....
55	Idaho	15.	15.	14.	16.	15.	14.	13.
56	Montana	....	....	....	....	....	12.	....
57	Nevada	3.	....	....	....	....	....	....
	Averages	5. 42	5. 16	4. 96	5. 18	4. 96	5. 07	5. 12

NOTE.—In the above table the redemption cities are not

capital and the ratios of dividends and of earnings to capital and surplus.

Ratios of dividends to capital and surplus, for six months ending—							Ratios of earnings to capital and surplus, for six months ending—							
Aug. 31, 1869.	Feb. 28, 1870.	Aug. 31, 1870.	Feb. 28, 1871.	Aug. 31, 1871.	Feb. 28, 1872.	Aug. 31, 1872.	Aug. 31, 1869.	Feb. 28, 1870.	Aug. 31, 1870.	Feb. 28, 1871.	Aug. 31, 1871.	Feb. 28, 1872.	Aug. 31, 1872.	
Per ct.	*Per ct.*	*Per ct.*	*Per ct.*	*Per ct.*	*Per ct.*	*Per ct.*	*Per ct.*	*Per ct.*	*Per ct.*	*Per ct.*	*Per ct.*	*Per ct.*	*Per ct.*	
4.53	4.45	4.49	4.43	4.37	4.28	4.40	6.08	6.	5.80	5.72	6.03	5.24	5.61	1
4.36	4.40	4.23	4.19	4.03	4.14	3.97	6.06	6.16	5.73	5.33	4.59	4.77	4.86	2
4.39	4.42	4.68	4.09	4.17	4.21	4.02	6.03	6.06	5.60	5.30	4.79	4.94	5.33	3
4.43	4.30	4.03	4.33	4.19	4.30	4.24	6.35	6.36	5.34	5.48	5.21	5.02	5.48	4
4.53	4.09	4.08	4.07	3.94	3.86	3.72	5.73	5.13	5.16	4.90	4.63	4.64	4.53	5
4.12	4.17	4.06	4.03	3.89	3.92	3.86	5.02	5.71	5.03	4.82	4.71	4.62	5.28	6
4.21	4.50	4.31	4.38	4.27	4.20	4.27	5.53	5.84	5.25	5.30	5.20	5.11	5.46	7
4.17	3.77	3.77	4.09	3.72	3.92	3.64	5.83	5.43	5.04	5.05	4.47	4.54	5.14	8
4.14	3.92	3.65	3.75	3.70	3.86	3.67	5.44	4.81	4.23	4.41	4.48	4.03	4.84	9
3.89	3.75	3.87	3.87	3.60	3.02	3.92	6.08	5.74	4.13	3.67	3.61	5.62	5.22	10
4.69	4.08	4.42	4.58	4.16	4.63	4.34	6.30	6.13	5.88	5.83	5.88	5.64	5.41	11
4.60	4.61	4.55	4.34	4.24	4.33	4.17	6.07	6.27	5.35	4.78	5.17	5.24	5.05	12
4.40	4.34	4.14	4.20	4.06	4.09	4.09	5.29	5.10	4.67	4.39	4.41	4.59	4.59	13
4.44	4.12	4.13	4.10	4.22	4.24	4.14	5.80	5.17	5.13	4.97	4.94	4.80	4.99	14
4.66	4.37	4.56	4.21	4.16	4.12	4.06	5.40	4.78	5.30	4.50	4.63	4.40	4.86	15
4.81	4.09	4.51	4.75	4.40	4.36	4.46	6.43	6.46	5.87	5.30	4.83	4.54	5.50	16
4.07	4.74	4.26	4.08	3.99	4.34	4.46	5.92	6.41	5.80	5.27	4.90	5.40	5.56	17
......	......	......	......	......	......	3.71	......	......	......	......	......	......	4.85	18
4.08	4.07	4.05	4.04	4.	2.12	3.70	4.78	5.18	4.35	5.22	7.64	3.04	5.26	19
4.68	5.09	4.51	4.31	3.08	4.22	4.24	6.45	6.82	6.39	6.81	6.62	5.30	5.97	20
4.65	4.44	4.42	4.70	3.72	4.87	4.76	6.47	5.86	5.66	5.33	3.52	5.76	5.91	21
6.85	5.32	3.85	3.94	4.19	5.66	4.83	10.04	8.93	5.46	5.91	6.17	7.27	3.72	22
5.39	12.47	5.07	5.40	5.03	5.05	4.76	7.76	9.82	8.75	7.47	5.93	6.72	6.46	23
5.76	5.09	5.02	8.22	4.78	4.36	4.74	7.59	7.91	8.20	6.70	5.83	5.95	6.70	24
......	......	......	4.58	5.24	3.28	6.18	......	1.69	......	11.35	5.70	4.34	9.39	25
4.72	5.84	5.78	5.69	5.	5.40	5.34	7.14	7.05	8.61	7.48	3.27	6.31	6.93	26
5.90	3.80	12.62	1.75	5.44	4.01	6.99	6.41	6.87	16.49	6.81	6.42	9.11	12.11	27
......	......	......	......	......	......	......	......	......	......	......	......	......	0.27	28
4.83	4.67	4.48	5.01	4.32	3.01	4.49	6.58	6.86	6.93	6.11	5.41	4.80	5.67	29
4.69	4.46	4.62	4.38	9.86	4.87	4.62	5.27	6.56	4.38	4.53	5.69	5.52	5.22	30
6.97	8.81	5.24	7.70	5.16	5.33	5.46	8.17	9.50	7.15	8.34	7.14	7.79	5.79	31
4.94	4.33	3.97	4.72	4.58	4.74	4.92	6.78	6.43	5.46	6.03	5.87	6.12	6.	32
5.17	4.83	4.93	4.18	4.56	4.22	4.61	7.91	6.30	4.80	6.67	4.39	4.84	5.35	33
4.56	4.71	3.45	2.67	3.46	3.71	4.52	5.	6.85	3.88	3.08	4.	5.70	5.27	34
4.62	4.43	4.21	4.82	4.52	4.37	4.79	6.50	6.42	5.94	6.30	5.43	5.40	5.25	35
5.52	5.01	5.14	4.97	4.92	4.68	4.54	7.98	7.90	6.70	6.77	6.65	6.07	6.50	36
5.35	2.20	2.06	3.50	3.81	......	5.	8.25	5.64	5.33	7.46	6.90	......	6.79	37
5.97	4.83	4.46	4.68	4.12	5.28	5.06	8.	7.88	6.89	7.06	6.26	6.57	7.15	38
3.85	4.12	4.10	4.10	4.10	4.32	3.80	6.27	6.80	5.85	6.09	6.58	6.90	6.66	39
5.18	5.01	4.76	8.07	3.45	4.20	4.09	7.75	8.13	6.91	9.01	5.27	6.67	5.49	40
4.46	3.59	3.76	4.16	3.74	3.76	15.22	7.81	3.97	5.39	6.65	6.28	4.89	13.04	41
6.42	5.19	4.92	4.78	4.24	4.01	9.63	8.96	7.80	5.66	6.31	5.53	5.90	11.80	42
6.13	6.05	4.70	6.92	5.05	4.56	5.09	7.08	8.	6.15	8.53	7.15	7.08	7.28	43
5.17	4.34	4.89	14.19	4.75	4.71	4.18	8.58	9.73	9.39	8.62	6.96	7.98	10.16	44
4.64	3.91	3.35	2.87	2.97	2.86	2.84	5.43	4.71	3.36	2.87	4.38	4.08	4.03	45
5.13	6.10	7.01	5.63	5.34	4.40	4.99	7.82	9.08	8.08	10.85	10.18	9.03	6.86	46
8.27	6.67	17.22	6.17	3.75	7.29	......	11.57	8.06	18.50	7.44	6.76	6.74	......	47
6.71	6.19	3.58	5.41	5.38	6.36	5.93	11.47	7.79	5.69	12.74	3.64	6.48	7.54	48
14.42	14.29	......	......	3.92	5.86	5.83	14.42	9.80	13.90	7.67	11.93	15.19	20.91	49
......	......	......	......	......	......	4.95	......	......	......	......	2.11	5.07	5.50	50
......	......	......	......	......	6.26	6.87	......	......	......	......	4.99	7.73	9.55	51
......	4.67	2.37	......	7.10	2.12	2.78	......	8.30	1.47	0.09	2.80	6.39	4.66	52
......	......	......	......	......	21.85	......	......	......	1.42	1.44	5.55	47.82	1.54	53
......	......	......	......	......	......	......	......	......	......	......	......	......	......	54
14.68	14.35	13.30	14.95	13.86	12.74	11.71	11.54	16.03	13.92	16.45	13.91	15.21	23.62	55
......	......	......	......	......	10.91	......	......	......	......	2.78	18.92	16.74	7.56	56
2.92	......	......	......	......	......	......	3.47	......	......	......	......	......	......	57
4.50	4.27	4.08	4.24	4.07	4.16	4.17	6.04	5.77	5.19	5.21	5.02	5.	5.36	

included with the States in which such cities are located.

Complete statistics, in detail, of the capital, surplus, earnings, and dividends by States and cities, will be found on pages 38–44 of the appendix.

The national banks are required to furnish to this office not less than five statements during each year of their assets and liabilities, and also to make specific returns to the Treasurer, semi-annually, of their circulation, deposits, and the average amount of capital not invested in United States bonds. The officers of the United States, and of the different States, whose duty it is to collect taxes, have, therefore, at all times at their command the *data* from which to ascertain the amount of taxes to be collected; and it is believed that there is no other species of capital upon which the tax can be so definitely assessed and so certainly collected as the tax upon the national banks of the country. There is no doubt that in some instances, owing to large deposits in proportion to capital, or to high rates of interest in the new States, large dividends have been declared; but it will be seen from the above table that the average earnings of the national banks, after making a proper allowance for bad debts, are not more than a fair remuneration upon capital. The dividends declared do not probably exceed in the aggregate the dividends under the old State systems, and are far less than the average annual dividends of the English banks.*

It is generally supposed that the circulation issued to the national

* The following statements of ten of the principal banks of London, including their branches, exhibiting the capital, reserve, deposits, net profits, and dividends of each, for the half-year previous to July 1, 1872, have been compiled from Abbott's tables in the London Bankers' Magazine for September:

No. of establishments.	Bank.	Paid-up capital.	Reserve fund.	Total deposits and acceptances.	Net profits.	Rate per cent. per annum of net profit on capital.	Amount of dividend for half year.	Rate per cent. per annum of dividend on capital.
8	London and Westminster	£2,000,000	£1,000,000	£26,773,829	£204,620	20.46	£200,000	20
6	London Joint Stock	1,200,000	454,890	20,935,302	140,923	23.49	120,000	20
114	London and County	1,000,000	500,000	19,327,458	103,086	20.62	100,000	20
5	Union	1,200,000	300,000	18,850,247	129,612	21.60	120,000	20
4	City	500,000	120,000	6,132,258	35,165	14.07	25,000	10
3	Imperial	450,000	65,000	2,631,925	23,744	10.55	18,000	8
23	London and South-western	166,180	5,000	681,963	5,578	6.71	4,154	5
3	Consolidated	800,000	66,000	3,082,791	39,645	9.91	32,000	8
4	Central	100,000	7,500	590,102	6,052	12.10	4,000	8
2	Alliance	800,000	110,000	2,522,771	29,920	7.48	24,000	6
	Total	8,216,180	2,628,390	101,526,646	718,345	17.49	647,154	15½
Aug. 31, 1872.	Bank of England	14,553,000	3,010,295	†126,974,008	716,375	8.32	727,650	10

†Public and other deposits, August 28.

The statistics of the Bank of England and its dividends were obtained from the report of the Bank of England, published in the London Bankers' Magazine for October, 1872. The usual dividends of this bank are 10 per cent. per annum, but the amount has varied for some years past from 8 to 13 per cent.

Similar statistics of 142 of the banks in Great Britain and Ireland, with an aggregate capital of £61,361,531, (or, $298,622,027,) compiled from a table in the London Economist of October 26, 1872, (pages 345–6,) give the average dividends for the four half-years prior to July 1, 1872, as, respectively, 5.71, 5.95, 6.25, and 6.41 per cent.

banks is a source of great profit; but if the premium upon bonds is considered as an ultimate loss, the profit upon circulation does not exceed 3 per cent. per annum. The chief source of profit in banking, under this as under all other systems, is from deposits, and upon this branch of business an annual tax is already fixed by law. If the system has the advantage of circulation, it is also subject to many restrictions which are considered burdensome, but which give steadiness and strength to the money transactions of the country. While the banks should contribute their proportion to the revenues of the country, they should not, under an imputation of extravagant profits, or an unfounded prejudice, be taxed to a greater degree than other corporations which are even less important to its prosperity.

The consolidation of the bank capital of the country in a sound and conservative system, with proper safeguards and restrictions, is of much greater importance than a penny-wise and pound-foolish imposition of excessive taxation, which will have a tendency to drive those banks that are not over-conscientious out of the system, with the purpose of evading all taxation whatever.

RESERVE.

A good deal of discussion has arisen during the recent stringency in the money market in the city of New York in reference to the provisions of the national currency act, requiring a reserve upon the liabilities of national banks.

The act requires that the country banks shall hold an amount of reserve equal to fifteen per cent. of the entire amount of their deposits and circulation, three-fifths of which reserve may be on deposit with national banks which are their agents in redemption cities. The national banks in the redemption cities must hold a reserve of twenty-five per cent., one-half of which may be on deposit with national banks in New York City.

The reserves of the nineteen hundred national banks located elsewhere than in the city of New York are held to a great extent in that city. For most of the time during the past year, an amount equal to more than one-fifth of the capital of all these national banks has been held on deposit by the national banks of the city of New York to the credit of their correspondents. In many cases these credits amount to twice the capital of the bank with which they are deposited; in other cases the amount of deposits is three, four, and even five times the capital, which amount has been attracted thither largely by the payment of interest on deposits. The failure of one of these New York City banks in a time of monetary stringency would embarrass, if not ruin, many banks in the redemption cities, and, in turn, the country correspondents of these banks would suffer from the imprudence of the New York bank, which would be responsible for wide-spread disaster. It is clear that a bank having such excessive liabilities has no right, even if there were no law, to increase its loans to such an unreasonable extent as to lead to embarrassment if unexpectedly called upon for the reserves of its correspondents. A provision of law prohibiting banks from extending their loans beyond three times their capital would seem to be not unreasonable, but such a provision would be much more restrictive than the present requirements of the law in reference to reserve.

The State laws of Massachusetts and Louisiana, which were in most respects models of a sound system of bank legislation, required an ample reserve to be kept on hand. The laws of the State of New York had no such restriction. The country banks of that State were, however, required to redeem their notes in the city of New York, in specie, and an examination of their returns will show that while the country banks usually held but a very small proportion (about 2½ per cent.) of circulation and deposits in their vaults, they were forced to keep on deposit with their city correspondents nearly as large a proportion of reserve as under the national system. An examination of the weekly returns made to the clearing-house in New York City will show that the State banks of established reputation in times of monetary stringency hold a sufficient reserve without such provision of law; while the larger proportion of banks, not included in the national system, are continually below a judicious limit. The truth is that the strong and well-managed banks do not need any law in reference to reserve, and do not, therefore, ask for a change of legislation in this respect. The weak banks and those already too largely extended wish to be free from all restrictions. It is the constant tendency of such banks to increase their liabilities. In times of excessive stringency loans are not made by such associations to business-men upon commercial paper, but to dealers in speculative securities upon short time at high rates of interest; and an increase of call-loans beyond the proper limit is more likely to afford facilities for unwarrantable stock speculations than relief to legitimate business transactions. The law is intended as a wholesome restriction upon national banks, organized in almost every city and village in the Union. Next to the absolute security provided for the crumpled bits of paper in the pockets of every citizen, no provision of the act has done so much to give character and standing to the national banking system as the assurance to the thousands of depositors throughout the country (who, after all, are the chief source of profit to every bank) that a reserve, equivalent to such a proportion of the liabilities of every bank as the experience of years and the fluctuations of business have shown to be necessary, will always be kept on hand to answer the extraordinary and unexpected calls of creditors.

The variations in the liabilities requiring reserve in the banks of the city of New York are very great. The banks outside of New York, during the dull season, send their surplus means to that city for deposit upon interest, to await the revival of business. The banks in the city of New York, at such periods of the year, have no legitimate outlet for these funds, and are therefore threatened with loss. The stock board takes advantage of this condition of affairs, speculation is stimulated by the cheapness of money, and a market is found for the idle funds upon doubtful collaterals, and the result is seen in the increased transactions at the clearing-house, which, during the past year, exceeded thirty-two thousand millions of dollars, or an average of more than one hundred millions of dollars daily—not one-half of which was the result of legitimate business; the total amount of transactions being greater than that of the bankers' clearing-house of the city of London. The evil arises largely from the payment, by the banks, of interest on deposits—an old-established custom which cannot easily be changed by legislation. A considerable portion of these deposits would remain at home if they could be used at a low rate of interest, and made available at any time upon the return of the season of active business. No sure investment of this kind is, however, open to the country banks; and the universal custom is to send forward the useless dollars from vaults comparatively insecure to their correspondents in the city, where they are supposed to be safer, and at the same time earning dividends for shareholders. A Government issue bearing a low rate of interest to be counted as a certain proportion of the reserve, and an increase of the amount which the country banks are required to keep on hand, is the proper remedy for such a state of things. Such an issue need not result in inflation, for the currency invested would be in the possession of the Government. If the currency is held, the objection is the loss of interest to the Government; but this loss would be no more than a just rebate upon the six millions of dollars of taxation annually paid by the banks to the Government, at a time when almost every kind of internal taxation has been discontinued. Such a reduction of taxation should not be grudgingly made, if the result shall be to give elasticity to the currency, to strengthen and steady the money market, to give additional security to seven hundred millions of dollars belonging to depositors by retaining in the vaults of the banks a large amount of funds for legitimate business purposes, which would otherwise be thrown upon the stock board to unsettle values throughout the country, and alternately increase and depress the price of every commodity.

For the information of those who do not believe that the banks usually hold the requisite amount of reserve, we have prepared tables showing that for the last five years, at from four to five different periods of the year, the banks organized in every State, and in the principal cities of the Union, have been found to hold, in almost every instance, a considerable amount beyond the requirements of law.

Table showing for twenty-two different dates during the five years, 1868–'72, the percentage

	States and Territories.	1868				1869			
		Jan. 6.	April 6.	July 6.	Oct. 5.	Jan. 4.	April 17.	June 12.	Oct. 9.
		Per ct.	*Per ct.*	*Per ct.*	*Per ct.*	*Per ct.*	*Per ct.*	*Per ct.*	*Per ct.*
1	Maine	23.6	22.6	21.5	22.7	20.7	18.3	21.	19.1
2	New Hampshire	28.8	24.1	23.6	25.6	23.9	21.4	23.7	22.
3	Vermont	20.9	21.	21.4	21.1	21.7	18.9	21.8	19.3
4	Massachusetts	24.5	22.8	24.5	23.2	23.3	21.1	20.7	20.6
5	Rhode Island	21.5	19.	22.	20.9	19.6	18.1	17.5	19.
6	Connecticut	22.9	20.8	22.8	21.4	20.9	19.6	23.1	21.4
7	New York	23.	22.3	22.7	22.5	22.1	20.3	19.6	19.9
8	New Jersey	26.8	24.3	24.9	24.5	23.3	24.2	23.6	21.4
9	Pennsylvania	22.8	23.7	22.9	22.8	22.2	21.	21.8	20.6
10	Delaware	23.3	22.8	24.3	23.6	25.1	23.5	22.3	25.7
11	Maryland	25.3	23.2	23.4	24.2	22.9	21.7	24.	26.3
12	District of Columbia	19.1	**14.8**	17.2	20.8	37.9	......	......	......
13	Virginia	19.2	18.9	20.8	19.3	19.1	**12.7**	15.3	**12.**
14	West Virginia	21.6	19.3	20.1	19.9	20.5	16.9	16.2	15.7
15	North Carolina	27.7	25.1	24.2	23.3	23.1	25.6	25.4	19.7
16	South Carolina	64.	64.8	61.	31.6	46.4	41.9	53.9	27.7
17	Georgia	37.9	34.9	36.4	38.1	38.4	31.2	41.7	30.9
18	Alabama	36.2	36.5	41.6	34.7	34.1	28.8	35.7	36.6
19	Mississippi	24.8	31.5	45.4	44.7	......	......	......	......
20	Texas	47.	54.6	51.2	39.8	50.1	42.7	52.7	40.7
21	Arkansas	21.3	**9.3**	19.2	16.8	**12.9**	21.9	22.3	**8.7**
22	Tennessee	22.	25.2	24.9	21.4	27.1	22.8	24.3	20.4
23	Kentucky	24.6	23.5	22.8	23.2	24.9	28.6	22.3	21.8
24	Ohio	22.9	21.1	21.9	21.1	22.1	19.	19.5	19.6
25	Indiana	22.2	22.3	21.2	20.7	21.2	19.2	19.3	19.7
26	Illinois	24.9	23.9	26.1	24.6	24.7	21.8	24.8	22.3
27	Michigan	25.4	24.3	26.5	24.9	24.2	23.2	21.4	21.8
28	Wisconsin	28.	24.2	27.5	23.1	27.4	23.2	25.1	20.4
29	Minnesota	21.9	19.6	22.	23.5	20.5	17.1	21.1	18.1
30	Iowa	26.3	24.2	32.4	21.9	23.7	21.3	24.7	20.3
31	Missouri	24.2	24.6	28.3	25.4	25.9	24.7	23.5	20.2
32	Kansas	15.5	32.7	30.	28.5	25.3	26.8	22.7	20.5
33	Nebraska	17.3	20.4	49.8	50.5	42.6	32.9	32.8	18.8
34	Nevada	24.	26.5	28.	31.9	29.	49.3	42.4	......
35	Oregon	38.2	37.3	40.5	30.1	38.1	28.4	25.5	30.1
36	California	......	......	......	......	......	......	......	......
37	Montana	42.4	41.9	31.	41.1	45.9	15.	34.7	22.2
38	Idaho	**12.3**	19.8	44.8	30.8	31.	21.7	25.8	25.1
39	Colorado	30.1	18.	28.9	33.9	25.5	24.5	31.1	34.9
40	Utah	17.1	**12.9**	18.4	16.7	18.9	......	......	......
41	Wyoming	......	......	......	......	......	......	......	......
42	New Mexico	......	......	......	......	......	......	......	......
	Averages	23.0	22.8	24.	22.9	22.9	20.9	21.6	20.5
	Redemption cities.								
1	New York	33.8	31.9	31.9	32.6	33.2	28.8	30.1	34.7
2	Boston	32.1	26.3	34.8	30.3	32.1	28.4	27.3	27.1
3	Philadelphia	36.9	32.3	36.8	31.9	32.9	30.2	30.4	29.9
4	Albany	36.2	34.3	31.1	35.9	42.1	41.5	37.9	36.5
5	Pittsburgh	29.2	30.6	27.9	29.4	29.3	25.1	**24.9**	27.3
6	Baltimore	32.4	27.8	31.2	28.2	30.9	28.4	25.5	**24.9**
7	Washington	26.8	24.2	27.5	26.1	28.6	27.8	27.5	26.4
8	New Orleans	36.3	42.5	34.8	38.9	31.4	36.5	44.3	31.4
9	Louisville	29.8	36.	31.	29.4	30.1	29.7	26.8	28.2
10	Cincinnati	23.4	**24.3**	26.6	25.1	28.4	**23.8**	**24.3**	28.5
11	Cleveland	29.2	26.4	**21.5**	27.7	30.6	25.	25.9	29.3
12	Chicago	32.6	30.6	34.2	35.3	35.1	30.2	33.4	30.5
13	Detroit	41.7	35.	29.9	36.7	32.1	27.6	31.7	32.7
14	Milwaukee	33.	30.6	32.2	33.4	34.7	28.7	30.7	28.
15	Saint Louis	26.5	26.8	28.9	**24.9**	28.3	**22.8**	27.4	25.2
16	Leavenworth	28.	**16.5**	**19.3**	**23.6**	**21.8**	**24.6**	**20.8**	32.2
17	San Francisco	......	......	......	......	......	......	......	......
	Averages	33.2	30.3	32.5	31.6	32.7	28.9	29.5	31.5

NOTE.—The reserve which the banks in the States and Territories are required to keep is 15 per "redemption cities" are required to keep is 25 per centum of the aggregate amount of their circulation printed in bold-face type.

of reserve to circulation and deposits, in each of the States and redemption cities of the Union.

1870					1871					1872				
Jan. 22.	Mar. 24.	June 9.	Oct. 8.	Dec. 28.	Mar. 18.	April 29.	June 10.	Oct. 2.	Dec. 16.	Feb. 27.	April 19.	June 10.	Oct. 3.	
Per ct.	*Per ct.*	*Per ct.*	*Per ct.*	*Per ct.*	*Per ct.*	*Per ct.*	*Per ct.*	*Per ct.*	*Per ct.*	*Per ct.*	*Per ct.*	*Per ct.*	*Per ct.*	
22.7	22.7	22.	20.7	22.5	22.1	22.4	22.7	21.7	18.3	22.	18.0	19.6	19.5	1
23.6	21.5	22.3	22.1	21.2	25.	22.7	25.5	23.7	21.2	22.3	20.3	20.3	21.6	2
21.7	19.5	20.7	19.7	20.6	20.6	20.7	21.3	20.8	18.4	18.7	17.	17.9	17.7	3
24.9	22.5	21.8	20.8	20.3	22.6	23.	22.2	20.7	18.7	20.6	19.5	20.	20.2	4
20.9	18.6	18.6	19.9	18.7	18.6	19.5	21.	18.9	17.1	18.2	17.2	18.	18.	5
26.1	24.3	24.8	22.1	22.8	24.4	26.	25.2	20.1	22.5	24.3	20.9	22.9	20.6	6
23.7	23.1	21.9	20.3	19.6	24.2	22.5	22.3	20.	18.4	21.1	20.	19.5	18.6	7
25.2	23.7	24.4	22.4	22.3	23.9	23.1	24.5	22.5	21.4	22.5	22.4	23.	20.9	8
22.4	24.	22.5	20.1	20.5	21.9	22.2	21.9	19.4	18.4	21.5	21.3	19.4	19.	9
25.1	24.6	19.5	23.	19.5	20.8	20.9	20.6	22.7	18.5	21.8	17.	20.2	20.5	10
27.5	28.2	30.6	27.3	27.5	26.	24.1	26.4	29.6	24.5	24.6	21.7	23.8	24.2	11
......	......	......	......	......	......	......	......	......	......	......	30.8	38.5	32.7	12
16.2	16.9	18.1	15.5	18.2	17.9	16.9	17.9	17.2	19.1	18.7	18.6	18.6	**14.4**	13
20.4	20.	18.9	17.4	17.1	16.2	16.9	17.4	20.3	20.2	19.8	16.3	16.5	17.	14
25.3	24.8	21.5	22.8	18.6	22.2	20.7	21.9	18.	21.4	22.	21.	19.5	18.7	15
26.6	21.5	23.9	21.1	21.6	26.6	31.9	23.1	20.1	18.7	23.2	20.4	22.5	17.8	16
30.1	30.8	28.1	20.6	28.	25.7	30.7	28.5	19.9	19.4	26.2	24.7	21.5	21.5	17
30.9	17.5	**10.7**	17.9	61.5	42.4	31.8	34.7	15.8	28.9	28.9	29.5	20.4	16.5	18
......	......	......	......	......	......	......	......	......	......	......	......	......	......	19
46.2	49.6	45.7	39.9	34.5	41.4	50.1	40.	38.	31.1	35.7	39.7	33.8	26.6	20
8.6	22.9	19.6	**10.5**	**13.8**	**14.4**	**9.7**	**10.5**	20.6	**11.4**	29.4	**11.6**	19.6	**14.6**	21
27.	24.7	24.1	22.3	25.4	22.1	21.	23.2	19.5	22.	21.4	21.6	21.9	16.6	22
27.2	27.5	24.2	20.9	22.4	20.	19.4	20.3	22.8	18.8	18.6	18.4	18.	18.1	23
21.2	21.3	20.8	19.9	20.9	21.1	21.4	22.4	21.6	21.	20.8	19.4	20.5	18.1	24
18.4	19.3	20.9	19.7	18.8	20.	22.3	23.9	23.	19.7	19.	20.6	22.2	19.4	25
22.3	24.7	26.2	20.3	23.3	22.2	21.4	24.8	22.5	22.3	22.8	20.6	24.	19.4	26
23.5	21.	22.5	19.6	22.1	24.6	24.6	24.1	24.4	22.4	21.2	19.5	19.2	19.	27
24.4	23.2	24.2	21.8	23.2	22.8	22.7	24.5	22.3	23.	22.4	20.1	21.1	22.1	28
16.8	20.1	24.9	23.4	19.2	17.1	19.6	21.6	25.4	19.4	17.1	16.5	21.7	19.8	29
22.9	24.6	24.4	21.5	22.9	21.9	22.6	24.7	24.1	21.6	22.	22.6	22.1	18.6	30
24.3	26.9	28.3	21.9	23.5	20.1	20.8	20.9	19.5	20.	19.9	19.6	22.9	17.6	31
21.9	18.9	23.8	20.6	19.6	21.8	22.4	15.8	22.	20.4	18.	22.	23.7	22.3	32
30.4	30.	33.3	28.	24.1	25.1	28.8	28.1	24.9	24.	16.9	21.	27.	22.5	33
......	......	......	......	......	......	......	......	......	......	......	......	......	......	34
29.2	22.	32.1	24.1	24.3	34.1	35.	33.1	30.3	23.3	25.3	23.7	28.4	27.6	35
......	......	......	......	......	......	......	......	......	......	......	......	......	20.5	36
15.1	18.	42.2	18.6	26.3	30.	**13.2**	22.2	15.5	18.2	**14.**	**14.2**	**13.7**	16.	37
13.6	15.3	17.8	27.9	29.4	15.8	17.2	17.9	20.3	16.	**13.6**	21.1	48.1	16.6	38
27.9	32.3	40.7	44.1	36.4	27.7	23.4	27.1	28.2	23.5	21.6	24.6	24.7	26.1	39
......	**6.4**	**3.5**	**13.5**	25.2	**10.4**	15.9	15.	**12.6**	16.3	**11.6**	**9.3**	**7.4**	**6.9**	40
......	......	......	......	......	......	27.3	30.5	40.	35.7	25.3	**14.9**	**10.7**	16.9	41
......	......	......	......	......	......	18.6	**9.9**	28.4	**13.2**	21.5	**7.8**	**12.1**	17.2	42
23.4	22.9	22.7	20.9	21.	22.6	22.6	22.9	21.2	19.9	21.3	20.2	20.8	19.3	

Jan. 22.	Mar. 24.	June 9.	Oct. 8.	Dec. 28.	Mar. 18.	April 29.	June 10.	Oct. 2.	Dec. 16.	Feb. 27.	April 19.	June 10.	Oct. 3.	
37.7	32.8	33.7	28.5	29.4	28.4	29.	30.9	26.7	27.6	25.7	26.7	29.1	**24.4**	1
31.8	30.	29.5	29.6	28.9	32.7	31.	29.9	27.1	26.6	26.1	26.2	27.4	**24.6**	2
32.3	33.5	35.	28.9	29.9	30.1	31.5	30.6	27.4	26.9	27.1	27.7	31.4	26.8	3
41.6	43.6	44.9	39.	41.6	40.	42.5	49.	36.1	34.	32.3	31.4	35.2	**24.8**	4
27.7	27.4	28.6	29.2	27.2	27.3	27.2	27.6	28.3	**24.3**	28.	**23.5**	25.9	**24.8**	5
31.3	31.1	31.5	26.1	29.2	28.1	29.	30.1	26.	27.2	25.8	26.8	27.1	26.6	6
26.6	27.5	27.4	27.3	26.2	30.3	30.2	34.5	27.5	**24.**	35.	34.4	34.9	**22.5**	7
43.2	28.6	28.8	**22.9**	35.9	35.6	35.2	33.2	**22.6**	**14.9**	31.6	28.9	27.2	**22.4**	8
28.4	31.4	27.6	32.	28.2	27.	30.	27.8	30.	25.8	25.6	**24.2**	25.9	25.1	9
28.4	29.1	28.9	27.9	30.8	28.9	32.7	34.1	35.8	27.5	26.	25.1	28.1	28.9	10
29.7	28.9	27.5	26.3	26.5	31.3	30.3	29.3	29.	28.7	27.8	39.9	**24.3**	27.8	11
30.4	30.6	29.4	30.7	30.1	29.4	32.	35.	31.7	38.5	30.5	29.2	29.4	27.2	12
29.9	28.3	33.3	32.2	30.4	36.7	35.3	36.2	33.6	29.5	28.2	25.	27.3	27.	13
32.1	31.5	37.4	32.9	26.8	**23.3**	34.6	41.	31.	25.3	26.9	**23.3**	26.7	29.6	14
31.5	31.6	32.5	27.1	27.7	25.	28.6	32.3	30.8	26.4	31.4	**24.8**	30.8	**23.5**	15
34.7	35.7	38.4	**23.8**	25.5	**22.2**	26.8	**19.2**	**18.7**	**22.6**	**20.3**	......	......	......	16
......	......	......	......	......	......	......	74.1	**18.4**	57.5	49.7	37.7	42.8	**16.4**	17
34.8	32.1	32.7	29.	29.4	29.7	30.4	31.3	27.7	27.8	26.9	27.1	29.	25.3	

centum of the aggregate amount of their circulation and deposits. The reserve which the banks in the and deposits. When the amount of reserve is less than the proportion required by law, the ratios are

A law which is so universally observed as to have become a rule with all the cautiously-managed banks of the country should not be repealed without full consideration. Carefully-prepared tables giving further information regarding the reserves of the National Banks will be found in the appendix to this report.

THE CHICAGO FIRE.

The great fire in Chicago, of October 8 to 11, 1871, should be mentioned among the noteworthy events of the year. The buildings occupied by the eighteen national banks in that city were all totally destroyed in the general conflagration, except one, and that one was rendered untenantable for some weeks.

The amount of bills receivable held by these banks at that time was more than twenty-one millions of dollars, and the indebtedness to correspondents nearly nine millions, and to individual depositors about seventeen millions. For a time it was thought that they were so seriously crippled that they would be unable to resume business, and it was proposed to open their doors with the offer of payment by installments to their creditors. The contents of their vaults were, however, rescued in good condition, and finally wise and prudent counsels prevailed, owing largely to the presence and advice of my predecessor. Eight days after the conflagration the banks obtained new offices in dwelling-houses distant from their former locations, and opened for the transaction of business. Instead of balances being largely drawn upon, deposits flowed in freely from dealers and correspondents, and at the close of the first day's business the receipts were found to be considerably larger than the disbursements. It was soon ascertained that the immense losses anticipated upon bills receivable would not be experienced, and confidence was restored. The total loss arising from the fire on discounted paper is estimated at about six hundred thousand dollars, and the loss from the destruction of bank-buildings, furniture, and fixtures, at about one hundred and seventy-six thousand dollars. The banks, at the time of this disaster, had accumulated a surplus fund exceeding one-fourth of their aggregate capital, and had at their command a reserve equal to more than thirty per cent. of their liabilities, and consequently were able to resume business without embarrassment. The wisdom of the sections of the law requiring an accumulation of surplus and the holding of reserve could not be better illustrated.

By reference to the abstract of the condition of the national banks of the city of Chicago, on page 38 of this volume, evidence will be found of the steady increase of business in these banks during the past year.*

---

* Since the above paragraph was written a great conflagration has taken place in Boston, resulting in the destruction of from seventy to eighty millions of property. The facts pertaining to the Boston banks were in many respects similar to those of Chicago. Their aggregate capital was $48,900,000; their surplus, $11,440,000; their bills receivable, $83,327,000; their deposits, $40,841,000; and their reserve, according to the latest official reports, about twenty-five per cent. of their liabilities. The buildings of seven national banks, out of forty-nine transacting business in the city, were destroyed by the fire, but their cash assets were subsequently recovered. On the second day after the commencement of the fire all the banks but one were represented at the clearing-house, and on the fourth day all of them had resumed business. The aggregate loss upon bills receivable is estimated at from two and a half to three millions of dollars. The losses of the banks are chargeable to surplus, which was in excess of the requirements of the law, and it is not supposed that the regular dividends to shareholders will be materially reduced by the disaster.

USURY.

Charges have been made against several national banks during the past year for receiving usurious rates of interest. These complaints have been made not only against banks in the South and West, where high rates of interest prevail, but also against banks organized in other States, where the usurious rate charged was but slightly in excess of the rate of six per cent., allowed by law. Section 30 of the act provides that when the amount of interest charged is greater than the rate authorized by State law, twice the interest paid may be recovered by the person paying the same; while section 53 provides that the franchises of an association may be forfeited if the directors of a bank knowingly violate the provisions of the act. The original national currency act of February 11, 1863, provided as a penalty for usury the forfeiture of the debt, and section 50 of the same act also subjected the rights, privileges, and franchises of an association to forfeiture for willful violations of the act. It may be doubted, therefore, whether Congress intended to impose a specific penalty involving the loss of the whole debt, and then, in addition, subject the same bank to a forfeiture of charter in a subsequent section, which is applicable to other violations of law. I am informed by gentlemen who participated in the framing of the present national currency act that the forfeiture of twice the amount of interest was regarded as a sufficient penalty for such violations of law, and, at the same time, a sufficient protection to borrowers.

These statements are confirmed by the act of April 22, 1870, "An act to amend the usury laws of the District of Columbia," which provides "that if any person or corporation in this District shall contract to receive a greater rate of interest than ten per cent. upon any contract in writing, or six per cent. upon any verbal contract, such person or corporation shall forfeit the whole of said interest so contracted to be received, and shall be entitled only to recover the principal sum due to such person or corporation." It will be observed that the forfeiture of the interest is the only penalty prescribed by Congress nearly six years after the passage of the national currency act for corporations and individuals in the District of Columbia.

The rates of interest fixed by State laws are not governed by any sound economical or business principles. In three of the New England States* usury laws are abolished, while in the remainder the rate has remained for half a century at a uniform standard, which is less than the present rate of the Bank of England. In Minnesota and Virginia, the rate is limited to twelve per cent.; in Illinois, Wisconsin, and Missouri, to ten per cent.; in Alabama and Ohio, to eight per cent., while in Pennsylvania, Maryland, and Kentucky, the rate is fixed at six per cent. In New York, the taking of an excess beyond the limit of seven per cent. forfeits the whole debt, and subjects the creditor to fine and imprisonment. It would be difficult to give any good reason why the rate of interest should be limited to ten per cent. in the city of Washington, to six per cent. in the neighboring cities of Philadelphia, Baltimore, Wilmington, and Raleigh, and to twelve per cent. across the Potomac, in Alexandria, and in the capital of Virginia. Many of the States have practically repealed their usury laws, while other neighboring States retain upon their statute-books laws which are so continually evaded that they have become obsolete. Savings-banks chartered by Congress, savings-banks, trust-

*The interest laws of Rhode Island, Massachusetts, and Connecticut will be found in the Appendix.

companies, and safe-deposit companies authorized by the legislatures of almost every State of the Union, as well as private bankers, offer for interest on deposits rates nearly equal, and sometimes exceeding the ruling rates allowed by law; and under such circumstances it is difficult to control by legislation the rates of the national banks.

Self-protection stimulates even the most conservative banks to control their own business and retain the accounts of dealers of long standing. The rates of interest charged must correspond in some degree to the supply of money and to the demand. If high rates are paid for deposits, it is with the expectation that the borrower will pay a rate correspondingly high. Hence loans are made to those dealers who will leave the largest proportion of the amount borrowed with the bank for the longest period in the guise of deposits. Banks in New York charge seven per cent., in Philadelphia and Baltimore, six per cent.; but their loans are made chiefly to dealers whose average accounts show balances continually on hand equal to one-eighth or one-fourth of the amount borrowed; while the banks in the South and the West not unfrequently charge the ruling rate without regard to the account of the customer. The expedients for violating the usury laws are so numerous that it may well be doubted whether it would not be better for all parties to allow the rate charged to be regulated by the state of the money market. Under existing laws, in an easy money market, the rate not unfrequently falls below that prescribed by law. If money is scarce, the rate is nominally within the limit, but really regulated in accordance with a previous understanding between borrower and lender.

There are no usury laws in Great Britain, or in the other commercial European states; and the commonwealth of Massachusetts, one of the most prosperous and enlightened States of the Union, has recently abolished* such laws; and it will be found, by reference to the table on page 16, that the earnings of the banks in that State for the four years since the passage of the act, have been even less than in many of the Eastern, Middle, and Southern States, where the rate is fixed at six per cent.

Mr. McCulloch, late Secretary of the Treasury, in his first report, as Comptroller of the Currency, recommended a uniform rate of interest, and expressed the opinion that Congress possessed the power to enact such a law, under the constitutional provision of regulating commerce among the several States. Congress alone has the power to coin money and regulate the value thereof; and if it alone has authority to issue and authenticate the paper currency of the country, there would seem to be no good reason why it should not also provide for its free circulation, which is now impeded by the ever-changing statutes of forty different legislatures.

The penalty for usury should at least be defined, and until this is done the Comptroller will not feel himself called upon to institute proceedings for forfeiture of the charter of a bank for usurious transactions, when it is evident that the business of the association is conducted legitimately and safely in other respects.

SAVINGS-BANKS.

The act of June 17, 1870, provides that savings-banks may be organized within the District of Columbia, under the provisions of section 4 of the act "to provide for the creation of corporations in the District

* Act of March 6, 1867.

of Columbia by general law;" and a subsequent act exempts from taxation the deposits of savings-banks in amounts less than $2,000. It is claimed that, under this legislation, savings-banks, with capital paid up in full or in part, may be established in the District of Columbia, to be conducted for the benefit of the shareholders. The legislatures of many of the States have authorized the establishment of similar institutions, which, under the act of Congress, are exempt from taxation on deposits, while these identical deposits, if placed to the credit of savings-banks in a national bank, as is frequently the case, are subject to a tax of one-half per cent. per annum. It is evident that Congress intended to discriminate in favor of those institutions which are organized for the purpose of receiving and investing savings for the benefit of depositors, and not of shareholders.

The official reports of the savings-banks in New England show the deposits at the close of the year 1871 to have been $312,333,479, or more than three times the amount of the aggregate deposits in the national banks. The deposits in the savings-banks of the State of New York, at the same date, were $267,905,866, a sum also considerably in excess of the deposits of the national banks in that state. A large portion of these are not properly savings-deposits. Savings-banks in some portions of New England, New York, and Pennsylvania, as well as other States, have recently become formidable competitors of the national banks by offering much larger rates of interest for deposits than is usual in well-managed banks.

The proper functions of savings-banks are to make safe and judicious investments of the funds intrusted to them, and at specified times to divide the earnings among the depositors; but for the purpose of attracting the deposits of business men and others, who would otherwise do business with regularly organized banking institutions, the custom prevails, to a large extent, of offering high rates of interest for deposits before dividends have been earned. The result is that savings-deposits are, to a considerable extent, endangered by investments in street-paper, in loans to the managers of such institutions, and in speculative securities.

The savings-banks are among the most important business institutions of the country, and they should be fostered and maintained; but at the same time they should be restricted to a legitimate savings-bank business, and not allowed to encourage violations of usury laws nor to be controlled by the personal interests of shareholders, managers, or trustees. Frequent publications of reports should be required and their affairs subjected to rigid scrutiny from time to time by competent examiners. Special charters, with special privileges for savings-banks and trust companies, should not be granted, but all such institutions should be organized under general laws. The passage of such a law for the District of Columbia, with judicious provisions, would be productive of beneficial results and would afford an example, not only for those States which have no enactments of this kind, but also for the older States, whose present savings-bank laws are liable to great abuses.

LOCKING UP OF GREENBACKS.

The act of February 19, 1869, provides "that no national banking association shall hereafter offer or receive United States notes or national bank notes as security, or as collateral security, for any loan of money, or for a consideration shall agree to withhold the same from use, or shall offer or receive the custody or promise of custody of such notes as security, or as collateral security or consideration, for any loan of money."

On the 5th of April last the Comptroller was advised that a bank in the city of New York, with a capital of $1,000,000, and whose average exchanges at the clearing-house did not exceed $300,000, was that morning creditor at the clearing-house for $4,770,000. As it was evident that this large credit was not the result of legitimate business, the examiner was directed to make an examination of the bank, which was immediately done, in connection with a member of the clearing-house committee. From the examination, which was thoroughly and carefully conducted, it appeared that deposits had been made in that bank, by one individual, upon the morning of April 5, to the amount of $4,100,000, the whole of which was drawn out upon the same day, upon the checks of the depositor, in legal-tender notes. The president of the bank denied that the bank had any interest in these transactions, and there was no evidence of any loan, or of advances in any shape, upon these deposits. These transactions were the subject, subsequently, of an investigation by the bank committee of the House of Representatives, and, although it was clear that the spirit of the law had been violated, no evidence could be obtained to warrant the commencement of a suit for the recovery of the penalty prescribed in the act referred to. The investigation undoubtedly had the effect to prevent the repetition of similar transactions; no offenses of this kind, on the part of any national bank, having since been brought to the attention of the Comptroller.

The New York clearing-house association subsequently passed a resolution declaring "that the clearing-house committee be and is hereby directed, whenever it appears, in its judgment, that legal-tender notes have been withdrawn from use through the agency of any bank, member of the association, to make an immediate examination of the bank in question, and should there appear to be complicity on the part of the bank or its officials, to suspend said bank from the clearing-house until action of the association shall be taken thereon."

The withdrawal of currency for illegitimate purposes has, however, since been accomplished without the assistance of the banks.

The rigid enforcement of the resolution of the clearing-house will prevent complicity on the part of the banks in such transactions; and if the New York stock-board and the leading banking-houses will unite with the clearing house, and refuse to transact business with unscrupulous men, who do not hesitate to embarrass legitimate business for the purpose of increasing or diminishing the values of stocks or bonds in which they are temporarily interested, they can do more to prevent such operations than any congressional enactment.

INSOLVENT BANKS.

Twenty-one national banks, organized in eleven different States, with an aggregate capital of $4,236,100, have failed since the organization of the system in 1863. The total circulation of these banks was $2,942,793, of which $2,441,430 has been redeemed in full, leaving a balance still outstanding of $501,363, which will also be redeemed, upon presentation to the Treasurer of the United States, from the avails of United States bonds held as security for that purpose. Of these banks, five have been finally closed, (two during the past year,) having paid dividends to their creditors, as follows:

Name and location of bank.	Appointment of receiver.	Capital stock.	Amount of claims proved.	Dividends paid.	Remarks.
				Per ct.	
First National Bank, Attica, New York.	Apr. 14, 1865	$50,000	$122,089	58	Finally closed.
First National Bank, Medina, New York.	Mar. 13, 1867	50,000	170,165	38¾	Finally closed
Tennessee National Bank, Memphis, Tennessee.	Mar. 21, 1867	100,000	376,932	17½	Finally closed.
Croton National Bank, New York City.	Oct. 1, 1867	200,000	170,752	88¼	Finally closed.
First National Bank Keokuk, Iowa.....	Mar. 3, 1868	100,000	205,256	68¼	Finally closed.

Six national banks have failed during the past year, as follows:

Name and location of bank.	Appointment of receiver.	Capital stock.	Amount of claims proved.	Dividends paid.	Remarks.
				Per ct.	
Ocean National Bank, New York City...	Dec. 13, 1871	$1,000,000	$1,280,328	70	
Union Square National Bank, New York City.	Dec. 15, 1871	200,000	157,120	100	Claims paid in full.
Eighth National Bank, New York City..	Dec. 15, 1871	250,000	373,936	50	Cash on hand, $28,474.62.
Fourth National Bank, Philadelphia.....	Dec. 20, 1871	200,000	645,558	100	Claims paid in full.
Waverly National Bank, Waverly, New York.	Apr. 23, 1872	106,100	54,878	100	Claims paid in full.
First National Bank, Fort Smith, Arkansas.	May 2, 1872	50,000	7,633	....	Cash on hand, $13,787.05.

Of these banks, the Union Square National Bank, New York, the Fourth National Bank, Philadelphia, and the Waverly National Bank, New York, have paid their creditors in full, a settlement, it is believed, without precedent prior to the establishment of the national system. The Eighth National Bank, New York, has paid a dividend of fifty per cent.; the Ocean National Bank, New York, a dividend of seventy per cent.; and the receivers of the Ocean National Bank, and of the First National Bank of Fort Smith, Arkansas, estimate that the creditors of both of these banks will ultimately receive a dividend of one hundred cents on the dollar. The remaining ten national banks which have failed are as follows:

Name and location of bank.	Appointment of receiver.	Capital stock.	Amount of claims proved.	Dividend paid.	Cash on hand.
				Per cent.	
Venango National Bank, Franklin, Pa ...	May 1, 1866	$300,000	$724,010	....	$100,347 58
Merchants' National Bank, Washington, D. C.	May 8, 1866	200,000	....	....	*37,371 00
First National Bank, Selma, Ala.........	Apr. 30, 1867	100,000	303,071	....	109,264 14
First National Bank, New Orleans, La...	May 20, 1867	500,000	1,116,631	35	187,670 78
National Unadilla Bank, Unadilla, N. Y..	Aug. 29, 1867	120,000	126,760	....	50,447 39
Farmers and Citizens' National Bank, Brooklyn, N. Y.	Sept. 6, 1867	300,000	1,180,000	92	13,937 89
First National Bank, Bethel, Conn.......	Feb. 28, 1868	60,000	68,986	70	11,668 43
National Bank of Vicksburgh, Miss......	Sept. 24, 1868	50,000	20,493	....	12,375 11
First National Bank, Rockford, Ill.......	Mar. 15, 1869	50,000	65,875	....	18,404 01
First National Bank, Nevada, Austin....	Oct. 14, 1869	250,000	169,314	50	53,159 65

* Also $50,000 United States six per cent. bonds, on deposit with Treasurer.

The aggregate amount of claims proved against the seventeen national banks which have failed, (excluding the four banks which were Government depositories,) is $5,205,068; the average dividends, 69½ per cent.; the additional dividends to be declared are estimated at $14\frac{8}{10}$ per cent.; making, in all, dividends in favor of creditors of $84\frac{3}{10}$ per cent., which would leave an average deficiency of $15\frac{7}{10}$ per cent. to be collected of shareholders, as provided in section 50 of the act.

A final dividend in favor of the Farmers and Citizens' National Bank, of Brooklyn, will be made during the present year, of about four per cent., making, in all, dividends from the assets of ninety-six per cent. A final dividend of about forty per cent. in favor of the creditors of the National Unadilla Bank is delayed by a claim in litigation for the value of the bonds deposited as security for circulation in excess of the amount required to redeem its circulating notes, which will probably go to the Supreme Court for final adjudication. An assessment has been made upon the shareholders of the National Bank of Bethel, of 15½ per cent., which, if collected, will pay the creditors in full, without interest, up to the date of the appointment of the receiver. A dividend of more than thirty per cent. will also soon be declared in favor of the creditors of the First National Bank of Nevada. The affairs of the Eighth National Bank of New York, and of the First National Bank of Rockford, Illinois, are involved in litigation, and the date of the final closing of their affairs is uncertain.

The Venango National Bank of Franklin, Pennsylvania; the Merchants' National Bank of Washington, District of Columbia; the First National Bank of Selma, Alabama, and the First National Bank of New Orleans, were United States depositories. The final dividend in favor of the creditors of the First National Bank of Vicksburg has been unexpectedly delayed by the recent presentation of a claim of the United States for money alleged to have been illegally deposited by the collector of internal revenue of that district, in the year 1868. Since that time no losses have occurred to the Government by deposits made in the national banks, although many millions of dollars have been continually on deposit with banks which are designated as depositories. The three first-named banks, at the time of their failure, had a large amount of Government funds on deposit.

The fifth section of the act of March 3, 1797, provides "that when any revenue officer or other person hereafter becoming indebted to the United States, by bond or otherwise, shall become insolvent; or where the estate of any deceased debtor, in the hands of executors or administrators, shall be insufficient to pay all the debts due from the deceased, the debt due to the United States shall be first satisfied; and the priority hereby established shall be deemed to extend as well to cases in which a debtor, not having sufficient property to pay all his debts, shall make a voluntary assignment thereof, or in which the estate and effects of an absconding, concealed, or absent debtor shall be attached by process of law, as to cases in which an act of legal bankruptcy shall be committed."

The Treasurer of the United States claims, under this act, that all deposits in these banks at the time of suspension, belonging to the United States, whether deposited to its credit directly, or to the credit of its disbursing officers, with interest thereon from the date of the failure of the bank, are entitled to priority of payment.

In the case of the First National Bank of New Orleans, other questions have arisen. At the date of its suspension the bank was in charge of officers of the Government, who were also engaged in the settlement of the accounts of a defaulting ex-assistant treasurer of the United

States. The nominal balance to the personal credit of this individual upon the books of the bank was $315,779.10, and a certified check for this amount was taken from him, and about $94,000 collected upon it. The Government holds this check, and claims that the balance uncollected shall have priority in payment, the same as if that amount had been on deposit to the credit of the United States. The creditors of the bank, on the other hand, claim that, at the time of the suspension, the bank held legal offsets, and that there was really no balance due upon the check held by the Government. The receiver concurs in this opinion, and if the claim should be presented to him in the usual way for settlement, it would be disallowed.

Unsuccessful attempts have been made to obtain a final decision in the Supreme Court of the United States upon these questions, owing, in part, as is believed, to defects in the present act. A large amount of funds has been on deposit with the Treasurer for the last three years, which will be distributed among the creditors as soon as a decision of the court can be obtained upon these points.

Section 50 of the national currency act provides that the Comptroller shall make a ratable dividend upon all claims which may be proved to his satisfaction or adjudicated in a court of competent jurisdiction; and this is the only existing provision in reference to the method of procedure in the proving of claims against an insolvent bank. The law should be so amended as to define the duties of the Comptroller and of the receiver in proving claims and in prescribing the mode and manner of referring conflicting interests to the proper tribunal for final arbitrament. A bill for this purpose was introduced into the last Congress, reported by the Bank Committee, and referred to the Judiciary Committee of the House of Representatives. The passage of this bill will facilitate the settlement of the affairs of these banks, and simplify the method of procedure in all cases of insolvent banks.

An amendment is also suggested giving authority for the return of the assets of an insolvent bank to an agent of the shareholders upon their unanimous request, after full payment shall have been made to the creditors of the bank.

Where dividends are delayed by reason of protracted litigation, provision should also be made for the investment of the funds on deposit with the Treasurer in interest-bearing securities.

SURPLUS AND SPECIE.

The law requires that every national bank shall carry one-tenth part of its profits to surplus-fund account before the declaration of a dividend, until the same shall amount to 20 per cent. of its capital stock. This wise provision has been generally observed, and the returns show that the banks now have a surplus of more than one hundred millions of dollars, and considerably more than one-fifth of their capital in surplus account. The act also limits the liabilities of any association, person, company, or corporation, for money borrowed, to one-tenth of the capital stock paid in. The Comptroller recommends that this limit be extended to one-tenth of the capital and surplus, which will have a tendency to increase the surplus fund beyond the limit required by the law.

Banks have hitherto been in the habit of reporting, as specie, checks payable in coin. The result is to give an erroneous aggregate of the amount of coin held by the banks, the same amount being reported by the bank holding the coin and the bank holding the check. In the present statement, and in all future statements, the item of coin will include only actual coin and United States coin certificates which are payable on demand at the Treasury.

The following table will exhibit the aggregate amount of specie held by the national banks at the dates mentioned, the coin, coin certificates, and checks payable in coin held by the national banks of the city of New York, being stated separately. The country banks have not heretofore separated coin and coin certificates in their reports:

Date.	Held by national banks in New York City.				Held by other national banks.	Aggregate.
	Coin.	U. S. coin certificates.	Checks payable in coin.	Total.		
Oct. 5, 1868....	$1,698,623 24	$6,390,140	$1,536,353 66	$9,625,116 90	$3,378,596 49	$13,003,713 39
Jan. 4, 1869....	1,902,769 48	18,038,520	2,348,140 49	22,289,429 97	7,337,320 29	29,626,750 26
April 17, 1869....	1,652,575 21	3,720,040	1,469,826 64	6,842,441 85	3,102,090 30	9,944,532 15
June 12, 1869....	2,542,533 96	11,953,680	975,015 82	15,471,229 78	2,983,860 70	18,455,090 48
Oct. 9, 1869....	1,792,740 73	16,897,900	1,013,948 72	19,704,589 45	3,297,816 38	23,002,405 83
Jan. 22, 1870....	6,196,036 29	28,501,460	2,190,644 74	36,888,141 03	11,457,242 69	48,345,383 72
Mar. 24, 1870....	2,647,908 39	21,872,480	1,069,094 30	25,589,482 69	11,507,060 75	37,096,543 44
June 9, 1870....	2,942,400 24	18,660,920	1,163,905 88	22,767,226 12	8,332,211 66	31,099,437 78
Oct. 8, 1870....	1,607,742 91	7,533,900	3,994,006 42	13,135,649 33	5,324,362 14	18,460,011 47
Dec. 28, 1870....	2,268,581 96	14,063,540	3,748,126 87	20,080,248 63	6,227,002 76	26,307,251 59
Mar. 18, 1871....	2,982,155 61	13,099,720	3,829,881 64	19,911,757 25	5,857,409 39	25,769,166 64
April 29, 1871....	2,047,930 71	9,845,080	4,382,107 24	16,275,117 95	6,456,909 07	22,732,027 02
June 10, 1871....	2,249,408 06	9,161,160	3,680,854 92	15,091,422 98	4,833,532 18	19,924,955 16
Oct. 2, 1871....	1,121,869 40	7,590,260	1,103,628 44	9,875,757 84	3,377,240 33	13,252,998 17
Dec. 16, 1871....	1,454,930 73	17,354,740	4,255,631 39	23,065,302 12	6,529,997 44	29,595,299 56
Feb. 27, 1872....	1,490,417 70	12,341,060	3,117,100 90	16,948,578 60	8,559,246 72	25,507,825 32
April 19, 1872....	1,828,659 74	10,102,400	4,718,364 25	16,646,423 99	7,787,475 47	24,433,899 46
June 10, 1872....	3,782,909 64	11,412,160	4,219,419 52	19,414,489 16	4,842,154 98	24,256,644 14
Oct. 3, 1872....	920,767 37	5,454,580	....	6,375,347 37	3,854,409 42	10,229,756 79

SHINPLASTERS.

The State of Alabama has issued for some years past, in the form and similitude of bank notes, of five different denominations, certificates which read as follows:

"The State of Alabama: Receivable as five dollars in payment of all dues to the State. Montgomery, May 1, 1867.

(Signed) ——— ——— *Governor.*

(Signed) ——— ——— *Comptroller of Public Accounts.*"

On the reverse:

"Receivable in payment of taxes and all dues to the State. Issued under the provisions of the act entitled 'An act to provide for the issue of certificates or receipts by the State,' approved February 19, 1867. The credit and faith of the State of Alabama are pledged for the redemption of this certificate or receipt, as provided for in such act."

A circular was also issued by the governor of Alabama, on July 24, 1867, and is still in circulation, which states that an opinion has been obtained from the Attorney-General of the United States that such receipts or certificates are not subject to the tax of ten per cent. imposed upon the notes of State banks by the act of March 3, 1865, and recommending the co-operation of banks and bankers in giving circulation to the issues referred to. The Constitution of the United States provides that no State shall emit bills of credit, and it has been held by the Supreme Court of the United States, in a famous case,*

* Briscoe *vs.* Bank of Kentucky, 11 Pet., 257.

that a note of circulation "issued by a State, involving the faith of the State, and designed to circulate as money on the credit of the State, in the ordinary course of business," is a bill of credit. Other decisions of the Supreme Court hold "that certificates issued by a State in sums not exceeding ten dollars nor less than fifty cents, receivable in payment of taxes, the faith and credit of the State being pledged for their redemption, are bills of credit within the prohibition of the Constitution."*

It is clear, therefore, that such certificates are bills of credit, and prohibited by the Constitution. Savings-banks, railroad, municipal, and other corporations in the States of Florida, Georgia, and other Southern States have followed the example of the State of Alabama, and have issued, and are still issuing, a large amount of similar circulation, some in the form of receipts and certificates, and others in the form of railroad tickets, but all issued in the form and similitude of bank notes, and intended to circulate as money. There is no law in existence to prevent the circulation, and no legislative provision for the enforcement of the constitutional prohibition of such issues. The act of July 17, 1862, makes it a penal offense "to make, issue, circulate, or pay any note, check, memorandum, token, or other obligation for a less sum than one dollar, intended to circulate as money, or be received or used in lieu of lawful money." It is recommended that this act be so amended as to prohibit, absolutely, the issue of such circulation, and thus prevent great ultimate loss to the people, among whom such notes are now obtaining extensive credit.

A few national banks have gone into liquidation and reorganized as State banks, retaining their national title. State savings-banks and private companies have also assumed the title of "national." These corporations and companies erect large signs over their doors, issue conspicuous advertisements, and obtain recognition in the counterfeit detectors among lists of national banks, thus transacting business under false colors, which, of itself, should be sufficient to put all business men upon their guard. Such abuses should, however, be prohibited, and the Comptroller recommends the passage of an act prohibiting the use of the word "national" as a title for banks other than those organized under the national currency act.

He also recommends that all officers of national banks, and all Government depositaries, be required to stamp the word "counterfeit" or "illegal" upon all counterfeit and unauthorized issues presented at their counters.

BANKS OF CIRCULATION.

The national currency act is, to a certain extent, deficient in a provision for the prompt closing up of national banks pursuing an illegitimate business. These banks are of two classes. One class organize or attempt to organize and pay up their capital stock with the notes of shareholders instead of cash capital, as required by law. A few such cases have been forced into liquidation by withholding the issue of circulation, and in one instance the Solicitor has been requested to bring a suit for the forfeiture of charter for willful violation of law, as provided in section 53 of the act. In all similar cases hereafter proceedings will be commenced for a like purpose. In other cases, banks which have lost a large portion of their capital refuse to go into liquidation, transacting no business, but in other respects conform to the requirements of

* Craig *vs.* Missouri, 4 Pet., 410; Byrne *vs.* Missouri, 8 Pet., 40.

the law, for the purpose of receiving the interest upon their bonds. The stockholders of these banks, in some instances, have the means to restore the capital, but refuse; in others, a portion of the shareholders desire to pursue a legitimate business, but another portion refuse to respond to assessments. The Comptroller respectfully recommends that in these cases authority be given to withhold the interest upon the bonds, and to commence proceedings for the forfeiture of charter, and that a penalty be imposed. These cases are not numerous, but a remedy is needed to terminate the existence of such associations, and no penalty is too severe for this evasion of the law. With proper legislation, and the co-operation of banks doing a legitimate business, an example may be made of illegitimate institutions, which will prevent the organization of banks without the full amount of capital paid up in cash, as required by law.

EXAMINATIONS.

It is the intention of the Comptroller that every national bank shall be thoroughly examined once a year by a competent bank examiner. Every director and shareholder is personally interested in these examinations, if properly conducted. No well-managed bank will object to a confidential scrutiny of its affairs, but will welcome at all times, as is generally the case, a competent and courteous agent of the Department. Many valuable suggestions may be obtained from the experience of an intelligent examiner, and, in not a few instances, banks have been saved from ruin by timely interference in the correction of abuses. In some instances information is received at this office of violations of law which call for special examinations, but which cannot be made because there is no means of paying the expense of conducting such examinations. If the bank is found in fault, it will respond to an assessment; if not, it should not be subjected to an expense not authorized by law. The Comptroller, therefore, respectfully asks for an appropriation of $3,000, in order that he may at all times be free to pursue such inquiries as he shall consider expedient for the protection of the creditors of such associations. Prompt action in cases of this kind is very desirable, and the expense incurred is trifling when compared with the public interests involved.

MUTILATED CURRENCY.

Section 24 of the act provides that the worn-out and mutilated circulating notes of the national banks "shall be burned to ashes in the presence of four persons, one to be appointed by the Secretary of the Treasury, one by the Comptroller of the Currency, one by the Treasurer of the United States, and one by the association, under such regulations as the Secretary of the Treasury may prescribe." From the organization of the system in 1863 to November 1, 1872, $86,695,305, more than one-fourth of the whole amount issued, has been returned to this office for destruction, as follows:

Previous to November 1, 1865	$175,490
During the year ended October 31, 1866	1,050,382
During the year ended October 31, 1867	3,401,423
During the year ended October 31, 1868	4,602,825
During the year ended October 31, 1869	8,603,729
During the year ended October 31, 1870	14,305,689
During the year ended October 31, 1871	24,344,047
During the year ended October 31, 1872	30,211,720

It is probable that the amount of mutilated currency to be returned hereafter for re-issue will exceed thirty millions of dollars annually, and that the whole amount of national-bank circulation will be re-issued as often as once in ten years. An additional force will be required for the careful performance of this duty.

No effort will be spared by the Comptroller to have the provision of the law in reference to the burning of mutilated notes and the prompt issue of new notes in their place strictly executed; and the national banks of the country are urged to send forward such notes as frequently as possible, in order that the currency of the country may be kept in the best possible condition. The officers and depositaries of the United States can render efficient service in purifying the currency, by sorting out all mutilated notes of the national banks and presenting the same to their agents in New York City and elsewhere, for redemption.

THE OFFICE.

The force of this office consists of the Deputy Comptroller, fifty-six male clerks, and twenty-eight female clerks. The work of the office is continually increasing. More than twelve thousand reports of national banks are received annually and carefully scrutinized. More than one hundred million dollars of United States bonds have been received, transferred and deposited with the Treasurer during the past year, and twenty-five millions of dollars of bonds have been withdrawn and surrendered to the banks. Thirty millions of dollars of mutilated currency have been received, counted, and destroyed, and fifty-two millions of dollars of new currency issued to the banks. Many thousands of communications are annually received and promptly answered. If any success shall attend the administration of the responsible duties of the office, the Comptroller will be in a large measure indebted to the industry and efficiency of the Deputy Comptroller, of the competent corps of examiners, and of the chiefs of the different divisions, and to the services of experienced clerks, who have assisted him in the discharge of these duties. A re-organization of the office, with increased pay corresponding to the responsibility of the different positions, would be a proper recognition of services which have too long been well performed without corresponding compensation.

APPENDIX.

Special attention is called to the carefully prepared tables contained in the appendix, exhibiting the aggregate resources and liabilities of all the national banks, yearly, for the last ten years; to tables showing their condition during the present year, for five different periods, arranged by States and redemption cities, and separate statements of every bank of the Union upon the third day of October ultimo; also to tables exhibiting the different kinds of funds held as reserve; the dividends and earnings of the national banks, by States and cities, semi-annually, from March 1, 1869, to August 31, 1872; together with lists of insolvent banks, and banks which have gone into voluntary liquidation, and the amounts and different kinds of United States bonds deposited with the Treasurer as security for circulating notes. The appendix also contains an exhibit of the capital and dividends, semi-annually, for two years, of one hundred and sixteen of the leading banks of Great Britain and Ireland; and the interest laws of Rhode Island, Massachusetts, and Connecticut.

A table of contents will be found on the succeeding page.

JOHN JAY KNOX,
Comptroller of the Currency.

HON. JAMES G. BLAINE,
Speaker of the House of Representatives.

APPENDICES.

APPENDICES.

Table of the dividends and earnings of the national banks, with their ratios to capital and capital and surplus-fund, for the six months from March 1, 1869, to August 31, 1869.

States, Territories, and cities.	Number of banks.	Capital paid in.	Surplus-fund.	Dividends paid.	Net earnings.	Ratios.		
						Dividends to capital.	Dividends to capital and surplus.	Earnings to capital and surplus.
						Per ct.	*Per ct.*	*Per ct.*
Maine	58	$8,925,000	$1,306,213	$463,034	$622,457	5.19	4.53	6.08
New Hampshire	40	4,785,000	506,787	233,550	324,138	4.88	4.36	6.06
Vermont	40	6,712,712	739,831	327,003	449,341	4.87	4.39	6.03
Massachusetts	159	36,572,000	8,138,185	1,977,300	2,837,983	5.41	4.43	6.35
Boston	45	42,500,000	9,024,398	2,332,500	2,950,649	5.49	4.53	5.73
Rhode Island	58	19,612,850	1,519,434	871,652	1,188,810	4.44	4.12	5.62
Connecticut	76	22,954,500	4,272,421	1,145,900	1,506,726	4.99	4.21	5.53
New York	203	32,259,150	5,626,092	1,581,499	2,207,920	4.90	4.17	5.83
New York City	51	70,785,000	17,494,679	3,651,750	4,801,466	5.16	4.14	5.44
Albany	7	2,650,000	975,000	141,000	220,503	5.32	3.89	6.08
New Jersey	52	11,083,350	2,382,505	632,252	848,656	5.70	4.69	6.30
Pennsylvania	146	23,355,020	4,810,860	1,296,060	1,709,036	5.55	4.60	6.07
Philadelphia	28	16,092,150	6,158,302	979,607	1,178,241	6.09	4.40	5.29
Pittsburgh	15	8,700,000	2,086,777	479,500	626,066	5.51	4.44	5.80
Delaware	10	1,373,185	308,698	78,335	90,750	5.70	4.66	5.40
Maryland	15	2,106,700	349,783	118,168	158,072	5.61	4.81	6.43
Baltimore	13	10,391,985	1,604,204	560,757	710,705	5.40	4.67	5.92
Washington	3	1,050,000	235,000	52,500	61,419	5	4.08	4.78
Virginia	14	1,823,300	166,449	93,165	128,427	5.11	4.68	6.45
West Virginia	14	2,116,400	250,580	110,125	153,143	5.20	4.65	6.47
North Carolina	4	650,000	43,392	47,500	69,671	7.31	6.85	10.04
South Carolina	3	823,500	64,398	47,880	68,908	5.81	5.39	7.76
Georgia	7	1,500,000	168,000	96,000	126,698	6.40	5.76	7.50
Alabama	....	....	....	....	....	....	....	....
New Orleans	1	1,000,000	60,000	50,000	75,650	5	4.72	7.14
Texas	2	300,000	39,250	20,000	21,763	6.67	5.90	6.41
Arkansas	....	....	....	....	....	....	....	....
Kentucky	11	1,885,000	159,970	98,750	134,512	5.24	4.83	6.58
Louisville	4	950,000	127,814	50,500	56,779	5.32	4.69	5.27
Tennessee	10	1,450,000	183,992	113,921	133,486	7.86	6.97	8.17
Ohio	118	15,109,700	2,774,165	886,475	1,217,074	5.83	4.94	6.78
Cincinnati	5	3,200,000	763,041	205,000	313,482	6.41	5.17	7.91
Cleveland	5	2,500,000	634,141	143,000	156,824	5.72	4.56	5
Indiana	63	12,037,000	2,504,519	671,780	945,886	5.58	4.62	6.50
Illinois	58	5,695,000	1,488,305	396,515	573,006	6.96	5.52	7.98
Chicago	5	8,395,000	1,534,500	531,515	819,086	6.33	5.35	8.25
Michigan	32	3,310,000	787,268	244,800	327,888	7.40	5.97	8
Detroit	3	1,750,000	330,000	80,000	130,484	4.57	3.85	6.27
Wisconsin	24	1,535,000	302,524	99,833	149,343	6.50	5.18	7.75
Milwaukee	3	650,000	179,372	37,000	64,602	5.69	4.46	7.81
Iowa	35	3,042,000	731,175	242,190	338,020	7.96	6.42	8.96
Minnesota	16	1,730,000	215,165	119,300	149,394	6.89	6.13	7.68
Missouri	9	900,000	183,969	56,000	93,013	6.22	5.17	8.58
Saint Louis	7	6,310,300	636,837	322,515	377,477	5.11	4.64	5.43
Kansas	2	170,000	9,348	9,200	14,025	5.41	5.13	7.82
Leavenworth	2	200,000	41,829	20,000	27,985	10	8.27	11.57
Nebraska	2	200,000	23,600	15,000	25,639	7.50	6.71	11.47
Oregon	1	100,000	4,000	15,000	15,000	15	14.42	14.42
Nevada	1	250,000	6,545	7,500	8,911	3	2.92	3.47
Idaho	1	100,000	2,251	15,000	11,800	15	14.68	11.54
	1,481	401,050,802	82,105,848	21,707,831	29,221,184	5.42	4.50	6.04

Dividends and earnings of the national banks, September 1, 1869, to February 28, 1870.

States, Territories, and cities.	Number of banks.	Capital paid in.	Surplus-fund.	Dividends paid.	Net earnings.	Ratios.		
						Dividends to capital.	Dividends to capital and surplus.	Earnings to capital and surplus.
						Per ct.	*Per ct.*	*Per ct.*
Maine	61	$9, 120, 000	$1, 307, 815	$468, 409	$630, 733	5. 14	4. 45	6
New Hampshire	41	4, 835, 000	612, 430	239, 950	335, 675	4. 96	4. 40	6. 16
Vermont	40	6, 842, 712	879, 109	341, 209	468, 308	4. 99	4. 42	6. 06
Massachusetts	160	38, 132, 000	8, 803, 870	2, 020, 075	2, 985, 244	5. 30	4. 30	6. 36
Boston	45	45, 050, 000	9, 485, 816	2, 229, 000	2, 797, 914	4. 95	4. 09	5. 13
Rhode Island	62	20, 364, 800	1, 672, 414	917, 942	1, 258, 919	4. 51	4. 17	5. 71
Connecticut	79	24, 191, 520	4, 484, 370	1, 286, 722	1, 671, 781	5. 33	4. 50	5. 84
New York	228	37, 992, 741	5, 903, 012	1, 654, 776	2, 381, 841	4. 36	3. 77	5. 43
New York City	52	71, 610, 000	17, 768, 668	3, 505, 566	4, 295, 704	4. 90	3. 92	4. 81
Albany	7	2, 650, 000	975, 000	136, 000	208, 088	5. 13	3. 75	5. 74
New Jersey	53	11, 365, 350	2, 451, 040	663, 743	846, 684	5. 84	4. 08	6. 13
Pennsylvania	149	23, 905, 240	4, 974, 496	1, 331, 635	1, 811, 543	5. 57	4. 61	6. 27
Philadelphia	29	16, 355, 150	6, 197, 217	978, 758	1, 150, 597	5. 98	4. 34	5. 10
Pittsburgh	15	8, 700, 000	2, 171, 125	447, 500	561, 638	5. 14	4. 12	5. 17
Delaware	10	1, 373, 175	317, 788	73, 935	80, 784	5. 38	4. 37	4. 78
Maryland	18	2, 348, 218	357, 643	135, 112	174, 769	5. 75	4. 99	6. 46
Baltimore	13	10, 391, 985	1, 686, 806	570, 509	773, 943	5. 49	4. 72	6. 41
Washington	3	1, 050, 000	241, 000	52, 500	66, 861	5	4. 07	5. 18
Virginia	15	2, 103, 300	169, 276	115, 705	154, 925	5. 50	5. 09	6. 82
West Virginia	14	2, 116, 400	286, 532	106, 620	140, 814	5. 04	4. 44	5. 86
North Carolina	6	846, 600	53, 185	47, 830	80, 382	5. 65	5. 32	8. 93
South Carolina	3	823, 500	73, 746	111, 880	88, 076	13. 59	12. 47	9. 82
Georgia	7	1, 500, 000	186, 900	86, 000	133, 358	5. 73	5. 09	7. 91
Alabama	1	300, 000	13, 873	....	5, 206	......	......	1. 69
New Orleans	2	1, 300, 000	70, 000	80, 000	96, 517	6. 15	5. 84	7. 05
Texas	2	300, 000	42, 100	13, 000	23, 486	4. 33	3. 80	6. 87
Arkansas	......	....	....	....	....	......	......	......
Kentucky	12	1, 935, 000	203, 260	99, 750	146, 656	5. 16	4. 67	6. 86
Louisville	2	500, 000	127, 814	28, 000	41, 170	5. 60	4. 46	6. 56
Tennessee	12	1, 125, 300	193, 309	116, 127	125, 258	10. 32	8. 81	9. 50
Ohio	119	15, 404, 700	2, 835, 134	789, 491	1, 172, 797	5. 13	4. 33	6. 43
Cincinnati	4	3, 200, 000	570, 813	182, 000	237, 666	5. 69	4. 83	6. 30
Cleveland	6	3, 100, 000	614, 827	175, 000	254, 456	5. 65	4. 71	6. 85
Indiana	68	12, 702, 000	2, 815, 440	687, 135	995, 499	5. 41	4. 43	6. 42
Illinois	67	6, 645, 000	1, 664, 910	415, 953	656, 139	6. 26	5. 01	7. 90
Chicago	8	3, 900, 000	1, 794, 500	135, 000	320, 900	3. 21	2. 20	5. 64
Michigan	37	3, 795, 000	916, 064	227, 550	371, 389	6. 10	4. 83	7. 88
Detroit	3	1, 750, 000	375, 000	87, 500	144, 719	5	4. 12	6. 80
Wisconsin	27	1, 760, 000	413, 817	108, 926	176, 742	6. 19	5. 01	8. 13
Milwaukee	5	850, 000	180, 129	37, 000	40, 896	4. 35	3. 59	3. 97
Iowa	39	3, 392, 000	812, 761	218, 112	327, 970	6. 43	5. 19	7. 80
Minnesota	17	1, 780, 000	280, 042	124, 900	165, 247	7. 02	6. 05	8
Missouri	10	1, 000, 000	210, 568	52, 500	117, 843	5. 25	4. 34	9. 73
Saint Louis	8	6, 810, 300	624, 765	290, 515	350, 372	4. 27	3. 91	4. 71
Kansas	3	220, 000	12, 848	14, 200	21, 151	6. 45	6. 10	9. 08
Leavenworth	1	100, 000	49, 814	10, 000	12, 069	10	6. 67	8. 06
Nebraska	3	350, 000	53, 600	25, 000	31, 447	7. 14	6. 19	7. 79
Oregon	1	100, 000	5, 000	15, 000	10, 285	15	14. 29	9. 80
Colorado	3	350, 000	78, 000	20, 000	35, 536	5. 71	4. 67	8. 30
Idaho	1	100, 000	4, 564	15, 000	16, 765	15	14. 35	16. 03
	1, 571	416, 366, 991	86, 118, 210	21, 479, 095	28, 996, 934	5. 16	4. 27	5. 77

Dividends and earnings of the national banks, continued, March 1, 1870, to August 31, 1870.

States, Territories, and cities.	Number of banks.	Capital paid in.	Surplus-fund.	Dividends paid.	Net earnings.	Ratios.		
						Dividends to capital.	Dividends to capital and surplus.	Earnings to capital and surplus.
						Per ct.	*Per ct.*	*Per ct.*
Maine	61	$9, 124, 000	$1, 484, 381	$476, 850	$615, 614	5. 23	4. 49	5. 80
New Hampshire	41	4, 835, 000	681, 918	233, 250	316, 022	4. 82	4. 23	5. 73
Vermont	40	6, 812, 713	993, 000	359, 709	437, 319	5. 28	4. 68	5. 60
Massachusetts	160	39, 022, 000	9, 359, 085	1, 947, 600	2, 585, 680	4. 99	4. 03	5. 34
Boston	46	47, 800, 000	9, 919, 412	2, 352, 500	2, 975, 954	4. 92	4. 08	5. 16
Rhode Island	62	20, 364, 800	1, 904, 672	905, 492	1, 120, 812	4. 45	4. 06	5. 03
Connecticut	81	24, 741, 520	4, 925, 724	1, 278, 680	1, 558, 413	5. 16	4. 31	5. 25
New York	230	36, 162, 741	6, 386, 205	1, 604, 840	2, 145, 885	4. 44	3. 77	5. 04
New York City	54	72, 910, 000	18, 657, 322	3, 345, 250	3, 870, 436	4. 59	3. 65	4. 23
Albany	7	2, 650, 000	990, 000	141, 000	150, 445	5. 32	3. 87	4. 13
New Jersey	54	11, 515, 350	2, 541, 090	621, 118	827, 467	5. 39	4. 42	5. 88
Pennsylvania	149	23, 920, 240	5, 370, 608	1, 334, 560	1, 566, 199	5. 58	4. 55	5. 35
Philadelphia	29	16, 255, 150	6, 498, 576	942, 058	1, 062, 048	5. 79	4. 14	4. 67
Pittsburgh	16	9, 000, 000	2, 235, 774	464, 500	575, 889	5. 16	4. 13	5. 13
Delaware	11	1, 428, 185	300, 211	79, 035	91, 912	5. 53	4. 56	5. 30
Maryland	18	2, 348, 217	378, 874	122, 869	160, 089	5. 23	4. 51	5. 87
Baltimore	13	10, 891, 985	1, 845, 709	543, 051	737, 387	4. 98	4. 26	5. 80
Washington	3	1, 050, 000	245, 000	52, 500	56, 353	5	4. 05	4. 35
Virginia	16	2, 225, 000	195, 248	109, 050	154, 738	4. 90	4. 51	6. 39
West Virginia	14	2, 116, 400	302, 638	106, 825	136, 972	5. 05	4. 42	5. 66
North Carolina	6	850, 000	65, 106	35, 250	50, 097	4. 15	3. 85	5. 46
South Carolina	3	1, 063, 803	95, 953	58, 828	101, 425	5. 53	5. 07	8. 75
Georgia	7	1, 750, 000	212, 000	98, 500	160, 815	5. 63	5. 02	8. 20
Alabama	1	....	....	....	....	.....	.....	.....
New Orleans	2	1, 300, 000	83, 550	80, 000	119, 107	6. 15	5. 78	8. 61
Texas	4	525, 000	49, 209	72, 500	94, 674	13. 81	12. 62	16. 49
Arkansas	.....	....	....	....	....	.....	.....	.....
Kentucky	12	2, 010, 700	226, 727	100, 250	155, 113	4. 99	4. 48	6. 93
Louisville	4	950, 000	143, 336	50, 500	47, 895	5. 32	4. 62	4. 38
Tennessee	13	1, 650, 300	212, 395	97, 735	133, 116	5. 92	5. 24	7. 15
Ohio	119	15, 244, 700	3, 139, 829	729, 457	1, 003, 912	4. 79	3. 97	5. 46
Cincinnati	5	3, 500, 000	555, 000	200, 000	194, 709	5. 71	4. 93	4. 80
Cleveland	6	3, 300, 000	350, 485	126, 000	141, 585	3. 82	3. 45	3. 88
Indiana	69	12, 777, 000	3, 039, 786	665, 610	940, 194	5. 21	4. 21	5. 94
Illinois	68	6, 570, 000	1, 840, 416	432, 665	563, 116	6. 59	5. 14	6. 70
Chicago	14	5, 900, 000	1, 987, 000	162, 500	420, 529	2. 75	2. 06	5. 33
Michigan	38	3, 835, 000	1, 057, 129	218, 050	337, 293	5. 68	4. 46	6. 89
Detroit	3	1, 750, 000	380, 000	87, 500	124, 552	5	4. 10	5. 85
Wisconsin	27	1, 715, 000	427, 101	101, 900	148, 036	5. 94	4. 76	6. 91
Milwaukee	4	750, 000	166, 461	34, 500	49, 358	4. 60	3. 76	5. 39
Iowa	41	3, 502, 000	875, 261	193, 100	252, 630	5. 38	4. 32	5. 66
Minnesota	17	1, 830, 000	306, 546	100, 400	131, 327	5. 49	4. 70	6. 15
Missouri	10	900, 000	255, 068	56, 500	108, 439	6. 28	4. 89	9. 39
Saint Louis	8	6, 810, 300	719, 291	252, 361	253, 222	3. 71	3. 35	3. 36
Kansas	3	220, 000	18, 268	16, 700	19, 250	7. 59	7. 01	8. 08
Leavenworth	2	200, 000	60, 359	44, 800	48, 175	22. 40	17. 22	18. 50
Nebraska	4	500, 000	57, 850	20, 000	32, 880	4	3. 58	5. 89
Oregon	1	100, 000	5, 000	....	14, 600	.....	.....	13. 90
Colorado	3	350, 000	72, 500	10, 000	6, 206	2. 86	2. 37	1. 47
Utah	1	100, 000	1, 437	....	1, 437	.....	.....	1. 42
Idaho	1	100, 000	5, 300	14, 000	14, 659	14	13. 30	13. 92
	1, 601	425, 317, 104	91, 630, 620	21, 080, 343	26, 813, 885	4. 96	4. 08	5. 19

of the national banks, continued, September 1, 1870, to February 28, 1871.

	Number of banks.	Capital paid in.	Surplus-fund.	Dividends paid.	Net earnings.	Ratios. Dividends to capital.	Ratios. Dividends to capital and surplus.	Ratios. Earnings to capital and surplus.
						Per ct.	Per ct.	Per ct.
...	61	$9,125,000	$1,544,445	$472,784	$610,752	5.18	4.43	5.72
...	41	4,835,000	735,110	233,250	296,963	4.82	4.19	5.33
...	41	7,312,713	1,025,440	340,700	442,244	4.66	4.09	5.30
...	160	38,922,000	9,821,227	2,109,850	2,671,817	5.42	4.33	5.48
...	46	47,800,000	10,278,664	2,361,500	2,843,041	4.94	4.07	4.90
...	62	20,364,800	2,035,065	902,062	1,079,977	4.43	4.03	4.82
...	81	25,059,520	5,207,790	1,326,922	1,603,128	5.30	4.38	5.30
...	220	36,212,741	6,632,118	1,751,688	2,164,117	4.84	4.09	5.05
...	54	73,435,000	18,882,707	3,457,547	4,069,305	4.71	3.75	4.41
...	7	2,650,000	990,000	141,000	133,511	5.32	3.87	3.67
...	54	11,590,050	2,632,541	650,807	827,840	5.62	4.58	5.83
...	151	24,205,240	5,577,481	1,293,860	1,424,050	5.35	4.34	4.78
...	29	16,255,150	6,537,247	957,258	1,000,230	4.90	4.20	4.39
...	16	9,000,000	2,297,158	463,500	561,177	5.15	4.10	4.97
...	11	1,428,175	313,709	73,284	78,332	5.13	4.21	4.50
...	18	2,348,217	404,906	130,722	145,818	5.57	4.75	5.30
...	13	10,891,985	1,899,814	522,177	674,142	4.79	4.08	5.27
...	3	1,050,000	251,000	52,500	67,843	5	4.04	5.22
...	16	2,275,000	231,011	108,050	170,751	4.75	4.31	6.81
...	14	2,120,500	258,462	112,190	126,898	5.29	4.70	5.33
...	6	850,000	69,760	36,250	54,322	4.27	3.94	5.91
...	3	1,090,774	121,017	65,446	90,484	6	5.40	7.47
...	7	1,750,000	239,600	163,500	133,300	9.34	8.22	6.70
...	2	400,000	14,570	19,000	47,035	4.75	4.58	11.35
...	2	1,300,000	107,100	80,000	105,239	6.15	5.69	7.48
...	4	525,000	50,499	10,000	39,195	1.90	1.75	6.81
...	......	......	......	......	......	......	......	......
...	12	2,010,000	252,731	113,250	138,356	5.63	5.01	6.11
...	4	950,000	146,879	48,000	49,639	5.05	4.38	4.53
...	13	1,950,300	241,538	168,700	182,848	8.65	7.70	8.34
...	117	15,104,700	3,313,914	868,554	1,110,153	5.75	4.72	6.03
...	5	3,500,000	566,779	170,000	271,306	4.86	4.18	6.67
...	6	3,300,000	366,048	98,000	112,890	2.97	2.67	3.08
...	69	12,827,000	3,304,555	776,872	1,016,870	6.06	4.82	6.30
...	67	6,660,000	1,779,280	419,937	572,361	6.29	4.97	6.77
...	14	6,200,000	2,086,528	297,500	618,053	4.80	3.59	7.46
...	38	3,873,000	1,195,599	237,300	357,719	6.13	4.68	7.06
...	3	1,750,000	383,000	87,500	129,830	5	4.10	6.09
...	28	1,785,000	403,774	175,550	197,272	9.83	8.07	9.01
...	4	650,000	179,512	34,500	55,159	5.31	4.16	6.65
...	43	3,902,000	832,079	226,179	298,711	5.80	4.78	6.31
...	17	1,780,000	305,601	144,250	177,838	8.11	6.92	8.53
...	12	1,300,000	282,525	224,500	136,351	17.27	14.19	8.62
...	7	6,610,300	623,222	207,361	207,573	3.14	2.87	2.87
...	3	230,000	21,737	14,161	27,319	6.16	5.63	10.85
...	2	200,000	59,544	16,000	20,307	8	6.17	7.44
...	3	400,000	62,000	25,000	58,868	6.25	5.41	12.74
...	1	250,000	5,000	....	10,506	......	......	7.67
...	3	350,000	72,500	....	395	......	......	0.09
...	1	100,000	11,616	....	1,612	......	......	1.44
...	1	100,000	7,000	16,000	17,600	16	14.95	16.45
...	1	100,000	10,000	....	3,055	......	......	2.78
	1,605	428,699,165	94,672,401	22,205,150	27,243,162	5.18	4.24	5.21

Dividends and earnings of the national banks, continued, March 1, 1871, to August 31, 1871.

States, Territories, and cities.	Number of banks.	Capital paid in.	Surplus-fund.	Dividends paid.	Net earnings.	Ratios. Dividends to capital.	Dividends to capital and surplus.	Earnings to capital and surplus.
						Per ct.	Per ct.	Per ct.
Maine	61	$9,125,000	$1,584,746	$467,659	$645,356	5.13	4.37	6.03
New Hampshire	41	4,835,000	772,094	226,150	257,575	4.68	4.03	4.59
Vermont	41	7,512,712	1,065,544	357,459	410,875	4.76	4.17	4.79
Massachusetts	160	39,222,000	10,237,612	2,074,350	2,579,051	5.29	4.19	5.21
Boston	47	48,100,000	10,657,436	2,315,500	2,721,391	4.81	3.94	4.63
Rhode Island	62	20,364,800	2,104,454	878,412	1,064,132	4.31	3.89	4.71
Connecticut	81	24,991,520	5,426,874	1,299,892	1,580,747	5.20	4.27	5.20
New York	231	36,507,741	6,905,177	1,619,651	1,943,189	4.44	3.72	4.47
New York City	54	73,235,000	19,186,169	3,415,050	4,143,813	4.66	3.70	4.48
Albany	7	2,650,000	990,000	131,000	131,296	4.94	3.60	3.61
New Jersey	56	12,240,350	2,809,897	626,555	884,205	5.12	4.16	5.88
Pennsylvania	151	24,545,240	5,781,467	1,284,381	1,568,270	5.23	4.24	5.17
Philadelphia	30	16,480,150	6,704,033	942,758	1,023,270	5.70	4.06	4.41
Pittsburgh	16	9,000,000	2,415,177	482,000	552,755	5.36	4.22	4.84
Delaware	11	1,528,185	351,484	78,184	86,982	5.12	4.16	4.63
Maryland	18	2,348,218	416,284	121,769	133,652	5.20	4.40	4.83
Baltimore	14	11,091,985	1,956,627	520,925	639,623	4.70	3.99	4.90
Washington	3	1,050,000	260,000	52,509	100,026	5	4	7.64
Virginia	22	3,080,000	274,882	133,639	222,152	4.34	3.98	6.62
West Virginia	15	2,374,000	295,143	99,330	94,073	4.18	3.72	3.52
North Carolina	9	1,300,000	76,787	57,750	84,935	4.44	4.19	6.17
South Carolina	4	1,591,200	143,454	87,174	102,851	5.48	5.03	5.93
Georgia	8	2,150,000	246,600	114,500	139,617	5.33	4.78	5.83
Alabama	3	500,000	34,642	28,000	30,468	5.60	5.24	5.70
New Orleans	6	2,880,000	121,153	150,000	98,285	5.21	5	3.27
Texas	5	625,000	54,799	37,000	43,647	5.92	5.44	6.42
Arkansas	...	...	...	...	...	...	...	...
Kentucky	20	4,051,963	289,707	187,623	234,648	4.63	4.32	5.41
Louisville	4	950,000	109,864	104,500	60,302	11	9.86	5.69
Tennessee	17	2,651,300	238,274	149,122	206,442	5.62	5.16	7.14
Ohio	118	15,460,700	3,530,347	869,762	1,114,436	5.63	4.58	5.87
Cincinnati	5	3,500,000	682,992	190,000	182,721	5.43	4.56	4.39
Cleveland	6	3,300,000	397,525	128,000	147,809	3.88	3.46	4
Indiana	70	14,262,000	3,333,366	795,480	956,111	5.58	4.52	5.43
Illinois	80	8,162,200	1,904,164	495,211	669,308	6.07	4.92	6.65
Chicago	16	6,950,000	2,279,000	351,250	636,532	5.05	3.81	6.90
Michigan	50	5,080,000	1,191,993	258,175	392,418	5.08	4.12	6.26
Detroit	3	1,750,000	386,000	87,500	140,543	5	4.10	6.58
Wisconsin	33	2,165,000	420,381	89,300	136,323	4.12	3.45	5.27
Milwaukee	4	750,000	198,823	34,500	59,631	4.60	3.74	6.28
Iowa	50	4,317,000	887,930	220,872	287,658	5.12	4.24	5.53
Minnesota	19	1,980,000	319,237	136,800	164,327	6.91	5.95	7.15
Missouri	15	1,650,700	203,039	88,035	128,976	5.33	4.75	6.96
Saint Louis	7	6,610,300	706,074	217,361	320,771	3.29	2.97	4.38
Kansas	6	430,000	23,212	24,200	46,115	5.63	5.34	10.18
Leavenworth	2	200,000	66,858	10,000	18,047	5	3.75	6.76
Nebraska	3	400,000	65,100	25,000	16,943	6.25	5.38	3.64
Oregon	1	250,000	5,000	10,000	30,416	4	3.92	11.93
San Francisco	1	1,000,000	...	...	21,068	...	...	2.11
New Mexico	1	150,000	...	6,000	7,489	4	...	4.99
Colorado	3	350,000	72,500	30,000	11,834	8.57	7.10	2.80
Utah	1	100,000	14,555	...	6,358	...	...	5.55
Wyoming	...	...	...	...	...	...	...	...
Idaho	1	100,000	8,100	15,000	15,040	15	13.86	13.91
Montana	1	100,000	10,000	...	20,809	...	...	18.92
	1,693	445,999,264	98,286,501	22,125,279	27,315,311	4.96	4.07	5.02

idends and earnings of the national banks, continued, September 1, 1871, to February 28, 1872.

tates, Territories, and cities.	Number of banks.	Capital paid in.	Surplus-fund.	Dividends paid.	Net earnings.	Ratios. Dividends to capital.	Ratios. Dividends to capital and surplus.	Ratios. Earnings to capital and surplus.
						Per ct.	*Per ct.*	*Per ct.*
ine	61	$9,125,000	$1,670,245	$462,204	$565,739	5.07	4.28	5.24
v Hampshire	41	4,835,000	815,670	231,900	269,579	4.80	4.14	4.77
mont	41	7,612,712	1,127,160	368,235	431,975	4.84	4.21	4.94
sachusetts	160	39,272,000	10,545,400	2,140,955	2,502,841	5.45	4.30	5.02
Boston	48	48,600,000	10,923,848	2,300,576	2,760,487	4.73	3.86	4.64
de Island	62	20,364,800	2,464,349	894,162	1,054,377	4.39	3.92	4.62
nectiont	81	25,059,520	5,617,278	1,315,395	1,567,735	5.25	4.29	5.11
v York	229	36,535,191	7,218,154	1,716,183	1,988,699	4.70	3.92	4.54
New York City	51	71,785,000	19,213,149	3,509,954	3,664,006	4.89	3.86	4.03
Albany	7	2,650,000	990,000	110,000	204,664	4.15	3.02	5.62
v Jersey	57	12,657,150	3,032,004	726,825	884,429	5.74	4.63	5.64
nsylvania	153	25,255,240	5,998,420	1,353,347	1,638,464	5.36	4.33	5.24
Philadelphia	30	16,935,000	6,804,709	971,750	1,068,461	5.74	4.09	4.50
Pittsburgh	16	9,000,000	2,481,622	487,000	557,482	5.41	4.24	4.86
aware	11	1,528,185	369,760	78,184	83,538	5.12	4.12	4.40
ryland	18	2,348,218	431,802	121,219	126,107	5.16	4.36	4.54
Baltimore	14	11,241,985	1,964,935	572,551	713,171	5.09	4.34	5.40
Washington	3	1,050,000	250,000	27,500	39,528	2.62	2.12	3.04
ginia	23	3,577,900	327,340	164,770	206,917	4.61	4.22	5.30
st Virginia	15	2,366,000	277,399	128,655	152,231	5.44	4.87	5.76
th Carolina	9	1,475,000	87,408	88,429	113,669	6	5.66	7.27
th Carolina	7	2,168,581	150,907	117,202	155,888	5.40	5.05	6.72
rgia	10	2,570,500	302,000	126,365	170,887	4.88	4.36	5.95
bama	6	908,000	37,517	31,000	41,039	3.41	3.28	4.34
New Orleans	6	3,300,000	144,532	186,000	217,382	5.64	5.40	6.31
as	5	625,000	57,999	27,400	62,250	4.38	4.01	9.11
ansas	...	...	...	...	...	...	...	...
tucky	25	4,970,000	353,097	208,152	255,316	4.19	3.91	4.80
Louisville	4	1,350,000	117,785	72,500	81,085	5.37	4.87	5.52
nessee	19	2,871,300	262,430	167,052	244,011	5.82	5.33	7.79
o	119	15,934,700	3,628,477	927,161	1,196,202	5.82	4.74	6.12
Cincinnati	5	4,000,000	691,315	198,000	227,194	4.95	4.22	4.84
Cleveland	6	3,300,000	416,460	138,000	212,001	4.19	3.71	5.70
iana	76	15,162,000	3,497,631	815,470	1,007,369	5.37	4.37	5.40
nois	93	9,573,000	2,079,521	545,865	707,731	5.71	4.68	6.07
Chicago	...	...	...	...	...	...	...	...
higan	56	5,580,000	1,249,294	360,751	449,607	6.47	5.28	6.57
Detroit	3	1,750,000	392,000	92,500	147,850	5.29	4.32	6.90
sconsin	36	2,525,000	448,043	124,722	198,231	4.94	4.20	6.67
Milwaukee	4	750,000	221,407	36,500	47,477	4.87	3.76	4.89
a	60	5,037,000	946,441	239,835	353,053	4.76	4.01	5.90
nesota	22	2,440,000	369,849	128,090	198,822	5.25	4.56	7.08
souri	22	2,085,000	234,033	109,277	185,085	5.24	4.71	7.98
Saint Louis	8	6,860,300	803,246	219,403	312,846	3.20	2.86	4.08
nsas	10	710,000	39,875	33,000	67,707	4.65	4.40	9.03
Leavenworth	2	200,000	74,905	20,000	18,541	10	7.29	6.74
raska	6	649,424	73,078	45,954	46,828	7.08	6.36	6.48
gon	1	250,000	6,000	15,000	38,898	6	5.86	15.19
San Francisco	1	1,000,000	...	8,333	56,704	0.83	...	5.67
v Mexico	1	150,000	1,489	10,500	11,707	7	6.26	7.73
orado	4	400,000	72,500	10,000	30,203	2.50	2.12	6.39
ah	1	100,000	128,800	50,000	109,404	50	21.85	47.82
oming	...	...	...	...	...	...	...	...
ho	1	100,000	9,900	14,000	16,717	14	12.74	15.21
ntana	1	100,000	10,000	12,000	18,415	12	10.91	16.74
	1,750	450,693,706	99,431,243	22,859,826	27,502,539	5.07	4.16	5

Dividends and earnings of the national banks, continued, March 1, 1872, to August 31, 1872.

States, Territories, and cities.	Number of banks.	Capital paid in.	Surplus-fund.	Dividends paid.	Net earnings.	Ratios.		
						Dividends to capital.	Dividends to capital and surplus.	Earnings to capital and surplus.
						Per ct.	Per ct.	Per ct.
Maine	62	$9,086,335	$1,737,090	$475,755	$607,246	5.23	4.40	5.61
New Hampshire	41	5,010,000	842,049	232,400	284,786	4.64	3.97	4.86
Vermont	41	7,612,912	1,172,223	353,236	468,009	4.64	4.02	5.33
Massachusetts	102	39,272,000	10,762,111	2,121,850	2,743,145	5.40	4.24	5.48
Boston	48	49,100,000	10,907,556	2,234,914	2,720,677	4.55	3.72	4.53
Rhode Island	62	20,079,800	2,738,189	881,712	1,204,796	4.39	3.86	5.28
Connecticut	81	25,059,520	5,953,817	1,325,682	1,692,717	5.29	4.27	5.46
New York	230	36,620,291	7,408,405	1,601,418	2,264,906	4.37	3.64	5.14
New York City	51	71,785,000	19,615,192	3,350,130	4,419,537	4.67	3.67	4.84
Albany	7	2,650,000	1,225,000	152,800	202,083	5.74	3.92	5.22
New Jersey	58	12,790,350	3,143,018	691,148	862,328	5.40	4.34	5.41
Pennsylvania	155	26,575,090	6,359,964	1,332,980	1,612,149	5.21	4.17	5.05
Philadelphia	29	16,735,000	6,821,824	964,250	1,081,428	5.76	4.09	4.59
Pittsburgh	16	9,000,000	2,570,277	479,000	576,970	5.32	4.14	4.99
Delaware	11	1,528,185	376,102	77,234	92,482	5.06	4.06	4.86
Maryland	19	2,398,218	442,362	126,619	156,197	5.28	4.46	5.50
Baltimore	14	11,241,985	2,060,230	592,800	739,954	5.27	4.46	5.56
District of Columbia	1	252,000	20,000	10,080	13,199	4	3.71	4.85
Washington	3	1,200,000	286,408	55,000	78,224	4.58	3.70	5.26
Virginia	23	3,730,000	368,028	173,675	244,518	4.66	4.24	5.97
West Virginia	17	2,546,000	298,134	135,274	168,001	5.31	4.76	5.91
North Carolina	9	1,950,000	87,683	98,500	75,866	5.05	4.83	3.72
South Carolina	8	2,320,702	165,749	118,335	160,681	5.10	4.76	6.46
Georgia	10	2,575,800	324,384	137,500	194,279	5.34	4.74	6.70
Alabama	7	1,068,000	45,320	68,800	104,580	6.44	6.18	9.39
New Orleans	9	4,850,000	171,253	268,024	348,015	5.53	5.34	6.93
Texas	5	625,000	61,302	48,000	83,119	7.68	6.99	12.11
Arkansas	2	183,000	20,000	....	554	......	......	0.27
Kentucky	27	5,143,333	393,580	248,825	313,744	4.84	4.49	5.67
Louisville	5	1,550,000	126,415	77,500	87,485	5	4.62	5.22
Tennessee	19	2,971,300	291,216	178,230	186,247	6	5.46	5.70
Ohio	133	17,474,700	3,804,378	1,046,804	1,277,622	5.99	4.92	6
Cincinnati	5	4,000,000	728,714	218,000	253,068	5.45	4.61	5.35
Cleveland	6	3,500,000	442,962	178,000	207,913	5.09	4.52	5.27
Indiana	84	15,951,100	3,664,895	938,666	1,030,229	5.88	4.79	5.25
Illinois	106	10,538,000	2,200,337	578,775	828,180	5.49	4.54	6.50
Chicago	16	8,200,000	1,987,885	509,583	691,333	6.21	5	6.79
Michigan	64	6,280,061	1,335,807	385,210	544,779	6.12	5.06	7.15
Detroit	3	1,750,000	550,000	87,500	153,139	5	3.80	6.66
Wisconsin	37	2,500,000	501,704	122,900	164,768	4.92	4.09	5.49
Milwaukee	4	750,000	185,725	142,500	121,998	19	15.22	13.04
Iowa	62	2,157,000	1,007,035	304,811	373,421	14.13	9.63	11.80
Minnesota	25	2,625,000	414,573	154,775	221,237	5.90	5.09	7.28
Missouri	25	2,235,000	295,401	105,750	257,088	4.73	4.18	10.16
Saint Louis	8	6,860,300	854,582	218,861	311,149	3.19	2.84	4.03
Kansas	20	1,235,041	124,341	67,854	93,297	5.49	4.99	6.86
Nebraska	8	800,000	94,200	52,879	67,207	6.61	5.93	7.54
Oregon	1	250,000	7,500	15,000	53,846	6	5.83	20.91
San Francisco	1	1,000,000	10,000	50,000	55,524	5	4.95	5.50
New Mexico	1	150,000	2,096	10,500	14,581	7	6.87	9.55
Colorado	5	400,000	75,500	15,000	24,933	3.26	2.78	4.06
Utah	2	250,000	77,010	....	5,035	......	......	1.54
Wyoming	......	....	....	....	....	......	......	......
Idaho	1	100,000	11,000	13,000	26,216	13	11.71	23.62
Montana	1	100,000	10,000	....	8,318	......	......	7.56
	1,852	465,676,023	105,181,942	23,827,289	30,572,891	5.12	4.17	5.36

Table showing the capital and last four semi-annual dividends of banking companies in the United Kingdom of England, Ireland, and Scotland, compiled from the Investor's Monthly Manual (appendix to London Economist) of October 26, 1872, pages 345 and 346.

	Capital.	*Amount of last four semi-annual dividends, payable in—				Rate per cent., semi-annual dividends, including bonus—			
		1871.	1871.	1872.	1872.	1871.	1871.	1872.	1872.
Aberdeen, Town and County	£182,000	£9,100	£9,100	£9,100	£9,100	5	5	5	5
Ashton, Stalybridge, Hyde, and Glossop	50,000	5,000	5,000	5,000	2,500	10	10	10	5
Bank of Australasia	1,200,000	60,000	48,000	60,000	48,000	5	4	5	4
Bank of Bolton	225,000	11,250	11,250	11,250	11,250	5	5	5	5
Bank of British Colombia	250,000	7,500	6,250	7,500	7,500	3	2½	3	3
Bank of British Colombia (new, issued at 2 per cent. premium)	48,000	1,440	1,200	1,440	1,440	3	2½	3	3
Bank of British North America	1,000,000	30,000	45,000	40,000	40,000	3	4½	4	4
Bank of Ireland	3,000,000	150,000	165,000	165,000	180,000	5	5½	5½	6
Bank of Leeds	151,300	3,782	3,782	3,782	4,539	2½	2½	2½	3
Bank of Liverpool	625,000	31,250	50,000	31,250	56,250	5	8	5	9
Bank of Scotland	1,000,000	60,000	60,000	60,000	60,000	6	6	6	6
Bank of Victoria	500,000	25,000	25,000	25,000	25,000	5	5	5	5
Bank of Whitehaven	73,460	6,428	5,510	6,428	5,510	8¾	7½	8¾	7½
Barnsley Banking Company	39,450	2,950	2,959	3,150	3,156	7½	7½	8	8
Belfast Banking Company	125,000	12,500	22,250	12,500	22,250	18	18	10	18
Belfast Banking Company (new shares, at 10 per cent. premium)	125,000	5,000	9,000	5,000	9,000	4	7 1-5	4	7 1-5
Bilston District	60,000	3,750	3,000	3,750	4,500	6¼	5	6¼	7½
Birmingham and Midland	275,000	27,500	27,500	27,500	27,500	10	10	10	10
Birmingham Banking	200,000	7,500	7,500	10,000	10,000	3¾	3¾	5	5
Birmingham Joint Stock	203,900	20,390	20,390	20,390	20,390	10	10	10	10
Birmingham, Town and District Banking	160,000	6,000	6,000	6,000	8,000	3¾	3¾	3¾	5
Bradford Commercial	200,000	18,000	17,000	17,500	18,000	9	8½	8¾	9
Bradford Banking Company	220,000	24,750	24,750	24,750	24,750	11¼	11¼	11¼	11¼
Bradford District	195,000	5,850	5,850	6,825	6,825	3	3	3½	3½
Bradford Old Bank	392,060	22,053	22,053	26,954	24,503	5⅝	5⅝	6⅞	6¼
British Linen Company	1,000,000	65,000	65,000	65,000	65,000	6½	6½	6½	6½
Burton, Uttoxeter, and Osbourn Union	130,000	9,750	8,450	9,750	9,100	7½	6½	7½	7
Bury Banking Company	109,080	10,908	13,635	10,908	13,635	10	12½	10	12½
Callidenlair Banking Company	125,000	6,875	7,500	7,500	8,750	5½	6	6	7
Carlisle and Cumberland	51,925	5,192	5,193	5,192	5,712	10	10	10	11
Central of London	100,000	2,500	3,000	3,000	4,000	2½	3	3	4
Carlisle, City and District	80,162	8,016	8,016	8,016	8,016	10	10	10	10
Chesterfield and North Derbyshire	35,000	1,750	1,750	1,750	1,750	5	5	5	5
City	500,000	17,500	20,000	22,500	25,000	3½	4	4½	5
City of Glasgow	870,000	39,150	39,150	39,150	43,500	4½	4½	4½	5
Clydesdale	900,000	54,000	54,000	54,000	54,000	6	6	6	6
Colonial	600,000	48,000	48,000	45,000	45,000	8	8	7½	7½
Commercial Bank of Liverpool	350,000	17,500	17,500	17,500	17,500	5	5	5	5
Commercial Bank of Scotland	1,000,000	70,000	70,008	70,000	70,000	7	7	7	7

Table showing the capital and last four semi-annual dividends of banking companies in the United Kingdom, &c.—Continued.

	Capital.	* Amount of last four semi-annual dividends, payable in—				Rate per cent., semi-annual dividends, including bonus—			
		1871.	1871.	1872.	1872.	1871.	1871.	1872.	1872.
Consolidated	£800,000	£28,000	£20,000	£30,000	£32,000	3½	2½	3¾	4
Coventry Union	56,000	2,800	2,800	2,800	3,080	5	5	5	5½
Cumberland Union	225,000	13,500	13,500	13,500	13,500	6	6	6	6
Darlington District	56,000	2,800	2,800	2,800	2,800	5	5	5	5
Delhi and London	500,000	6,250	8,750	8,750	7,500	1¼	1¾	1¾	1½
Derbys and Derbyshire Banking Company	62,500	2,500	2,575	2,500	2,500	4	4⅛	4	4
Devon and Cornwall Banking Company	128,000	6,000	8,320	8,480	8,480	6¼	6½	6⅝	6⅝
Dudley and West Bromwich Banking Company	85,200	2,130	2,130	2,130	2,130	2½	2½	2½	2½
Exchange and Discount (Leeds)	85,000	2,550	3,187	4,250	4,250	3	3¾	5	5
Gloucestershire	450,000	29,531	30,000	30,000	29,531	6 9-16	6⅔	6⅔	6 9-16
Halifax Commercial	120,000	6,000	10,800	6,000	10,800	5	9	5	9
Halifax Joint Stock	150,000	11,250	3,750	15,750	11,250	7½	2½	10½	7½
Huddersfield	315,000	15,750	15,750	15,750	15,750	5	5	5	5
Hull Banking Company	90,990	7,279	7,279	7,279	8,189	8	8	8	9
Imperial	562,500	16,875	16,875	16,875	22,500	3	3	3	4
Lancaster Banking	225,000	36,562	22,500	45,000	25,032	16¼	10	20	11⅛
Land and Mortgage Bank of India, 5 per cent. debenture, 1864, 30 years	500,000	12,500	12,500	12,500	12,500	2½	2½	2½	2½
Leamington, Priors, and Warwickshire	30,000	1,125	1,125	1,125	1,275	3¾	3¾	3¾	4¼
Leeds and County	230,000	6,900	6,900	6,900	8,050	3	3	3	3½
The Leicestershire Banking Company	187,500	12,056	12,187	12,187	12,187	6⅜	6½	6½	6½
Lloyds' Banking—at 5 and 7½ pounds premium	304,560	19,035	22,842	22,842	22,842	6¼	7½	7½	7½
London and County	1,000,000	90,000	90,000	95,000	100,000	9	9	9½	10
London and San Francisco	600,000	30,000	30,000	42,000	36,000	5	5	7	6
London and Southwestern	166,180	2,493	3,323	4,154	4,154	1½	2	2½	2½
London and Westminster	2,000,000	180,000	180,000	180,000	200,000	9	9	9	10
London Joint Stock	1,200,000	110,000	120,000	150,000	120,000	9 1-6	10	12 11-12	10

Northern Banking Company, (Ireland)	150,000	11,250	13,750	11,250	13,750	7½	9 1-6	7½	9 1-6
Northern Banking Company, (new shares)	150,000	5,625	6,875	5,625	6,875	3¾	4 7-12	3¾	4 7 12
North of Scotland	320,000	16,000	16,000	16,000	16,000	5	5	5	5
Northwestern, (Liverpool)	405,000	10,125	12,150	12,150	12,150	2½	3	3	3
North Wilts	70,000	5,230	6,300	7,000	7,000	7½	9	10	10
Nottingham Joint Stock	100,000	2,500	2,500	2,500	3,500	2½	2½	2½	3½
Oriental Bank Corporation	1,500,000	90,000	90,000	90,000	90,000	6	6	6	6
Pans Banking Company	150,000	6,000	6,000	7,500	7,500	4	4	5	5
Pares Leicestershire Banking Company	250,000	15,000	20,000	15,000	20,000	6	8	6	8
Preston Banking Company, (new A. shares)	£50,000	£2,500	£2,500	£2,500	£2,500	5	5	5	5
Provincial Bank of Ireland	500,000	50,000	50,000	50,000	50,000	10	10	10	10
Provincial Bank of Ireland, (new)	40,000	4,000	4,000	4,000	4,000	10	10	10	10
Royal Bank of Ireland	300,000	18,000	18,000	18,000	21,000	6	6	6	7
Royal Bank of Scotland	2,000,000	80,000	80,000	85,000	85,000	4	4	4¼	4¼
Sheffield and Rotherham	160,704	13,057	14,062	15,066	15,066	8⅛	8¾	9⅜	9⅜
Sheffield and Hallamshire	183,200	9,160	11,450	9,160	12,505	5	6¼	5	6⅞
Sheffield Banking Company	210,000	12,000	13,650	13,125	13,650	6	6½	6¼	6½
Sheffield Banking Company	105,000	6,300	6,825	6,562	6,825	6	6½	6¼	6½
Sheffield Union Banking Company	150,000	6,562	7,500	8,437	7,500	4⅜	5	5⅝	5
Shropshire Banking Company	45,000	1,125	1,125	1,687	1,687	2½	2½	3¾	3¾
Staffordshire Joint Stock	200,000	7,500	7,500	7,500	7,500	3¾	3¾	3¾	3¾
Stanford, Spalding, and Boston Banking	150,000	11,250	11,250	11,250	11,250	7½	7½	7½	7½
Stonebridge and Kidderminster	100,000	6,250	10,000	7,500	10,000	6¼	10	7½	10
Ulster Banking Company	250,000	22,500	27,500	22,500	27,500	9	11	9	11
Union Bank of Australia	1,250,000	75,000	81,250	81,250	81,250	6	6½	6½	6½
Union Bank of Liverpool	525,000	26,250	26,250	35,000	26,250	5	5	6⅔	5
Union Bank of London	1,200,000	90,000	120,000	120,000	120,000	7½	10	10	10
Union Bank of Manchester	440,000	23,650	23,650	23,650	23,650	5⅜	5⅜	5⅜	5⅜
Union Bank of Scotland	1,000,000	60,000	60,000	60,000	65,000	6	6	6	6½
West of England and South Wales District	750,000	30,000	30,000	37,500	37,500	4	4	5	5
West Riding Union	160,000	14,000	14,000	15,600	15,600	8¾	8¾	9¾	9¾
Whitehaven Joint Stock	45,000	4,200	4,500	5,250	5,625	9⅓	10	11⅔	12½
Wilts and Dorset Banking Company	200,000	21,000	22,000	22,000	23,000	10½	11	11	11½
Wolverhampton and Staffordshire	100,000	3,750	3,750	3,750	3,750	3¾	3¾	3¾	3¾
Worcester City and County Banking Company	250,000	12,500	12,500	12,500	15,469	5	5	5	6 3-16
York City and County	125,000	8,750	8,750	8,750	10,000	7	7	7	8
Yorkshire Banking Company	250,000	25,000	25,000	25,000	25,000	10	10	10	10
York Union Banking Company	132,000	9,900	9,900	9,900	9,900	7½	7½	7½	7½

* The date of payment of dividends varies, the last being payable October 1, 1872.

Statement exhibiting the number and amount of notes issued, redeemed, and outstanding November 1, 1872.

	Number of notes issued.	Number of notes redeemed.	Number of notes outstanding.	Amount issued.	Amount redeemed.	Amount outstanding.
Ones	14, 297, 360	7, 919, 389	6, 377, 971	$14, 297, 360	$7, 919, 389 00	$6, 377, 971 00
Twos	4, 782, 628	2, 408, 389	2, 374, 239	9, 565, 256	4, 816, 778 00	4, 748, 478 00
Fives	31, 933, 348	5, 960, 667	25, 972, 681	159, 666, 740	29, 803, 335 00	129, 863, 405 00
Tens	11, 253, 452	1, 699, 702	9, 553, 750	112, 534, 520	16, 997, 020 00	95, 537, 500 00
Twenties	3, 225, 688	438, 852	2, 786, 836	64, 513, 760	8, 777, 040 00	55, 736, 720 00
Fifties	497, 199	126, 180	371, 019	24, 859, 950	6, 309, 000 00	18, 550, 950 00
One-hundreds	367, 797	110, 989	256, 808	36, 779, 700	11, 098, 900 00	25, 680, 800 00
Five-hundreds	15, 621	7, 867	7, 754	7, 810, 500	3, 933, 500 00	3, 877, 000 00
One-thousands	4, 933	4, 315	618	4, 933, 000	4, 315, 000 00	618, 000 00
					93, 969, 962 00	
Deduct for fragments of notes lost or destroyed.					2, 646 30	
Add for fragments of notes lost or destroyed.						2, 646 30
Totals	66, 378, 026	18, 676, 350	47, 601, 676	434, 960, 786	93, 967, 315 70	340, 993, 470 30

Amount of gold bank notes issued, not included in above, $1,601,100.

Statement showing the amount and kind of United States registered bonds held by the Treasurer of the United States to secure the redemption of the circulating notes of national banks, on the 1st day of November, 1872.

Title of loan.	Authorizing act.	Rate of interest.	Amount.
Loan of 1858	June 14, 1858	5 per cent.	$640, 000
Loan of February 8, 1861, (81's)	February 8, 1861	6 per cent.	4, 009, 000
Loan of July and August, 1861, (81's)	July 17 and August 5, 1861	do	58, 778, 250
Five-twenties of 1862	February 25, 1862	do	8, 680, 500
Loan of 1863, (81's)	March 3, 1863	do	32, 030, 450
Ten-forties, 1864	March 3, 1864	5 per cent.	104, 867, 950
Five-twenties, of March 3, 1864	March 3, 1864	6 per cent.	2, 054, 000
Five-twenties, of June, 1864	June 30, 1864	do	16, 201, 150
Five-twenties of 1865	March 3, 1865	do	11, 743, 100
Consols of 1865	do	do	7, 978, 250
Consols of 1867	do	do	14, 013, 000
Consols of 1868	do	do	3, 715, 500
Funded loan of 1881	July 14, 1870, and January 20, 1871	5 per cent.	106, 157, 850
United States bonds issued to the Pacific Railway Companies.	July 1, 1862, and July 2, 1864	6 per cent.	14, 100, 000
Total			384, 968, 900

Statement showing the national banks in voluntary liquidation that have deposited lawful money with the Treasurer of the United States to redeem their circulation, withdrawn their bonds, and voluntarily closed business under the provisions of section 42 of the act; their capital, circulation issued, circulation surrendered, circulation redeemed by the Treasurer of the United States, and circulation outstanding on the 1st day of November, 1872.

Name and location of bank.	Capital.	Circulation delivered.	Circulation surrendered.	Circulation redeemed by the Treasurer of the United States.	Circulation outstanding.
First National Bank of Columbia, Mo	$100,000	$90,000	$78,010	$10,425 00	$1,565 00
First National Bank of Carondelet, Mo	30,000	25,500	....	24,348 75	1,151 25
National Union Bank of Rochester, N. Y	400,000	192,500	2,550	162,108 25	27,841 75
Farmers' National Bank of Waukesha, Wis	100,000	90,000	....	84,820 25	5,179 75
First National Bank of Bluffton, Ind	50,000	45,000	3,770	34,946 25	6,283 75
First National Bank of Jackson, Miss	100,000	40,500	....	33,515 00	6,985 00
First National Bank of Skaneateles, N. Y	150,000	135,000	6,585	110,472 20	17,942 80
Appleton National Bank of Appleton, Wis	50,000	45,000	....	38,383 85	6,616 15
National Bank of Whitestown, N. Y	120,000	44,500	....	38,513 25	5,986 75
First National Bank of Cedarburgh, Wis	100,000	90,000	18,000	59,997 00	12,003 00
Commercial National Bank of Cincinnati, Ohio	500,000	345,950	....	300,955 00	44,995 00
First National Bank of South Worcester, N. Y.	175,000	157,400	4,500	131,838 75	21,061 25
National Mechanics' and Farmers' Bank of Albany, N. Y.	350,000	314,950	48,410	229,292 75	37,247 25
Second National Bank, Des Moines, Iowa	50,000	42,500	2,200	34,147 00	6,153 00
First National Bank, Oskaloosa, Iowa	75,000	67,500	3,755	56,427 85	7,317 15
Merchants' and Mechanics' National Bank, Troy, N. Y.	300,000	184,750	13,900	148,941 20	21,908 80
First National Bank of Marion, Ohio	125,000	109,850	4,017	89,415 85	16,417 15
National Bank, Lansingburgh, N. Y	150,000	135,000	12,000	104,191 85	18,808 15
Nat'l Bank of North America, New York, N. Y.	1,000,000	333,000	65,800	222,660 65	44,539 35
First National Bank of Hallowell, Me	60,000	53,350	2,500	43,643 75	7,206 25
Pacific National Bank, New York, N. Y	422,700	134,990	4,715	113,862 25	16,412 75
Grocers' National Bank, New York, N. Y	390,000	85,250	45,810	33,076 00	6,364 00
Savannah National Bank, Savannah, Ga	100,000	85,000	....	72,255 25	12,744 75
First National Bank, Frostburgh, Md	50,000	45,000	4,250	34,322 75	6,427 25
First National Bank, Vinton, Iowa	50,000	42,500	885	36,023 75	5,591 25
First National Bank, Decatur, Ill	100,000	85,250	....	73,974 30	11,275 70
First National Bank, Berlin, Wis	50,000	44,000	3,923	33,985 80	6,091 20
First National Bank, Dayton, Ohio	150,000	135,000	2,900	112,381 05	19,718 95
National Bank of Chemung, Elmira, N. Y	100,000	90,000	....	80,593 25	9,406 75
First National Bank, Saint Louis, Mo	200,000	179,990	....	154,289 05	25,700 95
First National Bank, Lebanon, Ohio	100,000	85,000	....	71,023 75	13,976 25
National Union Bank, Owego, N. Y	100,000	88,250	5,400	19,904 00	62,946 00
Chemung Canal National Bank, Elmira, N. Y.	100,000	90,000	3,500	73,139 00	13,361 00
National Insurance Bank, Detroit, Mich	200,010	85,000	9,500	65,013 75	10,486 25
State National Bank, Saint Joseph, Mo	100,000	90,000	3,813	69,458 20	16,728 80
National Exchange Bank Lansingburgh, N. Y.	100,000	90,000	4,308	69,557 30	16,134 70
Saratoga County Nat'l Bank, Waterford, N. Y.	150,000	135,000	8,000	101,363 55	25,636 45
Farmers' National Bank, Richmond, Va	100,000	85,000	8,500	50,083 25	26,416 75
First National Bank, Des Moines, Iowa	100,000	90,000	700	70,551 25	18,748 75
First National Bank, Trenton, Mich	100,000	49,000	....	40,523 25	8,476 75
National State Bank, Dubuque, Iowa	150,000	127,500	14,900	*85,943 75	26,656 25
First National Bank of Cuyahoga Falls, Ohio.	50,000	45,000	12,600	22,904 75	9,495 25
Ohio National Bank, Cincinnati, Ohio	500,000	450,000	45,100	272,240 00	132,660 00
First National Bank, Clarksville, Va	50,000	27,000	....	14,655 00	12,345 00
Central National Bank, Cincinnati, Ohio	500,000	445,000	105,130	204,095 00	135,775 00
United National Bank, Winona, Minn	50,000	45,000	875	29,875 00	14,250 00
Muskingum National Bank, Zanesville, Ohio.	100,000	90,000	3,800	51,000 00	35,200 00
Fourth National Bank, Indianapolis, Ind	100,000	85,700	10,100	48,800 00	26,800 00
First National Bank, Wellsburgh, W. Va	100,000	90,000	500	58,768 00	30,732 00
National Exchange Bank, Richmond, Va	200,000	180,000	7,880	113,700 00	58,420 00
National Savings' Bank, Wheeling, W. Va	100,000	90,000	22,300	42,000 00	25,700 00
First National Bank, New Ulm, Minn	60,000	54,000	11,800	25,710 00	16,490 00
Merchants' National Bank, Milwaukee, Wis.	100,000	90,000	....	54,500 00	35,500 00
National Bank of Maysville, Ky	300,000	270,000	....	146,000 00	124,000 00
Miners' National Bank of Salt Lake City, Utah.	150,000	135,000	45,000	54,232 00	25,768 00
Commercial National Bank, Oshkosh, Wis	100,000	90,000	....	48,000 00	42,000 00
Fourth National Bank, Syracuse, N. Y	105,500	91,700	....	44,332 00	47,368 00
Port Madison National Bank, Port Madison, Iowa.	75,000	67,500	....	31,500 00	36,000 00
First National Bank, La Salle, Ill	50,000	45,000	11,800	14,000 00	19,200 00
First National Bank, Danville, Va	50,000	45,000	10,000	10,000 00	25,000 00
Nat'l Bank of Commerce, Georgetown, D. C.	100,000	90,000	4,600	19,000 00	66,400 00
Clarke National Bank, Rochester, N. Y	200,000	180,000	26,100	37,900 00	116,000 00
First National Bank, Rochester, N. Y	400,000	206,100	....	48,600 00	157,500 00
Merchants' and Farmers' National Bank, Quincy, Ill.	150,000	135,000	....	19,500 00	115,500 00
Lawrenceburgh National Bank, Lawrenceburgh, Ind.*	200,000	180,000	500	....	179,500 00

* Lawful money deposited in part.

Statement showing the national banks in voluntary liquidation, &c.—Continued.

Name and location of bank.	Capital.	Circulation delivered.	Circulation surrendered.	Circulation redeemed by the Treasurer of the United States.	Circulation outstanding.
Pittston National Bank, Pittston, Pa	$200, 000	(†)	....	....	....
Berkshire National Bank, Adams, Mass	100, 000	(†)	....	....	....
Kittanning National Bank, Kittanning, Pa.	200, 000	(†)	....	....	....
City National Bank, Savannah, Ga	100, 000	(†)	....	....	....
Central National Bank, Omaha, Nebr	100, 000	(†)	....	....	....
*American National Bank, New York, N. Y	500, 000	$450, 000	$30, 600	....	$419, 400 00
National Bank of Crawford County, Meadville, Pa.	300, 000	(†)	....	....	....
Total	12, 098, 210	8, 160, 980	735, 786	$4, 831, 680 70	2, 593, 513 30

* Lawful money not yet deposited.

† No circulation.

Statement showing the national banks in liquidation for the purpose of consolidating with other banks, their capital, bonds on deposit to secure circulation, circulation delivered, circulation surrendered and destroyed, and circulation outstanding November 1, 1872.

Name and location of bank.	Capital.	United States bonds on deposit.	Circulation delivered.	Circulation surrendered.	Circulation outstanding.
First National Bank of Leonardsville, N. Y	$50, 000	$50, 500	$45, 000	....	$45, 000
National Bank of the Metropolis, Washington, D. C.	200, 000	134, 000	180, 000	$60, 400	119, 600
First National Bank of Providence, Pa	100, 000	87, 000	90, 000	13, 750	76, 250
First National Bank of Newton, Newtonville, Mass.	150, 000	94, 000	130, 000	45, 400	84, 600
First National Bank of Kingston, N. Y	200, 000	150, 000	180, 000	45, 000	135, 000
First National Bank of Downingtown, Pa	100, 000	76, 000	89, 500	23, 000	66, 500
First National Bank of Titusville, Pa	100, 000	74, 000	86, 750	23, 400	63, 350
First National Bank of New Brunswick, N. J	100, 000	83, 000	90, 000	17, 000	73, 000
Second National Bank of Watertown, N. Y	100, 000	90, 000	90, 000	9, 000	81, 000
First National Bank of Steubenville, Ohio	150, 000	150, 000	135, 000	....	135, 000
First National Bank of Plumer, Pa	100, 000	90, 000	87, 500	13, 300	74, 200
First National Bank of Dorchester, Mass	150, 000	110, 000	132, 500	33, 800	98, 700
First National Bank of Clyde, N. Y	50, 000	49, 500	44, 000	6, 000	38, 000
National Exchange Bank, Philadelphia, Pa	300, 000	150, 000	175, 750	48, 000	127, 750
First National Bank, Burlington, Vt	300, 000	255, 500	270, 000	431, 100	226, 900
Carroll County National Bank, Sandwich, N. H	50, 000	49, 000	45, 000	1, 300	43, 700
Second National Bank, Portland, Me	100, 000	90, 000	81, 000	....	81, 000
Jewett City National Bank, Jewett City, Conn	60, 000	55, 000	48, 750	....	48, 750
Total	2, 360, 000	1, 837, 500	2, 000, 750	382, 450	1, 618, 300

Schedule of insolvent banks that have been placed in the hands of receivers, their capital, lawful money deposited to redeem circulation, circulation issued, circulation redeemed by the Treasurer of the United States, and the outstanding circulation, November 1, 1872.

Name and location of bank.	Capital paid in.	Lawful money deposited to redeem circulation.	Circulation issued.	Circulation redeemed by Treasury United States.	Circulation outstanding.
First National Bank of Attica, N. Y*	$50,000	$44,000	$44,000	$42,906 50	$1,093 50
Venango National Bank of Franklin, Pa	300,000	85,000	85,000	82,628 50	2,371 50
First National Bank of Medina, N. Y *	50,000	40,000	40,000	38,806 75	1,193 25
Merchants' National Bank of Washington, D.C.†	200,000	180,000	180,000	173,904 00	6,096 00
Tennessee National Bank of Memphis, Tenn.*	100,000	90,000	90,000	87,278 75	2,021 25
First National Bank of Selma, Ala	100,000	85,000	85,000	81,816 75	3,183 25
First National Bank of New Orleans, La	500,000	180,000	180,000	173,175 50	6,824 50
National Unadilla Bank of Unadilla, N. Y	120,000	100,000	100,000	97,014 50	2,985 50
Farmers' and Citizens' Bank of Brooklyn, N. Y.	300,000	253,900	253,900	244,050 25	9,849 75
Croton Nat'l Bank of the City of New York *	200,000	180,000	180,000	174,790 75	5,209 25
First National Bank of Bethel, Conn	60,000	26,300	26,300	23,839 50	2,460 50
First National Bank of Keokuk, Iowa*	100,000	90,000	90,000	87,149 00	2,851 00
National Bank of Vicksburgh, Miss	50,000	25,500	25,500	23,608 75	1,891 25
First National Bank of Rockford, Ill	50,000	45,000	45,000	41,483 00	3,517 00
First National Bank of Nevada, at Austin, Nev.	250,000	129,700	129,700	108,336 50	21,363 50
Ocean Nat'l Bank of the City of New York	1,000,000	800,000	800,000	575,035 00	224,965 00
Union Square National Bank of the City of New York.	200,000	50,000	50,000	33,947 00	16,053 00
Eighth National Bank of the City of New York.	250,000	243,393	243,393	173,099 00	70,294 00
Fourth National Bank of Philadelphia, Pa	200,000	179,000	179,000	125,000 00	54,000 00
Waverly National Bank of Waverly, N. Y	106,100	71,000	71,000	33,960 00	37,040 00
First National Bank of Fort Smith, Ark	50,000	45,000	45,000	19,500 00	25,500 00
Total	4,236,100	2,942,793	2,942,793	2,441,430 00	501,363 00

* Finally closed.
† $50,000 United States registered 5-20 bonds still on deposit with the Treasurer of the United States.

Table of the state of the lawful money reserve of the national banks of the United States, as

Number.	States and Territories.	Number of banks.	Liabilities to be protected by reserve.	Reserve required: 15 per cent. of liabilities.	Reserve held.	Per cent. of reserve to liabilities.
1	Maine	61	$12, 805, 236	$1, 920, 785	$2, 338, 274	18. 3
2	New Hampshire	42	6, 765, 471	1, 014, 821	1, 433, 360	21. 2
3	Vermont	41	9, 529, 794	1, 429, 469	1, 758, 050	18. 4
4	Massachusetts	160	53, 645, 435	8, 046, 815	10, 047, 573	18. 7
5	Rhode Island	62	20, 292, 636	3, 043, 895	3, 466, 447	17. 1
6	Connecticut	81	32, 358, 006	4, 853, 701	7, 279, 846	22. 5
7	New York	231	76, 469, 350	11, 470, 404	14, 005, 399	18. 4
8	New Jersey	57	26, 438, 420	3, 965, 763	5, 665, 475	21. 4
9	Pennsylvania	153	48, 007, 086	7, 201, 063	8, 836, 019	18. 4
10	Delaware	11	2, 701, 748	405, 262	498, 539	18. 5
11	Maryland	19	4, 367, 738	655, 161	1, 069, 128	24. 5
12	Virginia	23	9, 422, 577	1, 413, 387	1, 797, 875	19. 1
13	West Virginia	17	4, 869, 645	730, 447	982, 583	20. 2
14	North Carolina	9	4, 126, 920	619, 038	883, 295	21. 4
15	South Carolina	7	2, 781, 792	417, 269	519, 371	18. 7
16	Georgia	10	3, 970, 313	595, 547	770, 237	19. 4
17	Alabama	7	1, 563, 615	234, 542	452, 488	28. 9
18	Texas	5	1, 802, 584	270, 388	560, 846	31. 1
19	Arkansas	2	371, 983	55, 797	42, 508	11. 4
20	Kentucky	25	6, 771, 389	1, 015, 708	1, 270, 985	18. 8
21	Tennessee	19	6, 778, 468	1, 016, 770	1, 492, 468	22. 0
22	Ohio	120	31, 841, 973	4, 776, 296	6, 699, 288	21. 0
23	Indiana	78	24, 845, 393	3, 726, 809	4, 898, 738	19. 7
24	Illinois	98	20, 316, 338	3, 047, 451	4, 537, 154	22. 3
25	Michigan	58	10, 989, 512	1, 648, 427	2, 466, 430	22. 4
26	Wisconsin	36	5, 866, 060	879, 909	1, 346, 984	23. 0
27	Iowa	61	11, 442, 246	1, 716, 337	2, 470, 735	21. 6
28	Minnesota	23	6, 101, 513	915, 227	1, 184, 729	19. 4
29	Missouri	22	4, 825, 970	723, 896	963, 141	20. 0
30	Kansas	10	1, 822, 223	273, 333	371, 551	20. 4
31	Nebraska	6	2, 656, 840	398, 526	636, 612	24. 0
32	Oregon	1	1, 040, 489	156, 073	242, 311	23. 3
33	Montana	1	432, 464	64, 870	78, 702	18. 2
34	Idaho	1	202, 961	30, 444	32, 496	16. 0
35	Wyoming	1	102, 645	15, 397	36, 688	35. 7
36	Utah	1	504, 271	75, 640	82, 313	16. 3
37	Colorado	4	1, 670, 600	250, 590	392, 482	23. 5
38	New Mexico	1	208, 500	31, 275	27, 505	13. 2
	Total	1, 564	460, 710, 213	69, 106, 532	91, 728, 026	19. 9

Table of the state of the lawful money reserve—Continued.

Number.	Cities of redemption.	Number of banks.	Liabilities to be protected by reserve.	Reserve required: 25 per cent. of liabilities.	Reserve held.	Per cent. of reserve to liabilities.
1	Boston	48	$79, 071, 889	$19, 767, 972	$21, 011, 587	26. 6
2	Albany	7	9, 102, 284	2, 275, 571	3, 091, 395	34. 0
3	Philadelphia	29	49, 609, 751	12, 402, 438	13, 346, 949	26. 9
4	Pittsburgh	16	15, 921, 712	3, 980, 428	3, 876, 158	24. 3
5	Baltimore	14	19, 507, 791	4, 876, 948	5, 309, 047	27. 2
6	Washington	3	2, 455, 810	613, 953	590, 356	24. 0
7	New Orleans	7	7, 687, 377	1, 921, 844	1, 142, 037	14. 9
8	Louisville	4	1, 766, 903	441, 726	455, 852	25. 8
9	Cincinnati	5	11, 584, 220	2, 896, 055	3, 183, 753	27. 5
10	Cleveland	6	6, 577, 169	1, 644, 292	1, 886, 152	28. 7
11	Chicago	18	27, 092, 631	6, 773, 158	10, 422, 231	38. 5
12	Detroit	3	4, 347, 639	1, 086, 909	1, 283, 917	29. 5
13	Milwaukee	4	2, 981, 825	745, 456	753, 252	25. 3
14	Saint Louis	8	9, 913, 963	2, 478, 491	2, 614, 249	26. 4
15	Leavenworth	2	809, 454	202, 363	182, 692	22. 6
	Total	174	248, 430, 418	62, 107, 604	69, 150, 527	27. 8
16	New York City	51	207, 635, 813	51, 908, 953	57, 388, 978	27. 6
17	San Francisco	1	655, 668	163, 917	376, 699	57. 5

shown by the reports of their condition at the close of business on the 16th day of December, 1871:

Funds available for reserve.					States and Territories.
Specie.	Legal tenders.	Clearing-house certificates.	Three per cent. certificates.	Due from redeeming agents.	
$73,907	$1,071,713	....	....	$1,192,654	Maine.
25,229	486,769	....	....	921,362	New Hampshire.
38,013	674,818	....	$35,000	1,010,219	Vermont.
159,736	4,175,730	....	45,000	5,667,098	Massachusetts.
59,883	1,403,279	....	25,000	1,978,285	Rhode Island.
218,304	2,367,162	....	80,000	4,614,380	Connecticut.
211,314	5,641,327	....	260,000	7,982,758	New York.
94,500	1,939,293	....	115,000	3,516,682	New Jersey.
99,629	4,152,283	....	210,000	4,374,107	Pennsylvania.
2,829	186,802	....	80,000	228,906	Delaware.
26,747	408,258	....	....	634,123	Maryland.
92,986	832,408	....	....	872,481	Virginia.
12,026	446,067	....	....	524,490	West Virginia.
20,951	309,222	....	....	553,122	North Carolina.
18,118	287,022	....	....	214,231	South Carolina.
81,063	424,646	....	50,000	214,528	Georgia.
17,105	202,011	....	....	233,372	Alabama.
175,144	231,232	....	....	154,470	Texas.
709	25,165	....	....	16,634	Arkansas.
11,751	627,756	....	....	631,478	Kentucky.
69,662	730,519	....	....	692,287	Tennessee.
90,814	3,136,993	....	95,000	3,376,482	Ohio.
68,471	2,567,732	....	20,000	2,242,535	Indiana.
83,772	2,036,969	....	10,000	2,406,413	Illinois.
48,585	1,179,497	....	25,000	1,213,346	Michigan.
16,414	591,398	....	....	739,172	Wisconsin.
47,954	1,341,118	....	10,000	1,071,663	Iowa.
14,737	640,655	....	....	529,337	Minnesota.
17,985	480,460	....	....	464,696	Missouri.
9,019	191,737	....	....	170,795	Kansas.
9,214	203,943	....	....	423,455	Nebraska.
30,261	123,208	....	....	88,842	Oregon.
707	13,500	....	....	64,495	Montana.
9,723	22,773	....	....	....	Idaho.
52	12,656	....	....	23,980	Wyoming.
53,572	28,241	....	....	500	Utah.
32,516	168,668	....	....	191,298	Colorado.
9	17,954	....	....	9,542	New Mexico.
2,043,411	39,380,993	....	1,060,000	40,244,222	

CITIES, *as shown by reports of the 16th of December,* 1871.

Funds available for reserve.					Cities of redemption.
Specie.	Legal tenders.	Clearing-house certificates.	Three per cent. certificates.	Due from redeeming agents.	
$2,492,701	$8,256,780	....	$1,820,000	$8,442,106	Boston.
9,900	1,108,945	....	60,000	1,912,541	Albany.
750,330	5,813,254	$1,780,000	1,725,000	3,278,365	Philadelphia.
38,802	1,973,728	....	35,000	1,828,628	Pittsburgh.
203,893	1,818,080	146,000	255,000	2,886,974	Baltimore.
24,976	296,395	....	80,000	188,985	Washington.
134,510	736,201	....	....	271,326	New Orleans.
691	261,883	....	....	193,278	Louisville.
18,971	1,445,825	....	100,000	1,618,957	Cincinnati.
12,214	840,000	2,026	20,000	1,011,912	Cleveland.
344,612	5,023,984	....	80,000	4,973,635	Chicago.
1,170	641,350	....	60,000	581,397	Detroit.
10,421	433,146	....	....	309,685	Milwaukee.
45,379	1,299,460	....	105,000	1,164,410	Saint Louis.
563	92,953	....	10,000	79,176	Leavenworth.
4,089,142	30,041,974	1,928,026	4,350,000	28,741,375	
18,809,671	22,580,307	14,705,000	1,285,000	....	New York City.
374,301	2,398	....	....	....	San Francisco.

Table of the state of the lawful money reserve—Continued;

Number.	States and Territories.	Number of banks.	Liabilities to be protected by reserve.	Reserve required; 15 per cent. of liabilities.	Reserve held.	Per cent. of reserve to liabilities.
1	Maine	61	$13, 052, 919	$1, 957, 938	$2, 823, 018	21. 6
2	New Hampshire	42	6, 907, 728	1, 036, 159	1, 536, 273	22. 3
3	Vermont	41	9, 859, 132	1, 478, 870	1, 830, 833	18. 7
4	Massachusetts	160	55, 102, 065	8, 265, 310	11, 358, 130	20. 6
5	Rhode Island	62	20, 536, 108	3, 080, 416	3, 727, 902	18. 2
6	Connecticut	81	33, 684, 989	5, 052, 748	8, 160, 218	24. 3
7	New York	231	80, 778, 653	12, 116, 798	17, 083, 270	21. 1
8	New Jersey	58	27, 231, 738	4, 084, 760	6, 121, 513	22. 5
9	Pennsylvania	153	49, 304, 204	7, 395, 631	10, 580, 504	21. 5
10	Delaware	11	2, 855, 770	428, 369	622, 370	21. 8
11	Maryland	19	4, 593, 948	689, 092	1, 129, 975	24. 6
12	Virginia	23	9, 645, 603	1, 446, 841	1, 805, 088	18. 7
13	West Virginia	17	5, 149, 407	772, 411	1, 018, 044	19. 8
14	North Carolina	9	4, 272, 928	640, 939	940, 886	22
15	South Carolina	7	3, 403, 906	510, 586	789, 897	23. 2
16	Georgia	10	4, 336, 655	650, 498	1, 138, 134	26. 2
17	Alabama	7	1, 871, 650	280, 749	541, 141	28. 9
18	Texas	5	1, 933, 302	289, 995	689, 418	35. 7
19	Arkansas	1	329, 673	49, 452	96, 979	29. 4
20	Kentucky	25	7, 017, 662	1, 052, 649	1, 306, 096	18. 6
21	Tennessee	19	7, 263, 261	1, 089, 489	1, 557, 245	21. 4
22	Ohio	126	33, 185, 630	4, 977, 844	6, 913, 800	20. 8
23	Indiana	79	25, 309, 151	3, 796, 373	4, 812, 055	19
24	Illinois	102	23, 447, 683	3, 517, 152	5, 337, 903	22. 8
25	Michigan	61	11, 325, 428	1, 698, 814	2, 401, 700	21. 2
26	Wisconsin	36	5, 946, 611	891, 992	1, 333, 049	22. 4
27	Iowa	61	12, 533, 376	1, 880, 006	2, 759, 777	22
28	Minnesota	24	6, 557, 171	983, 576	1, 118, 213	17. 1
29	Missouri	23	5, 235, 945	785, 392	1, 042, 236	19. 9
30	Kansas	14	2, 087, 388	313, 108	375, 270	18
31	Nebraska	8	2, 793, 052	418, 958	472, 021	16. 9
32	Oregon	1	1, 080, 201	162, 030	273, 736	25. 3
33	Montana	1	413, 307	61, 996	58, 013	14
34	Idaho	1	187, 173	28, 076	25, 456	13. 6
35	Wyoming	1	87, 967	13, 195	22, 261	25. 3
36	Utah	1	385, 442	57, 816	44, 804	11. 6
37	Colorado	4	1, 584, 509	237, 672	342, 000	21. 6
38	New Mexico	1	215, 601	32, 340	46, 291	21. 5
	Total	1, 586	481, 506, 936	72, 226, 040	102, 275, 001	21. 3

Table of the state of the lawful money reserve—Continued;

	Cities of redemption.	Number of banks.	Liabilities to be protected by reserve.	Reserve required; 25 per cent. of liabilities.	Reserve held.	Per cent. of reserve to liabilities.
1	Boston	48	$81, 423, 348	$20, 355, 837	$21, 225, 410	26. 1
2	Albany	7	11, 278, 892	2, 819, 723	3, 644, 476	32. 3
3	Philadelphia	29	49, 913, 955	12, 478, 489	13, 537, 740	27. 1
4	Pittsburgh	16	16, 865, 241	4, 216, 310	4, 725, 075	28
5	Baltimore	14	20, 383, 244	5, 095, 811	5, 265, 719	25. 8
6	Washington	3	2, 289, 061	572, 265	800, 035	35
7	New Orleans	8	8, 830, 347	2, 207, 588	2, 790, 308	31. 6
8	Louisville	5	2, 055, 057	513, 764	525, 796	25. 6
9	Cincinnati	5	12, 181, 695	3, 045, 424	3, 173, 641	26
10	Cleveland	6	6, 740, 379	1, 685, 095	1, 872, 777	27. 8
11	Chicago	18	30, 325, 595	7, 581, 399	9, 236, 605	30. 5
12	Detroit	3	4, 164, 907	1, 041, 227	1, 175, 813	28. 2
13	Milwaukee	4	3, 003, 434	750, 858	809, 350	26. 9
14	Saint Louis	8	9, 462, 853	2, 365, 713	2, 972, 272	31. 4
15	Leavenworth	2	780, 076	195, 018	158, 407	20. 3
	Total	176	259, 698, 084	64, 924, 521	71, 912, 424	27. 7
16	New York City	51	210, 271, 963	52, 567, 991	54, 071, 079	25. 7
17	San Francisco	1	919, 224	229, 806	456, 562	49. 7

STATES, *as shown by reports of the 27th of February*, 1872.

Funds available for reserve.					States and Territories.
Specie.	Legal-tenders.	Clearing-house certificates.	Three per cent. certificates.	Due from redeeming agents.	
$97, 885	$986, 767			$1, 738, 366	Maine.
41, 255	437, 146			1, 058, 572	New Hampshire.
32, 255	717, 964		$35, 000	1, 054, 614	Vermont.
723, 803	3, 800, 539		35, 000	6, 798, 707	Massachusetts.
57, 507	1, 384, 930		15, 000	2, 270, 465	Rhode Island.
115, 508	2, 441, 489		45, 000	5, 587, 221	Connecticut.
198, 177	5, 075, 059		140, 000	11, 070, 034	New York.
96, 776	2, 038, 910		75, 000	3, 910, 827	New Jersey.
114, 150	4, 226, 303		205, 000	6, 035, 051	Pennsylvania.
2, 777	216, 209		60, 000	343, 384	Delaware.
20, 801	498, 356			610, 818	Maryland.
80, 201	842, 703			882, 184	Virginia.
15, 312	422, 120			580, 612	West Virginia.
69, 680	390, 815			480, 391	North Carolina.
15, 058	455, 870			318, 963	South Carolina.
189, 774	543, 416		50, 000	354, 944	Georgia.
26, 624	275, 370			239, 147	Alabama.
333, 478	188, 004			167, 936	Texas.
315	31, 500			65, 157	Arkansas.
7, 750	613, 568			685, 378	Kentucky.
69, 850	780, 135			707, 260	Tennessee.
49, 817	3, 323, 692		85, 000	3, 455, 291	Ohio.
55, 265	2, 433, 010		20, 000	2, 303, 760	Indiana.
99, 436	2, 160, 818		10, 000	3, 067, 739	Illinois.
51, 152	1, 082, 401		25, 000	1, 243, 147	Michigan.
13, 348	587, 138			732, 563	Wisconsin.
69, 104	1, 372, 529		10, 000	1, 308, 144	Iowa.
13, 732	504, 072			540, 409	Minnesota.
30, 658	487, 403			524, 175	Missouri.
9, 970	223, 887			141, 413	Kansas.
6, 875	188, 173			276, 973	Nebraska.
60, 662	114, 463			98, 611	Oregon.
2, 398	34, 600			21, 015	Montana.
10, 609	14, 847				Idaho.
193	12, 476			9, 592	Wyoming.
10, 600	33, 794			500	Utah.
23, 932	172, 275			145, 793	Colorado.
84	19, 362			26, 845	New Mexico.
2, 816, 771	39, 792, 119		810, 000	58, 856, 111	

CITIES, *as shown by reports of the 27th of February*, 1872.

Funds available for reserve.					Cities of redemption.
Specie.	Legal-tenders.	Clearing-house certificates.	Three per cent. certificates.	Due from redeeming agents.	
$4, 062, 195	$5, 533, 596		$1, 835, 000	$9, 794, 619	Boston.
8, 302	1, 314, 858		60, 000	2, 261, 256	Albany.
361, 412	5, 759, 941	$2, 800, 000	1, 345, 000	3, 271, 387	Philadelphia.
61, 911	2, 438, 741		35, 000	2, 189, 423	Pittsburgh.
216, 112	2, 294, 139	155, 000	215, 000	2, 385, 468	Baltimore.
21, 973	422, 710		80, 000	275, 352	Washington.
219, 569	1, 743, 362			877, 377	New Orleans.
2, 044	241, 920			281, 832	Louisville.
59, 785	1, 361, 000		100, 000	1, 651, 856	Cincinnati.
12, 818	873, 000		20, 000	966, 959	Cleveland.
116, 920	4, 872, 845		65, 000	4, 181, 840	Chicago.
13, 329	577, 883		60, 000	524, 601	Detroit.
21, 946	414, 047			373, 357	Milwaukee.
40, 468	1, 164, 411		105, 000	1, 662, 393	Saint Louis.
92	103, 818		10, 000	44, 497	Leavenworth.
5, 218, 936	29, 116, 271	2, 955, 000	3, 930, 000	30, 692, 217	
13, 831, 478	25, 999, 601	13, 240, 000	1, 000, 000		New York City.
454, 153	2, 409				San Francisco.

Table of the state of the lawful money reserve—Continued.

Number.	States and Territories.	Number of banks.	Liabilities to be protected by reserve.	Reserve required; 15 per cent. of liabilities.	Reserve held.	Per cent. of reserve to liabilities.
1	Maine	62	$12, 496, 673	$1, 874, 501	$2, 322, 024	18. 6
2	New Hampshire	42	6, 769, 919	1, 015, 488	1, 372, 532	20. 3
3	Vermont	41	9, 792, 528	1, 468, 879	1, 655, 682	17
4	Massachusetts	161	55, 922, 034	8, 388, 305	10, 884, 088	19. 5
5	Rhode Island	62	20, 799, 997	3, 120, 000	3, 584, 837	17. 2
6	Connecticut	81	33, 266, 646	4, 989, 997	6, 952, 129	20. 9
7	New York	231	78, 246, 650	11, 736, 998	15, 647, 148	20
8	New Jersey	58	28, 214, 790	4, 232, 219	6, 307, 167	22. 4
9	Pennsylvania	155	51, 980, 750	7, 797, 113	11, 057, 477	21. 3
10	Delaware	11	2, 792, 808	418, 921	473, 356	17
11	Maryland	10	4, 287, 878	643, 182	931, 068	21. 7
12	District of Columbia	1	589, 514	88, 427	181, 681	30. 8
13	Virginia	23	9, 608, 075	1, 441, 211	1, 783, 991	18. 6
14	West Virginia	17	5, 097, 013	764, 552	828, 542	16. 3
15	North Carolina	9	4, 224, 542	633, 681	882, 505	21
16	South Carolina	8	3, 398, 977	509, 847	694, 799	20. 4
17	Georgia	10	4, 193, 370	629, 006	1, 037, 042	24. 7
18	Alabama	7	1, 840, 323	276, 048	542, 916	29. 5
19	Texas	5	2, 020, 435	303, 065	801, 649	39. 7
20	Arkansas	1	313, 569	47, 035	36, 452	11. 6
21	Kentucky	26	6, 782, 061	1, 017, 309	1, 228, 452	18. 4
22	Tennessee	19	7, 245, 726	1, 086, 859	1, 566, 541	21. 6
23	Ohio	131	32, 918, 736	4, 937, 810	6, 401, 868	19. 4
24	Indiana	83	26, 533, 055	3, 979, 958	5, 464, 920	20. 6
25	Illinois	105	22, 854, 715	3, 428, 207	4, 710, 821	20. 6
26	Michigan	63	11, 632, 394	1, 744, 859	2, 273, 009	19. 5
27	Wisconsin	37	5, 879, 981	881, 997	1, 181, 903	20. 1
28	Iowa	62	12, 841, 868	1, 926, 280	2, 900, 592	22. 6
29	Minnesota	24	6, 631, 968	994, 795	1, 097, 316	16. 5
30	Missouri	24	5, 394, 615	809, 192	1, 061, 118	19. 6
31	Kansas	19	3, 323, 562	498, 534	731, 925	22
32	Nebraska	8	2, 849, 028	427, 354	599, 867	21
33	Oregon	1	998, 151	149, 723	236, 721	23. 7
34	Montana	1	400, 967	60, 145	58, 080	14. 2
35	Idaho	1	161, 051	24, 157	33, 982	21. 1
36	Wyoming	1	91, 906	13, 786	13, 672	14. 9
37	Utah	2	628, 314	94, 247	58, 358	9. 3
38	Colorado	4	1, 626, 831	244, 025	400, 793	24. 6
39	New Mexico	1	202, 705	30, 406	15, 732	7. 8
	Total	1, 616	484, 854, 125	72, 728, 118	98, 012, 845	20. 2

Table of the state of the lawful money reserve—Continued.

Number.	Cities of redemption.	Number of banks.	Liabilities to be protected by reserve.	Reserve required: 25 per cent. of liabilities.	Reserve held.	Per cent. of reserve to liabilities.
1	Boston	48	$79, 938, 875	$19, 984, 719	$20, 937, 782	26. 2
2	Albany	7	11, 345, 164	2, 836, 291	3, 567, 437	31. 4
3	Philadelphia	29	49, 889, 443	12, 472, 361	13, 824, 727	27. 7
4	Pittsburgh	16	16, 740, 322	4, 185, 080	3, 940, 332	23. 5
5	Baltimore	14	20, 261, 958	5, 065, 490	5, 438, 850	26. 8
6	Washington	3	2, 218, 942	554, 735	763, 885	34. 4
7	New Orleans	9	9, 582, 744	2, 395, 686	2, 771, 830	28. 9
8	Louisville	5	2, 196, 990	549, 248	530, 576	24. 2
9	Cincinnati	5	11, 428, 270	2, 857, 068	2, 873, 470	25. 1
10	Cleveland	6	9, 131, 181	2, 282, 795	3, 643, 860	39. 9
11	Chicago	18	30, 490, 789	7, 622, 697	8, 917, 799	29. 2
12	Detroit	3	4, 320, 717	1, 080, 179	1, 082, 460	25
13	Milwaukee	4	2, 747, 544	686, 886	639, 171	23. 3
14	Saint Louis	8	9, 014, 781	2, 253, 695	2, 235, 793	24. 8
		175	259, 307, 720	64, 826, 930	71, 167, 972	27. 4
15	New York City	51	200, 701, 665	50, 175, 416	53, 491, 399	26. 6
16	San Francisco	1	744, 991	186, 248	280, 874	37. 7

STATES, *as shown by reports of the 19th of April*, 1872.

Funds available for reserve.					States and Territories.
Specie.	Legal-tenders.	Clearing-house certificates.	Three per cent. certificates.	Due from redeeming agents.	
$85, 341	$939, 405	....	....	$1, 297, 278	Maine.
59, 474	413, 572	....	....	899, 486	New Hampshire.
51, 032	702, 155	....	$25, 000	877, 495	Vermont.
565, 952	3, 807, 831	....	35, 000	6, 385, 305	Massachusetts.
31, 753	1, 491, 205	....	15, 000	2, 046, 879	Rhode Island.
69, 850	2, 425, 973	....	45, 000	4, 411, 306	Connecticut.
252, 458	5, 916, 218	....	130, 000	9, 348, 472	New York.
96, 524	2, 156, 723	....	55, 000	3, 993, 920	New Jersey.
103, 878	5, 223, 902	....	165, 000	5, 564, 697	Pennsylvania.
2, 940	214, 266	....	50, 000	206, 150	Delaware.
21, 661	425, 321	....	....	484, 086	Maryland.
3, 749	130, 500	....	....	47, 432	District of Columbia.
77, 659	875, 570	....	....	830, 762	Virginia.
9, 559	395, 139	....	....	423, 844	West Virginia.
53, 011	387, 066	....	....	441, 618	North Carolina.
14, 175	479, 934	....	....	200, 690	South Carolina.
138, 280	498, 828	....	50, 000	349, 925	Georgia.
20, 147	227, 872	....	....	294, 897	Alabama.
360, 094	249, 134	....	....	191, 521	Texas.
425	27, 036	....	....	8, 091	Arkansas.
7, 692	616, 700	....	....	604, 060	Kentucky.
54, 262	836, 414	....	....	675, 865	Tennessee.
37, 352	3, 578, 048	....	60, 000	2, 725, 568	Ohio.
68, 131	2, 655, 897	....	10, 000	2, 730, 842	Indiana.
86, 765	2, 209, 276	....	10, 000	2, 404, 780	Illinois.
40, 271	1, 188, 150	....	20, 000	1, 018, 588	Michigan.
12, 405	621, 710	....	....	547, 788	Wisconsin.
61, 203	1, 561, 018	....	10, 000	1, 268, 371	Iowa.
22, 050	626, 907	....	....	448, 350	Minnesota.
22, 864	552, 440	....	....	485, 814	Missouri.
8, 097	372, 577	....	10, 000	341, 251	Kansas.
9, 398	219, 811	....	....	370, 658	Nebraska.
74, 054	85, 320	....	....	77, 347	Oregon.
2, 882	22, 000	....	....	33, 198	Montana.
11, 572	22, 410	....	....	....	Idaho.
228	7, 338	....	....	6, 106	Wyoming.
10, 431	46, 927	....	....	1, 000	Utah.
45, 089	173, 283	....	....	182, 421	Colorado.
47	10, 856	....	....	4, 829	New Mexico.
2, 600, 614	42, 485, 632	....	690, 000	52, 236, 599	

CITIES, *as shown by reports of the 19th of April*, 1872.

Funds available for reserve.					Cities of redemption.
Specie.	Legal-tenders.	Clearing-house certificates.	Three per cent. certificates.	Due from redeeming agents.	
$4, 002, 819	$5, 925, 400	....	$1, 240, 000	$9, 769, 563	Boston.
8, 276	1, 396, 538	....	60, 000	2, 102, 623	Albany.
226, 482	6, 930, 152	$2, 230, 000	970, 000	3, 468, 093	Philadelphia.
48, 385	2, 463, 957	....	....	1, 427, 790	Pittsburgh.
119, 893	2, 279, 503	194, 000	90, 000	2, 755, 454	Baltimore.
28, 447	445, 484	....	80, 000	209, 954	Washington.
176, 565	1, 301, 848	....	....	1, 293, 417	New Orleans.
1, 647	365, 991	....	....	162, 936	Louisville.
40, 336	1, 489, 500	....	....	1, 343, 634	Cincinnati.
4, 126	941, 000	....	20, 000	2, 678, 734	Cleveland.
103, 869	5, 676, 201	....	35, 000	3, 102, 729	Chicago.
644	667, 217	....	20, 000	394, 599	Detroit.
22, 444	345, 687	....	....	271, 040	Milwaukee.
41, 017	1, 206, 928	....	85, 000	902, 849	Saint Louis.
4, 825, 150	31, 435, 406	2, 424, 000	2, 600, 000	29, 863, 416	
11, 931, 060	29, 385, 330	11, 485, 000	590, 000	....	New York City.
278, 796	2, 078	....	....	....	San Francisco.

Table of the state of the lawful money reserve—Continued.

Number.	States and Territories.	Number of banks.	Liabilities to be protected by reserve.	Reserve required; 15 per cent. of liabilities.	Reserve held.	Per cent. of reserve to liabilities.
1	Maine	62	$12, 938, 178	$1, 940, 727	$2, 532, 987	19. 6
2	New Hampshire	41	7, 023, 905	1, 053, 586	1, 420, 730	20. 3
3	Vermont	41	9, 988, 892	1, 498, 338	1, 785, 129	17. 9
4	Massachusetts	162	55, 831, 694	8, 374, 754	11, 190, 947	20.
5	Rhode Island	62	20, 830, 426	3, 124, 564	3, 759, 765	18.
6	Connecticut	81	33, 386, 307	5, 007, 946	7, 636, 982	22. 9
7	New York	230	77, 274, 797	11, 591, 219	15, 068, 869	19. 5
8	New Jersey	58	27, 855, 792	4, 178, 368	6, 409, 548	23.
9	Pennsylvania	155	51, 360, 756	7, 705, 463	9, 969, 361	19. 4
10	Delaware	11	2, 888, 173	433, 226	582, 950	20. 2
11	Maryland	19	4, 276, 875	641, 531	1, 016, 689	23. 8
12	District of Columbia	1	684, 718	102, 708	263, 445	38. 5
13	Virginia	23	9, 728, 202	1, 459, 230	1, 810, 687	18. 6
14	West Virginia	17	5, 026, 268	753, 940	836, 858	16. 5
15	North Carolina	9	4, 022, 829	603, 424	782, 509	19. 5
16	South Carolina	8	3, 545, 550	531, 832	795, 981	22. 5
17	Georgia	10	4, 036, 837	605, 525	867, 343	21. 5
18	Alabama	7	1, 900, 579	285, 086	558, 553	29. 4
19	Texas	5	1, 869, 963	280, 494	631, 834	33. 8
20	Arkansas	2	352, 534	52, 880	69, 034	19. 6
21	Kentucky	27	6, 778, 322	1, 016, 748	1, 221, 241	18.
22	Tennessee	19	7, 140, 590	1, 071, 089	1, 561, 728	21. 9
23	Ohio	133	34, 394, 366	5, 159, 155	7, 056, 086	20. 5
24	Indiana	84	26, 918, 346	4, 037, 752	5, 973, 424	22. 2
25	Illinois	106	23, 994, 453	3, 599, 168	5, 763, 551	24
26	Michigan	64	11, 733, 582	1, 760, 037	2, 249, 922	19. 2
27	Wisconsin	37	6, 010, 635	901, 598	1, 270, 171	21. 1
28	Iowa	62	13, 984, 554	2, 097, 683	3, 089, 757	22. 1
29	Minnesota	25	7, 407, 621	1, 111, 143	1, 610, 439	21. 7
30	Missouri	25	5, 578, 260	836, 739	1, 277, 393	22. 9
31	Kansas	20	3, 821, 312	573, 197	903, 830	23. 7
32	Nebraska	8	3, 132, 190	469, 829	816, 641	27
33	Oregon	1	1, 118, 395	167, 759	317, 762	28. 4
34	Montana	1	458, 435	68, 765	62, 662	13. 7
35	Idaho	1	173, 242	25, 986	42, 352	48. 1
36	Wyoming	1	102, 474	15, 371	10, 937	10. 7
37	Utah	2	861, 689	129, 253	63, 418	7. 4
38	Colorado	5	1, 967, 900	295, 185	486, 109	24. 7
39	New Mexico	1	199, 771	29, 966	24, 096	12. 1
	Total	1, 626	490, 608, 432	73, 591, 264	101, 821, 650	20. 8

Table of the state of the lawful money reserve—Continued.

Number	Cities of redemption.	Number of banks.	Liabilities to be protected by reserve.	Reserve required; 25 per cent. of liabilities.	Reserve held.	Per cent. of reserve to liabilities.
1	Boston	48	$81, 754, 299	$20, 438, 575	$22, 373, 760	27. 4
2	Albany	7	11, 107, 171	2, 776, 793	3, 904, 555	35. 2
3	Philadelphia	29	58, 061, 381	14, 515, 345	18, 231, 324	31. 4
4	Pittsburgh	16	17, 599, 215	4, 399, 804	4, 565, 648	25. 9
5	Baltimore	14	21, 255, 801	5, 313, 950	5, 752, 257	27. 1
6	Washington	3	2, 757, 264	689, 316	962, 734	34. 9
7	New Orleans	9	9, 430, 625	2, 357, 656	2, 564, 527	27. 2
8	Louisville	5	2, 440, 470	610, 117	631, 664	25. 9
9	Cincinnati	5	11, 506, 030	2, 876, 507	3, 233, 281	28. 1
10	Cleveland	6	7. 335, 129	1, 833, 782	1, 786, 399	24. 3
11	Chicago	18	32, 897, 819	8, 224, 455	9, 653, 635	29. 4
12	Detroit	3	4, 384, 521	1, 096, 130	1, 195, 448	27. 3
13	Milwaukee	4	3. 018, 729	754, 683	807, 431	26. 7
14	Saint Louis	8	9, 543, 997	2, 385, 999	2, 936, 059	30. 8
	Total	175	273, 092, 451	68, 273, 112	78, 600, 731	28. 8
15	New York	51	225, 156, 173	56, 289, 043	65, 578, 711	29. 1
16	San Francisco	1	1, 149, 676	287, 419	492, 843	42. 8
		227	499, 398, 300	124, 849, 574	144, 672, 285	....

STATES, *as shown by reports of the 10th of June*, 1872.

Funds available for reserve.					States and Territories.
Specie.	Legal-tenders.	Clearing-house certificates.	Three per cent. certificates.	Due from redeeming agents.	
$22, 778	$1, 002, 497	.....	.....	$1, 507, 712	Maine.
24, 039	457, 990	.....	.....	938, 692	New Hampshire.
30, 948	766, 586	.....	$10, 000	975, 595	Vermont.
296, 835	4, 002, 155	.....	35, 000	6, 856, 957	Massachusetts.
26, 308	1, 347, 963	.....	15, 000	2, 370, 404	Rhode Island.
62, 782	2, 484, 828	.....	45, 000	5, 038, 312	Connecticut.
156, 703	5, 602, 063	.....	85, 000	9, 225, 043	New York.
105, 460	2, 084, 209	.....	55, 000	4, 164, 879	New Jersey.
94, 188	4, 650, 479	.....	155, 000	5, 009, 694	Pennsylvania.
2, 853	234, 519	.....	50, 000	295, 578	Delaware.
20, 672	489, 110	.....	.....	506, 907	Maryland.
4, 365	155, 000	.....	.....	104, 060	District of Columbia.
77, 674	827, 773	.....	.....	905, 240	Virginia.
13, 030	433, 843	.....	.....	389, 985	West Virginia.
45, 096	375, 562	.....	.....	361, 051	North Carolina.
12, 828	495, 515	.....	.....	287, 638	South Carolina.
68, 011	406, 072	.....	50, 000	343, 260	Georgia.
33, 723	276, 158	.....	.....	248, 671	Alabama.
262, 935	226, 660	.....	.....	148, 239	Texas.
1, 704	26, 500	.....	.....	40, 770	Arkansas.
5, 515	601, 499	.....	.....	614, 227	Kentucky.
40, 176	608, 733	.....	.....	822, 819	Tennessee.
39, 901	3, 537, 851	.....	60, 000	3, 418, 334	Ohio.
57, 200	2, 621, 457	.....	5, 000	3, 259, 677	Indiana.
71, 725	2, 182, 825	.....	10, 000	3, 499, 001	Illinois.
44, 677	1, 155, 405	.....	20, 000	1, 029, 840	Michigan.
10, 758	601, 866	.....	.....	657, 547	Wisconsin.
40, 249	1, 463, 109	.....	10, 000	1, 576, 399	Iowa.
21, 553	709, 115	.....	.....	879, 771	Minnesota.
18, 701	593, 818	.....	.....	664, 874	Missouri.
4, 789	402, 677	.....	.....	496, 364	Kansas.
21, 605	220, 013	.....	.....	605, 023	Nebraska.
44, 242	69, 038	.....	.....	204, 482	Oregon.
2, 418	19, 350	.....	.....	40, 894	Montana.
21, 202	21, 150	.....	.....	.....	Idaho.
355	10, 582	.....	.....	.....	Wyoming.
20, 588	40, 463	.....	.....	2, 367	Utah.
54, 360	185, 150	.....	.....	246, 509	Colorado.
246	19, 928	.....	.....	3, 922	New Mexico.
1, 890, 282	41, 495, 381	.....	605, 000	57, 830, 847	

CITIES, *as shown by reports of the 10th of June* 1872.

Funds available for reserve.					Cities of redemption.
Specie.	Legal-tenders.	Clearing-house certificates.	Three per cent. certificates.	Due from redeeming agents.	
$1, 040, 330	$8, 906, 325	.....	$925, 000	$10, 893, 105	Boston.
8, 259	1, 416, 100	.....	60, 000	2, 420, 196	Albany.
124, 155	8, 802, 568	$3, 365, 000	900, 000	4, 979, 605	Philadelphia.
38, 077	2, 573, 868	.....	.....	1, 953, 103	Pittsburgh.
128, 542	2, 655, 633	130, 000	90, 000	2, 748, 082	Baltimore.
16, 661	380, 244	.....	80, 000	465, 829	Washington.
170, 672	1, 108, 667	.....	.....	1, 285, 188	New Orleans.
498	380, 546	.....	.....	259, 620	Louisville.
64, 542	1, 351, 200	.....	.....	1, 827, 539	Cincinnati.
2, 468	900, 000	2, 577	20, 000	801, 334	Cleveland.
115, 029	5, 602, 545	.....	25, 000	3, 823, 061	Chicago.
1, 197	667, 710	.....	20, 000	506, 541	Detroit.
5, 238	465, 498	.....	.....	336, 695	Milwaukee.
29, 332	1, 409, 204	.....	75, 000	1, 422, 523	Saint Louis.
2, 354, 625	36, 820, 108	3, 497, 577	2, 195, 000	33, 733, 421	
15, 195, 070	41, 178, 641	8, 595, 000	610, 000	.....	New York City.
490, 333	2, 510	.....	.....	.....	San Francisco.
18, 040, 028	78, 001, 259	12, 092, 577	2, 805, 000	.....	

Table of the state of the lawful money reserve—Continued.

Number.	States and Territories.	Number of banks.	Liabilities to be protected by reserve.	Reserve required: 15 per cent. of liabilities.	Reserve held.	Per cent. of reserve to liabilities.
1	Maine	61	$13, 565, 837	$2, 034, 876	$2, 643, 929	19.5
2	New Hampshire	42	7, 439, 641	1, 115, 946	1, 606, 726	21.6
3	Vermont	41	10, 286, 060	1, 542, 909	1, 815, 565	17.7
4	Massachusetts	162	58, 735, 106	8, 810, 266	11, 863, 328	20.2
5	Rhode Island	62	20, 889, 298	3, 133, 395	3, 751, 731	18
6	Connecticut	81	32, 291, 194	4, 843, 679	6, 650, 806	20.6
7	New York	229	78, 377, 476	11, 756, 622	14, 562, 920	18.6
8	New Jersey	59	28, 980, 403	4, 347, 061	6, 058, 344	20.9
9	Pennsylvania	156	52, 795, 061	7, 919, 259	10, 021, 663	19
10	Delaware	11	3, 146, 615	471, 992	644, 588	20.5
11	Maryland	19	4, 579, 138	686, 871	1, 110, 091	24.2
12	District of Columbia	1	705, 635	105, 845	230, 794	32.7
13	Virginia	24	10, 429, 201	1, 564, 380	1, 496, 465	14.4
14	West Virginia	17	5, 191, 738	778, 761	883, 909	17
15	North Carolina	10	4, 191, 502	628, 725	782, 680	18.7
16	South Carolina	8	3, 382, 461	507, 369	602, 477	17.8
17	Georgia	11	4, 182, 743	627, 411	900, 580	21.5
18	Alabama	8	2, 014, 602	302, 190	333, 119	16.5
19	Texas	5	1, 815, 779	272, 367	482, 659	26.6
20	Arkansas	2	330, 280	49, 542	48, 113	14.6
21	Kentucky	28	7, 446, 331	1, 116, 949	1, 345, 175	18.1
22	Tennessee	22	7, 008, 152	1, 051, 223	1, 162, 095	16.6
23	Ohio	147	36, 694, 915	5, 504, 237	6, 657, 763	18.1
24	Indiana	87	27, 176, 941	4, 076, 541	5, 283, 667	19.4
25	Illinois	113	23, 361, 947	3, 504, 292	4, 524, 183	19.4
26	Michigan	68	13, 198, 615	1, 979, 793	2, 503, 681	19
27	Wisconsin	38	6, 878, 135	1, 031, 720	1, 522, 072	22.1
28	Iowa	70	13, 109, 816	1, 966, 472	2, 441, 815	18.6
29	Minnesota	29	7, 904, 290	1, 185, 644	1, 563, 976	19.8
30	Missouri	28	6, 073, 988	911, 098	1, 069, 551	17.6
31	Kansas	24	4, 429, 432	664, 415	985, 640	22.3
32	Nebraska	9	3, 227, 574	484, 136	725, 078	22.5
33	Oregon	1	1, 201, 821	180, 273	331, 275	27.6
34	California	1	909, 235	136, 385	186, 436	20.5
35	Montana	4	850, 375	127, 556	136, 117	16
36	Idaho	1	184, 671	27, 701	30, 596	16.6
37	Wyoming	1	107, 772	16, 166	18, 259	16.9
38	Utah	2	811, 900	121, 785	55, 711	6.9
39	Colorado	6	2, 581, 561	387, 234	674, 375	26.1
40	New Mexico	1	225, 906	33, 886	38, 922	17.2
	Total	1, 689	506, 713, 150	76, 006, 972	97, 765, 876	19.3

Table of the state of the lawful money reserve—Continued.

	Cities of redemption.	Number of banks.	Liabilities to be protected by reserve.	Reserve required: 25 per cent. of liabilities.	Reserve held.	Per cent. of reserve to liabilities.
1	Boston	49	$74, 735, 681	$18, 683, 920	$18, 368, 516	24.6
2	Albany	7	10, 611, 162	2, 652, 791	3, 447, 125	24.8
3	Philadelphia	29	50, 117, 037	12, 529, 259	13, 417, 584	26.8
4	Pittsburgh	16	16, 689, 278	4, 172, 319	4, 142, 534	24.8
5	Baltimore	14	20, 737, 270	5, 184, 318	5, 504, 949	26.6
6	Washington	4	3, 067, 151	766, 788	688, 913	22.5
7	New Orleans	9	9, 717, 597	2, 429, 399	2, 174, 312	22.4
8	Louisville	5	2, 460, 974	615, 243	617, 001	25.1
9	Cincinnati	5	11, 364, 760	2, 841, 190	3, 285, 432	28.9
10	Cleveland	6	7, 069, 312	1, 767, 328	1, 963, 729	27.8
11	Chicago	19	30, 586, 912	7, 646, 728	8, 327, 506	27.2
12	Detroit	3	4, 746, 734	1, 186, 683	1, 282, 519	27
13	Milwaukee	4	3, 213, 015	803, 254	951, 066	29.6
14	Saint Louis	8	8, 346, 919	2, 086, 730	1, 964, 962	23.5
		178	253, 463, 802	63, 365, 950	66, 136, 148	26.1
15	New York City	50	186, 105, 072	46, 526, 268	45, 394, 832	24.4
16	San Francisco	2	3, 780, 431	945, 108	621, 076	16.4

STATES, *as shown by reports of the 3d of October*, 1872.

Funds available for reserve.						States and Territories.
Specie.	Legal tenders.	Clearing-house certificates.	Three per cent. certificates.	U.S. certificates of deposit.	Due from redeeming agents	
$25,908	$1,151,159	....	....	....	$1,466,862	Maine.
8,978	524,288	....	....	....	1,072,400	New Hampshire.
35,577	747,094	....	$10,000	....	1,022,894	Vermont.
140,731	4,461,213	....	35,000	$110,000	7,136,384	Massachusetts.
37,304	1,467,464	....	....	....	2,246,963	Rhode Island.
106,711	2,608,391	....	20,000	....	3,915,706	Connecticut.
147,407	5,667,034	....	50,000	110,000	8,588,479	New York.
76,452	2,217,772	....	10,000	....	3,754,120	New Jersey.
86,004	4,704,807	....	45,000	....	5,125,852	Pennsylvania.
2,943	252,452	....	30,000	....	359,193	Delaware.
20,828	463,003	....	....	....	626,260	Maryland.
4,001	122,000	....	....	....	104,793	District of Columbia.
64,597	848,233	....	....	....	583,635	Virginia.
9,970	424,502	....	....	....	449,437	West Virginia.
60,503	304,355	....	....	....	417,822	North Carolina.
10,608	331,162	....	....	....	210,707	South Carolina.
67,964	582,785	....	50,000	....	199,831	Georgia.
22,166	207,505	....	....	....	103,448	Alabama.
226,990	171,344	....	....	....	84,319	Texas.
1,857	29,623	....	....	....	46,633	Arkansas.
11,476	550,860	....	....	....	773,839	Kentucky.
33,833	700,691	....	....	....	427,571	Tennessee.
37,908	3,556,811	....	60,000	....	3,093,044	Ohio.
46,470	2,578,691	....	5,000	....	2,653,506	Indiana.
72,359	2,120,243	....	10,000	....	2,321,581	Illinois.
59,917	1,232,941	....	....	....	1,210,823	Michigan.
19,557	662,015	....	....	....	840,500	Wisconsin.
40,870	1,431,626	....	10,000	....	959,319	Iowa.
15,796	722,085	....	....	....	826,095	Minnesota.
25,633	558,559	....	....	....	485,359	Missouri.
12,918	424,168	....	....	....	548,554	Kansas.
6,742	267,940	....	....	....	450,396	Nebraska.
106,464	65,901	....	....	....	158,910	Oregon.
186,436	....	....	....	....	....	California.
9,551	94,528	....	....	....	32,038	Montana.
0,656	20,940	....	....	....	....	Idaho.
133	14,330	....	....	....	3,796	Wyoming.
2,089	51,966	....	....	....	1,656	Utah.
93,458	230,191	....	....	....	341,726	Colorado.
1,371	18,622	....	....	....	18,929	New Mexico.
1,950,142	42,717,294	....	335,000	220,000	52,543,440	

CITIES, *as shown by reports of the 3d of October*, 1872.

Funds available for reserve.						Cities of redemption.
Specie.	Legal tenders.	Clearing-house certificates.	Three per cent. certificates.	U. S. certificates of deposit.	Due from redeeming agents.	
$804,592	$8,098,422	$135,000	$300,000	$265,000	$8,765,502	Boston.
7,852	1,167,174	....	30,000	200,000	2,042,099	Albany.
124,314	5,868,621	2,760,000	260,000	70,000	4,334,649	Philadelphia.
33,137	2,574,576	....	....	....	1,534,821	Pittsburgh.
84,378	2,387,494	152,000	30,000	....	2,851,077	Baltimore.
24,614	349,087	....	....	100,000	214,612	Washington.
73,369	1,304,493	....	....	....	796,450	New Orleans.
647	402,175	....	....	....	214,179	Louisville.
8,130	1,766,784	....	....	....	1,510,518	Cincinnati.
3,305	1,085,000	....	....	....	875,424	Cleveland.
137,349	5,294,822	....	25,000	....	2,870,335	Chicago.
1,589	641,968	....	....	....	638,962	Detroit.
2,834	401,688	....	....	....	546,544	Milwaukee.
24,030	962,471	....	....	....	978,461	Saint Louis.
1,330,140	32,305,375	3,047,000	645,000	635,000	28,173,633	
6,375,347	27,004,485	5,585,000	575,000	5,855,000	....	New York City
574,126	46,950	....	....	....	....	San Francisco.

Table of the state of the lawful money reserve of the national banks of the United States at condition made to the

STATES AND

Dates.	Number of banks.	Circulation and deposits.	Reserve required.	Reserve held.	Ratio of reserve to circulation and deposits.
					Per ct.
Jan. 6, 1868	1,418	$405, 322, 306	$60, 798, 353	$96, 873, 050	23.9
April 6, 1868	1,418	412, 251, 361	61, 837, 703	94, 143, 672	23.8
July 6, 1868	1,414	419, 787, 829	62, 968, 177	100, 782, 520	24
Oct. 5, 1868	1,422	414, 776, 428	62, 216, 475	95, 252, 448	22.9
Jan. 4, 1869	1,408	406, 128, 844	60, 919, 326	92, 909, 217	22.9
April 17, 1869	1,400	394, 615, 851	59, 192, 376	82, 523, 406	20.9
June 12, 1869	1,400	395, 378, 414	59, 306, 761	85, 673, 334	21.6
Oct. 9, 1869	1,398	394, 376, 119	59, 156, 419	80, 965, 648	20.5
Jan. 22, 1870	1,396	399, 041, 348	59, 856, 202	93, 426, 468	23.4
Mar. 24, 1870	1,397	403, 873, 222	60, 580, 977	92, 383, 755	22.9
June 9, 1870	1,396	406, 140, 873	60, 921, 131	92, 037, 332	22.7
Oct. 8, 1870	1,400	404, 337, 512	60, 650, 626	84, 777, 956	20.9
Dec. 28, 1870	1,430	406, 311, 675	60, 946, 750	85, 723, 389	21
Mar. 18, 1871	1,465	423, 793, 830	63, 569, 073	95, 615, 960	22.6
April 29, 1871	1,484	436, 412, 072	65, 461, 811	98, 696, 874	22.6
June 10, 1871	1,497	443, 155, 183	66, 473, 276	101, 706, 605	22.9
Oct. 2, 1871	1,536	467, 619, 031	70, 142, 854	98, 946, 184	21.2
Dec. 16, 1871	1,564	460, 710, 213	69, 106, 532	91, 728, 620	19.9
Feb. 27, 1872	1,586	481, 506, 936	72, 226, 040	102, 275, 001	21.3
April 19, 1872	1,616	484, 854, 125	72, 728, 118	98, 012, 845	20.2
June 10, 1872	1,626	490, 608, 432	73, 591, 264	101, 821, 660	20.8
Oct. 3, 1872	1,689	506, 713, 150	76, 006, 972	97, 765, 8	19.3

NOTE.—The reserve which the banks in the States and Territories are required to

REDEMPTION

Dates.	Number of banks.	Circulation and deposits.	Reserve required.	Reserve held.	Ratio of reserve to circulation and deposits.
					Per ct.
Jan. 6, 1868	224	$439, 653, 338	$109, 913, 335	$146, 041, 738	33.2
April 6, 1868	225	429, 084, 929	107, 271, 231	130, 148, 347	30.3
July 6, 1868	225	493, 814, 023	123, 453, 505	160, 352, 080	32.5
Oct. 5, 1868	223	440, 170, 650	110, 042, 664	139, 227, 396	31.6
Jan. 4, 1869	220	428, 310, 661	107, 077, 665	140, 320, 761	32.7
April 17, 1869	220	400, 006, 281	100, 001, 571	115, 570, 842	28.9
June 12, 1869	219	425, 263, 320	106, 315, 832	125, 468, 496	29.5
Oct. 9, 1869	219	403, 632, 332	100, 908, 081	127, 256, 666	31.5
Jan. 22, 1870	218	447, 831, 836	111, 957, 959	155, 894, 999	34.8
Mar. 24, 1870	218	445, 759, 265	111, 439, 813	143, 139, 798	32.1
June 9, 1870	216	460, 166, 341	115, 041, 582	150, 572, 350	32.7
Oct. 8, 1870	215	409, 060, 815	102, 265, 204	118, 633, 295	29
Dec. 28, 1870	218	420, 796, 417	105, 199, 105	123, 816, 297	29.4
Mar. 18, 1871	223	466, 973, 869	116, 743, 467	138, 772, 908	29.7
April 29, 1871	225	476, 104, 067	119, 026, 015	144, 809, 917	30.4
June 10, 1871	226	510, 018, 734	127, 504, 683	159, 603, 896	31.3
Oct. 2, 1871	230	484, 634, 132	121, 158, 533	134, 463, 827	27.7
Dec. 16, 1871	226	456, 721, 899	114, 180, 474	126, 916, 204	27.8
Feb. 27, 1872	228	470, 889, 271	117, 722, 318	126, 440, 065	26.9
April 19, 1872	227	460, 754, 376	115, 188, 594	124, 949, 109	27.1
June 10, 1872	227	499, 398, 300	124, 849, 574	144, 672, 283	29
Oct. 3, 1872	230	443, 349, 305	110, 837, 326	112, 152, 056	25.3

NOTE.—The reserve which the banks in the redemption cities above are required to *various dates, from January 6, 1868, to October 3, 1872, as shown by the reports of their Comptroller of the Currency.*

TERRITORIES.

Funds available for reserve.						
Specie.	Legal-tenders.	Compound-interest notes.	Clearing-house certificates.	Three per cent. certificates.	Due from redeeming agents.	United States certificates of deposit.
$2,565,221	$36,138,801	$12,933,550	....	$1,440,000	$43,795,478	....
1,804,017	34,735,700	11,806,040	....	2,905,000	42,892,915	....
2,058,989	36,247,168	6,478,600	....	4,265,000	51,732,763	....
1,781,317	39,034,570	2,131,020	....	5,245,000	47,060,541	....
2,819,665	40,724,681	....	....	4,815,000	44,639,871	....
1,705,877	37,213,372	....	....	4,595,000	39,009,157	....
1,597,541	36,232,475	....	....	4,235,000	43,608,318	....
1,573,300	36,215,334	....	....	3,795,000	39,382,014	....
3,146,141	36,855,868	....	....	3,370,000	50,054,459	....
3,329,055	35,659,362	....	....	3,265,000	50,130,338	....
2,912,275	36,992,740	....	....	3,115,000	49,017,317	....
2,357,856	35,465,915	....	....	2,890,000	44,064,185	....
2,359,126	36,842,257	....	....	2,545,000	43,977,006	....
2,420,987	35,589,817	....	....	2,245,000	55,360,156	....
2,504,655	38,506,524	....	....	2,040,000	55,647,695	....
2,032,371	38,481,550	....	....	1,885,000	59,307,684	....
1,814,927	40,139,433	....	....	1,355,000	55,636,824	....
2,043,411	39,320,993	....	....	1,060,000	49,244,222	....
2,816,771	39,792,119	....	....	810,000	53,856,111	....
2,600,614	42,465,032	....	....	690,000	52,236,599	....
1,890,232	41,495,581	....	....	605,000	57,830,847	....
1,950,142	42,717,294	....	....	335,000	52,543,440	$220,000

keep is 15 per centum of the aggregate amount of their circulation and deposits.

CITIES.

Funds available for reserve.						
Specie.	Legal-tenders.	Compound-interest notes.	Clearing-house certificates.	Three per cent. certificates.	Due from redeeming agents.	United States certificates of deposit.
$15,338,758	$78,167,600	$27,063,480	....	$6,805,000	$18,466,810	....
13,575,641	49,654,519	27,111,450	....	21,350,000	18,456,737	....
18,696,932	63,918,032	12,904,620	....	40,640,000	24,101,596	....
9,686,044	53,418,905	2,382,710	....	53,835,000	19,904,737	....
24,458,946	47,514,619	....	....	47,260,000	21,087,196	....
6,768,826	43,661,789	....	....	46,595,000	18,545,227	....
15,882,535	44,701,644	....	....	45,580,000	19,304,317	....
20,415,157	47,503,961	....	....	42,050,000	17,287,548	....
43,005,329	49,256,634	....	$17,956,000	24,090,000	21,587,027	....
32,703,399	44,720,616	....	19,881,000	22,530,000	23,304,783	....
27,023,254	53,718,011	....	21,403,000	22,810,000	25,618,085	....
12,108,149	41,737,662	....	19,136,000	23,440,000	22,211,484	....
19,949,751	41,680,488	....	20,498,000	20,860,000	20,828,058	....
19,516,341	53,253,532	....	20,599,000	16,955,000	28,449,035	....
15,788,996	65,006,031	....	21,581,572	13,020,000	29,413,318	....
14,171,225	81,923,110	....	19,248,000	11,290,000	33,061,561	....
10,226,739	66,648,233	....	20,322,070	5,825,000	31,241,785	....
23,273,114	52,633,689	....	16,633,026	5,635,000	28,741,375	....
19,504,567	55,118,281	....	16,195,000	4,930,000	30,692,217	....
17,142,870	60,822,823	....	13,909,000	3,190,000	29,883,416	....
18,049,028	78,001,250	....	12,092,577	2,805,000	33,733,421	....
8,279,613	59,356,810	....	8,632,000	1,220,000	28,173,633	$6,490,000

keep is 25 per centum of the aggregate amount of their circulation and deposits.

INTEREST LAWS OF RHODE ISLAND, MASSACHUSETTS, AND CONNECTICUT.

RHODE ISLAND.

AN ACT in relation to interest.

Be it enacted, &c., as follows:

SECTION 1. Interest in rendition of judgments, and in all business transactions where interest is secured or paid, shall be computed at the rate of six dollars on a hundred dollars for one year, *unless a different rate is expressly stipulated.*

SEC. 2. All acts or parts of acts inconsistent herewith are hereby repealed.

Approved March 17, 1865.

MASSACHUSETTS.

AN ACT concerning the rate of interest.

Be it enacted, &c., as follows:

SECTION 1. When there is no agreement for a different rate of interest of money, the same shall continue to be at the rate of six dollars upon one hundred dollars for a year, and at the same rate for a greater or less sum, and for a longer or shorter time.

SEC. 2. It shall be lawful to contract to pay or reserve discount at any rate, and to contract for payment and receipt of any rate of interest: *Provided, however,* That no greater rate of interest than six per centum per annum shall be recovered in any action, except when the agreement to pay such greater rate of interest is in writing.

SEC. 3. Sections three, four, and five of chapter fifty-three of the General Statutes, and all acts and parts of acts inconsistent herewith, are hereby repealed.

SEC. 4. This act shall not affect any existing contract or action pending, or existing right of action, and shall take effect on the first day of July next.

Approved March 6, 1867.

CONNECTICUT.

AN ACT concerning the rate of interest.

Be it enacted, &c., as follows:

SECTION 1. When there is no agreement for a different rate of interest of money, the same shall be at the rate of six dollars upon one hundred dollars for one year, and at the same rate for a greater or less sum, and for a longer or shorter time.

SEC. 2. It shall be lawful to contract or pay or reserve any discount at any rate, and to contract for payment and receipt of any rate of interest: *Provided, however,* That no greater rate of interest than six per centum per annum shall be recovered in any action, except when the agreement to pay such greater rate of interest is in writing.

SEC. 3. That the first, second, third, and fourth sections of an act entitled "An act to restrain the taking of usury," and all acts inconsistent herewith, are hereby repealed.

SEC. 4. This act shall not affect any existing contract or suit now pending.

Approved July 2, 1872.

Names and compensation of officers and clerks in the office of the Comptroller of the Currency.

Name.	Class.	Salary.
COMPTROLLER.		
Jno. Jay Knox		$5,000
DEPUTY COMPTROLLER.		
John S. Langworthy		2,500
CLERKS.		
J. Franklin Bates	Fourth class	1,800
Edward Wolcott	do	1,800
John D. Patton, jr	do	1,800
George W. Martin	do	1,800
John W. Magruder	do	1,800
John W. Griffin	do	1,800
John Burroughs	do	1,800
Charles A. Jewett	do	1,800
Edward S. Peck	do	1,800
George H. Wood	do	1,800
Charles H. Norton	Third class	1,600
Edward Myers	do	1,600
Fernando C. Cate	do	1,600
William H. Milstead	do	1,600
Frank A. Miller	do	1,600
John A. Kayser	do	1,600
Albert A. Miller	do	1,600
C. Burr Vickery	do	1,600
Charles H. Cherry	do	1,600
F. A. Simkins	do	1,600
George Wallace, jr	do	1,600
Watson W. Eldridge	do	1,600
Leonard Whitney	do	1,600
Theodore O. Ebaugh	do	1,600
William A. Page	Second class	1,400
John Joy Edson	do	1,400
Charles Scott	do	1,400
William Cruikshank	do	1,400
R. T. J. Falconer	do	1,400
William D. Swan	do	1,400
William Sinclair	do	1,400
Nathaniel O. Chapman	do	1,400
Miss Frances R. Sprague	do	1,400
Alanson T. Kinney	do	1,400
John J. Patton	First class	1,200
Philip T. Snowden	do	1,200
Isaac C. Miller	do	1,200
Walter Taylor	do	1,200
William B. Greene	do	1,200
Edw. W. Moore	do	1,200
John J. Sanborn	do	1,200
William H. Glascott	do	1,200
Moses C. Bayles	do	1,200
Mrs. Mary L. McCormick	Female clerk	900
Mrs. Sarah F. Fitzgerald	do	900
Mrs. Etha E. Poole	do	900
Mrs. Sophy C. Harrison	do	900
Mrs. Fayette C. Snead	do	900
Mrs. Maria L. Sturgus	do	900
Mrs. Maggie B. Miller	do	900
Mrs. C. F. B. Stevens	do	900
Mrs. Julia R. Donoho	do	900
Miss Celia N. French	do	900
Miss Louise W. Knowlton	do	900
Miss Anna W. Story	do	900
Miss Christina Hinds	do	900
Miss Maggie L. Simpson	do	900
Miss Eliza R. Hyde	do	900
Miss Clara J. Fenno	do	900
Miss Eliza M. Barker	do	900
Miss Amelia P. Stockdale	do	900
Miss Love L. Bursley	do	900
Miss Harriet M. Black	do	900
Miss Margaret E. Gooding	do	900
Miss Julia Greer	do	900
Miss Lizzie Henry	do	900
Miss Augusta Fox	do	900
Miss Margaret L. Browne	do	900
Miss Alice M. Kennedy	do	900

Names and compensation of officers and clerks, &c.—Continued.

Name.	Class.	Salary.
Miss Nellie M. Fletcher	Female clerk	$900
Miss Gertrude A. Massey	do	900
Miss Maggie B. Wilson	do	900
Edmund E. Schreiner	Messenger	840
Harry R. Hughes	do	840
J. E. De Saules	do	840
Charles B. Hinckley	Assistant messenger	720
Philo Burr	Watchman	720
William J. Martin	do	720
Henry Saunders	Laborer	720
Charles McTaylor	do	720
R. Le Roy Livingston	do	720
James D. Burke	do	720

Expenses of the office of the Comptroller of the Currency for the fiscal year ended June 30, 1872.

For special dies, plates, paper, printing, &c.	$72,653 72
For salaries	103,140 00
Total	175,793 72

The contingent expenses of the office were paid out of the general appropriation for contingent expenses of the Treasury Department, and as separate accounts are not kept for the different Bureaus, the amount cannot be stated.

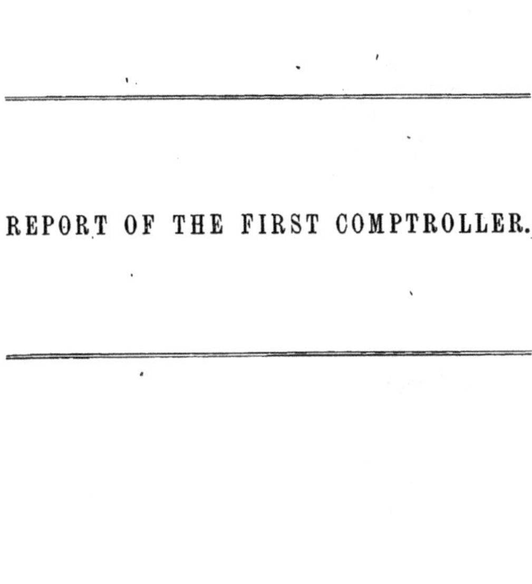

REPORT OF THE FIRST COMPTROLLER.

REPORT

OF

THE FIRST COMPTROLLER OF THE TREASURY.

TREASURY DEPARTMENT,
First Comptroller's Office, October 24, 1872.

SIR: I have the honor to submit the following report of the operations of this office during the fiscal year ended June 30, 1872.

Number of warrants examined, countersigned, entered upon blotters, and posted in ledgers, viz:

Treasury, proper	1,825
Public debt	247
Quarterly salary	1,737
Diplomatic	2,333
Customs	4,327
Internal revenue	6,008
Judiciary	1,642
War, civil	60
War, pay	3,756
War, repay	761
Navy, pay	1,376
Navy, repay	197
Interior, civil	1,801
Interior, pay	1,874
Interior, repay	112
Appropriation	105
Internal revenue, (covering)	3,791
Customs, (covering)	1,359
Land, (covering)	640
Miscellaneous, (covering)	5,831

Number of accounts received from the First and Fifth Auditors of the Treasury, and Commissioner of the General Land-Office, revised and certified, viz:

Judiciary, embracing the accounts of United States marshals for their fees and for the expenses of the United States courts, of the United States district attorneys, and of the commissioners and clerks of United States courts	1,927
Diplomatic and consular, embracing the accounts arising from our intercourse with foreign nations, expenses of consuls for sick and disabled seamen, and of our commercial agents in foreign countries	1,983
Public lands, embracing the accounts of the registers and receivers of land-offices, and surveyors-general and their deputies, and of lands erroneously sold	2,289
Steamboats, embracing accounts for the expenses of the inspection of steamboats and salaries of inspectors	1,458
Mint and its branches, embracing accounts of gold, silver, and cent coinage, of bullion, of salaries of the officers, and of the expenses	119
Public debt, embracing the accounts of the United States Treasurer, and the accounts of the assistant treasurers for the redemption of United States stocks and notes, and for payment of interest on the public debt	488
Public printing, embracing accounts for printing, for paper, and for binding	102
Territorial, embracing accounts for the legislative expenses of the several Territories, and the incidental expenses of their government	286

Congressional, embracing accounts for contingent expenses and other expenses of the United States Senate and House of Representatives	133
Internal-revenue collectors' accounts of the revenue collected, the expenses of collecting the same, their own compensation, and the expenses of their offices	3,271
Internal-revenue assessors' accounts for the expenses of levying the taxes, and for their own compensation	987
Internal-revenue stamp agents' accounts for the sale of stamps	1,185
Internal-revenue miscellaneous accounts for salaries of supervisors, surveyors, detectives, &c.	1,817
Other miscellaneous accounts, embracing accounts for the contingent expenses of all Executive Departments at Washington, salaries of judges, marshals, district attorneys, &c., &c.	2,046
Number of letters written on official business	11,082
Number of receipts given by collectors for tax-lists examined, registered, and filed	3,097
Number of requisitions examined, entered, and reported, viz:	
Diplomatic and consular	750
Collectors of internal revenue	2,822
Marshals	260

In addition to that specified in the foregoing items, a large amount of other work has been done in the examination, registering, and filing of official bonds; the examination and approval of bonds of indemnity; the examination and decision of application for the re-issue of securities in place of those lost or destroyed, and of conflicting claims to Government securities, and the examination and approval of all powers of attorney for the collection of interest and the collection of moneys from the Department.

The accounts of receipts and disbursements kept in this office correspond with those of the Secretary and of the Register, and therefore need not be repeated in this report.

The business of the office continues to be quite as large as formerly, and requires that the force of the office now authorized should be continued.

The aggregate of the items stated in this report is 3,771 greater than that of similar items in the report of last year.

Respectfully submitted.

R. W. TAYLER,
Comptroller.

HON. GEO. S. BOUTWELL,
Secretary of the Treasury.

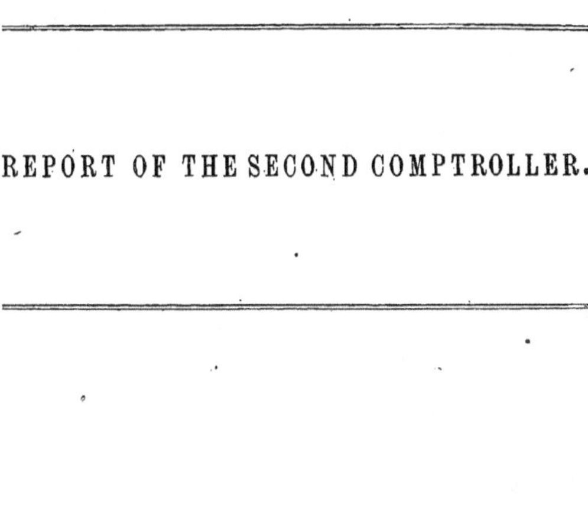

REPORT OF THE SECOND COMPTROLLER.

REPORT

OF

THE SECOND COMPTROLLER OF THE TREASURY.

TREASURY DEPARTMENT,
Second Comptroller's Office, October 26, 1872.

SIR: I have the honor to submit the following detailed statement of the business operations of this office for the fiscal year ending June 30, 1872:

The aggregate number of accounts of disbursing officers and agents which have been received, as well as those which have been finally adjusted, is as follows:

	Received.	Revised.	Amount.
From the Second Auditor	5,176	4,450	$176,290,896 64
From the Third Auditor	3,285	2,810	170,955,764 76
From the Fourth Auditor	452	443	23,689,462 00
Total	8,913	7,703	370,945,123 40

The above accounts have been duly entered, revised, and the balances found thereon certified to the Secretary of the Department in which the expenditure has been incurred, viz, those from the Second and Third Auditors to the Secretary of War, (excepting the accounts of Indian agents, which are certified to the Secretary of the Interior,) and those from the Fourth Auditor to the Secretary of the Navy.

Character of accounts.	Received.	Revised.	Amount.
FROM THE SECOND AUDITOR.			
Embracing accounts of disbursing officers of the War Department for collecting, organizing, and drilling volunteers.	46	42	$751,448 04
Paymasters' accounts for the pay of officers and the pay and rations of soldiers of the Army.	2,516	1,794	132,789,140 83
Special and referred accounts	730	730	10,051,429 79
Accounts of Army recruiting officers for clothing, equipments, and bounty to recruits, &c.	126	120	262,287 14
Ordnance, embracing the accounts of disbursing officers of the the Ordnance Department, for arsenals, armories, armaments, for fortifications, arming militia, &c.	102	102	4,742,446 61
Indian Department: Accounts of Indian agents, including the pay of Indian annuities, presents to Indians, expenses of holding treaties, pay of interpreters, pay of Indian agents, &c., and the settlement of personal claims for miscellaneous services of agents and others in connection with Indian affairs.	1,097	1,094	24,042,904 00
Medical and hospital accounts, including the purchase of medicines, drugs, surgical instruments, hospital stores, the claims of private physicians for services, and surgeons employed under contract.	422	422	429,816 64
Contingent expenses of the War Department, including expenses for military convicts, secret service, &c.	82	82	235,729 40

Character of accounts.	Received.	Revised.	Amount.
FROM THE SECOND AUDITOR—Continued.			
Freedmen's Bureau: Pay and bounty	12	12	$2, 143, 284 00
Soldiers' Home	31	31	432, 694 00
National Volunteer Asylum	12	12	417, 713 19
Total	5, 176	4, 450	176, 299, 896 64
FROM THE THIRD AUDITOR.			
Quartermaster's accounts for transportation of the Army, and the transportation of all descriptions of Army supplies and ordnance, and for the settlement of personal claims for services in the Quartermaster's Department.	1, 637	1, 144	$125, 380, 593 90
Commissaries' accounts for rations or subsistence of the Army, and for the settlement of personal claims for services in the Commissary Department.	1, 323	1, 372	7, 015, 145 32
Accounts of pension agents for the payment of military pensions, including the entries of the monthly reports of new pensioners added to the rolls, and the statements from the Commissioner of Pensions respecting the changes arising from deaths, transfers, &c., and for pension claims presented for adjustment.	222	190	34, 327, 896 11
Accounts of the Engineer Department for military surveys, the construction of fortifications, for river and harbor surveys and improvements.	72	72	2, 670, 474 43
Accounts for the relief of freedmen and refugees	32	32	1, 561, 655 00
Total	3, 285	2, 810	170, 955, 764 76
FROM THE FOURTH AUDITOR.			
Marine Corps accounts: 1st, quartermasters of the Marine Corps, embracing accounts for the expenses of officers' quarters, fuel, forage for horses, attendance on courts-martial and courts of inquiry, transportation of officers and marines, supplies of provisions, clothing, medical stores and military stores, for barracks, and all incidental supplies for marines on shore; 2d, accounts of paymasters of the Marine Corps for pay of the officers and the pay and rations of the marines.	4	4	$609, 594 00
Paymasters of the Navy: Accounts for the pay and rations of officers and crew of the ship, supplies of provisions, of clothing, and repairs of vessels on foreign stations.	277	274	5, 494, 161 00
Paymasters at navy-yards: Accounts for the pay of officers on duty at navy-yards, or on leave of absence, and the pay of mechanics and laborers on the various works.	110	106	10, 040, 264 00
Paymasters acting as navy-agents: Accounts for their advances to paymasters, purchases of timber, provisions, clothing, and naval stores.	40	39	7, 203, 866 00
Navy pension-agents' accounts for the payment of pensions of officers and seamen, &c., of the Navy, and officers and privates of the Marine Corps.	21	20	341, 577 00
Total	452	443	23, 689, 462 00
Naval prize-lists	28	28	....
CLAIMS REVISED DURING THE YEAR.			
Soldiers' pay and bounty	8, 419	8, 205	$1, 202, 754 31
Sailors' pay and bounty	2, 572	2, 391	482, 020 00
Prize-money	1, 252	1, 252	110, 003 00
Quartermaster's stores, under the act of July 4, 1864; property lost, or destroyed, or captured, &c., under the act of March 3, 1849; rent of buildings and land for the use of the Army, and for other miscellaneous military claims against the War Department.	2, 330	2, 258	1, 695, 246 09
Oregon and Washington Territory war claims	38	38	12, 157 93
Claims of States for enrolling, subsisting, clothing, supplying, arming, equipping, paying, and transporting their troops in defense of the United States.	3	3	239, 643 43
Subsistence	250	259	82, 228 83
Total	15, 132	14, 665	3, 904, 282 42
Referred cases	2, 740	2, 740	....

Settlements for the fiscal year ending June 30, 1872	$7, 702
Accounts on hand at the commencement of the fiscal year, July 1, 1871	1, 952
Accounts on hand at the close of the fiscal year, June 30, 1872	824
Letters written on official business	824

Number of requisitions recorded during the year.

Requisitions.	War.	Navy.	Interior.
Accountable	1,162	1,113	941
Refunding	819	260	118
Settlement	2,459	251	963
Transfer	284	24	60
Total	4,724	1,648	2,082

Number of contracts, classified as follows:

Quartermaster's Department	502
Engineer's Department	88
Indian Department	125
Freedmen's Bureau	1
Ordnance	8
Navy Department	152
Adjutant-General	106
Surgeons'	5
Leases	8
Commissary of Subsistence	315
	1,310
Official bonds filed	68

Respectfully submitted.

J. M. BRODHEAD,
Comptroller.

Hon. GEORGE S. BOUTWELL,
Secretary of the Treasury.

REPORT OF THE COMMISSIONER OF CUSTOMS.

REPORT

OF

THE COMMISSIONER OF CUSTOMS.

TREASURY DEPARTMENT,
Office of Commissioner of Customs, September 20, 1872.

SIR: I submit herewith, for your information, a statement of the work performed in this office during the fiscal year ending June 30, 1872:

The number of accounts on hand July 1, 1871		199
The number of accounts received from First Auditor during the year		6,309
		6,508
The number of accounts adjusted during the year	6,230	
The number of accounts returned during the year	40	
		6,270
The number of accounts on hand June 30, 1872		238

There was paid into the Treasury of the United States from sources the accounts of which are settled in this office—

On account of customs	$216,370,286 77
On account of fines, penalties, and forfeitures	674,232 77
On account of steamboat inspections	248,416 45
On account of storage, drayage, &c.	461,409 12
On account of marine-hospital tax	319,823 16
On account of fees, &c.	603,808 01
Total	218,677,976 28

And there was paid out of the Treasury—

On account of expenses of collecting the revenue from customs	$6,950,189 81
On account of refunding excess of deposits	2,557,770 83
On account of debentures	591,240 71
On account of building and maintenance of revenue-cutters	1,084,998 79
On account of public buildings	1,510,911 39
On account of construction and maintenance of lights	3,166,461 93
On account of marine hospitals, relief of sick seamen	421,897 03
On account of distributive shares, fines, penalties, and forfeitures	353,427 42
On account of life-saving stations	55,660 16
On account of captured and abandoned property	34,450 01
On account of miscellaneous accounts	125,247 29
Total	16,832,255 37

The number of estimates received	2,590
The number of requisitions issued	2,472
Amount involved in said requisitions	$9,365,001 61
The number of letters received	10,110
The number of letters written	11,369
The number of letters recorded	10,975
The number of returns received and examined	4,878
The number of oaths examined and registered	4,274
The number of appointments registered	3,088
The average number of clerks employed	25
The amount involved in this statement	$245,075,233 26

Very respectfully, your obedient servant,

W. T. HAINES,
Commissioner of Customs.

HON. GEO. S. BOUTWELL,
Secretary of the Treasury.

Statement of warehouse transactions at the several districts and ports of the United States for the year ending June 30, 1872.

Districts.	WAREHOUSE BONDS.									
	Balance due July 1, 1871.	Warehoused and bonded.	Rewarehoused and bonded.	Constructively warehoused.	Increase of duties ascertained on liquidations.	Withdrawal duty paid.	Withdrawal for transportation.	Withdrawal for exportation.	Allowances and deficiencies.	Balance of bonds not due.
Albany				$122,610 30		$122,610 30				
Alexandria	$1,423 89	$2,670 47	$682 86			2,891 20				$1,706 02
Aroostook		1,538 40				920 31		$258 74		350 35
Baltimore	1,588,965 82	6,585,582 69	44,189 32	64,027 13	$498,493 97	5,994,880 12	$538,774 60	81,379 44	$234,003 54	1,032,241 23
Buffalo Creek	8,493 21	42,041 11	1,507 58	93,298 93	75 75	43,497 07	77,997 73	1,604 50	504 03	21,603 16
Belfast	2,132 09	7,296 77	931 14		19 11	3,158 40		1,741 10		5,479 61
Bangor	24,855 74	12,897 08	2,752 20	579 40	29,92	29,082 60				12,031 74
Bath	22,020 39	12,052 80	3,635 32	21 24		33,307 88		2,475 45		7,946 42
Bristol and Warren	1,135 25	1,151 70				2,286 95				
Barnstable			10,952 28					8,816 22		2,136 06
Boston*	3,397,555 90	1,024,408 37	18,209 37	21,787 05	28,717 87	790,299 70	17,772 22	39,146 60	70,049 03	3,507,411 10
Burlington, N. J				644 80		644 80				
Brunswick	50,093 58				166 11	50,200 16			59 53	
Brazos de Santiago†	98,480 94	22,291 66	499,248 32	73,772 58	4 38	6,384 34	1,088 80	581,168 07		105,156 61
Chicago	91,433 11	537,098 67	532,212 93	123,806 88	161 95	798,321 16	70,603 21	2,472 82	42,069 15	371,187 20
Champlain				104,888 40			104,888 40			
Cuyahoga	9,218 52	29,756 72	30,625 52	15,846 08	57 85	39,550 24	9,439 18	352 00	627 17	35,536 10
Charleston	26,047 54	29,549 35	1,688 70	3,039 32	447 68	35,685 65	268 15	190 00	1,998 34	23,730 45
Castine	2,873 72	2,186 10	607 29		14 41	369 61	144 18	2,970 71	12	2,196 90
Cincinnati	35,545 59	28,780 24	246,665 45	120,063 10	236 76	324,297 62			2,383 78	104,609 67
Cape Vincent				5,549 65			5,549 65			
Cairo				1,575 00		1,575 00				
Corpus Christi	2,533 73	162,946 39	156 10		336 75	6,880 11		153,462 38	4 00	5,625 88
Detroit	8,659 22	10,312 39	24,865 71	598,955 53	295 88	62,618 92	74,771 93	489,372 09	153 05	11,102 74
Delaware			37,576 29			37,576 29				
Dubuque	1,222 04		1,447 12			2,026 00				643 16
Evansville	61 88		573 33	116,692 95		116,754 83				573 33
Erie		1,981 10		76 00		2,057 10				
Frenchman's Bay	145 45		658 53	104 37		52 08		599 84		256 43
Fall River				59,518 29	502 85	59,921 18			99 96	
Genesee	1,599 79	133 60	1,002 00	11,525 64	57 39	5,282 45	7,602 89		126 13	1,307 16
Gloucester	28,190 56	19,873 56	1,896 84		332 49	2,260 55	939 48	37,866 28	928 47	8,306 07
Georgetown, D. C	9,674 54	1,579 20	3,320 22	224 82	148 37	4,028 66			405 39	4,113 10
Galena			46 05							46 05
Huron				272,077 20		3,263 20	168,055 06	100,758 94		
Kennebunk				1,776 04			853 12	922 92		
Louisville	2,237 72	1,540 61	27,415 07	88,914 07	228 13	101,654 35			1,015 80	17,665 45
Milwaukee	9,519 56	21,413 48	57,686 81	36,208 31	350 21	104,776 86	5,719 70	458 03	332 00	13,891 78
Mobile	71,710 90	439,842 15	669 04	3,368 23	1,281 32	291,924 30	110,609 08		5,834 47	109,083 70

Memphis	29,521 54		9,054 07	74,450 30	38 94	85,071 34			429 65	97,564 76
Minnesota	19,333 36		1,022 10	149,412 00	9 63	132,065 44	986 28	25,770 25		11,855 12
Niagara				1,654,347 85			1,654,187 55	160 30		
New Haven	36,992 71	210,599 22	4,781 50		9 74	173,370 07	11,384 76	709 83	305 08	72,612 83
New London		56,204 09		11,542 27		43,692 26	5,495 06	314 13		18,244 91
Newburyport†	20,490 60	14,893 04	322 00	134 78		29,608 32		754 80		5,617 30
New Bedford	2,815 00			21,422 04		1,500 85	19,921 19	2,815 00		
Norfolk and Portsmouth	23,034 21	1,750 42	830 74	7,046 32	2,233 08	28,822 26	5,703 99			968 52
Nashville	2,353 05		28,786 50	16,134 88		40,393 72				6,880 71
New Orleans‡	895,372 29	1,093,144 80	97,435 90	1,050,026 42	89,786 05	1,277,121 33	1,279,271 34	119,432 26	154,375 35	905,565 18
Newark				708 20		708 20				
New York§										
Oswego	5,282 60	581,248 85		52,420 65	3,318 70	250,875 85	385,144 20			6,256 75
Oswegatchie	9,618 91	17,119 35		21,313 38	67 74	18,219 31	23,011 19	198 50	1,118 18	5,572 20
Providence	62,790 47	84,118 65	25,370 54	2,815 68	251 02	138,669 95	19,816 39	60 00	809 21	75,900 81
Passamaquoddy	581 00	307 70		153,387 07		581 00	130,408 73	22,979 24		307 70
Philadelphia‖	1,171,070 53	874,694 25	105,249 00	38,143 29	69,542 54	1,301,650 68	4,052 25	5,993 31	76,321 06	930,682 11
Portsmouth, N. H.	1,776 03	16,126 20	2,041 94	935 50		17,015 64		861 81		2,422 22
Portland and Falmouth¶	83,032 60	127,635 83	72,274 89	8,773,622 20	905 67	156,335 07	523,085 79	8,338,352 71	5,585 72	34,111 90
Pensacola				500 00				500 00		
Petersburgh	648 56	6,511 83	2,824 36	1,883 13		9,143 96				2,723 02
Plymouth	7,346 94		13,263 42	3,517 92		6,735 42		3,512 88	1,629 99	10,249 99
Pittsburgh	705 08		16,204 53	78,876 95	22 82	82,915 03	323 60		347 96	12,282 19
Puget's Sound				1,104 70				1,104 70		
Perth Amboy				76,679 43			76,679 43			
Quincy		14,382 20	56,965 44			71,347 64				
Richmond	3,072 23	20,818 52	15,800 42	20,465 83	70 08	37,848 45	506 22		241 24	21,631 19
San Francisco§										
Salem and Beverly	522 25	7,818 03	10,054 31	1,457 48		10,614 50		3,576 02	40 46	5,621 09
Savannah	9,924 54	20,087 41	8,400 69	6,361 29	2,825 31	17,123 54	1,278 50	4,982 59	3,815 99	20,398 62
Saint Louis	135,746 24	18,400 87	515,942 53	1,147,138 20	1,210 27	1,653,482 19			10,133 79	154,822 13
Saluria	1,428 65		359 31	2,450 60	81 63	1,707 59	385 20	1,176 91	694 24	359 31
Sandusky				15,086 30		15,686 30				
Saint John's¶		183 50	42 66			87 50				138 66
Superior				7,470 56			7,470 56			
Texas	19,269 78	100,214 02	12,719 06	8,251 46	436 63	112,909 95	699 40		1,035 87	26,253 66
Vermont	2,218 20	7,089 50		704,340 47	72 02	6,506 87	352,448 40	442,734 72		1,970 20
Wiscasset	190 52		345 76		16 91	186 02		251 61		115 56
Waldoborough				439 43		439 43				
Willamette	12,621 18	44,520 99	6,656 67	20,529 21	124 29	65,607 20	1,042 58	2,021 18	720 94	15,060 44
Total	8,057,004 51	12,922,734 08	2,668,480 53	16,155,565 18	703,668 32	14,875,973 32	5,701,187 53	10,484,370 97	624,584 89	8,821,344 91

* For July, 1871. † To February, 1872. ‡ To January 31, 1872. § No returns. ‖ To November 30, 1871. ¶ To March 31, 1872.

Statement of warehouse transactions at the several districts and ports of the United States, &c.—Continued.

RECAPITULATION.

Balance due July 1, 1871	$8,057,004 51	Withdrawal duty paid	$14,875,973 32
Warehoused and bonded	12,922,734 08	Withdrawal for transportation	5,701,187 53
Rewarehoused and bonded	2,068,489 53	Withdrawal for exportation	10,484,370 97
Constructively warehoused	10,155,565 18	Allowances and deficiencies	624,584 89
Increase of duties ascertained on liquidation	703,668 32	Balance of bonds not due June 30, 1872	8,821,344 91
Total	40,507,461 62	Total	40,507,461 62

OFFICE OF COMMISSIONER OF CUSTOMS, *October* 28, 1872.

W. T. HAINES, *Commissioner.*

REPORT OF THE FIRST AUDITOR.

REPORT

OF

THE FIRST AUDITOR OF THE TREASURY.

TREASURY DEPARTMENT,
First Auditor's Office, October 18, 1872.

SIR: I have the honor to transmit herewith a statement of the business transactions of this Office for the fiscal year ended June 30, 1872:

Accounts adjusted.	Number of accounts.	Amounts.
RECEIPTS.		
Collectors of customs	1,191	$218,319,775 69
Collectors under steamboat act	612	235,615 99
Mints and assay offices	102	58,635,727 87
Fines, penalties, and forfeitures	429	673,271 61
Wages of seamen forfeited	22	1,675 31
Marine hospital money collected	1,180	312,874 10
Miscellaneous receipts	25	9,120 48
Official emoluments of collectors, naval officers, and surveyors received	918	682,087 67
Moneys received from captured and abandoned property	11	10,368,777 72
Treasurer of the United States for moneys received	3	622,925,702 12
Proceeds of sale of old public buildings	18	35,519 22
	4,511	912,200,147 78
DISBURSEMENTS.		
Expenses of collecting the revenue from customs	1,124	$7,297,937 86
Official emoluments of collectors, naval officers, and surveyors	918	2,473,577 52
Excess of deposits for unascertained duties	111	2,175,148 73
Debentures, drawbacks, bounties, and allowances	91	765,409 68
Light-house establishment	319	746,457 88
Marine-hospital service	596	427,574 94
Revenue-cutter disbursements	374	965,703 13
Additional compensation to collectors, naval officers, and surveyors	2	401 79
Distribution of fines, penalties, and forfeitures	273	629,084 07
Accounts for duties illegally exacted, fines remitted, judgments satisfied, and net proceeds of unclaimed merchandise paid	945	453,652 65
Judiciary expenses, embracing accounts of United States marshals, district attorneys, commissioners and clerks, rent of court-rooms, support of prisoners, &c	2,275	3,432,158 71
Mints and assay offices	102	58,655,558 48
Territorial accounts	96	177,164 57
Salaries of the civil list paid directly from the Treasury	2,207	734,344 77
Disbursements on account of captured and abandoned property	11	5,901,146 76
Defense of suits in relation to captured and abandoned property	70	32,407 05
Treasurer of the United States for general expenditures	3	646,644,351 64
Salaries and mileage of members of the Senate and House of Representatives	3	3,082,062 27
Salaries of officers of the Senate	8	150,477 38
Contingent expenses of the Senate	31	153,047 68
Contingent expenses of the House of Representatives	43	253,947 32
Salaries of officers of the House of Representatives	4	113,377 79
Survey of the coast of the United States	20	822,320 25
Redemption of the public debt	116	311,294,430 77
Payment of interest on the public debt	260	120,033,455 10
Reimbursement of the Treasurer of the United States for United States demand-notes, legal-tender notes, fractional currency, and gold-certificates destroyed by burning	71	145,812,172 42
Construction of State, War, and Navy Departments	11	632,761 06
Construction of court-houses and post-offices	180	1,472,949 26
Construction of custom-houses	320	442,347 50
Construction of branch mint at San Francisco	18	121,395 55
Construction of barge-office at New York	5	53,712 94
Construction of penitentiaries in Territories	12	30,044 69
Construction of light-houses	564	1,308,761 88

Accounts adjusted.	Number of accounts.	Amounts.
DISBURSEMENTS—Continued.		
Construction of heating-apparatus for public buildings	36	$103, 156 26
Fuel, lights, and water for public buildings	131	154, 187 32
Repairs and preservation of public buildings	240	352, 720 28
Furniture and repairs of same	36	86, 460 94
Government Hospital for the Insane—for support, extension of buildings, and purchase of land	25	186, 430 74
Providence Hospital—for care, support, and medical treatment of transient paupers	12	12, 000 00
Maryland Institution for the Blind	2	600 00
National Association for Colored Women	1	2, 110 50
Humane Society of Massachusetts	3	3, 045 29
Columbia Hospital for Women and Lying-in Asylum, and other charities for support, purchase of buildings, &c	4	28, 288 45
Public printing and binding	116	2, 127, 988 56
Supervising and local inspectors of steam-vessels, for traveling and incidental expenses	348	45, 372 00
Disbursing-clerks for paying the salaries of the several Departments of the Government at Washington	346	5, 308, 542 79
Contingent expenses of said Departments	421	1, 249, 865 18
Expenses of national loan	36	1, 781, 267 02
Commissioner of Public Buildings and Grounds	220	601, 331 06
Commissioner of Agriculture	52	100, 632 15
Warehouse and bond accounts	812	....
Miscellaneous accounts	1, 271	9, 632, 766 32
Life-saving stations on the Atlantic coast	8	39, 522 90
	15, 293	1, 339, 778, 632 45

Reports and certificates recorded	12, 900
Letters written	2, 356
Letters recorded	2, 356
Powers of attorney for collecting interest on the public debt registered and filed	5, 672
Acknowledgments of accounts written	9, 356
Requisitions answered	584
Judiciary emolument accounts registered and filed	508
Total	33, 732

Very respectfully, your obedient servant,

D. W. MAHON,
Auditor.

Hon. GEO. S. BOUTWELL,
Secretary of the Treasury.

REPORT OF THE SECOND AUDITOR.

REPORT

OF

THE SECOND AUDITOR OF THE TREASURY.

TREASURY DEPARTMENT,
Second Auditor's Office, November 1, 1872.

SIR: I have the honor to transmit herewith the annual report of this office for the fiscal year ended June 30, 1872, showing in detail the condition of business in each division at the commencement of the year, its progress during the year, and its condition at the end thereof.

BOOK-KEEPER'S DIVISION.

The following statement shows the amount and nature of the work performed by this division during the year:

Requisitions registered, journalized, and posted.

On what account drawn.	No.	Amount.
DEBIT REQUISITIONS.		
Pay.		
Advances in favor of Pay Department	131	$13,572,343 00
Advances in favor of Adjutant-General's Department	55	198,177 86
Advances in favor of Ordnance Department	152	1,846,507 51
Advances in favor of Medical Department	25	418,050 00
Advances under direction of the Secretary of War	5	41,572 79
Advances in favor of Indian Department	354	2,964,768 90
Advances under direction of the General of the Army	2	5,000 00
Claims paid under appropriations of Pay Department	149	25,896 99
Claims paid under appropriations of Adjutant-General's Department	14	738 07
Claims paid under appropriations of Ordnance Department	16	153,078 47
Claims paid under appropriations of Medical Department	236	25,149 39
Claims paid under appropriations in charge of the Secretary of War	50	63,519 78
Claims paid under appropriations of Quartermaster's Department	1	42 50
Claims paid under appropriations of Indian Department	948	3,067,903 92
Claims paid under special acts of relief by Congress	5	17,257 92
Payments to Treasurer United States, (internal revenue fund)	8	4,313 02
Payments to National Asylum for Disabled Volunteer Soldiers	14	418,324 19
Payments to Soldiers' Home	31	396,868 83
Total payments	2,196	23,219,513 14
TRANSFER.		
Requisitions issued for the purpose of adjusting appropriations:		
Transferring amounts from appropriations found to be chargeable to such as are entitled to credit on the books of the Second Auditor's Office	32	$11,319,115 09
Transferring amounts as above to the books of the Third Auditor's Office	116	1,484,156 90
Transferring amounts as above to the books of the Fourth Auditor's Office	1	150 00
Transferring amounts as above to the books of the Register's Office	22	15,504 15
Total transfers	171	12,818,926 14
Aggregate debits	2,367	$36,038,439 28
CREDIT REQUISITIONS.		
Deposit.		
In favor of Pay Department	148	$663,704 89
In favor of Ordnance Department		1,672,196 37
In favor of Adjutant-General's Department		16,665 15
In favor of Medical Department		115,897 38
In favor of Quartermaster's Department		279 49
In favor of Commanding General's Office		590 25
In favor of Indian Department	29	230,216 38
Total deposit	177	2,699,549 91

Requisitions registered, journalized, and posted—Continued.

On what account drawn.	No.	Amount.
Counter.		
Requisitions issued for the purpose of adjusting appropriations:		
Transferring amounts to appropriations entitled to credit from appropriations found to be chargeable on the books of the Second Auditor's Office	33	$11,319,310 03
Transferring amounts as above from appropriations on the books of the First Auditor's Office to the books of the Second Auditor's Office	2	936 66
Transferring amounts as above from the books of the Third Auditor's Office to those of the Second Auditor's Office	24	15,793 20
Transferring amounts as above from the books of the Fourth Auditor's Office to those of the Second Auditor's Office	3	215,421 15
Total counter	62	11,551,461 04
Aggregate credits	239	14,251,010 95
Aggregate debits and credits	2,606	50,289,450 23
Deducting the credits from the debits shows the net amount drawn out to be	....	21,787,428 33
APPROPRIATION WARRANTS.		
Credits.		
In favor of appropriations of Pay Department	7	17,377,009 63
In favor of appropriations of Adjutant-General's Department		125,580 00
In favor of appropriations of Ordnance Department		2,022,804 00
In favor of appropriations of Medical Department		227,000 00
In favor of appropriations in charge of Secretary of War		448,713 97
In favor of appropriations in charge of General of the Army		5,000 00
In favor of appropriations of the Quartermaster's Department		650,000 00
In favor of appropriations of the Indian Department	50	7,496,659 03
Under special acts of relief by Congress	2	18,992 51
Total credits	59	28,371,759 14
Debits.		
Surplus fund warrants	4	25,435,806 74
Total debits	4	25,435,806 74
Aggregate debits and credits	63	53,807,565 88
Excess of credits over debits	....	2,935,952 40

CONDENSED BALANCE-SHEET OF APPROPRIATIONS.

	War Department.	Indian Department.
Credit.		
Balance to credit of all appropriations on the books of this office June 30, 1871	$45,784,358 29	$9,999,848 03
Amount credited by appropriation warrants during fiscal year ended June 30, 1872	20,875,100 11	7,496,659 03
Amount credited by deposit and transfer requisitions during same period	14,007,255 68	243,755 27
Amount credited in Third Auditor's Office to appropriations used in common by both offices	1,993,946 43	....
Total	82,660,660 51	17,740,262 33
Debit.		
Amount debited to appropriations by surplus-fund warrants during the fiscal year ended June 30, 1872	24,905,129 40	530,677 34
Amount drawn from appropriations by requisition during same period	28,753,619 34	7,284,819 94
Amount drawn in Third Auditor's Office from appropriations used in common by both offices	2,501,305 61	....
Balance remaining to the credit of all appropriations on books of this office June 30, 1872	26,500,606 16	9,924,765 05
Total	82,660,660 51	17,740,262 33

SETTLEMENTS MADE.

During the year the following settlements, of a miscellaneous character, were made by this division:

On what account.	No.	Amount.
Transfer settlements for the adjustment of appropriations	4	$11, 112, 912 39
Transfer to books of Third Auditor's Office	1	212 47
Total	5	11, 113, 124 86

SETTLEMENTS ENTERED.

Paymasters'	485
Recruiting	141
Ordnance	66
Medical	70
Treasurer United States, internal revenue fund	1
Soldiers' Home	32
National Asylum for Disabled Volunteer Soldiers	12
Charges and credits to officers for overpayments, refundments, &c	315
Arrears of pay	32
Transfers to credit of disbursing officers on books of Third Auditor's Office	65
Transfers to credit of disbursing officers on books of Fourth Auditor's Office	1
Transfer settlements, Second Auditor's Office	4
Special acts of relief	5
Indian	137
Claims—Indians	956
Claims—war	386
Miscellaneous	23
Total	2, 731

Number of certificates given to the Third Auditor's Office and the various divisions of this office 1, 262

Number of letters written 809

PAYMASTER'S DIVISION.

The number of accounts examined and settlements made during the year is 3,531, as follows:

Paymasters' accounts examined and reported to the Second Comptroller	2, 336
Old settlements of paymasters' accounts revised	517
Charges against officers on account of overpayments	38
Charges against officers on account of double payments	178
Credits to officers for overpayments refunded	7
Credits to officers for double payments refunded	52
Draft-rendezvous accounts examined	14
Paymasters' accounts balanced and closed	148
Paymasters' accounts finally adjusted, on which balances remain due the United States	75
Miscellaneous	166
Total	3, 531

The amounts involved in the above are as follows:

Paymasters' accounts $131, 057, 413 02

Amount of fines by sentence of courts-martial, forfeitures by desertion, arrears of pay, and bounties disallowed, for the support of the National Asylum for Disabled Volunteer Soldiers, ascertained to be due: first, in the current examination of paymasters' accounts, $51,129.93; secondly, in a special examination, $181,969.62; and, thirdly, the examination of draft-rendezvous accounts, commenced May, 1871, $167,765.34. The amount found due has been paid to the asylum, in accordance with the act of Congress of March 21, 1866, as follows:

1871.		
July 19	$15 00	
August 1	24,705 69	
September 1	10,035 73	
October 2	8,268 78	
November 1	2,772 86	
November 18	596 00	
December 2	37,142 16	
1872.		
January 2	23,228 40	
February 2	27,141 63	
March 2	71,647 88	
April 1	27,645 19	
May 1	93,512 67	
June 3	36,208 93	
June 30	37,925 83	
		$400,864 89
Amount of fines, forfeitures, &c., for the support of the Soldiers' Home, found to be due in the examination of paymasters' accounts, and paid to said Soldiers' Home in accordance with the act of Congress of March 3, 1859, as follows:		
1871		
July 22	$152 33	
August 3	525 32	
September 1	2,578 55	
October 5	3,889 51	
November 2	5,064 11	
November 21	10 53	
December 2	23,392 11	
1872.		
January 4	44,467 94	
February 2	51,662 78	
March 4	93,286 46	
April 2	72,968 68	
May 3	58,516 06	
June 4	33,260 49	
June 30	76,879 40	
		466,654 27
Amount credited to the Treasurer of the United States on account of tax on salaries		92,029 73
Amount transferred from the appropriation for "pay to the Army" to that for "ordnance, ordnance-stores, and supplies," on account of deductions from the pay of officers and soldiers for ordnance and ordnance-stores, in accordance with Par. 1380, Revised Army Regulations of 1863		27,904 80
Amount transferred from the appropriation for "pay of the Army" to the books of the Third Auditor's Office, on account of deductions from the pay of soldiers for tobacco, pursuant to General Orders No. 63, War Department, Adjutant-General's Office, June 11, 1867		173,395 95
Amount transferred to the books of the Third Auditor's Office, on account of stoppages against officers for subsistence stores, quartermasters' stores, transportation, &c		7,837 47
Amount charged to officers on account of overpayments		4,781 66
Amount charged to officers on account of double payments		47,346 16
Amount credited to officers for overpayments refunded		343 73
Amount credited to officers for double payments refunded		9,619 41
Amount deposited by paymasters to close their accounts, being balances due United States on final settlement		57,315 46
Amount of balances found due paymasters, and paid them to close accounts		17,868 74
Amount paid to civilians under "reconstruction acts"		2,460 50
Amount of "lost checks" paid, in accordance with the act of February 2, 1872		2,047 35
Miscellaneous credits		1,827 48
Total		132,369,710 62

Accounts of paymasters on hand, June 30, 1871	3,071
Daft-rendezvous accounts on hand, June 30, 1871	30
Accounts of paymasters received during the year	376
Total	3,477
Accounts of paymasters audited and reported to the Second Comptroller during the year	2,336
Draft-rendezvous accounts examined and reported	14
	2,350
Accounts of paymasters remaining unexamined, June 30, 1872	1,111
Draft-rendezvous accounts on hand, under examination	16
Total number of accounts on hand, June 30, 1872	1,127
Number of letters written	29,593

During the year the accounts of one hundred and forty-eight paymasters were finally settled under the acts of March 16, 1868, and June 23, 1870. In one hundred and four cases balances amounting to $57,315.46 were found due to the United States, and were collected and turned into the Treasury. In the remaining forty-four cases, balances aggregating $17,868.74 were found due the paymasters, and were paid to them.

The accounts of seventy-five paymasters were finally settled, on which there is due the United States $667,031.35, including $463,712.79, the amount of J. L. Hodge's defalcation.

The accounts of five paymasters have been prepared for suit, involving an indebtedness of $38,810.62.

MISCELLANEOUS DIVISION.

The following statement shows the number of money-accounts on hand in this division at the commencement of the fiscal year, the number received and settled during the year, and the number remaining unsettled at the close of the year, together with the expenditure embraced in the settlement:

Ordnance, medical, and miscellaneous accounts on hand, June 30, 1871	618
Recruiting accounts on hand, June 30, 1871	955
Number of accounts received during the year	2,060
Total	3,633
Number of accounts settled during the year	1,805
Number of accounts remaining unsettled, June 30, 1871	1,828

The amounts involved in the above settlements are as follows:

Ordnance, medical, and miscellaneous:	
Ordnance Department	$686,096 18
Medical Department	484,891 72
Expended by disbursing officers out of the quartermasters' funds, not chargeable to said funds, but to certain appropriations on the books of this office	130,567 27
Secret-service fund	112,890 40
Expenses of military convicts	60,720 05
Contingencies of the Army	30,734 49
Telegraph-line from Yankton to Fort Sully, Dakota Territory, per act of March 3, 1871	16,000 00
Providing for the comfort of sick and discharged soldiers	13,016 24
Bronze equestrian statue of Lieutenant General Winfield Scott	10,000 00

Army Medical Museum and Library	$8,272 97	
Expenses of the Commanding General's Office	5,185 92	
Medical and surgical history and statistics	1,448 08	
Arming and equipping militia	1,273 86	
Contingencies of the Adjutant General's Department	1,206 45	
Library of the Surgeon General's Office	1,028 58	
Pay of the Army	691 75	
Expenses of recruiting	233 85	
Medals of honor	4 00	
Relief of Alexander J. McMillan, act March 3, 1871	1,017 57	
Relief of Mrs. Cecelia Barr, act May 31, 1872	1,000 00	
Relief of David L. Wright, act June 10, 1872	286 84	
Relief of John E. Wheeler, act April 19, 1871	247 74	
Relief of Granville M. Dodge, act May 6, 1870	111 00	
		$1,566,924 96
Regular recruiting:		
Expenses of recruiting	$89,292 42	
Bounty to volunteers and regulars	5,900 00	
Pay of the Army	978 51	
Subsistence of officers	652 20	
Medical and Hospital Department	139 97	
Pay in lieu of clothing for officers' servants	73 41	
		$97,036 51
Volunteer recruiting:		
Collecting, drilling, and organizing volunteers	401,302 24	
Bounty to volunteers and regulars	152,205 49	
Draft and substitute fund	6,633 15	
Medical and Hospital Department	77 28	
Ordnance, ordnance stores, &c	11 35	
		560,229 51
Local bounty:		
Pay of two and three years volunteers		2,134 75
Total		2,226,325 73

Three hundred and ninety-seven paymasters' accounts were examined for the necessary data as to double payments to officers, and two hundred and twenty-one double payments were discovered and reported. Several clerks have been temporarily withdrawn from this work for the purpose of expediting the examination of the voluminous accounts of General George W. Ballock, late chief disbursing officer of the Freedmen's Bureau.

Total number of letters written, 1,897.

INDIAN DIVISION.

General report of the Indian division for the fiscal year ended June 30, 1871:

Money-accounts of agents on hand June 30, 1871	521
Property-accounts of agents on hand June 30, 1871	577
Claims on hand June 30, 1871	7
Money-accounts of agents received during the year	912
Property-accounts received during the year	473
Claims received during the year	1,049
Total	3,539
Money-accounts of agents audited during the year	653
Property-accounts examined during the year	321
Claims settled during the year	996
Total	1,970

Money-accounts of agents on hand June 30, 1872	780
Property-accounts of agents on hand June 30, 1872	729
Claims on hand June 30, 1872	60
Total number of accounts, &c., on hand June 30, 1872	1,569
Amount involved in money-accounts audited	$2,243,655 83
Amount involved in claims settled	3,108,160 49
Total	5,351,816 32
Number of letters written	1,421

Transcripts of the accounts of two superintendents of Indian affairs were made during the year, for the purpose of entering suit against them for the recovery of $29,839.09 due United States.

There was also prepared a report to Congress of receipts and expenditures of the Indian Department during the fiscal year.

PAY AND BOUNTY DIVISION.

The following tabular statements exhibit in detail the operation of the two branches of this division during the year, together with the condition of the business, both at the commencement and close of the year.

EXAMINING BRANCH.

The work performed by the examining branch is shown by the four following tables:

Claims in cases of white soldiers.

Date.	Additional bounty, act July 28, 1866, and amendments.												Arrears of pay and original bounty.											
	Original claims.					Suspended claims.							Original claims.					Suspended claims.						
	Whole number examined.	Number found correct.	Number found incomplete and suspended.	Number rejected.	Number of duplicate applications found.	Whole number examined.	Number completed by additional evidence received.	Number again suspended: additional evidence insufficient.	Number rejected.	Total number of claims examined.	Number of letters written.		Whole number examined.	Number found correct.	Number found incomplete and suspended.	Number rejected.	Number of duplicate applications found.	Whole number examined.	Number completed by additional evidence received.	Number again suspended: additional evidence insufficient.	Number rejected.	Total number of claims examined.	Number of letters written.	
1871.																								
July	9	1	4	4	......	235	34	120	81	244	509		681	29	412	60	180	2,776	310	1,910	556	3,457	4,134	
August	7	4	......	......	3	347	66	221	60	354	509		692	48	377	109	158	2,460	310	1,836	314	3,152	3,854	
September	3	1	1	......	1	464	81	238	145	467	908		482	26	280	40	136	2,509	229	1,722	558	2,991	3,371	
October	7	3	4	......	1	458	84	247	127	465	......		474	75	219	58	122	1,485	201	1,058	226	1,959	3,537	
November	1	......	......	......	1	472	94	252	126	473	590		675	95	399	73	108	2,262	311	1,556	395	2,937	3,702	
December	5	......	5	......	......	412	75	257	80	417	731		567	44	372	60	91	2,381	349	1,522	510	2,948	3,547	
1872.																								
January	1	......	1	......	......	502	77	318	107	503	875		533	43	297	71	122	2,242	357	1,579	306	2,775	3,426	
February	6	1	4	......	1	596	68	336	192	602	879		520	36	287	57	140	1,966	263	1,477	226	2,486	3,017	
March	1	......	1	......	......	609	95	355	159	610	828		540	25	292	67	156	1,956	237	1,476	243	2,496	2,968	
April	233	32	172	29	......	500	73	327	100	733	1,276		777	45	437	58	237	2,063	242	1,505	316	2,840	3,386	
May	753	72	444	77	160	281	43	163	75	1,034	1,534		874	22	482	41	329	29,324	342	28,729	253	30,198	2,648	
June	577	109	285	100	83	8,689	68	8,602	19	9,266	1,539		336	33	96	34	173	24,334	201	24,066	47	24,670	1,810	
Total	1,603	223	921	210	249	13,565	858	11,436	1,271	15,168	10,178		7,151	521	3,950	728	1,952	75,758	3,352	68,456	3,950	82,909	39,406	

Bounty-claims under act of April 22, 1872.

Date.	Original claims.					Suspended claims.				Total number of claims examined.	No. of letters written.
	Whole number examined.	No. found correct.	No. found incomplete and suspended.	No. rejected.	No. of duplicate applications found.	Whole number examined.	No. completed by additional evidence received.	No. again suspended; additional evidence incomplete.	No. rejected.		
1872.											
May	1, 323	143	998	157	25	.....	.....	.....	.....	1, 323	.....
June	2, 290	511	1, 335	403	41	860	200	599	61	3, 150	3, 929
Total	3, 613	654	2, 333	560	66	860	200	599	61	4, 473	3, 929

Claims in cases of colored soldiers including both arrears of pay and bounties.

Date.	Original claims.					Suspended claims.				Total number of claims examined.	No. of letters written.
	Whole number examined.	No. found correct.	No. found incomplete and suspended.	No. rejected.	No. of duplicate applications found.	Whole number examined.	No. completed by additional evidence received.	No. again suspended; additional evidence incomplete.	No. rejected.		
1871.											
July	406	3	92	131	180	1, 030	189	796	45	1, 436	1, 368
August	259	1	93	7	158	1, 622	175	1, 327	120	1, 881	2, 098
September	143	2	87	6	48	1, 270	132	867	271	1, 413	1, 616
October	152	6	94	5	47	958	144	665	149	1, 110	1, 147
November	100	......	55	3	42	890	152	615	123	990	1, 074
December	106	2	68	8	28	1, 138	194	839	105	1, 244	1, 353
1872.											
January	134	1	81	2	50	1, 419	130	1, 032	257	1, 553	1, 578
February	124	1	87	2	34	1, 181	142	915	124	1, 305	1, 301
March	137	3	73	8	53	1, 211	119	854	238	1, 348	1, 328
April	126	......	76	3	47	1, 208	98	989	121	1, 334	1, 349
May	96	......	59	8	29	1, 054	133	878	43	1, 150	1, 342
June	167	2	90	14	61	856	87	739	30	1, 023	1, 044
Total	1, 950	21	955	197	777	13, 837	1, 695	10, 516	1, 626	15, 787	16, 798

SUMMARY.

Claims in cases of colored soldiers including both arrears of pay and bounty.

1871.											
July	1, 096	33	508	195	360	4, 041	533	2, 826	682	5, 137	6, 011
August	958	53	470	116	319	4, 429	551	3, 384	494	5, 387	6, 451
September	628	29	368	46	185	4, 243	442	2, 827	974	4, 871	5, 895
October	633	84	317	63	169	2, 901	429	1, 970	502	3, 534	4, 684
November	776	95	454	76	151	3, 624	557	2, 423	644	4, 400	5, 366
December	678	46	445	68	119	3, 931	618	2, 618	695	4, 609	5, 631
1872.											
January	668	44	379	73	172	4, 163	564	2, 929	670	4, 831	5, 879
February	650	38	378	59	175	3, 743	473	2, 728	542	4, 393	5, 197
March	678	28	366	75	209	3, 776	451	2, 685	640	4, 454	5, 324
April	1, 136	77	685	90	284	3, 771	413	2, 821	537	4, 907	6, 011
May	3, 046	237	1, 983	283	543	30, 659	518	29, 770	371	33, 705	5, 524
June	3, 370	655	1, 806	551	358	34, 739	556	34, 026	157	38, 109	8, 328
Total	14, 317	1, 419	8, 159	1, 695	3, 044	104, 020	6, 105	91, 007	6, 908	118, 337	70, 301

SETTLING BRANCH.

The following tables show the work performed by the settling branch of this division during the year:

Claims in cases of white soldiers.

Date.	Additional bounty, act July 28, 1866.					Arrears of pay, &c., act July 22, 1861.				
	Number of claims.				Amount involved.	Number of claims.				Amount involved.
	Received.	Allowed.	Rejected.	Whole number disposed of.		Received.	Allowed.	Rejected.	Whole number disposed of.	
1871.										
July	9	173	50	223	$15, 090 00	728	281	73	354	$39, 746 20
August	10	83	22	105	14, 050 00	672	437	156	593	62, 352 94
September	13	108	77	185	13, 850 00	840	333	357	690	48, 544 93
October	7	119	52	171	14, 157 14	628	352	194	546	65, 394 88
November	6	105	9	114	13, 150 00	479	399	83	482	87, 794 12
December	9	94	17	113	12, 600 00	485	447	27	474	80, 290 72
1872.										
January	7	126	73	199	16, 269 60	548	501	73	574	76, 098 77
February	13	69	35	104	9, 091 84	544	382	80	462	61, 467 76
March	9	98	11	109	11, 619 93	650	345	119	464	48, 038 82
April	1, 838	109	6	115	13, 400 00	1, 173	364	17	381	49, 246 51
May	1, 052	128	53	181	15, 722 12	890	281	20	301	36, 642 38
June	475	121	14	135	16, 731 80	830	236	55	291	41, 277 22
Total	3, 448	1, 333	421	1, 754	166, 652 43	8, 473	4, 358	1, 254	5, 612	696, 895 25

Bounty-claims under act April 22, 1872.

Date.	Number of claims.				Amount involved.
	Received.	Allowed.	Rejected.	Whole number disposed of.	
1872.					
May	*11, 163	65	40	105	$9, 200 00
June	577	335	5	340	27, 750 00
Total	11, 740	400	45	445	36, 950 00

* In this number are included 10,306 claims filed prior to the passage of the act of April 22, 1872, but not acted upon.

Claims in cases of colored soldiers, including both arrears of pay and bounties.

Date.	Number of claims.				Amount involved.
	Received.	Allowed.	Rejected.	Whole number disposed of.	
1871.					
July	94	221	125	346	$39, 459 55
August	90	168	74	242	29, 536 47
September	103	160	127	287	26, 782 55
October	70	178	22	200	32, 378 60
November	89	210	34	244	35, 717 70
December	55	192	59	251	34, 053 76
1872.					
January	96	164	5	169	27, 113 34
February	88	163	12	175	26, 464 68
March	86	227	3	230	41, 116 68
April	105	148	12	160	25, 490 09
May	37	205	13	218	32, 709 53
June	113	170	20	190	26, 839 66
Total	1, 026	2, 206	506	2, 712	377, 662 61

SUMMARY.

Date.	Number of claims.				Amount involved.	No. of letters written.
	Received.	Allowed.	Rejected.	Total number disposed of.		
1871.						
July	831	675	248	923	$95, 195 75	3, 790
August	772	688	252	940	105, 939 41	3, 039
September	956	601	561	1, 162	89, 177 48	2, 418
October	705	649	268	917	111, 930 62	2, 411
November	574	714	126	840	136, 661 82	2, 352
December	549	733	105	838	126, 944 48	2, 360
1872.						
January	651	791	151	942	119, 501 71	2, 898
February	645	614	127	741	97, 024 28	2, 247
March	751	670	133	803	100, 775 43	2, 506
April	3, 116	621	35	656	88, 136 60	2, 431
May	13, 142	679	126	805	94, 274 03	2, 760
June	1, 995	862	94	956	112, 598 68	1, 488
Total	24, 687	8, 297	2, 226	10, 523	1, 278, 160 29	30, 700

Consolidated statement showing the operation of the entire division for the fiscal year ended June 30, 1872.

Date.	Number of claims.			Whole number disposed of.	Amount involved.	Number of letters written.	Number of certificates issued.
	Received.	Allowed.	Rejected, including duplicates.				
1871.							
July	831	675	1,485	2,160	$95,195 75	9,801	761
August	772	688	1,181	1,869	105,939 41	9,490	707
September	956	601	1,766	2,367	89,177 48	8,313	611
October	705	649	1,002	1,651	111,930 62	7,095	705
November	574	714	997	1,711	136,661 82	7,718	732
December	549	733	987	1,720	126,944 48	7,991	558
1872.							
January	651	791	1,066	1,857	119,501 71	8,777	724
February	645	614	903	1,517	97,024 28	7,444	831
March	751	670	1,057	1,727	100,775 43	7,830	661
April	3,116	621	946	1,567	88,136 60	8,442	760
May	13,142	679	1,323	2,002	94,274 03	8,284	730
June	1,995	862	1,160	2,022	112,598 68	9,816	562
Total	24,687	8,207	13,873	22,170	1,278,160 29	101,001	8,342

In addition to the above there have been made in this division nineteen settlements on account of fines, forfeitures, stoppages, &c., against soldiers of the Regular Army, embracing $38,673.64, paid to the treasurer of the Soldiers' Home in accordance with the acts of Congress of March 3, 1851, and March 3, 1859, making the total number of settlements 8,316 and the total disbursements $1,316,833.93.

Number of claims under act July 28, 1866, (white,) on hand June 30, 1871	7,364
Number of claims for arrears of pay and original bounty, (white,) on hand June 30, 1871	23,960
Number of colored claims on hand June 30, 1871	8,171
Total number of claims on hand June 30, 1871	39,495

Number of claims under act of July 28, 1866, (white,) on hand June 30, 1872	7,321
Number of claims for arrears of pay and bounty (white) on hand June 30, 1872	19,337
Number of colored claims on hand June 30, 1872	4,171
Number of bounty-claims under act of April 22, 1872, on hand June 30, 1872	11,183
Total number of claims on hand June 30, 1872	42,012

The following statement shows the condition of the claims on hand:

Number of claims suspended awaiting evidence to be filed by claimants or their attorneys	27,428
Number of claims ready for settlement	3,587
Number of claims unexamined June 30, 1872	10,997
Total	42,012

PROPERTY DIVISION.

The following statement shows the progress and condition of business in this division:

Number of property-returns of officers on hand June 30, 1872 ... 34,558

Number of property-returns of officers received during the year:

Ordnance, ordnance stores, &c.	Regulars	96	
	Volunteers	1,355	

Clothing, camp and garrison equipage.	Regulars	4,024	
	Volunteers	87	
			5,562
Total			40,120
Number of returns settled during the year			23,265
Number of returns on hand June 30, 1872			16,855

Number of certificates of non-indebtednes issued to officers	723
Amount charged to officers for property not accounted for	$2,749 63
Number of returns registered	5,562
Number of letters written	9,332
Number of letters recorded	5,077

In addition to the above, 214,410 returns rendered by officers of volunteers in previous years, but not heretofore reported, have been settled under the provisions of the act of Congress approved June 23, 1870.

DIVISION OF INQUIRIES AND REPLIES.

The work performed in the division of inquiries and replies during the year ended June 30, 1872, is as follows:

Number of inquiries on hand unanswered June 30, 1871 3,666

Officers making inquiry.	Number received.	Number answered.
Adjutant General	7,048	5,901
Paymaster General	310	309
Quartermaster General	175	174
Commissary General of Subsistence	224	224
Commissioner of Pensions	1,025	1,039
Third Auditor	1,511	1,488
Fourth Auditor	18	25
Freedmen's Bureau	118	118
Other sources	35,376	20,031
Total	45,805	29,309

Number of inquiries on hand June 30, 1872	20,162
Rolls and vouchers copied for the Adjutant-General, Paymaster-General, and Department of Justice	1,116
Rolls and vouchers copied for preservation in this office	1,719
Rolls and vouchers partially copied and traced for preservation in this office	2,891
Signatures verified	3,300
Number of letters written	22,152

In addition to the work above reported, a large amount of miscellaneous copying has been done, and the general business of the division has quadrupled since the last report.

DIVISION FOR THE INVESTIGATION OF FRAUDS.

During the year 4,697 cases have been under examination, investigation, and prosecution by this division. Abstracts of facts have been prepared in 476 cases, 316 have been finally disposed of, and 148 cases have been prepared for suit and prosecution through the various United States district courts.

The amounts recovered by suit and otherwise are as follows:

Money recovered by draft, certificate of deposit, and current funds, and turned into the Treasury to be credited to the proper appropriations	$6,521 88
Amount recovered from the Freedmen's Bureau and parties implicated in the prosecution of fraudulent colored claims and turned into the Treasury	6,049 09

Money unlawfully withheld by claim-agents and secured to the proper claimants by the interposition of this office	$4,945 04
Money recovered as interest	1,225 50
Amount of Treasury certificates and checks issued in fraudulent claims recovered and canceled	519 69
Money recovered on forged checks and turned over to United States disbursing officers for appropriate credit	707 13
Money secured to United States Assistant Treasurer, New York, by reclamation upon the bank through which a forged check was negotiated	100 00
Money recovered as fines, but carried to the credit of the judiciary fund	300 00
Total	20,368 33
Amount of bond of indemnity on hand	$1,700 00

There are now under examination and investigation 4,381 cases, involving forgery, fraud, unlawful withholding of money, overpayments, &c., as follows:

Fraudulent and contested claims in cases of white soldiers, in which settlements had been made prior to notice of fraud or receipt of adverse claims.	1,271
Fraudulent and contested unsettled claims in cases of white soldiers	535
Fraudulent and contested claims in cases of colored soldiers, in which settlements had been made prior to notice of fraud or receipt of adverse claims.	707
Unsettled claims of widows of colored soldiers involving fraud in the marriage evidence	204
Unsettled contested claims in cases of colored soldiers	276
Unsettled claims in cases of colored soldiers, in which the evidence of heirship is believed to have been manufactured by claim-agents and their abettors	1,064
Cases alleged to have been paid by the Pay Department upon fraudulent papers, and awaiting the action of the Court of Claims	76
Cases involving overpayments to United States Army officers in which civil actions are being instituted for the recovery of the money	248
Total	4,381

Number of claims on hand June 30, 1871	4,036	
Number of claims received during the year	661	
		4,697
Number of claims finally disposed of during the year		316
Number of claims on hand June 30, 1872		4,381
Number of letters written		4,975

There are also filed in this division a large number of letters and informal complaints regarding the malpractice and swindling operations of attorneys, which have so far been acted upon only with a view of debarring such attorneys from further practice in the prosecution of claims, but which are to be fully acted upon whenever the question of liability shall have been determined by the United States courts in cases of a similar character.

ARCHIVES DIVISION.

The following statement shows the work performed by this division:

Number of accounts received from the Paymaster-General		376
Number of accounts on file awaiting settlement		1,111
Number of confirmed settlements received from the Second Comptroller, verified, briefed, and transferred to permanent files:		
Paymasters'	485	
Indian	1,093	
Miscellaneous	1,153	
		2,731
Number of paymasters' settlements re-examined		2,209

Number of settlements withdrawn and returned to files 3,371
Number of vouchers withdrawn and returned to accounts 43,954
Number of abstracts of accounts bound in covers 323
Number of duplicate bounty vouchers examined for certificates of payment .. 92,062
Number of mutilated muster and pay rolls repaired 16,794
Number of letters written 375

REGISTRY AND CORRESPONDENCE DIVISION.

Statement of work performed by the registry and correspondence division during the fiscal year:

Number of letters received 27,808
Number of letters written 31,103
Number of letters recorded 2,123
Number of letters referred to other bureaus 1,709
Number of dead-letters received and registered 3,247
Number of claims received, briefed, and registered 22,023
Number of miscellaneous vouchers received, stamped, and distributed 61,211
Number of letters, with additional evidence in the case of suspended claims, received, briefed, and registered 19,668
Number of pay and bounty certificates examined, registered, and mailed 7,657
Number of pay and bounty certificates examined, registered, and sent to the Paymaster General, in accordance with joint resolution of April 10, 1869 ... 5,353
Number of reports calling for requisitions sent to the War Department....... 454

For convenience of reference, I annex the following consolidated statement, showing the various classes of accounts settled in the office, the number of each class on hand at the beginning of the year, the number received and disposed of during the year, and the number on hand at the end of the year; also, the amount involved in settlements:

Description of accounts.	On hand June 30, 1871.	Received during the year.	Disposed of during the year.	On hand June 30, 1872.	Am't involved in settlements.	Number of letters written.
Paymasters	3,101	376	2,350	1,127	$131,502,191 46	29,593
Indian agents	521	912	653	780	2,243,655 83	
Indian agents, (property)	577	473	321	729	....	1,421
Indian claims	7	1,049	996	60	3,108,160 49	
Bounty, arrears of pay, &c	39,495	24,687	22,170	42,012	1,278,160 29	101,001
Ordnance, medical, and miscellaneous	618				1,506,924 96	
Regular recruiting					97,036 51	
Volunteer recruiting	955	2,060	1,805	1,828	560,229 51	1,697
Claims for return of local bounty					2,134 75	
Ordnance and Quartermaster's Department, (property.)	34,556	5,562	23,265	16,855	....	9,332
Soldiers' Home	....	33	33	....	....	....
National Asylum	....	14	14	....	....	....
Total	79,832	35,166	51,607	63,391	141,264,686 60	143,244

Besides the number of letters stated in the above table, there have been written 59,414 relating to the miscellaneous business of the office, making a total of 202,658.

The average number of clerks employed during the year was 269.

The following statements and reports were prepared and transmitted during the year:

Annual report to the Secretary of the Treasury of the transactions of the office during the fiscal year.

Annual statement of the recruiting fund, prepared for the Adjutant General of the Army.

Annual statement of the contingencies of the Army, prepared for the Secretary of War.

Annual report of balances on the books of this office remaining unaccounted for more than one year, transmitted to the First Comptroller.

Annual report of balances on the books of this office remaining unaccounted for more than two years, transmitted to the First Comptroller.

Annual statement of the clerks and other persons employed in this office during the year 1871, or any part thereof, showing the amount paid to each on account of salary, with place of residence, &c., in pursuance of the eleventh section of the act of August 26, 1842, and resolution of the House of Representatives of January 13, 1846, transmitted to the Secretary of the Treasury.

List of employés in this office on September 30, 1871, showing the State or Territory from which each person was appointed to office, the State or country in which he was born, and the compensation given to each, transmitted to the Register of the Treasury in accordance with the acts of Congress of September 5, 1859, and March 2, 1861.

Monthly tabular statement, showing the business transacted in the office during the month and the number of accounts remaining unsettled at the close of the month, transmitted to the Secretary of the Treasury.

Monthly report of absence from duties of employés of this office, with reasons therefor, transmitted to the Secretary of the Treasury.

Pay-rolls, upon which payment was made to the employés of this office, prepared semi-monthly.

Earnest effort has been made to keep up the general work of the office and dispose of the large number of claims for bounty that have been presented under the two acts of April 22, 1872, without an increase of the clerical force. All that was desired has not been accomplished, but there is good reason to expect that those bounty-claims will soon be disposed of.

Much credit is due the gentlemen of the office for their faithful performance of duty.

I have the honor to be, very respectfully,

E. B. FRENCH,
Auditor.

Hon. GEORGE S. BOUTWELL,
Secretary of the Treasury.

REPORT OF THE THIRD AUDITOR.

REPORT

OF

THE THIRD AUDITOR OF THE TREASURY.

TREASURY DEPARTMENT,
Third Auditor's Office, August 30, 1872.

SIR: In compliance with instructions from your office and the requirements of law, I have the honor to transmit herewith the following report of the business operations of this office for the fiscal year ended June 30, 1872:

BOOK-KEEPER'S DIVISION.

The duties devolving upon this division are, in general, to keep the appropriation and money accounts of the office.

The annexed statement of the financial operations of the office during the fiscal year ended June 30, 1872, exhibits the amounts drawn on specific apppropriations, except those under direction of the Chief of Engineers of the Army, which are aggregated and entered under the general heading "Engineer Department." It also shows the repayments into the Treasury for the same period.

The average number of clerks engaged in this division during the period embraced in this report has been nine, and that number now constitutes the active force of the division.

The number of requisitions drawn on the Secretary of the Treasury by the Secretaries of War and of the Interior for the fiscal year ended June 30, 1872, was 3,341, amounting to $58,498,475.02, as follows, viz:

	Advances to officers and agents.	Claims paid during the year.	Second and Third Auditor's transfers during the year.	Totals.
Quartermaster's Department, (regular supplies)	$4,315,744 94	$285,995 93	$204,991 15	$4,806,732 02
Incidental expenses Quartermaster's Department	1,225,417 95	38,566 09	4,113 88	1,268,097 92
Barracks and quarters	1,605,876 95	123,240 69	2,093 79	1,731,211 43
Army transportation	3,697,459 20	1,131,257 75	42,801 50	4,871,518 45
Officers' transportation	....	1,471 58	36,778 52	38,250 10
Cavalry and artillery horses	450,876 88	73,191 00	....	524,067 88
Clothing of the Army	654,946 91	3,622 78	1,823,782 17	2,482,351 86
National cemeteries	261,636 84	55 00	....	261,691 84
Subsistence of the Army	2,667,372 39	83,552 60	2,583 05	2,753,508 04
Engineer Department, (sundry appropriations)	6,981,657 70	1,640 12	23,915 84	7,007,213 66
Pensions, invalid	9,532,400 00	198 67	....	9,532,598 67
Pensions, widows' and others	18,323,600 00	2,334 39	203,915 75	18,529,850 14
Pensions, war of 1812	3,115,500 00	....	....	3,115,500 00
Relief of destitute in District of Columbia	12,000 00	....	....	12,000 00
Commutation of rations to prisoners of war	5,000 00	....	....	5,000 00
Support of the Bureau of Refugees, Freedmen, &c.	173,919 21	....	269 90	174,189 11
Contingencies of the Army	1,675 11	....	....	1,675 11
Gun-boats on western rivers	....	....	26,695 68	26,695 68
Collecting, organizing, and drilling volunteers	....	372 65	....	372 65

	Advances to officers and agents.	Claims paid during the year.	Second and Third Auditor's transfers during the year.	Totals.
Mexican hostilities			$44 35	$44 35
Purchase of heating and cooking stoves	$5,080 40	$186 74	30,094 13	35,361 27
Signal-service	5,000 00			5,000 00
Observation and report of storms	163,501 00			163,501 00
Current and ordinary expenses Military Academy	60,814 00			60,814 00
Miscellaneous items and incidental expenses Military Academy	26,180 00			26,180 00
Horses and other property lost in the military service, act March 3, 1849		80,437 19		80,437 19
Pay of Washington and Oregon Indian-war claims		30 89		30 89
Services of Washington and Oregon volunteers		300 00		300 00
Pay for the use of the Corcoran gallery of art, &c		125,000 00		125,000 00
Payment of members of certain military organizations		307,771 82	703 46	308,475 28
Reimbursing Ohio and Indiana for expenses incurred in suppressing rebellion		13 40	22 60	36 00
Reimbursing Nebraska for expenses incurred in suppressing rebellion		6,529 02		6,529 02
Payment of Iowa for advances, &c., in 1857 and 1859		871 84		871 84
Refunding to States expenses incurred, &c		296,145 61		296,145 61
Refunding to California expenses incurred		538 11		538 11
Act for the relief of Robert Kirkpatrick		20,523 00		20,523 00
Act for the relief of Noah Fisher		420 00		420 00
Act for the relief of Shadrack Saunders and others		33 60		33 60
Act for the relief of Joseph Segar, of Virginia		15,000 00		15,000 00
Act for the relief of Robert B. Williamson		2,567 00		2,567 00
Act for the relief of Henry Otis		3,000 00		3,000 00
Act for the relief of Charles and Henry Spencer		8,196 50		8,196 50
Act for the relief of L. B. Mitchell and other		466 50		466 50
Act for the relief of L. Merchant & Co		3,700 00		3,700 00
Claims of loyal citizens for supplies, &c., act March 3, 1871		191,707 17		191,707 17
Payment of tax on salaries			1,072 23	1,072 23
	53,285,659 48	2,808,937 54	2,403,878 00	58,498,475 02

REPAYMENTS.

The number of credit and counter requisitions drawn by the Secretaries of War and of the Interior on sundry persons in favor of the Treasurer of the United States is 709, on which repayments into the Treasury during the fiscal year ended June 29, 1872, have been made through the office of the Third Auditor as follows:

On account of deposits	$5,943,883 43
On account of Third Auditor's transfers	2,382,409 04
On account of Second Auditor's transfers	273,509 51
On account of War Department transfers	1,212,231 82
Total	9,812,033 80

The aggregate amount of $3,392,992.90, standing to the credit of 95 "specific appropriations" respectively, has been carried to the surplus fund, by warrant No. 130, dated June 29, 1872.

Report of business transacted in the Third Auditor's Office, United States Treasury, in the year ended June 30, 1872.

Description of accounts.	Number of accounts remaining on hand June 30, 1871.	Number of accounts received in the year ended June 30, 1872.	Number of accounts settled in the year ended June 30, 1872.		Number of accounts unsettled June 30, 1872.	
	Monthly.	Monthly.	Monthly.	Amount involved.	Monthly.	Amount involved.
Quartermasters' money	284	6,164	5,616	$43,329,640 02	832	$17,863,150 52
Quartermasters' property	3,766	12,433	12,332	....	3,867	....
Commissaries' money	1,264	1,677	2,524	4,644,159 78	417	501,941 83
Pension agents' money	861	684	900	40,000,205 68	645	21,319,856 47
Engineers' money	141	160	212	4,387,022 36	89	4,918,071 84
Refugees, Freedmen, and Abandoned Lands' money.	45	37	72	1,700,556 39	10	49,802 02
Refugees, Freedmen, and Abandoned Lands' property.	35	60	95	....	....	....
Signal-officers' money	....	80	....	....	80	207,102 88
Signal officers' property	91	5	96	....	....	....
Total	6,487	21,300	21,847	94,061,584 23	5,940	44,859,925 56
Claims for horses lost	5,331	214	386	$65,629 57	5,159	$930,425 05
steamboats destroyed	70	7	8	108,400 00	69	560,873 07
Oregon war	822	169	149	15,725 04	842	65,797 51
miscellaneous	5,024	5,523	3,761	3,097,973 21	6,786	4,190,774 57
State war	7	10	11	384,830 25	6	661,457 81
Total	11,254	5,923	4,315	3,672,558 07	12,862	6,409,328 01

QUARTERMASTER'S DIVISION.

The accounts of quartermasters cover a wide and varied range of disbursements and property accountability, embracing disbursements for barracks, quarters, hospitals, store-houses, offices, stables, forage and transportation of all Army supplies, Army clothing, camp and garrison equipage; the purchase of cavalry and artillery horses, fuel, forage, straw, material for bedding, stationery; hired men; per diem to extra-duty men; of the pursuit and apprehension of deserters; of the burial of officers and soldiers; of hired escorts; of expresses, interpreters, spies, and guides; of veterinary surgeons and medicines for horses; of supplying posts with water, and generally the proper and authorized expenses for the movements and operations of an army not expressly assigned to any other department. The "returns" are an account of the disposition made of all property paid for by the Quartermaster's Department, (except clothing, camp and garrison equipage, which are accounted for to the Second Auditor.)

The tabular statement herewith exhibits in a condensed form the results of the labors of the force employed in this division.

	Money accounts.		Property returns.	Supplemental settlements.		
	No.	Amount involved.		Property.	Money.	Amount involved.
On hand, per last report, June 30, 1871	284	$16,362,177 00	3,766	....	....	....
Received during the current year	6,164	44,830,613 54	12,433	11,095	613	$3,220,900 19
Total	6,448	61,192,790 54	16,199	11,095	613	3,220,900 19
Reported during the current year	5,616	$43,329,640 02	12,332	11,095	613	$3,220,900 19
Remaining unsettled June 30, 1872	832	17,863,150 52	3,867	....	....	....
Total	6,448	61,192,790 54	16,199	11,095	613	3,220,900 19

	Signal-accounts.			Total.	
	Property.	Money.	Amount involved.	No.	Amount involved.
On hand, per last report, June 30, 1871	91			4,141	$16,362,177 00
Received during the current year	5	80	$207,102 88	30,390	48,258,616 61
Total	96	80	207,102 88	34,531	64,620,793 61
Reported during the current year	96			29,752	$46,550,540 21
Remaining unsettled June 30, 1872		80	$207,102 88	4,779	18,070,253 40
Total	96	80	207,102 88	34,531	64,620,793 61

Number of letters sent out from the division during the year, 17,444; average number of clerks employed, $94\frac{8}{12}$.

A comparison of the above with my last annual report will show a large increase in the number of accounts and returns received and settled, without a corresponding increase in the amounts involved. This increase is accounted for in this way: Prior to the rebellion, accounts and returns were rendered quarterly, and after administrative action was had by the proper military bureau. Generally each account and return as rendered was transmitted to this office by a separate letter, and in making entries of receipts it became customary to consider a letter of transmittal and an account or return as numerically the same. In consequence of inadequate clerical force to dispose of the largely increased business accumulated in the Quartermaster-General's Office, all the accounts or returns of any one officer which had been examined at the time of transmittal were forwarded with one letter, which circumstance appears to have been overlooked in entering the receipt by this office, as the letters continued to be considered as synonymous with an account, when, in point of fact, the letter covered several accounts—so that the record of receipts really showed the number of letters of transmittal of the Quartermaster-General instead of the number of accounts and returns received. When this was discovered all the unexamined accounts and returns on file in this office were counted, and showed the following result on 31st August, 1871: Quartermaster accounts, per count, 2,683; quartermaster accounts, per register, 465; quartermaster returns, per count, 7,165; quartermaster returns, per register, 2,095; signal-returns, per count, 6; signal-returns per register, 2—so that the number actually on hand exceeded the number as shown by the register as follows: Quartermaster accounts, excess 2,218; quartermaster returns, excess 5,070; signal-returns, excess 4. The accounts of the officers are rendered monthly, and each monthly account is regarded and counted as one account.

SUBSISTENCE DIVISION.

This division audits the accounts of all commissaries and acting commissaries of subsistence in the Army, whose duties are to purchase the provisions and stores necessary for the feeding of the Army, and see to their proper distribution. These commissaries render monthly money-accounts, with proper vouchers, for disbursements of the funds intrusted to them, together with a provision-return, and vouchers showing the disposition of provisions and stores purchased and received during each month. These accounts are received monthly through the office of the Commissary-General of Subsistence, and are every six months (or oftener, if the officer ceases to disburse) examined and audited in this division, and the money-accounts and vouchers, together with a certified statement of their condition, referred to the Second Comptroller of the Treasury for his decision thereon. Upon their receipt back from the Comptroller with the statement approved, the officers are then officially notified of the result of said examinations and are called upon by this office to adjust or explain any omissions or errors that may have been discovered. The money and provision accounts, together with vouchers and papers belonging thereto, are, after examination, placed in the settled files of this division for future reference and remain permanently in the custody of this office.

Annual report of the subsistence division for the fiscal year ended June 30, 1872.

	Subsistence accounts.			Refugees, Freedmen and Abandoned Lands accounts.		
	Money accounts.		Provision returns.			Property returns.
	No.	Amount involved.		No.	Amount involved.	
On hand, per last report, June 30, 1871	1,264	$973,405 39	155	45	$1,334,156 83	35
Received during fiscal year	1,677	4,172,696 22	3,043	37	415,201 58	60
Total	2,941	5,146,101 61	3,198	82	1,749,358 41	95
Audited during fiscal year	2,524	4,644,159 78	2,793	72	1,699,556 39	95
Remaining on hand June 30, 1872	417	501,941 83	405	10	49,802 02	.....

Number of vouchers examined, 78,772; difference-sheets written, 860; letters written, 1,069; queries answered, 1,591. Average number of clerks employed, 8.

ENGINEER DIVISION.

This division is employed in the examination of the accounts of the officers and agents of the Engineer Department, who, under direction of the Chief of Engineers of the Army, (except the Superintendent of the Military Academy at West Point, whose disbursements are directed by the Inspector-General,) disburse moneys out of various appropriations—now 248 in number—made from time to time by Congress, for works of a public nature, which may be classed under the following general heads, viz:

The purchase of sites and materials for, and construction and repairs of, the various fortifications throughout the United States;

Construction and repairs of roads, bridges, bridge-trains, &c., for armies in the field;

Surveys on the Atlantic and Pacific coasts;

Examination and surveys of the northern and western lakes and rivers;

Construction and repairs of breakwaters;

Repairs and improvement of harbors, both on sea and lake coasts;

Improvement of rivers and purchase of snag and dredge-boats for the same; and

The expenses of the Military Academy at West Point.

The average number of clerks employed on the division for the year ended June 30, 1872, was three; and the transactions of the division for the same period are shown by the following statement, viz:

	Accounts.		Supplemental and transfer settlements.	
	Number of quarters.	Amount involved.	No.	Amount admitted.
On hand per last report, June 30, 1871	141	$3,405,999 77	...	...
Received during the year	160	5,899,094 43	...	...
Total	301	9,305,094 20	...	...
Reported during the year	212	4,387,022 36	59	$5,600 24
Remaining on hand June 30, 1872	89	4,918,071 84	...	...
Total	301	9,305,094 20	59	5,600 24

There are now on hand only five quarters of engineer officers' money accounts for periods prior to 1871 unsettled, viz, five of the fourth quarter, 1870.

All of the balances on old accounts (some of them dating back from twenty to forty years) have been re-examined during the year, and either "closed," or where any considerable balance has been found due the United States, the officer, if alive, has been notified; or, if dead, out of the service, or not to be found, the papers have been forwarded to the collection-division.

STATE WAR-CLAIMS DIVISION.

The duties of this division embrace the settlement, under the various acts and resolutions of Congress, of all claims of the several States for costs, charges, and expenses properly incurred by them for enrolling, subsisting, clothing, supplying, arming, equipping, paying, and transporting their troops employed by the United States in aiding to suppress the recent insurrection against the United States. Also, claims on account of Indian and other border invasions.

	Original accounts.		Suspended account, special settlements.	
	No.	Amount.	No.	Amount.
On hand June 30, 1871	7	$284,701 73	86	$4,420,166 50
Received during the fiscal year ended June 30, 1872	10	761,526 33	11	227,303 95
Total	17	1,046,288 06	97	4,647,470 45
Reported during the fiscal year ended June 30, 1872	11	384,830 25	21	468,533 94
Balance remaining June 30, 1872	6	661,457 81	76	4,178,936 51

Number of letters written during the year, 119.
Number of clerks employed during the year, 3.

CLAIMS DIVISION.

The duties of this division embrace the settlement of claims of a miscellaneous character, arising in the various branches of service in the War Department, growing out of the purchase or appropriation of supplies and stores for the Army; the purchase, hire, or appropriation of water-craft, railroad stock, horses, wagons, and other means of transportation; the transportation contracts of the Army; the occupation of real estate for camps, barracks, hospitals, fortifications, &c.; the hire of employés, mileage, court-martial fees, traveling-expenses, communications, &c.; claims for compensation for vessels, railroad-cars, and engines, &c., lost in the military service; claims growing out of the Oregon and Washington war of 1855 and 1856, and other Indian war claims; claims of various descriptions under special acts of Congress, and claims not otherwise assigned.

The following statements show the business transacted by this division during the fiscal year ended June 30, 1872, and the condition of the business at the commencement and at the end thereof.

1.—*Miscellaneous claims.*

	Number.	Amount claimed.	Amount allowed.
On hand July 1, 1871	5,024	*$4,140,073 80	
Received during the year	5,523	†3,148,673 98	
Total	10,547	7,288,747 78	
Disposed of during the year	3,761	‡3,097,973 21	$2,217,724 01
On hand June 30, 1872	6,786	§4,190,774 57	

* This is the amount claimed in 3,753 cases, the amounts claimed in the others (1,271) not being stated.
† This is the amount claimed in 5,322 cases, the amounts claimed in the others (201) not being stated.
‡ This is the amount claimed in 3,613 cases, the amounts claimed in the others (148) not being stated.
§ This is the amount claimed in 5,462 cases, the amounts claimed in the others (1,324) not being stated.

2.—*Oregon and Washington Indian war claims.*

	Number.	Amount claimed.	Amount allowed.
On hand July 1, 1871	822	*$65,615 19	
Received during the year	169	†15,907 36	
Total	991	81,522 55	
Disposed of during the year	149	‡15,725 04	$12,503 25
On hand June 30, 1872	842	§65,797 51	

* This is the amount claimed in 412 cases, the amounts claimed in the others (410) not being stated. In the report for the year ended June 30, 1871, the cases remaining on hand in which the amounts claimed were stated were entered as 407, and those in which the amounts claimed were not stated as 415; but the correct numbers are as above stated.
† This is the amount claimed in 77 cases, the amounts claimed in the others (92) not being stated.
‡ This is the amount claimed in 84 cases, the amounts claimed in the others (65) not being stated.
§ This is the amount claimed in 405 cases, the amounts claimed in the others (437) not being stated.

3.—*Lost vessels, act of March* 3, 1849.

	No.	Amount claimed.	Amount allowed.
On hand July 1, 1871	70	$604,682 11	
Received during the year	7	64,590 96	
Total	77	669,273 07	
Disposed of during the year	8	108,400 00	$61,755 69
On hand June 30, 1872	69	560,873 07	

HORSE-CLAIMS DIVISION.

This division is engaged in settling claims for compensation for the loss of horses and equipage sustained by officers or enlisted men while in the military service of the United States, and for the loss of horses, mules, oxen, wagons, sleighs, and harness, while in said service by impressment or contract.

The number of claims received and docketed during the year is 205, in which the aggregate amount claimed is $44,790.56. The number settled and finally disposed of during the same period (including those received prior to, as well as during the year) is 386, in which the aggregate amount claimed is $65,629.57, and on which the aggregate amount allowed is $44,447.77.

There have been during the year 419 briefs made; 3,016 claims examined and suspended, and 357 claims preliminarily reported to the Second Comptroller.

The following table presents the condition of the business of this division at the commencement and close of the year, as well as its progress through the year:

	Number.	Amount.	Number.	Amount.
Claims on hand July 1, 1871			5,331	$949,896 66
Claims received during the year			205	44,790 56
Claims reconsidered during the year			9	1,367 40
Total			5,545	996,054 62
Claims allowed during the year	311	$44,447 77		
Rejected on same		7,839 03		
Amount claimed		52,286 80		
Claims disallowed during the year	75	13,342 77		
Deduct as finally disposed of during the year			386	65,629 57
Claims on hand unsettled July 1, 1872			5,159	930,425 05

PENSION DIVISION.

The duties devolving upon this division are keeping an account with each Army pensioner of the United States, recording the name, rate, date of commencement, noting every increase, reduction, transfer, remarriage, death and expiration, whether by limitation under existing laws, or on account of the disability having ceased. Also, keeping an account with each pension agent, (of whom there are 59,) charging him with all moneys advanced by the Government, under the several appropriations to pay pensions, receive and register the accounts as sent each month direct to this office, by the agents who have disbursed the money, and properly file them for settlement.

Each voucher is properly examined, and the payment made by the agent is entered on the roll-book opposite the pensioner's name. The act of June 17, 1870, provided that every soldier who lost a limb in the service of the United States might be furnished with an artificial limb, or, if he should so elect, may receive money commutation in lieu thereof. The bills for limbs furnished and the transportation, with the vouchers for money commutation, are all paid by the agents, and are rendered in the same manner as pension vouchers.

Congress under act July 8, 1870, changed the mode of paying pensioners, and authorized payments to be made quarterly, instead of semi-annually as theretofore. This more than doubled the labor of this division, as twice as many vouchers are received, examined, entered, filed and reported to the Second Comptroller.

Congress under act July 12, 1870, required that all accounts shall be settled for each fiscal year, separately, and the balance unexpended shall be covered into the Treasury. So far as it relates to pension agents' accounts, I think this one of the best laws enacted; but, of course, great care has to be exercised to keep the accounts correct. The act of February 14, 1871, granted pensions to the survivors and certain widows of the war of 1812. This has increased the roll during the past year 20,127.

Congress under act June 8, 1872, amended act 6th June, 1866, which granted to certain disabled soldiers fifteen, twenty, and twenty-five dollars per month, so that now they are entitled to receive eighteen, twenty-four, and thirty-one $\frac{25}{100}$ dollars per month. This necessitates the change and increase of about seventeen thousand pensioners.

Number of pensioners on the rolls at present, as follows:

Revolutionary, half-pay, act 1848, &c	1,732
Invalids and widows, not including children, act July 14, 1862	208,923
War 1812, act February 14, 1871	20,127
Total	230,782
Number of pensioners who received limbs	1,332
Number of pensioners who received commutation	8,115

Amount drawn from the Treasury to pay pensions during the year ended June 30, 1872.

Invalids	$9,532,400
Widows and others	18,323,600
War of 1812, act February 14, 1871	3,115,500
Total	30,971,500

The difference of $2,309,902.74 between the amounts charged and the amounts reported as disbursed has been deposited and will be placed to the credit of the appropriation.

The following tabular statement shows the amount of business disposed of by this division during the fiscal year ended June 30, 1872:

	Number.	Amount involved.
Accounts on hand July 1, 1871	861	$32,658,464 89
Accounts received during the year	684	28,661,597 26
Total	1,545	61,320,062 15
Accounts reported during the year	900	40,000,205 68
Accounts remaining unsettled June 30, 1872	645	21,319,856 47
Total	1,545	61,320 062 15

The accounts on file unsettled are divided as follows, viz:

Accounts of 1871	390
Accounts of 1872	255
Total	645

Pensioners recorded, increased including additional for children of $2 per month	52,980
Pensions transferred	2,298
Pension vouchers examined	885,154
Payments entered on roll-books	791,603
Pages of difference and miscellaneous copied	3,515
Copies of surgeons' certificates furnished Commissioner	1,619

The force in this division July 1, 1871, was 31 clerks and 2 copyists. During the year there were added 10 clerks and 1 copyist, which made the whole force June 30, 1872, 41 clerks and 3 copyists.

It is my desire that the work on this division shall be brought up to current work, and with that view 8 more will be added by transfer from another division of the office.

The following tabular statement exhibits the amount paid at the several agencies during the year endedJune 30, 1872:

State.	Agency.	Agent.	Invalids.		Act of February 14, 1871. "1812."	Widows and others.	Total.
			Artificial limbs.	Invalid.			
Arkansas	Little Rock	James Coates	$200 00	$20,052 95	$10,370 38	$105,336 67	$135,960 00
Connecticut	Hartford	D. C. Rodman	813 34	118,152 92	25,800 27	302,372 64	447,139 17
California	San Francisco	H. C. Bennett	1,026 20	25,314 97	5,436 16	23,693 24	55,470 57
District of Columbia	Washington	W. T. Collins	1,578 34	101,201 55	27,218 74	140,824 21	270,822 84
Do	do	D. C. Cox	289 62	127,954 97	93,245 17	109,510 21	330,999 97
Delaware	Wilmington	E. D. Porter	251 80	26,903 23	3,151 65	47,231 59	77,538 27
Indiana	Fort Wayne	Hiram Iddings	1,096 30	192,412 62	19,988 27	281,166 29	494,663 48
Do	Indianapolis	C. W. Brouse	2,915 15	473,330 66	76,570 42	798,764 90	1,351,581 13
Do	Madison	Mark Tiltou	535 60	134,418 66	27,792 07	275,187 80	437,934 13
Illinois	Chicago	D. Blakely	2,218 85	350,819 17	28,319 78	366,453 01	747,810 81
Do	Quincy	B. M. Prentiss	772 10	175,215 78	23,256 71	245,174 19	444,418 78
Do	Springfield	William Jayne	1,944 64	222,055 06	27,917 29	338,211 52	590,128 51
Do	Salem	James S. Martin	1,520 06	228,970 39	29,580 54	583,795 54	843,866 53
Iowa	Des Moines	Stewart Goodrell	390 00	109,366 78	15,095 45	192,948 82	317,801 05
Do	Fairfield	D. B. Wilson	1,389 00	129,318 74	16,644 88	215,165 56	362,518 18
Do	Marion	J. B. Young	1,311 78	145,034 79	16,242 23	226,933 13	389,521 93
Kansas	Topeka	C. B. Lines	812 94	110,217 93	6,186 24	138,803 49	256,020 60
Kentucky	Lexington	A. H. Adams	995 25	66,407 56	48,119 91	279,200 32	394,723 04
Do	Louisville	W. D. Gallagher	350 00	120,291 03	57,944 81	405,836 57	584,423 01
Louisiana	New Orleans	R. H. Isabelle	375 00	22,940 77	13,649 40	55,055 63	92,020 80
Maine	Augusta	H. Boynton	843 05	114,259 22	21,213 95	182,952 62	319,268 84
Do	do	F. M. Drew	330 55	37,578 87	9,975 87	59,055 86	106,941 15
Do	Bangor	S. B. Morison	449 70	135,277 30	17,296 77	226,505 59	379,529 36
Do	Portland	M. A. Blanchard	882 00	133,902 44	25,474 84	200,186 45	360,445 73
Do	do	George L. Beal	68 00	37,348 18	8,496 45	51,871 87	97,784 50
Massachusetts	Boston	C. A. Phelps	2,623 34	514,106 95	52,875 27	871,228 31	1,440,833 87
Maryland	Baltimore	H. Adreon	1,125 35	129,737 94	54,370 24	211,010 88	396,244 41
Michigan	Detroit	A. Kaichen	3,000 84	376,505 22	67,147 99	610,488 70	1,057,142 75
Do	Grand Rapids	T. Foote	958 90	92,154 44	11,132 24	129,915 58	234,161 16
Missouri	Macon City	William C. Ebert	661 80	130,884 37	36,182 95	258,523 27	426,252 39
Do	Saint Louis	James Lindsay	2,040 95	170,794 46	43,557 12	460,050 93	676,442 76

Ohio	Cincinnati	William E. Davis	3,001 70	343,401 60	54,292 58	567,900 02	968,595 90
Do	......do	Charles E. Brown	582 65	112,631 73	29,103 86	178,097 89	320,416 13
Do	Cleveland	Seth M. Barber	1,989 01	296,845 26	61,472 98	398,663 03	758,970 30
Do	Columbus	John A. Norris	2,272 10	286,959 42	72,949 40	518,660 56	880,841 57
Oregon	Oregon City	Henry Warren	75 00	4,955 07	2,528 46	3,940 71	11,499 24
Pennsylvania	Philadelphia	William T. Forbes	4,008 92	257,194 62	21,415 26	4,511 18	287,129 98
Do	......do	H. G. Sickel	2,977 35	636,303 01	89,956 59	11,084 13	740,312 08
Do	......do	A. R. Colhoun	....	....	9,672 72	418,695 99	428,368 71
Do	......do	L. R. B. Nevin	....	....	27,822 39	993,322 12	1,021,144 51
Do	Pittsburgh	James McGregor	3,577 56	358,039 09	46,916 03	531,684 69	940,217 37
Rhode Island	Providence	C. R. Brayton	312 00	44,493 54	7,251 03	101,089 31	153,145 88
Tennessee	Knoxville	D. T. Boynton	491 25	87,294 59	53,040 69	369,218 79	510,045 32
Do	Nashville	W. J. Stokes	676 15	28,940 98	69,697 27	207,661 78	306,976 18
Vermont	Burlington	J. L. Barstow	62 80	85,456 89	16,041 71	135,109 41	236,670 81
Do	Montpelier	S. Thomas	656 65	113,249 56	25,282 27	154,655 76	293,844 24
Virginia	Richmond	A. Washburn	198 00	26,351 29	135,057 35	62,036 31	223,642 95
West Virginia	Wheeling	T. M. Harris	1,700 35	147,896 03	66,413 41	302,752 79	518,762 58
Wisconsin	La Crosse	J. A. Kellogg	384 62	55,454 47	7,007 82	105,836 59	168,685 50
Do	Milwaukee	E. Ferguson	2,159 44	166,948 38	14,689 08	274,062 44	457,859 34
Do	Madison	Thomas Reynolds	1,798 30	110,759 60	12,843 65	202,811 99	328,213 54
Washington Territory	Vancouver	S. W. Brown	50 00	3,442 74	124 53	560 12	4,177 39
Total			74,249 40	10,052,726 28	2,309,961 43	17,297,363 42	29,734,300 53

SOLDIERS' CLAIMS BOUNTY-LAND, AND PENSION DIVISION, WAR OF 1812.

During the fiscal year ended 30th June, 1872, 30,721 pension claims, "act of February 14, 1871," have been examined, certified, and returned to the Commissioner of Pensions for his action.

Eight hundred and ninety-nine bounty-land claims have been examined and returned to the Commissioner of Pensions as above.

COLLECTION DIVISION.

The following statement shows the work of this division during the months named, viz:

Month.	Delinquents recorded.	Delinquents examined.	Entries on register.	Cases examined.	Accounts referred to.	Vouchers examined.	Letters written.	Pages manuscript copied.	Cases referred for suit.
1871.									
September	82	142	75	81	....	....	29	31	......
October	261	130	101	58	35	....	118	34	......
November	103	45	219	79	72	....	153	76	......
December	44	93	88	109	95	....	115	24	......
1872.									
January	....	....	158	116	270	189	66	....	......
February	....	70	113	223	591	1,300	183	36	......
March	518	60	158	292	611	1,139	303	39	......
April	931	127	201	210	413	692	347	32	......
May	410	290	129	134	269	530	350	8	2
June	....	302	216	134	294	559	126	16	......
Total	2,349	1,259	1,458	1,436	2,650	4,409	1,790	296	2

A reference to previous reports will show that the amount involved in the accounts of quartermasters received in the year 1869 was $31,816,235.59; in 1870, $8,154,912.33; in 1871, $23,126,666.31, and in 1872, $44,830,613.54. The amount involved in the settlements made in the years named was as follows, viz: in 1869, $117,504,508.64; in 1870, $31,045,231.69; in 1871, $13,984,186.97, and in 1872, $43,329,640.02. The excess in the amount of settlements in this division in 1872, reported over the previous year, was $22,752,853.49; nearly 100 per cent. greater, though the force employed was only about 77 per cent. as great as the force then employed. A large number of property-returns of officers of the Army have been settled under the act of June 23, 1870, authorizing the settlement of the accounts of officers of the Army and Navy. Prior to the rebellion it was customary to examine money-accounts and property-returns together; but, by reason of the immense amounts disbursed by officers of the Army during the war, and the possible injuries which might result should settlements be deferred until the returns could be received and examined, they were transmitted to this office separately and examined and adjusted separately in this office. The necessity of such separation does not now seem to exist, and as soon as the accounts and returns now on file are settled, it is proposed to return to the old system and settle the accounts and returns of disbursing officers together, thus insuring greater accuracy and enabling the accounting officers to examine more readily the returns of property in connection with the money-accounts disbursed in its purchase.

Your attention is again respectfully invited to the *absolute* necessity for more file-room in this office. The shelving-room suitable for accounts has long been filled, and there are now some six thousand settlements lying upon the floors of the large file-room. These papers are of great value to the Government, and should be properly taken care of.

On the 30th of June last, the force of this office was reduced thirty-five clerks, in accordance with recommendation contained in my report of 23d of August, 1871.

Some changes have also been made for the better in the organization of the office, and the work in all the divisions is progressing in a satisfactory manner.

It affords me great pleasure to speak of the interest manifested in its business by all the clerks now employed here, and to commend their general ability, industry, and faithfulness.

Respectfully submitted.

ALLAN RUTHERFORD,
Third Auditor.

Hon. GEORGE S. BOUTWELL,
Secretary of the Treasury.

REPORT OF THE FOURTH AUDITOR

REPORT

OF

THE FOURTH AUDITOR OF THE TREASURY.

TREASURY DEPARTMENT,
Fourth Auditor's Office, September 25, 1872.

SIR: In accordance with your request of August 8, 1872, that I should forward to you the annual report of the operations of this office for the fiscal year ending June 30, 1872, I have the honor to transmit the following tabular statements in which is embraced the information desired:

I. PAYMASTERS' DIVISION—WILLIAM CONARD, CHIEF.

Statement of accounts, including marine, received and settled in the Paymasters' Division from July 1, 1871, to June 30, 1872, with the amount of cash disbursed in those settled and the number of letters received and written in relation to the same.

PAYMASTERS' AND MARINE ACCOUNTS.

Date.	Accounts received.	Accounts settled.	Letters received.	Letters written.	Cash disbursements.
1871.					
July	50	37	130	142	$434,576 02
August	19	18	138	148	1,192,550 67
September	11	16	139	90	694,951 42
October	34	19	121	102	944,101 44
November	34	39	107	103	1,391,666 85
December	10	25	68	126	1,386,285 43
1872.					
January	37	20	95	90	1,365,935 72
February	37	32	106	145	1,177,850 02
March	16	27	89	101	882,531 07
April	40	33	121	126	2,596,213 83
May	29	34	110	106	1,378,090 47
June	12	27	67	115	1,824,397 68
Total	329	333	1,291	1,394	15,270,059 62

Number of unsettled accounts on hand July 1, 1871, 13; number of unsettled accounts on hand June 30, 1872, 9; average number of clerks employed in the division, 15.

II.—PENSION DIVISION—RICHARD GOODHART, CHIEF.

Statement showing the amount disbursed at the different agencies on account of Navy pensions and the work performed by the Navy pension division during the fiscal year ending June 30, 1872.

PENSION ACCOUNTS.

Location.	Number of Navy invalid pensioners.	Number of Navy widows and orphans.	Amount disbursed to invalids.	Amount disbursed to widows and orphans.	Total disbursements.
Baltimore, Maryland	52	70	$5,614 99	$13,939 04	$19,554 03
Boston, Massachusetts	238	276	30,629 56	49,096 62	79,726 18
Brooklyn, New York	302	347	36,722 90	70,295 31	107,018 21
Cincinnati, Ohio	36	73	4,532 55	15,999 40	20,531 95
Chicago, Illinois	37	26	5,199 52	5,140 05	10,339 57
Detroit, Michigan	10	22	1,320 73	2,788 27	4,109 00
Hartford, Connecticut	12	23	1,319 87	8,909 55	10,229 42
Louisville, Kentucky	5	14	509 70	2,903 08	3,412 78
Milwaukie, Wisconsin	11	12	1,021 60	1,620 53	2,642 13
New Orleans, Louisiana	13	7	2,712 27	1,308 07	4,020 34
Pittsburgh, Pennsylvania	14	30	714 47	4,185 81	4,900 28
Philadelphia, Pennsylvania	165	295	19,461 55	48,737 98	68,199 53
Portland, Maine	64	62	7,325 19	8,151 87	15,477 06
Portsmouth, New Hampshire	34	28	3,697 72	5,295 74	8,993 46
Providence, Rhode Island	13	23	1,163 22	4,311 40	5,474 62
Richmond, Virginia	20	39	2,060 06	10,587 11	12,647 17
San Francisco, California	10	6	1,156 24	1,451 80	2,608 04
Saint Louis, Missouri	13	14	2,632 29	2,098 80	4,731 09
Saint Paul, Minnesota	....	1	....	540 00	540 00
Trenton, New Jersey	22	28	2,502 77	8,088 34	10,591 11
Washington, District of Columbia	75	133	10,474 46	29,679 49	40,153 95
Total	1,148	1,529	140,771 66	295,128 26	435,899 92

During this time there were 206 accounts received and 185 settled, involving an expenditure of those settled of $327,072.28. Also there were 402 letters received and 326 written. Number of clerks employed, 1.)

III.—RECORD DIVISION—CHARLES COOK, CHIEF.

Statement of correspondence of the Fourth Auditor's Office for the fiscal year ending June 30, 1872, *and the work of the record division.*

Date.	Letters received.	Letters written.	Letters recorded.	Letters filed.	Letters referred to other bureaus.	Letters indexed.	Names indexed and double indexed.	Reports of settled accounts recorded and indexed.	Dead letters registered.	Letters written by record division.
1871.										
July	1,092	1,269	1,438	715	15	2,613	4,502	72	19	53
August	1,077	1,193	1,255	1,043	19	4,052	14,793	207	18	95
September	1,085	1,110	1,218	772	11	4,768	6,594	125	19	77
October	914	962	690	649	....	3,489	6,215	450	9	15
November	1,028	1,184	930	781	18	6,097	10,103	264	8	53
December	982	1,101	1,252	747	14	6,900	11,488	86	5	49
1872.										
January	1,128	1,489	1,579	803	6	6,462	11,945	192	13	57
February	1,188	1,350	1,291	889	13	4,387	8,378	25	16	75
March	1,238	1,546	2,165	886	28	1,114	1,897	188	9	104
April	1,236	1,651	1,598	884	18	2,943	5,206	56	15	124
May	1,291	1,336	1,465	805	25	2,719	5,828	251	11	96
June	1,218	1,440	1,351	836	22	1,341	2,229	196	18	44
Total	13,477	15,631	16,232	9,810	189	46,945	91,178	2,112	160	842

Average number of clerks employed, 7.

IV.—PRIZE-MONEY DIVISION—S. M. B. SERVOSS, CHIEF.

Statement of the work performed by the prize-money division during the fiscal year ending June 30, 1872.

Date.	Prize-lists.			Letters.		Claims.		Amount paid.
	Number received.	Lists apportioned.	Amount appropriated.	Letters received.	Letters written.	Claims received.	Claims settled.	Prize-money.
1871.								
July				187	306	38	20	$2,173 29
August				218	277	39	39	2,287 68
September				222	247	32	22	1,321 37
October				165	193	24	22	1,495 45
November	15	15	$121,560 55	159	168	27	23	10,250 24
December				148	168	94	91	15,548 85
1872.								
January				231	437	506	482	36,171 87
February				238	234	235	217	27,936 47
March				270	427	45	33	3,439 80
April				259	558	27	22	2,749 02
May				288	298	61	42	2,756 81
June	2	1	7,500 00	217	324	109	55	7,926 74
Total	17	16	129,060 55	2,602	3,637	1,237	1,068	114,057 59

Average number of clerks employed, 3⅓.

V.—GENERAL-CLAIM DIVISION—A. C. ADAMSON, CHIEF.

Annual report of the general-claim division for the year ending June 30, 1872.

Date.	Claims received.	Claims adjusted.	Amount involved.	Letters written.	Number of reports on applications for pensions.	Number of reports on applications for bounty-land.	Number of reports on applications for admission to Naval Asylum.
1871.							
On hand July 1	124						
July	87	124	$12,191 92	491	31	7	
August	97	108	21,195 13	429	49		1
September	72	56	6,350 35	336	28		3
October	103	115	8,045 38	419	28	3	1
November	141	137	11,318 11	444	31	16	
December	98	104	18,037 53	401	36	1	
1872.							
January	121	116	25,841 67	547	90		1
February	136	135	26,457 15	544	111	11	
March	130	120	11,520 49	512	40	26	
April	113	110	12,559 11	464	43	2	
May	111	122	11,138 64	475	40	9	3
June	120	114	70,365 43	527	60		1
Total	1,453	1,361	235,020 91	5,589	587	75	10

Average number of clerks employed, 6⅔.

VI.—NAVY AGENTS' DIVISION—WILLIAM F. STIDHAM, CHIEF.

Annual report of the Navy agents' division for the fiscal year ending June 30, 1872.

Date.	Accounts received.	Accounts settled.	Amount involved.	Letters written.	Letters received.
1871.					
July	46	47	$1,077,304 75	102	131
August	16	11	152,334 99	101	116
September	4	6	1,524,170 84	130	139
October	11	8	456,532 93	120	127
November	6	7	1,329,845 52	168	153
December	21	23	261,072 10	126	121
1872.					
January	77	73	288,274 65	110	114
February	90	91	1,400,741 68	124	125
March	64	67	488,931 40	123	125
April	114	114	1,396,333 20	128	140
May	30	28	343,686 13	140	141
June	20	23	1,594,260 37	189	188
Total	499	498	10,313,488 56	1,561	1,620

ALLOTMENT ACCOUNTS.

Date.	Allotments registered.	Allotments discontinued.	Date.	Allotments registered.	Allotments discontinued.
1871.			1872.		
July	39	88	January	22	110
August	49	48	February	57	90
September	19	71	March	165	77
October	36	99	April	59	85
November	143	156	May	53	76
December	70	119	June	89	94
Total	356	581	Total	295	532

Statement of amounts paid by Navy agents for allotments during the year 1871.

New York	$78,874 50
Boston	55,068 00
Philadelphia	53,292 75
Washington	20,423 00
Portsmouth	10,795 50
Baltimore	9,464 50
San Francisco	1,847 00
	209,865 25

Accounts remaining on hand June 30, 1872, 3; average number of clerks employed, 6½; number of vouchers examined, 25,135.

VII.—BOOK-KEEPERS' DIVISION—PARIS H. FOLSOM, CHIEF.

Statement of the work performed in the book-keepers' division for the fiscal year ending June 30, 1872.

Date.	Number of pay-requisitions.	Cash pay-requisitions—amount.	Number of repay-requisitions.	Cash repay-requisitions—amount.	Letters received.	Letters written.	Accounts journalized, entered, and balanced.	Extracts from ledgers.	Accounts settled.	Summary statements entered.	Accounts received.
1871.											
July	124	$1,614,276 93	16	$40,067 17	118	187	66	110	178	39	178
August	129	2,121,821 25	9	55,352 79	113	153	253	126	92	......	92
September	135	1,816,157 41	32	141,002 19	143	230	173	32	163	77	163
October	68	1,400,419 55	1	296,160 40	104	113	161	42	65	17	65
November	137	3,285,309 52	18	77,401 42	110	201	337	36	62	52	62
December	117	1,578,304 57	13	224,161 02	117	199	75	31	117	62	117
1872.											
January	129	2,575,640 09	14	81,212 50	123	209	247	156	1	40	1
February	110	2,081,858 53	7	602,443 66	111	206	103	274	63	58	63
March	126	1,487,528 08	26	405,827 75	133	237	56	116	114	80	114
April	105	1,349,826 96	13	443,854 46	153	198	141	412	50	60	50
May	90	1,418,867 80	16	113,388 70	137	161	277	61	67	71	67
June	147	1,266,285 01	4	5,210 12	148	106	198	36	229	22	229
Total	1,437	21,996,304 70	169	2,486,082 18	1,510	2,290	2,087	1,432	1,201	578	1,201

Average number of clerks employed, 5½.

VIII.—DISBURSEMENT AND MISCELLANEOUS DIVISION—B. P. DAVIS IN CHARGE.

Statement of the work performed during the fiscal year ending June 30, 1872.

Number of letters written	452
Number of dead-letters registered	160
Number of checks against accounts ordered	365

In addition to the above, Mr. Davis has made up various tabular statements and miscellaneous reports called for by Congress and the Secretary of the Treasury; kept the record of appointments, resignations, removals, and absences; received and distributed the stationery used by the office, and discharged the duties of disbursing-clerk.

The amount of work performed by the office is very satisfactory. The same valuable assistance which I have acknowledged during previous years, on the part of my chief clerk, William B. Moore, esq., I have also received from him during the past fiscal year.

Very truly and respectfully, your obedient servant,

STEPHEN J. W. TABOR,
Auditor.

Hon. GEORGE S. BOUTWELL,
Secretary of the Treasury.

REPORT OF THE FIFTH AUDITOR.

REPORT

OF

THE FIFTH AUDITOR OF THE TREASURY.

TREASURY DEPARTMENT,
Fifth Auditor's office, October 29, 1872.

SIR: Herewith are submitted the tabular statements of the operations of this office for the year ended June 30, 1872. There have been eleven thousand five hundred and sixty-six letters written, and fifteen thousand four hundred and six accounts adjusted, involving $720,071,-736.40.

Very respectfully,

J. H. ELA,
Auditor.

Hon. GEORGE S. BOUTWELL,
Secretary of the Treasury.

A.—*Statement of the expenses of all missions abroad for salaries, contingencies, and loss by exchange, from July 1, 1871, to June 30, 1872, as shown by accounts adjusted in this office.*

No.	Mission.	Salary.	Contingencies.	Loss by exchange.	Total.
	ARGENTINE REPUBLIC.				
1	R. C. Kirk, minister	$4,306 32	$235 12	....	$4,541 44
	AUSTRIA.				
2	John Jay, minister	12,000 00	903 95	....	
3	J. F. Delaplaine, secretary of legation	1,800 00	....	....	
		13,800 00	903 95	....	14,703 95
	BELGIUM.				
4	J. R. Jones, minister	7,500 00	717 17	....	8,217 17
	BOLIVIA.				
5	L. Markbreit, minister	7,500 00	535 85	$655 75	8,691 60
	BRAZIL.				
6	J. R. Partridge, minister	12,000 00	426 01	....	
7	R. C. Shannon, secretary of legation	1,800 00	....	....	
		13,800 00	426 01	....	14,226 01
	CHILI.				
8	J. P. Root, minister	10,000 00	....	....	10,000 00

A.—*Statement of the expenses of all missions abroad, &c.*—Continued.

No	Mission.	Salary.	Contingencies.	Loss by exchange.	Total.
	COLOMBIA.				
9	S. A. Hurlbut, minister	$7,500 00	....	....	$7,500 00
	CHINA.				
10	F. F. Low, minister	12,000 00	$918 76	$73 09	
11	S. W. Williams, secretary of legation	5,000 00	....	308 39	
		17,000 00	918 76	381 48	18,300 24
	COSTA RICA.				
12	J. B. Blair, minister	7,500 00	299 11	358 07	8,157 18
	DENMARK.				
13	M. J. Cramer, minister	7,500 00	365 91	227 53	8,093 44
	ECUADOR.				
14	E. R. Wing, minister	7,500 00	283 27	452 55	8,235 82
	FRANCE.				
15	E. B. Washburne, minister	17,500 00	4,379 28	4 92	
16	W. Hoffman, secretary of legation	2,625 00	....	....	
17	F. Moore, assistant secretary of legation	2,000 00	....	....	
18	G. Washburne, assistant secretary of legation	1,500 00	....	....	
		22,625 00	4,379 28	4 92	27,009 20
	GERMAN EMPIRE.				
19	George Bancroft, minister	17,500 00	2,771 56	65 98	
20	A. Bliss, secretary of legation	2,500 00	....	....	
21	N. Fish, assistant secretary of legation	1,800 00	....	....	
		21,800 00	2,771 56	65 98	24,637 54
	GREECE.				
22	C. K. Tuckerman, late minister	3,199 73	60 22	260 31	
23	J. M. Francis, minister	4,368 13	178 72	5 92	
		7,567 86	238 94	266 23	8,073 23
	GREAT BRITAIN.				
24	Robert C. Schenck, minister	17,500 00	2,985 63	....	
25	Benjamin Moran, secretary of legation	2,625 00	....	....	
26	M. Woodhull, assistant secretary	2,000 00	....	....	
		22,125 00	2,985 63	....	25,110 63
	GUATEMALA.				
27	S. A. Hudson, minister	7,500 00	....	....	7,500 00
	HAWAIIAN ISLANDS.				
28	H. A. Peirce, minister	7,500 00	176 46	....	7,676 46
	HAYTI.				
29	E. D. Bassett, minister	7,500 00	368 99	....	7,868 99
	HONDURAS.				
30	Henry Baxter, minister	7,500 00	....	....	7,500 00
	ITALY.				
31	G. P. Marsh, minister	12,000 00	488 65	31 08	
32	G. W. Wurts, secretary of legation	1,800 00	....	....	
		13,800 00	488 65	31 08	14,319 73

A.—*Statement of the expenses of all missions abroad, &c.*—Continued.

No.	Mission.	Salary.	Contingencies.	Loss by exchange.	Total.
	JAPAN.				
33	C. E. Delong, minister	$10,000 00	$604 38	....	
34	J. C. Hepburn, interpreter	2,500 00	....	....	
		12,500 00	604 38	....	$13,104 38
	LIBERIA.				
35	J. M. Turner, minister	4,000 00	252 74	....	4,252 74
	MEXICO.				
36	T. H. Nelson, minister	12,000 00	1,773 60	....	
37	P. C. Bliss, secretary of legation	1,800 00	....	....	
		13,800 00	1,773 60	....	15,573 60
	NETHERLANDS.				
38	C. T. Gorham, minister	7,500 00	417 10	$4 57	7,921 67
	NICARAGUA.				
39	C. N. Riotte, minister	7,500 00	445 48	....	7,945 48
	PARAGUAY AND URUGUAY.				
40	J. L. Stevens, minister	11,250 00	84 58	300 00	11,634 58
	PERU.				
41	Thomas Settle, minister	10,000 00	129 20	....	
42	H. M. Brent, secretary of legation	1,500 00	....	....	
		11,500 00	129 20	....	11,629 20
	PORTUGAL.				
43	C. H. Lewis, minister	7,500 00	352 79	45 88	7,898 67
	RUSSIA.				
44	A. G. Curtin, minister	12,000 00	1,521 25	....	
45	E. Schuyler, secretary of legation	1,800 00	....	....	
		13,800 00	1,521 25	....	15,321 25
	SALVADOR.				
46	Thomas Biddle, minister	5,074 73	165 22	....	5,239 95
	SPAIN.				
47	D. E. Sickles, minister	12,000 00	2,834 62	325 46	
48	A. A. Adee, secretary of legation	1,800 00	....	....	
		13,800 00	2,834 62	325 46	16,960 08
	SWEDEN.				
49	C. C. Andrews, minister	7,500 00	864 23	362 99	8,727 22
	SWITZERLAND.				
50	H. Rublee, minister	7,500 00	369 65	....	7,869 65
	TURKEY.				
51	George H. Boker, minister, (from Dec. 11, 1871)	4,175 82	968 12	....	
52	J. P. Browne, late chargé	1,875 00	1,409 63	65 37	
		6,050 82	2,377 75	65 37	8,493 94
	VENEZUELA.				
53	William A. Pile, minister	7,500 00	409 18	108 81	8,017 99

A.—*Statement of the expenses of all missions abroad, &c.*—Continued.

No.	Mission.	Salary.	Contingencies.	Loss by exchange.	Total.
	UNITED STATES BANKERS, LONDON.				
54	Baring Bros & Co.			$1,778 14	
55	Clews, Habicht & Co.			981 65	
				2,759 79	$2,759 79
	UNITED STATES DISPATCH AGENTS.				
56	B. F. Stevens, agent	$2,000 00	$18,085 79		20,085 79
	Total	360,599 73	46,782 22	6,416 46	413,798 41

REMARKS.

8. No accounts for contingencies received.
9. Accounts incomplete.
10. Accounts for first and second quarter of 1872 not received.
18. Salary commences April 1, 1872.
23. Salary from December 11, 1871.
24. Second quarter of 1872 not yet received.
27. No contingent accounts received.
30. No accounts received for over two years.
33. Contingent accounts for first and second quarter, 1872, not received.
46. Salary from October 21, 1871.
51. Salary from December 11, 1871.

B.—*Statement of consular salaries, fees, and loss by exchange for the fiscal year ended June 30, 1872, as shown by accounts adjusted.*

Consulate.	Salaries.	Fees.	Loss.	Remarks.
Acapulco	$2,000 00	$501 55		
Aix-la-Chapelle	2,500 00	2,937 50	$0 91	
Agency	2,120 04	2,600 00		
Alexandria	3,667 58	85 58	50 84	Inclusive of salary of consular clerk, from May 1 to June 30.
Algiers	1,500 00	95 01	115 86	
Amoor River	500 00	43 12		Accounts for first and second quarters, 1872, not received.
Amsterdam	1,000 00	1,306 27		
Agency	173 78	173 78		
Amoy	3,818 58	1,576 33	377 53	Inclusive of home transit of late consul.
Antwerp	2,500 00	2,908 69	4 96	
Apia	750 00	91 83	176 12	Account for second quarter, 1872, not received.
Aspinwall	2,500 00	2,574 59		
Aux Cayes	250 00	281 56		Accounts for first and second quarters, 1872, not received.
Bahia	1,000 00	800 60		
Bangkok	3,000 00	178 22	824 32	
Barcelona	1,500 00	312 54	72 74	
Barmen	2,000 00	7,496 00	86 59	Inclusive of additional compensation allowed when fees reach $3,000.
Agencies	3,083 71	5,560 50		
Basle	2,109 89	3,954 00	32 43	Inclusive of home transit of late consul.
Agency	2,000 00	3,100 00		
Batavia	1,068 68	1,038 24	30	
Bay of Islands	1,000 00	478 53	12 74	
Beirut	2,380 49	446 41	49 59	Inclusive of salary of consular clerk to November 17, 1871.
Belfast	2,000 00	12,175 71		
Berlin	3,787 35	9,315 50		
Birmingham	2,500 00	12,325 50		
Agencies	5,000 00	6,021 50		
Bordeaux	2,000 00	6,777 49		
Boulogne	1,500 00	110 00	51 18	
Bradford	3,939 31	10,488 50		
Bremen	3,000 00	4,365 50		
Brindisi	1,310 42	6 50		Partial returns. Inclusive of instruction and transit salaries.
Brussels	3,819 16	5,437 00	73 54	
Buenos Ayres	2,508 00	4,961 03		
Cadiz	1,500 00	1,068 70	37 48	
Calcutta	6,100 54	6,120 84	39 68	Inclusive of consul-general's transit to his post of duty.
Callao	3,500 00	2,419 11		
Canea	1,000 00	2 00	99 80	
Canton	4,000 00	1,075 70	357 22	
Cape Haytien	1,000 00	498 89		
Cape Town	1,473 84	307 20	63 01	Inclusive of instruction and transit salaries.
Agency	1,047 37	1,047 37		

B.—*Statement of consular salaries, fees, and loss by exchange, &c.*—Continued.

Consulate.	Salaries.	Fees.	Loss.	Remarks.
Carthagena	$500 00	$513 22		
Ceylon	651 09	300 85	$2 18	Partial returns for the year.
Chemnitz	2,000 00	9,813 00		
Chin Kiang	3,880 41	2,043 40	397 42	Inclusive of instruction, transit, and exequatur salaries.
Clifton	2,000 00	5,137 50		Inclusive of the additional compensation allowed when fees reach $3,000.
Agency	217 00	217 00		
Coaticook	2,000 00	7,144 00	3 75	Do.
Agencies	2,745 50	2,745 50		
Constantinople	3,000 00	550 38	180 75	
Cork	2,054 35	1,363 56		Inclusive of home transit of late consul.
Agency	37 57	37 57		
Cyprus	1,000 00		65 00	
Demerara	2,000 00	2,298 03		
Dresden	2,163 07	3,337 00		No returns received since Dec. 31, 1871.
Dundee	2,260 87	7,349 75	2 18	Inclusive of instruction and transit salaries.
Agency	581 25	381 25		
Elsinore	1,500 00	44 00	54 24	
Agency	4 00	4 00		
Fayal	750 00	565 87		
Foo-Chow	3,500 00	1,458 83	334 60	
Fort Erie	1,500 00	2,892 25		
Agencies	657 00	657 00		Partial returns.
Frankfort-on-the-Main	3,190 22	3,466 50		Inclusive of consular clerk's salary to September 8, 1871. Fee returns not complete.
Funchal	1,500 00	134 17	114 06	
Gaboon	1,000 00	37 03		
Geneva	1,500 00	1,402 25	7 52	
Genoa	1,500 00	1,711 52		
Gibraltar	1,500 00	773 50		
Glasgow	3,000 00	12,878 21		
Goderich	1,500 00	585 37		
Agency	2,107 88	2,077 00		
Guaymas	1,000 00	840 89		
Guayaquil	750 00	628 47		
Hakodadi	3,994 55	357 22	368 39	Inclusive of instruction and transit salaries.
Halifax	2,000 00	3,468 20	2 91	
Agencies	586 72	586 72		
Hamburg	2,000 00	8,918 00	70 44	
Agencies	1,928 54	1,928 54		
Hamilton	2,555 16	4,110 50		Account for expenses second quarter, 1872, not received.
Agencies	2,185 00	2,185 00		
Hankow	3,000 00	1,044 06	412 57	
Havana	7,082 38	20,108 04		Inclusive of salary of consular clerks.
Agency	858 14	858 14		
Havre	6,000 00	5,888 01	4 55	
Hong-Kong	2,625 00	7,024 46		Account for second quarter, 1872, not received.
Honolulu	4,000 00	4,957 48		
Jerusalem	1,125 00	28 00	121 89	Account for second quarter, 1872, not received.
Kanagawa	3,000 00	5,480 21	1,203 47	Inclusive of $1,110.14 paid late consul for loss by exchange.
Kingston, Canada	1,500 00	1,674 18		
Agencies	3,057 00	3,057 00		
Kingston, Jamaica	2,000 00	2,218 87	3 54	
Laguayra	750 00	270 50		Returns incomplete.
Lanthala	1,000 00	80 44	177 69	
La Rochelle	1,500 00	304 00	79 21	
Agencies	2,923 06	2,923 06		
Leeds	2,000 00	2,570 48		
Agencies	1,248 68	2,225 57		
Leghorn	1,500 00	2,228 94	60	
Leipsic	3,000 00	7,680 00		Inclusive of consular clerk's salary and additional compensation when fees reach $3,000.
Leith	3,169 21	3,169 21		
Agency	2,100 00	2,100 00		
Lisbon	750 00	587 02	65, 88	Half year's report to December 31, 1871.
Liverpool	8,141 31	40,244 96		Inclusive of consular clerk's pay from November 10, 1871.
Agency	2,034 91	3,731 00		
London	7,500 00	58,027 21		
Lyons	2,000 00	10,649 75	111 97	
Agency	2,105 05	3,758 50		
Malaga	1,500 00	1,772 75		
Malta	1,500 00	140 28	75 29	
Manchester	3,000 00	33,326 47		
Maranham	1,000 00	266 08		
Marseilles	3,019 23	3,958 99	41 23	Inclusive of consular clerk's salary from October 1, 1871, to April 7, 1872.

B.—*Statement of consular salaries, fees, and loss by exchange, &c.*—Continued.

Consulate.	Salaries.	Fees.	Loss.	Remarks.
Agencies	$1,290 49	$1,290 49	....	
Matamoras	2,000 00	882 25	$17 92	
Agency	1,660 00	1,660 00	....	
Mantanzas	2,500 00	4,755 66	....	
Agencies	3,090 05	5,189 47	....	
Mauritius	2,500 00	342 59	107 76	
Mayence	....	....	....	Accounts imperfect.
Melbourne	4,000 00	2,674 26	23 57	
Messina	1,500 00	2,611 27	....	
Mexico	950 54	499 00	....	Accounts received up to June 12, 1872.
Montevideo	1,205 36	1,291 39	....	Inclusive of transit and instruction salaries.
Montreal	4,000 00	6,222 17	....	
Agencies	3,526 25	3,526 25	....	
Munich	1,500 00	1,253 50	34 68	
Nagasaki	3,000 00	914 34	343 57	
Nantes	1,500 00	270 50	32 04	
Naples	1,125 00	1,575 34	....	Account for second quarter, 1872, not received.
Nassau, N. P	2,000 00	1,505 74	....	
Newcastle-upon-Tyne	1,500 00	1,604 50	....	
Agencies	1,660 60	1,660 60	....	
Nice	1,500 00	517 50	42 03	
Nuremberg	4,003 44	7,377 50	....	
Odessa	2,000 00	115 85	281 52	
Omoa and Truxillo	750 00	11 42	....	Account for second quarter, 1872, not received.
Oporto	1,125 00	228 96	59 96	Do.
Osaca and Hiogo	3,651 11	2,161 99	101 27	Inclusive of instruction and transit salaries.
Palermo	1,500 00	1,765 45	....	
Agencies	410 64	410 64	....	
Panama	3,500 00	2,136 04	....	
Para	1,000 00	2,164 52	....	
Paris	8,000 00	54,826 00	....	
Agency	1,023 00	1,023 00	....	
Paso del Norte	500 00	34 50	....	
Payta	500 00	336 09	....	
Pernambuco	2,000 00	1,200 14	95 35	
Picton	....	....	....	No returns received.
Piræus	1,245 32	15 25	54 31	Inclusive of instruction and transit salaries.
Port Mahon	1,500 00	181 01	44 14	
Agency	5 00	5 00	....	
Port Said	2,000 00	....	105 00	
Port Stanley	750 00	258 63	....	Account for second quarter, 1872, not received.
Prescott	1,500 00	1,521 00	1 05	
Agencies	4,085 44	4,371 50	....	
Prince Edward Island	1,500 00	820 94	13 93	
Agencies	134 65	134 65	....	
Quebec	1,500 00	1,350 26	2 72	
Rio de Janeiro	1,780 21	....	60 45	Accounts unsettled; the consulate in charge of an alien.
Rio Grande do Sul	1,082 42	568 27	....	Inclusive of instruction salary.
Rome	1,703 80	1,330 55	42 63	Inclusive of $203.80, consular clerk's salary.
Rotterdam	2,000 00	2,088 41	20 92	
Agencies	2,002 00	2,239 81	....	
Sabanilla	....	....	....	Returns incomplete.
St. Catharine's	1,500 00	99 01	....	
St. Domingo	1,500 00	416 19	12 82	
St. Helena	1,500 00	553 92	18 29	
St. John's, Canada	2,000 00	3,544 00	....	
St. John's, New Brunswick.	3,797 94	6,318 81	....	
Agencies	2,873 09	2,873 09	....	
St. Paul de Loando	250 00	....	....	Accounts for the fourth quarter, 1871, and first and second quarters, 1872, not received.
St. Petersburg	1,500 00	304 00	149 03	Account for third quarter, 1871, not received.
St. Thomas	4,250 36	1,671 81	6 51	Inclusive of transit salary.
San Juan del Norte	2,103 30	423 28	....	Inclusive of instruction salary.
San Juan, Porto Rico	2,000 00	986 50	....	
Agencies	4,816 16	4,816 16	....	
San Juan del Sur	1,500 00	381 40	....	Account for second quarter, 1872, not received.
Santa Cruz	1,527 17	283 06	9 52	
Agency	376 67	376 67	....	
Santiago, Cape Verde	750 00	110 34	70 08	

B.—*Statement of consular salaries, fees, and loss by exchange, &c.*—Continued.

Consulate.	Salaries.	Fees.	Loss.	Remarks.
Santiago de Cuba	$2,500 00	$914 62	....	
Sarnia	1,500 00	1,872 75	....	
Agency	15 00	15 00	....	
Seychelles	662 87	22 66	$25 96	
Shanghai	6,000 00	11,022 45	....	Inclusive of consular clerks' salaries.
Sheffield	4,461 49	9,496 00	....	
Agencies	2,754 35	10,388 25	....	
Singapore	3,525 81	1,700 45	232 01	Inclusive of transit salaries.
Agency	250 93	250 93	....	
Smyrna	2,000 00	1,767 15	27 53	
Sonneberg	3,875 63	6,004 00	....	
Southampton	1,000 00	314 50	....	Accounts for first and second quarters 1872, not received.
Spezia	1,500 00	10 67	111 57	
Stettin	1,073 37	290 35	34 56	
Agencies	222 65	222 65	....	
Stuttgart	2,000 00	3,070 00	19 06	Inclusive of additional componsation allowed when fees reach $3,000.
Swatow	3,500 00	566 02	584 63	
Tabasco	500 00	377 35	....	
Tahiti	1,271 73	856 02	23 61	Inclusive of instruction and transit salaries.
Talcahuano	1,000 00	596 70	....	
Tamatave	2,000 00	32 19	252 79	
Tampico	1,586 50	333 24	....	Inclusive of instruction salary.
Tangier	5,655 61	10 00	226 07	Inclusive of accounts suspended in 1870 and 1871.
Toronto	2,000 00	4,766 00	....	Inclusive of additional compensation allowed when fees reach $3,000.
Agencies	3,904 56	4,257 50	....	
Trieste	2,000 00	1,428 04	....	
Agency	22 00	22 00	....	
Trinidad de Cuba	2,500 00	409 38	....	
Tripoli	3,000 00	....	111 39	
Tumbez	676 62	205 94	....	Inclusive of transit salary.
Tunis	3,000 00	....	....	
Tunstall	2,146 75	8,851 27	....	Inclusive of additional compensation and transit salaries.
Turk's Islands	2,000 00	548 32	74 29	
Agencies	404 94	404 94	....	
Valencia	1,162 07	17 50	....	Returns imperfect.
Valparaiso	3,000 00	1,787 65	....	
Venice	750 00	470 71	31 20	
Vera Cruz	3,500 00	1,845 36	....	
Vienna	2,000 00	6,572 50	66 63	Inclusive of additional compensation allowed when fees reach $3,000.
Agencies	570 50	570 50	....	
Windsor	1,500 00	2,504 00	....	
Agencies	1,423 00	1,423 00	....	
Winnipeg	1,500 00	362 00	....	
Yedo	750 00	23 50	80 72	Settled to September 30, 1871.
Zanzibar	1,140 81	134 10	148 96	Account for second quarter of 1872 not received.
Zurich	2,000 00	4,149 85	4 28	Inclusive of additional compensation allowed when fees reach $3,000.
Agency	2,085 00	2,842 25	....	
Agents to examine consular affairs.	5,000 00	....	....	
Total	472,990 11	706,907 95	10,235 00	

RECAPITULATION.

Total fees received		$706,907 95
salaries paid	$472,990 11	
loss by exchange	10,235 00	
		483,225 11
Excess of fees over salaries and loss by exchange		223,682 84

B 1.—*Expenditures on account of sundry appropriations from July 1, 1871, to June 30, 1872, as shown by adjustments in this office.*

For interpreters to the consulates in China, Japan, and Siam	$7,214 64
For salaries of the marshals of the consular courts in Japan, including that at Nagasaki, and in China, Siam, and Turkey	5,591 44
For rent of prisons for American convicts in Japan, China, Siam, and Turkey	8,011 93
For expenses of the consulates in the Turkish dominions, viz: Interpreters, guards, and other expenses of the consulates at Constantinople, Smyrna, Candia, Alexandria, Jerusalem, and Beirut	3,104 04

C.—*Statement showing the amount expended by the consular officers of the United States for the relief of American seamen, the money received by said officers for extra wages, &c., and the loss by exchange incurred by them during the fiscal year ended June 30, 1872.*

Consulate.	Expended.	Received.	Loss by exchange.
Acapulco	$710 75		
Amoy		$44 00	
Amsterdam	1,316 80		$54 78
Antigua	54 00		
Antwerp	1,298 59	179 15	
Aspinwall	1,087 00	575 00	
Bangkok	44 40		
Barbados	189 16	283 60	
Batavia	3,253 68	61 28	279 24
Bathurst	76 49	49 25	
Bay of Islands, New Zealand	813 95	518 20	11 01
Belfast		63 97	
Bermuda	39 36	237 20	
Bombay	154 27	61 98	
Bordeaux		27 92	
Bradford	2 90		
Bremen	76 69	76 55	
Bristol	62 52	33 38	46
Buenos Ayres	749 82	197 66	
Cadiz	668 70	63 76	53 04
Calcutta	501 62	775 52	
Callao	3,176 75	1,979 55	
Canton	12 00		
Cape Haytien	24 85		
Cape Town	203 03	211 67	
Cardiff	74 88	196 48	
Constantinople	7 65	25 00	
Cork	131 28	109 37	4 09
Corunna	30 10		
Curaçoa	74 70		
Demerara	28 59	607 47	
Dublin	96 30		
Dundee	19 35		
Elsinore	101 07	293 12	
Fayal	3,953 04	451 99	
Gaboon	27 00		
Geestemunde	119 11	1,757 95	
Genoa	233 29	170 43	
Gibraltar	91 36	154 78	
Glasgow	5 77		
Guayaquil	661 20		
Guaymas		5 20	
Hakodadi	36 00		4 00
Halifax	360 59		
Hamburg	2 16	1,086 39	11 78
Havana	612 00	1,814 20	186 04
Havre	365 82	138 99	6 63
Hilo			31 81
Hong-Kong, (quarter ended June 30, 1872, not received)	988 50	358 20	
Honolulu*	120,425 85	961 14	1,689 34
Kanagawa	408 50	368 10	
Kingston, Jamaica	142 56	683 21	
La Paz	60 00		
Leeds	7 56		
Leghorn		133 08	
Lisbon	25 92	40 00	
Liverpool	440 98	3,509 34	
London	845 63	440 00	
Madagascar	5 00		

* Inclusive of $116,452.00 expended on account of the destruction, by ice, of the whaling-fleet in the Arctic Ocean.

C.—*Statement showing the amount expended by the consular officers, &c.*—Continued.

Consulate.	Expended.	Received.	Loss by exchange.
Malaga	$2,474 44	$304 35	$165 14
Manchester	9 68		
Manila	795 05	380 24	
Marseilles	478 30	60 00	
Matanzas	134 07	181 36	70 53
Mauritius	1,192 63	80 00	53 00
Melbourne	133 04	106 57	
Minatitlan	14 88		
Monrovia	47 00		
Montevideo	880 21		
Nagasaki		57 40	
Naples	50 45		
Nassau, Bahamas	2,251 66	139 00	
Panama	907 85	257 00	
Para		71 36	
Paramaribo	975 80		19 80
Paris	3 86		
Payta	4,216 43	120 00	
Pernambuco	744 02		63 03
Piræus	3 62		
Quebec	484 00		3 65
Rio de Janeiro	71 45	213 19	
Rio Grande, Brazil	1,617 60	70 00	
Rotterdam	230 36	63 06	
St. Catherine's, Brazil	103 97	20 00	
St. Croix, West Indies	21 00	36 04	
St. Domingo City	53 76		
St. Helena	359 71	813 50	
St. John's, New Brunswick	45 00	94 35	
St. John's, Newfoundland	288 11		4 32
San Juan, Porto Rico	521 45	15 34	
St. Martin, West Indies	88 42		
St. Pierre, Miquelon	367 95		
St. Thomas, West Indies	676 50		93
San Andres	46 80		
San Juan del Norte	101 40		
Santiago, Cape Verde Islands	763 94	131 11	70 24
Santiago de Cuba	180 23		1 71
Seychelles		20 00	
Shanghai	789 17	1,682 33	
Sheffield	5 21		
Singapore	869 05	1,075 86	
Stettin	13 40		54
Stockholm	8 53		
Swatow	50 00	421 51	8 82
Sydney, Australia	1,122 08	205 68	78 67
Talcahuano	4,349 65	400 00	
Tahiti	1,432 10	417 40	95 19
Tampico	61 00		
Teneriffe	232 50	67 02	40 54
Toronto	41 50		
Trieste	66 25	40 25	
Trinidad de Cuba		28 20	
Tumbez	148 00	321 00	
Valparaiso	386 26	852 15	
Venice	23 81	3 86	2 09
Vera Cruz	112 00		
Victoria, Vancouver's Island	184 00	25 00	

RECAPITULATION.

Total amount of expenditures and loss by exchange	$179,147 66
Amount of extra wages received	27,548 22
Excess of disbursements over receipts	151,599 44

D.—*Statement of the number of destitute American seamen sent to the United States, and the amount paid for their passage, from the following consulates, during the fiscal year ended June* 30, 1872.

Consulates.	Number of seamen.	Amount.	Consulates.	Number of seamen.	Amount.
Acapulco	17	$170 00	Padang	1	$10 00
Antigua	4	40 00	Palermo	6	75 00
Aribo	3	30 00	Panama	35	350 00
Aspinwall	81	810 00	Paramaribo	4	60 00
Auckland	4	40 00	Pernambuco	3	30 00
Bahia	1	10 00	Point-a-Pitre	1	10 00
Barbados	8	80 00	Port Hastings	5	50 00
Batavia	2	20 00	Port Louis	23	900 00
Bay of Islands	5	50 00	Ponce	1	10 00
Bermuda	2	20 00	Porto Rico	2	22 00
Buenos Ayres	1	10 00	Puenta Arenas	1	10 00
Cadiz	3	30 00	Rio de Janeiro	9	90 00
Callao	7	70 00	Rio Grande do Sul	4	40 00
Cape Town	1	10 00	Rivatan	1	10 00
Cardenas	3	30 00	Sagua la Grande	3	30 00
Cardiff	2	20 00	San José	2	20 00
Cow Bay	6	60 00	San Juan	18	190 00
Cronstadt	2	20 00	Santiago, C. V	7	110 00
Curaçoa	6	120 00	Santiago de Cuba	2	20 00
Demerara	3	30 00	Scammon's Lagoon	32	320 00
Fayal	77	1,582 00	Shanghai	3	30 00
Gaboon	3	30 00	Sydney	9	90 00
Genoa	2	20 00	Singapore	6	60 00
Geestemünde	2	79 20	Sourabaya	1	10 00
Hakodadi	16	160 00	St. Ann's Bay	1	10 00
Halifax	28	167 00	St. Croix	4	40 00
Hamburg	3	30 00	San Domingo	1	10 00
Havana	38	380 00	St. Helena	8	105 00
Havre	1	10 00	St. John's	3	30 00
Honolulu	211	2,110 00	St. Kitt's	4	64 00
Inagua	5	50 00	St. Martin	4	40 00
Kanagawa	26	260 00	St. Thomas	28	280 00
Kingston	9	90 00	Tabasco	4	50 00
La Paz	3	30 00	Tahiti	12	135 00
Liverpool	26	260 00	Talcahuana	8	80 00
London	5	50 00	Tampico	5	95 00
Long Cay, C. I	3	30 00	Teneriffe	4	40 00
Malaga	3	30 00	Trinidad	2	20 00
Manila	6	60 00	Tumacoa	1	10 00
Manzanillo	4	40 00	Vera Cruz	3	30 00
Maranham	2	20 00	Victoria	11	125 00
Minatitlan	4	40 00	Yamsk	3	30 00
Mazatlan	6	82 00	Zanzibar	2	20 00
Merida	1	10 00			
Montevideo	1	10 00	Total	1,012	12,069 20
Nassau, New Providence	95	950 00			

American seamen picked up in the Arctic Ocean from the wreck of the whaling-fleet, in September, 1871, and taken into Honolulu, 1,172	$41,020 00
American seamen picked up at sea and taken into the United States by different vessels, 37	736 00

D 1.—*Statement showing the amount expended in bringing to the United States American seamen charged with crime during the fiscal year ended June* 30, 1872.

Consulates.	Number of seamen.	Amount.
Monrovia	3	$595 81
Palermo	1	75 00
Rio de Janeiro	8	900 00
St. Thomas	1	20 00
Tahiti	12	483 51
Total	.....	2,074 32

E.—*Statement showing the amount refunded to citizens, seamen, or their representatives, directly from the United States Treasury, the several sums having been previously paid therein by consular officers, during the fiscal year ended June 30, 1872.*

J. H. Bartlett & Sons, owners bark Canton Packet	$245 90
Edward Cornes, citizen, estate of	1,297 80
James H. Crutchett, citizen, estate of	105 89
Gilbert L. Huson, seaman, estate of	40 27
J. W. Ruggles, citizen, estate of	291 36
Robert Sellars, citizen, estate of	5,477 04
Lewis Stinson, seaman, estate of	49 31
Nunzio Virzini, citizen, estate of	29 50
G. H. Wilson, seaman, estate of	695 57
Total	8,232 64

F.—*Department accounts received and settled for the fiscal year ended June 30, 1872.*

State Department:		
Publishing laws in pamplet form		$57,505 80
Proof-reading and packing		2,998 00
Copper-plate printing, books, maps, &c		2,078 00
Rescue of American citizens from shipwreck		2,448 52
Expenses under the neutrality act		243 41
Stationery, furniture, &c		3,351 30
Contingent expenses of foreign intercourse and missions abroad	$26,326 38	
The same settled on Department of State approval	7,216 21	
		33,542 59
Contingent expenses of consuls	37,818 47	
The same settled on Department of State approval	52,807 74	
		90,626 21
Salary and expenses of United States and British claim commission		69,614 57
Salary and expenses of United States and Spanish claim commission		9,532 27
Salary and expenses of United States and Mexican claim commission		19,423 63
Salary and expenses of United States commissioner to Texas		1,607 00
Award to Hudson's Bay and Puget Sound		325,000 00
		617,971 85
Interior Department:		
Expenses of taking ninth census		$914,366 93
Expenses of taking eighth census		6,139 79
Miscellaneous and contingent expenses of Patent-Office		98,416 70
Publishing Patent-Office Official Gazette		5,425 00
Plates for Patent-Office Official Gazette		3,327 76
Expenses for copies of drawings in the Patent-Office		39,972 26
Expenses of packing and distributing congressional documents		6,979 90
Expenses of building hall in Smithsonian Institute		10,000 00
Preservation of collections of United States exploring expeditions		10,000 00
		1,094,628 34
Post-Office Department:		
Contingent expenses of Post-Office Department		$58,626 31
Contingent expenses for stationery, fuel, gas, &c		12,268 26
		70,894 57

G.—*Statement showing the expenses of assessing the internal-revenue taxes in the several collection districts, including the salaries, commissions, and allowances of the assessors, their contingent expenses, and the compensation of assistant assessors and store-keepers, from July 1, 1871, to June 30, 1872.*

District.	Gross compensation.	Tax.	Compensation.	Clerk-hire.	Stationery.	Printing and advertising.	Postage and express.	Rent of assessors.	Survey of distilleries.	Net compensation of assistant assessors.	Net compensation of store-keepers.	Tax on compensation of ass't. assessors and store-keepers.	Total.
ALABAMA.													
First district†	....	....	$2,492 66	$1,800 00	$199 87	$17 75	$97 72	....	....	$8,848 53	$1,140 00	....	$14,596 53
Second district	....	....	2,500 00	1,800 00	192 29	33 50	119 44	$270 00	....	10,118 58	....	....	15,033 81
Third district*	....	....	2,500 00	915 33	35 78	30 25	17 60	90 00	$108 30	4,399 10	....	....	8,108 36
Total	....	....	7,492 66	4,515 33	427 94	87 50	234 76	360 00	108 30	23,336 21	1,140 00	....	37,732 70
ARIZONA.†													
Arizona	....	....	2,500 00	....	58 77	84 00	19 32	300 00	....	1,637 19	....	....	4,599 28
ARKANSAS.													
First district*	....	....	3,512 16	1,375 00	190 20	120 91	135 55	180 00	....	6,161 63	132 00	$24 82	11,807 45
Second district	$2,609 58	$5 47	2,604 11	1,200 00	156 75	8 25	15 14	480 00	....	4,364 81	....	....	8,829 06
Third district*	....	....	2,500 00	541 66	53 99	5 00	34 47	150 00	....	4,018 44	....	8 56	7,303 56
Total	....	....	8,616 27	3,116 66	400 94	134 16	185 16	810 00	....	14,544 88	132 00	....	27,940 07

CONNECTICUT.													
First district			3,784 77	900 00	24 75	13 34	71 15	267 50		6,509 26	6,051 52		17,572 29
Second district			2,747 43	1,200 00	44 83	8 50	80 48	100 00		6,280 69			10,461 93
Third district			1,723 63	800 00	16 55	3 00	46 09	300 00		4,526 83	1,084 00		8,500 10
Fourth district			1,860 65	800 00	51 69	9 50	45 57	75 00		6,347 32			9,189 73
Total			10,066 48	3,700 00	137 82	34 34	243 29	742 50		23,664 10	7,135 52		45,724 05
DAKOTA.													
Dakota*	3,392 85	69 64	3,323 21		79 37		13 02	139 84		2,005 13			5,560 57
DELAWARE.													
Delaware			2,985 90	1,400 00	83 18		60 67		38 50	7,053 92			11,622 17
DISTRICT OF COLUMBIA.													
District of Columbia*	2,031 41	13	2,031 28	1,500 00	54 32	20 00	3 00	420 00		5,953 13			9,981 73
FLORIDA.													
Florida*			2,500 00	1,325 00	137 41	63 75	136 10	300 00		10,390 10			14,852 36
GEORGIA.													
First district			2,051 61	1,587 12	93 42		38 25	500 00		9,982 68			14,253 08
Second district*			2,637 83	1,500 00	136 16	12 90	103 90	375 00		11,238 78		29 23	16,004 57
Third district*			2,821 84	1,500 00	90 99	16 25	152 31	192 50		12,769 61		35 99	17,543 50
Fourth district*			2,882 14	1,800 00	70 87	19 00	90 43	341 25		10,923 20	569 00	14 05	16,695 89
Total			10,393 42	6,387 12	391 44	48 15	384 89	1,408 75		44,914 27	569 00		64,497 04
IDAHO.													
Idaho			2,517 47		31 01	59 00	18 00	600 00		2,241 12	1,565 00		7,031 60
ILLINOIS.													
First district			9,789 20	4,196 32	388 21	48 95	73 91	271 92		17,036 10	17,302 50		49,107 11
Second district			1,749 37	720 00	71 71	9 80	70 52	140 00		3,894 36	488 00		7,143 76
Third district*			5,063 55	1,433 33	89 48	19 00	37 95	180 00		6,019 32	2,139 00		14,981 63
Fourth district			5,575 00	1,200 00	19 36	9 25	100 73	150 00	8 65	4,672 10	9,048 00		20,783 09
Fifth district*	9,383 51	28 18	9,355 33	1,500 00	148 84		48 95	258 40	18 50	10,450 14	14,476 00		36,265 16
Sixth district†			2,733 17	400 00	1 00	7 75	12 40	200 00		3,660 45	2,156 00		8,570 77
Seventh district*	3,250 54	11 28	3,239 26	900 00	55 66	14 50	30 72	90 62		4,788 59	2,109 92		11,229 27
Eighth district*	5,649 50	5 17	5,644 33	1,599 98	103 15	28 45	79 69		26 30	8,393 44	5,787 09	21 87	21,662 43
Ninth district			2,926 59	540 00	16 24		43 50	100 00	29 90	3,512 33	2,656 00		9,824 56

*Including items belonging to previous fiscal years not before adjusted.

†Complete returns for the district not received at this office.

G.—*Statement showing the expenses of assessing the internal-revenue taxes in the several collection districts, &c.*—Continued.

District.	Gross compensation.	Tax.	Compensation.	Clerk-hire.	Stationery.	Printing and advertising.	Postage and express.	Rent of assessors.	Survey of distilleries.	Net compensation of assistant assessors.	Net compensation of store-keepers.	Tax on compensation of ass't assessors and store-keepers.	Total.
ILLINOIS—Continued.													
Tenth district*	$1,586 53	$4 32	$1,582 21	$300 00	$34 41	$12 25	$17 00	$200 00	....	$4,398 95	....	....	$6,544 82
Eleventh district*	....	....	1,500 00	300 00	61 25	6 60	34 79	78 00	....	3,703 69	....	....	5,684 33
Twelfth district*	3,905 85	2 51	3,903 34	980 10	64 03	34 23	48 00	179 00	$12 50	5,002 30	$1,076 00	$5 85	11,299 61
Thirteenth district*	....	....	1,492 85	300 00	28 72	14 25	....	72 00	21 15	4,722 00	....	4 51	6,650 97
Total	....	....	54,554 20	14,369 73	1,082 06	205 05	598 16	1,919 94	117 60	79,662 86	57,238 51	....	209,747 51
INDIANA.													
First district*	5,420 82	2 89	5,417 93	1,200 00	33 57	85 95	68 77	160 00	178 80	6,090 58	6,892 00	....	20,127 60
Second district	....	....	1,570 36	533 30	109 28	50 00	36 70	100 00	168 75	3,461 30	1,272 00	....	7,301 69
Third district	....	....	3,730 62	800 00	53 57	38 55	32 06	100 00	....	3,485 95	2,698 00	....	10,938 75
Fourth district*	8,184 11	45 07	8,139 04	1,000 00	24 67	23 50	43 37	120 00	24 85	3,141 54	9,540 00	....	22,056 97
Fifth district*	1,569 30	2 41	1,566 89	375 00	88 73	10 00	19 18	181 50	....	3,172 52	297 00	....	5,710 82
Sixth district	....	....	3,090 14	956 94	29 89	7 70	74 69	....	31 90	3,163 50	1,890 00	....	9,844 76
Seventh district*	....	....	3,839 16	614 98	69 32	32 00	22 00	75 00	22 20	3,589 88	2,613 00	....	10,877 54
Eighth district*	4,201 99	16 75	4,185 24	909 96	19 53	....	....	166 25	....	2,354 89	1,252 00	....	8,977 87
Ninth district	2,059 89	2 16	2,057 73	39 00	....	14 00	12 45	42 00	7 45	3,706 08	1,252 00	....	7,130 71
Tenth district	....	....	1,500 00	....	28 40	26 50	18 00	70 00	....	2,782 54	....	....	4,425 44
Eleventh district	....	....	1,555 57	60 00	....	....	60 50	137 50	....	2,651 88	1,252 00	....	5,717 45
Total	....	....	37,252 08	6,579 18	456 96	288 20	387 72	1,152 25	433 95	37,600 66	28,958 00	....	113,109 60
IOWA.													
First district*	1,973 96	2 00	1,971 96	720 00	88 13	37 00	52 36	110 00	....	4,032 08	....	....	7,011 53
Second district*	....	....	2,704 98	600 00	48 53	36 50	49 00	85 00	14 35	4,674 68	1,356 00	....	9,569 04
Third district	....	....	3,462 42	743 24	42 26	36 40	76 07	....	....	4,211 67	3,206 00	....	11,778 66
Fourth district†	....	....	1,408 85	490 92	29 94	55 75	93 46	120 00	....	3,267 90	....	....	5,475 82
Fifth district*	....	....	1,883 30	571 58	141 27	....	2 15	90 00	....	3,303 17	290 00	4 79	6,251 56
Sixth district	....	....	1,500 00	400 00	62 90	93 00	90 90	144 00	....	3,208 57	....	....	5,500 27
Total	....	....	12,931 60	3,534 74	383 03	259 55	364 54	549 00	14 35	22,698 07	4,852 00	....	45,586 68

* Including items belonging to previous fiscal years not before adjusted.

† Complete returns for the district not received at this office.

KANSAS.													
Kansas			1,872 39	1,200 00	117 40	112 15	279 49	360 00	55 55	10,686 73	120 00		14,803 71
KENTUCKY.													
First district*			2,090 99	975 15	104 85	6 00	22 60	150 00	45 05	6,675 38	2,775 20		12,846 12
Second district			3,005 08	999 96	9 37		35 97	150 00	12 30	6,983 38	9,552 00		20,748 06
Third district*	1,797 67	4 35	1,793 32	900 00	55 42		41 80	140 00	113 70	4,314 18			7,358 51
Fourth district*	3,323 49	22 21	3,301 28	1,466 68	118 92	27 50	42 69	200 00	21 30	8,920 11	19,737 92	3 08	33,836 40
Fifth district*			4,880 98	2,499 96	203 13	27 00	69 78			9,518 77	12,862 50	4 56	30,062 12
Sixth district*	6,961 20	6 82	6,954 38	1,800 00	164 69	10 00	79 58	250 00	48 45	7,461 46	17,598 00		34,366 56
Seventh district†*	4,926 17	30 45	4,895 72	1,550 00	161 18	7 50	65 71	360 00		6,865 21	22,120 00		36,025 32
Eighth district			1,608 66	800 00	114 79		20 91	110 00	24 75	4,293 39	3,352 00		10,324 50
Ninth district			1,727 24	570 15	16 15	12 50	96 20	237 50	73 85	3,216 85	1,912 00		7,862 44
Total			30,257 65	11,561 90	948 50	90 50	475 33	1,597 50	340 30	58,248 73	89,909 62		193,430 03
LOUISIANA.													
First district*	4,842 43	89	4,841 54	3,838 52	7 50	50 00	7 00			17,657 49	8,925 00	38 79	35,336 05
Second district*	2,671 70	5 15	2,666 55	1,500 00	110 05	6 75	24 89	300 00		12,212 12		43 57	16,820 36
Third district*			2,349 53	933 03	109 90	90 25	50 50	299 16		10,144 68		53 28	13,977 05
Total			9,857 62	6,271 55	227 45	156 00	82 39	599 16		40,014 29	8,925 00		66,133 46
MAINE.													
First district*	1,257 27	4 71	1,252 56	1,000 00	188 62	16 92	20 42			2,627 70	1,188 00		6,293 42
Second district			1,500 00	240 00	26 18	11 25	66 50	100 00		3,010 81			4,954 74
Third district			1,500 00	188 00	20 20	7 55	27 06	44 00		2,025 61			3,812 42
Fourth district			1,500 00	240 00	36 98	10 75	28 79	72 00		2,616 89			4,505 41
Fifth district*			1,500 00		1 80	14 50	27 32	100 00		2,249 96			3,893 58
Total			7,252 56	1,668 00	273 78	60 17	170 09	316 00		12,530 97	1,188 00		23,459 57
MARYLAND.													
First district*			2,509 14	600 00	26 38	88 52		468 33	13 70	10,036 58	1,240 00	14 63	14,982 65
Second district*	1,187 16	33	1,186 83		25 94	13 00	50	291 67		2,723 77	1,255 00	2 40	5,496 71
Third district			4,142 40	3,000 00	120 05	51 50	10 00			21,145 88	4,105 00		32,575 73

* Including items belonging to previous fiscal years not before adjusted.

† Complete returns for the district not received at this office.

G.—*Statement showing the expenses of assessing the internal-revenue taxes in the several collection districts, &c.*—Continued.

District.	Gross compensation.	Tax.	Compensation.	Clerk-hire.	Stationery.	Printing and advertising.	Postage and express.	Rent of assessors.	Survey of distilleries.	Net compensation of assistant assessors.	Net compensation of store-keepers.	Tax on compensation of ass't assessors and store-keepers.	Total.
MARYLAND—Continued.													
Fourth district			$1, 054 72	$600 00	$60 70	$33 50	$22 20	$50 00	$24 30	$5, 793 63	$2, 120 00		$10, 350 05
Fifth district			4, 517 32	833 33	23 27	81 62	22 25	45 00	8 25	6, 961 87	3, 968 00	$9 56	16, 460 91
Total			14, 010 41	5, 033 33	257 24	268 14	54 95	855 00	46 25	46, 661 73	12, 088 00		79, 875 05
MASSACHUSETTS.													
First district			1, 806 33	720 00	46 20	26 00	49 53	200 00		5, 012 12			7, 860 18
Second district			2, 121 54	360 00	56 36	12 00	42 27	200 00		4, 479 25			7, 271 42
Third district			4, 849 55	3, 124 99	67 52	51 25	73 49	1, 000 00		18, 560 68	5, 577 50		33, 304 98
Fourth district*			4, 921 49	2, 000 00	70 79	14 50	46 00	550 00		12, 515 20	5, 591 06	6 70	25, 709 04
Fifth district			3, 320 94	1, 200 00	63 11	23 50	24 00	175 00		6, 826 97	1, 252 00		12, 886 12
Sixth district			4, 478 25	1, 399 92	73 28	30 00	72 32	300 00		5, 405 84	2, 492 00		14, 251 61
Seventh district			2, 255 00	1, 200 00	75 52	19 88	49 38	250 00		5, 528 26			9, 378 04
Eighth district			2, 101 53	1, 367 00	67 95	12 25	47 33	400 00		5, 854 40			90, 850 46
Ninth district			1, 600 90	720 00	73 30	19 25	91 63	200 00	4 00	7, 311 74			10, 020 82
Tenth district			2, 874 99	1, 249 99	41 61	15 62	65 62	250 00		8, 399 68	2, 504 00		15, 401 51
Total			30, 330 52	13, 341 90	635 64	224 25	562 17	3, 525 00	4 00	79, 894 14	17, 416 56		145, 934 18
MICHIGAN.													
First district			4, 262 17	1, 692 00	70 47	25 75	15 00	500 00		7, 736 17	1, 240 00		15, 541 56
Second district*	$1, 584 56	$2 54	1, 582 02	600 00		17 95	25 05	200 00		3, 470 98			5, 896 00
Third district*			1, 529 81	720 00	42 37	18 25	31 70	150 00		4, 845 39			7, 337 52
Fourth district			1, 574 75	600 00	69 06	30 70	9 07	125 00		4, 451 43			6, 860 61
Fifth district			1, 500 00	480 00	70 22	22 55	47 78	150 00		3, 875 85			6, 146 40
Sixth district*			1, 946 01	646 64	53 40	28 85	104 52	52 00		8, 252 28		2 88	11, 083 70
Total			12, 394 76	4, 738 64	305 52	144 05	233 72	1, 177 00		32, 632 10	1, 240 00		52, 805 79
MINNESOTA.													
First district*			1, 500 00	400 00			71 87	100 00		5, 060 29		5 92	7, 132 16
Second district			1, 945 79	799 80	64 66	40 62	138 87	225 00		7, 807 48			11, 022 22
Total			3, 445 79	1, 199 80	64 66	40 62	210 74	325 00		12, 867 77			18, 154 38

MISSISSIPPI.													
First district*			2,497 64	1,308 33	26 33	9 00	49 91	300 00		7,399 97		29 50	11,591 18
Second district*			2,500 00	999 97	156 05	65 75	37 95	300 00	97 60	9,403 19		48 89	13,560 51
Third district*			2,499 99	720 00	135 03	33 50	144 55	200 00	132 75	10,089 13	145 00	39 06	14,099 95
Total			7,497 63	3,028 30	317 41	108 25	232 41	800 00	230 35	26,892 29	145 00		39,251 64
MISSOURI.													
First district*			5,686 30	3,720 00	238 22	21 00	10 00	1,000 00		15,396 80	8,115 00		34,187 32
Second district*	1,406 60	1 50	1,405 10	825 00	33 29	49 50	241 11	180 00	237 90	5,648 27	1,920 00		10,540 17
Third district			1,798 96	999 96	115 43	56 25	76 52	100 00	31 50	3,602 51	72 00		6,853 13
Fourth district			2,202 24	49 30		30 50	3 50	114 00		4,669 44			7,068 98
Fifth district*			2,168 35	1,200 00	162 25	59 10	180 26	253 00	106 35	8,839 84	156 64		13,125 79
Sixth district*	3,544 65	3 02	3,541 63	1,599 97	196 26	48 35	307 29	420 00	6 45	12,006 87	2,880 00		21,006 82
Total			16,802 58	8,394 23	745 45	264 70	818 68	2,067 00	382 20	50,163 73	13,143 64		92,782 21
MONTANA.													
Montana			2,500 00	999 98			32 00	500 00		7,358 83			11,390 81
NEBRASKA.													
Nebraska			1,500 00	900 00	160 13		36 83	180 00		5,974 93	1,044 00		9,795 89
NEVADA.													
Nevada			2,500 00	1,015 00	26 56	192 70	27 05	180 00	108 20	5,363 30			9,412 81
NEW HAMPSHIRE.													
First district			2,050 20	594 00		18 50	32 00	60 00		3,595 18	772 00		7,121 88
Second district			1,520 69	700 00	6 10	18 90	40 80	150 00		2,684 81			5,121 30
Third district			1,372 26	407 00	8 16	15 25	48 17	80 00		2,113 08			4,043 92
Total			4,943 15	1,701 00	14 26	52 65	120 97	290 00		8,393 07	772 00		16,287 10
NEW JERSEY.													
First district			1,500 13	720 00	59 52			150 00		8,300 57	124 00		10,854 22
Second district*	2,682 15	29 38	2,652 77	1,200 00	164 70	24 75	38 99	200 00		6,697 19			10,978 49
Third district			3,494 60	1,200 00	66 49	8 55	45 01	200 00		11,129 05	1,586 00		17,729 70
Fourth district			2,576 49	999 96	70 27	20 70	30 00	200 00	31 50	9,993 15			13,931 07
Fifth district			3,914 86	2,845 00	109 65	13 90	8 87			14,357 33			21,249 61
Total			14,138 85	6,964 96	470 72	67 90	131 87	750 00	31 50	50,477 29	1,710 00		74,743 09

* Including items belonging to previous fiscal years not before adjusted.

G.—*Statement showing the expenses of assessing the internal-revenue taxes in the several collection districts, &c.*—Continued.

District.	Gross compensation.	Tax.	Compensation.	Clerk-hire.	Stationery.	Printing and advertising.	Postage and express.	Rent of assessors.	Survey of distilleries.	Net compensation of assistant assessors.	Net compensation of store-keepers.	Tax on compensation of ass't assessors and store-keepers.	Total.
NEW MEXICO.													
New Mexico			$2,248 64	$770 83	$144 12	$82 00	$35 25	$205 60		$7,717 27	$558 36	$5 64	$11,762 07
NEW YORK.													
First district			4,937 71	4,999 94	145 36	75 00	23 05	1,000 00		78,387 76	6,535 00		96,103 82
Second district*			4,000 00	6,000 00	263 27	58 00	28 05	1,617 50		34,362 61		3 60	46,329 43
Third district*	$5,981 93	$4 14	5,977 79	6,199 98	149 00	72 00	9 00	3,000 00		37,182 39			52,590 16
Eighth district*			4,000 00	3,199 92	132 96	26 00	14 75	1,200 00		15,084 77			23,658 40
Ninth district			4,131 96	3,000 00	57 97	30 00	40 00	840 00		18,753 83	230 00		27,083 76
Tenth district			3,194 65	1,500 00	60 54	22 00	19 46	300 00		9,273 86	880 00		15,250 51
Eleventh district*			1,609 69	720 00	158 86	5 00	51 82	175 00		10,148 87		2 17	12,869 24
Twelfth district*			2,276 42	1,200 00	47 67	25 30	1 80	156 25	$1 50	8,707 22		5 78	12,416 16
Thirteenth district			1,917 71	876 00	35 64	7 52	25 50	150 00	2 64	4,241 29		9	7,256 30
Fourteenth district			3,828 95	2,119 50	63 24	27 25	64 73	500 00		8,010 23			14,613 90
Fifteenth district			2,533 69	1,500 00	117 35	17 50	69 51	400 00		8,082 06			12,720 11
Sixteenth district*			1,324 50	300 00	98 60	19 00	70 91			3,163 13		1 45	5,035 14
Seventeenth district			1,500 00	153 00	48 43	20 75	21 76	100 00		2,262 05			4,105 99
Eighteenth district*	1,870 24	2 43	1,867 81	720 00	62 50	6 75	6 00	153 32		6,479 32	1,008 00		10,305 70
Nineteenth district*			1,500 00	360 00	64 34	21 37	59 17	100 00		2,969 73			5,134 61
Twentieth district			1,558 19	483 86	37 34	22 00	18 75	100 00		2,643 23			4,863 37
Twenty-first district*			3,173 62	885 00	92 75	8 50	78 13	241 67		7,091 08		20 70	12,170 75
Twenty-second district*	5,338 94	48 31	5,290 63	1,200 00	38 04	19 25	15 68			4,869 78	2,344 00		13,777 38
Twenty-third district*			3,513 93	1,447 00	56 48	18 75	43 12	500 00		7,003 61	2,720 00		15,302 89
Twenty-fourth district*			3,563 26	1,200 00	62 14	11 00	35 20	100 00		5,024 76	1,604 00		11,600 36
Twenty-fifth district*	1,751 20	10 99	1,740 21	720 00	35 03	13 63	44 88	85 00		3,574 57			6,213 32
Twenty-sixth district*			1,885 07	630 00	159 14	12 75	43 48	200 00	8 40	4,821 29			7,760 13
Twenty-seventh dist., (old)	1,517 53	50	1,517 03	660 00	33 11	11 74	59 05	91 66		4,216 96			6,589 35
Do (new)							18 30	3 50		586 61			608 41
Twenty-eighth district			3,171 16	1,041 66	100 97	17 75	13 90	500 00		7,393 63			12,230 07
Twenty-ninth district*			1,501 69	840 00	111 47	17 50	4 50	120 00		4,704 42			7,299 58
Thirtieth district*			5,770 63	2,683 34	178 82	4 00	43 70	525 00		13,636 00	7,350 00		30,191 49
Thirty-first district*			1,500 00	478 62	36 29		65 51	43 82		2,876 82			5,001 06
Thirty-second district			4,000 00	5,913 65	414 93	38 40	37 56			33,249 04	7,700 00		51,354 48
Total			82,786 30	51,091 47	2,862 24	629 71	1,027 27	12,262 72	12 54	349,401 82	30,371 00		530,445 07

NORTH CAROLINA.													
First district	2,045 66	42	2,045 24	600 00	117 62	2 50	26 51	150 00	....	10,146 26	....	....	13,088 13
Second district	2,079 77	40	2,079 37	1,000 01	104 85	19 75	9 50	120 00	....	6,186 54	....	....	9,520 02
Third district	....	....	2,000 00	499 00	25 24	88 75	18 99	68 75	....	6,074 98	....	....	8,775 71
Fourth district*	3,239 74	6 64	3,233 10	1,500 00	58 43	16 00	60 86	250 00	17 75	17,983 33	698 00	....	23,807 47
Fifth district*	4,189 74	28 06	4,161 68	1,261 96	162 03	12 00	79 15	300 00	....	14,320 20	1,599 56	77 24	21,896 58
Sixth district*	....	....	2,892 40	1,500 00	....	9 25	46 98	150 00	....	8,467 49	1,540 00	....	14,606 12
Seventh district	1,672 39	39	1,672 33	300 00	130 92	....	1 00	94 08	....	7,490 49	....	....	9,688 82
Total	....	....	18,084 12	6,660 97	599 09	148 25	242 99	1,132 83	17 75	70,669 29	3,827 56	....	101,382 85
OHIO.													
First district	....	....	8,699 03	4,200 00	238 17	30 00	1 54	1,500 00	....	25,897 05	17,010 00	....	57,575 79
Second district, (old)*	2,306 16	48	2,305 68	125 00	55 98	....	....	....	....	678 37	198 00	14 63	3,363 03
Third district*	6,336 09	12 48	6,323 61	1,800 00	97 92	18 00	73 09	108 00	9 75	7,679 84	13,995 70	20 49	30,105 91
Fourth district*	5,051 11	15 30	5,035 81	1,200 00	51 47	32 00	17 35	150 00	....	2,481 23	5,684 00	....	14,651 86
Fifth district*	....	....	3,074 49	600 00	52 62	37 50	29 88	60 00	....	3,488 07	1,834 00	81	9,176 56
Sixth district*	4,137 69	45 73	4,091 96	880 29	42 81	6 00	37 07	86 18	....	2,862 87	3,056 00	....	11,063 18
Seventh district*	4,786 35	11 53	4,775 02	1,446 20	103 86	48 00	61 12	150 00	....	5,845 15	5,366 66	....	17,796 01
Eighth district	....	....	1,500 00	300 00	45 78	16 25	3 35	100 00	....	3,407 53	....	....	5,372 91
Ninth district	....	....	4,724 41	731 16	98 99	76 50	57 18	100 00	26 60	4,791 13	6,008 00	....	16,613 97
Tenth district	....	....	4,668 67	1,610 00	135 55	22 00	42 47	....	....	5,844 66	3,008 00	2 93	15,331 35
Eleventh district*	4,919 86	48 13	4,871 73	....	34 70	35 00	23 50	131 25	....	4,346 18	1,704 00	16 47	11,146 36
Twelfth district	....	....	3,446 76	699 96	35 19	27 25	23 90	60 00	....	4,237 32	1,972 00	....	10,502 38
Thirteenth district*	....	....	1,580 73	473 33	72 38	14 50	71 85	125 00	....	4,186 36	135 00	....	6,650 15
Fourteenth district	....	....	1,523 08	330 00	16 34	16 00	22 57	100 00	7 00	2,869 47	1,124 00	....	6,008 46
Fifteenth district*	....	....	1,500 00	600 00	36 13	18 50	38 69	100 00	....	2,779 29	....	....	5,072 61
Sixteenth district*	....	....	1,544 35	297 00	57 31	24 00	47 20	50 00	8 20	4,260 29	3,588 00	....	9,876 35
Seventeenth district	....	....	3,028 03	262 40	54 52	....	49 75	150 00	11 85	3,375 77	2,892 00	....	9,824 32
Eighteenth district	....	....	3,732 63	2,000 00	69 27	16 00	33 45	750 00	....	9,568 74	1,016 00	....	17,186 09
Nineteenth district*	....	....	1,500 00	131 00	1 35	10 50	24 00	100 00	....	2,525 84	1,017 20	....	5,309 89
Total	....	....	67,925 99	17,686 34	1,300 34	448 00	657 96	3,820 43	63 40	101,125 16	69,608 56	....	262,636 18
OREGON.													
Oregon	....	....	2,588 33	206 00	42 22	21 50	63 92	360 00	16 62	6,066 25	....	....	9,364 84
PENNSYLVANIA.													
First district*	....	....	4,298 35	4,850 00	163 18	....	103 86	700 00	....	31,527 07	4,850 00	4 41	46,492 46
Second district	....	....	4,129 40	3,599 99	227 22	83 21	21 36	540 00	....	23,138 86	6,422 50	....	38,162 54
Third district, (old)*	....	....	49 68	....	....	....	....	....	....	....	....	....	49 68
Fourth district*	....	....	1,896 40	1,445 98	69 06	45 90	93 50	300 00	....	9,233 52	1,460 00	....	14,544 36
Fifth district*	....	....	2,681 90	1,800 00	51 57	10 85	30 00	500 00	....	10,916 21	....	....	15,990 53
Sixth district	2,726 22	5 69	2,720 53	999 96	79 38	25 57	9 98	250 00	5 00	8,158 22	....	....	12,248 64
Seventh district	....	....	1,500 00	550 00	70 22	....	50 76	225 00	....	4,499 37	....	....	6,895 35
Eighth district*	....	....	2,162 84	1,200 00	38 01	8 05	16 32	200 00	1 20	4,542 34	2,475 04	96	10,643 80
Ninth district*	2,439 17	03	2,439 14	1,216 00	147 22	14 00	24 68	250 00	11 41	7,719 67	1,492 00	50	13,314 32

* Including items belonging to previous fiscal years not before adjusted.

G.—*Statement showing the expenses of assessing the internal-revenue taxes in the several collection districts, &c.*—Continued.

District.	Gross compensation.	Tax.	Compensation.	Clerk-hire.	Stationery.	Printing and advertising.	Postage and express.	Rent of assessors.	Survey of distilleries.	Net compensation of assistant assessors.	Net compensation of store-keepers.	Tax on compensation of ass't assessors and store-keepers.	Total.
PENNSYLVANIA—Cont'd.													
Tenth district			$1,649 92	$999 96	$51 71	$19 00	$34 17	$200 00		$5,807 33			$8,762 09
Eleventh district*			1,816 48	720 00	3 50	46 50	51 25	110 00		5,377 52			8,125 25
Twelfth district*	$2,167 62	$0 84	2,166 78	900 00	142 81	8 00	117 51	250 00	$10 00	4,566 53	$1,736 00		9,897 63
Thirteenth district†			1,500 00	480 00	15 17		4 65	45 00		3,671 40	1,526 00		7,242 22
Fourteenth district*			1,705 93	900 00	131 98		16 45	150 00		6,996 02	1,224 00	$3 85	11,124 35
Fifteenth district*	2,508 43	9 99	2,498 44	1,500 00	22 01	12 50	11 62	200 00		9,834 30	5,060 00		19,138 87
Sixteenth district*	2,312 71	12 78	2,299 93	866 60	154 41	17 87		56 94		5,832 09	10,771 50	46	19,999 34
Seventeenth district			1,875 00	450 00	42 18	11 90	6 81	75 00		4,206 99	284 00		6,951 88
Eighteenth district			1,500 00	330 00	99 00	13 75	73 56	100 00	19 75	5,330 20	816 00		8,282 26
Nineteenth district*	1,517 58	95	1,516 63	419 46	99 50		10 99	120 00	4 00	6,703 17	368 00		9,241 75
Twentieth district*			1,678 48	374 40	78 13		48 26	150 00	1 67	5,797 66	1,712 00		9,840 60
Twenty-first district*	7,148 97	175 13	6,973 84	1,200 00	54 66	6 50	46 92	93 00	89 36	6,386 11	11,720 00		26,570 39
Twenty-second district			4,443 02	2,409 98	66 60	7 75	87 74	800 00		9,445 77	3,748 00		21,099 76
Twenty-third district*			3,258 40	1,750 00	51 24	12 00	10 08	300 00		6,953 28	5,732 00	5 51	18,067 00
Twenty-fourth district*			1,791 87	799 92	84 03	13 20	66 92	132 00	130 20	5,383 81	7,464 00	2 25	15,874 95
Total			58,553 86	20,852 25	1,942 79	356 55	937 50	5,746 94	281 59	192,027 44	68,861 04		358,560 05
RHODE ISLAND.													
First district			3,409 14	1,600 00	82 47	35 99	30 60			11,273 36	880 00		17,311 56
Second district			1,500 00	360 00	14 22	13 00	8 84	200 00		4,082 99			6,179 05
Total			4,909 14	1,960 00	96 69	48 99	39 44	200 00		15,356 35	880 00		23,490 61
SOUTH CAROLINA.													
First district*			2,500 00		81 06		85 05	100 00		5,299 03		4 01	8,065 14
Second district			2,500 00		32 25	14 05	89 70			5,852 73			8,488 73
Third district			2,521 10	840 00	84 06	4 00	52 15	240 00		6,076 43			9,817 74
Total			7,521 10	840 00	197 37	18 05	226 90	340 00		17,228 19			26,371 61
TENNESSEE.													

Third district			1,999 96	999 96	88 86		80 50	195 00	174 00	4,871 57			8,409 85
Fourth district*			1,726 73	501 10	115 32	32 20	11 68	144 00	138 85	4,343 39	1,928 00		8,941 27
Fifth district*			3,373 95	1,800 00	52 04	26 35	45 00	360 00	35 45	8,969 45	5,696 00		20,358 24
Sixth district			2,000 00	878 60	32 57	10 00	3 00	92 50	29 95	4,776 25	1,008 00		8,830 87
Seventh district			2,000 00	900 00	67 40	22 40	12 80	96 00		3,470 69			6,569 29
Eighth district			2,392 08	1,800 00	73 01	32 75	89 50	600 00		6,788 41			11,775 75
Total			17,501 94	7,959 66	503 81	138 70	280 50	1,769 50	397 50	38,710 34	9,516 00		76,777 95
TEXAS.													
First district*			2,502 76	1,500 00	151 76	4 00	90 74	400 00	71 25	11,903 08		46 71	16,623 59
Second district			2,500 00	1,200 00	56 56		76 36	360 00		7,753 29			11,946 21
Third district*			2,497 64	1,000 00	274 14	4 00	136 52	399 99		9,365 58			13,677 87
Fourth district*			2,500 00	1,200 00	101 91	151 00	115 20	480 00	315 80	9,385 33		3 50	14,249 24
Total			10,000 40	4,900 00	584 37	159 00	418 82	1,639 99	387 05	38,407 28			56,496 91
UTAH.													
Utah			2,495 89	600 00	106 17		131 92	599 20		4,803 87			8,737 05
VERMONT.													
First district			1,499 32	16 62	25 48	17 25	53 00	149 90		1,551 87			3,313 44
Second district*			1,500 00	174 00	44 91	13 50	81 94	76 23		1,536 08			3,426 60
Third district*			1,500 00	221 67	38 57	17 40	65 91	200 00		3,252 17			5,295 72
Total			4,499 32	412 29	108 96	48 15	200 85	426 13		6,340 12			12,035 82
VIRGINIA.													
First district*			1,464 30	161 50	18 20		5 25	72 20		5,260 62			6,982 07
Second district*	4,079 76	12 31	4,067 45	1,509 96	117 43	25 60	124 17			12,865 99	752 00		19,552 60
Third district*	4,283 22	11 38	4,271 84	2,158 29	194 66	68 50	118 27			9,652 77	928 00	11 83	17,392 33
Fourth district			1,500 00	799 92	218 56		185 64	240 00		10,084 69			13,028 81
Fifth district	4,127 74	3 83	4,123 91	1,899 98	178 51	30 75	62 95	222 00	103 75	11,979 79		30 54	18,601 64
Sixth district			1,742 65	1,500 00	49 75	17 40	155 05	125 00	29 55	10,338 69	7,822 00		21,780 09
Seventh district			1,550 45	900 00	105 03	18 50	21 00	150 00		4,920 75	1,403 00		9,068 73
Eighth district			1,550 53	360 00	108 75		104 41	250 00		4,362 99	1,252 00		7,988 68
Total			20,271 13	9,379 65	990 89	160 75	776 74	1,059 20	133 30	69,466 29	12,157 00		114,394 95
WASHINGTON.													
Washington*	2,527 45	1 37	2,526 08	600 00	69 92	27 10	42 78	300 00		2,345 76			5,911 64
WEST VIRGINIA.													
First district*	2,740 37	14	2,740 23	1,200 00	140 05		59 06		16 25	6,379 19		1 63	10,534 78

* Including items belonging to previous fiscal years not before adjusted.

† Complete returns for the district not received at this office.

G.—*Statement showing the expenses of assessing the internal-revenue taxes in the several collection districts, &c.*—Continued.

District.	Gross compensation.	Tax.	Compensation.	Clerk-hire.	Stationery.	Printing and advertising.	Postage and express.	Rent of assessors.	Survey of distilleries.	Net compensation of assistant assessors.	Net compensation of store-keepers.	Tax on compensation of ass't assessors and store-keepers.	Total.
WEST VIRGINIA—Cont.													
Second district*	....	....	$1, 585 29	$600 00	$36 35	$107 00	$4 00	$50 00	....	$4, 472 52	$946 00	$2 48	$7, 801 16
Third district*†	....	....	1, 254 40	291 67	16 16	13 00	39 54	60 00	....	3, 325 41	....	36 72	5, 000 18
Total	....	....	5, 579 92	2, 091 67	192 56	120 00	102 60	110 00	$16 25	14, 177 12	946 00	....	23, 336 12
WISCONSIN.													
First district*	$5, 183 76	$3 15	5, 180 61	2, 499 97	154 45	12 75	84 59	500 00	....	10, 495 12	7, 452 00	....	26, 379 49
Second district*	....	....	1, 958 61	1, 000 00	143 18	44 50	145 28	....	....	7, 772 55	1, 372 00	....	12, 436 12
Third district, (new)*	....	....	502 74	260 00	64 31	27 60	49 69	48 00	....	5, 374 36	400 00	....	6, 726 70
Fourth district	....	....	907 26	325 00	53 43	....	22 51	53 33	50	1, 187 81	....	....	2, 639 84
Fifth district*	....	....	907 26	333 34	2 20	....	38 79	28 33	....	2, 544 49	....	2 50	3, 944 41
Sixth district*	1, 487 87	09	1, 487 78	360 00	46 52	31 30	140 61	240 00	....	6, 455 12	....	1 59	8, 761 33
Total	....	....	11, 124 26	4, 778 31	464 09	116 15	481 47	869 66	50	33, 829 45	9, 224 00	....	60, 887 89
WYOMING.													
Wyoming	....	....	2, 499 90	....	85 22	....	58 00	300 00	....	755 09	....	....	3, 698 30

RECAPITULATION.

District.	...nsation.	...hire.	...nery.	...ng and ...tising.	...e and ...ress.	...f assess...rs.	...of dis...eries.	...mpensa... f assist... ssessors.	...mpensa... of store...ers.	

Colorado	2,500 00.	1,500 00	54 34	69 00	49 00*	480 00	....	4,265 78	....	8,918 12
Connecticut	10,086 48	3,700 00	137 82	34 34	243 29	742 50	....	23,664 10	7,135 52	45,724 05
Dakota†	3,323 21	....	79 37	....	13 02	139 84	....	2,005 13	....	5,560 57
Delaware	2,985 90	1,400 00	83 16	....	60 67	....	38 50	7,053 92	....	11,622 17
District of Columbia	2,031 28	1,500 00	54 32	20 00	3 00	420 00	....	5,953 13	....	9,981 73
Florida	2,500 00	1,325 00	137 41	63 75	136 10	300 00	....	10,390 10	....	14,852 36
Georgia	10,393 42	6,387 12	391 44	48 15	384 89	1,408 75	....	44,914 27	569 00	64,497 04
Idaho	2,517 47	....	31 01	59 00	18 00	600 00	....	2,241 12	1,565 00	7,031 60
Illinois	54,534 20	14,369 73	1,082 06	205 05	598 16	1,919 94	117 00	79,602 86	57,238 51	209,747 51
Indiana	37,252 68	6,579 18	456 06	288 20	387 72	1,152 25	433 95	37,600 66	28,958 00	113,109 60
Iowa	12,931 60	3,534 74	383 03	250 55	304 54	549 00	14 35	22,698 07	4,852 00	45,580 88
Kansas	1,872 39	1,200 00	117 40	112 15	279 49	360 00	55 55	10,686 73	120 00	14,803 71
Kentucky	30,257 65	11,561 90	948 50	90 50	475 33	1,597 50	340 30	58,248 73	89,909 62	193,430 03
Louisiana	9,857 62	6,271 55	227 45	156 00	82 39	599 16	....	40,014 29	8,925 00	66,133 46
Maine	7,252 56	1,668 00	273 78	60 17	170 09	316 00	....	12,530 97	1,188 00	23,459 57
Maryland	14,010 41	5,033 33	257 24	268 14	54 95	855 00	46 25	46,661 73	12,688 00	79,875 05
Massachusetts	30,330 52	13,341 90	635 64	224 25	562 17	3,525 00	4 00	79,894 14	17,410 56	145,934 18
Michigan	12,394 76	4,738 64	305 52	144 05	233 72	1,177 00	....	32,632 10	1,240 00	52,865 79
Minnesota	3,445 79	1,199 80	64 66	40 62	210 74	325 00	....	12,867 77	....	18,154 38
Mississippi	7,497 63	3,028 30	317 41	108 25	232 41	800 00	230 35	26,892 29	145 00	39,251 64
Missouri	16,802 58	8,469 23	745 45	264 70	818 68	2,067 00	382 20	50,163 73	13,143 64	92,980 84
Montana	2,500 00	999 98	....	....	32 00	500 00	....	7,358 63	....	11,390 31
Nebraska	1,500 00	900 00	160 13	....	36 83	180 00	....	5,974 93	1,044 00	9,795 89
Nevada	2,500 00	1,015 00	26 56	192 70	27 05	180 00	108 20	5,363 30	....	9,412 81
New Hampshire	4,943 15	1,701 00	14 26	52 65	120 97	290 00	....	8,393 07	772 00	16,287 10
New Jersey	14,138 85	6,964 96	470 72	67 90	137 87	750 00	31 50	50,477 29	1,710 00	74,743 09
New Mexico	2,248 64	770 83	144 12	82 00	35 25	205 60	....	7,717 27	558 36	11,762 07
New York	82,786 30	51,091 47	2,862 24	629 71	1,027 27	12,262 72	12 54	349,401 82	30,371 00	530,445 07
North Carolina	18,084 12	6,660 97	599 09	148 25	242 90	1,132 83	17 75	70,669 29	3,827 56	101,382 85
Ohio	67,925 99	17,686 34	1,300 34	448 00	657 96	3,820 43	63 40	101,125 16	69,608 56	262,636 18
Oregon	2,588 33	206 00	42 22	21 50	63 92	360 00	16 02	6,066 25	....	9,364 84
Pennsylvania	58,553 86	20,852 25	1,942 79	356 55	937 59	5,746 94	281 59	192,027 44	68,861 04	358,560 05
Rhode Island	4,000 14	1,960 00	96 69	48 99	39 44	200 00	....	15,356 35	880 00	23,490 61
South Carolina	7,521 10	840 00	197 37	18 05	226 90	340 00	....	17,228 19	....	26,371 61
Tennessee	17,501 94	7,959 66	503 81	138 70	280 50	1,769 50	397 50	38,710 34	9,516 00	76,777 95
Texas	10,000 40	4,900 00	584 37	150 00	418 82	1,639 99	387 65	38,407 28	....	56,496 91
Utah	2,495 89	600 00	106 17	....	131 92	599 20	....	4,803 87	....	8,737 05
Vermont	4,499 32	412 29	108 96	48 15	200 85	426 13	....	6,340 12	....	12,035 82
Virginia	20,271 13	9,379 65	890 89	160 75	776 74	1,059 20	133 30	69,466 29	12,157 00	114,394 95
Washington	2,526 08	600 00	60 92	27 10	42 78	300 00	....	2,345 76	....	5,911 64
West Virginia	5,579 02	2,091 67	192 56	120 00	102 60	110 00	16 25	14,177 12	946 00	23,336 12
Wisconsin	11,124 26	4,778 31	464 09	116 15	481 47	869 66	50	33,829 45	9,224 00	60,887 89
Wyoming	2,499 99	....	85 22	....	58 00	300 00	....	755 09	....	3,696 30
Grand total	654,398 36	265,696 97	10,234 56	5,841 59	12,161 58	57,014 92	3,503 20	1,748,763 29	462,911 37	3,229,525 90
Add amount of taxes	....	....	....	....	....	....	....	....	....	1,587 55
										3,231,113 45

* Including items belonging to previous fiscal years not before adjusted.

† Complete returns for the district not received at this office.

NOTE.—The districts where the gross compensation and tax are stated include payments for services prior to August 1, 1870.

H.—*Statement showing the expenses of collecting the internal-revenue taxes in the several collection districts, including the commissions, salaries, and extra allowances of the collectors; the office expenses which are paid out of the commissions and extra allowances; and the assessments and collections, from July 1, 1871, to June 30, 1872.*

District.	Compensation.	Stationery and blank-books.	Postage.	Express and dep. money.	Advertising.	Total expense of collecting.	Expenses of administering office.	Assessments.	Collections.
ALABAMA.									
First district	$8,000 00	$96 46	$41 91	$5 05	$4 00	$8,147 42	$5,244 00	$168,665 85	$130,283 60
Second district	9,000 00	106 09	85 00	....	....	9,191 09	6,080 84	95,243 55	78,705 20
Third district	6 980 80	34 36	95 25	....	51 75	7,162 16	4,480 80	30,714 89	25,272 12
Total	23,980 80	236 91	222 16	5 05	55 75	24,500 67	15,004 64	294,624 29	234,260 92
ARIZONA.									
Arizona†	1,800 00	41 16	12 00	....	45 50	1,898 66	684 59	3,936 17	14,406 14
ARKANSAS.									
First district*	9,014 29	38 47	122 00	84 33	14 50	9,273 59	3,449 94	36,593 56	44,492 06
Second district*	8,056 73	161 37	143 56	4 45	....	8,366 11	4,104 62	44,153 62	34,785 95
Third district*	5,135 89	112 13	40 86	....	5 00	5,293 88	1,495 00	59,584 79	20,576 90
Total	22,206 91	311 97	306 42	88 78	19 50	22,933 58	9,049 56	140,331 97	99,854 91
CALIFORNIA.									
First district*	24,955 00	160 75	273 35	265 84	70 96	25,725 90	19,955 00	2,157,994 64	2,493,203 08
Second district*	10,954 23	....	....	....	....	10,954 23	....	80	16,498 52
Third district*	9,000 00	197 68	99 90	752 67	31 00	10,081 25	6,000 00	211,791 89	198,676 20
Fourth district*	9,765 32	104 16	350 50	338 46	199 00	10,757 44	6,717 03	272,115 79	286,835 76
Fifth district*	9,000 00	185 95	217 00	149 08	107 51	9,659 54	6,006 00	88,587 22	78,366 71
Total	63,674 55	648 54	940 75	1,506 05	408 47	67,178 36	38,678 03	2,730,490 34	3,073,580 27
COLORADO.									
Colorado*	8,750 00	88 54	76 80	8 90	184 70	9,108 94	5,000 00	76,546 14	63,047 42
CONNECTICUT.									
First district	8,636 07	33 15	67 00	....	31 45	8,768 27	3,272 54	563,559 07	544,049 26
Second district*	6,957 50	49 02	144 00	2 03	23 32	7,175 87	2,658 49	354,329 81	345,749 96
Third district	4,963 84	86 63	137 00	....	9 35	5,196 82	1,400 00	143,522 43	144,726 52
Fourth district	5,211 12	50 05	136 00	3 99	16 50	5,417 66	1,046 64	175,608 27	170,067 70

DAKOTA.									
Dakota	2,000 00	20 94	27 00	8 00	10 75	2,066 69	252 99	6,431 33	6,924 52
DELAWARE.									
Delaware*	7,901 44	76 78	96 97		47 21	8,122 40	2,000 00	469,770 41	482,091 38
DISTRICT OF COLUMBIA.									
District of Columbia	5,669 99	48 54	96 00		54 00	5,868 53	1,378 60	230,910 38	216,999 56
FLORIDA.									
Florida*	11,114 78	137 34	209 50	9 04	99 00	11,569 66	5,308 00	102,352 72	98,723 52
GEORGIA.									
First district*	5,319 93	90 03	71 75		22 00	5,503 71	4,166 09	97,898 97	115,872 54
Second district	7,108 70	94 57	164 17	7 14	25 50	7,400 08	4,108 70	111,836 91	100,014 90
Third district*	10,068 80	83 52	97 29		10 00	10,259 61	4,968 75	124,700 85	131,324 72
Fourth district	7,500 00	108 66	90 02	4 55	24 50	7,727 73	7,073 43	265,968 84	245,397 39
Total	29,997 43	376 78	423 23	11 69	82 00	30,891 13	20,316 97	600,405 57	592,609 55
IDAHO.									
Idaho*	4,010 18	58 04	30 48	147 00	10 00	5,164 70	1,910 18	25,185 22	35,636 98
ILLINOIS.									
First district*	25,928 98	168 92	172 30	4 83	23 75	26,298 78	11,108 00	6,990,935 58	6,139,880 48
Second district*	5,101 60	79 09	85 36		31 20	5,296 65	1,042 91	118,372 22	147,511 81
Third district	10,707 76	37 68	99 68			10,845 12	3,185 21	815,034 80	751,763 03
Fourth district*	13,403 33	155 20	109 27		81 00	13,748 80	2,322 50	1,936,911 93	1,726,186 72
Fifth district*	25,674 38	146 37	128 98	7 70	50 25	26,007 68	7,367 91	4,449,487 36	4,112,597 97
Sixth district †*	6,150 70	85 85	42 24	3 02		6,281 81	1,414 54	403,540 51	407,067 76
Seventh district*	6,226 48	53 63	174 00		14 65	6,468 76	1,465 47	226,327 51	245,121 76
Eighth district*	12,642 95	309 03	195 00		51 60	13,198 58	6,196 66	1,440,427 89	1,107,684 33
Ninth district*	7,458 00	70 26	88 55		17 75	7,634 56	1,864 69	474,863 80	350,645 63
Tenth district*	3,806 38	44 03	94 17	4 05	51 25	4,000 78	2,272 08	64,386 39	76,373 75
Eleventh district*	3,906 47	37 45	239 78		4 00	4,187 70	1,164 41	23,405 54	27,270 46
Twelfth district*	8,268 97	123 95	354 19		48 70	8,795 81	4,512 82	527,261 38	496,535 18
Thirteenth district*	8,119 51	84 90	50 00		44 00	8,298 41	1,395 71	53,667 14	58,518 19
Total	137,304 91	1,397 26	1,833 52	19 60	418 15	141,063 44	45,822 91	17,524,562 05	15,647,157 07
INDIANA.									
First district*	11,888 63	95 61	75 00		61 00	12,120 24	3,135 17	1,034,858 84	992,574 80
Second district*	4,131 93	107 22	127 00		49 00	4,416 05	1,144 26	91,972 09	103,389 70

Inding items which belong to previous fiscal years not before adjusted.

† Complete returns not received from collector.

H.—*Statement showing the expenses of collecting the internal-revenue taxes, &c.*—Continued.

District.	Compensation.	Stationery and blank-books.	Postage.	Express and dep. money.	Advertising.	Total expense of collecting.	Expenses of administering office.	Assessments.	Collections.
INDIANA—Continued.									
Third district*	$8,715 89	$127 80	$73 78	$4 00	$33 15	$8,955 52	$4,976 33	$582,874 33	$476,664 75
Fourth district*	17,228 78	232 95	555 00	31 00	....	18,047 73	5,642 86	2,072,322 33	1,971,593 95
Fifth district*	3,338 02	28 81	47 22	....	....	3,434 05	701 50	50,673 14	51,470 02
Sixth district	8,855 35	124 49	138 02	....	48 85	9,166 71	1,553 69	623,699 11	563,778 38
Seventh district*	8,856 97	55 88	25 58	....	29 00	8,967 43	1,845 56	597,777 32	508,978 32
Eighth district	8,738 43	64 63	75 00	2 18	29 10	8,909 34	1,704 08	477,930 56	477,419 52
Ninth district	5,358 42	49 68	31 42	....	6 00	5,445 52	1,452 03	175,811 18	167,330 67
Tenth district	3,847 90	23 58	25 50	....	44 55	3,941 53	848 17	85,918 72	78,263 55
Eleventh district*	13,305 83	128 90	193 45	....	....	13,628 18	1,379 27	77,820 54	72,921 21
Total	94,286 15	1,039 55	1,367 87	38 08	300 65	97,032 30	24,382 94	5,871,658 16	5,464,384 85
IOWA.									
First district	5,358 02	71 21	90 00	....	31 50	5,551 63	1,608 85	182,346 73	185,791 93
Second district*	6,787 78	95 96	130 50	....	46 13	7,060 37	2,488 78	333,104 55	303,168 53
Third district	8,233 37	210 15	180 45	5 03	41 60	8,670 60	2,400 00	472,526 58	442,265 25
Fourth district	2,555 00	47 50	106 04	....	4 50	2,713 04	599 65	53,024 04	42,412 13
Fifth district	4,000 00	82 31	138 25	4 70	....	4,225 26	2,298 58	52,794 66	48,416 03
Sixth district*	4,346 92	171 66	132 80	14 05	116 76	4,782 19	2,232 78	41,657 42	37,409 67
Total	31,281 99	678 79	778 04	23 78	240 49	33,003 09	11,628 63	1,145,453 98	1,059,463 54
KANSAS.									
Kansas*	7,500 00	117 49	378 00	4 46	182 00	8,181 95	4,576 85	259,469 77	238,932 32
KENTUCKY.									
First district*	5,577 00	249 20	145 00	....	32 15	6,003 44	2,266 70	287,585 94	199,376 62
Second district*	10,826 16	111 32	188 44	585 37	....	11,711 29	3,081 67	357,782 85	325,977 68
Third district*	2,772 24	72 36	78 02	46 80	18 50	2,987 92	465 00	32,673 18	33,578 78
Fourth district*	7,870 90	67 15	247 94	521 80	39 65	8,747 44	2,911 50	317,838 52	339,232 93
Fifth district	12,081 40	243 99	105 00	....	158 85	12,589 24	4,485 99	1,980,828 68	1,971,674 11
Sixth district*	14,588 02	246 82	73 96	4 80	28 50	14,942 10	4,901 92	2,073,332 68	1,845,969 71
Seventh district*	8,154 63	249 04	125 00	....	....	8,528 67	4,257 49	821,716 76	617,146 26
Eighth district	2,996 74	80 85	131 28	7 20	5 00	3,221 07	1,158 71	137,046 46	47,543 78
Ninth district*	6,571 72	93 54	60 54	....	34 25	6,760 05	3,350 00	99,200 61	106,299 44

LOUISIANA.									
First district*	20, 245 22	108 45	46 75	12 38	58 50	20, 571 30	11, 796 67	1, 599, 874 59	1, 523, 702 01
Second district*	14, 654 05	90 58	52 87	141 00	42 85	14, 981 35	6, 015 45	88, 406 23	50, 283 73
Third district*	10, 420 04	20 75	48 24	87 83	53 25	10, 630 11	4, 996 21	54, 569 09	50, 043 35
Total	45, 419 31	219 78	147 86	241 21	154 60	46, 182 76	22, 808 33	1, 742, 849 91	1, 624, 029 09
MAINE.									
First district	5, 290 49	11 84	82 00	....	14 75	5, 399 08	340 17	167, 306 52	168, 552 86
Second district	2, 672 51	37 21	62 00	....	17 50	2, 789 22	630 00	38, 694 12	39, 083 67
Third district	2, 501 38	26 92	69 08	....	15 15	2, 612 53	568 00	34, 142 64	33, 379 52
Fourth district*	2, 599 91	66 80	54 55	4 31	....	2, 725 57	150 00	34, 960 02	36, 663 80
Fifth district	2, 277 36	....	41 95	....	23 75	2, 343 06	859 58	24, 547 96	25, 911 81
Total	15, 341 65	142 77	309 58	4 31	71 15	15, 869 46	2, 539 75	299, 651 26	303, 591 86
MARYLAND.									
First district*	5, 232 27	33 90	75 00	....	18 75	5, 359 92	1, 374 42	559, 150 68	351, 979 16
Second district*	3, 612 76	8 00	56 68	2 00	13 75	3, 693 19	898 34	289, 548 49	212, 557 95
Third district*	16, 414 38	228 27	103 00	1 00	32 13	16, 868 78	8, 470 66	3, 343, 000 60	3, 326, 549 85
Fourth district*	4, 639 47	51 48	28 03	2 50	121 15	4, 842 63	1, 510 15	117, 414 64	99, 836 56
Fifth district*	12, 130 41	107 15	167 54	7 67	47 96	12, 460 73	3, 356 63	684, 422 08	594, 963 01
Total	42, 020 29	428 80	520 25	13 17	233 74	43, 225 25	15, 610 20	4, 993, 536 49	4, 585, 886 53
MASSACHUSETTS.									
First district	5, 117 29	63 97	69 79	2 60	59 25	5, 312 90	2, 030 00	185, 535 34	161, 728 89
Second district	5, 742 42	54 04	115 90	....	19 00	5, 931 36	2, 120 00	161, 735 79	224, 242 17
Third district*	16, 419 11	205 97	351 80	6 91	42 63	17, 026 42	6, 317 53	3, 174, 693 92	2, 860, 406 64
Fourth district	12, 121 96	104 93	156 00	....	53 25	12, 436 14	5, 494 38	1, 374, 610 05	1, 478, 716 49
Fifth district	7, 818 42	....	84 00	....	29 00	7, 931 42	1, 135 98	416, 669 68	395, 971 62
Sixth district	10, 041 99	68 42	116 00	....	34 00	10, 260 41	5, 365 00	785, 510 83	728, 565 75
Seventh district	6, 009 64	50 78	122 32	6 54	43 00	6, 232 28	1, 565 32	365, 670 60	250, 964 19
Eighth district	5, 705 25	113 41	306 28	....	26 00	6, 150 94	1, 036 16	175, 890 21	220, 308 64
Ninth district	4, 710 18	51 72	194 00	2 75	17 25	4, 975 90	1, 465 00	132, 615 10	120, 217 12
Tenth district	8, 008 66	105 29	154 00	3 58	21 00	8, 292 53	2, 655 35	451, 585 94	429, 579 98
Total	81, 694 92	818 53	1, 670 09	22 38	344 38	84, 550 30	29, 184 72	7, 224, 517 46	6, 870, 701 49
MICHIGAN.									
First district*	11, 904 25	96 72	159 68	....	65 00	12, 225 65	3, 532 00	1, 872, 445 66	1, 917, 394 48
Second district	3, 024 14	37 19	93 49	....	....	3, 154 82	1, 790 83	65, 566 95	50, 804 40
Third district	4, 640 93	63 08	230 25	....	27 00	4, 961 26	1, 271 65	109, 103 56	114, 092 60
Fourth district	4, 648 08	42 72	85 00	....	50 40	4, 826 20	1, 487 43	117, 496 11	114, 785 34

* Including items which belong to previous fiscal years not before adjusted.

Complete returns not received from collector.

H.—*Statement showing the expenses of collecting the internal-revenue taxes, &c.*—Continued.

District.	Compensation.	Stationery and blank-books.	Postage.	Express and dep. money.	Advertising.	Total expense of collecting.	Expenses of administering office.
MICHIGAN—Continued.							
Fifth district*	$2,982 50	$58 62	$136 74	$24 20	$13 50	$3,215 56	$3,391 48
Sixth district	5,071 65	145 20	116 32	6 15	15 70	5,355 02	1,702 95
Total	32,271 55	443 53	821 48	30 35	171 60	33,738 51	13,176 34
MINNESOTA.							
First district*	4,464 44	42 95	206 16	....	25 00	4,738 55	1,882 29
Second district*	6,000 00	33 14	193 00	....	40 00	6,266 14	3,500 00
Total	10,464 44	76 09	399 16	....	65 00	11,004 69	5,382 29
MISSISSIPPI.							
First district*	6,000 00	84 10	19 20	23 15	....	6,126 45	3,527 58
Second district*	8,290 00	17 50	161 08	....	6 00	8,474 58	5,790 00
Third district*	6,220 53	243 07	172 64	....	19 50	6,715 74	5,066 13
Total	20,570 53	344 67	352 92	23 15	25 50	21,316 77	14,383 71
MISSOURI.							
First district	18,000 00	273 47	221 00	4 07	38 50	18,537 04	13,060 78
Second district	8,465 06	172 22	333 78	50 59	59 75	9,081 40	5,965 06
Third district*	6,618 16	16 63	128 71	....	24 50	6,788 00	1,350 00
Fourth district	5,581 77	136 59	126 00	4 64	86 50	5,935 50	570 45
Fifth district*	8,549 79	115 60	264 27	14 96	98 25	9,042 87	4,719 59
Sixth district	11,000 00	216 01	326 25	....	91 55	11,633 81	8,370 96
Total	58,214 78	930 52	1,400 01	74 26	399 05	61,018 62	34,036 84
MONTANA.							
Montana*	9,000 00	55 00	43 44	....	35 00	9,133 44	6,019 00
NEBRASKA.							
Nebraska*†	9,797 43	130 62	37 23	....	....	9,965 28	2,822 75

15 F

NEVADA.									
Nevada*	11,208 67	25 92	90 20	110 54	223 83	11,659 16	9,118 85	65,801 04	36,710 75
NEW HAMPSHIRE.									
First district	5,301 25	2 70	116 70	....	27 25	5,447 90	959 56	194,880 92	175,337 65
Second district	4,502 21	89 62	70 43	....	23 00	4,685 28	1,328 75	123,518 01	100,220 96
Third district	2,391 49	67 87	86 00	....	36 50	2,581 86	215 00	28,376 40	29,716 46
Total	12,194 95	160 19	273 13	....	86 75	12,715 02	2,503 31	346,775 33	305,275 07
NEW JERSEY.									
First district*	4,600 38	14 90	83 11	24 45	2 00	4,724 84	1,869 79	126,634 90	110,024 02
Second district*	5,453 93	10 00	186 73	3 40	44 50	5,698 56	1,960 00	172,784 66	191,543 24
Third district	8,688 95	95 47	243 86	....	22 60	9,050 88	3,350 80	573,187 82	559,955 62
Fourth district*	6,854 95	92 44	148 00	81 83	30 83	7,208 05	1,949 06	276,092 10	317,929 21
Fifth district*	10,913 60	316 92	239 60	112 50	....	11,582 62	7,140 00	1,412,529 36	1,330,882 01
Total	36,511 81	529 73	901 30	222 18	99 93	38,264 95	16,269 65	2,561,228 84	2,510,334 10
NEW MEXICO.									
New Mexico*	5,969 90	....	48 05	10 55	236 64	6,265 14	3,470 60	32,081 43	38,219 11
NEW YORK.									
First district*	22,375 00	368 16	229 99	....	96 50	23,069 65	17,375 00	4,928,550 79	4,427,810 99
Second district	22,092 40	387 22	234 00	....	124 20	22,837 82	18,592 40	3,171,769 74	3,084,597 69
Third district*	11,855 68	188 08	105 60	63 68	90 00	12,303 04	5,103 17	2,235,985 04	2,296,344 85
Eighth district*	13,336 95	78 46	194 70	1 95	344 55	13,956 61	8,576 95	1,754,751 09	2,207,743 80
Ninth district	11,709 42	147 36	128 75	....	75 20	12,060 73	6,736 89	1,366,860 83	1,353,618 79
Tenth district*	13,037 38	46 72	157 61	2 82	48 75	13,293 28	4,315 26	332,607 64	463,009 00
Eleventh district	4,915 69	246 45	65 65	8 81	53 50	5,290 10	1,560 71	132,189 39	130,768 02
Twelfth district*	9,767 88	116 69	163 00	4 90	42 50	10,094 97	1,739 28	318,704 70	258,475 74
Thirteenth district*	3,875 66	83 66	94 26	50	63 88	4,117 96	822 07	190,746 16	82,938 20
Fourteenth district	10,057 66	135 78	148 60	13 04	70 75	10,425 83	3,432 80	953,874 62	911,501 49
Fifteenth district*	6,565 67	36 74	97 50	2 00	69 00	6,770 91	2,019 38	324,331 38	306,567 33
Sixteenth district*	2,753 60	71 91	72 47	6 47	8 50	2,912 95	612 50	44,834 18	41,839 11
Seventeenth district	2,410 51	83 11	64 52	....	32 50	2,590 64	1,485 20	32,358 27	30,350 38
Eighteenth district*	5,619 95	82 11	237 55	18 65	37 38	5,995 64	1,600 00	238,915 52	192,926 01
Nineteenth district	2,714 58	38 77	50 41	15 18	41 25	2,860 19	1,296 15	38,758 14	40,485 87
Twentieth district*	4,150 95	18 24	108 30	....	26 75	4,304 24	800 00	77,176 06	88,374 23
Twenty-first district*	7,513 38	37 56	164 00	....	97 45	7,812 39	1,120 00	399,912 80	404,295 99
Twenty-second district	8,258 37	72 59	203 50	....	33 75	8,568 21	2,298 94	377,907 05	404,249 39
Twenty-third district	8,000 12	60 13	90 00	2 79	30 75	8,183 79	2,477 40	507,844 66	425,425 22
Twenty-fourth district*	8,472 08	106 70	245 83	7 26	25 25	8,857 12	1,246 17	385,283 48	448,631 73
Twenty-fifth district*	4,039 70	....	74 25	....	....	4,113 95	1,049 50	61,142 77	60,322 54

* Including items which belong to previous fiscal years not before adjusted.

† Complete returns not received from collector.

H.—*Statement showing the expenses of collecting the internal-revenue taxes, &c.*—Continued.

District.	Compensation.	Stationery and blank-books.	Postage.	Express and dep. money.	Advertising.	Total expense of collecting.	Expenses of administering office.	Assessments.	Collections.
NEW YORK—Continued.									
Twenty-sixth district*	$5,279 11	$112 81	$43 50	$6 06	$22 18	$5,463 68	$1,850 19	$155,622 01	$177,910 99
Twenty-seventh district, (old)	4,520 79	43 49	76 25	....	25 39	4,665 92	1,909 50	137,167 51	128,478 16
Do. (new)	575 69	....	17 00	6 55	3 88	603 12	279 58	32,759 85	28,722 77
Twenty-eighth district*	8,030 40	45 74	41 71	....	19 00	8,136 85	2,983 11	492,498 89	486,317 80
Twenty-ninth district*	3,502 26	40 01	71 95	....	....	8,614 22	599 50	85,626 54	66,953 18
Thirtieth district*	15,887 10	135 27	94 79	2 72	54 50	16,174 47	5,119 25	1,871,526 43	1,754,027 38
Thirty-first district*	2,544 44	25 06	158 00	....	....	2,727 50	550 00	28,772 57	38,936 10
Thirty-second district*	22,701 24	340 26	327 60	3 28	23 60	23,395 98	17,126 19	3,240,449 60	3,303,483 59
Total	246,467 01	3,358 26	3,603 68	163 86	1,512 21	255,105 02	114,877 09	23,918,928 61	23,651,306 34
NORTH CAROLINA.									
First district*	5,559 56	75 15	71 28	....	12 50	5,718 49	1,914 17	22,180 16	24,507 03
Second district*	9,801 78	102 64	129 04	....	10 00	10,043 46	5,392 95	45,035 31	51,610 43
Third district	6,500 00	38 06	42 22	....	15 00	6,595 28	3,426 83	40,671 36	57,342 55
Fourth district	10,000 00	87 06	84 11	5 38	8 00	10,184 55	7,193 30	387,928 91	376,109 63
Fifth district*	16,781 40	115 67	191 90	4 83	24 56	17,118 36	11,610 98	412,450 24	398,763 81
Sixth district*	9,426 80	211 48	83 00	13 44	....	9,734 72	5,585 49	235,554 67	200,319 47
Seventh district*	12,733 44	87 63	48 00	....	....	12,869 07	5,454 02	20,782 35	22,067 65
Total	70,802 98	717 69	649 55	23 65	70 06	72,263 93	40,577 74	1,164,603 00	1,130,720 57
OHIO.									
First district	24,167 19	235 17	138 00	....	13 00	24,553 36	9,930 07	6,359,239 63	6,079,487 83

Seventeenth district*	7,519 28	111 74	89 00	....	9 00	7,729 02	1,171 75	377,028 37	351,265 43
Eighteenth district*	10,957 53	*109 80	102 00	....	52 40	11,221 73	4,350 00	911,232 98	890,914 79
Nineteenth district*	3,673 98	27 43	96 65	30	31 50	3,829 86	1,258 22	78,469 51	72,201 37
Total	165,891 10	1,622 96	1,641 64	11 31	501 00	169,668 01	49,243 81	15,678,820 86	15,128,908 42
OREGON.									
Oregon*	6,474 96	49 19	58 54	5 60	32 05	6,620 34	2,974 06	114,120 00	125,547 12
PENNSYLVANIA.									
First district	12,188 12	191 42	5 00	1 60	21 00	12,407 14	4,493 67	1,893,932 84	1,938,599 01
Second district*	11,615 21	88 03	10 50	....	22 50	11,736 24	5,983 00	2,138,850 69	1,857,487 37
Third district*	332 38	205 57	....	....	....	537 95	5,654 00	824 24	1,535 38
Fourth district	5,773 94	85 83	20 00	....	36 50	5,916 27	2,357 50	417,578 56	419,413 98
Fifth district*	6,862 02	55 85	140 20	....	23 10	7,081 17	673 06	345,581 63	368,907 85
Sixth district	6,658 70	55 04	32 79	....	18 50	6,765 03	1,072 50	260,682 26	315,869 86
Seventh district	2,963 20	43 45	68 56	....	7 40	3,082 61	715 00	49,634 27	48,773 37
Eighth district*	5,817 93	34 12	33 00	....	9 75	5,894 80	900 00	235,712 81	249,801 30
Ninth district	6,320 53	73 01	85 71	....	19 50	6,498 75	1,500 00	232,031 49	274,320 68
Tenth district	5,051 87	45 25	72 46	1 49	9 75	5,180 82	2,189 22	147,946 21	154,616 14
Eleventh district*	4,848 61	102 63	128 20	....	114 00	5,193 44	1,360 00	145,898 07	139,979 06
Twelfth district	5,722 32	163 35	182 20	7 49	24 50	6,099 86	2,252 95	231,782 60	197,002 89
Thirteenth district*	2,940 42	91 50	97 21	....	15 00	3,144 13	1,029 55	50,303 14	49,043 74
Fourteenth district*	4,845 33	80 80	134 80	6 56	78 50	5,154 99	1,039 09	125,577 86	135,824 02
Fifteenth district*	6,486 11	73 12	114 40	1 35	30 25	6,705 23	3,084 09	238,150 46	247,988 62
Sixteenth district	5,162 19	101 90	151 45	40 54	32 25	5,488 33	1,812 69	143,284 24	144,635 28
Seventeenth district*	2,960 68	....	61 00	....	19 50	3,041 18	550 53	50,360 79	48,689 48
Eighteenth district*	4,042 73	14 85	120 45	....	19 00	4,197 03	2,002 72	81,115 36	87,017 00
Nineteenth district*	10,214 66	57 38	163 30	....	20 50	10,455 84	3,689 95	171,691 56	158,382 75
Twentieth district*	9,285 62	7 50	222 00	....	10 50	9,525 62	2,470 42	155,498 98	168,826 71
Twenty-first district*	9,668 28	123 10	161 45	1 85	8 00	9,962 68	3,379 03	516,793 81	486,018 30
Twenty-second district*	11,411 50	152 90	118 48	....	....	11,682 88	5,018 80	1,182,242 50	1,171,480 41
Twenty-third district*	8,943 14	79 01	80 00	....	35 50	9,137 65	3,442 50	544,960 25	523,336 75
Twenty-fourth district	4,988 30	99 02	137 72	....	9 93	5,234 97	2,346 93	143,394 86	141,523 44
Total	155,103 79	2,033 63	2,340 88	60 88	585 43	160,124 61	59,017 80	9,503,829 48	9,329,073 58
RHODE ISLAND.									
First district	8,179 61	86 47	113 00	2 18	38 00	8,419 26	2,250 00	584,603 47	580,196 89
Second district*	3,201 90	18 61	37 00	....	24 50	3,282 01	438 15	68,685 36	57,994 85
Total	11,381 51	105 08	150 00	2 18	62 50	11,701 27	2,688 15	653,288 83	638,191 74

* Including items which belong to previous fiscal years not before adjusted.

H.—*Statement showing the expenses of collecting the internal-revenue taxes, &c.*—Continued.

District.	Compensation.	Stationery and blank-books.	Postage.	Express and dep. money.	Advertising.	Total expense of collecting.	Expenses of administering office.	Assessments.	Collections.
SOUTH CAROLINA.									
First district*	$7,316 25	$65 29	$211 30	$5 75	$25 50	$7,624 09	$3,358 00	$141,918 01	$105,107 06
Second district	6,062 88	51 58	89 30	....	52 80	6,256 56	3,062 88	91,363 16	94,991 15
Third district	5,844 81	155 90	101 97	6 25	23 00	6,131 93	3,420 52	77,032 37	68,630 47
Total	19,223 94	272 77	402 57	12 00	101 30	20,012 58	9,841 40	310,313 54	268,728 68
TENNESSEE.									
First district*	3,981 09	26 49	35 07	2 75	28 50	4,073 90	2,031 09	10,406 06	14,803 96
Second district*	6,575 35	20 17	35 00	....	14 00	6,644 52	5,150 32	77,791 42	62,819 63
Third district*	5,626 71	200 92	60 50	....	....	5,888 13	3,146 57	39,883 45	32,302 28
Fourth district	5,000 00	107 80	43 80	....	24 50	5,176 10	3,051 86	41,815 42	46,547 59
Fifth district	7,500 00	81 69	104 00	1 50	11 20	7,698 39	4,830 73	330,816 17	322,961 29
Sixth district*	9,014 10	172 92	20 08	....	50	9,207 60	5,065 34	148,673 74	188,562 70
Seventh district*	4,250 00	149 76	59 50	....	14 50	4,473 76	2,250 00	68,656 45	57,092 19
Eighth district	6,982 25	84 68	155 33	4 90	32 00	7,259 16	3,982 25	156,576 50	167,649 99
Total	48,929 50	844 43	513 28	9 15	125 20	50,421 56	29,508 16	874,619 21	893,339 63
TEXAS.									
First district†*	7,766 76	147 78	35 84	2 75	10 00	7,963 13	5,454 16	190,335 05	105,449 20
Second district*	10,403 25	109 63	160 24	40 00	95 85	10,808 97	7,228 15	84,632 26	65,197 62
Third district	8,000 00	22 50	73 61	13 90	46 55	8,156 56	5,054 75	91,293 45	52,439 23
Fourth district†*	16,472 85	186 73	137 19	99 30	....	16,896 07	3,980 04	51,900 88	68,304 66
Total	42,642 86	466 64	406 88	155 95	152 40	43,824 73	21,717 10	418,161 64	291,390 71
UTAH.									
Utah*	5,311 54	93 81	194 00	85 20	....	5,684 55	2,611 54	55,389 30	46,186 07
VERMONT.									
First district	5,143 01	4 95	45 00	....	45 50	3,238 46	....	39,346 19	54,767 13
Second district*	3,168 94	2 40	88 79	....	37 50	5,297 63	1,033 60	29,449 28	38,661 93
Third district*	3,140 31	28 55	103 78	....	38 00	3,310 64	1,088 57	47,461 21	53,616 12
Total	11,452 26	35 90	237 57	....	121 00	11,846 73	2,122 17	116,256 68	147,045 18

VIRGINIA.									
First district*	684 66	182 43	16 34	5 75	104 46	993 64	414 00	35, 231 59	15, 809 54
Second district	9, 072 96	80 90	80 50	....	16 65	9, 251 01	3, 261 92	822, 089 92	713, 081 00
Third district*	13, 311 99	266 47	99 47	2 55	60 25	13, 740 73	4, 980 42	2, 020, 230 63	2, 004, 286 C9
Fourth district*	5, 826 68	105 00	109 98	6 47	....	6, 048 13	2, 671 20	81, 674 79	80, 583 66
Fifth district	11, 250 50	329 41	129 95	7 25	20 00	11, 737 11	4, 443 09	1, 645, 397 15	1, 600, 407 77
Sixth district*	8, 287 80	168 44	237 55	....	32 75	8, 726 54	4, 699 25	148, 110 61	148, 856 99
Seventh district	4, 353 62	66 27	141 28	....	38 00	4, 599 17	1, 425 00	109, 814 69	91, 465 93
Eighth district	2, 744 45	76 37	139 60	....	....	2, 960 42	598 50	26, 803 71	25, 721 19
Total	55, 532 66	1, 275 29	954 67	22 02	272 11	58, 056 75	22, 502 38	4, 889, 353 09	4, 680, 272 17
WASHINGTON.									
Washington*	7, 994 93	411 81	83 99	174 43	48 55	8, 713 71	4, 740 46	37, 793 37	23, 200 27
WEST VIRGINIA.									
First district	6, 966 01	....	92 02	1 10	32 00	7, 091 13	1, 980 00	313, 548 06	345, 049 65
Second district*	4, 528 70	66 39	84 51	20 40	32 00	4, 732 00	510 00	135, 450 75	103, 211 40
Third district*	2, 320 63	32 51	61 27	....	....	2, 414 41	209 72	19, 830 66	22, 984 54
Total	13, 815 34	98 90	237 80	21 50	64 00	14, 237 54	2, 699 72	468, 829 47	471, 245 59
WISCONSIN.									
First district*	12, 608 66	56 92	91 01	2 29	38 85	12, 797 73	3, 000 00	1, 669, 634 74	1, 601, 413 76
Second district*	5, 310 84	49 73	143 65	....	70 50	5, 574 72	1, 200 00	230, 491 63	171, 902 28
Third district*	4, 000 69	45 09	90 17	12 97	27 75	4, 176 67	1, 848 62	135, 144 39	66, 737 76
Fourth district	2, 118 62	19 46	50 00	....	....	2, 188 08	691 66	40, 924 79	37, 378 68
Fifth district*	3, 859 62	24 31	44 80	4 01	....	3, 932 74	1, 766 42	32, 055 16	63, 791 67
Sixth district*	11, 164 79	89 33	91 50	....	18 40	11, 364 02	2, 577 25	64, 898 04	65, 316 89
Total	39, 016 42	284 84	511 13	19 27	155 50	39, 987 16	11, 063 95	2, 173, 148 75	2, 006, 541 04
WYOMING.									
Wyoming	3, 026 02	139 40	50 35	31 77	17 40	3, 264 94	1, 026 02	7, 595 77	6, 777 16

* Including items which belong to previous fiscal years not before adjusted. † Complete returns not received from collector.

NOTE.—The districts marked "old" and "new" are those that have been consolidated, and show the amount of expense previous and subsequent to consolidation.

H.—*Statement showing the expenses of collecting the internal-revenue taxes, &c.*—Continued.

RECAPITULATION.

District.	Compensation.	Stationery and blank-books.	Postage.	Express and dep. money.	Advertising.	Total expense of collecting.	Expenses of administering office.	Assessments.	Collections.
Alabama	$23,980 80	$236 91	$222 16	$5 05	$55 75	$24,500 67	$15,004 64	$294,624 29	$234,260 92
Arizona	1,800 00	41 16	12 00	....	45 50	1,898 66	684 59	3,936 17	14,406 14
Arkansas	22,206 91	311 97	306 42	88 78	19 50	22,933 58	9,049 56	140,331 97	99,854 91
California	63,674 55	648 54	940 75	1,506 05	408 47	67,178 36	38,678 03	2,730,490 34	3,073,580 27
Colorado	8,750 00	88 54	76 80	8 90	184 70	9,108 94	5,000 00	76,546 14	63,047 42
Connecticut	25,769 13	218 85	484 00	6 02	80 62	26,558 62	8,377 67	1,237,019 58	1,204,613 44
Dakota	2,000 00	20 94	27 00	8 00	10 75	2,066 69	252 99	6,431 33	6,924 52
Delaware	7,901 44	76 78	96 97	....	47 21	8,122 40	2,000 00	469,770 41	482,091 38
District of Columbia	5,669 99	48 54	96 00	....	54 00	5,868 53	1,378 60	230,910 38	216,999 56
Florida	11,114 78	137 34	209 50	9 04	99 00	11,569 66	5,308 00	102,352 72	98,723 52
Georgia	29,997 43	376 78	423 23	11 69	82 00	30,891 13	20,316 97	600,405 57	592,609 55
Idaho	4,910 18	58 04	39 48	147 00	10 00	5,164 70	1,910 18	25,185 22	35,636 98
Illinois	137,394 91	1,307 26	1,833 52	19 60	418 15	141,063 44	45,622 91	17,524,562 05	15,647,157 07
Indiana	94,286 15	1,039 55	1,367 87	38 08	300 65	97,032 30	24,382 94	5,871,658 16	5,464,384 85
Iowa	31,281 99	678 70	778 04	23 78	240 49	33,003 09	11,628 63	1,145,453 98	1,059,463 54
Kansas	7,500 00	117 49	378 00	4 46	182 00	8,181 95	4,576 85	259,469 77	238,932 32
Kentucky	71,438 90	1,414 27	1,155 18	1,165 97	316 90	75,491 22	26,969 18	6,108,005 08	5,486,799 31
Louisiana	45,419 31	219 78	147 86	241 21	154 60	46,182 76	22,808 33	1,742,849 91	1,624,029 09
Maine	15,341 65	142 77	309 58	4 31	71 15	15,869 46	2,539 75	299,651 26	303,591 86
Maryland	42,029 29	428 80	520 25	13 17	233 74	43,225 25	15,610 20	4,993,536 49	4,585,886 53
Massachusetts	81,694 92	818 53	1,670 09	22 38	344 38	84,550 30	29,184 72	7,224,517 46	6,870,701 49
Michigan	32,271 55	443 53	821 48	30 35	171 60	33,738 51	13,176 34	2,375,401 75	2,401,970 58
Minnesota	10,464 44	76 09	399 16	....	65 00	11,004 69	5,382 29	272,198 30	247,398 41
Mississippi	20,570 53	344 67	352 92	23 15	25 50	21,316 77	14,383 71	781,188 35	678,501 11
Missouri	58,214 78	930 52	1,400 01	74 26	309 05	61,018 62	34,036 64	5,101,960 45	4,687,455 96
Montana	9,000 00	55 60	43 44		35 00	9,133 44	6,019 00	[illegible]	[illegible]

Utah	5,311 54	93 81	104 00	85 20	....	5,684 55	2,811 54	55,389 30	46,188 07
Vermont	11,452 26	35 90	237 57	....	121 00	11,846 73	2,122 17	116,256 68	147,045 18
Virginia	55,532 66	1,275 29	954 67	22 02	272 11	58,056 75	22,502 38	4,889,353 09	4,680,272 17
Washington	7,994 93	411 81	83 99	174 43	48 55	8,713 71	4,740 46	37,793 37	23,200 27
West Virginia	13,815 34	98 90	237 80	21 50	64 00	14,237 54	2,699 72	468,829 47	471,245 50
Wisconsin	39,016 42	284 84	511 13	19 27	155 50	39,987 16	11,083 95	2,173,148 75	2,006,541 04
Wyoming	3,026 02	139 40	50 35	31 77	17 40	3,264 94	1,026 02	7,595 77	6,777 16
Grand total	1,843,433 21	23,028 50	27,498 15	4,593 29	8,523 57	1,907,076 72	776,100 52	123,079,983 73	117,329,127 93

I.—*Statement of accounts of revenue-stamp agents from April 1, 1871, to December 31, 1871.*

DR.

To amount outstanding in agents' hands April 1, 1871	$3,104,771 51
To amount of stamps received from Commissioner	9,177,744 44
To amount charged T. J. West as interest	104 33
To amount charged Ault & Bachtel as costs of suit	37 56
To amount commissions charged back to Ault & Bachtel	11 25
	12,282,669 09

CR.

By amount of cash deposited with the United States Treasurer	$8,376,285 39
By amount allowed as commissions	507,348 36
By amount of stamps returned to Commissioner	159,536 62
By amount allowed L. L. Merry by act of Congress, private, No. 2, approved December 20, 1870	3,696 73
By amount outstanding in agents' hands December 31, 1871 to be accounted for	3,235,801 99
	12,282,669 09

Amount overpaid by agents in settlement of their accounts	$920 04

K.—*Statement of amounts paid for printing stamps and for stamp-paper for the Office of Internal Revenue for the fiscal year ending June 30, 1872.*

To the Continental Bank Note Company	$208,675 96
To the American Phototype Company	4,035 48
To Joseph R. Carpenter	94,628 54
To the Bureau of Printing and Engraving	117,257 01
To the National Bank Note Company	10,106 75
To Henry Skidmore	6,335 60
To James M. Willcox & Co., (paper)	68,059 97
	509,099 31

L.—*Statement of accounts of the Commissioner of Internal Revenue for internal revenue beer-stamps for the fiscal year ending June 30, 1872.*

DR.

To amount of stamps in hands of Commissioner June 30, 1870, as per last report	$218,526 67
To amount of stamps received from printer	10,450,683 33
To amount of stamps returned by collectors	8,379 70
	10,677,589 70

CR.

By amount of stamps sent to collectors	$8,973,647 50
By amount of stamps destroyed	6,379 70
By amount of stamps remaining in hands of Commissioner June 30, 1872	1,697,562 50
	10,677,589 70

M.—*Statement of accounts of the Commissioner of Internal Revenue for internal revenue stamps for distilled spirits for the fiscal year ending June 30, 1872.*

DR.

To amount of stamps in hands of Commissioner June 30, 1871, as per last report	$15,297,050 00
To amount of stamps received from printers	45,299,200 00
To amount of stamps returned by collectors	171,575 00
	60,767,825 00

CR.

By amount of stamps sent to collectors	$37,498,075 00
By amount of stamps destroyed	8,563,575 00
By amount of stamps remaining in hands of Commissioner June 30, 1872	14,706,175 00
	60,767,825 00

N.—*Statement of accounts of the Commissioner of Internal Revenue for internal revenue tobacco, snuff, and cigar stamps for the fiscal year ending June 30, 1872.*

DR.

To amount of stamps in hands of Commissioner June 30, 1871, as per last report	$6,750,980 75
To amount of stamps received from printers	38,043,699 05
To amount of stamps returned by collectors	476,961 43
	45,271,640 93

CR.

By amount of stamps sent to collectors	$39,852,800 74
By amount of stamps destroyed	2,550,637 47
By amount of stamps remaining in hands of Commissioner June 30, 1872	2,868,202 72
	45,271,640 93

O.—*Statement of accounts of the Commissioner of Internal Revenue for internal revenue stamps (adhesive) for the fiscal year ending June 30, 1872.*

DR.

To amount of stamps in hands of Commissioner June 30, 1871, as per last report	$2,329 82
To amount of stamps ordered from printers	16,915,017 01
To amount of stamps returned by agents	224,055 21
To amount of discount withheld in exchange	1,832 33
	17,143,234 37

CR.

By amount of cash deposited with the United States Treasurer	$3,875,548 73
By amount allowed as commission	232,851 34
By amount of stamps sent to agents	12,683,631 73
By amount of stamps destroyed	325,161 14
By amount allowed on affidavits of loss	20,791 39
By amount allowed under decision of Court of Claims reversing decision of C. Delano, late Commissioner, as commissions	5,150 04
By amount of stamps remaining in hands of Commissioner June 30, 1872	100 00
	17,143,234 37

P.—*Statement of accounts of the Commissioner of Internal Revenue for internal revenue stamped foil wrappers for tobacco for the fiscal year ending June 30, 1872.*

DR.

To amount of stamped foil wrappers received from printer.............. $828, 321 78

CR.

By amount of stamped foil wrappers sent to collectors.................. $828, 321 78

Q.—*Statement showing the amounts paid for salaries in the office of the Commissioner of Internal Revenue; also, salaries and expenses of supervisors, detectives, and surveyors of distilleries; miscellaneous expenses, counsel-fees, &c., drawbacks on rum and alcohol, and taxes erroneously assessed and collected, refunded during the fiscal year ended June 30, 1872.*

Supervisors.	Salary.	Expenses.	Clerk-hire.	Furniture.	Rent.	Total.
James R. Bayley	$2, 539 40	$1, 152 90	....	....	$300 00	$3, 992 30
E. W. Barber	3, 000 00	663 23	$1, 125 00	....	105 40	4, 893 63
S. J. Conklin	3, 000 00	633 07	1, 798 30	....	920 00	6, 351 37
K. R. Cobb	2, 997 56	2, 658 36	1, 626 54	....	252 00	7, 534 46
R. G. Corwin	3, 000 00	1, 160 85	4, 129 63	$10 50	369 99	8, 670 97
S. B. Dutcher	3, 000 00	1, 271 93	3, 547 19	138, 35	....	7, 957 47
J. W. Dwyer	3, 000 00	1, 093 69	1, 200 00	....	54 00	5, 347 69
G. W. Emery*	2, 029 87	1, 179 95	2, 468 00	....	240 00	5, 917 82
Speed S. Fry*	2, 959 78	1, 335 76	2, 135 45	68 95	147 98	6, 647 92
Alexander Fulton	3, 000 00	391 42	1, 879 01	....	....	5, 270 43
L. M. Foulke	3, 000 00	1, 406 63	2, 028 42	28 00	994 93	7, 457 98
Wolcott Hamlin	2, 497 76	596 48	799 54	....	89 00	3, 982 78
J. M. Hedrick	2, 997 19	2, 503 99	1, 502 94	83 00	100 02	7, 187 14
Dana E. King	3, 000 00	638 56	1, 198 85	193 25	225 00	5, 255 66
W. Krzyzanowski*	1, 051 63	2, 961 55	401 09	....	50 00	4, 464 27
George Marston*	1, 842 39	787 50	1, 158 91	....	166 33	3, 955 13
John McDonald	3, 000 00	5, 156 11	6, 866 97	....	720 00	15, 743 08
D. W. Munn*	1, 605 96	530 75	1, 335 05	127 45	150 00	3, 749 21
John O'Donnell	2, 999 97	337 01	1, 899 89	....	158 29	5, 395 16
Otis F. Presbrey	3, 000 00	1, 653 68	2, 871 69	....	550 56	8, 075 93
P. W. Perry	2, 999 98	1, 954 53	1, 491 24	....	275 00	6, 720 75
Simon T. Powell	2, 999 28	1, 021 33	1, 329 33	32 25	247 50	5, 629 69
N. D. Stanwood	3, 000 00	1, 095 05	873 18	74 50	153 33	5, 196 06
W. A. Simmons	3, 000 00	1, 250 22	2, 052 00	....	1, 074 96	7, 377 18
J. B. Sweitzer	3, 000 00	339 96	1, 351 41	....	....	4, 691 37
Benj. J. Sweet*	1, 394 02	474 94	572 28	257 50	75 00	2, 773 74
W. B. Stokes*	969 24	188 01	501 35	....	104 00	1, 762 60
Alexander P. Tutton	3, 000 00	889 37	1, 874 99	....	....	5, 764 36
Total	73, 884 03	35, 326 83	50, 018 25	1, 013 75	7, 523 29	167, 766 15
Add to this amount for stationery furnished supervisors, and allowed in contractors' accounts.						1, 821 24
Total						169, 587 39

* In office a fraction of the year.

DETECTIVES.

Name.	Salary.	Expenses.	Total.
O. J. Averell	$672 00	$498 50	$1,170 50
George C. Alden	1,722 00	1,303 74	3,025 74
J. N. Bench	2,019 00	1,328 95	3,347 95
B. P. Brasher	2,163 00	1,616 68	3,779 68
James J. Brooks	2,448 00	338 73	2,786 73
James T. Bryer	1,134 00	642 79	1,776 79
A. E. Burpee	1,848 00	707 44	2,555 44
Willard Bhilard	208 00	19 00	227 00
John B. Brownlow	805 00	397 40	1,202 40
Matthew Berry	1,878 00	1,455 85	3,333 85
E. T. Bridges	2,191 00	914 80	3,105 80
S. C. Boynton	520 00	22 15	542 15
H. Bowman	352 00	24 36	376 36
John C. Bowyer	1,398 00	471 77	1,869 77
T. K. Church	670 00	609 28	1,279 28
George L. Douglass	110 00	....	110 00
R. J. Easton	1,442 00	904 40	2,346 40
William A. Gavett	2,037 00	1,714 62	3,751 62
Arthur Gunther	1,866 00	2,968 25	4,834 25
Lucian Hawley	2,630 00	1,223 82	3,853 82
Thomas Hammond, jr	976 00	156 10	1,132 10
C. M. Horton	1,495 00	974 40	2,469 40
W. Huffman	300 00	149 40	449 40
D. W. Ives	1,453 00	265 00	1,718 00
James H. Kelly	....	35 60	35 60
J. J. Lamoree	275 00	575 84	850 84
D. H. Lyman	2,110 00	1,355 68	3,465 66
J. H. Manley	1,825 00	1,248 08	3,073 08
H. S. McCollum	285 00	286 20	571 20
John Murray	126 00	7 00	133 00
Henry W. Purvis	228 00	118 40	346 40
Charles Parker	924 00	537 25	1,461 25
J. W. Reams	295 00	186 65	481 65
J. E. Simpson	1,729 00	1,590 45	3,319 45
S. A. Sixbury	588 00	408 94	996 94
Thomas Waters	861 00	673 95	1,534 95
J. W. Wood	775 00	519 50	1,294 50
H. T. Yaryan	1,555 00	1,674 15	3,229 15
Total	43,913 00	27,925 10	71,838 10

SURVEYORS OF DISTILLERIES.

Salaries	$15,129 63
Expenses	13,355 07
Total	28,484 70

Salary, &c., of Office of Commissioner of Internal Revenue.

Salary, (thirteen months,)		$409,397 48
Traveling expenses, &c		394 80
		409,792 28

MILCELLANEOUS EXPENSES.

Salary	$4,454 00	
Traveling expenses	10,744 91	
Expenses	19,615 88	
Telegrams	3,105 05	
Rent	8,000 00	
Stationery	43,044 22	
Expressage	61,826 41	
		150,790 47

COUNSEL FEES AND EXPENSES MOIETIES, AND REWARDS.

Fees and expenses	$16,381 56	
Moieties	2,714 38	
Rewards	12,790 00	
		31,885 94
		592,468 69

Drawbacks on rum and alcohol	$553,002 00
Taxes, erroneously assessed and collected, refunded	570,005 34
	1,123,007 34

Statement of fines, penalties, and forfeitures.

Balance on deposit to credit of the Secretary of the Treasury July 1, 1871.	$280,249 72
Amount deposited	149,749 09
	429,998 81
Amount disbursed	206,056 24
Balance on deposit to credit of the Secretary of the Treasury July 1, 1872	223,942 57

Statement of disbursements for salaries of United States direct-tax commissioners in insurrectionary districts during the fiscal year ended June 30, 1872.

State.	Salary.
South Carolina	$538 01

Moneys refunded on lands sold for taxes and redeemed.

State.	Amount.
Virginia	$4,281 31

Moneys illegally collected in the insurrectionary districts refunded during the fiscal year ended June 30, 1872.

Amount refunded	$3,497 28

Statement of certificates issued and allowed for drawbacks on merchandise exported, as provided for under section 171 of the act of June 30, 1864, for the fiscal year ended June 30, 1872.

Number of certificates received and allowed	150
Amount allowed	$15,004 76

REPORT OF THE SIXTH AUDITOR.

REPORT

OF

THE SIXTH AUDITOR OF THE TREASURY.

OFFICE OF THE AUDITOR OF THE TREASURY
FOR THE POST-OFFICE DEPARTMENT,
Washington, D. C., October 17, 1872.

SIR: I have the honor to submit the following report of the business operations of this office for the fiscal year ended June 30, 1872. My forthcoming report to the Postmaster-General will exhibit in detail all that pertains to the financial transactions of the Post-Office Department for the past fiscal year.

Pursuing the plan adopted in presenting my last annual report, I have, as far as practicable, made quarterly exhibits of the work performed, with a view of showing the increase of business.

A comparison of the tables and statements in the present report with those contained in my report for the fiscal year ended June 30, 1871, will show a steady increase of business in every division of the Bureau.

EXAMINING DIVISION—BENJAMIN LIPPINCOTT, PRINCIPAL EXAMINER.

This division receives and audits the quarterly accounts-current of all post-offices in the United States. It is divided into four subdivisions, viz, the opening-room, the stamp-rooms, the examining corps proper, and the error-rooms.

1. *The opening-room.*—All returns, as soon as received, are opened, and, if found in order, according to regulations, are entered on the register, carefully folded and tied, and then forwarded to the stamp-rooms.

The number of quarterly accounts-current received during each quarter of the fiscal year ended June 30, 1872, was as follows:

Third quarter, 1871	29,218
Fourth quarter, 1871	29,846
First quarter, 1872	30,021
Second quarter, 1872	30,119
Total	119,204

2. *The stamp-rooms.*—The quarterly returns received from the opening-room are divided alphabetically among eight stamp-clerks, whose duties consist in comparing the stamp-statements of the postmasters in the accounts-current with their own books and the returns made to them from the stamp-division of the finance office, whence stamp-orders are issued and receipts for the same received and forwarded to the stamp-clerks. The returns thus approved or corrected are passed to the examiners. All accounts from offices of the first and second classes are passed through the various subdivisions of the office in advance of

other returns, so that they may reach the chief examiner and his assistant with as little delay as possible.

The number of accounts examined and settled by the stamp-clerks for each quarter of the fiscal year ended June 30, 1872, was as follows:

Third quarter, 1871	28,378
Fourth quarter, 1871	28,806
First quarter, 1872	29,713
Second quarter, 1872	29,920
Total	116,817

3. The examining corps proper is composed of seventeen clerks, among whom the returns received from the stamp-rooms are divided by sections, each comprising several States or parts of States.

The average number to each section is about 1,700. After the examination of the accounts-current and the stamp-account, reviewing and refooting the transcript of mails received, and examining all vouchers belonging to that portion of the work, the balance is drawn on all accounts of the third, fourth, and fifth classes. The returns thus examined and completed are forwarded to the registering division to be entered upon its books.

The number of accounts examined and sent to the registering division for the fiscal year ended June 30, 1872, was as follows:

Third quarter, 1871	28,378
Fourth quarter, 1871	28,806
First quarter, 1872	29,713
Second quarter, 1872	29,920
Total	116,817

4. The error-rooms contain six clerks, who review and re-examine the error-accounts received from the registering division, and forward to each postmaster a copy of his account as stated by him and as audited and corrected by this office.

The number of accounts so corrected and copied for the fiscal year ended June 30, 1872, was as follows:

Third quarter, 1871	6,092
Fourth quarter, 1871	7,928
First quarter, 1872	6,818
Second quarter, 1872	6,683
Total	27,521

Each subdivision reports weekly to the chief examiner, and monthly, through that officer, to the chief clerk, the progress of the work, so that the exact amount of work done by each clerk is clearly ascertained.

All vouchers relative to allowances made by the Post-Office Department for clerk-hire, lights, fuel, rent, stationery, &c., at post-offices of the first and second classes, are forwarded at the beginning of each quarter to the chief examiner and his assistant for examination. A statement is then prepared showing the vouchers received, the amount allowed, and the amount suspended when found to be in excess of the allowance.

On receipt of the returns from the examiners, these accounts are received, and the amount allowable added, and the balance drawn by the chief examiner.

The number of post-offices of the first and second classes which have received allowances for clerk-hire, rent, &c., was 344.

The number of offices of the second class having an allowance for clerk-hire only, was 159.

The number of offices having an allowance for clerk-hire to aid in separating the mails, (independent of the number above stated,) was 348.

Total number of offices of all classes receiving allowances, and approved by the chief examiner, was 851.

The expense-accounts of the offices of the first and second classes were regularly entered by the chief examiner and his assistant on the expense-register, and show quarterly the amount of vouchers received, amount allowed and amount suspended, copies of which were forwarded to each postmaster.

Attached to the examining division is a corresponding clerk, whose duty consists in corresponding with postmasters relative to errors in their accounts-current, and in making day-book entries, &c.

The amount involved in the settlement of the quarterly accounts-current of postmasters during the fiscal year, was as follows:

Third quarter, 1871	$5,090,791 21
Fourth quarter, 1871	5,407,570 98
First quarter, 1872	5,668,583 18
Second quarter, 1872	5,394,917 30
Total	21,561,862 67

The labors of the examining division for the fiscal year ended June 30, 1872, have been fully completed. All accounts received in proper form have been examined and passed to the registering division. At no period has the work been more perfect in all its details. Not only has there been a decided improvement in the preparation of returns by postmasters, particularly those of first and second class offices, but, by judicious changes in the office, the efficiency of the examining corps has been greatly increased.

REGISTERING DIVISION—F. I. SEYBOLT, PRINCIPAL REGISTER.

This division receives from the examining division the quarterly accounts-current of postmasters, and re-examines and registers them, placing each item of revenue and expenditure under its appropriate head; noting also, in books prepared for the purpose, corresponding with each register, the amount of letter-postage and stamps reported as remaining on hand in each account. The same books also show the proper amount of newspaper-postage and box-rents chargeable to and compensation allowed each office contained therein, and afford a complete check in the settlement of every account.

Upon this division thirteen clerks are employed, and during the fiscal year the number of accounts registered and amount involved therein were as follows:

Third quarter, 1871	29,313	$5,119,153 41
Fourth quarter, 1871	29,479	5,439,572 17
First quarter, 1872	29,696	5,689,904 58
Second quarter, 1872	30,076	5,417,146 35
Total	118,564	21,665,776 51

During the fiscal year, 6,022 circulars were sent to postmasters who had failed to render their quarterly returns.

The number of changes of postmasters, establishment, re-establishment, discontinuance, and change of name of post-office, reported from the appointment office during the fiscal year and noted by the registers, was as follows:

Third quarter, 1871	1,975
Fourth quarter, 1871	2,235
First quarter, 1872	2,662
Second quarter, 1872	2,975
Total	9,847

The work of this division is fully up to the requirements of the office, the quarterly accounts-current received from every office having been registered to the 30th day of June, 1872, the footings and recapitulations made, and the books prepared for the registration of the accounts for the quarter ended September 30, 1872, as well as the new salary-books for the two years ending 1874.

BOOK-KEEPERS' DIVISION—F. B. LILLEY, PRINCIPAL CLERK.

This division has in charge the ledger-accounts of postmasters, late postmasters, contractors, late contractors, and the general, special, and miscellaneous accounts of the Department.

The work of this division requires the services of fourteen clerks, viz, one principal book-keeper in charge of ledger of general accounts, one assistant principal in charge of cash-book, register of deposits, stamp-journal, ledger of warrants and deposits, and day-book entries on reports approved by the Auditor; eight book-keepers of postmasters accounts, and four of contractors' accounts. The number of ledgers is 52, averaging over 575 pages each, and containing 37,307 current accounts.

The auxiliary, books from which the postings are made quarterly, are as follows: 13 registers of postmasters' accounts, 35 pay-books, 8 journals, 1 register of warrants, 3 registers of Postmaster-General's drafts, 1 stamp-journal, 1 cash-book, 1 deposit-book, 1 Auditor's draft-book, 1 money-order transfer book, 6 mail-messengers' registers, 6 registers of special mail-service, 1 route-agents' book, 1 letter-carriers' book, 1 special agents' fare-book; total, 80 books.

Accounts of offices of the first, second, and third classes, and all contractors' accounts, are balanced quarterly; all others at the end of the fiscal year.

It affords me pleasure to state that the work of this division is in a satisfactory condition, fully up to the requirements of the office.

Ledgers of postmasters' accounts.

Sections.	Number of ledgers.	Current accounts.	Late accounts.
Number 1	5	3,593	694
Number 2	4	3,509	300
Number 3	4	3,645	733
Number 4	4	4,633	742
Number 5	5	3,857	853
Number 6	5	4,113	902
Number 7	5	4,118	908
Number 8	4	4,333	703
Total	36	31,801	5,835

Ledgers of mail-contractors' accounts.

Sections.	Number of ledgers.	Current accounts.	Day-book entries journalized.	Acc'ts journalized from transfer-sheets.
1	3	1,512	1,519	5,432
2	3	1,642	1,927	8,897
3	3	1,159	1,926	7,667
4	3	1,193	2,088	4,477
Total	12	5,506	7,460	26,473

Miscellaneous.

Number of entries on stamp-journal	6,567
Number of day-book entries	1,205
Number of certificates of deposit entered in deposit-book	8,011
Number of certificates of deposit entered in cash-book	2,982
Total	18,765

STATING DIVISION—WILLIAM H. GUNNISON, PRINCIPAL CLERK.

This division has charge of more than thirty-two thousand general postal accounts of present postmasters, and more than eight thousand of late postmasters, subdivided into thirteen sections, varying in number from twenty-eight hundred to twenty-two hundred of the former, and from one thousand to four hundred of the latter.

Each account is stated quarterly from the various records of the office, a comparison of the items made with those of any statements of general accounts rendered by the postmasters, and with the ledgers of the bookkeepers, the differences investigated, if possible adjusted, and instructions sent, according to the classification of the office, as to the disposition of the balances as audited. Other duties of the division are, to correspond with postmasters in special cases; to cause drafts to be issued for balances due the United States in cases of continued neglect or refusal to pay, in order that demand for payment may be made on sureties; to record "changes" reported weekly from the appointment office; to have "special" offices made "deposit" also, whenever the quarterly proceeds sufficiently exceed payments for the special mail service; to make reports to the Postmaster-General of failures—to pay quarterly proceeds on collection-orders, to render accounts-current for two or more quarters, to order stamps from the Department, and of new appointees to qualify within a reasonable time.

Accounts of "draft," "deposit," and "collection" offices of the first, second, and third classes have been stated much earlier during the past year than ever before, viz, from the 1st of the second month to the 20th of the third month, in the quarter succeeding that to which the items pertain, owing both to the efficiency of the clerks and the increased facilities for obtaining the various data, thus allowing statements and instructions to reach postmasters in time for examination, and any necessary entries on their own records, before rendering their general accounts for the current quarter. Accounts of postmasters at "collection" offices of the fourth and fifth classes, showing balances of $10 or more, as stated from the ledgers each quarter, have had the items of the succeeding quarter added from later records; and, whenever the accounts continued to show such indebtedness, special instructions were sent that such amounts be included in the payments for the current quarter. The remaining accounts of present postmasters at offices of the fourth and fifth classes were stated and balanced with the ledgers to the close of the last fiscal year, before the 31st of January, and where balances of more than $1 were found due the United States, or balances of more than $25 due the postmaster, instructions were sent to include the former amounts in their payments at the close of the current quarter, and giving authority to retain the latter from subsequent proceeds of their offices.

Accounts of late postmasters have been fully stated to latest dates audited, in advance of the time usually allowed for adjustment, that the results may be used in the annual report of the office to the Postmaster-General.

By the foregoing system a complete revision of all the general postal accounts, as recorded in the office, is secured each quarter, an adjustment had once a quarter with all postmasters at "draft" and "deposit" offices, and "collection" offices of the first, second, and third classes, numbering forty-five hundred and fifty-five, and at least once a year with all other postmasters, twenty-seven thousand five hundred and ten in number, when their accounts differ materially from those of the office.

Statement of the number of the general accounts of present postmasters, the increase in the number, and the classification of the offices for the fiscal year ended June 30, 1872.

Number of section.	States and Territories.	Draft-offices.		Deposit-offices.		Collection-offices.		Special offices.	Number in each State and Territory.	Number in each section.	Increase in each State and Territory.	Increase in each section.
		First, second, and third classes.	Fourth and fifth classes.	First, second, and third classes.	Fourth and fifth classes.	First, second, and third classes.	Fourth and fifth classes.	Fourth and fifth classes.				
1	Maine	6	3	7	127	11	673	37	864	....	18	....
	New Hampshire	7	......	7	51	6	341	12	424	....	9	....
	Vermont	10	4	2	79	6	353	19	473	....	4	....
	Massachusetts	12	1	36	133	35	471	19	707	....	5	....
	Total	35	8	52	390	58	1,838	87	....	2,468	......	36
2	New York, A to S	31	4	34	329	61	1,672	242	....	2,373	......	69
3	Pennsylvania, A to R	8	3	34	180	35	1,976	41	....	2,277	......	68
4	Connecticut	9	2	12	88	13	265	32	421	....	19	....
	Rhode Island	2	......	2	15	5	75	3	102	....	1	....
	West Virginia	1	......	1	25	3	582	16	628	....	16	....
	Wisconsin	3	1	8	72	32	965	64	1,145	....	60	....
	Total	15	3	23	200	53	1,887	115	....	2,296	......	96
5	North Carolina	2	......	......	58	9	756	14	839	....	37	....
	South Carolina	1	......	3	9	5	372	4	394	....	36	....
	Georgia	2	......	9	141	9	377	26	564	....	60	....
	Alabama	3	......	1	46	7	601	20	678	....	96	....
	Total	8	......	13	254	30	2,106	64	....	2,475	......	229
6	Kansas	1	......	6	33	20	615	114	789	....	114	....
	Minnesota	2	......	7	38	8	620	47	722	....	48	....
	California	1	......	4	36	13	506	32	592	....	23	....
	Utah	......	......	......	1	3	146	6	156	....	12	....
	Colorado	1	......	......	4	6	111	12	134	....	22	....
	Washington	......	......	......	2	2	105	7	110	....	10	....

Statement of the number of the general accounts of present postmasters in charge of the division, &c.—Continued.

Number of section.	States and Territories.	Draft-offices.		Deposit-offices.		Collection-offices.		Special offices.	Number in each State and Territory.	Number in each section.	Increase in each State and Territory.	Increase in each section.
		First, second, and third classes.	Fourth and fifth classes.	First, second, and third classes.	Fourth and fifth classes.	First, second, and third classes.	Fourth and fifth classes.	Fourth and fifth classes.				
	Montana				1	4	78	9	92		23	
	Dakota				2	1	59	16	78		26	
	New Mexico					2	43	1	46		*3	
	Idaho				1	2	39	2	44		9	
	Arizona					1	26	2	29		3	
	Wyoming				2	2	18	4	26		2	
	Alaska				4				4			
	Total	5		17	124	64	2,366	252		2,828		295
7	Ohio	12		8	228	67	1,667	88	2,070		37	
	Oregon				6	2	192	16	216		31	
	Nevada			1	2	6	57	6	72		9	
	Total	12		9	236	75	1,916	110		2,358		77
8	Illinois	7		14	369	84	1,238	41	1,753		66	
	New Jersey	2		13	87	23	438	32	595		29	
	Total	9		27	456	107	1,676	73		2,348		95
9	Missouri			2	45	34	1,258	142	1,481		114	
	Tennessee	3		7	116	4	734	68	932		54	
	Louisiana			1	16	5	256	7	285		57	
	Total	3		10	177	43	2,248	217		2,698		225
10	Kentucky	3		9	108	10	752	106	990		55	
	Texas	2			61	17	561	38	679		36	
	Arkansas	1		1	23	3	515	30	572		54	
	Mississippi			11	86	7	325	37	466		*27	
	Total	6		21	277	37	2,153	213		2,707		118
11	Virginia	2		5	85	13	1,047	34	1,186		26	
	Maryland	1		3	43	5	488	22	562			
	New York, T to Z	2	1	4	57	12	262	33	371		10	
	Nebraska	1			11	6	312	43	373		79	
	Total	6	1	12	106	36	2,109	132		2,492		115
12	Indiana	11	2	8	214	33	1,110	64	1,442		81	
	Pennsylvania, S to Z	4		7	33	14	592	17	667		*15	
	Delaware	1		1	9	1	80	2	94		2	
	District of Columbia			2			5		7		3	
	Total	16	2	18	256	48	1,787	83		2,210		71
13	Iowa	19		15	113	21	1,026	84	1,278		135	
	Michigan	11		4	148	41	850	53	1,107		100	
	Florida	1		2	12	1	129	5	150		12	
	Total	31		21	273	63	2,005	142		2,535		247

* Decrease.

Whole number of general postal accounts	32,065
Whole number of general postal accounts for fiscal year ended June 30, 1871	30,324
Increase during fiscal year ended June 30, 1872	1,741

Statement showing the number of changes, and the condition of general postal accounts of "late" postmasters for and during the fiscal year ended June 30, 1872.

Changes reported to this office weekly by the First Assistant Postmaster-General, recorded for the fiscal year.	Third quarter, 1871.	Fourth quarter, 1871.	First quarter, 1872.	Second quarter, 1872.	No. of changes during the year.	Total number during the year.
Established	473	419	598	655	2, 145	....
Re-established	105	116	176	153	610	....
Discontinued	211	396	237	226	1, 070	....
New bonds	137	123	156	439	855	....
Miscellaneous, removals, resignations, &c	1, 197	1, 428	1, 654	1, 666	5, 945	....
Total	2, 183	2, 482	2, 821	3, 139	....	10, 625

Condition of general accounts of postmasters becoming "late" during the year.	Quarters prior to third quarter, 1871.	Third quarter, 1871.	Fourth quarter, 1871.	First quarter, 1872.	Second quarter, 1872.	Total.
Suspended accounts stated to latest dates audited	157	51	102	....	....	310
Accounts stated finally	....	1, 551	1, 711	....	....	3, 262
Accounts stated to latest dates audited	....	....	....	2, 078	2, 388	4, 466
						8, 038
Deducting the number of accounts suspended						310
Leaves the number settled finally for and during the year						7, 728

Miscellaneous statement.

Letters, reports, &c.	Third quarter, 1871.	Fourth quarter, 1871.	First quarter, 1872.	Second quarter, 1872.	Total.
Entries of credits authorized by the weekly reports of the Third Assistant Postmaster-General	560	531	579	1, 130	2, 800
Entries of debits for stamps unaccounted for on orders from the stamp division	101	1, 450	651	761	2, 963
Entries of miscellaneous debits and credits on orders from the stamp-division	214	244	249	195	902
Entries made in day-books to close "late" accounts	165	127	133	120	545
Reports of postmasters delinquent in paying quarterly proceeds of offices	38	14	19	22	93
Reports of postmasters delinquent in rendering quarterly accounts-current for more than two successive quarters	9	25	79	23	136
Reports of failures of appointees to qualify within ninety days	78	100	168	11	357
Reports made to Third Assistant Postmaster-General of failures to order stamps	11	26	4	5	46
Letters written, correspondence in special cases	128	197	167	110	602
Circulars sent in answer to letters received, special cases	333	236	528	403	1, 500

COLLECTING DIVISION—E. J. EVANS, PRINCIPAL CLERK.

The duties of this division are to collect balances due from late and present postmasters throughout the United States, and to attend to the final settlement of the same. The number of clerks employed at this time is twenty, apportioned as follows:

On correspondence, 4. The duties of these gentlemen are to correspond in relation to postmasters', late postmasters' and contractors' accounts, with a view to the collection of balances due the Department, and to prepare for submission for suit accounts of defaulting postmasters and contractors.

On drafts, 1. His duties are to locate and issue drafts for the collection of balances due by postmasters and contractors, and record the same in the draft-register; and to report to the Post-Office Department for payment all balances due to late postmasters, and record the same in a book kept for that purpose.

On changes, 1. His duties are to record all changes of postmasters reported to this office from the Post-Office Department; to enter drafts paid and file them away; to record all accounts of late postmasters in the book of balances, and to state the final action thereon.

On letter-books, 2. Their duties are to record all letters written, and address and transmit the same; also, to transmit all circulars received by them from the corresponding clerks.

On miscellaneous, 1. His duties are to examine and compare with the ledgers all accounts of late postmasters, and close the same as "uncollectible" or by "suspense," and to assist in the preparation of the Postmaster-General's annual report.

On copying, 11. Their duties are to copy all accounts of postmasters and others, and transmit the same in their respective circulars; to copy changes of postmasters; to prepare salary-books of the various post-offices in the country, and to assist in the adjustment of salaries.

I most respectfully ask your attention to the statement in the accompanying table, exhibiting the aggregate amount of balances due to late postmasters reported to the Post-Office Department. The system adopted by this office of paying credit balances is of recent origin, having been inaugurated under our present management, and is regarded as but just and equitable between the Government and its employés. The large number of cases which appears in this and last year's report explained by the fact that it is the accumulation of many years. Hereafter it is the intention of this office, as far as practicable, to pay all balances due to late postmasters annually. The gentleman to whom this work is assigned is capable and faithful, and, for the manner in which he discharges the business of his desk, is, I think, worthy of special mention.

It gives me pleasure to state that the regulations of the Department requiring current business to be dispatched on the day received are observed by the division generally, but particularly by the men on correspondence, and that they are indefatigable in the performance of the duties intrusted to them, I beg leave to refer to the annexed table as evidence, although it but imperfectly exhibits the actual labor performed.

Statement of business transacted by collecting division.

Accounts of postmasters and contractors.	No.	Amount.
Accounts of postmasters becoming late during the period from July 1, 1869, to June 30, 1871, in charge of the division	16,129	....
Accounts of postmasters becoming late during the fiscal year:		
Quarter ended September 30, 1871	2,011	....
Quarter ended December 31, 1871	1,892	....
Quarter ended March 31, 1872	1,833	....
Quarter ended June 30, 1872	1,683	....
Total	23,548	$217,359 54
Accounts of contractors received from the pay-division for collection upon which drafts were issued:		
Quarter ended September 30, 1871	19	2,189 05
Quarter ended December 31, 1871	11	2,004 45
Quarter ended March 31, 1872	26	9,962 60
Quarter ended June 30, 1872	16	9,627 76
Total	72	23,783 86

Statement of business transacted by collecting division—Continued.

Accounts of postmasters and contractors.	No.	Amount.
Drafts issued on present and late postmasters during fiscal year:		
Quarter ended September 30, 1871	857	$112,470 18
Quarter ended December 31, 1871	1,115	137,271 95
Quarter ended March 31, 1872	1,145	122,042 77
Quarter ended June 30, 1872	898	106,350 47
Total	4,015	478,135 37
Accounts of postmasters becoming late during the fiscal year, showing balances in their favor, and closed by "suspense:"		
Quarter ended September 30, 1871	857	3,857 79
Quarter ended December 31, 1871	1,676	12,292 40
Quarter ended March 31, 1872	837	24,325 10
Quarter ended June 30, 1872	97	1,985 69
Total	3,467	42,461 00
Accounts of postmasters becoming late during the fiscal year, showing balances due the United States, and closed by "suspense:"		
Quarter ended September 30, 1871	17	146 88
Quarter ended December 31, 1871	501	195 40
Quarter ended March 31, 1872	35	30 96
Quarter ended June 30, 1872	97	812 68
Total	650	1,185 92
Accounts of postmasters becoming late during the fiscal year, showing balances due the United States found uncollectible:		
Quarter ended September 30, 1871	21	9,589 14
Quarter ended December 31, 1871	1	34 15
Quarter ended March 31, 1872	18	1,577 61
Quarter ended June 30, 1872	17	9,744 25
Total	57	20,945 15
Accounts showing balances due late and present postmasters, and reported to the Post-Office Department for payment:		
Quarter ended September 30, 1871	241	16,176 68
Quarter ended December 31, 1871	337	18,046 25
Quarter ended March 31, 1872	527	32,038 76
Quarter ended June 30, 1872	365	26,418 43
Total	1,470	92,680 12
Accounts of late postmasters and contractors submitted for suit:		
Quarter ended September 30, 1871	17	6,118 69
Quarter ended December 31, 1871	22	10,397 31
Quarter ended March 31, 1872	32	19,639 67
Quarter ended June 30, 1872	31	10,498 99
Total	103	46,654 66

Letters received during the fiscal year:	
Quarter ended September 30, 1871	58,668
Quarter ended December 31, 1871	57,916
Quarter ended March 31, 1872	69,402
Quarter ended June 30, 1872	68,141
Total	254,127

Letters sent during the fiscal year:	
Quarter ended September 30, 1871	33,665
Quarter ended December 31, 1871	39,791
Quarter ended March 31, 1872	44,482
Quarter ended June 30, 1872	35,468
Total	153,406

Letters recorded during the fiscal year:	
Quarter ended September 30, 1871	2,131
Quarter ended December 31, 1871	2,258
Quarter ended March 31, 1872	2,906
Quarter ended June 30, 1872	2,180
Total	9,475

Letters written to postmasters and others during the fiscal year:

Quarter ended September 30, 1871	1,790
Quarter ended December 31, 1871	1,856
Quarter ended March 31, 1872	2,400
Quarter ended June 30, 1872	2,166
Total	8,212

Accounts copied during the fiscal year and sent in their appropriate circulars:

Quarter ended September 30, 1871	9,164
Quarter ended December 31, 1871	6,701
Quarter ended March 31, 1872	7,008
Quarter ended June 30, 1872	5,737
Total	28,610

Pages of post-office changes reported by the Post-Office Department during the fiscal year, recorded in the change-books:

Quarter ended September 30, 1871	2,442
Quarter ended December 31, 1871	2,574
Quarter ended March 31, 1872	2,970
Quarter ended June 30, 1872	3,168
Total	11,154

Pages of stamp-journal added and recapitulated:

Quarter ended September 30, 1871	154
Quarter ended December 31, 1871	47
Quarter ended March 31, 1872	109
Quarter ended June 30, 1872	72
Total	382

Pages of draft-register recorded:

Quarter ended September 30, 1871	46
Quarter ended December 31, 1871	58
Quarter ended March 31, 1872	62
Quarter ended June 30, 1872	44
Total	210

Pages of book of balances recorded:

Quarter ended September 30, 1871	137
Quarter ended December 31, 1871	158
Quarter ended March 31, 1872	175
Quarter ended June 30, 1872	164
Total	634

Pages of letter-book recorded:

Quarter ended September 30, 1871	945
Quarter ended December 31, 1871	928
Quarter ended March 31, 1872	1,350
Quarter ended June 30, 1872	1,153
Total	4,376

LAW DIVISION—J. BOZMAN KERR, PRINCIPAL CLERK.

To this division is assigned the duty of preparing and transmitting to the Department of Justice, for suit, accounts of late postmasters and contractors who fail to pay their indebtedness to the United States upon the drafts of the Department.

The number of accounts and accompanying papers certified for suit during the fiscal year was as follows:

Quarter ended September 30, 1871	17	$6,118 69
Quarter ended December 31, 1871	22	10,397 31
Quarter ended March 31, 1872	32	19,639 67
Quarter ended June 30, 1872	31	10,498 99
Total	102	46,654 66

Judgments obtained during the fiscal year, as reported by the Department of Justice	106
Amount of collections on judgments, including interest	$56,040 94

All accounts received from the collecting division have been prepared for suit and sent to the Department of Justice.

FOREIGN-MAIL DIVISION—ISAAC W. NICHOLLS, PRINCIPAL CLERK.

This division has charge of the postal accounts with foreign governments, and making up the accounts for steamship companies for ocean transportation of mails, when not paid by subsidy.

Number of accounts settled during the fiscal year, with amounts involved.

Name of country.	Number of quarterly accounts.	Amount.
United Kingdom of Great Britain and Ireland	4	$910,314 69
German Union	4	621,153 51
Belgium	4	16,419 15
Netherlands	4	24,258 50
Switzerland	4	36,878 68
Italy	4	27,463 93
Total	24	1,636,488 46

Number of duplicates registered during the fiscal year.

Received from—	Third quarter, 1871.	Fourth quarter, 1871.	First quarter, 1872.	Second quarter, 1872.	Sent to—	Third quarter, 1871.	Fourth quarter, 1871.	First quarter, 1872.	Second quarter, 1872.
United Kingdom	339	322	347	336	United Kingdom	300	249	203	253
German Union	183	158	168	178	German Union	196	135	128	171
France	38	44	49	55	France	32	40	33	40
Belgium	104	100	111	109	Belgium	103	98	76	93
Netherlands	40	36	42	37	Netherlands	52	50	41	44
Switzerland	48	48	56	51	Switzerland	52	50	41	44
Italy	40	37	42	38	Italy	52	50	41	44
Denmark	1	2	43	52	Denmark	2	3	27	44
Spain	......	......	......	......	Spain	......	2	4	1
West Indies	96	101	114	128	West Indies	75	78	96	101
Nova Scotia	50	34	15	45	Nova Scotia	61	18	13	42
Total received	939	882	987	1,029	Total sent	925	773	703	877

Total number registered, 7,115.

Amounts reported for payment on account of balances due to foreign countries.

To—	Quarter ended—	Amount in gold.
United Kingdom of Great Britain and Ireland	Sept. 30, 1870	$22, 602 54
	Dec. 31, 1870	21, 209 53
	Mar. 31, 1871	19, 834 94
Total		63, 647 01
Costing in currency		70, 542 96
German Union	Sept. 30, 1870	22, 837 16
	Dec. 31, 1870	28, 197 60
	Mar. 31, 1871	33, 330 92
	June 30, 1871	29, 338 49
Total		113, 704 17
Costing in currency		126, 886 93
Belgium	Dec. 31, 1870	1, 623 38
	Mar. 31, 1871	1, 366 92
Total		2, 990 30
Costing in currency		3, 302 60
Total amount reported		180, 341 48
Costing in currency		200, 732 49

The following amounts have been paid in gold by the goverments named :

By—	Quarter ended—	Amount in gold.
Switzerland	June 30, 1871	$1, 641 04
	Sept. 30, 1871	2, 465 06
	Dec. 31, 1871	1, 835 03
	Total	5, 941 13
Netherlands	Mar. 31, 1871	546 68
	June 30, 1871	308 69
	Sept. 30, 1871	674 86
	Dec. 31, 1871	734 22
	Total	2, 324 45
Italy	Mar. 31, 1871	1, 318 02
	June 30, 1871	934 30
	Sept. 30, 1871	824 72
	Total	3, 067 04
Total amount received in gold		11, 392 92

Number of reports of ocean postages to the Postmaster-General, and amounts reported.

Third quarter, 1871.		Fourth quarter, 1871.		First quarter, 1872.		Second quarter, 1872.	
Number of reports.	Amounts.	Number of reports.	Amounts.	Number of reports.	Amounts.	Number of reports.	Amounts.
1	$17,090 43	1	$19,377 32	1	$18,646 58	1	$18,718 51
1	11,382 48	1	11,545 22	1	14,678 46	1	12,345 02
1	10,404 07	1	10,509 09	1	10,536 41	1	11,708 27
1	8,318 13	1	8,628 03	1	10,189 22	1	9,058 94
1	7,580 42	1	5,719 20	1	6,037 52	1	6,671 45
1	5,521 53	1	5,492 42	1	5,394 11	1	5,278 35
1	2,131 77	1	2,310 50	1	3,129 00	1	3,601 31
1	1,361 63	1	1,398 36	1	1,291 28	1	1,896 88
1	1,332 79	1	788 83	1	875 66	1	1,669 40
1	1,214 27	1	682 56	1	684 67	1	1,555 05
1	1,101 34	1	538 37	1	452 41	1	1,247 83
1	1,095 93	1	395 29	1	353 85	1	1,089 89
1	994 55	1	326 27	1	296 08	1	800 78
1	848 24	1	313 60	1	209 24	1	768 42
1	759 70	1	299 60	1	173 83	1	750 00
1	683 57	1	286 12	1	161 52	1	721 77
1	657 20	1	212 92	1	155 12	1	718 76
1	521 65	1	208 11	1	125 79	1	489 27
1	414 40	1	194 81	1	106 23	1	423 71
1	354 40	1	151 90	1	101 15	1	410 75
1	352 59	1	99 00	1	95 41	1	404 39
1	328 34	1	73 51	1	90 02	1	397 52
1	284 06	1	71 63	1	55 72	1	356 30
1	280 16	1	59 29	1	53 76	1	251 03
1	277 22	1	46 02	1	19 18	1	236 17
1	261 10	1	29 41	1	12 60	1	233 38
1	254 31	1	24 29	1	10 36	1	181 15
1	245 04	1	24 29	1	48	1	172 62
1	243 07	1	22 66	1	36	1	154 39
1	226 81	1	3 91			1	143 15
1	226 73	1	2 05			1	118 40
1	219 96	1	1 17			1	110 67
1	202 99					1	102 55
1	202 60					1	99 47
1	196 53					1	75 47
1	186 13					1	74 02
1	181 72					1	36 92
1	166 53					1	32 36
1	153 30					1	31 68
1	139 21					1	30 32
1	137 97					1	25 05
1	114 56					1	19 03
1	112 21					1	16 37
1	80 84					1	14 80
1	71 70						
1	69 49						
1	63 15						
1	59 19						
1	47 12						
1	36 68						
1	35 46						
1	30 85						
1	30 03						
1	25 25						
1	17 70						
1	16 47						
1	12 36						
1	8 23						
1	7 73						
1	5 58						
1	27						
61	70,322 74	32	69,841 75	29	73,936 24	44	83,241 57

Total number of reports made, 166. Total amount reported, $306,402.30.

The foregoing statement will in no wise indicate the amount of labor performed by each clerk, or of the division as a whole; 239 letters and reports were written, and each of the 7,115 duplicates was briefed, and the necessary examinations and calculations made on the same.

The number of clerks regularly employed on this division is 4.

PAY DIVISION—C. HAZLETT, PRINCIPAL CLERK.

This division has in charge the settlement and payment of all accounts for transportation of the mails, including railroad companies, steamboat companies, and other mail contractors, special mail-carriers, mail-messengers, railway postal clerks, route agents, special agents, letter-carriers, and all miscellaneous payments.

To this division are also assigned the registration of all warrants and drafts countersigned by the Auditor, and the custody of the archives pertaining to all the branches of the office.

Accounts of contractors settled during the fiscal year ended June 30, 1872.

Quarter.	Number.	Amount.
In the quarter ended September 30, 1871	7,069	$2,916,740 42
In the quarter ended December 31, 1871	7,073	3,092,790 17
In the quarter ended March 31, 1872	7,075	3,250,646 51
In the quarter ended June 30, 1872	7,147	2,533,758 11
	28,364	11,793,935 21
Foreign mail accounts settled during the fiscal year	168	1,022,816 28

Mail-messenger service.

Number of mail-messengers in service June 30, 1872 3,018

Accounts settled during the fiscal year, as follows:

	Number.	Amount.
In the quarter ended September 30, 1871	2,683	$108,729 17
In the quarter ended December 31, 1871	2,790	110,347 41
In the quarter ended March 31, 1872	2,906	115,885 51
In the quarter ended June 30, 1872	3,052	128,127 91
Total	11,431	463,090 00

Accounts of mail-messengers and special mail-carriers:

	Number.	Amount.
In the quarter ended September 30, 1871	1,376	$12,259 15
In the quarter ended December 31, 1871	1,543	13,369 20
In the quarter ended March 31, 1872	1,480	12,365 30
In the quarter ended June 30, 1872	1,538	13,143 03
Total	5,937	51,136 68

Accounts of special agents:

	Number.	Amount.
In the quarter ended September 30, 1871	150	$43,675 00
In the quarter ended December 31, 1871	155	41,011 80
In the quarter ended March 31, 1872	165	43,773 44
In the quarter ended June 30, 1872	156	40,851 39
Total	626	169,311 63

Accounts of letter-carriers:

	Number.	Amount.
In the quarter ended September 30, 1871	1,723	$346,259 78
In the quarter ended December 31, 1871	1,520	346,594 60
In the quarter ended March 31, 1872	1,509	347,411 78
In the quarter ended June 30, 1872	1,506	343,127 53
Salary of special agent, paid out of appropriation for letter-carriers		2,572 07
Total	6,258	1,385,965 76

Railway postal clerks, route and other agents:

	Number.	Amount.
In the quarter ended September 30, 1871	1,526	$367,488 56
In the quarter ended December 31, 1871	1,654	375,454 67
In the quarter ended March 31, 1872	1,739	407,989 59
In the quarter ended June 30, 1872	1,745	419,036 50
Total	6,664	1,569,969 32

Miscellaneous accounts:

	Number.	Amount.
In the quarter ended September 30, 1871	104	$205,992 13
In the quarter ended December 31, 1871	152	206,722 14
In the quarter ended March 31, 1872	187	228,393 08
In the quarter ended June 30, 1872	191	242,263 78
Total	634	883,371 13

Collection orders sent out to postmasters:

	Number.	Amount.
In the quarter ended September 30, 1871	23,707	$622,076 78
In the quarter ended December 31, 1871	24,085	745,183 49
In the quarter ended March 31, 1872	24,394	831,500 30
In the quarter ended June 30, 1872	23,991	726,599 30
Total	96,177	2,925,359 87

Warrants issued by the Postmaster-General and countersigned by the Auditor, passed and registered:

	Number.	Amount.
In the quarter ended September 30, 1871	1,654	$2,199,518 91
In the quarter ended December 31, 1871	1,603	2,076,805 04
In the quarter ended March 31, 1872	1,774	2,216,070 49
In the quarter ended June 30, 1872	1,675	2,169,711 08
Total	6,706	8,662,105 52

Drafts issued by the Postmaster-General and countersigned by the Auditor, passed and registered:

	Number.	Amount.
In the quarter ended September 30, 1871	4,031	$678,727 47
In the quarter ended December 31, 1871	4,413	665,648 56
In the quarter ended March 31, 1872	4,656	785,311 98
In the quarter ended June 30, 1872	4,543	802,048 08
Total	17,643	2,931,736 09

Report of the archives clerk for the fiscal year.

Quarter.	Reports received and filed.	Postmasters' accounts received and filed.	Receipts for drafts received and filed.	Certificates of deposit received and filed.
In the quarter ended September 30, 1871	5,720	489	3,877	1,941
In the quarter ended December 31, 1871	6,091	535	4,085	2,163
In the quarter ended March 31, 1872	6,576	7,983	4,369	2,228
In the quarter ended June 30, 1872	6,641	465	4,538	2,396
Total	25,028	9,472	16,869	8,728

MONEY-ORDER DIVISION—JOHN LYNCH, PRINCIPAL CLERK.

I regret to state that, in consequence of the great pressure of business in this division, I am unable to present an exhibit of the work performed *by quarters*, and in lieu of such statement the aggregates for the fiscal year ended June 30, 1872, are here given, and a comparison made with the aggregates for the fiscal year ended June 30, 1871:

Number of money-order statements received, examined, and registered during the fiscal year ended June 30, 1872		164, 996
Number of money-order statements received, examined, and registered during the fiscal year ended June 30, 1871		109, 221
Increase		55, 775
Aggregate of money-orders issued and paid during the fiscal year ended June 30, 1872		$93, 432, 008 50
Aggregate of money-orders issued and paid during the fiscal year ended June 30, 1871		83, 920, 276 10
Increase		9, 511, 732 40
Number of paid money-orders received, examined, checked, and filed during the fiscal year ended June 30, 1872		2, 568, 350
Number of paid money-orders received, examined, checked, and filed during the fiscal year ended June 30, 1871		2, 122, 081
Increase		446, 269
Number and amount of certificates of deposit registered, compared, and entered during the fiscal year ended June 30, 1872	157, 706	$41, 120, 100 71
Number and amount of certificates of deposit registered, compared, and entered during the fiscal year ended June 30, 1871	125, 636	30, 356, 300 51
Increase	32, 070	10, 763, 800 20
Number and amount of transfers and re-transfers registered and filed during the fiscal year ended June 30, 1872	6, 124	$1, 006, 172 50
Number and amount of transfers and re-transfers registered and filed during the fiscal year ended June 30, 1871	5, 686	793, 492 58
Increase	438	212, 679 92
Number and amount of drafts registered during the fiscal year ended June 30, 1872	8, 802	$4, 052, 011 00
Number and amount of drafts registered during the fiscal year ended June 30, 1871	7, 348	3, 850, 238 00
Increase	1, 454	201, 773 00
Number of money-orders returned for correction during the fiscal year ended June 30, 1872		8, 000
Number of money-orders returned for correction during the fiscal year ended June 30, 1871		6, 803
Increase		1, 197
Number of letters written by this division during the fiscal year		1, 495

In conclusion, it affords me pleasure to state that the clerks and other employés of this Bureau have discharged the duties assigned to them faithfully and efficiently; and the business of the office in every branch is in a very satisfactory condition.

I have the honor to be, sir, your obedient servant,

J. J. MARTIN,
Auditor.

Hon. GEORGE S. BOUTWELL,
Secretary of the Treasury.

REPORT OF TREASURER OF THE UNITED STATES.

TABLE OF CONTENTS.

REPORT.

APPENDIX.

REPORT

OF

THE TREASURER OF THE UNITED STATES.

TREASURY OF THE UNITED STATES,
Washington, October 29, 1872.

SIR: In obedience to statutory provisions, and in compliance with departmental regulations, I have the honor to submit to you, herewith, a statement of the condition of the Treasury of the United States, as it stood at the close of the business of the fiscal year ending with the month of June, 1872, and of its movement during the year preceding that time, together with remarks in regard to the past, and suggestions touching its needs, conduct, and management in the future.

INCREASE OF WORK.

During the past year the labor of the office has been, and continues to be, largely increased. This is due, mainly, to the following causes: To the redemption of old loans, and the change of the mode of paying interest. Payment of the interest on the registered part of the old loans, was made only *semi-annually*, and then on the *simple signing of a prepared list*. On the new loan, it is paid *quarterly* by a *separate draft* for the amount, and payable to *the order of each stockholder:*

To a new requirement, directing the weekly examination, and the giving of an official certificate as to the condition of the accounts of every disbursing officer of the Government, certifying to the Heads of Departments, or the Chiefs of Bureaus thereof, to which such officer may belong, the balance standing to the credit of such officer at the end of each week with the Treasurer, any Assistant Treasurer, designated depositary, or national bank, designated as a depositary of the United States. This necessitates the examination of one hundred and forty-five lists of reports of the weekly condition of the accounts of these officers, from these various depositaries; and of eleven hundred and thirty-five weekly reports of disbursing officers, located in all parts of the Union. A critical comparison is made of the one with the other, and a statement of the condition of the account of each disbursing officer, as reported by the depositary, is indorsed upon the back of each disbursing officer's report, stating the difference, if less than the amount reported by him. This statement is then officially certified, and returned to the head of the Department, or the chief of the bureau to which it belongs.

From present indications the work, in addition to the above, will be still further increased in consequence of the more rapid, than heretofore, redemption of mutilated currency of all kinds, superinduced by an act of Congress, that permits the registration of letters to and from this office *free of charge* for either *postage or registration*, that contain mutilated currency to, or new currency in return therefor from, the Treasury; and also, by a new arrangement with Adams Express Company, including all companies connecting with that company, by which *five dollars* or more in *fractional currency*, or *fifty dollars* or more in *legal-tender United States notes*, or *mixed of both legal-tenders and fractional currency*, may be forwarded to the Treasury by any corporation, association, officer, or private citizen, and return therefor be made by new currency, or by draft, free of charge to the sender, the whole being at the sole proper charge and expense of the Government. There are still other causes for the increase of the work of the office. Among these is the larger return of the notes of national banks in liquidation.

As new loans will probably be placed, necessitating the redemption of old stocks, there will probably be no decrease of work in the immediate future. It may therefore become necessary to ask for an increase of the working force of the office within the current year. This will, however, not be done if it shall be found possible to conduct the business of the office correctly, and with safety and dispatch, with the force now employed.

CIVIL SERVICE REFORM AND PAY OF EMPLOYÉS.

No matter what plans may be adopted, or what expedients may be resorted to, for reform in the civil service of the Government, the opinion is ventured that there will be no *real reform* until adequate pay is by law provided for those engaged in that service. While the price of everything else, including the wages of labor, whether skilled or otherwise, has advanced enormously, the salaries of nearly all Government officials, save those of the Army and Navy, and of all the clerks, have remained as they were fixed by law when the purchasing power of the dollar was more than double, if not triple, what it now is.

Take, for example, the inspectors of customs—not that their case is a peculiarly hard one, for their wages have been raised one-third, while those of others have remained unchanged, but because this class of men are employed to watch the fountains, and stand sentry at the very portals of our principal sources of revenue. They are now paid only four dollars a day. This is less than is paid to many journeymen mechanics. Does any one, possessing an ordinary portion of brains, believe that under such circumstances the requisite number of honest and competent men can be procured to faithfully perform the arduous and very responsible duties required of these officers? These men have, or should have, families, for the family is ordinarily the greatest security for the man's honesty. With the present pay of these officers, it is barely possible to support a family. What is the probable result? Rather than see their wives and children suffer for the want of the comforts of life, they yield to the temptation that the Government forces upon them; and thus the revenue is defrauded to amounts many-fold that which it would cost for salaries commensurate to the services performed, and the duties required of these important officers. What is said of this class, is true to a degree of almost every civil officer and employé of the Government.

Until demagogues and a hypocritical party press shall cease their clamor for a reduction of salaries, and until legislators shall learn not to be "penny-wise and pound-foolish," there will be little hope for a thorough reform in the civil service of the Government. Another evil is the cry for a reduction of the working force in the public offices. The truth is, that the number of clerks in many of the offices is inadequate to the safe conduct of the public business.

The requirement of too many and various duties of one and the same person, prevents the application of the proper safeguards that prudence demands for the safe transaction of official business. The losses sustained in this office, and the large and more recent one in the office of the Assistant Treasurer in the city of New York, are almost, if not entirely, due to the fact that there was not sufficient help in the offices to secure the necessary checks afforded by the supervision of one man over the acts of another. The want of these needed checks has been the real cause of most if not all of the defalcations that have occurred. The large loss, last year, in the pay-bureau of the Army would not have occurred if the checks of this office that have since been placed upon that had existed at that time. The attempted reform in the reduction of the force of the offices, like that to reduce the pay of those employed therein, is in the direction directly opposite that believed to be the true one for the correct, economical, and safe transaction of the public business.

There is a class of offices that *rich men* will take, for the honor they are supposed to confer upon the holder. There is another class that *dishonest men* strive for and struggle to obtain, because of the "stealings" they hope to "make off" them. As matters are now arranged, an honest, competent *poor man* is debarred and virtually disqualified and disfranchised from holding places of public trust. None but rich men or rascals can now afford to hold any of the public offices that were formerly considered places of high honor. Then offices were conferred upon persons of distinguished honesty and ability, and were coveted by the purest and best men in the land; and office-holders were treated with respect, and were looked up to by whole communities as exemplars of private and public virtue. Now they are looked upon with suspicion and distrust.

It has become fashionable for persons who believe themselves to be reformers, to talk flippantly of the degeneracy of the public morals. It would be well for all such should they set themselves seriously to the examination of the cause, and of themselves as well, and see if they themselves are not to blame for the state of things they so much deplore.

My official life will soon end; I have no personal motives to serve, and can therefore afford, and feel constrained, without fear of demagogues, who hope to make party capital at the people's expense, to tell the honest truth as it has forced conviction upon my mind, after long experience and close observation of the workings of the public service. The conclusion arrived at is, that no real, radical reform in the civil service can be hoped for until the holding of a public office shall be considered as conferring honor upon the possessor, and the office-holder be an honor to the people he represents and serves. This, it is believed, can only be brought about by the payment of such salaries as will draw into the public service, from the more lucrative pursuits of private life, competent and honest men, every way fit for and worthy of places of honor and trust.

If our form of government is to fail, it is hoped that it may be by a bloody revolution, rather than by the corruption that it is feared will be brought into its system by the payment of low salaries to a low order of men holding its public offices. And, just here, I desire again to call attention to and reiterate all that has heretofore been said on this subject in my last and in former reports, and in an especial manner so far as the pay of the *personnel* of this office is concerned. Another year's experience has more than ever satisfied me of the correctness of the views therein set forth. But for an annual extra compensation allowed to certain employés in this office, it would not be practicable to transact the public business pertaining thereto.

LOSSES.

In my annual report for 1869 it was stated that in the eight years and more that the Treasury of the United States had "been in my charge, during which time money transactions were had that foot on the books of the office at a sum exceeding forty-four thousand million dollars," and that "notwithstanding the fact that vast sums of money have been, and are every day, handled by hundreds of persons in this office, yet not one cent has, up to this time, been lost to the people of the United States on account of the management of the Treasury, or on account of the conduct of any employés in this office." And I went on to say that I felt "that such good fortune cannot last always. The bark of the most fortunate and skillful mariner may at last be wrecked on some hidden rock. The law of chances is now strongly against me. I therefore now, more than ever, feel an anxious desire to retire from the perilous position that I hold." The painful forebodings that then oppressed me have been verified, and came to pass within the past year.

Soon after my return from Europe, where you had sent me to aid in the negotiation of the new loan, the dreadful discovery was made that two of the officers attached to this Bureau had robbed the Government of $62,000. Both these men had been in the office for many years. They came in with the highest recommendations for capacity, honesty, and integrity. Both of them had families of their own, and they were connected with families of the highest respectability and character. Both were members of Christian churches. Their personal behavior, conduct, and bearing in the office were such as to place them above suspicion, and to induce their promotion, through all the four grades of clerkships, to the responsible offices which they held when they yielded to temptation and fell.

Frederick A. Marden, the chief of the division of accounts, whose duty it was, in part, to pay the salaries of all the employés of this office, with the connivance of Seth Johnson, the assistant paying-teller, managed to embezzle $12,000. Seth Johnson not only assisted Marden in perpetrating the fraud, by taking his checks on the Treasury where he had no funds, and concealing the fact by counting the checks as cash, but he himself purloined $50,000, and covered it up by making false entries in his books. The accounts of these two defalcations now stand as follows:

Frederick A. Marden's defalcation		$12,000 00	
Recovered from back salary	$134 24		
Cash returned	322 98		
Proceeds of United States bond	128 81		
		586 03	
			$11,413 97
Seth Johnson's defalcation		50,000 00	
Recovered from back salary	111 95		
Lockwood & Co., New York	1,868 04		
Fant, Washington & Co., Washington	10,125 81		
		12,105 80	
			37,894 20
Unrecovered aggregate of both defalcations			49,308 17

It came out, on the investigation, that Seth Johnson had lent John F. Cowen a sum of money, which, at the time of the exposure, with interest, amounted to $3,700. To secure the payment of that sum, Mr. Cowen left with the Assistant Treasurer bonds of the Cincinnati and Terre Haute Railroad Company, of the par value of $4,000. Default having been made in payment of the notes to which these bonds were collateral, they are now the property of the United States. The market value of the bonds is not known. Whatever amount is realized from their sale will be deducted, and will reduce Johnson's defalcation by that amount.

Mortifying as all this is, yet, when compared with other ordinary money transactions, and by the laws of chances, the wonder is that it has not been much worse. When it is considered that the money transactions of the Treasury foot many millions of dollars every business day in the year, and that the losses, as compared with the footings of the books, do not amount to one ten-thousandth of one per cent. on the gross amount, it will be believed that this is a less percentage of loss by defalcations and through dishonesty than occurs from the same causes in the ordinary transactions of private business. The defalcations in banks and other moneyed institutions for the same time would show a percentage vastly in excess of those that have happened in the Treasury during the last eleven years. As an instance, a bank with a capital of only $150,000, that was for many years in charge of myself as its executive officer, and during all that time never lost a cent, has, since I came here, lost by the defalcation of its cashier, a sum nearly equal to all the losses by defalcations that have occurred in this office since it has been in my control. I do not make this statement in excuse for my misfortunes from the acts of others, but to show that, in large business transactions, losses are inevitable.

COMPARISON OF RECEIPTS AND EXPENDITURES.

By an examination of the tables of receipts and of expenditures by warrants, that immediately follow this report, and by a comparison with the like tables of the preceding fiscal year, it will be found that the payments for the reduction of the Public Debt, and for the payments of the interest on the same, have fallen off, for this, as compared with the preceding year, $39,199,719.29. It will also be found that there has been a decrease of gross receipts, as follows: On account of Internal Revenue, of $12,455,975.91; from sales of war *materiel*, $2,138,079.69; and from miscellaneous sources, of $4,989,055.45. And that there has been an increase of gross receipts from the Interior Department, of $2,546,310.41; from the Navy Department, of $52,544.86; from sale of lands, of $187,067.51, and from customs, in gold, of $10,099,878.72. It will be found that there has been an increase of gross expenditures for pay of the Judiciary, of $767,857.66; on account of foreign intercourse, of $303,442.54; for expenditure for the Treasury proper, of $420,604.86; for the collection of customs, of $612,215.94; for quarterly salaries, of $7,944.01; for the civil branch of the War Department, of $195,665.42; on account of the Navy, of $1,871,327.64. And that there has been a decrease of gross expenditures for the Army of $2,565,914.31; for the Interior Department, of $3,729,450.33; for the Treasury Interior, of $140,403.09; for collection of the internal revenue, $1,457,922.49.

The duty collected from national banks on their capital, circulation, and deposits, in addition to taxes collected by the collectors of internal revenue, amounted in this fiscal year to $6,505,812 21
In the preceding fiscal year to 6,017,460 34

The increase of duty collected this year over last was .. 488,351 87

The securities left on deposit with the Treasurer, by national banks, at the close of the fiscal year, were as follows:

To secure the redemption of circulating notes	$380,440,700
To secure public deposits	15,759,000
To secure subscriptions to the funded loan	3,878,300
Total par value of securities held	400,078,000

The last item has since been entirely withdrawn, as all the subscriptions to the loan of 1881 have been paid. On November 28, 1871, the deposits on account of the subscriptions, in United States stocks, amounted to $57,267,400. On that day, the face-value of the United States bonds belonging to national banks, deposited in a single vault of the Treasury, was over four hundred and fifty millions, and their market value over five hundred million dollars.

The "conscience fund" was increased during the year in various sums, aggregating $2,997.42; and now amounts to $129,144.77. These contributions have been made by persons who thus acknowledged not only their indebtedness, but their willingness to pay the Government what they owed it. On the other hand, the United States is indebted to individuals on various accounts, but principally for unclaimed interest on bonds. Governments should set an example of honesty to the people. The withholding of the amount of an honest indebtedness is as dishonest as, and more mean than, an absolute refusal to pay. It is therefore recommended that there shall be prepared and published, after the close of every fiscal year, a list of all unclaimed balances due from the Government that have remained upon the books of the Department for two years or more; said list to state the names of the persons to whom moneys are due, and the amount due each respectively.

In the tables that are hereunto appended will appear, in gross and in detail, the business and work of this office for the last fiscal year, and, to some extent, for former years; together with the amounts of funds received, and the particular sources of income, and the money expended, and on what account, and for what purpose paid out. Also, the issue of new and the redemption of old paper money; as well as the securities held in trust for national banks, and the notes of such banks as are in liquidation, that have been redeemed; together with various other matters of interest relating to the business operations of the Treasury of the United States.

All of which is submitted by,

Your obedient servant,

F. E. SPINNER,

Treasurer of the United States.

Hon. GEORGE S. BOUTWELL,

Secretary of the Treasury.

APPENDIX.

A.—GENERAL TREASURY.

I.—RECEIPTS AND EXPENDITURES.

1.—*Receipts and expenditures by warrant.*

The books of the office were closed June 30, 1872, after the entry of all moneys received and disbursed on authorized warrants within the fiscal year, as follows:

Receipts.

Received from—	Net receipts.	Counter-warrants.	Repayments.	Totals.
Loans	$305,047,054 00	$161,030 00		$305,208,084 00
Internal revenue	130,642,177 72			130,642,177 72
Customs	216,370,286 77			216,370,286 77
Lands	2,575,714 19			2,575,714 19
Miscellaneous	24,518,688 88	545,790 12	$2,711,692 44	27,776,171 44
War		15,202,243 61	5,496,768 74	20,699,012 35
Navy		2,148,797 95	1,107,395 33	3,256,193 28
Interior		217,454 64	3,143,534 68	3,360,989 32
	679,153,921 56	18,275,316 32	12,459,391 19	709,888,629 07
Late depositary United States, Mobile, Alabama, formerly credited as unavailable				18,228 35
Late depositary United States, Saint Croix, Wisconsin, formerly credited as unavailable				1,014 48
Balance from June 30, 1871				109,917,477 24
Gross receipts for fiscal year				819,825,349 14

Expenditures.

Paid on account of—	Net expenditures.	Repayments.	Counter-warrants.	Totals.
War	$35,372,157 20	$5,496,768 74	$15,202,243 61	$56,071,169 55
Navy	21,249,809 99	1,107,395 33	2,148,797 95	24,506,003 27
Interior	35,595,131 58	3,143,534 68	217,454 64	38,956,120 90
Public debt	529,323,414 02	1,422,408 30	161,030 00	530,906,852 32
Treasury	24,376,883 42	161,121 83	142,451 59	24,680,456 84
Customs	16,832,255 37	541,919 60	275,493 37	17,649,668 34
Interior civil	5,228,072 77	110,771 68		5,338,844 45
Internal revenue	7,418,118 41	245,814 14	6,309 19	7,670,241 74
Diplomatic	1,855,142 53	69,360 98	40,007 25	1,964,510 76
Quarterly salaries	716,692 85			716,692 85
War civil	1,091,447 96	28,603 57		1,120,051 53
Judiciary	3,466,144 11	131,692 34	81,528 72	3,679,365 17
	682,525,270 21	12,459,391 19	18,275,316 32	713,259,977 72
Carried to unavailable late depositary United States, Mobile, Alabama				10,625 54
Carried to unavailable late depositary United States, Baltimore, Maryland				3,104 64
Balance in Treasury June 30, 1872				106,551,641 24
Gross expenditures for fiscal year				819,825,349 14

NOTE.—The above balance in Treasury June 30, 1872, differs from that of the Secretary and Register as follows:

Balance as above		$106,551,641 24
Deduct amount received from United States depositary, St. Croix, not charged by Secretary in this fiscal year		1,014 48
		106,550,626 76
Add amounts credited to unavailable in above statement, not credited in the account of the Secretary—		
Late United States depositary, Mobile	$10,625 54	
Late United States depositary, Baltimore	3,104 64	
		13,730 18
Balance as per statement of Secretary		106,564,356 94

Repay covering-warrants represent repayments of money advanced to disbursing officers, and proceeds of sales of stores, both of which are credited to the appropriations from which the moneys were advanced.

Counter-warrants represent moneys returned to appropriations, which moneys had previously been expended on some other account.

2.—*Warrants.*

The receipts, as stated in the foregoing table, were carried into the Treasury by 12,450 covering warrants, which is 1,127 more than were issued during the preceding year. The payments were made on 27,020 authorized warrants, for the payment of which there were issued 31,757 drafts on the Treasury and the various branches thereof. This is an increase of warrants issued over the number issued during the preceding year of 1,309, but a decrease of 2 in drafts drawn.

3.—*Receipts and Expenditures by Ledger.*

The actual receipts and expenditures during the fiscal year, as per Cash Ledger were as follows:

Cash, Dr.

Cash Ledger Balance, June 30, 1871		$112,685,027 73
Semi-annual Bank Duty	6,521,875 80	
Five-Twenty Bonds	5,000 00	
Bonds, Funded Loan of 1881	138,876,950 00	
Interest, on Funded Loan of 1881	1,182,550 71	
Conscience Money	2,997 42	
Coin Certificates	63,229,500 00	
Customs	216,375,291 24	
Legal-Tender Notes	69,599,804 00	
Fractional Currency	31,816,900 00	
Internal Revenue	130,642,418 33	
Sales of Public Lands	2,589,113 21	
Premium on sales of Coin	9,692,209 99	
Patent fees	706,978 26	
Fines and penalties	726,524 18	
Indian Trust fund	362,447 80	
Miscellaneous Interest	281,949 21	
Miscellaneous Revenue	4,054,160 61	
War	6,349,083 27	
Navy	1,119,723 22	
Prize Captures	187,386 96	
Profits on Coinage	192,301 97	
Pacific Railroad repayments	749,861 87	
Repayments, (chiefly pension agents)	4,242,062 29	
Three per cent. certificates	65,000 00	
Total cash receipts		689,572,110 33
Received, formerly credited as unavailable:		
From late Depositary United States, Mobile, Alabama	$18,228 35	
From late Depositary United States, Saint Croix, Wisconsin	1,014 48	
		19,242 83
Total		802,276,380 89

Cash, Cr.

The actual expenditures, as per Cash Ledger, were as follows:

Public Debt		$530,745,822 32
War proper		42,306,054 30
War, (civil branch)		1,120,051 53
Navy		22,150,939 22
Interior		37,517,527 69
Quarterly Salaries		715,227 81
Judiciary		3,598,631 09
Customs		17,316,889 49
Treasury proper		24,635,985 43
Treasury Interior		5,338,844 45
Diplomatic		1,619,585 22
Internal Revenue		7,609,922 91
Total actual expenditures		694,675,481 46
Carried to unavailable:		
On account of late Depositary United States, Mobile, Alabama	$10,625 54	
On account of late Depositary United States, Baltimore, Maryland	3,104 64	
		13,730 18
Balance of cash in Treasury		107,587,169 25
		802,276,380 89
Total cash balance at the close of the year		107,587,169 25
This balance consists of gold and silver	$89,764,599 87	
Other lawful money	17,822,569 38	
Total cash		$107,587,169 25
Deduct cash not covered by warrants		1,035,528 01
Balance as per Warrant Ledger, see above		106,551,641 24

II.—BALANCES AND OVERDRAFTS.

Balances and overdrafts to the credit and debit of the Treasurer United States, June 30, 1872.

	Balances.	Overdrafts.
Treasurer United States, Washington	$20,075,923 42	
Assistant Treasurer, New York	45,723,712 83	
Assistant Treasurer, Philadelphia	5,634,940 15	
Assistant Treasurer, Boston	5,438,229 19	
Assistant Treasurer, Saint Louis	1,251,390 71	
Assistant Treasurer, San Francisco	1,761,389 78	
Assistant Treasurer, New Orleans	2,350,604 74	
Assistant Treasurer, Baltimore	990,338 69	
Assistant Treasurer, Charleston		$18,186 12
Depositary United States, Cincinnati	544,345 15	
Depositary United States, Chicago	1,684,043 07	
Depositary United States, Louisville	63,021 92	
Depositary United States, Buffalo	267,485 41	
Depositary United States, Pittsburgh	358,548 07	
Depositary United States, Olympia	817 44	
Depositary United States, Oregon City	44 52	
Depositary United States, Mobile	223,815 43	
Depositary United States, Santa Fé		45,508 89
Depositary United States, Tucson	336,020 19	
National Banks	7,777,873 00	
National Banks, Funded Loan of 1881	5,001,091 53	
Assay Office, New York	3,752,513 00	
United States Mints	4,090,479 19	
Mint, Philadelphia, Nickel account	327,177 47	
Suspense account		2,940 14
Balance as per Ledger		107,587,169 25
Total	107,653,804 40	107,653,804 40

III.—DISBURSING OFFICERS.

1. *Balances.*

Balances to the credit of disbursing officers of the United States, June 30, 1872.

Treasurer United States, Washington, D. C	....	$1,884,455 59
Assistant Treasurer, Boston	$591,213 32	....
Assistant Treasurer, New York	4,706,381 31	....
Assistant Treasurer, Philadelphia	715,382 63	....
Assistant Treasurer, Charleston	135,208 95	....
Assistant Treasurer, Saint Louis	628,503 39	....
Assistant Treasurer, New Orleans	601,334 32	....
Assistant Treasurer, San Francisco	1,866,761 47	....
Assistant Treasurer, Baltimore	323,097 04	....
With Assistant Treasurers United States	....	9,567,882 43
Depositary United States, Buffalo	72,505 37	....
Depositary United States, Chicago	604,299 96	....
Depositary United States, Cincinnati	232,904 79	....
Depositary United States, Louisville	210,654 37	....
Depositary United States, Pittsburgh	140,512 36	....
Depositary United States, Mobile	68,881 70	....
Depositary United States, Santa Fé	298,745 19	....
Depositary United States, Tucson	37,346 48	....
With Depositaries		1,665,850 22
With 128 National Bank Depositaries		4,239,603 92
Total amount in all offices to credit of disbursing officers		17,357,792 16

2.—*Reports.*

Statement of the reports of disbursing officers United States, received and examined at the Treasurer's office, and returned to the various Departments to which the disbursing officers belong.

From December 2, 1871, to June 29, 1872, inclusive, there were received at this office 13,929 reports of 1,135 disbursing officers, for examination, as follows:

244 Quartermasters United States Army.
296 Commissaries United States Army.
62 Paymasters United States Army.
96 Officers of the Engineer Corps, United States Army.
54 Recruiting Officers United States Army.
29 Ordnance Officers United States Army.
6 Surgeons United States Army.
1 Superintendent Military Academy.
2 Officers of the Signal Corps.
4 Officers of the Freedmen's Bureau.
34 Paymasters and Pay Inspectors United States Navy.
208 Collectors of Internal Revenue.
88 Collectors of Customs.
3 Disbursing Clerks.
8 Disbursing Agents.

IV.—TRANSFERS OF FUNDS.

To facilitate payments at points where the moneys were needed for disbursements, transfer letters, transfer orders, and bills of exchange were issued during the fiscal year, as follows:

2,178 letters on National Banks	$41,876,960 38
359 transfer orders on National Banks	6,745,302 89
64 bills of exchange on Collectors of Customs	300,000 00
792 transfer orders on Treasurer, Assistant Treasurers, and Depositaries	227,228,575 00
3,393 transfers, amounting to	276,150,838 27

Of which amount there was in coin		$86,803,000 00
And in currency		189,347,838 27
Total		276,150,838 27

V.—UNAVAILABLE FUNDS, JUNE 30, 1872.

Currency:		
First National Bank, Selma, Alabama	$59,978 07	
Venango National Bank, Franklin, Pennsylvania	217,391 38	
Total amount with National Banks		$277,369 45
Deficit at New Orleans, (Whitaker's)	675,270 22	
Deficit at Louisville, (stolen)	9,000 00	
Deficit at Louisville, (Bloomgart's)	11,083 52	
Deficit at Santa Fé, (J. L. Collins')	30,058 83	
Total with Assistant Treasurers and Depositaries		725,412 57
Total Currency		1,002,782 02
Coin:		
Balances from previous to the outbreak of the rebellion:		
United States Branch Mint, Charlotte, North Carolina	32,000 00	
United States Branch Mint, Dahlonega, Georgia	27,950 03	
Depositary United States, Galveston, Texas	778 66	
Total Coin		60,728 69
Total		1,063,510 71

This amount has been reduced since the close of the fiscal year, by $20,073.52, being the amount of the deficits at Louisville, Kentucky, (less $10 additional deficit at New Orleans,) from which the Depositary United States at Louisville was relieved by act of Congress.

VI.—NATIONAL BANK DEPOSITARIES.

The business transactions between the Treasury and National Banks as depositaries have been for the fiscal year as follows:

Balances brought from last year's account	$7,197,115 04
Receipts during the last fiscal year	106,104,855 16
Receipts during the same period for fractional currency	2,994,444 10
Total	116,296,414 30
Payments during the last fiscal year	$108,518,541 30
Balance due the United States, June 30, 1872	7,777,873 00
Total	116,296,414 30
Payments through expresses, at Government expense	$6,745,302 89
Payments without expense to the Government	101,773,238 41
Total	108,518,541 30

VII.—OUTSTANDING LIABILITIES.

Amount covered into the Treasury to July 1, 1871	$241,975 19
And in the last fiscal year	21,974 92
Total	263,950 11
There has been paid to various parties entitled to receive the same, to July 1, 1872	$38,633 05
Unclaimed balance remaining in the Treasury	225,317 06
Total	263,950 11

VIII.—CONSCIENCE FUND.

Amount received from various persons from December 1, 1863, to July 1, 1871	$126,147 35
And in the last fiscal year	2,997 42
Total amount received since November 30, 1863	129,144 77

IX.—OPEN ACCOUNTS.

With Assistant Treasurers	9
With Designated Depositaries	10
With United States Mints	10
With National Bank Depositaries	157
With Disbursing Officers	107
Impersonal Accounts	169

B.—POST-OFFICE DEPARTMENT.

I.—RECEIPTS AND EXPENDITURES.

The receipts and expenditures for and on account of the Post-Office Department for the fiscal year have been as follows:

Cash, Dr.

Balance from last year's account		$297,539 43
Receipts:		
At Washington	$92,867 42	
At Boston	518,275 94	
At Baltimore	130,572 64	
At Charleston	58,358 72	
At New York	7,557,962 96	
At New Orleans	128,025 07	
At Philadelphia	467,748 56	
At Saint Louis	175,375 03	
At San Francisco	236,655 61	
Depositary, Buffalo, New York	3,560 25	
Depositary, Louisville, Kentucky	122 48	
Depositary, Cincinnati, Ohio	50 00	
Depositary, Mobile, Alabama	42,271 64	
Depositary, Pittsburgh, Pennsylvania	1,160 89	
First National Bank, Galveston, Texas	2,637 25	
First National Bank, Helena, Montana Territory	256 00	
First National Bank, Knoxville, Tennessee	329 92	
First National Bank, Leavenworth, Kansas	102 74	
First National Bank, Nashville, Tennessee	54 15	
First National Bank, Memphis, Tennessee	2,598 02	
First National Bank, Portland, Oregon	756 00	
First National Bank, Richmond, Virginia	5,345 66	
First National Bank, Springfield, Illinois	7,216 56	
Second National Bank, Detroit, Michigan	12,185 77	
Second National Bank, Leavenworth, Kansas	132 89	
Second National Bank, Utica, New York	108 70	
Merchants' National Bank, Cleveland, Ohio	1,358 61	
Merchants' National Bank, Little Rock, Arkansas	1,330 90	
Merchants' National Bank, Portland, Maine	19 26	
Merchants' National Bank, Savannah, Georgia	26,762 76	
Atlanta National Bank, Atlanta, Georgia	1,894 20	
Indianapolis National Bank, Indianapolis, Indiana	35 15	
Kansas Valley National Bank, Topeka, Kansas	24 68	
Lynchburgh National Bank, Lynchburgh, Virginia	50 00	
Planters' National Bank, Richmond, Virginia	566 13	
City National Bank, Grand Rapids, Michigan	656 46	
National State Bank, Des Moines, Iowa	55 29	
Total receipts during the year		9,477,484 31
Total		9,775,023 74

Warrants were issued on the various offices for the payment of the aggregate amounts as follows:

Cash, Cr.

On Washington	$345,314 03
On New York	5,543,146 60
On Boston	433,487 11
On Baltimore	194,605 72
On Charleston	229,968 17
On New Orleans	496,645 22
On Saint Louis	655,014 18
On Philadelphia	479,159 97
On San Francisco	283,962 43
Depositary, Mobile, Alabama	1,399 51
Total issued during year	8,662,702 94
Balance, Cash on hand to new account	1,112,320 80
Total	9,775,023 74

II.—APPROPRIATIONS FROM TREASURY FOR POST-OFFICE DEPARTMENT.

Moneys included in the above receipts were drawn from the Treasury on account of the Post-Office Department, that were not receipts from the Department, but were appropriated for its use by Congress, under the several laws as specified, at the times, and for amounts as follows:

To supply deficiencies in the revenues of the Post-Office Department, Act March 3, 1871:		
July 3, 1871, paid Treasury warrant No. 881	$1,000,000	
October 4, 1871, paid Treasury warrant No. 1313	1,200,000	
December 28, 1871, paid Treasury warrant No. 6	900,000	
March 28, 1872, paid Treasury warrant No. 428	1,200,000	
		$4,300,000
For Mail-Steamship service between San Francisco, Japan, and China:		
July 6, 1871, paid Treasury warrant No. 944	125,000	
October 4, 1871, paid Treasury warrant No. 1325	125,000	
December 28, 1871, paid Treasury warrant No. 6	125,000	
March 28, 1872, paid Treasury warrant No. 428	125,000	
		500,000
For Mail-Steamship service between San Francisco and the Sandwich Islands:		
July 11, 1871, paid Treasury warrant No. 969	18,750	
October 7, 1871, paid Treasury warrant No. 1326	18,750	
January 18, 1872, paid Treasury warrant No. 111	18,750	
March 28, 1872, paid Treasury warrant No. 428	18,750	
June 21, 1872, paid Treasury warrant No. 907	18,750	
		93,750
For Mail-Steamship service between the United States and Brazil:		
September 13, 1871, paid Treasury warrant No. 1231	37,500	
December 9, 1871, paid Treasury warrant No. 1699	37,500	
March 16, 1872, paid Treasury warrant No. 395	37,500	
June 13, 1872, paid Treasury warrant No. 842	37,500	
		150,000
For free mail matter, Act March 3, 1847, and March 3, 1851:		
December 28, 1871, paid Treasury warrant No. 6		350,000
Total amount received from Government		5,393,750

III.—RECEIPTS AND PAYMENTS BY POSTMASTERS.

Receipts by Postmasters, on account of postage on letters, newspapers, and pamphlets, registered letters, emoluments, &c., disbursed by the Post-Office Department without being paid into the Treasury, but afterward carried into and out of the Treasury by warrant, were as follows:

For quarter ended September 30, 1871	$4,203,258 12
For quarter ended December 31, 1871	4,485,369 40
For quarter ended March 31, 1872	4,647,510 84
For quarter ended June 30, 1872	4,553,668 04
Total	17,889,806 40

IV.—TOTAL RECEIPTS AND EXPENDITURES, (INCLUDING AMOUNTS RECEIVED AND PAID BY POSTMASTERS.)

Cash, Dr.

Balance from last year		$297,539 43
From Postmasters and others	$4,083,734 31	
From Treasury on warrants to supply deficiencies of Post-Office Department	4,300,000 00	
From Treasury on warrants for subsidies to steamships	1,093,750 00	
		9,477,484 31
For amount received and paid by Postmasters		17,889,806 40
Total		27,664,830 14

Cash, Cr.

Paid on 6,707 Post-Office warrants	$8,662,702 94
Received and paid by Postmasters	17,889,806 40
Balance to new account	1,112,320 80
Total	27,664,830 14

C.—NATIONAL BANKS.

I.—NUMBER OF NATIONAL BANKS.

The number of National Banks on the 30th June, 1871, that had deposited securities of the United States with this Office preliminary to their organization, was	1,839
The number of new banks organized during the last fiscal year, was	168
Total number of banks June 30, 1872	2,007

The number of banks that had paid duty and deposited securities for their circulating notes, and were doing business on the 30th of June last, as appears from the books of this Office, was	1,914
Failed prior to June 30, 1871—securities sold	15
Failed prior to June 30, 1871—securities in part sold	1
Failed in last fiscal year	6
Having no circulation—securities withdrawn	12
In voluntary liquidation—money deposited to redeem circulation prior to June 30, 1871	55
In voluntary liquidation—money deposited and securities withdrawn in the last fiscal year	4
Number of banks organized	2,007

II.—NEW NATIONAL BANKS.

The following National Banks were organized during the last fiscal year:
The First National Bank of Wyandotte, Kansas.
The First National Bank of Greenville, Illinois.
The Second National Bank of Winona, Minnesota.
The Bates County National Bank of Butler, Missour.
The National Bank of Newberry, South Carolina.
The Cook County National Bank of Chicago, Illinois.
The First National Bank of Brownville, Nebraska.

The German National Bank of Covington, Kentucky.
The National Bank of Spartausburgh, South Carolina.
The First National Bank of Grand Haven, Michigan.
The First National Bank of Mason City, Illinois.
The Second National Bank of Charleston, Illinois.
The First National Bank of Marseilles, Illinois.
The First National Bank of Tuscaloosa, Alabama.
The First National Bank of Frankfort, Indiana.
The Nebraska City National Bank of Nebraska.
The First National Bank of Warrensburgh, Missouri.
The First National Bank of Port Huron, Michigan.
The Valley National Bank of Saint Louis, Missouri.
The Covington City National Bank of Covington, Kentucky.
The National Exchange Bank of Augusta, Georgia.
The First National Bank of Newman, Georgia.
The Mills County National Bank of Glenwood, Iowa.
The Citizens' National Bank of Faribault, Minnesota.
The First National Bank of Paola, Kansas.
The First National Bank of Rolla, Missouri.
The National Bank of Illinois, at Chicago, Illinois.
The First National Bank of Saint Joseph, Michigan.
The First National Bank of Jefferson, at Charlestown, West Virginia.
The Rush County National Bank of Rushville, Indiana.
The First National Bank of Marengo, Illinois.
The Knoxville National Bank of Iowa.
The Union National Bank of Macomb, Illinois.
The First National Bank of Vincennes, Indiana.
The First National Bank of Webster City, Iowa.
The National Bank of Kutztown, Pennsylvania.
The First National Bank of Paxton, Illinois.
The First National Bank of Knob Noster, Missouri.
The Meridian National Bank of Indianapolis, Indiana.
The Citizens' National Bank of Peru, Indiana.
The First National Bank of Tama City, Iowa.
The Dixon National Bank of Illinois.
The Will County National Bank of Joliet, Illinois.
The National Bank of Piedmont, West Virginia.
The Wellsburgh National Bank of West Virginia.
The Littleton National Bank of New Hampshire.
The Citizens' National Bank of Niles, Michigan.
The First National Bank of Olean, New York.
The First National Bank of Bloomington, Indiana.
The Rock Island National Bank of Rock Island, Illinois.
The Citizens' National Bank of Greensburgh, Indiana.
The First National Bank of Pella, Iowa.
The Bedford National Bank of Bedford, Indiana.
The Citizens' National Bank of Hagerstown, Maryland.
The Farmers' National Bank of Greensburgh, Pennsylvania.
The Merchants' National Bank of Toledo, Ohio.
The Sycamore National Bank of Sycamore, Illinois.
The First National Bank of Newport, Indiana.
The Mutual National Bank of New Orleans, Louisiana.
The State National Bank of Lincoln, Nebraska.
The First National Bank of Cynthiana, Kentucky.
The Kansas City National Bank of Kansas City, Missouri.
The First National Bank of Chetopa, Kansas.
The First National Bank of Jackson, Ohio.
The First National Bank of Plymouth, Ohio.
The First National Bank of Hackensack, New Jersey.
The Defiance National Bank of Defiance, Ohio.
The Rochelle National Bank of Rochelle, Illinois.
The Kentucky National Bank of Louisville, Kentucky.
The Second National Bank of Aurora, Illinois.
The People's National Bank of Ottawa, Kansas.
The First National Bank of Owatonna, Minnesota.
The National Bank of Wooster, Ohio.
The First National Bank of Wichita, Kansas.
The First National Bank of Plattsmouth, Nebraska.
The First National Bank of Emporia, Kansas.
The First National Bank of Plymouth, Michigan.

The First National Bank of Napoleon, Ohio.
The Second National Bank of East Saginaw, Michigan.
The Manufacturers' National Bank of Three Rivers, Michigan.
The First National Bank of Coshocton, Ohio.
The Salt Lake City National Bank of Salt Lake City, Utah.
The First National Bank of Rochelle, Illinois.
The First National Bank of Millersburgh, Ohio.
The Southern Michigan National Bank of Coldwater, Michigan.
The First National Bank of Liberty, Indiana.
The De Witt County National Bank of Clinton, Illinois.
The Merchants' National Bank of Fort Scott, Kansas.
The Farmers and Mechanics' National Bank of Georgetown, District of Columbia.
The First National Bank of Shelby, Ohio.
The First National Bank of Minerva, Ohio.
The National Bank of Monticello, Kentucky.
The First National Bank of Sullivan, Indiana.
The First National Bank of Burlington, Wisconsin.
The Nokomis National Bank of Nokomis, Illinois.
The National Bank of Greenville, South Carolina.
The Farmers and Mechanics' National Bank of Phœnixville, Pennsylvania.
The Crescent City National Bank of New Orleans, Louisiana.
The National Bank of Gloversville, New York.
The Holyoke National Bank of Holyoke, Massachusetts.
The First National Bank of Clinton, Missouri.
The Moline National Bank of Moline, Illinois.
The Guernsey National Bank of Cambridge, Ohio.
The First National Bank of Wyoming, Iowa.
The First National Bank of Bellaire, Ohio.
The Topeka National Bank of Topeka, Kansas.
The Third National Bank of Scranton, Pennsylvania.
The Merchants' National Bank of Fort Dodge, Iowa.
The Iron National Bank of Portsmouth, Ohio.
The First National Bank of Delphi, Indiana.
The National Bank of Western Arkansas, Fort Smith, Arkansas.
The First National Bank of Parsons, Kansas.
The First National Bank of Rochester, Indiana.
The Lansing National Bank of Lansing, Michigan.
The First National Bank of Duluth, Minnesota.
The City National Bank of Denver, Colorado.
The Norway National Bank of Norway, Maine.
The First National Bank of El Dorado, Kansas.
The Kinney National Bank of Portsmouth, Ohio.
The National Bank of Rising Sun, Indiana.
The Montana National Bank of Helena, Montana.
The First National Bank of Flora, Illinois.
The Lawrence National Bank of Lawrence, Massachusetts.
The National Bank of Owen, at Owenton, Kentucky.
The Miners' National Bank of Braidwood, Illinois.
The Merchants' National Bank of Holly, Michigan.
The First National Bank of Trenton, Missouri.
The Indiana National Bank of Lafayette, Indiana.
The First National Bank of Prophetstown, Illinois.
The First National Bank of Oregon, Illinois.
The Citizens' National Bank of Des Moines, Iowa.
The Citizens' National Bank of Sedalia, Missouri.
The Fayette County National Bank of Washington, Ohio.
The First National Bank of Adrian, Michigan.
The First National Bank of Fremont, Nebraska.
The First National Bank of Deer Lodge, Montana.
The Citizens' National Bank of Sioux City, Iowa.
The First National Bank of Junction City, Kansas.
The Scandinavian National Bank of Chicago, Illinois.
The Burlington National Bank of Burlington, Kansas.
The Pomeroy National Bank of Pomeroy, Ohio.
The First National Bank of New London, Ohio.
The Manchester National Bank of Manchester, Ohio.
The Emporia National Bank of Emporia, Kansas.
The Citizens' National Bank of Galion, Ohio.
The Planters' National Bank of Danville, Virginia.
The Marion County National Bank of Knoxville, Iowa.

The First National Bank of Fairbury, Illinois.
The Second National Bank of Richmond, Indiana.
The Quaker City National Bank of Quaker City, Ohio.
The Giles National Bank of Pulaski, Tennessee.
The First National Bank of Georgetown, Colorado.
The Keokuk National Bank of Keokuk, Iowa.
The Eleventh Ward National Bank of Boston, Massachusetts.
The National Gold Bank and Trust Company of San Francisco, California.
The Commercial National Bank of Kansas City, Missouri.
The Mount Vernon National Bank of Mount Vernon, Ohio.
The Clinton County National Bank of Wilmington, Ohio.
The First National Bank of Grand Rapids, Michigan.
The Citizens' National Bank of New Philadelphia, Ohio.
The Stones River National Bank of Murfreesborough, Tennessee.
The First National Bank of Council Grove, Kansas.
The Citizens' National Bank of Winterset, Iowa.
The People's National Bank of Fayetteville, North Carolina.
The First National Bank of Berea, Ohio.
The Citizens' National Bank of Mankato, Minnesota.
The North Western National Bank of Minneapolis, Minnesota.
The Union National Bank of Liberty, Indiana.

III.—NATIONAL BANKS THAT HAVE FAILED.

The First National Bank of Attica, New York, in 1865.
The Merchants' National Bank of Washington, D. C., in 1866.
The Venango National Bank of Franklin, Pa., in 1866.
The First National Bank of Medina, New York, in 1867.
The Tennessee National Bank of Memphis, Tennessee, in 1867.
*The First National Bank of Newton, Newtonville, Massachusetts, in 1867.
The First National Bank of New Orleans, Louisiana, in 1867.
The First National Bank of Selma, Alabama, in 1867.
The National Unadilla Bank, of Unadilla, New York, in 1868.
The Farmers and Citizens' National Bank of Brooklyn, New York, in 1868.
The Croton National Bank of the City of New York, in 1868.
The First National Bank of Bethel, Connecticut, in 1868.
The First National Bank of Keokuk, Iowa, in 1868.
The National Bank of Vicksburgh, Mississippi, in 1868.
The First National Bank of Rockford, Illinois, in 1869.
The First National Bank of Nevada, Austin, Nevada, in 1869.
The Fourth National Bank of Philadelphia Pennsylvania, in 1871.
The Eighth National Bank of the City of New York, New York, in 1871.
The Ocean National Bank of the City of New York, New York, in 1871.
The Union Square National Bank of the City of New York, New York, in 1871.
The Waverly National Bank of Waverly, New York, in 1872.
The First National Bank of Fort Smith, Arkansas, in 1872.
Whole number failed, 22.

IV.—NATIONAL BANKS IN VOLUNTARY LIQUIDATION.

1.—*Before July* 1, 1871.

The National Farmers and Mechanics' Bank of Albany, New York.
The Appleton National Bank of Appleton, Wisconsin.
The First National Bank of Berlin, Wisconsin.
The First National Bank of Bluffton, Indiana.
The First National Bank of Carondelet, Missouri.
The First National Bank of Cedarburgh, Wisconsin.
The Central National Bank of Cincinnati, Ohio.
The Commercial National Bank of Cincinnati, Ohio.
The Ohio National Bank of Cincinnati, Ohio.
The First National Bank of Cuyahoga Falls, Ohio.
The First National Bank of Clarksville, Virginia.
The First National Bank of Columbia, Missouri.
The First National Bank of Dayton, Ohio.
The First National Bank of Decatur, Illinois.
The First National Bank of Des Moines, Iowa.

* The National Security Bank, of Boston, Massachusetts, has assumed the circulation of this bank.

The Second National Bank of Des Moines, Iowa.
The National Insurance Bank of Detroit, Michigan.
The National State Bank of Dubuque, Iowa.
The National Bank of Chemung, Elmira, New York.
The Chemung Canal National Bank of Elmira, New York.
The First National Bank of Fenton, Michigan.
The First National Bank of Frostburgh, Maryland.
The First National Bank of Hallowell, Maine.
The Fourth National Bank of Indianapolis, Indiana.
The Frst National Bank of Jackson, Mississippi.
The National Bank of Lansingburgh, New York.
The National Exchange Bank of Lansingburgh, New York.
The First National Bank of Lebanon, Ohio.
The First National Bank of Marion, Ohio.
The National Bank of Maysville, Kentucky.
The Merchants' National Bank of Milwaukee, Wisconsin.
The First National Bank of New Ulm, Minnesota.
The Grocers' National Bank of the City of New York, New York.
The Pacific National Bank of the City of New York, New York.
The National Bank of North America, City of New York, New York.
The First National Bank of Oskaloosa, Iowa.
The National Bank of Owego, New York.
The National Exchange Bank of Richmond, Virginia.
The Farmers' National Bank of Richmond, Virginia.
The National Union Bank of Rochester, New York.
The Savannah National Bank of Savannah, Georgia.
The Miners' National Bank of Salt Lake City, Utah.
The First National Bank of South Worcester, New York.
The First National Bank of Skaneateles, New York.
The First National Bank of Saint Louis, Missouri.
The State National Bank of Saint Joseph, Missouri.
The Merchants and Mechanics' National Bank of Troy, New York.
The First National Bank of Vinton, Iowa.
The Farmers' National Bank of Waukesha, Wisconsin.
The Saratoga County National Bank of Waterford, New York.
The First National Bank of Wellsburgh, West Virginia.
The United National Bank of Winona, Minnesota.
The National Savings Bank of Wheeling, West Virginia.
The National Bank of Whitestown, New York.
The Muskingum National Bank of Zanesville, Ohio.

2.—*In the last fiscal year.*

The Commercial National Bank of Oshkosh, Wisconsin.
The Fort Madison National Bank of Iowa.
The First National Bank of La Salle, Illinois.
The Fourth National Bank of Syracuse, New York.

All the preceding banks have paid money into the Treasury for the redemption of their circulating notes.

V.—REDEMPTION OF CIRCULATING NOTES OF NATIONAL BANKS FAILED AND IN LIQUIDATION.

Names of Banks.	Redeemed to July 1, 1871.	Redeemed in fiscal year.	Total redemptions, less discounts.
National Mechanics and Farmers' Bank, Albany, New York	$114,527 75	$99,670 00	$214,197 75
Appleton National Bank, Appleton, Wis	17,476 50	17,807 35	35,283 85
First National Bank, Attica, New York	40,897 50	1,509 00	42,406 50
First National Bank of Nevada, Austin, Nevada	56,714 00	45,007 50	101,721 50
First National Bank, Berlin, Wisconsin	14,147 10	16,428 70	30,575 80
First National Bank, Bethel, Connecticut	20,339 50	3,000 00	23,339 50
First National Bank, Bluffton, Indiana	15,433 00	17,013 25	32,446 25

V.—REDEMPTION OF CIRCULATING NOTES, ETC.—Continued.

Names of Banks.	Redeemed to July 1, 1871.	Redeemed in fiscal year.	Total redemptions, less discounts.
Farmers and Citizens' National Bank, Brooklyn, New York	$223,753 00	$15,410 25	$239,163 25
First National Bank, Carondelet, Mo	23,348 75	1,000 00	24,348 75
First National Bank, Cedarburgh, Wis.	23,969 50	32,527 50	56,497 00
Central National Bank, Cincinnati, Ohio	....	142,000 00	142,000 00
Commercial National Bank, Cincinnati, Ohio	153,445 50	132,009 50	285,455 00
Ohio National Bank, Cincinnati, Ohio	....	192,000 00	192,000 00
First National Bank, Cuyahoga Falls, O	....	16,804 75	16,804 75
First National Bank, Clarksville, Va.	....	10,000 00	10,000 00
First National Bank, Columbia, Mo	9,425 00	1,000 00	10,425 00
First National Bank, Dayton, Ohio	51,676 70	53,011 35	104,688 05
First National Bank, Decatur, Illinois	33,741 15	35,933 15	69,674 30
First National Bank, Des Moines, Iowa	....	64,551 25	64,551 25
Second National Bank, Des Moines, Iowa	15,142 50	16,004 50	31,147 00
National Insurance Bank, Detroit, Mich	....	58,513 75	58,513 75
National State Bank, Dubuque, Iowa	....	69,518 75	69,518 75
National Bank of Chemung, Elmira, N. Y	36,083 75	39,009 50	75,093 25
Chemung Canal National Bank, Elmira, New York	17,342 15	50,239 85	67,582 00
First National Bank, Fenton, Michigan	....	35,523 25	35,523 25
Fort Madison National Bank, Fort Madison, Iowa	....	7,500 00	7,500 00
First National Bank, Fort Smith, Ark	....	3,500 00	3,500 00
Venango National Bank, Franklin, Penn	78,628 50	4,000 00	82,628 50
First National Bank, Frostburgh, Md	16,804 00	16,018 75	32,822 75
First National Bank, Hallowell, Maine	19,486 00	20,204 75	39,690 75
Fourth National Bank, Indianapolis, Ind	....	33,500 00	33,500 00
First National Bank, Jackson, Miss	13,515 00	18,000 00	31,515 00
First National Bank, Keokuk, Iowa	79,139 50	7,009 50	86,149 00
National Bank of Lansingburgh, N. Y	47,487 65	49,525 20	97,012 85
National Exchange Bank, Lansingburgh, New York	501 90	62,952 40	63,454 30
First National Bank, La Salle, Illinois	....	....	....
First National Bank, Lebanon, Ohio	27,523 75	39,500 00	67,023 75
First National Bank, Marion, Ohio	43,455 15	39,621 70	83,076 85
National Bank of Maysville, Kentucky	....	73,800 00	73,800 00
First National Bank, Medina, New York	36,806 75	1,500 00	38,306 75
Tennessee National Bank, Memphis, Tennessee	82,198 75	2,500 00	84,698 75
Merchants' National Bank, Milwaukee, Wisconsin	....	36,500 00	36,500 00
First National Bank, New Orleans, La	159,510 50	10,000 00	169,510 50
First National Bank, New Ulm, Minn	....	14,000 00	14,000 00
Croton National Bank, New York, N. Y	162,517 65	10,214 10	172,731 75
Eighth National Bank, New York, N. Y	....	126,400 00	126,400 00
Grocers' National Bank, New York, N. Y	5,208 00	23,063 00	28,271 00
Ocean National Bank, New York, N. Y	....	451,500 00	451,500 00
Pacific National Bank, New York, N. Y	54,537 50	44,004 75	98,542 25
Union Square National Bank, New York, New York	....	26,500 00	26,500 00
National Bank of North America, New York, New York	109,299 65	93,740 00	203,039 65
First National Bank, Oskaloosa, Iowa	26,635 05	24,814 80	51 449 85
National Union Bank, Owego, N. Y	200 00	3,400 00	3,600 00
Commercial National Bank, Oshkosh, Wisconsin	....	10,000 00	10,000 00
Fourth National Bank, Philadelphia, Pennsylvania	....	95,000 00	95,000 00
National Exchange Bank, Richmond, Va.	....	64,500 00	64,500 00

V.—REDEMPTION OF CIRCULATING NOTES, ETC.—Continued.

Names of Banks.	Redeemed to July 1, 1871.	Redeemed in fiscal year.	Total redemptions, less discounts.
Farmers' National Bank, Richmond, Va	....	$31,533 25	$31,533 25
National Union Bank, Rochester, N. Y	$69,513 75	79,004 50	148,518 25
First National Bank, Rockford, Illinois	28,983 00	11,000 00	39,983 00
Savannah National Bank, Savannah, Ga	32,806 25	35,519 00	68,325 25
Miners' National Bank, Salt Lake, Utah	....	28,300 00	28,300 00
First National Bank, Selma, Alabama	75,316 75	5,500 00	80,816 75
First National Bank, South Worcester, New York	68,805 75	56,033 00	124,838 75
Fourth National Bank, Syracuse, N. Y	....	11,000 00	11,000 00
First National Bank, Skaneateles, N. Y	52,174 30	51,820 90	103,995 20
First National Bank, St. Louis, Mo	64,274 50	78,416 55	142,691 05
State National Bank, St. Joseph, Mo	....	61,158 20	61,158 20
Merchants and Mechanics' National Bank, Troy, New York	67,674 60	71,947 60	139,622 20
National Unadilla Bank, Unadilla, N. Y	91,005 25	3,514 25	94,519 50
National Bank of Vicksburgh, Miss	18,708 75	2,500 00	21,208 75
First National Bank, Vinton, Iowa	11,523 75	21,000 00	32,523 75
Merchants' National Bank, Washington, District of Columbia	163,829 25	7,504 75	171,334 00
Farmers' National Bank, Waukesha, Wis	69,320 25	12,500 00	81,820 25
Waverly National Bank, Waverly, N. Y	....	9,300 00	9,300 00
Saratoga County National Bank, Waterford, New York	....	88,322 55	88,322 55
First National Bank, Wellsburgh, W. Va	....	37,503 00	37,503 00
United National Bank, Winona, Minn	....	19,000 00	19,000 00
National Savings Bank, Wheeling, West Virginia	....	28,000 00	28,000 00
National Bank of Whitestown, N. Y	18,649 00	17,514 25	34,163 25
Muskingum National Bank, Zanesville, Ohio	....	28,000 00	28,000 00
Total	2,661,503 80	3,374,153 90	6,035,657 70

NOTE.—The above total is $2,198.25 less than that given for the same item under the title "Redemptions," the difference being the amount of notes of the First National Bank of Newton, Newtonville, Massachusetts, redeemed and destroyed by the Treasury, but for which it was afterward reimbursed, upon the consolidation of that bank with another.

VI.—DEPOSITS MADE AND BALANCES REMAINING TO CREDIT OF NATIONAL BANKS FAILED AND IN LIQUIDATION.

Names of Banks.	Deposits to redeem notes.	Balance remaining.
National Mechanics and Farmers' Bank, Albany, New York	$266,540 00	$52,342 25
Appleton National Bank, Appleton, Wisconsin	45,000 00	9,716 15
First National Bank, Attica, New York	44,000 00	1,593 50
First National Bank of Nevada, Austin, Nevada	129,700 00	27,978 50
First National Bank, Berlin, Wisconsin	40,077 00	9,501 20
First National Bank, Bethel, Connecticut	26,300 00	2,960 50
First National Bank, Bluffton, Indiana	41,230 00	8,783 75
Farmers and Citizens' National Bank, Brooklyn, New York	253,900 00	14,736 75
First National Bank, Carondelet, Missouri	25,500 00	1,151 25

VI.—DEPOSITS MADE AND BALANCES REMAINING, ETC.—Continued.

Names of Banks.	Deposits to redeem notes.	Balance remaining.
First National Bank, Cedarburgh, Wisconsin	$72,000 00	$15,503 00
Central National Bank, Cincinnati, Ohio	265,000 00	123,000 00
Commercial National Bank, Cincinnati, Ohio	345,950 00	60,495 00
Ohio National Bank, Cincinnati, Ohio	300,000 00	108,000 00
First National Bank, Cuyahoga Falls, Ohio	32,400 00	15,595 25
First National Bank, Clarksville, Virginia	27,000 00	17,000 00
First National Bank, Columbia, Missouri	11,990 00	1,565 00
First National Bank, Dayton, Ohio	132,100 00	27,411 95
First National Bank, Decatur, Illinois	85,250 00	15,575 70
First National Bank, Des Moines, Iowa	89,300 00	24,748 75
Second National Bank, Des Moines, Iowa	40,300 00	9,153 00
National Insurance Bank, Detroit, Michigan	75,500 00	16,986 25
National State Bank, Dubuque, Iowa	112,600 00	43,081 25
National Bank of Chemung, Elmira, New York	90,000 00	14,906 75
Chemung Canal National Bank, Elmira, New York	86,500 00	18,918 00
First National Bank, Fenton, Michigan	49,500 00	13,976 75
Fort Madison National Bank, Fort Madison, Indiana	67,500 00	60,000 00
First National Bank, Fort Smith, Arkansas	45,000 00	41,500 00
Venango National Bank, Franklin, Pa	85,000 00	2,371 50
First National Bank, Frostburgh, Maryland	40,750 00	7,927 25
First National Bank, Hallowell, Maine	50,850 00	11,159 25
Fourth National Bank, Indianapolis, Indiana	75,100 00	41,600 00
First National Bank, Jackson, Mississippi	40,500 00	8,985 00
First National Bank, Keokuk, Iowa	90,000 00	3,851 00
National Bank of Lansingburgh, New York	123,000 00	25,987 15
National Exchange Bank, Lansingburgh, New York	85,692 00	22,237 70
First National Bank, La Salle, Illinois	33,200 00	33,200 00
First National Bank, Lebanon, Ohio	85,000 00	17,976 25
First National Bank, Marion, Ohio	105,833 00	22,756 15
National Bank, Maysville, Kentucky	270,000 00	196,200 00
First National Bank, Medina, New York	40,000 00	1,693 25
Tennessee National Bank, Memphis, Tennessee	90,000 00	5,301 25
Merchants' National Bank, Milwaukee, Wisconsin	90,000 00	53,500 00
First National Bank, New Orleans, Louisiana	180,000 00	10,489 50
First National Bank, New Ulm, Minnesota	30,000 00	16,000 00
Croton National Bank, New York, New York	180,000 00	7,268 25
Eighth National Bank, New York, New York	243,393 00	116,993 00
Grocers' National Bank, New York, New York	39,440 00	11,169 00
Ocean National Bank, New York, New York	800,000 00	348,500 00
Pacific National Bank, New York, New York	130,275 00	31,732 75
Union Square National Bank, New York, New York	50,000 00	23,500 00
National Bank of North America, New York, New York	267,200 00	64,160 35
First National Bank, Oskaloosa, Iowa	63,745 00	12,295 15
National Union Bank, Owego, New York	82,850 00	79,250 00
Commercial National Bank, Oshkosh, Wisconsin	90,000 00	80,000 00
Fourth National Bank, Philadelphia, Pennsylvania	179,000 00	84,000 00
National Exchange Bank, Richmond, Virginia	72,120 00	7,620 00
Farmers' National Bank, Richmond, Virginia	76,500 00	44,966 75
National Union Bank, Rochester, New York	189,950 00	41,431 75
First National Bank, Rockford, Illinois	45,000 00	5,017 00
Savannah National Bank, Savannah, Georgia	85,000 00	16,674 75
Miners' National Bank, Salt Lake, Utah	90,000 00	61,700 00
First National Bank, Selma, Alabama	85,000 00	4,183 25
First National Bank, South Worcester, New York	152,900 00	28,061 25
Fourth National Bank, Syracuse, New York	91,700 00	80,700 00
First National Bank, Skaneateles, New York	128,415 00	24,419 80
First National Bank, St. Louis, Missouri	179,990 00	37,298 95
State National Bank, St. Joseph, Missouri	86,187 00	25,028 80
Merchants and Mechanics' National Bank, Troy, N. Y	170,850 00	31,227 80
National Unadilla Bank, Unadilla, New York	100,000 00	5,480 50
National Bank of Vicksburgh, Mississippi	25,500 00	4,291 25
First National Bank, Vinton, Iowa	41,615 00	9,091 25
Merchants' National Bank, Washington, D. C	180,000 00	8,666 00

VI.—DEPOSITS MADE AND BALANCES REMAINING, ETC.—Continued.

Names of Banks.	Deposits to redeem notes.	Balance remaining.
Farmers' National Bank, Waukesha, Wisconsin	$90,000 00	$8,179 75
Waverly National Bank, Waverly, New York	71,000 00	61,700 00
Saratoga County National Bank, Waterford, New York	127,000 00	38,677 45
First National Bank, Wellsburgh, West Virginia	89,500 00	51,997 00
United National Bank, Winona, Minnesota	44,125 00	25,125 00
National Savings Bank, Wheeling, West Virginia	67,700 00	39,700 00
National Bank of Whitestown, New York	44,500 00	10,336 75
Muskingum National Bank, Zanesville, Ohio	86,200 00	58,200 00
Total	8,861,717 00	2,826,059 30

VII.—SECURITIES HELD IN TRUST FOR NATIONAL BANKS.

1.—*To assure the redemption of circulating notes, June* 30, 1872.

Registered United States bonds, 6 per cent. coin	$158,649,450
Registered United States bonds, 5 per cent. coin	207,189,250
Registered United States bonds, 6 per cent. currency	14,602,000
Amount June 30, 1872	380,440,700
Amount received in last fiscal year	$87,032,300
Amount withdrawn in last fiscal year	66,477,150
Increase in the last fiscal year	20,555,150
Amount held June 30, 1871	359,885,550
Total	380,440,700

2.—*To assure Public deposits with National Bank Depositaries, June* 30, 1872.

Registered United States bonds, 6 per cent. coin	$6,554,800
Registered United States bonds, 5 per cent. coin	6,377,700
Registered United States bonds, 6 per cent. currency	784,000
Coupon United States bonds, 6 per cent. coin	684,000
Coupon United States bonds, 5 per cent. coin	1,028,500
Personal bonds	330,000
	15,759,000
Amount withdrawn in last fiscal year	$2,783,500
Amount received in last fiscal year	2,676,000
Decrease within fiscal year	107,500
Total June 30, 1872	15,759,000
Amount held June 30, 1871	15,866,500

3.—*Recapitulation.*

To assure the redemption of circulating notes of National Banks	$380,440,700
To assure Public deposits with National Banks	15,759,000
To assure subscriptions to the Funded Loan of 1881	3,878,300
Total securities of National Banks at par	400,078,000

4.—*Depositaries.*

On the 30th June, 1871, the number of Banks, Depositaries of the United States, was		159
Number designated and reinstated in last fiscal year	11	
Number discontinued in last fiscal year	7	4
Number of Depositaries June 30, 1872		163

5.—*Statement by Loans of United States bonds held in trust for National Banks.*

Bonds.	Rate of interest.	When redeemable.	Amount.
REGISTERED.			
Title.			
Loan of June, 1858	5 per cent. Coin	January 1, 1874	$640,000
Loan of February, 1861, (1881s)	6 per cent. Coin	December 31, 1880	4,148,000
Loan of July and August, 1861, (1881s)	6 per cent. Coin	June 30, 1881	59,536,500
5-20s of 1862	6 per cent. Coin	April 30, 1867	8,879,800
Loan of 1863, (1881s)	6 per cent. Coin	June 30, 1881	32,193,350
10-40s of 1864	5 per cent. Coin	February 28, 1874	105,505,150
5-20s of March, 1864	6 per cent. Coin	October 31, 1869	2,104,000
5-20s of 1865	6 per cent. Coin	October 31, 1869	12,515,900
Consols of 1865	6 per cent. Coin	July 1, 1870	8,810,450
Consols of 1867	6 per cent. Coin	July 1, 1872	16,756,900
Consols of 1868	6 per cent. Coin	July 1, 1873	3,695,000
Funded loan of 1881	5 per cent. Coin	May 1, 1881	107,421,800
Pacific Railway July 1, 1862, and July 2, 1864	6 per cent. Currency	January, 1895–'98	15,386,000
5-20s of 1864	6 per cent. Coin	October 31, 1869	16,564,350
COUPON.			
Title.			
Oregon War Debt	6 per cent. Coin	July 1, 1881	16,000
Loan of July and August, 1861	6 per cent. Coin	June 30, 1881	50,000
5-20s of 1862	6 per cent. Coin	April 30, 1867	109,500
Loan of 1863, (1881s)	6 per cent. Coin	June 30, 1881	211,000
10-40s of 1864	5 per cent. Coin	February 28, 1874	1,028,500
5-20s of June, 1864	6 per cent. Coin	October 31, 1869	80,000
5-20s of 1865	6 per cent. Coin	October 31, 1870	60,000
Consols of 1865	6 per cent. Coin	July 1, 1870	109,500
Consols of 1867	6 per cent. Coin	July 1, 1872	48,000
Personal bonds held for public deposits			330,000
Total securities			396,199,700

6.—*Special deposits of bonds by National Banks designated by the Department as Coin Depositaries for subscriptions to the "Funded Loan of 1881."*

From August 18, 1871, to June 30, 1872, sixty-three National Banks made deposits of United States bonds with the Department as security for subscriptions to said loan, which were placed in custody of this office, namely:

Number of deposits made	301
Number of withdrawals made	641
Largest aggregate amount, November 28, 1871	$57,267,400

On the 30th June last these deposits stood at $3,878,300, which last-named amount has since been withdrawn.

7.—*Receipts and withdrawals of United States bonds held for circulation, in fiscal year.*

Loan.	Received.	Withdrawn.
Amount held for circulation July 1, 1871	$359,885,550	....
Loan of February, 1861	413,000	$188,000
Loan of July and August, 1861, (1881s)	1,999,550	5,392,350
5-20s of 1862	122,500	27,560,350
Loan of 1863, (1881s)	1,177,500	2,953,200
10-40s of 1864	7,294,300	6,523,400
5-20s of 1864	352,500	9,064,350
5-20s of 1865	271,100	6,757,100
Consols of 1865	1,645,200	2,981,800
Consols of 1867	4,306,250	2,517,250
Consols of 1868	1,218,000	219,000
5-20s of March 1864	1,000	156,500
Pacific Railway	105,000	1,089,000
Funded Loan of 1881	68,126,400	1,072,850
10-40s of 1864 coupon	....	2,000
Amount on hand June 30, 1872	....	380,440,700
Total	446,917,850	446,917,850

8.—*Receipts and withdrawals of United States bonds held for Public deposits, in fiscal year.*

Loan.	Received.	Withdrawn.
Amount bonds on hand July 1, 1871	$15,866,500	....
Oregon War Debt	....	$25,000
Loan of February, 1861, (1881s)	10,000	12,000
Loan of July and August 1861, (1881s)	202,000	183,500
5-20s of 1862	....	365,300
Loan of 1863 (1881s)	92,000	170,000
10-40s of 1864	380,000	240,500
5-20s of June, 1864	100,000	229,000
5-20s of 1865	8,000	655,200
Consols of 1865	105,000	314,000
Consols of 1867	185,000	344,000
Consols of 1868	1,000	....
Pacific Railway	....	125,000
Funded Loan of 1881	1,593,000	120,000
Amount held June 30, 1872	....	15,759,000
Total	18,542,500	18,542,500

9.—*Coupon Interest.*

Payment of coin interest on coupon bonds held in trust was made by the issue of 208 coin checks, amounting to $292,731.69.

10.—*Examination of securities.*

The number of banks that have made an examination of their securities held here in trust, in compliance with the 25th section of the National Currency act, during the last fiscal year, is 1,091.

VIII.—SEMI-ANNUAL DUTY.

1.—Semi-annual Duty paid by National Banks during the year preceding January 1, 1872, under section 41 of the National Currency act.

For the term of six months preceding July 1, 1871:		
On circulation	$1,517,355 28	
On deposits	1,478,752 31	
On capital	193,659 02	
		$3,189,766 61
For the term of six months preceding January 1, 1872:		
On circulation	1,575,442 28	
On deposits	1,549,015 27	
On capital	191,588 05	
		3,316,045 60
Total duty for the calendar year		6,505,812 21

2.—Comparison of duties for 1870 and 1871.

Amount received in the year preceding January 1, 1872	$6,505,812 21
Amount received in year preceding January 1, 1871	6,017,460 34
Increase of duty in last calendar year	488,351 87

D.—UNITED STATES PAPER CURRENCY.

I.—ISSUED, REDEEMED, AND OUTSTANDING TO JULY 1, 1872.

Old Demand Notes.

Denominations.	Issued.	Redeemed.	Outstanding.
Five Dollars	$21,800,000 00	$21,776,285 50	$33,714 50
Ten Dollars	20,030,000 00	19,998,783 75	31,216 25
Twenty Dollars	18,200,000 00	18,176,634 50	23,365 50
Totals	60,030,000 00	59,941,703 75	88,296 25
Deduct discounts for mutilations			2,128 75
Total amount actually outstanding			86,167 50

Legal-Tender Notes, new issue.

Denominations.	Issued.	Redeemed.	Outstanding.
One Dollar	$28,351,348 00	$25,318,766 55	$3,032,581 45
Two Dollars	34,071,128 00	30,058,475 95	4,012,652 05
Five Dollars	101,000,000 00	75,420,761 75	25,579,238 25
Ten Dollars	118,010,000 00	81,432,772 25	36,577,227 75
Twenty Dollars	102,920,000 00	68,445,237 00	34,474,763 00
Fifty Dollars	30,055,200 00	26,005,684 50	4,049,515 50
One Hundred Dollars	40,000,000 00	33,508,235 00	6,491,765 00
Five Hundred Dollars	58,986,000 00	54,785,475 00	4,200,525 00
One Thousand Dollars	155,928,000 00	151,074,700 00	4,853,300 00
Totals	669,321,676 00	546,050,108 00	123,271,568 00
Deduct discounts for mutilations			98,410 50
Total amount actually outstanding			123,173,157 50

Legal-Tender Notes, series of 1869.

Denominations.	Issued.	Redeemed.	Outstanding.
One Dollar	$31,984,000 00	$3,915,478 75	$28,068,521 25
Two Dollars	39,240,000 00	4,937,187 50	34,302,812 50
Five Dollars	36,700,000 00	216,215 75	36,483,784 25
Ten Dollars	72,480,000 00	837,387 00	71,642,613 00
Twenty Dollars	53,520,000 00	248,386 50	53,271,613 50
Fifty Dollars	30,200,000 00	232,172 50	29,967,827 50
One Hundred Dollars	28,720,000 00	168,595 00	28,551,405 00
Five Hundred Dollars	34,800,000 00	1,032,500 00	33,767,500 00
One Thousand Dollars	54,800,000 00	282,000 00	54,518,000 00
Totals	382,444,000 00	11,869,923 00	370,574,077 00
Deduct for new notes not put in circulation			136,345,645 00
			234,228,432 00
Deduct discounts for mutilations			2,529 00
Total amount actually outstanding			234,225,903 00

Legal-Tender Notes, new issue, and series of 1869.

Denominations.	Issued.	Redeemed.	Outstanding.
One Dollar	$60,335,348 00	$29,234,245 30	$31,101,102 70
Two Dollars	73,311,128 00	34,995,663 45	38,315,464 55
Five Dollars	137,700,000 00	75,636,977 50	62,063,022 50
Ten Dollars	190,490,000 00	82,270,159 25	108,219,840 75
Twenty Dollars	156,440,000 00	68,693,623 50	87,746,376 50
Fifty Dollars	60,255,200 00	26,237,857 00	34,017,343 00
One Hundred Dollars	68,720,000 00	33,676,830 00	35,043,170 00
Five Hundred Dollars	93,786,000 00	55,817,975 00	37,968,025 00
One Thousand Dollars	210,728,000 00	151,356,700 00	59,371,300 00
Totals	1,051,765,676 00	557,920,031 00	493,845,645 00
Deduct for new notes not yet put in circulation			136,345,645 00
			357,500,000 00
Deduct discounts for mutilations			100,939 50
Total amount actually outstanding			357,399,060 50
"New Issue," less discount, outstanding			$123,173,157 50
"Series of 1869," less discount, outstanding			234,225,903 00
Total as above			357,399,060 50

One-Year Notes of 1863.

Denominations.	Issued.	Redeemed.	Outstanding.
Ten Dollars	$6,200,000 00	$6,179,589 00	$20,411 00
Twenty Dollars	16,440,000 00	16,387,434 00	52,566 00
Fifty Dollars	8,240,000 00	8,221,745 00	18,255 00
One Hundred Dollars	13,640,000 00	13,621,175 00	18,825 00
Totals	44,520,000 00	44,409,943 00	110,057 00
Deduct for unknown denominations destroyed			90 00
			109,967 00
Deduct discounts for mutilations			237 00
Total amount actually outstanding			109,730 00

Two-Year Notes of 1863.

Denominations.	Issued.	Redeemed.	Outstanding.
Fifty Dollars	$6,800,000 00	$6,779,487 50	$20,512 50
One Hundred Dollars	9,680,000 00	9,664,110 00	15,890 00
Totals	16,480,000 00	16,443,597 50	36,402 50
Deduct discounts for mutilations			152 50
Total amount actually outstanding			36,250 00

Two-Year Coupon Notes of 1863.

Denominations.	Issued.	Redeemed.	Outstanding.
Fifty Dollars	$5,905,600 00	$5,900,347 50	$5,252 50
One Hundred Dollars	14,484,400 00	14,473,800 00	10,600 00
Five Hundred Dollars	40,302,000 00	40,298,500 00	3,500 00
One Thousand Dollars	89,308,000 00	89,285,000 00	23,000 00
Totals	150,000,000 00	149,957,647 50	42,352 50
Deduct for unknown denominations destroyed			10,500 00
			31,852 50
Deduct discounts for mutilations			2 50
Total amount actually outstanding			31,850 00

Compound-Interest Notes.

Denominations.	Issued.	Redeemed.	Outstanding.
Ten Dollars	$23,285,200 00	$23,179,923 00	$105,277 00
Twenty Dollars	30,125,840 00	29,973,917 00	151,923 00
Fifty Dollars	60,824,000 00	60,614,820 00	209,180 00
One Hundred Dollars	45,094,400 00	44,982,270 00	112,130 00
Five Hundred Dollars	67,846,000 00	67,812,500 00	33,500 00
One Thousand Dollars	39,420,000 00	39,409,000 00	11,000 00
Totals	266,595,440 00	265,972,430 00	623,010 00
Deduct discounts for mutilations			480 00
Total amount actually outstanding			622,530 00
Outstanding June 30, 1871			$813,800 00
Redeemed within the fiscal year			191,270 00
Outstanding as above			622,530 00

Fractional Currency, First Issue.

Denominations.	Issued.	Redeemed.	Outstanding.
Five Cents	$2,242,889 00	$1,203,025 25	$1,039,863 75
Ten Cents	4,115,378 00	2,845,401 12	1,269,976 88
Twenty-Five Cents	5,225,696 00	4,159,786 38	1,065,909 62
Fifty Cents	8,631,672 00	7,616,123 16	1,015,548 84
Totals	20,215,635 00	15,824,335 91	4,391,299 09
Deduct discounts for mutilations			13,925 04
Total amount actually outstanding			4,377,374 05

Fractional Currency, Second Issue.

Denominations.	Issued.	Redeemed.	Outstanding.
Five Cents	$2,794,826 10	$2,084,336 51	$710,489 59
Ten Cents	6,176,084 30	5,238,585 19	937,499 11
Twenty-Five Cents	7,648,341 25	6,884,524 42	763,816 83
Fifty Cents	6,545,232 00	5,766,754 02	778,477 98
Totals	23,164,483 65	19,974,200 14	3,190,283 51
Deduct discounts for mutilations			9,470 86
Total amount actually outstanding			3,180,812 65

Fractional Currency, Third Issue.

Denominations.	Issued.	Redeemed.	Outstanding.
Three Cents	$601,923 90	$507,375 29	$94,548 61
Five Cents	657,002 75	519,419 69	137,583 06
Ten Cents	16,976,134 50	15,686,366 68	1,289,767 82
Fifteen Cents	*1,352 40	2 70	1,349 70
Twenty-Five Cents	31,143,188 75	29,918,248 48	1,224,940 27
Fifty Cents	36,735,426 50	35,443,660 70	1,291,765 80
Totals	86,115,028 80	82,075,073 54	4,039,955 26
Deduct discounts for mutilations			95,257 95
Total amount actually outsanding			3,944,697 31

*Specimens.

Fractional Currency, Fourth Issue, First Series.

Denominations.	Issued.	Redeemed.	Outstanding.
Ten Cents	$21,520,600 00	$14,844,407 42	$6,676,192 58
Fifteen Cents	4,201,416 00	2,594,616 26	1,606,799 74
Twenty-Five Cents	31,748,500 00	22,403,087 46	9,345,412 54
Fifty Cents	9,576,000 00	8,724,494 25	851,505 75
Totals	67,046,516 00	48,566,605 39	18,479,910 61
Deduct discounts for mutilations			4,532 86
Total amount actually outstanding			18,475,377 75

Fractional Currency, Fourth Issue, Second Series.

Denominations.	Issued.	Redeemed.	Outstanding.
Fifty Cents	$27,084,000 00	$16,329,613 20	$10,754,386 80
Deduct discounts for mutilations			477 80
Total amount actually outstanding			10,753,909 00
Fourth issue, First series, outstanding, less discount			$18,475,377 75
Fourth issue, Second series, outstanding, less discount			10,753,909 00
Total Fourth issue outstanding, less discount			29,229,286 75

Fractional Currency—Résumé.

Denominations.	Issued.	Redeemed.	Outstanding.
Three Cents	$601,923 90	$507,375 29	$94,548 61
Five Cents	5,694,717 85	3,806,781 45	1,887,936 40
Ten Cents	48,788,196 80	38,614,760 41	10,173,436 39
Fifteen Cents	4,202,768 40	2,594,618 96	1,608,149 44
Twenty-Five Cents	75,756,726 00	63,365,646 74	12,400,079 26
Fifty Cents	88,572,330 50	73,880,645 33	14,691,685 17
Totals	223,625,663 45	182,769,828 18	40,855,835 27
Deduct discounts for mutilations			123,664 51
Total amount actually outstanding			40,732,170 76
Of the above-stated amount there was held in the Office at the close of business, June 30, 1872			2,919,050 00
Leaving the actual circulation at			37,813,120 76

II.—LEGAL-TENDER NOTES ISSUED DURING FISCAL YEAR.

One-Dollar notes	$6,284,000
Two-Dollar notes	8,216,000
Five-Dollar notes	4,560,000
Ten-Dollar notes	5,160,000

Twenty-Dollar notes	$3,080,000
Fifty-Dollar notes	....
One-Hundred-Dollar notes	....
Five-Hundred-Dollar notes	....
One-Thousand-Dollar notes	....
Total	27,300,000

III.—NEW LEGAL-TENDER NOTES ON HAND NOT YET PUT IN CIRCULATION.

One Dollar	$6,353,145
Two Dollars	10,944,000
Five Dollars	15,297,500
Ten Dollars	32,450,000
Twenty Dollars	20,124,000
Fifty Dollars	9,065,000
One Hundred Dollars	9,402,000
Five Hundred Dollars	10,242,000
One Thousand Dollars	22,468,000
Total	136,345,645

IV.—FRACTIONAL CURRENCY ISSUED DURING FISCAL YEAR.

Ten Cents	$8,507,600
Fifteen Cents	1,288,800
Twenty-Five Cents	11,960,500
Fifty Cents	10,060,000
Total	31,816,900

V.—SPECIMEN FRACTIONAL CURRENCY.

There has been received from the sale of the various kinds of fractional currency, with faces and backs printed on separate pieces of paper, and mostly pasted on cards, as follows:

Up to and including June 30, 1871	$15,061 95
During fiscal year ended June 30, 1872	113 83
Total amount sold	15,175 78

VI.—CURRENCY OUTSTANDING AT THE CLOSE OF EACH FISCAL YEAR FOR THE LAST ELEVEN YEARS.

June 30, 1862:	
Old Demand Notes	$51,105,235 00
Legal-Tender Notes, new issue	96,620,000 00
Total	147,725,235 00
June 30, 1863:	
Old Demand Notes	$3,384,000 00
Legal-Tender Notes, new issue	387,646,589 00
Fractional Currency, first issue	20,192,456 00
Total	411,223,045 00
June 30, 1864:	
Old Demand Notes	$789,037 50
Legal-Tender Notes, new issue	447,300,203 10
Compound-Interest Notes	6,060,000 00
One-Year Notes of 1863	44,520,000 00
Two-Year Notes of 1863	16,480,000 00
Two-Year Coupon Notes of 1863	111,620,550 00
Fractional Currency, first issue	14,819,156 00
Fractional Currency, second issue	7,505,127 10
Total	649,094,073 70

	Dollars	Cts.
June 30, 1865:		
Old Demand Notes	$472,603	50
Legal-Tender Notes, new issue	431,066,427	99
Compound-Interest Notes	191,721,470	00
One-Year Notes of 1863	8,467,570	00
Two-Year Notes of 1863	7,715,950	00
Two-Year Coupon Notes of 1863	34,441,650	00
Fractional Currency, first issue	9,915,408	66
Fractional Currency, second issue	12,798,130	60
Fractional Currency, third issue	2,319,589	50
Total	698,918,800	25
June 30, 1866:		
Old Demand Notes	$272,162	75
Legal-Tender Notes, new issue	400,780,305	85
Compound-Interest Notes	172,369,941	00
One-Year Notes of 1863	2,151,465	50
Two-Year Notes of 1863	5,209,522	50
Two-Year Coupon Notes of 1863	1,078,552	50
Fractional Currency, first issue	7,030,700	78
Fractional Currency, second issue	7,937,024	57
Fractional Currency, third issue	12,041,150	01
Total	608,870,825	46
June 30, 1867:		
Old Demand Notes	$208,432	50
Legal-Tender Notes, new issue	371,783,597	00
Compound Interest Notes	134,774,981	00
One-Year Notes of 1863	794,687	00
Two Year Notes of 1863	396,950	00
Two-Year Coupon Notes of 1863	134,252	50
Fractional Currency, first issue	5,497,534	93
Fractional Currency, second issue	4,975,827	08
Fractional Currency, third issue	18,001,261	01
Total	536,567,523	02
June 30, 1868:		
Old Demand Notes	$143,912	00
Legal-Tender Notes, new issue	356,000,000	00
Compound-Interest Notes	54,608,230	00
One-Year Notes of 1863	458,557	00
Two-Year Notes of 1863	188,402	50
Two-Year Coupon Notes of 1863	69,252	50
Fractional Currency, first issue	4,881,091	27
Fractional Currency, second issue	3,924,075	22
Fractional Currency, third issue	23,922,741	98
Total	444,196,262	47
June 30, 1869:		
Old Demand Notes	$123,739	25
Legal-Tender Notes, new issue	356,000,000	00
Compound-Interest Notes	3,063,410	00
One-Year Notes of 1863	220,517	00
Two-Year Notes of 1863	84,752	50
Two-Year Coupon Notes of 1863	42,502	50
Fractional Currency, first issue	4,605,708	52
Fractional Currency, second issue	3,528,163	65
Fractional Currency, third issue	23,980,765	19
Total	391,649,558	61
June 30, 1870:		
Old Demand Notes	$106,256	00
Legal-Tender Notes, new issue	289,145,032	00
United States Notes, series of 1869	66,854,968	00

Compound-Interest Notes	$2,191,670 00
One-Year Notes of 1863	160,347 00
Two-Year Notes of 1863	56,402 50
Two-Year Coupon Notes of 1863	37,202 50
Fractional Currency, first issue	4,476,995 87
Fractional Currency, second issue	3,273,191 03
Fractional Currency, third issue	10,666,556 52
Fractional Currency, fourth issue	21,461,941 06
Total	398,430,562 48
June 30, 1871:	
Old Demand Notes	$96,505 50
Legal-Tender Notes, new issue	181,806,518 00
United States Notes, series of 1869	174,193,482 00
Compound-Interest Notes	814,280 00
One-Year Notes of 1863	128,037 00
Two-Year Notes of 1863	44,502 50
Two-Year Coupon Notes of 1863	33,452 50
Fractional Currency, first issue	4,414,025 04
Fractional Currency, second issue	3,218,156 37
Fractional Currency, third issue	5,617,535 75
Fractional Currency, fourth issue	27,333,157 40
Total	397,699,652 06
June 30, 1872:	
Old Demand Notes	$88,296 25
Legal-Tender Notes, new issue	123,271,568 00
United States Notes, series of 1869	234,228,432 00
Compound-Interest Notes	623,010 00
One-Year Notes of 1863	109,967 00
Two-Year Notes of 1863	36,402 50
Two-Year Coupon-Notes of 1863	31,852 50
Fractional Currency, first issue	4,391,299 09
Fractional Currency, second issue	3,190,283 51
Fractional Currency, third issue	4,039,955 26
Fractional Currency, fourth issue	29,234,297 41
Total	399,245,363 52

VII.—COMPARATIVE STATEMENT OF TOTAL OUTSTANDING FOR THE LAST ELEVEN YEARS.

Outstanding June 30, 1862	$147,725,235 00
Outstanding June 30, 1863	411,223,045 00
Outstanding June 30, 1864	649,094,073 70
Outstanding June 30, 1865	698,918,800 25
Outstanding June 30, 1866	608,870,825 46
Outstanding June 30, 1867	536,567,523 02
Outstanding June 30, 1868	444,196,262 47
Outstanding June 30, 1869	391,649,558 61
Outstanding June 30, 1870	398,430,562 48
Outstanding June 30, 1871	397,699,652 06
Outstanding June 30, 1872	399,245,363 52

E.—REDEMPTIONS.

I.—REDEMPTION AND DESTRUCTION OF MONEYS AND SECURITIES DURING FISCAL YEAR.

Old Demand Notes		$8,209 25
Legal-Tender Notes, new issue	$58,534,950 00	
Legal-Tender Notes, new issue (burned at Chicago)	135,000 00	
		58,669,950 00
Legal-Tender Notes, series of 1869	9,564,854 00	
Legal-Tender Notes, series of '69 (burned at Chicago)	865,000 00	
		10,429,854 00
One-Year Notes of 1863		18,070 00
Two-Year Notes of 1863		8,100 00
Two-Year Coupon Notes of 1863		1,600 00
Compound Interest Notes		191,270 00
Fractional Currency, first issue		22,725 95
Fractional Currency, second issue		27,872 86
Fractional Currency, third issue		1,577,580 49

Fractional Currency, fourth issue, first series	$19,886,751 04
Fractional Currency, fourth issue, second series	10,029,008 95
Fractional Currency, (burned at Chicago)	32,000 00
Coin Certificates, old issue	957,000 00
Coin Certificates, series of 1870	50,947,500 00
Coin Certificates, series of 1871	274,500 00
Coin Certificates, (burned at Chicago)	2,200 00
Discounts on above	22,165 48
Total amount destroyed as money	153,106,358 02
National Bank Notes, (including discounts)	3,374,234 00
Total	156,480,592 02
Statistical matter destroyed	222,879,983 49
Balance on hand July 1, 1872	1,158,834 86
Total amount for fiscal year	380,519,410 37

Cash Account, Dr.

Balance from last year	$915,133 74
Amount received	153,327,893 66
Total	154,243,027 40

Contra, Cr.

Amount destroyed during the year	$153,084,192 54
Balance on hand July 1, 1872	1,158,834 86
Total	154,243,027 40
Amount brought down	$153,106,358 02
National Bank Notes, (broken and in liquidation)	3,374,234 00
Balance on hand July 1, 1872	1,158,834 86
Statistical matter destroyed	222,879,983 49
Total amount for fiscal year	380,519,410 37

Destroyed as money during the year	$153,106,358 02	
As per last Report	1,655,208,117 67	
Total amount destroyed as money		$1,803,314,475 69
Destroyed statistically during year	222,879,983 49	
As per last Report	2,738,256,945 24	
		2,961,136,928 73
Total		4,769,451,404 42
Certificate of indebtedness		592,905,350 26
National Bank Notes destroyed during year	$3,374,234 00	
As per last Report	2,663,995 00	
		6,038,229 00
Total amount destroyed to July 1, 1872		5,368,394,983 68
Total of all destroyed during the year	$379,360,575 51	
Total of all destroyed before	4.989,034,408 17	$5,368,394,983 68

II.—DISCOUNTS ON MUTILATED CURRENCY.

1.—*Discounts for missing parts of mutilated currency destroyed to July 1, 1872.*

On Old Demand Notes	$2,128 75
On Legal-Tender Notes, new issue	98,410 50
On Legal-Tender Notes, series of 1869	2,529 00
On One-Year Notes of 1863	237 00
On Two-Year Notes of 1863	152 50
On Two-Year Coupon Notes of 1863	2 50
On Compound-Interest Notes	480 00
On Fractional Currency, first issue	13,925 04
On Fractional Currency, second issue	9,470 86
On Fractional Currency, third issue	95,257 95

On Fractional Currency, fourth issue, first series	$4,532 86
On Fractional Currency, fourth issue, second series	477 80
	227,604 76
On moneys redeemed but not destroyed	127 57
Total discounts from the beginning	227,732 33

2.—*Discounts by years.*

These discounts were made for the amounts and in the years as follows:

In the year 1863	$615 27
In the year 1864	11,393 93
In the year 1865	13,108 09
In the year 1866	17,813 36
In the year 1867	24,767 69
In the year 1868	31,671 54
In the year 1869	38,543 56
In the year 1870	44,622 43
In the year 1871	32,995 52
In the year 1872	12,200 94
	227,732 33

3.—*Discount Account.*

On moneys destroyed to July 1, 1872		$227,604 76
On moneys destroyed to July 1, 1871		205,439 28
Discounts for last fiscal year		22,165 48
Discount on moneys on hand July 1, 1871	$10,092 11	
Discount on moneys on hand July 1, 1872	127,57	
		9,964 54
Total discounts for fiscal year		12,200 94
Amount discounted before July 1, 1871		$215,531 39
Amount discounted for last fiscal year		12,200 94
Total amount of discounts to July 1, 1872, as above		227,732 33

III.—DESTRUCTION OF PAPER MONEY.

1.—*Number of notes destroyed.*

There have been destroyed, since the commencement of the rebellion, paper representing moneys, as follows:

Old Demand Notes:	
Five Dollars	4,353,353½
Ten Dollars	1,999,922½
Twenty Dollars	908,892
Total number of notes destroyed	7,262,168

Legal-Tender Notes, new issue:	
One Dollar	25,348,743½
Two Dollars	15,039,741
Five Dollars	15,087,976½
Ten Dollars	8,144,545
Twenty Dollars	3,422,788
Fifty Dollars	520,152
One Hundred Dollars	335,106
Five Hundred Dollars	109,572
One Thousand Dollars	151,075
Total number of notes destroyed	68,159,699

Legal-Tender Notes, series of 1869:	
One Dollar	3, 916, 470
Two Dollars	2, 469, 116
Five Dollars	43, 256
Ten Dollars	83, 761
Twenty Dollars	12, 423
Fifty Dollars	4, 644
One Hundred Dollars	1, 687
Five Hundred Dollars	2, 065
One Thousand Dollars	282
Total number of notes destroyed	6, 533, 704
One-Year Notes of 1863:	
Ten Dollars	617, 962
Twenty Dollars	819, 378
Fifty Dollars	164, 436
One Hundred Dollars	136, 212
Total number of notes destroyed	1, 737, 988
Two-Year Notes of 1863:	
Fifty Dollars	135, 591
One Hundred Dollars	96, 642
Total number of notes destroyed	232, 233
Two-Year Coupon Notes of 1863:	
Fifty Dollars	118, 007
One Hundred Dollars	144, 738
Five Hundred Dollars	80, 597
One Thousand Dollars	89, 285
Total nnmber of notes destroyed	432, 627
Compound-Interest Notes:	
Ten Dollars	2, 318, 006
Twenty Dollars	1, 498, 702½
Fifty Dollars	1, 212, 300
One Hundred Dollars	449, 823
Five Hundred Dollars	135, 625
One Thousand Dollars	39, 409
Total number of notes destroyed	5, 653, 865½
Fractional Currency, First Issue:	
Five Cents	24, 091 063
Ten Cents	28, 476, 213
Twenty-Five Cents	16, 662, 758
Fifty Cents	15, 240, 794
Total number of notes destroyed	84, 470, 828
Fractional Currency, Second Issue:	
Five Cents	41, 726, 362
Ten Cents	52, 424, 389
Twenty-Five Cents	27, 545, 314
Fifty Cents	11, 537, 171
Total number of notes destroyed	133, 233, 236
Fractional Currency, Third Issue:	
Three Cents	16, 917, 923
Five Cents	10, 397, 293
Ten Cents	157, 098, 717
Fifteen Cents	18
Twenty-Five Cents	119, 796, 336
Fifty Cents	70, 967, 942
Total number of notes destroyed	375, 178, 229

Fractional Currency, Fourth Issue, first series:	
Ten Cents	148,454,941
Fifteen Cents	17,300,891
Twenty-Five Cents	89,617,302
Fifty Cents	17,452,370
Total number of notes destroyed	272,825,504
Fractional Currency, Fourth Issue, Second Series:	
Fifty Cents	32,660,182
Coin Certificates, old issue:	
Twenty Dollars	45,290
One Hundred Dollars	113,971
Five Hundred Dollars	17,984
One Thousand Dollars	59,961
Five Thousand Dollars	64,583
Ten Thousand Dollars	2,500
Total number of notes destroyed	304,289
Coin Certificates, series of 1870:	
Five Hundred Dollars	7,911
One Thousand Dollars	15,356
Five Thousand Dollars	5,794
Ten Thousand Dollars	5,190
Total number of notes destroyed	34,251
Coin Certificates, series of 1871:	
One Hundred Dollars	2,745
Notes of National Banks, failed and in liquidation:	
One Dollar	98,224
Two Dollars	35,140
Five Dollars	581,649
Ten Dollars	151,793
Twenty Dollars	42,740
Fifty Dollars	4,625
One Hundred Dollars	3,575
Total number of notes destroyed	917,746

2.—*Number of notes of each kind destroyed during the fiscal year.*

Old Demand Notes	965
Legal-Tender Notes, new issue	8,695,581
Legal-Tender Notes, series of 1869	5,285,762
One-Year Notes of 1863	854
Two-Year Notes of 1863	125
Two-Year Coupon Notes of 1863	18
Compound-Interest Notes	6,607
Fractional Currency, first issue	140,505
Fractional Currency, second issue	197,737
Fractional Currency, third issue	6,941,603
Fractional Currency, fourth issue, first series	120,762,138
Fractional Currency, fourth issue, second series	20,058,704
Coin Certificates, old issue	5,791
Coin Certificates, series of 1870	17,886
Coin Certificates, series of 1871	2,745
Total	162,117,021
National Bank Notes	489,449
Total	162,606,470
Number as per last Report	827,032,822½
Total number to July 1, 1872	989,639,292½

IV.—DESTRUCTION ACCOUNT.

Statement of face value of money destroyed since 1861.

Old Demand Notes	$59,943,832 50
Legal-Tender Notes, new issue	546,283,518 50
Legal-Tender Notes, series of 1869	12,737,452 00
One-Year Notes of 1863	44,410,270 00
Two-Year Coupon Notes of 1863	16,443,750 00
Two-Year Notes of 1863	149,968,150 00
Compound-Interest Notes	265,972,910 00
Fractional Currency, first issue	15,838,260 95
Fractional Currency, second issue	19,983,671 00
Fractional Currency, third issue	82,170,331 49
Fractional Currency, fourth issue, first series	48,571,138 25
Fractional Currency, fourth issue, second series	16,330,091 00
Fractional Currency, (burned at Chicago)	32,000 00
Coin Certificates, old issue	429,170,900 00
Coin Certificates, series of 1870	100,181,500 00
Coin Certificates, series of 1871	274,500 00
Coin Certificates, (burned at Chicago, issue not known)	2,200 00
Total amount destroyed as money	1,808,314,475 69
Total amount destroyed statistically	2,961,136,928 73
National Bank Notes	6,038,229 00
Certificates of indebtedness	592,905,350 26
Total amount destroyed to July 1, 1872	5,368,394,983 68

V.—REDEMPTION ACCOUNT.

Statement of redemptions of moneys since 1861.

Moneys destroyed before July 1, 1871		$1,655,208,117 67
Moneys destroyed within the year		153,084,192 54
Discounts on same		22,165 48
Total		1,808,314,475 69
National Bank Notes before July 1, 1871	$2,663,995 00	
During the year	3,374,234 00	
		6,038,229 00
Statistical matter destroyed before July 1, 1871	2,738,256,945 24	
During the year	222,879,983 49	
		2,961,136,928 73
Certificates of indebtedness		592,905,350 26
Total amount destroyed to July 1, 1872		5,368,394,983 68
Balance on hand but not destroyed		1,158,834 86
Total amount redeemed to July 1, 1872		5,369,553,818 54

VI.—REDEMPTIONS AND DISCOUNTS.

Amounts paid, discounts, and amounts retired to July 1, 1872.

Old Demand Notes.

Denominations.	Amount paid.	Amount discounted.	Total amount retired.
Five Dollars	$21,766,285 50	$482 00	$21,766,767 50
Ten Dollars	19,998,783 75	441 25	19,999,225 00
Twenty Dollars	18,176,634 50	1,205 50	18,177,840 00
Totals	59,941,703 75	2,128 75	59,943,832 50

Legal-Tender Notes, new issue.

Denominations.	Amount paid.	Amount discounted.	Total amount retired.
One Dollar	$25,318,766 55	$29,977 45	$25,348,744 00
Two Dollars	30,058,475 95	21,006 05	30,079,482 00
Five Dollars	75,420,761 75	19,120 75	75,439,882 50
Ten Dollars	81,432,772 25	12,677 75	81,445,450 00
Twenty Dollars	68,445,237 00	10,523 00	68,455,760 00
Fifty Dollars	26,005,684 50	1,915 50	26,007,600 00
One Hundred Dollars	33,508,235 00	2,365 00	33,510,600 00
Five Hundred Dollars	54,785,475 00	525 00	54,786,000 00
One Thousand Dollars	151,074,700 00	300 00	151,075,000 00
Totals	546,050,108 00	98,410 50	546,148,518 50

Legal-Tender Notes, series of 1869.

Denominations.	Amount paid.	Amount discounted.	Total amount retired.
One Dollar	$3,915,478 75	$991 25	$3,916,470 00
Two Dollars	4,937,187 50	1,044 50	4,938,232 00
Five Dollars	216,215 75	64 25	216,280 00
Ten Dollars	837,387 00	223 00	837,610 00
Twenty Dollars	248,386 50	73 50	248,460 00
Fifty Dollars	232,172 50	27 50	232,200 00
One Hundred Dollars	168,595 00	105 00	168,700 00
Five Hundred Dollars	1,032,500 00	....	1,032,500 00
One Thousand Dollars	282,000 00	....	282,000 00
Totals	11,869,923 00	2,529 00	11,872,452 00

One-Year Notes of 1863.

Denominations.	Amount paid.	Amount discounted.	Total amount retired.
Ten Dollars	$6,179,589 00	$31 00	$6,179,620 00
Twenty Dollars	16,387,434 00	126 00	16,387,560 00
Fifty Dollars	8,221,745 00	55 00	8,221,800 00
One Hundred Dollars	13,621,175 00	25 00	13,621,200 00
Unknown	90 00		90 00
Totals	44,410,033 00	237 00	44,410,270 00

Two-Year Notes of 1863.

Denominations.	Amount paid.	Amount discounted.	Total amount retired.
Fifty Dollars	$6,779,487 50	$62 50	$6,779,550 00
One Hundred Dollars	9,664,110 00	90 00	9,664,200 00
Totals	16,443,597 50	152 50	16,443,750 00

Two-Year Coupon Notes of 1863.

Denominations.	Amount paid.	Amount discounted.	Total amount retired.
Fifty Dollars	$5,900,347 50	$2 50	$5,900,350 00
One Hundred Dollars	14,473,800 00	....	14,473,800 00
Five Hundred Dollars	40,298,500 00	....	40,298,500 00
One Thousand Dollars	89,285,000 00	....	89,285,000 00
Unknown	10,500 00	....	10,500 00
Totals	149,968,147 50	2 50	149,968,150 00

Compound-Interest Notes.

Denominations.	Amount paid.	Amount discounted.	Total amount retired.
Ten Dollars	$23,179,923 00	$137 00	$23,180,060 00
Twenty Dollars	29,973,917 00	133 00	29,974,050 00
Fifty Dollars	60,614,820 00	180 00	60,615,000 00
One Hundred Dollars	44,982,270 00	30 00	44,982,300 00
Five Hundred Dollars	67,812,500 00	....	67,812,500 00
One Thousand Dollars	39,409,000 00	....	39,409,000 00
Totals	265,972,430 00	480 00	265,972,910 00

Fractional Currency, First Issue.

Denominations.	Amount paid.	Amount discounted.	Total amount retired.
Five Cents	$1,203,025 25	$1,527 90	$1,204,553 15
Ten Cents	2,845,401 12	2,220 18	2,847,621 30
Twenty-Five Cents	4,159,786 38	5,903 12	4,165,689 50
Fifty Cents	7,616,123 16	4,273 84	7,620,397 00
Totals	15,824,335 91	13,925 04	15,838,260 95

Fractional Currency, Second Issue.

Denominations.	Amount paid.	Amount discounted.	Total amount retired.
Five Cents	$2,084,336 51	$1,981 59	$2,086,318 10
Ten Cents	5,238,585 19	3,853 71	5,242,438 90
Twenty-Five Cents	6,884,524 42	1,804 08	6,886,328 50
Fifty Cents	5,766,754 02	1,831 48	5,768,585 50
Totals	19,974,200 14	9,470 86	19,983,671 00

Fractional Currency, Third Issue.

Denominations.	Amount paid.	Amount discounted.	Total amount retired.
Three Cents	$507,375 29	$162 40	$507,537 69
Five Cents	519,419 69	444 96	519,864 65
Ten Cents	15,686,366 68	23,505 02	15,709,871 70
Fifteen Cents	2 70	....	2 70
Twenty-Five Cents	29,918,248 48	30,835 52	29,949,084 00
Fifty Cents	35,443,660 70	40,310 05	35,483,970 75
Totals	82,075,073 54	95,257 95	82,170,331 49

Fractional Currency, Fourth Issue, First Series.

Denominations.	Amount paid.	Amount discounted.	Total amount retired.
Ten Cents	$14,844,407 42	$1,086 68	$14,845,494 10
Fifteen Cents	2,594,616 26	517 39	2,595,133 65
Twenty-Five Cents	22,403,087 46	1,238 04	22,404,325 50
Fifty Cents	8,724,494 25	1,690 75	8,726,185 00
Totals	48,566,605 39	4,532 86	48,571,138 25

Fractional Currency, Fourth Issue, Second Series.

Denominations.	Amount paid.	Amount discounted.	Total amount retired.
Fifty Cents	$16,329,613 20	$477 80	$16,330,091 00

VII.—DESTRUCTION OF NOTES OF NATIONAL BANKS IN LIQUIDATION.

1.—*Notes destroyed, by denominations.*

Denominations.	Amount paid.	Amount discounted.	Total amount retired.
One Dollar	$98,171 85	$52 15	$98,224 00
Two Dollars	70,260 60	19 40	70,280 00
Five Dollars	2,908,012 50	232 50	2,908,245 00
Ten Dollars	1,517,887 00	43 00	1,517,930 00
Twenty Dollars	854,789 00	11 00	854,800 00
Fifty Dollars	231,240 00	10 00	231,250 00
One Hundred Dollars	357,495 00	5 00	357,500 00
Totals	6,037,855 95	373 05	6,038,229 00

2.—*Destruction Account.*

Total amount destroyed during the year		$3,374,153 90
As per last Report		2,663,702 05
Total from the beginning		6,037,855 95
Discounts during the fiscal year	$80 10	
As per last Report	292 95	373 05
Total destruction to July 1, 1872		6,038,229 00

F.—STATISTICAL DESTRUCTIONS.

1.—DESTRUCTION OF STATISTICAL MATTER DURING FISCAL YEAR.

Coin Certificates, series of 1871:		
One Hundred Dollars		$200,000 00
Fractional Currency, Fourth Issue, First Series:		
Ten Cents	$152,366 40	
Fifteen Cents	35,112 00	
Twenty-Five Cents	601,506 25	
Fifty Cents	1,800 00	
		790,784 65
Fractional Currency, Fourth Issue, Second Series:		
Fifty Cents		246,200 00
Five-Twenty Coupon Bonds:		
Fifty Dollars	$76,750 00	
One Hundred Dollars	366,200 00	
Five Hundred Dollars	2,029,500 00	
One Thousand Dollars	8,985,000 00	
Three Thousand Dollars	42,000 00	
		11,499,450 00
Ten-Forty Registered Bonds:		
Fifty Dollars	24,950 00	
One Hundred Dollars	99,900 00	
Five Hundred Dollars	524,500 00	
One Thousand Dollars	622,000 00	
Five Thousand Dollars	8,245,000 00	
Ten Thousand Dollars	19,990,000 00	
		29,506,350 00
Registered Bonds, Loan of 1842:		
One Hundred Dollars	16,500 00	
Five Hundred Dollars	18,000 00	
One Thousand Dollars	76,000 00	
Two Thousand Dollars	22,000 00	
Three Thousand Dollars	216,000 00	
Five Thousand Dollars	175,000 00	
Ten Thousand Dollars	1,950,000 00	
		2,473,500 00
Registered Bonds, Loan of 1847:		
Fifty Dollars	36,150 00	
One Hundred Dollars	362,300 00	
Two Hundred Dollars	46,400 00	
Three Hundred Dollars	38,100 00	
Five Hundred Dollars	147,500 00	
One Thousand Dollars	638,000 00	
Two Thousand Dollars	428,000 00	
Three Thousand Dollars	426,000 00	
Five Thousand Dollars	1,490,000 00	
Ten Thousand Dollars	1,580,000 00	
		5,192,450 00

Registered Bonds, Loan of 1848:		
Fifty Dollars	$92,350 00	
One Hundred Dollars	320,900 00	
Two Hundred Dollars	83,600 00	
Three Hundred Dollars	165,000 00	
Five Hundred Dollars	1,317,000 00	
One Thousand Dollars	159,000 00	
Two Thousand Dollars	654,000 00	
Three Thousand Dollars	258,000 00	
Five Thousand Dollars	1,595,000 00	
Ten Thousand Dollars	1,080,000 00	
		$5,724,850 00
Five per cent. Registered Bonds:		
Fifty Dollars	1,050 00	
One Hundred Dollars	7,400 00	
Five Hundred Dollars	9,000 00	
One Thousand Dollars	977,000 00	
Five Thousand Dollars	6,880,000 00	
Ten Thousand Dollars	1,200,000 00	
		9,074,450 00
Registered Central Pacific Railway Bonds:		
One Thousand Dollars		3,390,000 00
Registered Union Pacific Railway Bonds:		
One Thousand Dollars	$4,713,000 00	
Five Thousand Dollars	12,015,000 00	
Ten Thousand Dollars	27,090,000 00	
		43,818,000 00
Registered Pacific Railway Bonds, Atchison and Pike's Peak:		
One Thousand Dollars	1,859,000 00	
Five Thousand Dollars	3,365,000 00	
Ten Thousand Dollars	6,170,000 00	
		11,394,000 00
Registered Kansas Pacific Railway Bonds:		
One Thousand Dollars		1,000 00
Registered Bonds, Loan of 1860:		
One Thousand Dollars	$1,407,000 00	
Five Thousand Dollars	2,740,000 00	
		4,147 000 00
Registered Bonds, Act July, 1861:		
Fifty Dollars	29,250 00	
One Hundred Dollars	101,900 00	
One Thousand Dollars	129,000 00	
Five Thousand Dollars	50,000 00	
		310,150 00
Six per cent. Registered Bonds:		
Fifty Dollars	53,300 00	
One Hundred Dollars	124,800 00	
Five Hundred Dollars	913,500 00	
One Thousand Dollars	4,392,000 00	
Five Thousand Dollars	20,760,000 00	
Ten Thousand Dollars	41,840,000 00	
		68,083,600 00
Five-Twenty Registered Bonds:		
Fifty Dollars	6,200 00	
One Hundred Dollars	23,000 00	
Five Hundred Dollars	168,000 00	
One Thousand Dollars	717,000 00	
Ten Thousand Dollars	1,890,000 00	
		2,804,200 00

Legal-Tender Notes, Series of 1869:		
One Dollar	$435,660 00	
Two Dollars	419,000 00	
Five Dollars	268,360 00	
Ten Dollars	342,720 00	
Twenty Dollars	111,520 00	
		$1,577,260 00
Registered Bonds Central Branch Union Pacific Railway:		
One Thousand Dollars	249,000 00	
Five Thousand Dollars	1,245,000 00	
		1,494,000 00
War-Bounty Stock:		
Twenty-Five Dollars	100 00	
One Hundred Dollars	200 00	
Five Hundred Dollars	7,500 00	
One Thousand Dollars	2,000 00	
Five Thousand Dollars	820,000 00	
		829,800 00
Registered Western Pacific Railway Bonds:		
One Thousand Dollars	249,000 00	
Ten Thousand Dollars	2,490,000 00	
		2,739,000 00
Internal-Revenue Stamps		17,583,938 84
Total for fiscal year		$222,879,983 49
Amount per last Report		2,738,256,945 24
Total to July 1, 1872		2,961,136,928 73

II.—NUMBER OF NOTES DESTROYED DURING FISCAL YEAR ON STATISTICAL ACCOUNT.

Coin Certificates, Series of 1871	2,000
Legal-Tender Notes, Series of 1869	738,680
Fractional Currency, Fourth Issue, First Series	3,880,345
Fractional Currency, Fourth Issue, Second Series	492,400
Five-Twenty Coupon Bonds	18,255
Six per cent. Registered Bonds	16,869
Five per cent. Registered Bonds	2,586
Five-Twenty Registered Bonds	1,596
Registered Bonds, Loan of 1842	590
Registered Bonds, Loan of 1847	6,450
Registered Bonds, Loan of 1848	9,657
Registered Bonds, Loan of 1860	1,955
Registered Bonds, Loan of 1861	1,743
Ten-Forty Registered Bonds	6,817
Registered Central Pacific Railway Bonds	3,888
Registered Union Pacific Railway Bonds	9,825
Registered Bonds Pacific Railway, Atchison and Pike's Peak Division	3,149
Registered Western Pacific Railway Bonds	498
Registered Bonds Kansas Pacific Railway	1
War-Bounty Stock	187
Registered Bonds Central Branch Union Pacific Railway	498
Total number for fiscal year	5,197,989
Number as per last Report	38,212,889
Total number of notes to July 1, 1872	43,410,878

G.—COIN CERTIFICATES.

I.—RECEIPTS AND REDEMPTIONS OF ALL ISSUES.

Coin Certificates of all issues received from Printing Bureau, exclusive of amount destroyed statistically:

Twenty-Dollar Notes	$960,160 00
One-Hundred-Dollar Notes	16,645,700 00
Five-Hundred-Dollar Notes	29,004,000 00
One-Thousand-Dollar Notes	110,008,000 00
Five-Thousand-Dollar Notes	523,040,000 00
Ten-Thousand-Dollar Notes	225,000,000 00
Total	904,657,860 00
Cash destructions of all issues:	
Twenty-Dollar Notes	$905,500 00
One-Hundred-Dollar Notes	11,671,900 00
Five-Hundred-Dollar Notes	12,948,500 00
One-Thousand-Dollar Notes	75,316,000 00
Five-Thousand-Dollar Notes	351,885,000 00
Ten-Thousand-Dollar Notes	76,900,000 00
Total destructions	529,626,900 00
Redeemed but not destroyed	1,063,200 00
	530,690,100 00
Amount on hand unissued	341,881,460 00
Amount outstanding	32,086,300 00
Total	904,657,860 00

II.—COIN CERTIFICATES, OLD ISSUE.

Denominations.	Received from Printing Bureau.	Issued.	On hand, unissued.
20s	$960,160 00	$960,000 00	$160 00
100s	11,645,700 00	11,644,900 00	800 00
500s	9,004,000 00	9,000,000 00	4,000 00
1,000s	60,008,000 00	60,000,000 00	8,000 00
5,000s	323,040,000 00	323,000,000 00	40,000 00
10,000s	25,000,000 00	25,000,000 00	
Totals	429,657,860 00	429,604,900 00	52,960 00

Denominations.	Issued.	Redeemed.	Outstanding.
20s	$960,000 00	$905,500 00	$54,500 00
100s	11,644,900 00	11,397,400 00	247,500 00
500s	9,000,000 00	8,993,000 00	7,000 00
1,000s	60,000,000 00	59,960,000 00	40,000 00
5,000s	323,000,000 00	322,915,000 00	85,000 00
10,000s	25,000,000 00	25,000,000 00	
Totals	429,604,900 00	429,170,900 00	434,000 00
Deduct redeemed but not destroyed			50,200 00
Total amount actually outstanding			383,800 00

III.—COIN CERTIFICATES, SERIES OF 1870 AND 1871.

Denominations.	Received from Printing Bureau.	Issued.	On hand, unissued.
100s	$5,000,000 00	$980,000 00	$4,020,000 00
500s	20,000,000 00	5,785,500 00	14,214,500 00
1,000s	50,000,000 00	19,756,000 00	30,244,000 00
5,000s	200,000,000 00	37,280,000 00	162,720,000 00
10,000s	200,000,000 00	69,370,000 00	130,630,000 00
Totals	475,000,000 00	133,171,500 00	341,828,500 00

Denominations.	Issued.	Redeemed.	Outstanding.
100s	$980,000 00	$274,500 00	$705,500 00
500s	5,785,500 00	3,955,500 00	1,830,000 00
1,000s	19,756,000 00	15,356,000 00	4,400,000 00
5,000s	37,280,000 00	28,970,000 00	8,310,000 00
10,000s	69,370,000 00	51,900,000 00	17,470,000 00
Totals	133,171,500 00	100,456,000 00	32,715,500 00
Deduct amount redeemed but not destroyed			1,013,000 00
Total amount actually outstanding			31,702,500 00

IV.—COIN CERTIFICATES, SERIES OF 1870, NOT NUMBERED, ON HAND IN TREASURER'S OFFICE.

500s	$161,000
1,000s	2,949,000
5,000s	985,000
10,000s	4,630,000
Total	8,725,000

V.—TOTAL REDEMPTIONS OF COIN CERTIFICATES.

At Washington	$625,480
At Boston	15,139,020
At New York	502,273,620
At Philadelphia	712,720
At Charleston	248,920
At New Orleans	771,420
At Saint Louis	440,620
At San Francisco	1,040
At Baltimore	9,520,520
At Buffalo	82,980
At Chicago	346,080
At Cincinnati	316,300
At Saint Paul	9,000
At Louisville	115,620
At Mobile	86,760
Total	530,690,100

NOTE.—Up to August 1, 1869, redemptions were made at the offices of the various Assistant Treasurers, and Depositaries, but subsequent to that date redemptions were made only at the offices of the Treasurer United States at Washington, and the Assistant Treasurer at New York.

VI.—MOVEMENT OF COIN CERTIFICATES.

Washington office Notes:		
Received from Printing Bureau		$3,200,000
Redeemed and destroyed	$3,193,400	
On hand as statistical matter (samples)	800	
		3,194,200
Outstanding of Washington issue		5,800
New York office Notes:		
Sent to New York previous to June 30, 1871	$509,700,000	
Sent to New York during fiscal year	72,410,000	
Total amount sent to New York	582,110,000	
Remaining on hand at New York June 30, 1872, never issued	19,378,500	
Total issued at New York office	562,731,500	
Total redeemed of New York issue	530,651,000	
Outstanding of New York issue		32,080,500
Total outstanding, as per Public Debt statement of July 1, 1872		32,086,300

VII.—ISSUES AND REDEMPTIONS BY FISCAL YEARS.

Issued:		
From November 13, 1865, to June 30, 1866, inclusive		$98,493,660
From July 1, 1866, to June 30, 1867, inclusive		109,121,620
From July 1, 1867, to June 30, 1868, inclusive		77,960,400
From July 1, 1868, to June 30, 1869, inclusive		80,663,160
From July 1, 1869, to June 30, 1870, inclusive		76,731,060
From July 1, 1870, to June 30, 1871, inclusive		56,577,000
From July 1, 1871, to June 30, 1872, inclusive		63,229,500
Total issued		562,776,400
Redeemed:		
From November 13, 1865, to June 30, 1866, inclusive	$87,545,800	
From July 1, 1866, to June 30, 1867, inclusive	101,295,900	
From July 1, 1867, to June 30, 1868, inclusive	79,055,340	
From July 1, 1868, to June 30, 1869, inclusive	65,255,620	
From July 1, 1869, to June 30, 1870, inclusive	75,270,120	
From July 1, 1870, to June 30, 1871, inclusive	71,237,820	
From July 1, 1871, to June 30, 1872, inclusive	51,029,500	
Total redeemed		530,690,100
Total outstanding as per books of this office		32,086,300

VIII.—ON HAND AT NEW YORK.

On hand at New York, July 1, 1871, (never issued)	$10,198,000
Sent to New York during fiscal year	72,410,000
Total	82,608,000
Less amount issued during fiscal year	63,229,500
On hand June 30, 1872, (never issued)	19,378,500
On hand redeemed, June 30, 1872, not returned to Washington	507,000
Total on hand at New York, as per statement of Assistant Treasurer United States, at New York	19,885,500

IX.—COIN CERTIFICATES, ALL ISSUES, OUTSTANDING, BY DENOMINATIONS.

20s	$54,500
100s	953,000
500s	1,837,000
1,000s	4,440,000
5,000s	8,395,000
10,000s	17,470,000
Total amount outstanding	33,149,500
Deduct amount redeemed but not destroyed	1,063,200
Actually outstanding, as per Public Debt statement	32,086,300

X.—RÉSUMÉ.

Amount received from Printing Bureau exclusive of amount destroyed statistically		$904,657,860
On hand		341,881,460
Amount issued		562,776,400
Amount redeemed and destroyed	$529,626,900	
Amount redeemed but not destroyed	1,063,200	
Total amount redeemed to close of fiscal year		530,690,100
Total amount outstanding at close of fiscal year		32,086,300

H.—THREE PER CENT. CERTIFICATES.

I.—RECEIPTS AND REDEMPTIONS.

Received from Printing Bureau		$160,000,000
Redeemed	$72,930,000	
Destroyed statistically	1,980,000	
		74,910,000
		85,090,000
On hand		72,870,000
Outstanding as per Public Debt statement		12,220,000

II.—MOVEMENT OF THREE PER CENT. CERTIFICATES.

Forwarded to Assistant Treasurer, New York		$93,000,000
Redeemed	$72,930,000	
On hand in New York	7,850,000	
		80,780,000
Outstanding, as above		12,220,000

I.—TEMPORARY-LOAN CERTIFICATES.

Outstanding 4 per cents:		
Payable at the Cincinnati office	$75,000	
Total of 4 per cents		$75,000
Outstanding 5 per cents:		
Payable at the New York office	$500	
Payable at the Washington office	405	
Total of 5 per cents		905

Outstanding 6 per cents:

Payable at the Cincinnati office	$1,400	
Payable at the Philadelphia office	1,000	
Payable at the Washington office	255	
Total of 6 per cents		$2,655
Total of all kinds outstanding		78,560

These certificates ceased bearing interest August 26, 1866.

K.—CERTIFICATES OF INDEBTEDNESS.

I.—ISSUED, REDEEMED, AND OUTSTANDING.

Old series issued:

Numbers 1 to 153,662, of $1,000		$153,662,000 00
Numbers 1 to 14,500, of $5,000		72,500,000 00
Numbers 15,001 to 31,010, of $5,000		80,050,000 00
Numbers 31,111 to 69,268, of $5,000		190,790,000 00
Numbers 1 to 13, of various amounts		1,591,241 65
Total of first series issued		498,593,241 65

New series issued:

Numbers 1 to 15,145, of $1,000	$15,145,000 00	
Numbers 1 to 9,603, of $5,000	48,015,000 00	
Total of second series issued		63,160,000 00
Total amount issued		561,753,241 65
*Redeemed to July 1, 1872		$561,748,241 65
Outstanding, as per Debt statement		5,000 00
		561,753,241 65

Five certificates, of the denomination of $1,000, are outstanding, two of which are caveated.

II.—PRINCIPAL AND INTEREST PAID.

Total amount of interest paid to July 1, 1872	$31,157,108 61
Principal paid as above stated	561,748,241 65
Total principal and interest paid to July 1, 1872	592,905,350 26

L.—TREASURY NOTES OF 1861.

Denominations.	Issued.	Redeemed.	Outstanding.
50s	$2,303,800	$2,302,050	$1,750
100s	4,495,800	4,494,400	1,400
500s	6,832,500	6,832,500	
1,000s	8,836,000	8,836,000	
Totals	22,468,100	22,464,950	3,150

*No redemptions during the year.

M.—SEVEN-THIRTIES OF 1861, AND OF 1864 AND 1865.

I.—CONVERSIONS AND REDEMPTIONS.

1.—*Conversions and redemptions during fiscal year by series and denominations, and in gross amounts during former years.*

Seven-Thirties of 1861:	
1 One Hundred	$100
3 One Thousands	3,000
Redeemed during fiscal year	3,100
Redeemed previous to July 1, 1871	140,071,650
Total amount redeemed	140,074,750
Outstanding July 1, 1872	20,000
Total original issue	140,094,750
First series, August 15, 1864:	
154 Fifties	$7,700
88 One Hundreds	8,800
14 Five Hundreds	7,000
3 One Thousands	3,000
Redeemed during fiscal year	26,500
Redeemed previous to July 1, 1871	299,864,650
Total amount redeemed	299,891,150
Outstanding July 1, 1872	101,350
Total original issue	299,992,500
Second series, June 15, 1865:	
95 Fifties	$4,750
125 One Hundreds	12,500
27 Five Hundreds	13,500
16 One Thousands	16,000
Redeemed during fiscal year	46,750
Redeemed previous to July 1, 1871	330,864,450
Total amount redeemed	330,911,200
Outstanding July 1, 1872	88,800
Total original issue	331,000,000
Third series, July 15, 1865:	
298 Fifties	$14,900
190 One Hundreds	19,000
17 Five Hundreds	8,500
5 One Thousands	5,000
Redeemed during fiscal year	47,400
Redeemed previous to July 1, 1871	198,810,600
Total amount redeemed	198,858,000
Outstanding July 1, 1872	142,000
Total original issue	199,000,000

2.—*Recapitulation of all the issues converted and redeemed.*

547 Fifties	$27,350
404 One Hundreds	40,400
58 Five Hundreds	29,000
27 One Thousands	27,000

Redeemed during fiscal year	$123,750
Redeemed previous to July 1, 1871	969,611,350
Total amount redeemed	969,735,100
Outstanding July 1, 1872	352,150
Total	970,087,250

II.—OUTSTANDING.

1.—*Statement by series and denominations of Seven-Thirties of* 1861, *and of* 1864 *and* 1865, *outstanding June* 30, 1872.

Seven-Thirties of 1861:

70 Fifties	$3,500
65 One Hundreds	6,500
6 Five Hundreds	3,000
7 One Thousands	7,000
Total	20,000

First series, August 15, 1864:

599 Fifties	$29,950
429 One Hundreds	42,900
39 Five Hundreds	19,500
9 One Thousands	9,000
Total	101,350

Second series, June 15, 1865:

157 Fifties	$7,850
264½ One Hundreds	26,450
69 Five Hundreds	34,500
20 One Thousands	20,000
Total	88,800

Third series, July 15, 1865:

725 Fifties	$36,250
662½ One Hundreds	66,250
37 Five Hundreds	18,500
21 One Thousands	21,000
Total	142,000

2.—*Recapitulation of the four series combined, outstanding.*

1,551 Fifties	$77,550
1,421 One Hundreds	142,100
151 Five Hundreds	75,500
57 One Thousands	57,000
Total	352,150

N.—RETIREMENT OF FIVE-TWENTY BONDS.

I.—PURCHASES.

1.—Purchased during fiscal year.

Loan.	Coupon.	Registered.	Total.	Premium paid.	Accrued interest paid.
5-20s, 1862	$9,040,050	$9,519,650	$18,559,700	$2,097,372 97	$205,452 19
5-20s, March, 1864	....	81,100	81,100	9,848 93	873 83
5-20s, June, 1864	4,861,850	2,886,100	7,747,950	915,350 19	102,585 31
5-20s, 1865	600,150	4,733,300	5,333,450	626,071 15	52,922 82
Consols, 1865	13,394,350	4,962,900	18,357,250	2,278,981 97	290,714 43
Consols, 1867	5,919,500	1,735,050	7,654,550	927,475 08	122,444 62
Consols, 1868	60,300	34,500	94,800	11,121 99	1,573 89
Total	33,876,200	23,952,600	57,828,800	6,866,222 28	776,567 09

2.—Purchased from May 11, 1869, (date of first purchase,) to July 1, 1872.

Loan.	Coupon.	Registered.	Total.	Premium paid.	Accrued interest paid.
5-20s, 1862	$11,663,200	$32,745,150	$44,408,350	$5,263,431 51	$496,690 29
5-20s, March, 1864	....	1,063,500	1,063,500	179,079 73	13,234 66
5-20s, June, 1864	24,213,650	11,568,950	35,782,600	4,371,856 35	441,901 95
5-20s, 1865	17,057,850	15,207,700	32,265,550	3,638,179 05	370,676 46
Consols, 1865	80,140,600	22,368,350	102,508,950	12,431,861 93	1,399,451 95
Consols, 1867	42,699,150	10,837,450	53,536,600	7,015,878 67	742,073 76
Consols, 1868	2,551,000	519,000	3,070,000	500,486 10	41,480 76
Total	178,325,450	94,310,100	272,635,550	33,400,773 34	3,505,509 83

3.—Sinking Fund.

(These bonds are all included in statement 2, above.)

a.—Condition of Sinking Fund, July 1, 1871.

Loan.	Principal.	Premium paid.	Accrued interest paid.
5-20s of 1862	$7,956,000 00	$975,752 62	$90,036 89
5-20s of March, 1864	184,500 00	29,757 55	1,687 97
5-20s of June, 1864	8,989,750 00	1,010,477 26	103,119 88
5-20s of 1865	10,023,850 00	1,011,632 67	132,056 65
Consols of 1865	22,215,350 00	2,386,985 01	255,402 61
Consols of 1867	16,703,600 00	2,152,126 24	258,889 79
Consols of 1868	706,100 00	107,591 06	13,984 84
Total	66,779,150 00	7,674,322 41	855,178 63

b.—Addition to Sinking Fund during the year.

Loan.	Principal.	Premium paid.	Accrued interest paid.
5-20s of 1862	$6,417,850 00	$764,055 21	$75,179 43
5-20s of March, 1864	127,100 00	14,959 03	1,338 70
5-20s of June, 1864	3,604,650 00	438,656 16	57,449 80
5-20s of 1865	3,635,200 00	436,838 70	37,817 37
Consols of 1865	11,788,900 00	1,436,989 46	149,248 21
Consols of 1867	6,958,900 00	833,600 15	108,487 92
Consols of 1868	85,850 00	9,951 63	1,386 95
Total	32,618,450 00	3,935,050 34	430,908 38

c.—Condition of Sinking Fund, July 1, 1872.

Loan.	Principal.	Premium paid.	Accrued interest paid.
5-20s of 1862	$14,373,850 00	$1,739,807 83	$165,216 32
5-20s of March, 1864	311,600 00	44,716 58	3,026 67
5-20s of June, 1864	12,594,400 00	1,449,133 42	160,569 68
5-20s of 1865	13,659,050 00	1,448,471 37	169,874 02
Consols of 1865	34,004,250 00	3,823,974 47	404,650 82
Consols of 1867	23,662,500 00	2,985,726 39	367,377 71
Consols of 1868	791,950 00	117,542 69	15,371 79
Total	99,397,600 00	11,609,372 75	1,286,087 01

II.—CONVERSIONS OF FIVE-TWENTIES INTO THE FUNDED LOAN OF 1881.

1.—*Conversions during fiscal year.*

Loan.	Coupon.	Registered.	Total.
5-20s of 1862	$439,850	$352,450	$792,300
5-20s of June, 1864	118,350	373,650	492,000
5-20s of 1865	489,850	130,250	620,100
Consols of 1865	842,850	371,800	1,214,650
Consols of 1867	105,250	181,850	287,100
Consols of 1868	3,050		3,050
Total	1,999,200	1,410,000	3,409,200

2.—*Total conversions to date.*

Loan.	Coupons.	Registered.	Total.
5-20s of 1862	$1,089,850	$25,081,550	$26,171,400
5-20s of March, 1864		380,500	380,500
5-20s of June, 1864	930,800	11,287,850	12,218,650
5-20s of 1865	1,449,600	8,137,000	9,586,600
Consols of 1865	2,685,650	6,017,950	8,703,600
Consols of 1867	1,897,350	3,908,500	5,805,850
Consols of 1868	24,750	187,000	211,750
Total	8,078,000	55,000,350	63,078,350

III.—REDEMPTIONS OF FIVE-TWENTIES.

1.—*Redemptions of 5-20s of 1862, designated by notices of Secretary dated September 1, December 7, and December 20, 1871.*

Under notice of—	Coupon.	Registered.	Total.
September 1, 1871, (first call)	$79, 643, 400	$18, 088, 300	$97, 731, 700
December 7, 1871, (second call)	12, 958, 550	2, 285, 650	15, 244, 200
December 20, 1871, (third call)	16, 304, 900	2, 317, 800	18, 622, 700
Total	108, 906, 850	22, 691, 750	131, 598, 600

2.—*Redemptions of 5-20s not included in above.*

Loan.	Coupon.	Registered.	Total.
5-20s of 1862	$17, 605, 700	$15, 875, 550	$33, 481, 250
5-20s of March, 1864		89, 000	89, 000
5-20s of June, 1864	9, 350	4, 844, 150	4, 853, 500
5-20s of 1865	50	2, 015, 800	2, 015, 850
Consols of 1868	150		150
Total	17, 615, 250	22, 824, 500	40, 439, 750

3.—*Total redemptions of 5-20s to date.*

Loan.	Coupon.	Registered.	Total.
5-20s of 1862	$126, 512, 550 00	$38, 567, 300 00	$165, 079, 850 00
5-20s of March, 1864		89, 000 00	89, 000 00
5-20s of June, 1864	9, 350 00	4, 844, 150 00	4, 853, 500 00
5-20s of 1865	50 00	2, 015, 800 00	2, 015, 850 00
Consols of 1868	150 00		150 00
Total	126, 522, 100 00	45, 516, 250 00	172, 038, 350 00

IV.—FIVE-TWENTY BONDS RETIRED DURING FISCAL YEAR.

Loan.	Coupon.	Registered.	Total.
5-20s of 1862	$135, 992, 450 00	$48, 439, 400 00	$184, 431, 850 00
5-20s of March, 1864		170, 100 00	170, 100 00
5-20s of June, 1864	4, 989, 550 00	8, 103, 900 00	13, 093, 450 00
5-20s of 1865	1, 090, 050 00	6, 879, 350 00	7, 969, 400 00
Consols of 1865	14, 237, 200 00	5, 334, 700 00	19, 571, 900 00
Consols of 1867	6, 024, 750 00	1, 916, 900 00	7, 941, 650 00
Consols of 1868	63, 500 00	34, 500 00	98, 000 00
Total	162, 397, 500 00	70, 878, 850 50	233, 276, 350 00

V.—TOTAL OF FIVE-TWENTY BONDS RETIRED TO JULY 1, 1872.

Loan.	Coupon.	Registered.	Total.
5-20s of 1862	$139,265,600 00	$96,394,000 00	$235,659,600 00
5-20s of March, 1864	....	1,533,000 00	1,533,000 00
5-20s of June, 1864	25,153,800 00	27,700,950 00	52,854,750 00
5-20s of 1865	18,507,500 00	25,360,500 00	43,868,000 00
Consols of 1865	82,826,250 00	28,386,300 00	111,212,550 00
Consols of 1867	44,596,500 00	14,745,950 00	59,342,450 00
Consols of 1868	2,575,900 00	706,000 00	3,281,900 00
Total	312,925,550 00	194,826,700 00	507,752,250 00

VI.—COST OF PURCHASED FIVE-TWENTIES.

1.—*Statement of purchase of Five-Twenty Bonds, showing their net cost in gold and currency, the average gold cost of each purchase, and the average gold cost of all the purchases made prior to the end of each month, from May, 1869, to July 1, 1872.*

Date of purchase.	Principal.	Net cost.	Net cost estimated in gold.	Av. gold cost of a $100 bond.	Av. gold cost of total purchase to date.
May 12, 1869	$1,000,000	$1,152,565 64	$832,177 36	$83.22	....
May 19, 1869	70,000	81,718 00	57,548 45	82.21	....
May 19, 1869	1,000,000	1,168,512 10	822,895 85	82.29	....
May 27, 1869	1,000,000	1,153,581 50	826,940 14	82.69	$82.72
June 3, 1869	1,000,000	1,164,770 68	842,510 43	84.25	....
June 10, 1869	1,000,000	1,161,967 00	838,208 84	83.82	....
June 16, 1869	1,000	1,155 00	835 44	83.54	....
June 17, 1869	1,000,000	1,152,950 00	833,960 21	83.40	....
June 23, 1869	1,620,000	1,870,402 50	1,364,012 76	84.20	....
June 26, 1869	1,000,000	1,158,228 25	842,347 82	84.23	83.55
July 1, 1869	1,000,000	1,158,098 75	842,253 63	84.22	....
July 3, 1869	3,000,000	3,496,474 00	2,552,170 80	85.07	....
July 9, 1869	3,000,000	3,518,044 00	2,586,797 06	86.23	....
July 14, 1869	3,000,000	3,607,622 90	2,626,113 12	87.54	....
July 15, 1869	1,000,000	1,201,850 00	877,262 77	87.73	....
July 21, 1869	3,000,000	3,600,028 80	2,664,221 12	88.81	....
July 28, 1869	3,000,000	3,604,859 00	2,640,922 34	88.03	....
July 29, 1869	1,000,000	1,201,570 55	885,134 84	88.51	85.93
August 4, 1869	2,000,000	2,431,136 80	1,787,600 59	89.38	....
August 11, 1869	2,000,000	2,422,038 27	1,787,482 12	89.37	....
August 12, 1869	1,000,000	1,198,931 70	887,276 00	88.73	....
August 18, 1869	2,000,000	2,378,781 81	1,788,557 75	89.43	....
August 25, 1869	2,000,000	2,389,539 01	1,793,275 07	89.66	....
August 26, 1869	1,000,000	1,196,247 80	893,555 78	89.36	86.87
September 1, 1869	2,000,000	2,401,991 00	1,800,930 46	90.05	....
September 8, 1869	2,000,000	2,356,000 00	1,732,352 94	86.62	....
September 9, 1869	1,000,000	1,183,972 53	871,368 92	87.14	....
September 15, 1869	2,000,000	2,369,639 55	1,740,782 04	87.04	....
September 22, 1869	2,000,000	2,337,657 62	1,697,029 12	84.85	....
September 23, 1869	1,000,000	1,165,548 50	822,982 17	82.30	....
September 25, 1869	3,000,000	3,537,158 16	2,647,078 14	88.24	....
September 29, 1869	3,000,000	3,473,533 12	2,599,463 51	86.65	86.90
October 6, 1869	2,000,000	2,319,139 18	1,783,953 22	89.20	....
October 7, 1869	1,000,000	1,159,945 10	884,610 18	88.46	....
October 7, 1869	153,500	178,187 69	135,891 47	88.53	....
October 13, 1869	2,000,000	2,318,883 53	1,782,043 06	89.10	....
October 20, 1869	2,000,000	2,314,079 00	1,780,060 77	89.00	....
October 21, 1869	1,000,000	1,152,000 00	885,302 59	88.53	....

1.—*Statement of purchase of Five-Twenty Bonds, &c.*—Continued.

Date of purchase.	Principal.	Net cost.	Net cost estimated in gold.	Av. gold cost of a $100 bond.	Av. gold cost of total purchase to date.
October 27, 1869	$2,000,000	$2,292,600 00	$1,761,844 38	$88.09	$87.20
November 3, 1869	2,000,000	2,257,255 21	1,768,662 26	88.43	....
November 4, 1869	1,000,000	1,126,843 74	889,906 21	88.99	....
November 4, 1869	1,000,000	1,129,090 29	891,680 39	89.17	....
November 5, 1869	201,300	227,413 00	179,773 12	89.31	....
November 5, 1869	433,000	489,241 07	386,751 83	89.32	....
November 10, 1869	2,000,000	2,259,000 00	1,780,492 61	89.02	....
November 17, 1869	2,000,000	2,256,513 69	1,775,035 35	88.75	....
November 17, 1869	1,000,000	1,129,039 02	888,132 95	88.81	....
November 24, 1869	3,000,000	3,382,483 67	2,671,200 54	89.04	87.48
December 1, 1869	2,000,000	2,206,992 21	1,807,158 41	90.36	....
December 2, 1869	1,000,000	1,102,659 61	901,971 06	90.20	....
December 8, 1869	2,000,000	2,248,236 56	1,818,593 78	90.93	....
December 15, 1869	2,000,000	2,239,710 90	1,839,598 27	91.98	....
December 16, 1869	1,000,000	1,118,412 34	919,557 94	91.96	....
December 22, 1869	2,000,000	2,215,985 83	1,844,733 26	92.24	....
December 29, 1869	2,000,000	2,220,427 12	1,852,285 40	92.61	....
December 30, 1869	1,000,000	1,110,507 80	926,388 15	92.64	88.20
January 5, 1870	2,000,000	2,246,595 03	1,876,071 01	93.80	....
January 11, 1870	451,700	517,400 49	422,367 75	93.51	....
January 11, 1870	1,342,550	1,539,794 35	1,256,974 98	93.63	....
January 13, 1870	1,000,000	1,141,010 09	938,137 79	93.81	....
January 19, 1870	2,000,000	2,281,555 49	1,877,823 45	93.89	....
January 27, 1870	1,000,000	1,142,872 27	936,780 55	93.68	88.55
February 10, 1870	1,000,000	1,126,500 00	932,919 25	93.30	....
February 11, 1870	50,000	56,325 00	46,888 66	93.78	....
February 24, 1870	1,000,000	1,115,764 80	948,577 94	94.86	....
February 24, 1870	1,000,000	1,117,488 85	950,043 66	95.04	88.73
March 2, 1870	1,000,000	1,107,377 50	951,559 61	95.16	....
March 10, 1870	1,000,000	1,067,347 35	961,574 19	96.16	....
March 17, 1870	1,000,000	1,067,480 27	953,107 39	95.31	....
March 24, 1870	1,000,000	1,060,440 34	942,613 63	94.26	....
March 30, 1870	1,000,000	1,069,985 26	956,411 41	95.64	89.04
April 7, 1870	1,000,000	1,070,574 91	955,870 46	95.59	....
April 13, 1870	1,000,000	1,073,953 37	954,625 22	95.46	....
April 21, 1870	1,000,000	1,078,778 18	951,513 28	95.15	....
April 27, 1870	1,000,000	1,100,490 79	966,402 45	96.64	....
April 30, 1870	345,400	383,020 40	333,423 63	96.53	....
April 30, 1870	758,800	840,929 55	732,038 78	96.47	89.36
May 5, 1870	2,000,000	2,215,447 70	1,932,778 80	96.64	....
May 12, 1870	1,850	2,070 46	1,794 55	97.00	....
May 12, 1870	1,000,000	1,118,370 86	969,335 52	96.93	....
May 19, 1870	2,000,000	2,230,611 87	1,943,888 34	97.19	....
May 26, 1870	1,000,000	1,108,910 71	970,600 18	97.06	89.76
June 2, 1870	2,000,000	2,223,786 41	1,942,171 53	97.11	....
June 9, 1870	1,000,000	1,109,976 64	977,952 99	97.79	....
June 16, 1870	2,000,000	2,217,755 94	1,960,447 24	98.02	....
June 23, 1870	1,000,000	1,104,612 10	989,574 11	98.96	....
June 30, 1870	2,000,000	2,218,005 71	1,987,015 19	99.35	90.31
July 7, 1870	1,000,000	1,107,000 00	987,290 97	98.73	....
July 11, 1870	690,400	758,749 60	659,065 88	95.46	....
July 11, 1870	1,683,150	1,848,423 98	1,605,580 00	95.39	....
July 14, 1870	2,000,000	2,182,332 89	1,933,406 77	96.67	....
July 21, 1870	1,000,000	1,070,136 00	878,961 81	87.90	....
July 28, 1870	2,000,000	2,162,085 83	1,777,665 64	88.88	90.52
August 4, 1870	1,000,000	1,085,712 21	891,755 41	89.17	....
August 11, 1870	2,000,000	2,191,414 93	1,885,088 11	94.25	....
August 18, 1870	1,000,000	1,097,329 29	939,896 61	93.99	....
August 25, 1870	2,000,000	2,181,093 02	1,850,344 02	92.52	90.62
September 1, 1870	1,000,000	1,091,038 65	937,519 78	93.75	....
September 8, 1870	3,000,000	3,272,957 77	2,871,015 58	$95.70	....

1.—*Statement of purchase of Five-Twenty Bonds, &c.*—Continued.

Date of purchase.	Principal.	Net cost.	Net cost estimated in gold.	Av. gold cost of a $100 bond.	Av. gold cost of total purchase to date.
September 15, 1870	$2,000,000	$2,183,503 11	$1,909,073 76	$95.45	....
September 22, 1870	3,000,000	3,281,789 74	2,881,922 93	96.06	....
September 29, 1870	2,000,000	2,177,057 86	1,911,796 14	95.59	$90.98
October 6, 1870	2,000,000	2,174,300 26	1,924,159 52	96.21	....
October 13, 1870	2,000,000	2,170,465 37	1,906,006 91	95.30	....
October 20, 1870	2,000,000	2,170,236 48	1,922,690 12	96.13	....
October 27, 1870	2,000,000	2,165,529 30	1,933,508 30	96.68	91.24
November 3, 1870	1,000,000	1,077,698 19	973,090 92	97.31	....
November 3, 1870	245,850	265,173 81	239,434 59	97.39	....
November 3, 1870	542,250	584,800 55	528,036 61	97.39	....
November 10, 1870	1,000,000	1,072,263 90	971,473 52	97.15	....
November 17, 1870	1,000,000	1,064,972 36	942,453 42	94.25	....
November 25, 1870	1,000,000	1,065,650 15	951,473 35	95.15	91.39
December 1, 1870	1,000,000	1,064,917 08	962,636 91	96.26	....
December 8, 1870	1,000,000	1,063,854 32	961,676 22	96.17	....
December 15, 1870	1,000,000	1,065,972 75	958,177 75	95.82	....
December 22, 1870	1,000,000	1,064,459 26	962,223 06	96.22	....
December 29, 1870	1,000,000	1,064,473 95	961,150 29	96.11	91.53
January 4, 1871	2,000,000	2,147,345 03	1,938,911 99	96.96	....
January 11, 1871	1,000,000	1,074,257 50	967,799 55	96.78	....
January 18, 1871	2,000,000	2,144,457 32	1,938,492 49	96.92	....
January 25, 1871	1,000,000	1,074,651 96	971,436 80	97.14	91.72
February 1, 1871	2,000,000	2,173,985 90	1,943,227 62	97.16	....
February 8, 1871	2,000,000	2,175,643 46	1,946,884 53	97.34	....
February 15, 1871	2,000,000	2,184,170 19	1,963,299 05	98.16	....
February 21, 1871	2,000,000	2,191,633 24	1,970,007 41	98.50	91.99
March 1, 1871	2,000,000	2,199,585 00	1,983,842 16	99.19	....
March 8, 1871	2,000,000	2,199,570 48	1,977,142 00	98.85	....
March 15, 1871	2,000,000	2,191,702 96	1,967,859 00	98.39	....
March 22, 1871	2,000,000	2,188,826 83	1,974,139 19	98.71	....
March 29, 1871	2,000,000	2,183,254 76	1,980,276 42	99.01	92.34
April 3, 1871	216,000	235,807 20	213,884 08	99.02	....
April 5, 1871	3,000,000	3,295,500 00	2,985,730 46	99.52	....
April 12, 1871	2,000,000	2,197,018 24	1,995,022 24	99.75	....
April 19, 1871	3,000,000	3,317,193 80	2,971,730 17	99.06	....
April 26, 1871	2,000,000	2,215,181 72	1,997,909 10	99.90	92.71
May 3, 1871	2,000,000	2,221,571 71	1,999,164 64	99.96	....
May 10, 1871	2,000,000	2,223,162 54	1,998,348 35	99.92	....
May 17, 1871	2,000,000	2,228,989 07	1,992,392 46	99.62	....
May 24, 1871	2,000,000	2,224,133 69	1,992,504 98	99.63	....
May 31, 1871	2,000,000	2,225,697 79	1,989,450 54	99.47	93.04
June 7, 1871	1,000,000	1,115,811 40	994,041 33	99.40	....
June 14, 1871	1,000,000	1,114,175 30	991,479 69	99.15	....
June 21, 1871	1,000,000	1,116,587 05	993,625 85	99.36	....
June 28, 1871	1,000,000	1,118,691 60	988,898 65	98.89	93.16
July 5, 1871	1,000,000	1,132,384 49	997,695 59	99.77	....
July 12, 1871	1,000,000	1,122,692 96	999,059 35	99.91	....
July 19, 1871	385,600	433,278 38	385,136 33	99.88	....
July 26, 1871	1,000,000	1,122,086 99	999,632 06	99.96	93.20
August 2, 1871	162,750	182,407 63	162,682 39	99.96	....
August 9, 1871	20,100	22,509 99	20,098 20	99.99	....
August 16, 1871	1,000,000	1,122,127 56	999,668 21	99.97	....
August 23, 1871	1,000,000	1,121,011 54	998,673 98	99.87	....
August 30, 1871	1,000,000	1,125,650 82	993,952 16	99.39	93.35
September 6, 1871	1,000,010	1,128,864 31	991,318 82	99.13	....
September 13, 1871	1,000,000	1,125,800 00	988,627 88	98.86	....
September 20, 1871	3,000,000	3,375,135 99	2,957,402 84	98.58	....
September 25, 1871	3,000,000	3,397,836 15	2,954,640 13	98.49	....
September 27, 1871	2,000,000	2,262,400 68	1,975,895 78	98.79	93.50
October 4, 1871	2,000,000	2,258,747 45	1,981,357 41	99.07	....
October 11, 1871	4,000,000	4,470,310 00	3,917,029 57	97.93	....

1.—*Statement of purchase of Five-Twenty Bonds, &c.*—Continued.

Date of purchase.	Principal.	Net cost.	Net cost estimated in gold.	Av. gold cost of a $100 bond.	Av. gold coin of total purchase to date.
October 18, 1871	$4,000,000	$4,414,343 08	$3,915,160 16	$97.88	....
October 18, 1871	50,000	55,160 00	48,922 39	97.84	....
October 25, 1871	2,000,000	2,217,901 51	1,986,921 84	99.35	$93.82
November 1, 1871	1,000,000	1,113,421 29	994,126 15	99.41	....
November 8, 1871	1,000,000	1,114,150 87	998,119 48	99.81	....
November 15, 1871	21,100	23,452 74	21,081 11	99.88	....
November 21, 1871	1,000,000	1,107,389 47	999,900 20	99.99	93.90
December 6, 1871	517,450	568,325 56	517,247 38	99.96	....
December 13, 1871	43,700	47,734 84	43,693 21	99.99	....
December 20, 1871	81,000	88,083 15	80,996 00	99.99	....
December 27, 1871	240,550	260,908 91	240,469 04	99.97	93.91
January 4, 1872	566,200	617,775 00	566,116 84	99.99	....
January 18, 1872	899,750	978,713 38	897,902 18	99.80	93.95
February 1, 1872	1,000,000	1,091,919 01	994,914 81	99.49	....
February 15, 1872	1,000,000	1,092,584 13	991,006 01	99.10	....
February 29, 1872	1,000,000	1,091,388 34	984,341 23	98.43	94.02
March 14, 1872	1,000,000	1,092,821 91	992,346 80	99.23	....
March 28, 1872	1,000,000	1,095,961 25	992,943 37	99.29	94.05
April 3, 1872	1,000,000	1,097,435 25	998,803 41	99.88	....
April 10, 1872	1,000,000	1,100,721 08	998,386 46	99.84	....
April 17, 1872	2,000,000	2,213,295 42	1,996,207 82	99.81	....
April 24, 1872	263,850	294,794 93	263,503 85	99.87	94.15
May 1, 1872	691,650	776,203 34	691,495 18	99.98	....
May 8, 1872	5,000	5,640 00	4,963 70	99.27	....
May 8, 1872	4,000,000	4,519,795 84	3,977,818 12	99.44	....
May 15, 1872	3,000,000	3,395,826 68	2,978,795 34	99.29	....
May 22, 1872	2,000,000	2,267,116 41	1,993,069 37	99.65	....
May 29, 1872	2,000,000	2,274,174 67	1,997,079 84	99.85	94.38
June 5, 1872	825,950	945,245 28	824,641 46	99.84	....
June 12, 1872	47,850	54,486 79	47,795 42	99.88	....
June 19, 1872	921,900	1,047,373 04	919,756 79	99.77	....
June 26, 1872	1,084,400	1,227,634 17	1,082,808 53	99.85	94.44

2.—*Statement by loans, showing net cost in currency and gold of bonds purchased, and average gold cost of all the purchases to July 1, 1872.*

Loan.	Principal.	Net cost.	Net cost estimated in gold.	Average cost in gold per $100 of total purchase to date.
5-20s, 1862	$44,408,350	$19,670,843 37	$42,499,932 16	$95.70
5-20s, March, 1864	1,063,500	1,242,567 25	974,024 23	91.59
5-20s, June, 1864	35,782,600	40,150,432 03	33,869,985 92	94.65
5-20s, 1865	32,265,550	35,903,675 57	30,899,527 94	95.77
Consols, 1865	102,508,950	114,915,828 25	97,061,222 67	94.69
Consols, 1867	53,536,600	60,551,733 75	49,431,326 47	92.33
Consols, 1868	3,070,000	3,570,394 20	2,737,278 78	89.16
Total	272,635,550	306,005,474 42	257,473,298 17	94.44

O.—INTEREST.

I.—COIN COUPONS.

1.—*Coupon interest paid in coin during the fiscal year, by loans and denominations.*

Number of coupons of each loan.	Denominations.	Amount.	Total.
Loans of 1858:			
28,009	Twenty-Five Dollars		$700,225 00
Loans of 1860:			
3	Twenty-Five Dollars		75 00
Loan of February 1861, (1881s:)			
9,551	Thirty Dollars		286,530 00
Oregon War Debt:			
376	Three Dollars	$1,128 00	
923	Six Dollars	5,538 00	
3,389	Fifteen Dollars	50,835 00	
			57,501 00
Loan of July and August, 1861, (1881s:)			
6,336	One Dollar and Fifty Cts.	9,504 00	
28,391	Three Dollars	85,173 00	
55,166	Fifteen Dollars	827,490 00	
99,743	Thirty Dollars	2,992,290 00	
			3,914,457 00
Five-Twenties, 1862:			
139,664	One Dollar and Fifty Cts.	209,496 00	
381,245	Three Dollars	1,143,735 00	
235,121	Fifteen Dollars	3,526,815 00	
496,679	Thirty Dollars	14,900,370 00	
7	Fractional	19 79	
			19,780,435 79
Loan of 1863, (1881s:)			
2,820	One Dollar and Fifty Cts.	4,230 00	
9,552	Three Dollars	28,656 00	
11,622	Fifteen Dollars	174,330 00	
36,596	Thirty Dollars	1,097,880 00	
			1,305,096 00
Ten-Forties of 1864:			
4,999	Two Dollars and Fifty Cts.	12,497 50	
16,675	Five Dollars	83,375 00	
49,602	Twelve Dollars and Fifty Cents	620,025 00	
86,047	Twenty-Five Dollars	2,151 175 00	
1,376	Fractional	3,029 28	
			2,870,101 78
Five-Twenties of June, 1864:			
5,645	One Dollar and Fifty Cts.	8,467 50	
26,430	Three Dollars	79,290 00	
25,547	Fifteen Dollars	383,205 00	
66,203	Thirty Dollars	1,986,090 00	
			2,457,052 50
Five-Twenties of 1865:			
1,163	One Dollar and Fifty Cts.	1,744 50	
35,987	Three Dollars	107,961 00	
68,476	Fifteen Dollars	1,027,140 00	
202,086	Thirty Dollars	6,062,580 00	
			7,199,425 50

1.—*Coupon interest paid in coin during the fiscal year, &c.*—Continued.

Number of coupons of each loan.	Denominations.	Amount.	Total.
Consols of 1865:			
109,047	One Dollar and Fifty Cts.	$163,570 50	
221,148	Three Dollars	663,444 00	
142,949	Fifteen Dollars	2,144,235 00	
243,437	Thirty Dollars	7,303,110 00	
50	Fractional	500 00	
			$10,274,859 50
Consols of 1867:			
173,194	One Dollar and Fifty Cts.	259,791 00	
347,510	Three Dollars	1,042,530 00	
191,808	Fifteen Dollars	2,877,120 00	
330,346	Thirty Dollars	9,910,380 00	
			14,089,821 00
Consols of 1868:			
20,395	One Dollar and Fifty Cts.	30,592 50	
51,760	Three Dollars	155,280 00	
20,805	Fifteen Dollars	312,075 00	
37,709	Thirty Dollars	1,131,270 00	
			1,629,217 50
Funded Loan of 1881:			
24,909	Sixty-Two Cents	15,443 58	
13,519	Sixty-Three Cents	8,516 97	
55,577	One Dollar and Twenty-Five Cents	69,471 25	
59,736	Six Dollars and Twenty-Five Cents	373,350 00	
219,197	Twelve Dollars and Fifty Cents	2,739,962 50	
			3,206,744 30
Seven-Thirties of 1861:			
1	Three Dollars and Sixty-Five Cents		3 65
Texas Indemnity Stock:			
9	Twenty-Five Dollars		225 00

2.—*Recapitulation by Loans.*

Title of loans.	No. of coupons.	Amount.
Loan of 1858	28,009	$700,225 00
Loan of 1860	3	75 00
Loan of February, 1861, (1881s)	9,551	286,530 00
Oregon War Debt	4,688	57,501 00
Loan of July and August, 1861, (1881s)	189,636	3,914,457 00
Five-Twenties of 1862	1,252,716	19,780,435 79
Loan of 1863, (1881s)	60,590	1,305,096 00
Ten-Forties of 1864	158,699	2,870,101 78
Five-Twenties of June, 1864	123,825	2,457,052 50
Five-Twenties of 1865	307,712	7,199,425 50
Consols of 1865	716,631	10,274,859 50
Consols of 1867	1,042,858	14,089,821 00
Consols of 1868	130,069	1,629,217 50
Funded Loan of 1881	372,938	3,206,744 30
Seven-Thirties of 1861	1	3 65
Texan Indemnity Stock	9	225 00
Total	4,399,535	67,771,770 52

II.—CURRENCY COUPONS.

There were paid in currency one thousand three hundred and sixty-six coupons, of twenty dollars each, from Certificates of Indebtedness of 1870, amounting to $27,320.

III.—QUARTERLY-INTEREST CHECKS FUNDED LOAN OF 1881.

Issued, paid, and outstanding July, 1872.

Amount of checks issued		$4,924,027 32
Paid by Treasurer, Washington	$42,379 97	
Paid by Assistant Treasurer, New York	3,513,650 11	
Paid by Assistant Treasurer, Philadelphia	358,857 45	
Paid by Assistant Treasurer, Boston	832,719 88	
Paid by Assistant Treasurer, Saint Louis	4,542 50	
Paid by Assistant Treasurer, New Orleans	96,997 50	
Paid by Assistant Treasurer, San Francisco	1,256 24	
Paid by Assistant Treasurer, Baltimore	24,457 50	
Paid by Depositary, Buffalo	8,293 75	
Paid by Depositary, Chicago	1,085 00	
Paid by Depositary, Cincinnati	6,103 75	
Paid by Depositary, Louisville	1,250 00	
Paid by Depositary, Pittsburgh	75 00	
Paid by Depositary, Mobile	1,250 00	
		4,892,918 65
Amount of checks outstanding		31,108 67

P.—TRUST FUNDS.

There remain in the custody of the Treasurer, held by the Secretary of the Treasury in trust for the Smithsonian fund, six per cent. stocks of the State of Arkansas, that matured in 1868, amounting at their par face value, interest excluded, to $538,000.

There are also held special deposits in sealed packages, the contents and value of which are unknown.

Q.—PAYMENTS BY CHECKS ON OTHER OFFICES.

There were drawn during the year transfer checks on Assistant Treasurers, as follows:

	Currency Checks:		
40,254	on New York	$35,594,737 28	
2,139	on Boston	2,928,134 46	
2,733	on Philadelphia	2,397,845 34	
662	on New Orleans	954,309 16	
207	on San Francisco	185,042 33	
45,995	Currency checks amounting to		$42,060,068 57
	Coin Checks:		
7,959	on New York	$173,232,961 46	
860	on Boston	2,829,437 37	
794	on Philadelphia	1,378,956 44	
8	on New Orleans	11,453 93	
15	on San Francisco	4,667 09	
9,636	Coin checks amounting to		177,457,476 29
55,631	Checks, coin and currency		219,517,544 86

R.—EMPLOYÉS.

1.—CHANGES IN THE EMPLOYÉS OF THE TREASURER'S OFFICE DURING FISCAL YEAR.

Total force of Treasurer's office June 30, 1871			346
Number of persons appointed during fiscal year ending June 30, 1872		62	
Deceased during same period	5		
Resigned during same period	15		
Transferred during same period	2		
Discharged during same period	12		
		34	
			28
Total force of Treasurer's office, June 30, 1872			374

R.—SALARIES PAID.

The amount disbursed for salaries to the employés of this office during the fiscal year, was as follows:

Regular Roll	$168, 102 93
Temporary Roll	228, 435 17
Additional compensation	8, 492 65
Total payments during the year	405, 030 75

S.—OFFICIAL CORRESPONDENCE.

LETTERS RECEIVED AND TRANSMITTED DURING FISCAL YEAR.

Received by mail, containing money	22, 120
Received by mail, containing no money	52, 585
Received by express, money-packages	38, 157
Total received	112, 862
Transmitted by mail, manuscript letters	4, 021
Transmitted by mail, printed forms filled in	74, 937
Transmitted by mail, drafts payable to order	23, 818
Transmitted by express, money-packages	32, 586
Total transmitted	135, 362

T.—RECEIPTS AND DISBURSEMENTS OF ASSISTANT TREASURERS OF THE UNITED STATES FOR THE FISCAL YEAR.

NEW YORK.

Balance June 30, 1871		$66, 556, 612 53
RECEIPTS.		
On account of Customs	$153, 615, 390 14	
On account of Gold Notes	63, 229, 500 00	
On account of Internal Revenue	6, 603, 666 93	
On account of Three Per Cent. Certificates	65, 000 00	
On account of Post-Office Department	7, 553, 093 41	
On account of Transfers	149, 902, 912 05	
On account of Patent Fees	32, 092 15	
On account of Miscellaneous	91, 066, 457 36	
On account of Disbursing Accounts	276, 382, 900 56	
On account of Bullion	3, 177, 482 90	
On account of Assay Office	126, 725 81	
On account of Interest, Coin	76, 497, 428 34	
On account of Interest, Currency	2, 690, 029 20	
		830, 942, 678 85
		897, 499, 291 38
DISBURSEMENTS.		
On account of Treasury Drafts	470, 100, 735 37	
On account of Post-Office Drafts	7, 304, 628 40	
On account of Disbursing Accounts	273, 982, 053 71	
On account of Bullion Account	3, 093, 036 72	
On account of Assay Office Account	144, 131 21	
On account of Interest, Coin	76, 527, 775 20	
On account of Interest, Currency	2, 690, 029 20	
		833, 842, 389 81
Balance June 30, 1872		63, 656, 901 57

BOSTON, MASSACHUSETTS.

Balance, June 30, 1871		$7,361,451 34
RECEIPTS.		
On account of Customs, (coin)	$25,522,478 30	
On account of Patent Fees	30,545 80	
On account of Sales of Internal-Revenue Stamps	946,343 00	
On account of Transfers	19,952,252 14	
On account of Miscellaneous	3,177,035 01	
On account of Interest Account, (registered)	6,673,674 72	
On account of Post-Office Department	518,275 94	
On account of Disbursing Officers' Accounts	18,872,593 81	
		75,693,298 72
		83,054,750 06
DISBURSEMENTS.		
On account of Treasury Drafts	$25,415,263 30	
On account of Transfers	15,386,320 88	
On account of Interest Account, (registered)	7,340,057 12	
On account of Interest Account, (coupon)	7,142,801 10	
On account of Post-Office Department	432,802 24	
On account of Disbursing Officers' Accounts	18,625,796 75	
		74,343,041 39
Balance June 30, 1872		8,711,708 67

PHILADELPHIA, PENNSYLVANIA.

Balance June 30, 1871		$8,217,514 12
RECEIPTS.		
On account of Customs	$8,498,688 76	
On account of Internal-Revenue Tax	334,190 30	
On account of Internal-Revenue Stamps	1,102,882 20	
On account of Transfers	19,419,040 60	
On account of Semi-Annual Duty	337,607 23	
On account of Patent Fees	13,999 10	
On account of Post-Offices	517,748 56	
On account of Disbursing Officers	13,426,074 43	
On account of Fractional Currency for Redemption	3,654,511 22	
On account of Interest Funds	3,467,404 00	
On account of Miscellaneous Funds	6,742,373 68	
		57,514,520 08
		65,732,034 20
DISBURSEMENTS.		
On account of Treasury Drafts	33,177,587 52	
On account of Post-Office Drafts	479,060 58	
On account of Disbursers' Checks	13,317,869 72	
On account of Fractional Currency Redeemed	3,647,927 22	
On account of Interest-Checks	6,979,289 16	
		57,601,734 20
Balance June 30, 1872		8,130,300 00

BALTIMORE MARYLAND.

Balance June 30, 1871		$2,493,126 22
RECEIPTS.		
On account of Disbursing Officers	$2,223,000 38	
On account of Internal Revenue	994,622 38	
On account of Duties on Imports	8,077,687 08	
On account of Customs	116,746 86	
On account of Gold Sales	5,067,828 97	

On account of Premiums	$599,202 33	
On account of Transfer of Funds	1,998,433 96	
On account of Post-Office Department	130,270 61	
On account of Currency Redemption	250,679 13	
On account of Semi-Annual Duties	59,936 50	
On account of Miscellaneous	129,667 94	
		$19,648,076 14
		22,141,202 36

DISBURSEMENTS.

On account of Disbursing-Officers' Checks	2,111,921 02	
On account of Drafts and Post-Office Warrants	4,067,032 71	
On account of Gold Sales	5,067,828 97	
On account of Interest on Public Debt, (Gold)	1,745,692 22	
On account of Interest on Public Debt, (Lawful Money)	48,240 00	
On account of Transfers	7,637,238 70	
On account of Five Per Cent. Notes and Interest	1,196 50	
On account of Currency Redemption	252,756 02	
On account of Miscellaneous	165 00	
		20,932,071 14
Balance June 30, 1872		1,209,131 22

SAN FRANCISCO, CALIFORNIA.

Balance June 30, 1871		$8,051,723 41

RECEIPTS.

On account of Customs	$8,425,130 35	
On account of Internal-Revenue Tax	3,132,691 37	
On account of Internal-Revenue Stamps	387,020 15	
On account of Sales of Land	505,456 26	
On account of Patent Fees	8,626 75	
On account of Loans	262,312 30	
On account of Various Sources	741,585 59	
On account of Transfers	4,029,960 20	
On account of Post-Office Department	280,819 73	
On account of Disbursing Officers	20,785,383 06	
		38,558,985 76
		46,610,709 17

DISBURSEMENTS.

On account of Treasury Drafts	9,936,299 45	
On account of Redemption Public Debt	26,969 50	
On account of Post-Office Department	326,301 20	
On account of Disbursing Officers	19,914,730 22	
On account of Transfers	9,486,000 00	
		39,690,300 37
Balance June 30, 1872		6,920,408 80

NEW ORLEANS, LOUISIANA.

Balance June 30, 1871		$2,920,308 06

RECEIPTS.

On account of Transfers	$5,995,362 15	
On account of Customs	5,732,489 60	
On account of Disbursing Officers	7,730,756 24	
On account of Post-Office Department	612,206 62	
On account of Miscellaneous	2,391,744 33	
		22,462,558 94
		25,382,867 00

DISBURSEMENTS.

On account of Disbursing Officers	$7,355,388 25	
On account of Post-Office Department	502,650 96	
On account of Treasurer United States, General Account,	9,791,121 05	
On account of Legal-Tender Notes Redeemed	3,217,000 00	
On account of Fractional Currency Redeemed	507,000 00	
On account of Interest	90,844 75	
		$21,464,005 01
Balance June 30, 1872		3,918,861 99

ST. LOUIS, MISSOURI.

Balance June 30, 1871		$2,730,887 99
RECEIPTS.		
On account of Transfers	$6,436,920 56	
On account of Duties	1,613,205 43	
On account of Revenue	632,558 47	
On account of Postal	673,974 42	
On account of Officers	5,682,397 57	
On account of Miscellaneous	2,116,105 63	
		17,155,162 08
		19,886,050 07
DISBURSEMENTS.		
On account of Treasurer's Drafts	9,066,858 09	
On account of Post-Office Warrants	640,636 94	
On account of Disbursing Officers	6,188,711 52	
On account of Coin Sales	928,487 59	
On account of Coin Interest and Drafts	1,118,605 07	
On account of Miscellaneous	8,578 26	
		17,951,877 47
Balance June 30, 1872		1,934,172 60

CHARLESTON, SOUTH CAROLINA.

Balance June 30, 1871		$395,958 01
RECEIPTS.		
On account of Customs, (Coin)	$146,128 59	
On account of Internal Revenue	488,027 97	
On account of Miscellaneous	1,291,647 37	
On account of Disbursing Officers	1,713,945 86	
On account of Post-Office Department	268,358 72	
On account of Interest, &c	9,921 09	
		3,918,029 60
		4,313,987 61
DISBURSEMENTS.		
On account of Treasury Drafts, &c	2,157,452 64	
On account of Disbursing Officers' Checks	1,655,986 58	
On account of Post-Office Drafts	231,781 59	
On account of Interest, &c	12,397 82	
		4,057,618 63
Balance June 30, 1872		256,368 98

Fractional currency received	$255,500 00
Fractional currency redeemed	94,320 49

U.—RECEIPTS AND DISBURSEMENTS OF DESIGNATED DEPOSITARIES OF THE UNITED STATES FOR THE FISCAL YEAR.

CHICAGO, ILLINOIS.

*Receipts from October 26, 1871, to June 30, 1872	$11,927,714 82
Disbursements from October 26, 1871, to June 30, 1872	10,956,528 03
Balance June 30, 1872	971,186 79

CINCINNATI, OHIO.

Balance June 30, 1871	$953,363 49
Receipts	19,425,116 98
Total	20,378,480 47
Disbursements	$19,878,058 89
Balance June 30, 1872	500,420 58
Total	20,378,480 47

LOUISVILLE, KENTUCKY.

Receipts	$4,273,392 67
Disbursements	$4,131,911 02
Balance June 30, 1872	141,481 65
Total	4,273,392 67

BUFFALO, NEW YORK.

Balance June 30, 1871	$208,932 04
Receipts	3,984,571 55
Total	4,193,503 59
Disbursements	$3,922,436 15
Balance June 30, 1872	271,067 44
Total	4,193,503 59

PITTSBURGH, PENNSYLVANIA.

Balance June 30, 1871	$626,535 47
Receipts	4,610,220 65
Total	5,236,756 12
Disbursements	$4,861,117 02
Balance June 30, 1872	375,639 10
Total	5,236,755 12

* As all the books, records, and papers of the Chicago Depositary were destroyed during the great fire, no complete report of the operations of that office from July 1, 1871, to October 26, 1871, can now be obtained.

SANTA FÉ, NEW MEXICO.

Balance June 30, 1871	$286,500 82
Receipts	3,421,180 64
Total	3,707,681 46
Disbursements	$3,417,970 80
Balance June 30, 1872	289,710 66
Total	3,707,681 46

TUCSON, ARIZONA.

Balance June 30, 1871	$14,533 11
Receipts	481,484 62
Total	496,017 73
Disbursements	$158,573 59
Balance June 30, 1872	337,444 14
Total	496,017 73

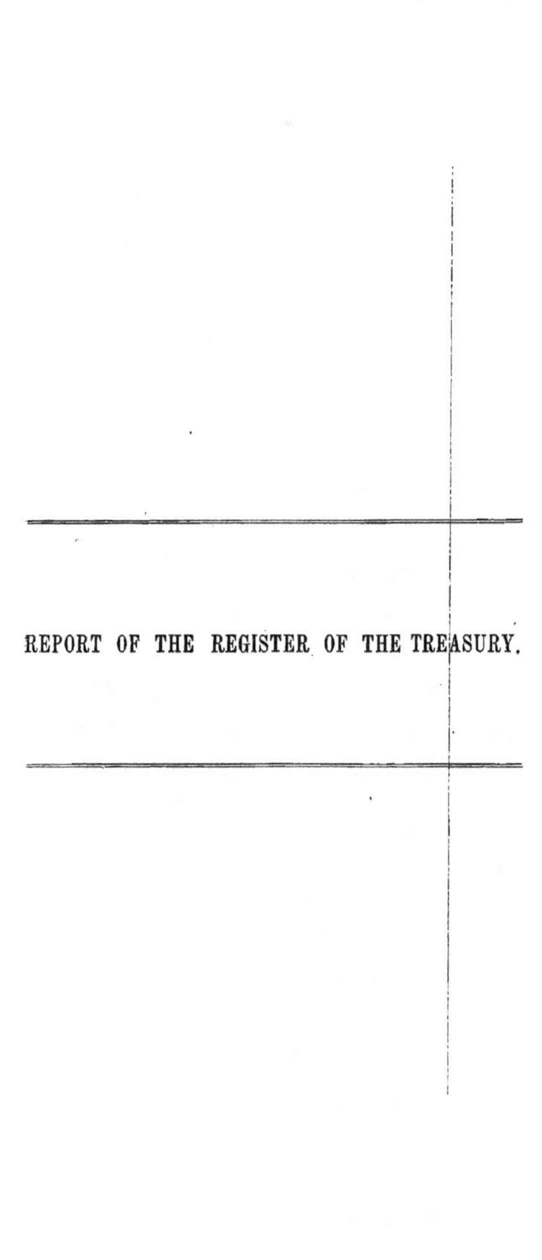

REPORT OF THE REGISTER OF THE TREASURY.

REPORT

OF

THE REGISTER OF THE TREASURY.

TREASURY DEPARTMENT,
Register's Office, November 15, 1872.

SIR: I have the honor to submit my annual report of the transactions of this Bureau for the last fiscal year.

Among the duties of this office, is that of furnishing the various and oftentimes voluminous statements from the books of this office required by the different Bureaus, members of Congress, and the public generally. These statements frequently embrace the transactions of previous years, sometimes running back even to the formation of the Government. As our centennial anniversary is at hand, it appears to me that a properly classified and arranged published statement of the receipts and expenditures of the Government, showing the amount expended under each head of appropriation, arranged in tabular form, from the inception of the Government, embracing the period of one hundred years, would be of incalculable advantage as a complete and accurate record of the fiscal transactions of the Government, as well as a statistical work of rare value.

I would respectfully suggest the following plan of the work:

RECEIPTS to be classified under two general heads, *current* or *ordinary*, and *extraordinary*.

FIRST.—Current or ordinary to embrace the current and usual annual sources of revenue under the following sub-classifications, viz:

CUSTOMS.—Receipts from each collection district, arranged by States, from customs, steamboat fees, fines, penalties, and forfeitures, surplus emoluments, coastwise intercourse, labor, drayage, and storage, &c.

LANDS.—Receipts from lands arranged by States, registers and receivers' fees, and all other receipts arising from the sales of lands.

DIPLOMATIC.—Receipts from consular fees, consular receipts, &c.

COURTS.—Receipts from fines, penalties, and forfeitures; surplus emoluments, &c.

TRUST FUNDS.—Receipts from interest on stocks and proceeds of sale of bonds held in trust.

MINTS AND ASSAY OFFICES.—Receipts from bullion deposits, profits on coinage, sweeps, &c.

SALES OF GOVERNMENT PROPERTY.—Receipts from sales of custom-houses, marine hospitals, waste paper, old materials, &c.

MISCELLANEOUS.—Embracing receipts from various current sources which cannot be readily classified.

SECOND.—*Extraordinary* to embrace receipts arising from extraordinary sources and intended to be applicable to meet certain emergencies that have arisen or may arise, under the following sub-classification:

LOANS.—Receipts from each loan, stating also for what purpose the loan was effected.

LOANS.—*Premiums* showing the amount of premium received from each loan.

LOANS.—*Interest* showing the amount of interest received from each loan.

INTERNAL REVENUE.—Receipts from each district, arranged by States, from internal revenue, from tax on circulation of national banks, from direct tax, and all other sources of internal revenue.

MILITARY.—Receipts from captured and abandoned property, from confiscations, from commutation from drafted persons, from deserters, &c.

NAVY.—Receipts from sales of prize-vessels, sales of vessels condemned for being engaged in the slave-trade, &c.

It is purposed to give only a general outline of the plan of classification. As the work progresses it will probably be found expedient to vary somewhat, to amplify, to condense, or otherwise modify any general plan laid down, in order that the largest and most varied amount of information may be classified in the most concise and satisfactory manner, aggregating, as far as practicable, the receipts from sources of a like character together.

Expenditures to be classified as follows:

CIVIL.—Embracing the legislative, executive, judiciary, and territorial, classifying first all compensation accounts, second all miscellaneous and contingent, and sub-classified as follows:

LEGISLATIVE.—Senate, House of Representatives, Library of Congress, Botanic Garden, Public Printing, and Court of Claims.

EXECUTIVE.—Executive proper, Department of State, Treasury Department, Independent Treasury, Interior, Internal Revenue, War Department, Navy Department, Post-Office Department, Agricultural Department, &c.

JUDICIARY.—Expenses of courts, compensation of judges, marshals, attorneys, &c.

TERRITORIAL.—Compensation of governor, judges, &c.; compensation and mileage of members, contingent expenses.

CUSTOMS:

GENERAL ACCOUNTS.—Expenses collecting revenue, revenue-cutter service, &c., arranged by ports.

REFUNDING ACCOUNTS.—Repayments to importers, debentures and drawbacks, and all other refunding accounts.

PUBLIC BUILDINGS.—Repairs, furniture, and repairs, fuel and miscellaneous items for public buildings.

CUSTOM-HOUSES.—Expenses for construction and repair, arranged by States.

MARINE HOSPITALS.—Expenses for construction and repair, arranged by States.

LIGHT-HOUSE ESTABLISHMENT.—Expenses for construction and repair, arranged by States.

MISCELLANEOUS, embracing such accounts as cannot readily be classified.

INTERNAL REVENUE:

GENERAL ACCOUNT.—Expenses collecting and assessing the internal revenue, arranged by districts.

REFUNDING ACCOUNTS.—Allowance or drawbacks, and all other refunding accounts.

MISCELLANEOUS, embracing such accounts as cannot readily be classified.

INTERIOR, (CIVIL:)

SURVEYS.—Expenses of surveys of public lands.

REFUNDING ACCOUNTS.—Repayment for lands erroneously sold, arranged by States; deposits by individuals for expenses of surveys, and all other refunding accounts.

FIVE PER CENT. FUND of the net proceeds for the sales of public lands arranged by States.

MISCELLANEOUS, embracing such accounts as cannot readily be classified.

PUBLIC BUILDINGS.—Expenditures on account of the public buildings in Washington; 1st, all compensation accounts; 2d, all for repairs; 3d, all construction accounts.

IMPROVEMENT OF AVENUES, STREETS, ETC.—1st, compensation accounts; 2d, all for repairs; 3d, all construction accounts.

PRESIDENTIAL.—1st, all compensation accounts; 2d, all for repairs; 3d, for refurnishing; 4th, for construction.

MISCELLANEOUS, embracing such accounts as cannot readily be classified.

MINT ESTABLISHMENT, expenses of buildings, compensation accounts, wages of workmen, contingent and miscellaneous.

COURT-HOUSE, POST-OFFICE, cost of sites, expenses of buildings, repairs, contingent and miscellaneous.

COAST SURVEY, classified under the appropriate heads.

INTERIOR, arranged under the general heads of *pensions* and *Indians*.

MILITARY ESTABLISHMENT, arranged by Bureaus, giving details of the expenditures for forts, improvement of harbors and rivers, arranged by States.

NAVAL ESTABLISHMENT, to be arranged by Bureaus.

PUBLIC DEBT.—Expenditures on account of the public debt, classified under the heads of *principal*, *premium*, and *interest*.

As in the receipts it is only proposed to give a general outline of the plan of classification, the detail of the work will necessarily modify any general plan that might be laid down. It would be the aim of those engaged in the compilation to so classify and arrange both the receipts and expenditures from 1776 to 1876, so as to condense such items as are of minor importance, and to amplify and enlarge upon such as are frequently required.

In connection with the foregoing I would respectfully suggest the propriety of establishing in this Bureau a division of reports and statements, the duties of which would be—

First. The compilation and preparation of the receipts and expenditures for publication annually in accordance with the law of Congress of December 30, 1871.

Second. Furnishing the statistical information annually required from this office for the estimates of appropriations, finance report, and Register's report.

Third. Compiling the various statements required by the governmental Departments, members of Congress, &c.

Fourth. The compilation, as above suggested, of the receipts and expenditures of the Government from 1776 to 1876, inclusive.

The want of a properly organized division, under the head of a competent person, to whom all letters of inquiry requiring statistical information could be referred, and whose duty it would be to furnish the multifold and valuable information annually required, has long been felt to be desirable instead of the present method of referring sometimes to one clerk and sometimes to another, resulting in frequent apparently incongruous and contradictory statements upon the same subject.

There are at present engaged upon the three first-mentioned objects a force of four clerks. Should this force be increased to six clerks, and a division, as suggested, established, the work could readily be accomplished without adding greatly to the expenses of the Bureau. It seems to me that the benefits to be derived are so apparent and so great that the additional expenses should not prevent the adoption of a plan which, if adopted, is calculated to secure uniformity and correctness in all reports emanating from this office.

Not presuming to assume that these suggestions are the best that could be devised to secure the object in view, I yet think them worthy of being submitted for your consideration, and hope they may meet your sanction and approval.

The report of business transacted is submitted under the head of the division to which it appertains.

DIVISION OF RECEIPTS AND EXPENDITURES—J. H. BEATTY, CHIEF OF DIVISION.

The following statement exhibits the work of the division for the year:

The number of warrants issued during the year for civil, diplomatic, miscellaneous, internal revenue, and public debt expenditures was	19,951
In the preceding year	19,032
Increase	919
The number of warrants issued for receipts from customs, lands, direct tax, internal revenue, and miscellaneous sources, was	11,330
In the preceding year	10,024
Increase	1,306
The number of warrants issued for payments and repayments in the War, Navy, and Interior (Pension and Indian) Departments, was	8,185
In the preceding year	7,977
Increase	208
The number of journal pages required for the entry of accounts relating to the civil, diplomatic, internal revenue, miscellaneous, and public debt receipts and expenditures was	4,236
In the preceding year	4,027
Increase	209
The number of drafts registered was	34,604
In the preceding year	29,186
Increase	5,418
The number of certificates furnished for the settlement of accounts was	10,464
In the preceding year	9,537
Increase	927
The number of accounts received from the offices of the First and Fifth Auditors and Commissioner of the General Land Office, was	24,448
In the preceding year	20,984
Increase	3,464

The work of compiling the receipts and expenditures of the Government is being kept up as far as the settlement of the public accounts will permit.

The manuscript for the fiscal year ending June 30, 1870, will be ready for the printer by the 1st of December next.

In the report for 1871 your attention was called to the fact that the work of this division has been materially increased by the act of July 12, 1870. The experience of the past year has demonstrated that this increase has been much greater than anticipated, involving nearly a third more labor to the division, while the force remains substantially the same as it was prior to the passage of the law.

LOAN DIVISION—HARTWELL JENISON, CHIEF OF DIVISION.

The amount of bonds issued during the fiscal year was:

Original issues	$133,433,730
Coupon-bonds converted into registered	36,919,800
Transfers	156,476,150
Total	326,829,680

The amount of bonds canceled during the year was:

Coupon-bonds exchanged for registered	$36,919,800
Registered bonds transferred	156,476,150
Coupon and registered bonds redeemed	208,693,500
Total	402,089,450

The total number of coupon and registered bonds issued during the year was	176,715
Total number canceled	324,323

This embraces only a portion of the actual redemptions during the year, as the bonds pass through the hands of the accounting officers before reaching this office.

About $50,000,000 coupon-bonds, purchased by the Secretary, have been received, registered, canceled, and turned over to the burning committee. These bonds are first canceled by the assistant treasurer, before transmittal to the Treasurer. They also receive additional cancellation in every stage of accountability, rendering any improper use of them impossible.

The vault account shows that there have been received from the Bureau of Printing and Engraving 44,766 sheets of registered bonds, amounting to $301,225,000; and 209,500 sheets of coupon-bonds of the funded loan of 1881, amounting to $142,300,000, of which there is $80,061,550 still on hand; 21,436,550 signed and sealed, and ready for delivery.

The payment of interest on the funded loan of 1881, by coin checks, meets with general approval.

Heretofore, only the names of the payees on the consolidated interest schedules have been printed, but for the next January dividend, payable at New York, the whole of the schedule will be printed, thus materially reducing the great amount of clerical work, heretofore necessary, both here and in the office of the assistant treasurer.

The following statement shows the number of cases, number and amount of registered and coupon-bonds issued and canceled during the fiscal year:

Statement showing the number of cases, number and amount of registered and coupon bonds issued and canceled during the year ending June 30, 1872.

Loans.	ISSUED.									
	Direct issues.			Exchanges.			Transfers.			Total issue.
	No. of cases.	Bonds issued.	Amount.	No. of cases.	Bonds issued.	Amount.	No. of cases.	Bonds issued.	Amount.	Amount.
1847										
1848										
1850, Texan indemnity										
1858							30	243	$647,000	$647,000
1860										
1861, February 8				16	35	$168,000	108	455	1,453,000	1,621,000
Oregon war							14	102	50,150	50,150
1861, July 17	2	4	$3,100	187	511	1,557,400	907	3,610	13,342,900	14,903,400
1862				108	322	715,400	764	5,695	33,850,950	34,566,350
1863				80	185	229,150	455	1,687	6,196,350	6,425,500
1864, 5-20s							29	109	447,200	447,200
1864, 10-40s				170	493	1,001,050	747	3,073	12,991,050	13,992,100
1864, June 30				65	150	346,450	388	1,995	10,586,300	10,932,750
1865				41	108	334,000	455	2,696	13,677,900	14,011,900
Consols of 1865				330	1,010	2,086,650	848	4,355	18,150,300	20,236,950
Consols of 1867	6	12	1,900	559	1,859	5,587,450	1,169	4,918	17,788,200	23,377,550
Consols of 1868				216	568	1,795,000	259	615	2,638,000	4,433,000
Pacific Railroad	2	6	4,680				645	3,673	19,537,000	19,541,680
Funded loan of 1881	1,217	131,606	133,424,050	656	4,669	23,099,250	283	1,951	5,119,850	161,643,150
War-bounty scrip										
Total	1,227	131,628	133,433,730	2,430	9,910	36,919,800	7,191	35,177	156,476,150	326,829,680

Statement showing the number of cases, &c.—Continued.

Loans.	CANCELED.							
	Redemptions.			Exchanges.		Transfers.		Total canceled.
	No. of cases.	Bonds canceled.	Amount.	No. of bonds.	Amount.	No. of bonds.	Amount.	Amount.
847	2	2	$500					$500
848								
850, Texan indemnity	2	68	68, 000					68, 000
858						243	$647, 000	647, 000
860	6	22	46, 000					46, 000
861, February 8				169	$168, 000	485	1, 453, 000	1, 621, 000
regon war						114	50, 150	50, 150
861, July 17				3, 084	1, 557, 400	3, 871	13, 342, 900	14, 900, 300
862	2, 970	125, 856	125, 065, 700	1, 543	715, 400	8, 761	33, 850, 950	159, 652, 050
863				610	229, 150	1, 608	6, 196, 350	6, 425, 500
64, 5-20s	19	145	645, 600			113	447, 200	1, 092, 800
864, 10-40s				4, 558	1, 001, 050	3, 686	12, 991, 050	13, 992, 100
864, June 30	387	11, 588	23, 821, 650	541	346, 450	2, 621	10, 586, 300	34, 754, 400
865	336	8, 865	18, 857, 700	400	334, 000	3, 277	13, 677, 900	32, 869, 600
onsols of 1865	330	36, 004	25, 986, 700	5, 561	2, 086, 650	6, 266	18, 150, 300	46, 223, 650
onsols of 1867	234	23, 924	13, 779, 750	26, 760	5, 587, 450	6, 740	17, 788, 200	37, 155, 400
onsols of 1868	75	1, 354	375, 550	4, 613	1, 795, 000	1, 020	2, 638, 000	4, 808, 550
acific Railroad						3, 954	19, 537, 000	19, 537, 000
unded loan of 1881	3	13	26, 300	24, 505	23, 090, 250	1, 380	5, 119, 850	28, 245, 400
ar bounty-scrip	2	2	50					50
Total	4, 366	207, 863	208, 693, 500	72, 344	36, 919, 800	44, 139	156, 476, 150	402, 089, 450

NOTE AND COUPON DIVISION—LEWIS D. MOORE, CHIEF OF DIVISION.

The following is a statement of the work performed in this division during the fiscal year:

Treasury notes (upper halves) counted, assorted, arranged, registered, and examined:

854	One-year five per cent. Treasury notes	$18,070
125	Two-year five per cent. Treasury notes	8,100
18	Two-year five per cent. (coupon) notes	1,600
997	Total	27,770

Three-year six per cent. Treasury notes:

216	notes act of March 3, 1863	$8,170
6,391	notes, act of June 30, 1864	183,100
6,607	Total	191,270

Gold certificates:

26,410 act of March 3, 1863 .... $52,179,000

Five and six per cent. interest notes (whole) received from the Comptroller, counted, verified, and delivered to the United States Treasurer:

7,604 notes, amounting to $219,040

Seven-thirty coupon Treasury notes received, counted, assorted, arranged, registered, examined, and compared:

5	notes act July 17, 1861	$3,200
199	notes act June 30, 1864, (1st series)	21,350
260	notes act March 3, 1865, (2d series)	47,900
568	notes act March 3, 1865, (3d series)	52,500
1,032	Total	124,950

Five-twenty and other bonds registered, examined, scheduled, compared, and delivered to the committee:

		Amount.	Coupons Attached.
1,339	bonds act June 14, 1858	$1,339,000	$10,200
1,016	bonds act June 22, 1860	1,016,000	936
1,098	bonds act February 8, 1861	1,098,000	24,151
9,756	bonds act July 17 and August 5, 1861	6,034,350	194,489
13,209	Total	9,487,350	229,776

Detached Coupons:

Number counted, assorted, and arranged numerically	4,880,624
Registered	4,431,806
Examined and compared	11,766,285

NOTES AND FRACTIONAL CURRENCY DIVISION—CHARLES NEALE, CHIEF OF DIVISION.

The following statement exhibits the number of notes and amount of fractional currency, Treasury notes, national-bank notes (of such banks as are broken or have gone into voluntary liquidation) counted, examined, canceled, and destroyed, by burning, during the fiscal year, viz:

	Number of notes.	Amount.
Legal-tender notes	8,645,319	$58,064,960
Legal-tender notes, (series of 1869)	4,956,173	9,313,118
National-bank notes	412,100	2,887,300
Demand notes	709	5,860
Postal currency	136,000	22,000
Fractional currency, (second issue)	192,000	27,200
Fractional currency, (third issue)	6,606,000	1,537,300
Fractional currency, (fourth issue)	118,672,000	18,492,000
Fractional currency, (fourth issue, second series)	19,446,000	9,724,000
Total	159,160,301	100,073,738

Discounted money, counted by the committee, and record kept in this office, viz:

Legal-tender notes	$107,958 00
Legal-tender notes, (series 1869)	15,768 00
Demand notes	24 25
Postal currency	197 00
Fractional currency, (second issue)	156 06
Fractional currency, (third issue)	25,237 09
Fractional currency, (fourth issue)	5,659 64
Fractional currency, (fourth issue, second series)	1,038 95
Total	156,038 99

The number of notes counted this year was	159,160,301 00
The number of notes counted last year was	152,837,601 00
Showing an increase of	6,322,700 00

The amount of the notes counted this year was	$100,073,738 00
The amount of the notes counted last year was	147,334,359 40
Showing a decrease of	47,260,621 40

TONNAGE DIVISION—W. P. TITCOMB, CHIEF OF DIVISION.

The tonnage employed in foreign trade has decreased 14,495 tons, and the tonnage employed in home trade has increased 169,634 tons, making a total increase in the tonnage of the country of 155,139 tons, as shown in the following table:

	1871.		1872.	
	Vessels.	Tons.	Vessels.	Tons.
Registered, (foreign trade)	2,721	1,425,142	2,699	1,410,647
Enrolled and licensed, (home trade)	26,930	2,857,465	28,415	3,027,099
Total	29,651	4,282,607	31,114	4,437,746

The comparison of the various classes of vessels is as follows:

	1871.		1872.	
	Vessels.	Tons.	Vessels.	Tons.
Sailing-vessels	17,298	2,286,155	17,655	2,325,375
Steam-vessels	3,567	1,087,637	3,753	1,111,552
Barges	1,472	260,343	1,621	296,106
Canal-boats	7,314	648,472	8,085	704,713
Total	29,651	4,282,607	31,114	4,437,746

This shows an increase in the number of vessels of each class as well as in the aggregate.

The proportion of the steam tonnage of the country employed in foreign trade is 15 per centum.

The increase in the aggregate tonnage of the country during the fiscal year—1,463 vessels, 155,139 tons—is made up as follows:

The sailing tonnage has increased 39,220 tons; the steam tonnage has increased 23,915 tons; the barge tonnage has increased 35,763 tons; and the canal tonnage has increased 56,241 tons.

SHIP-BUILDING.

The total amount of tonnage built in the country during the last two years, with the numbers of vessels and amount of tonnage of each class, is shown below:

	1871.		1872.	
	Vessels.	Tons.	Vessels.	Tons.
Sailing-vessels	756	97, 176	645	76, 291
Steam-vessels	302	87, 842	292	62, 216
Barges	229	46, 822	168	24, 534
Canal-boats	468	41, 386	538	46, 017
Total	1, 755	273, 226	1, 643	209, 052

The amount of tonnage built during the year ended June 30, 1872, was 64,174 tons less than during the preceding year. The number of vessels built was smaller by 112.

The number of vessels built, and the amount of tonnage of each class, (with the exception of canal-boats,) are less than in 1871.

The canal-boat tonnage built is greater by 70 boats—4,631 tons.

The following statement exhibits the amount of tonnage built within the several grand divisions of the country during the past two years:

	1871.	1872.
Atlantic and Gulf coasts	$150, 925	$125, 820
Pacific coast	5, 324	2, 276
Northern lakes	43, 897	44, 612
Western rivers	73, 080	36, 344
Total	273, 226	209, 052

The number of iron vessels built during the year is the same as during the preceding year, but the tonnage is less.

Below is shown the tonnage of iron vessels built in the United States from 1868 to 1872:

	Tonnage built.				
	1868.	1869.	1870.	1871.	1872.
Sailing-vessels	None.	1, 039	679	2, 067	None.
Steam-vessels	2, 801	3, 545	7, 602	13, 412	12, 766
Total	2, 801	4, 584	8, 281	15, 479	12, 766

Of the iron vessels built during the past year one, a propeller of 1,156 tons, built at New York, was designed for foreign trade, and one iron steamer was built at Wilmington, Delaware, destined for Brazil. The remainder were for the home trade.

THE FISHERIES.

The tonnage engaged in the cod and mackerel fisheries and whale fisheries during the years 1869, 1870, 1871, and 1872 is as follows:

	1869.		1870.		1871.		1872.	
	Vessels.	Tons.	Vessels.	Tons.	Vessels.	Tons.	Vessels.	Tons.
Cod and mackerel	1,714	62,704	2,292	91,460	2,426	92,865	2,385	97,546
Whale fisheries	311	70,202	209	67,954	249	61,480	217	51,608

The tonnage employed in the cod and mackerel fisheries has increased somewhat for the past three years.

The following table shows the amount of tonnage employed in the cod and mackerel fisheries, with the percentage belonging in each State:

State.	Tons.	Per cent.
Massachusetts	68,263	70
Maine	18,780	19.2
Connecticut	4,392	4.5
New Hampshire	3,419	3.5
New York	1,815	1.9
Rhode Island	867	0.9
Total	97,546	100

The amount of tonnage employed in the whale fisheries continues to decline. The whole amount on the 30th day of June, 1872, was 217 vessels, 51,608 tons; a decrease since 1871 of 32 vessels, 9,881 tons, as shown below:

Ports.	1871.		1872.	
	Vessels.	Tons.	Vessels.	Tons.
New Bedford	187	51,442	166	44,320
New London	22	3,877	19	3,113
Barnstable	20	1,939	19	1,671
Edgartown	5	1,854	4	1,296
Nantucket	5	729	3	467
Salem and Beverly	5	785	2	348
Sag Harbor, N. Y	2	261	2	261
San Francisco	3	602	2	132
Total	249	61,489	217	51,608

From the above statement it will be seen that 85 per cent. of the tonnage employed in the whale fisheries hails from New Bedford.

In closing I deem it proper to state that the organization of the Bureau remains substantially the same as at the date of my last report, except in the tonnage division. Joseph Nimmo, jr., esq., having resigned to accept of the office of supervising inspector of steamboats, W. P. Titcomb, esq., of the loan division, has been promoted to that office.

The aggregate number of persons employed in this Bureau at this date is 223, showing a reduction of 12 since June, 1871, and it will be my aim to keep the number as low as may be consistent with the prompt performance of official duties.

I take great pleasure in bearing testimony to the general good conduct and efficiency of those engaged in the public service in this Bureau.

I remain, with great respect, your obedient servant,

JOHN ALLISON.

Hon. GEORGE S. BOUTWELL,
Secretary of the Treasury.

Statement of the number of persons employed in each district of the United States for the collection of customs, during the fiscal year ending June 30, 1872, with their occupation and compensation, per act of March 3, 1849.

District, number of persons, and occupation.	Agg. compensation.
AROOSTOOK, ME.	
1 collector	$1,500 00
1 deputy collector	1,400 00
4 deputy collectors	4,380 00
2 special inspectors	2,920 00
2 inspectors	1,400 00
PASSAMAQUODDY, ME.	
1 collector	3,000 00
1 surveyor	2,000 00
1 deputy collector and inspector	2,000 00
1 deputy collector and inspector	1,464 00
1 deputy collector and inspector	973 00
3 deputy collectors and inspectors	3,294 00
1 deputy collector and inspector	915 00
1 deputy collector and inspector	732 00
3 inspectors	3,294 00
3 inspectors	2,745 00
1 inspector	975 00
1 inspector	732 00
1 inspector	729 00
1 aid to the revenue	1,098 00
1 aid to the revenue	400 00
1 watchman	915 00
2 watchmen	1,464 00
1 watchman	452 00
1 clerk	339 00
1 janitor	360 00
MACHIAS, ME.	
1 collector	1,861 37
1 special deputy collector	1,095 00
1 deputy collector	912 50
1 deputy collector	730 00
3 inspectors	2,190 00
FRENCHMAN'S DAY.	
1 collector	850 00
1 special deputy collector	1,200 00
3 deputy collectors	1,800 00
1 deputy collector	744 00
1 inspector	1,116 00
1 inspector	500 00
1 United States store-keeper	360 00
BANGOR, ME.	
1 collector	2,439 00
1 deputy collector	1,800 00
1 deputy collector	1,277 00
1 deputy collector	1,095 00
3 inspectors	3,285 00
BANGOR, ME.—Continued.	
1 inspector	$368 00
1 temporary inspector	800 00
1 occasional inspector	160 00
1 weigher, gauger, &c	1,500 00
1 night-watchman	730 00
1 janitor	720 00
CASTINE, ME.	
1 collector	1,769 13
1 special deputy collector and inspector	1,460 00
1 special deputy collector and inspector	912 50
3 special deputy collectors & inspector	3,285 00
1 special inspector	1,460 00
BELFAST, ME.	
1 collector	1,315 70
1 inspector	1,460 00
1 deputy collector	1,460 00
1 deputy collector	1,156 52
1 deputy collector	1,402 24
1 deputy collector	500 00
1 deputy collector	400 00
1 temporary inspector	200 00
1 janitor	400 00
WALDOBOROUGH, ME.	
1 collector	2,285 59
1 special deputy collector	1,464 00
1 deputy collector, inspector, &c	1,238 00
1 deputy collector, inspector, &c	1,223 86
1 deputy collector, inspector, &c	1,114 00
1 deputy collector, inspector, &c	1,036 23
1 deputy collector, inspector, &c	870 89
1 deputy collector, inspector, &c	732 00
1 deputy collector, inspector, &c	355 24
WISCASSET, ME.	
2 deputy collectors and inspectors	2,196 00
1 inspector, &c	1,098 00
1 temporary inspector	52 50
BATH, ME.	
1 collector	2,512 26
1 deputy collector, inspector, weigher, gauger, and measurer.	1,500 00
1 inspector, weigher, gauger, and measurer.	1,500 00
2 inspectors	2,928 00
1 deputy collector and inspector	1,261 00

Statement of the number of persons employed for the collection of customs, &c.—Continued.

District, number of persons, and occupation.	Agg. compensation.
BATH, ME.—Continued.	
1 inspector	$600 00
1 inspector	500 00
1 inspector	350 00
1 inspector	147 00
PORTLAND AND FALMOUTH.	
1 collector	6,400 00
3 deputy collectors	9,000 00
3 clerks	4,500 00
1 clerk	1,319 06
2 clerks	2,400 00
1 clerk	1,100 00
3 clerks	3,000 00
1 surveyor	4,500 00
1 deputy surveyor	2,500 00
1 superintendent warehouses and clerk	1,500 00
2 store-keepers	2,928 00
3 store-keepers	3,844 50
1 appraiser	3,000 00
1 assistant appraiser	2,500 00
1 examiner	1,800 00
2 weighers, gaugers, and measurers	4,000 00
2 occasional weighers, gaugers, and measurers.	3,430 04
3 inspectors	4,372 00
19 inspectors	23,754 00
5 inspectors	5,490 00
2 inspectors	1,464 00
1 inspector	628 00
10 temporary inspectors	2,946 00
2 boatmen	1,464 00
1 porter, appraiser's office	428 00
1 porter, custom-house	550 00
1 marker	720 00
SACO, ME.	
1 collector	344 45
1 deputy collector	450 00
1 inspector	500 00
1 inspector	100 00
1 store-keeper	92 00
KENNEBUNK, ME.	
1 collector	Fees 192 00
1 inspector	600 00
3 inspectors	468 00
YORK, ME.	
1 collector, for salary, fees, &c	269 23
1 inspector	100 00
PORTSMOUTH, N. H.	
1 collector	1,248 22
1 surveyor	438 68
1 deputy collector and inspector	1,460 00
1 deputy collector and inspector	250 00
1 inspector, weigher, gauger, and measurer.	1,500 00
3 inspectors	4,380 00
1 inspector	650 00
1 janitor	500 00
VERMONT, VT.	
1 collector of customs	2,500 00
1 deputy collector	2,000 00
1 deputy collector	1,800 00
1 deputy collector	1,600 00
2 deputy collectors	3,000 00
7 deputy collectors	8,400 00
7 deputy collectors	7,000 00
1 deputy collector	900 00
VERMONT, VT.—Continued.	
1 deputy collector	$800 00
5 deputy collectors	3,000 00
1 deputy collector	500 00
4 deputy collectors	3,650 00
1 customs clerk	1,200 00
1 customs clerk	1,000 00
1 bond clerk	1,000 00
30 inspectors	27,375 00
1 inspector	1,095 00
1 inspector	548 00
1 inspector	800 00
10 inspectors and tally boys	3,650 00
3 watchmen	2,190 00
1 revenue boatman	684 00
1 revenue boatman	450 00
NEWBURYPORT, MASS.	
1 collector	1,637 00
1 surveyor	508 00
1 deputy collector and inspector	1,095 00
1 inspector	1,095 00
1 weigher, gauger, measurer, and inspector.	1,095 00
1 inspector	250 00
2 store-keepers	....
1 janitor	720 00
GLOUCESTER, MASS.	
1 collector	3,000 00
1 deputy collector	1,500 00
1 clerk	1,000 00
2 inspectors	2,920 00
2 inspectors	2,190 00
2 inspectors	1,460 00
2 inspectors	600 00
1 janitor	885 00
1 surveyor	250 00
7 weighers and store-keepers	....
SALEM AND BEVERLY, MASS.	
1 collector	1,166 00
1 surveyor	780 00
1 deputy collector and inspector	1,460 00
1 clerk and inspector	1,460 00
1 weigher and gauger	1,500 00
1 inspector	1,000 00
6 inspectors	6,570 00
1 inspector	774 00
1 inspector	285 00
1 boatman	480 00
1 boatman	300 00
1 janitor	480 00
MARBLEHEAD, MASS.	
1 inspector and special deputy collector.	915 00
1 inspector	420 00
1 inspector, acting temporary weigher, gauger, and measurer.	672 00
1 inspector	366 00
1 boatman	100 00
1 collector	380 62
BOSTON AND CHARLESTOWN, MASS.	
1 collector	6,400 00
1 auditor	3,500 00
2 deputy collectors	6,000 00
1 deputy collector, Hingham	700 00
1 deputy collector, Cohasset	700 00
1 cashier	3,000 00
1 assistant cashier	2,200 00
1 clerk	2,500 00

Statement of the number of persons employed for the collection of customs, &c.—Continued

District, number of persons, and occupation.	Agg. compensation.
BOSTON AND CHARLESTOWN—Cont'd.	
1 clerk	$2,400 00
2 clerks	4,400 00
4 clerks	8,000 00
4 clerks	7,200 00
7 clerks	11,900 00
8 clerks	12,000 00
23 clerks	32,200 00
8 clerks	10,400 00
6 clerks	7,200 00
9 clerks	9,900 00
5 clerks	5,000 00
1 janitor	1,200 00
4 messengers	3,000 00
6 messengers	4,212 00
1 engineer	1,100 00
1 assistant engineer	702 00
1 superintendent of warehouses	1,800 00
4 store-keepers paid by Government	5,840 00
21 store-keepers paid by merchants	30,660 00
4 assistant store-keepers	3,200 00
9 weighers	18,000 00
4 gaugers	5,940 00
4 measurers	5,940 00
19 foremen to weighers and gaugers	19,0[illegible]0 00
15 foremen to measurers	15,000 00
59 inspectors	86,140 00
35 temporary inspectors	44,712 50
50 night inspectors	54,750 00
4 revenue boatmen	3,650 00
1 revenue boat messenger	1,095 00
175 laborers	48,100 00
30 laborers	15,800 00
1 naval officer	5,000 00
1 deputy naval officer	2,500 00
1 deputy naval officer	2,000 00
6 clerks	10,800 00
4 clerks	6,400 00
2 clerks	2,400 00
1 messenger	800 00
1 surveyor	4,500 00
1 deputy surveyor	2,500 00
1 clerk	1,800 00
1 clerk	1,500 00
1 clerk	1,400 00
1 messenger	850 00
1 general appraiser	3,000 00
2 appraisers	6,000 00
2 assistant appraisers	5,000 00
8 clerks	6,000 00
7 clerks	12,600 00
2 clerks	3,200 00
1 clerk	1,500 00
4 clerks	5,600 00
6 clerks	7,200 00
1 examiner of drugs	1,000 00
1 messenger	950 00
1 messenger	850 00
2 laborers	1,600 00
10 laborers	8,250 00
PLYMOUTH, MASS.	
1 collector	579 95
1 inspector	1,098 00
1 inspector	600 00
1 inspector	400 00
1 inspector	300 00
1 inspector	200 00
BARNSTABLE, MASS.	
1 collector	1,750 00
1 deputy collector and inspector	1,095 00
1 deputy collector and inspector	900 00
2 deputy collectors and inspector	1,500 00
1 deputy collector and inspector	800 00
1 deputy collector and inspector	500 00
1 deputy collector and inspector	400 00
1 inspector	400 00
BARNSTABLE, MASS.—Continued	
1 aid to the revenue	$300 00
1 clerk	3[illegible]0 00
1 janitor	350 00
1 boatman	150 00
FALL RIVER, MASS.	
1 collector	3,715 52
1 deputy collector, inspector, weigher, gauger, and measurer.	1,500 00
1 permanent inspector, weigher, and measurer.	1,500 00
1 permanent inspector, weigher, gauger, and measurer.	1,275 82
1 temporary inspector	250 00
3 temporary night inspectors	669 00
1 weigher, gauger, and measurer	421 52
NEW BEDFORD, MASS.	
1 collector	3,054 00
1 deputy collector and inspector	1,4[illegible]0 00
1 inspector	1,460 00
1 inspector, weigher, measurer, and gauger.	1,460 00
1 clerk	1,000 00
1 janitor	900 00
1 inspector	300 00
1 inspector	120 00
1 inspector	1,000 00
2 inspectors	160 00
1 inspector	125 00
EDGARTOWN, MASS.	
1 collector	1,008 78
2 deputy collectors and inspectors	2,445 00
3 temporary inspectors	1,600 00
2 night inspectors	1,330 00
1 revenue boatman	420 00
NANTUCKET, MASS.	
1 collector	174 89
1 deputy collector and inspector	833 33
1 inspector	600 00
PROVIDENCE, R. I.	
1 collector	5,000 00
1 deputy collector, inspector, and measurer.	1,500 00
4 inspectors, weighers, gaugers, and measurers.	5,816 57
1 inspector, weigher, gauger, and measurer.	1,500 00
2 inspectors, coastwise	1,460 00
2 inspectors, foreign	2,832 00
3 inspectors for measuring lumber	892 00
1 inspector, permanent	1,460 00
1 inspector at Pawtucket	456 00
1 inspector at Pawtuxet	1,095 00
1 inspector at East Greenwich	500 00
1 boatman at Providence	412 89
1 boatman at Pawtuxet	600 00
1 messenger and store-keeper	1,200 00
1 store keepers	808 22
1 appraiser	3,000 00
1 messenger to appraiser	915 00
BRISTOL AND WARREN, R. I.	
1 collector	257 67
1 permanent inspector	1,095 00
1 permanent inspector	250 00
2 temporary inspectors	80 00
1 temporary inspector	36 00
2 gaugers	78 36
1 measurer	47 14

Statement of the number of persons employed for the collection of customs, &c.—Continued.

District, number of persons, and occupation.	Agg. compensation.
Bristol and Warren, R. I.—Cont'd.	
1 boatman	$216 00
2 store-keepers	42 00
NEWPORT, R. I.	
1 collector	1,062 30
1 superintendent of lights	....
1 agent marine hospital	....
1 deputy collector	1,200 00
2 permanent inspectors	2,196 00
1 inspector at Dutch Island	600 00
1 inspector at New Shoreham	200 00
1 inspector at North Kingston	300 00
4 occasional inspectors	1,124 00
1 weigher, gauger, and measurer	....
1 boatman	27 18
1 janitor and boatman	472 82
STONINGTON, R. I.	
1 inspector	500 00
1 inspector	400 00
1 temporary inspector	15 00
1 boat-keeper	144 00
1 surveyor	150 00
1 weigher	1,125 00
1 deputy collector	....
1 collector	1,726 15
NEW LONDON, CONN.	
1 collector and disbursing agent	2,984 62
1 clerk	1,800 00
2 inspectors	1,000 00
1 inspector	200 00
1 inspector, weigher, gauger, and measurer.	985 32
MIDDLETOWN, CONN.	
1 collector	1,169 81
1 deputy collector	1,200 00
2 inspectors	739 00
1 store-keeper	100 00
1 janitor	600 00
NEW HAVEN, CONN.	
1 collector	3,000 00
1 deputy collector	2,000 00
2 inspectors and clerks	3,000 00
2 weighers, measurers, and gaugers	3,000 00
1 inspector	1,277 50
1 inspector	1,186 23
1 inspector	1,095 00
1 inspector	1,095 00
1 night-watchman	1,095 00
1 boatman and night-watchman	650 00
1 night-watchman	400 00
1 messenger and porter	500 00
1 janitor	660 00
1 inspector	72 00
1 inspector	60 00
1 inspector	48 00
FAIRFIELD, CONN.	
1 collector	1,767 66
1 deputy collector, inspector, weigher, gauger, and measurer.	1,500 00
2 inspectors	325 00
1 night-inspector	27 00
SAG HARBOR, N. Y.	
1 collector	502 77
1 deputy collector	300 00
1 surveyor	253 25

District, number of persons, and occupation.	Agg. compensation.
Sag Harbor, N. Y.—Continued.	
1 inspector	$234 00
1 inspector	180 00
1 inspector	120 00
1 inspector	....
NEW YORK CITY, N. Y.	
1 collector	6,400 00
1 assistant collector	5,000 00
1 auditor	7,000 00
1 assistant auditor	4,000 00
1 assistant auditor	3,500 00
1 cashier	5,000 00
1 assistant cashier	3,500 00
8 deputy collectors	24,000 00
4 clerks	12,000 00
1 clerk	2,800 00
9 clerks	22,500 00
12 clerks	26,400 00
33 clerks	66,000 00
38 clerks	68,400 00
2 clerks	3,400 00
36 clerks	57,600 00
45 clerks	67,500 00
50 clerks	70,000 00
71 clerks	85,200 00
1 clerk	1,100 00
28 clerks	28,000 00
9 clerks	8,100 00
1 clerk	850 00
34 clerks	27,200 00
1 clerk	600 00
3 messengers	1,413 00
2 ushers	2,200 00
2 carpenters	2,362 00
1 engineer	1,500 00
4 foremen	2,880 00
8 watchmen	8,000 00
4 Sunday-watchmen	520 00
13 porters	9,360 00
266 inspectors	389,424 00
7 inspectresses	7,686 00
1 captain night-inspectors	1,600 00
2 lieutenants night-inspectors	2,400 00
116 night-inspectors	127,368 00
19 weighers	47,500 00
8 gaugers	16,000 00
1 assistant collector, Jersey City	2,000 00
1 inspector at Troy	1,464 00
1 surveyor at Troy	250 00
97 store-keepers	142,008 00
1 assistant store-keeper	1,000 00
9 inspectors for measuring vessels	13,176 00
1 measurer of marble	2,000 00
1 superintendent, Castle Garden	2,000 00
2 inspectors, Castle Garden	2,928 00
1 store-keeper, Castle Garden	1,464 00
1 assistant store-keeper, Castle Garden	1,000 00
1 appraiser at large	3,000 00
1 appraiser	4,000 00
10 assistant appraisers	30,000 00
1 clerk to general appraisers	2,500 00
18 examiners	45,000 00
10 examiners	22,000 00
13 examiners	26,000 00
12 examiners	21,600 00
2 examiners	3,200 00
8 examiners	12,000 00
1 examiner of marble	1,500 00
6 clerks	8,400 00
39 clerks	46,800 00
1 clerk	1,100 00
8 clerks	8,000 00
8 messengers	7,200 00
2 openers and packers	2,355 00
96 openers and packers	80,103 00
1 naval officer	5,000 00
3 deputies	7,500 00

Statement of the number of persons employed for the collection of customs, &c.—Continued.

District, number of persons and occupation.	Agg. compensation.
NEW YORK CITY, N. Y.—Continued.	
1 auditor	$2,500 00
1 chief clerk	2,500 00
9 clerks	19,800 00
2 clerks	4,400 00
16 clerks	28,800 00
25 clerks	40,000 00
12 clerks	16,800 00
5 clerks	6,000 00
3 messengers	3,000 00
1 messenger	800 00
1 surveyor	4,500 00
4 deputies	10,000 00
6 clerks	9,000 00
5 clerks	7,000 00
3 messengers	2,700 00
4 clerks	5,200 00
1 porter	720 00
ALBANY, N. Y.	
1 surveyor	3,000 00
1 deputy surveyor	1,460 00
1 inspector	1,095 00
1 clerk	480 00
CHAMPLAIN, N. Y.	
1 collector	2,500 00
1 deputy collector and cashier	1,800 00
1 deputy collector and clerk	1,600 00
1 deputy collector and clerk	1,350 00
1 deputy collector and clerk	1,100 00
1 deputy collector and inspector	1,200 00
8 deputy collectors and inspectors	7,200 00
4 inspectors	3,600 00
1 inspector	450 00
1 deputy collector and inspector	700 00
1 deputy collector and inspector	572 50
6 inspectors	2,870 00
1 inspector and night-watch	535 00
1 inspectress	357 50
1 boatman	250 00
OSWEGATCHIE, N. Y.	
1 collector	2,500 00
1 deputy collector	1,800 00
2 deputy collectors and clerks	3,000 00
1 deputy collector	1,500 00
1 deputy collector and inspector	1,200 00
6 deputy collectors	4,800 00
1 deputy inspector	1,200 00
2 inspectors	2,196 00
5 inspectors	4,575 00
1 inspector	732 00
1 inspectress	314 00
CAPE VINCENT, N. Y.	
1 collector	2,500 00
1 special deputy collector and inspector	1,500 00
1 deputy collector and inspector	1,200 00
9 deputy collectors and inspectors	7,875 00
2 inspectors	2,150 00
5 inspectors	4,115 00
OSWEGO, N. Y.	
1 collector	4,500 00
1 special deputy collector	2,000 00
1 deputy collector and clerk	1,416 49
1 deputy collector and inspector	1,464 00
5 inspectors	5,490 00
5 inspectors	3,900 00
2 inspectors	1,370 00
1 deputy collector and inspector	915 00
OSWEGO, N. Y.—Continued.	
2 deputy collectors and inspectors	$1,300 00
1 clerk	1,000 00
2 clerks	2,600 00
2 clerks	2,400 00
1 clerk	697 28
1 clerk	850 00
1 clerk	732 00
1 janitor	550 00
5 store-keepers	3,660 00
1 store-keeper	368 00
1 store-keeper	548 00
1 warehouse superintendent	1,464 00
GENESEE, N. Y.	
1 collector	2,500 00
1 special deputy collector	1,800 00
8 deputy collectors	5,986 50
11 inspectors	5,471 50
4 temporary inspectors	480 00
1 inspectress	720 00
1 clerk	900 00
NIAGARA, N. Y.	
1 collector	2,500 00
1 deputy collector and inspector	1,800 00
1 deputy collector and inspector	1,500 00
13 deputy collectors and inspectors	11,895 00
4 deputy collectors and inspectors	2,200 00
1 deputy collector and inspector	687 50
1 deputy collector and inspector	1,098 00
1 deputy collector and watchman	1,200 00
1 deputy collector and watchman	915 00
1 special inspector	1,464 00
1 live-stock inspector	1,200 00
7 inspectors	6,405 00
1 inspector	732 00
1 inspector	687 50
1 inspector	564 00
2 inspectors	1,494 00
1 clerk	900 00
1 female examiner	549 00
BUFFALO CREEK, N. Y.	
1 collector	2,500 00
1 deputy collector	2,000 00
1 deputy collector at Grand Trunk Railroad.	1,464 00
3 deputies	3,294 00
1 deputy	1,200 00
1 deputy	1,281 00
1 cashier United States depository	1,800 00
1 clerk	1,500 00
1 clerk	1,200 00
1 clerk and inspector	1,464 00
1 clerk	900 00
2 inspectors	2,928 00
18 inspectors	19,764 00
2 inspectors	1,758 00
1 watchman United States depository	836 00
1 night-clearance deputy	642 00
1 janitor	600 00
1 fireman	600 00
DUNKIRK, N. Y.	
1 collector	1,317 63
1 special deputy collector	912 50
2 inspectors	1,825 00
NEWARK, N. J.	
1 collector	1,705 27
1 deputy collector	1,460 00
1 inspector	1,460 00

Statement of the number of persons employed for the collection of customs, &c.—Continued.

District, number of persons, and occupation.	Agg. compensation.
PERTH AMBOY, N. J.	
1 collector	$1,848 19
1 deputy collector	1,200 00
3 inspectors	2,058 60
1 inspector	730 00
2 inspectors	1,200 00
6 boatmen	1,068 60
LITTLE EGG HARBOR, N. J.	
4 inspectors	1,686 00
2 boatmen	1,395 00
GREAT EGG HARBOR, N. J.	
1 collector	664 87
1 inspector	549 00
1 boatman	402 00
BRIDGETOWN, N. J.	
1 collector	621 54
2 deputy collectors	150 00
BURLINGTON, N. J.	
1 collector	447 11
1 deputy collector	....
PHILADELPHIA, PA.	
1 collector	6,000 00
2 deputy collectors	6,000 00
1 cashier	2,500 00
1 assistant cashier	1,350 00
1 assistant cashier	350 00
1 clerk	2,300 00
1 clerk	1,800 00
1 clerk	49 45
2 clerks	3,156 04
9 clerks	12,623 08
11 clerks	14,300 00
1 clerk	23 08
1 assistant collector, Camden	1,500 00
1 messenger	912 50
1 fireman	912 50
1 porter	912 50
2 night-watchmen	2,190 00
1 surveyor at Chester	500 00
54 day inspectors	78,512 00
11 temporary inspectors	15,872 00
3 temporary inspectors	3,980 00
2 temporary inspectors	336 00
4 temporary inspectors	610 00
1 messenger	912 50
1 inspector at Bristol	547 50
1 inspector at Marcus Hook	547 50
1 inspector at Lazaretto	500 00
30 night-inspectors	32,607 00
7 night-inspectors, temporary	7,587 00
2 night-inspectors, temporary	788 00
1 night-inspector, captain	1,460 00
1 night-inspector, lieutenant	1,200 00
1 chief weigher	2,000 00
3 assistant weighers	3,600 00
10 beamsmen	6,610 00
2 beamsmen, temporary	342 00
1 beamsman, temporary	162 00
15 assistant weighers	3,650 40
1 weigher's clerk	1,384 62
1 weigher's clerk	164 84
1 weigher's clerk	98 90
1 weigher's clerk	1,400 00
1 foreman to laborers	912 50
2 gaugers	1,485 00
1 gauger, temporary	1,485 00
1 measurer	1,485 00
1 measurer, assistant	1,095 00
1 naval officer	5,000 00
1 deputy naval officer	2,500 00
PHILADELPHIA, PA.—Continued.	
1 clerk	$1,900 00
1 clerk	1,600 00
2 clerks	2,800 00
4 clerks	5,200 00
1 messenger	912 50
1 surveyor	5,000 00
1 deputy surveyor	2,500 00
1 clerk	1,500 00
1 clerk	1,346 61
1 clerk	975 00
1 clerk	400 00
3 clerks, admeasurement	3,285 00
1 messenger	912 50
1 marker	912 50
1 general appraiser	3,000 00
1 clerk	1,400 00
1 messenger	912 50
1 local appraiser	3,000 00
2 assistant appraisers	5,000 00
1 examiner	1,800 00
2 examiners	3,000 00
2 examiners	2,800 00
1 clerk	1,600 00
3 clerks	4,200 00
9 packers	9,033 75
1 watchman	821 25
1 messenger	912 50
1 store-keeper, port	1,500 00
1 clerk	1,400 00
1 first foreman	352 50
1 first foreman	900 00
1 second foreman	912 50
2 watchmen	1,825 00
1 marker	900 00
1 sampler	1,000 00
1 superintendent warehouses	1,600 00
9 assistant store-keepers	13,140 00
4 bargemen	3,650 00
1 janitor appraiser's stores	1,046 76
1 janitor custom-house	803 16
1 examiner of drugs	1,000 00
ERIE, PA.	
1 collector	1,000 00
2 deputy collectors and inspectors	2,700 00
1 temporary inspector	1,128 50
1 temporary inspector	855 50
1 temporary inspector	489 00
1 temporary inspector	246 50
1 temporary inspector	231 00
1 temporary inspector	192 50
1 temporary inspector	186 41
PITTSBURGH, PA.	
1 surveyor	4,500 00
1 deputy surveyor	1,400 00
1 clerk	900 00
1 janitor and messenger	940 00
DELAWARE, DEL.	
1 collector	2,370 77
3 deputy collectors and inspectors	2,900 00
3 inspectors	2,400 00
4 oarsmen	1,200 00
BALTIMORE, MD.	
2 deputy collectors	6,000 00
1 deputy collector at Havre de Grace	1,200 00
1 auditor	2,500 00
1 cashier	2,500 00
1 deputy cashier	1,800 00
1 clerk	2,000 00
10 clerks, (8 part of year)	14,850 00
4 clerks, (3 part of year)	5,311 84
3 clerks, (4 part of year	5,866 67

Statement of the number of persons employed for the collection of customs, &c.—Continued.

District, number of persons, and occupation.	Agg. compensation.
BALTIMORE, MD.—Continued.	
4 clerks	$6,766 52
1 clerk	1,300 00
11 clerks, (7 and 10 part of year)	11,071 98
1 superintendent of building	1,200 00
1 janitor of building	912 50
2 messengers, (366 days)	1,830 00
1 messenger, (part of year)	587 06
1 porter, (366 days)	915 00
2 messengers, (part of year)	561 00
49 inspectors, (45 part of year)	68,868 00
1 inspectress	800 00
1 inspector at Havre de Grace	400 00
Special day-inspectors during year	1,714 00
1 captain of the watch, (365 days)	1,464 00
1 lieutenant of the watch	1,200 00
6 watchmen	6,588 00
3 watchmen, (additional, building)	2,040 00
43 night-inspectors, (40 part of year)	44,100 00
Special night-inspectors during year	2,898 00
2 debenture markers	1,830 00
1 secret aid to the revenue	1,098 00
1 messenger, (barge-office, 366 days)	915 00
1 United States weigher	2,000 00
1 clerk to weigher	1,400 00
1 clerk to weigher	1,200 00
16 assistant weighers, (14 part of year.)	17,128 49
Markers, laborers, and messenger, weigher's department, during year.	33,675 31
1 United States measurer	1,500 00
2 assistant measurers	2,196 00
Special measurers and laborers, during year.	353 03
2 United States gaugers	3,000 00
1 clerk and store-keeper, (No. 1)	1,800 00
1 clerk	1,200 00
1 foreman	1,200 00
5 porters, (4 part of year)	4,40[illegible] 00
1 messenger, (part of year,) at $3 per diem.	1,032 00
1 engineer	1,000 00
1 fireman, (366 days)	915 00
1 superintendent at $1,800 per annum, and 22 store-keepers private bonded warehouse at $1,400 per annum, $32,758; paid monthly by proprietors of private bonded warehouses.	
1 general appraiser	3,000 00
1 clerk to general appraiser	1,400 00
2 local appraisers	6,000 00
1 clerk	1,800 00
6 examiners, (4 part of year)	7,475 80
6 clerks, (4 part of year)	6,983 16
1 clerk	1,200 00
1 foreman, openers and packers	1,200 00
6 openers and packers, (4 part of year.)	5,010 50
6 porters, (4 part of year)	5,010 50
1 messenger	915 00
1 deputy naval officer	2,500 00
1 clerk	1,800 00
1 clerk	1,6[illegible]0 00
5 clerks	7,500 00
1 clerk	1,200 00
1 messenger, (366 days)	915 00
1 deputy surveyor	2,500 00
1 clerk	1,600 00
1 clerk	1,500 00
1 aid to surveyor	1,460 00
1 clerk, (366 days)	1,317 60
1 clerk	1,200 00
1 messenger, (366 days)	915 00
1 collector, (compensation not reported)	....
ANNAPOLIS, MD.	
1 collector	1,141 57
1 surveyor	262 15
ANNAPOLIS, MD.—Continued.	
1 surveyor	$127 09
1 temporary inspector	132 00
1 permanent inspector	240 00
1 boatman	180 00
1 boatman	45 00
1 boatman	80 00
1 boatman	73 20
TOWN CREEK, MD.	
1 surveyor	150 00
EASTERN, MD.	
2 deputy collectors and inspectors	2,555 00
1 collector	1,200 00
GEORGETOWN, D. C.	
1 collector	1,702 25
2 deputy collectors and inspectors	2,400 00
1 deputy collector and inspector	1,228 75
1 inspector	163 67
1 laborer and janitor	885 86
ALEXANDRIA, VA.	
1 collector	730 67
1 deputy collector	1,500 00
1 deputy collector	1,000 00
2 inspectors	2,160 00
1 janitor	600 00
TAPPAHANNOCK, VA.	
1 collector	379 70
1 special deputy collector	350 00
YORKTOWN, VA.	
1 collector	565 00
1 deputy collector and inspector	730 09
1 special deputy collector	1,460 00
RICHMOND, VA.	
1 collector	3,291 69
1 deputy collector	1,800 00
1 clerk	1,460 00
3 inspectors	4,380 00
1 inspector	100 00
1 janitor	900 00
1 watchman	760 50
PETERSBURGH, VA.	
1 collector	1,253 81
1 deputy and clerk	1,800 00
1 inspector	1,460 00
1 porter and messenger, &c	594 50
1 revenue boatman	180 00
1 janitor	900 00
NORFOLK AND PORTSMOUTH, VA.	
1 collector	3,331 12
1 deputy collector	1,800 00
2 clerks	3,000 00
1 clerk	1,200 00
8 inspectors	11,080 00
1 night-inspector	1,095 00
2 night-inspectors	1,200 00
1 United States weigher	1,500 00
1 watchman	912 50
4 boatmen	1,920 00
1 janitor	600 00
1 United States measurer	411 92

Statement of the number of persons employed for the collection of customs, &c.—Continued.

District, number of persons, and occupation.	Agg. compensation.
CHERRYSTONE, VA.	
1 collector	$1, 134 89
1 inspector and deputy collector	1, 095 00
1 inspector and deputy collector	1, 038 00
1 boatman	333 50
2 boatmen	55 00
3 temporary watchmen	312 00
WHEELING, WEST VA.	
1 surveyor	1, 292 05
1 janitor	540 00
PARKERSBURGH, WEST VA.	
1 surveyor	350 00
ALBEMARLE, N. C.	
1 collector	1, 312 00
1 special deputy collector	1, 000 00
1 deputy collector	1, 098 00
1 deputy collector	1, 464 00
2 boat hands	480 00
1 coast inspector	366 00
PAMLICO, N. C.	
1 collector, Newberne	1, 431 94
1 deputy collector, weigher, gauger, &c., Newberne.	1, 460 00
1 deputy collector and inspector, Newberne.	1, 460 00
1 deputy collector and inspector, Washington.	1, 460 00
1 deputy collector and inspector, Portsmouth.	730 00
2 revenue boatmen, Portsmouth	600 00
1 inspector, Hatteras	360 00
2 revenue boatmen, Hatteras	600 00
BEAUFORT, N. C.	
1 collector	1, 214 67
1 inspector	747 00
1 temporary inspector	30 00
1 weigher	39 60
1 boatman	300 00
WILMINGTON, N. C.	
1 collector	2, 900 00
1 deputy collector	2, 000 00
1 clerk	1, 500 00
7 inspectors	10, 220 00
1 weigher, gauger, and measurer	1, 500 00
1 store-keeper	511 00
4 boatmen	1, 440 00
GEORGETOWN, S. C.	
1 collector	548 80
1 inspector	1, 095 00
2 boatmen	1, 200 00
CHARLESTON, S. C.	
1 collector	6, 400 00
1 deputy collector	2, 200 00
2 clerks	3, 089 35
2 clerk	2, 800 00
1 clerk	1, 500 00
1 clerk	1, 300 00
8 day-inspectors	11, 680 00
1 day inspector, temporary	120 00
5 night-inspectors	4, 502 50
1 night inspector	692 50
3 watchmen	2, 190 00
1 watchman	642 00
1 weigher and measurer	1, 500 00
CHARLESTON, S. C.—Continued.	
1 gauger	$334 32
1 store-keeper paid by proprietors	1, 460 00
1 store-keeper of bonded warehouses	1, 095 00
1 messenger	1, 000 00
2 porters	1, 460 00
1 porter	600 00
4 bargemen	2, 920 00
1 appraiser	1, 500 00
1 appraiser	1, 487 50
BEAUFORT, S. C.	
1 collector	1, 336 07
1 inspector	1, 098 00
2 boatmen	690 00
SAVANNAH, GA.	
1 collector, (compensation as collector, compensation from shares, fines, &c., and in other capacities, not reported.)	4, 000 00
1 deputy collector	2, 500 00
2 clerks	4, 000 00
1 clerk	1, 600 00
4 clerks	6, 000 00
1 clerk	1, 200 00
1 clerk	1, 000 00
2 appraisers	3, 000 00
1 appraiser's clerk	1, 500 00
1 weigher and gauger	1, 500 00
13 inspectors	18, 980 00
1 inspector	1, 095 00
3 inspectors, temporary	3, 2[illegible]5 00
21 inspectors, night	19, 162 50
1 store-keeper	1, 200 00
1 store-keeper	900 00
1 janitor	1, 000 00
2 porters	720 00
4 boatmen	2, 880 00
1 surveyor	1, 363 50
1 surveyor's clerk	1, 500 00
BRUNSWICK, GA.	
1 collector	2, 700 00
2 deputy collectors and inspectors	2, 190 00
1 inspector	1, 095 00
6 boatmen	2, 520 00
SAINT MARY'S, GA.	
1 collector	983 50
1 deputy collector and inspector	1, 460 00
1 boatman	420 00
1 boatman	360 00
FERNANDINA, FLA.	
1 collector	1, 263 15
1 deputy collector and inspector	1, 460 00
1 inspector	1, 095 00
1 inspector	7[illegible]0 00
1 boatman and porter	420 00
1 boatman	360 00
1 boatman	322 00
1 boatman	305 00
SAINT JOHN'S, FLA.	
1 collector	1, 137 82
3 inspectors	3, 660 00
4 boatmen	1, 440 00
SAINT AUGUSTINE, FLA.	
1 collector	542 77
2 deputy collectors and inspectors	2, 920 00
1 inspector	1, 095 00
6 boatmen	2, 160 00

Statement of the number of persons employed for the collection of customs, &c.—Continued.

District, number of persons, and occupation.	Agg. compensation.
KEY WEST, FLA.	
1 collector	$3,400 00
1 special deputy collector and clerk	1,800 00
1 chief clerk and accountant	1,500 00
2 clerks	1,500 00
3 inspectors	4,380 00
1 inspector and night-watchman	1,460 00
1 janitor	567 93
1 messenger	300 00
4 boatmen	1,440 00
SAINT MARK'S FLA.	
1 collector	1,250 00
3 deputy collectors	4,380 00
6 revenue boatmen	2,160 00
APPALACHICOLA, FLA.	
1 collector	1,200 00
1 deputy collector, at $4 per day	....
1 messenger	300 00
4 temporary boatmen at $2.50 per day, each.	....
PENSACOLA, FLA.	
1 collector	3,000 00
3 deputy collectors	3,955 00
7 inspectors	7,065 00
1 night inspector	1,095 00
4 revenue boatmen	1,920 00
1 janitor	600 00
MOBILE, ALA.	
1 collector	6,250 00
1 deputy collector	2,500 00
1 cashier and book-keeper	3,000 00
1 auditor	1,800 00
1 weigher and gauger	1,800 00
1 entrance and collector's clerk	1,800 00
2 auditor's clerks	3,000 00
1 superintendant public warehouses	1,464 00
1 admeasurer	1,464 00
8 inspectors	11,712 00
3 inspectors	3,294 00
2 night-inspectors	1,830 00
1 night-watchman	1,098 00
1 day-watchman	203 00
1 messenger	600 00
1 bargeman	600 00
5 oarsmen	2,700 00
3 store-keepers	4,392 00
1 store-keeper	1,088 00
1 temporary inspector	342 00
1 appraiser of merchandise	3,000 00
PEARL RIVER, MISS.	
1 collector	500 00
1 deputy collector and inspector	678 00
2 boatmen	660 00
VICKSBURGH, MISS.	
1 collector	532 20
1 deputy collector	....
NATCHEZ, MISS.	
1 collector	501 80
NEW ORLEANS, LA.	
1 collector	6,000 00
1 special deputy	2,505 00
2 deputy collectors	5,505 00
1 auditor	2,505 00
1 cashier	2,500 00
NEW ORLEANS, LA.—Continued.	
1 entry clerk	$2,500 00
1 assistant cashier	2,000 00
2 clerks	4,000 00
16 clerks	28,578 28
10 clerks	16,959 93
9 clerks	13,991 31
9 clerks	13,351 88
2 clerks	2,800 00
2 clerks	2,599 86
3 clerks	3,547 82
1 clerk	918 70
1 custom-house superintendent	1,099 98
1 messenger	1,100 02
2 messengers	2,000 00
1 messenger	475 00
3 messengers	2,136 30
1 messenger	800 01
2 messengers	1,080 00
1 messenger	659 97
3 messengers	1,457 88
1 clerk	187 50
1 engineer	1,459 97
1 carpenter	1,459 97
7 laborers	7,140 00
8 watchmen	6,975 00
1 deputy collector	358 51
1 general appraiser	3,000 00
2 appraisers	5,505 50
1 assistant appraiser	2,500 00
6 examiners	10,800 00
1 sampler	1,500 00
4 chief laborers	4,000 00
18 laborers	15,846 68
1 special examiner of drugs	1,000 00
1 warehouse superintendent	2,500 00
17 store-keepers	24,490 61
12 laborers	8,565 61
1 weigher	2,000 00
8 deputy weighers	11,212 90
2 gaugers	2,869 56
1 measurer	1,500 00
37 laborers	24,331 02
4 laborers	4,196 50
59 inspectors	86,048 00
5 boarding-officers	5,334 00
2 night-inspectors and lookout	2,196 00
15 river inspectors	15,639 00
39 night-inspectors	42,267 00
21 boatmen	14,878 84
TECHE, LA.	
1 collector	750 00
6 inspectors	6,348 00
TEXAS.	
1 collector	4,500 00
1 clerk	2,000 00
1 clerk	1,800 00
5 clerks	8,000 00
2 deputy collectors and inspectors	3,000 00
1 weigher, gauger, &c	1,500 00
1 surveyor	1,000 00
1 surveyor	350 00
8 boatmen	7,200 00
1 boatman	600 00
2 store-keepers bonded warehouses	2,928 00
16 inspectors	23,424 00
1 assistant in appraiser's store	1,252 00
1 assistant weigher, gauger, &c	939 00
1 night-watchman	1,098 00
1 messenger	732 00
SALURIA, TEXAS.	
1 collector	2,089 70
1 surveyor	600 00
1 deputy collector and clerk	2,090 00

Statement of the number of persons employed for the collection of customs, &c.—Continued.

District, number of persons, and occupation.	Agg. compensation.
SALURIA, TEX.—Continued.	
1 deputy collector	$1,500 00
1 clerk	1,460 00
3 mounted inspectors	4,380 00
2 inspectors	2,920 00
1 porter and messenger	250 00
1 revenue boatman	600 00
CORPUS CHRISTI, TEX.	
1 collector	2,500 00
1 special deputy collector and clerk	1,800 00
1 clerk	1,500 00
6 deputy collectors and inspectors	8,784 00
2 inspectors	2,928 10
2 inspectors	1,830 00
1 inspector	762 50
1 inspector	25 00
4 mounted inspectors	5,856 00
1 mounted inspector	1,220 00
1 mounted inspector	244 00
1 mounted inspector	248 00
1 mounted inspector	1,004 00
1 mounted inspector	432 00
1 mounted inspector	932 00
1 mounted inspector	728 00
1 store-keeper	900 00
1 porter	420 00
BRAZOS DE SANTIAGO, TEX.	
1 collector	4,500 00
1 deputy collector and cashier	2,500 00
1 deputy collector and book-keeper	2,500 00
1 deputy collector and inspector	2,400 00
1 deputy collector and inspector	2,000 00
1 entry clerk	2,000 00
1 bond clerk	2,000 00
1 store-keeper, weigher, gauger, &c	1,800 00
1 statistical clerk	1,600 00
1 clerk and inspector	1,600 00
8 mounted inspectors	14,640 00
6 inspectors	8,760 00
1 inspectress	1,098 00
1 messenger	600 00
1 revenue boatman	480 00
PASO DEL NORTE, TEX.	
1 collector	2,000 00
3 deputies	4,500 00
4 deputies	4,000 00
1 deputy	300 00
5 mounted inspectors	6,347 50
1 night-watchman	600 00
MEMPHIS, TENN.	
1 surveyor	3,000 00
1 appraiser	3,000 00
1 clerk	1,200 00
2 store-keepers	157 31
1 messenger	600 00
NASHVILLE, TENN.	
1 surveyor	1,714 10
PADUCAH, KY.	
1 surveyor	652 18
LOUISVILLE, KY.	
1 surveyor	3,000 00
1 appraiser	3,000 00
1 customs clerk	1,500 00
1 recording clerk	1,100 00
1 inspector, customs	1,460 00
LOUISVILLE, KY.—Continued.	
1 clerk	$1,200 00
1 inspector	912 50
1 laborer, bonded warehouse	46 00
CINCINNATI, OHIO.	
1 surveyor	3,000 00
1 appraiser	3,000 00
1 deputy surveyor	2,000 00
1 entry clerk	1,500 00
1 warehouse clerk	1,000 00
2 inspectors	2,095 00
1 invoice clerk	1,000 00
1 weigher and measurer	1,460 00
3 store-keepers	2,550 00
1 admeasuring clerk	1,252 00
1 porter for appraiser	600 00
1 janitor	480 00
CUYAHOGA, OHIO.	
1 collector	2,500 00
1 deputy collector	1,400 00
1 special collector and clerk	1,600 00
1 special collector and clerk	1,200 00
1 special collector and clerk	930 00
1 United States appraiser	3,000 00
1 deputy collector and inspector	1,464 00
1 deputy collector and inspector	1,098 00
1 deputy collector and inspector	1,098 00
1 deputy collector and inspector	1,098 00
1 night deputy collector and inspector	1,098 00
1 night deputy collector and inspector	575 00
1 weigher and gauger	915 00
1 deputy collector at Fairport	480 00
1 deputy collector at Ashtabula	300 00
1 deputy collector at Conneaut	300 00
1 deputy collector at Black River	300 00
1 night-watchman	915 00
1 janitor and porter	720 00
1 fireman	640 00
1 lumber measurer and inspector	1,140 00
1 lumber measurer and inspector	644 00
1 lumber measurer and inspector	644 00
SANDUSKY, OHIO.	
1 collector	1,960 00
1 deputy collector	1,000 00
1 deputy collector and inspector	913 00
1 deputy collector and inspector	600 00
1 deputy collector and inspector	300 00
3 deputy collectors and inspectors	600 00
1 clerk	600 00
MIAMI, OHIO.	
1 collector	2,500 00
1 special deputy collector	1,500 00
1 deputy collector	1,300 00
4 inspectors	4,380 00
DETROIT, MICH.	
1 collector	3,573 50
1 special deputy collector	2,250 00
1 deputy collector and clerk	1,500 00
1 deputy collector and inspector	1,467 02
1 deputy collector and clerk	1,433 50
1 deputy collector and inspector	1,400 54
1 deputy collector and inspector	1,367 02
1 deputy collector and inspector	1,300 00
2 deputy collectors and inspectors	2,425 00
2 deputy collectors and inspectors	2,000 00
2 deputy collectors and inspectors	1,600 00
1 deputy collector and inspector	700 00
1 deputy collector and inspector	600 00
1 deputy collector and inspector	533 33

Statement of the number of persons employed for the collection of customs, &c.—Continued.

District, number of persons, and occupation.	Agg. compensation.
DETROIT, MICH.—Continued.	
1 deputy collector and inspector	$300 00
4 deputy collectors and inspectors	800 00
1 deputy collector and inspector	120 00
1 deputy collector and inspector	90 00
1 inspector	1,460 00
1 inspector	1,003 75
4 inspectors	4,000 00
1 inspector	949 00
1 inspector	912 50
2 inspectors	1,760 00
4 inspectors	2,800 00
3 inspectors	1,800 00
2 inspectors	1,000 00
1 inspector	360 00
2 inspectors	600 00
1 inspector	240 00
3 inspectors	360 00
1 deputy collector	753 00
1 deputy collector	240 00
1 deputy collector	200 00
1 inspectress	300 00
1 janitor	800 00
1 appraiser	2,046 19
HURON, MICH.	
1 collector	2,500 00
1 special deputy collector	2,000 00
1 cashier and book-keeper	1,500 00
1 bond and entry clerk	1,200 00
1 marine clerk	1,095 00
1 general clerk	1,095 00
1 deputy in charge of Grand Trunk Crossing	1,460 00
1 deputy in charge of Grand Trunk warehouse	1,229 00
3 inspectors at Grand Trunk Crossing*	3,285 00
1 inspector at Grand Trunk Crossing*	821 25
4 inspectors at Grand Trunk Crossing*	4,380 00
1 deputy at Great Western Crossing†	972 00
1 deputy at Great Western Crossing†	587 50
1 deputy at Great Western Crossing†	470 00
1 inspector at London, Ontario†	366 00
1 deputy at Sarnia Ferry	912 50
1 night deputy at Sarnia Ferry	825 00
1 inspectress at Sarnia Ferry	240 00
1 special inspector	996 50
2 special inspectors	1,825 00
1 special inspector	575 00
1 watchman and porter	730 00
1 deputy collector at Bay City	1,005 00
1 deputy collector at Saint Clair	200 00
1 deputy collector at Marine City	800 00
1 deputy collector at East Saginaw	600 00
1 deputy collector at Algonac	420 00
1 deputy collector at Alpena	360 00
1 deputy collector at Lexington	180 00
1 deputy collector at Sand Beach	100 00
1 inspector at Toronto, Ontario, (coin)*	1,460 00
1 inspector at Toronto, Ontario, (coin)*	912 50
1 inspector at Stratford, Ontario, (coin)*	1,460 00
SUPERIOR, MICH.	
1 collector	2,900 00
2 deputy collectors	2,400 00
1 deputy collector	800 00
1 deputy collector	500 00
1 deputy collector	400 00
1 deputy collector	300 00
2 deputy collectors	720 00
1 deputy collector	1,098 00
3 deputy collectors	1,464 00
1 deputy collector	849 00
1 special inspector	90 00
1 aid to the revenue	849 00
inspector of the revenue	849 00
MICHIGAN, MICH.	
1 collector	$2,500 00
1 deputy collector and clerk	1,200 00
2 deputy collectors and inspectors	1,200 00
2 deputy collectors and inspectors	960 00
2 deputy collectors and inspectors	720 00
1 deputy collector and inspector	520 00
1 deputy collector and inspector	319 56
1 deputy collector and inspector	284 68
2 deputy collectors and inspectors	600 00
2 deputy collectors and inspectors	480 00
1 deputy collector and inspector	180 00
1 deputy collector and inspector	120 00
1 deputy collector and inspector	35 50
1 deputy collector and inspector	33 67
1 deputy collector and inspector	30 00
NEW ALBANY, IND.	
1 surveyor	350 00
EVANSVILLE, IND.	
1 surveyor	2,634 60
1 clerk	1,000 00
1 appraiser	3,000 00
1 store-keeper	850 00
CHICAGO, ILL.	
1 collector	4,624 09
1 deputy collector	3,000 00
1 deputy collector	2,266 03
2 deputy collectors	3,000 00
1 deputy collector	1,000 00
1 deputy collector	107 33
1 auditor	1,800 00
1 cashier	1,800 00
1 accountant and disbursing clerk	1,482 98
1 corresponding clerk	1,482 98
1 clerk	1,375 00
1 clerk	1,099 44
1 clerk	1,383 52
1 clerk	325 00
4 clerks	671 44
2 clerks	107 16
1 surveyor	350 00
1 appraiser	3,000 00
1 examiner	1,235 86
1 clerk	300 00
1 opener and packer	280 00
1 special inspector	1,464 00
2 inspectors	2,928 00
10 inspectors	12,810 00
3 inspectors	3,561 99
6 inspectors	6,138 00
3 inspectors	277 50
2 inspectors	119 00
1 watchman	915 00
1 watchman	460 00
1 porter	600 00
1 janitor	600 00
GALENA, ILL.	
1 surveyor	593 50
1 clerk	500 00
QUINCY, ILL.	
1 surveyor	2,574 30
ALTON, ILL.	
1 surveyor	350 00
1 deputy surveyor	....

* Paid by Grand Trunk Railway.

† Paid by Great Western Railway.

Statement of the number of persons employed for the collection of customs, &c.—Continued.

District, number of persons, and occupation.	Agg. compensation.
CAIRO, ILL.	
1 surveyor and acting collector	$971 71
1 inspector	942 00
MILWAUKEE, WIS.	
1 collector	2,700 00
1 appraiser of merchandise	3,000 00
1 deputy collector	1,600 00
1 deputy collector	1,500 00
1 deputy collector	600 00
2 deputy collectors	600 00
1 deputy collector	200 00
1 deputy collector	150 00
3 inspectors	3,285 00
1 inspector	714 00
DU LUTH, MINN.	
1 surveyor	354 75
MINNESOTA, MINN.	
1 collector	1,000 00
1 special deputy collector, clerk, and inspector	1,277 50
1 deputy collector	1,200 00
1 inspector	730 00
1 inspector	912 50
4 mounted inspectors	3,351 00
DUBUQUE, IOWA.	
1 surveyor	598 67
1 janitor	600 00
1 fireman	435 25
BURLINGTON, IOWA.	
1 surveyor	350 00
KEOKUK, IOWA.	
1 surveyor	410 00
1 deputy surveyor	....
SAINT LOUIS, MO.	
1 surveyor and acting collector	6,000 00
1 clerk and special deputy	2,800 00
1 cashier and deputy	2,300 00
1 clerk and deputy	2,100 00
1 clerk and deputy	2,000 00
1 clerk and deputy	1,700 00
2 clerks	3,000 00
3 clerks	1,330 00
5 inspectors	5,200 00
2 store-keepers	1,569 00
1 appraiser	3,000 00
SAINT JOSEPH, MO.	
1 surveyor	394 70
OMAHA, NEBR.	
1 collector	411 50
MONTANA AND IDAHO.	
1 collector	1,005 48
PUGET SOUND, WASH.	
1 collector	3,400 00
3 deputy collectors	5,700 00
1 clerk and inspector	1,600 00
8 inspectors	11,680 00
1 inspectress	913 00
1 watchman	900 00
4 revenue boatmen	3,000 00

District, number of persons, and occupation.	Agg. compensation.
OREGON, OREG.	
1 collector	$3,019 51
1 deputy collector	1,800 00
1 deputy collector	1,500 00
1 deputy collector	1,150 00
1 inspector	1,200 00
4 inspectors	4,000 00
1 inspector	527 17
1 special inspector	500 00
WILLAMETTE, OREG.	
1 collector	3,000 00
1 deputy collector	2,000 00
1 deputy collector	1,900 00
1 appraiser	3,000 00
1 clerk	1,540 00
1 weigher and gauger	1,500 00
2 inspectors	2,700 00
1 night-inspector	1,229 00
1 porter and messenger	1,200 00
Sundry temporary inspectors	495 25
Sundry temporary night-inspectors	354 00
SAN FRANCISCO, CAL.	
1 collector, &c	6,000 00
3 deputy collectors	9,000 00
1 deputy collector and auditor	3,625 00
3 deputy collectors	4,500 00
2 clerks	6,000 00
4 clerks	8,432 97
5 clerks	10,000 00
4 clerks	7,500 00
10 clerks	18,000 00
5 clerks	8,000 00
3 messengers	3,240 00
3 watchmen	3,240 00
1 porter	1,080 00
1 deputy collector and store-keeper	3,000 00
3 clerks	6,000 00
5 clerks	9,000 00
1 clerk	1,600 00
1 superintendent of laborers	1,200 00
2 messengers	2,160 00
2 watchmen	2,160 00
7 laborers	7,560 00
8 assistant store-keepers	13,140 00
2 appraisers	4,994 50
2 assistant appraisers	5,000 00
1 examiner	2,250 00
2 examiners	4,000 00
1 clerk	1,800 54
1 packer and superintend't of laborers	1,200 00
1 messenger	1,080 00
5 laborers	5,400 00
1 surveyor	4,000 00
1 deputy surveyor	3,000 00
1 deputy surveyor	2,500 00
1 clerk	1,800 00
1 messenger	1,080 00
3 district officers	5,400 00
29 inspectors	45,240 00
2 inspectors	2,400 00
6 inspectors	6,000 00
6 inspectors	3,600 00
1 inspector	300 00
1 night-inspector	1,560 00
1 night-inspector	1,400 00
17 night-inspectors	20,400 00
4 weighers	8,000 00
10 assistant weighers	12,000 00
1 gauger	2,000 00
2 laborers	2,200 00
2 boarding-officers	3,200 00
6 bargemen	6,480 00
1 naval officer	4,500 00
1 deputy naval officer	3,125 00
1 clerk	2,200 00
1 clerk	2,100 00

Statement of the number of persons employed for the collection of customs, &c.—Continued.

District, number of persons, and occupation.	Agg. compensation.	District, number of persons, and occupation.	Agg. compensation.
SAN FRANCISCO, CAL.—Continued.		ALASKA.	
2 clerks	$3,750 00	1 collector	$2,870 15
1 clerk	1,800 00	1 deputy collector at Sitka	1,500 00
1 clerk	1,750 00	1 deputy collector at Kodiac	1,500 00
4 clerks	6,400 00	1 deputy collector at Ounalaska	1,500 00
1 messenger	1,080 00	1 deputy collector at Wraugel	1,5[illegible]0 00
		1 inspector at Sitka	1,460 00
		1 entrance and clearance clerk at Sitka	1,200 00
		1 deputy collector at Tongas	1,200 00

Statement showing the amount of moneys expended for collecting the revenue from customs at each custom-house in the United States previous to June 30, 1872, not heretofore reported, per act of March 3, 1869, as per settlements received in this office.

District or port.	Period reported. From—	Period reported. To—	Amount.
Aroostook, Me	April 1, 1870	Mar. 31, 1872	$12,370 66
Passamaquoddy, Me	April 1, 1870	Mar. 31, 1872	28,442 68
Machias, Me	Mar. 1, 1871	Mar. 31, 1872	6,729 64
Frenchman's Bay, Me	Jan. 1, 1871	Sept. 30, 1871	6,155 76
Castine, Me	April 1, 1871	Mar. 31, 1872	7,656 15
Waldoborough, Me	Feb. 13, 1871	Mar. 31, 1872	11,880 97
Wiscasset, Me	Jan. 1, 1871	Mar. 31, 1872	4,508 47
Bath, Me	Jan. 1, 1871	Mar. 31, 1872	16,059 07
Portland and Falmouth, Me	April 1, 1871	Mar. 31, 1872	85,292 39
Saco, Me	Mar. 19, 1871	June 30, 1871	616 53
Kennebunk, Me	Jan. 1, 1871	Dec. 31, 1871	943 94
York, Me	Apr. 1, 1871	Mar. 31, 1872	370 98
Belfast, Me	Mar. 15, 1871	Dec. 31, 1871	5,858 56
Bangor, Me	Mar. 15, 1871	Dec. 31, 1871	11,872 41
Portsmouth, N. H	April 1, 1871	Mar. 31, 1872	9,424 76
Burlington, Vt	July 1, 1871	Mar. 31, 1872	80,302 50
Newburyport, Mass*			
Gloucester, Mass	Jan. 1, 1871	Dec. 31, 1871	13,069 14
Salem and Beverly, Mass	June 30, 1871	June 30, 1872	14,502 20
Marblehead, Mass	Feb. 1, 1871	Mar. 31, 1872	3,620 82
Boston and Charlestown, Mass	Jan. 1, 1871	Dec. 31, 1871	595,609 82
Plymouth, Mass	April 1, 1871	June 30, 1871	683 88
Fall River, Mass	April 1, 1871	Mar. 31, 1872	9,871 90
Barnstable, Mass	Jan. 1, 1871	Mar. 31, 1872	13,698 36
New Bedford, Mass	April 1, 1871	June 30, 1872	16,349 15
Edgartown, Mass	April 1, 1871	Mar. 31, 1872	6,300 06
Nantucket, Mass	April 1, 1871	Dec. 31, 1871	1,716 50
Providence, R. I	Jan. 1, 1871	Dec. 31, 1871	30,403 32
Bristol and Warren, R. I	April 5, 1871	Mar. 31, 1872	2,428 98
Newport, R. I	April 1, 1871	June 30, 1872	7,563 23
Middletown, Conn	Jan. 1, 1871	Mar. 31, 1872	2,994 76
New London, Conn	April 1, 1871	Mar. 31, 1872	4,602 34
Fairfield, Conn	April 1, 1871	Dec. 31, 1871	1,681 21
New Haven, Conn	Aug. 1, 1870	Mar. 31, 1872	20,246 37
Stonington, Conn	July 1, 1871	Mar. 31, 1872	3,131 97
Genesee, N. Y	April 1, 1871	Dec. 31, 1871	17,637 87
Oswego, N. Y	May 1, 1871	Mar. 31, 1872	47,673 49
Niagara, N. Y	Jan. 1, 1871	Mar. 31, 1872	59,234 51
Buffalo Creek, N. Y	April 1, 1871	Dec. 31, 1871	35,039 94
Oswegatchie	July 1, 1871	Mar. 31, 1872	22,139 85
Sag Harbor, N. Y	April 1, 1871	Mar. 31, 1872	2,112 16
New York, N. Y	July 1, 1870	Mar. 31, 1872	2,127,550 25
Champlain, N. Y	April 1, 1871	Mar. 31, 1872	32,778 95
Cape Vincent, N. Y	Mar. 14, 1871	Mar. 31, 1872	17,237 89
Dunkirk, N. Y	April 1, 1871	Mar. 31, 1872	4,264 40
Albany, N. Y	April 1, 1871	Mar. 31, 1872	7,133 54
Bridgeton, N. J	July 1, 1871	Mar. 31, 1872	313 93
Burlington, N. J	July 1, 1871	June 30, 1872	281 14
Perth Amboy, N. J	Jan. 1, 1871	Mar. 31, 1872	11,402 46
Great Egg Harbor, N. J	Jan. 1, 1871	Dec. 31, 1871	1,892 25
Little Egg Harbor, N. J	Oct. 1, 1870	June 30, 1871	2,425 48
Newark, N. J	Jan. 1, 1871	Dec. 31, 1871	3,544 89

* Nothing.

Statement showing the amount of moneys expended for collecting the revenue, &c.—Continued.

District or port.	Period reported.		Amount.
	From—	To—	
Philadelphia, Pa	July 1, 1870	Dec. 31, 1871	$417,018 80
Erie, Pa	April 1, 1871	Mar. 31, 1872	8,035 33
Pittsburgh, Pa	April 1, 1871	Mar. 31, 1872	4,991 37
Delaware, Del	April 1, 1871	Mar. 31, 1872	9,068 27
Baltimore, Md	April 1, 1871	Mar. 31, 1872	355,208 87
Annapolis, Md	April 1, 1871	Mar. 31, 1872	3,095 44
Eastern, Md	Mar. 8, 1871	Mar. 31, 1872	3,422 51
Town Creek, Md	July 1, 1869	June 30, 1871	300 41
Georgetown, D. C	April 1, 1871	Mar. 31, 1872	4,825 83
Alexandria, Va	April 1, 1871	June 30, 1872	5,459 61
Cherrystone, Va	Mar. 21, 1871	Mar. 31, 1872	4,657 79
Norfolk and Portsmouth, Va	Jan. 1, 1871	Dec. 31, 1871	28,087 76
Tappahannock, Va	Sept. 19, 1870	June 30, 1871	699 05
Richmond, Va	Jan. 1, 1871	Dec. 31, 1871	10,491 51
Petersburgh, Va	July 1, 1870	Mar. 31, 1872	7,527 82
Yorktown, Va	April 1, 1871	Mar. 31, 1872	2,539 74
Wheeling, W. Va	July 1, 1871	Mar. 31, 1872	304 52
Parkersburgh, W. Va	July 1, 1871	Mar. 31, 1872	267 73
Albemarle, N. C	July 1, 1870	Mar. 31, 1872	9,875 88
Pamlico, N. C	July 1, 1871	Dec. 31, 1871	12,569 02
Beaufort, N. C	April 1, 1871	Mar. 31, 1872	9,705 46
Wilmington, N. C	July 1, 1870	Dec. 31, 1871	33,663 85
Charleston, S. C	Jan. 1, 1871	Mar. 31, 1872	61,589 45
Georgetown, S. C	July 1, 1870	Mar. 31, 1872	5,145 67
Beaufort, S. C	April 1, 1870	Feb. 29, 1872	4,378 75
Savannah, Ga	Mar. 31, 1870	Mar. 31, 1872	152,604 54
St. Mary's, Ga	April 1, 1871	Mar. 31, 1872	2,482 59
Brunswick, Ga	Jan. 1, 1871	Mar. 31, 1872	12,925 65
Mobile, Ala	April 1, 1871	Feb. 8, 1872	56,206 35
Selma, Ala	....	....	....
Pearl River, Miss	....	....	....
Natchez, Miss	April 1, 1871	June 30, 1871	125 00
Vicksburgh, Miss	Jan. 30, 1871	June 30, 1872	1,241 97
Pensacola, Fla	Jan. 1, 1871	Mar. 31, 1872	22,256 84
Saint Augustine, Fla	Apr. 1, 1871	Mar. 31, 1872	6,645 86
Key West, Fla	Jan. 1, 1871	Dec. 31, 1871	13,962 88
Saint Mark's, Fla	Apr. 1, 1871	Mar. 31, 1872	8,154 63
Saint John's, Fla	Apr. 1, 1871	Mar. 31, 1872	6,205 54
Apalachicola, Fla	Jan. 1, 1871	Dec. 31, 1872	3,345 14
Fernandina, Fla	Apr. 1, 1871	Mar. 31, 1872	5,941 30
New Orleans, La	July 1, 1870	Mar. 31, 1872	829,270 17
Teche, La	Jan. 1, 1871	Mar. 31, 1872	8,761 62
Galveston, Tex	July 1, 1871	Mar. 31, 1872	43,284 17
Saluria, Tex	Apr. 1, 1871	Mar. 31, 1872	18,884 57
Brazos de Santiago, Tex	Nov. 8, 1870	Mar. 31, 1872	63,840 66
Paso del Norte	Jan. 1, 1871	Mar. 31, 1872	23,137 67
Corpus Christi, Tex	Apr. 1, 1871	Mar. 31, 1872	34,696 93
Memphis, Tenn	Jan. 1, 1871	Sept. 30, 1871	7,735 91
Nashville, Tenn	Sept. 7, 1870	Mar. 31, 1872	3,797 67
Paducah, Ky	Sept. 1, 1870	June 30, 1871	446 53
Louisville, Ky	Apr. 1, 1871	Mar. 31, 1872	16,095 06
Saint Louis, Mo	July 1, 1871	Dec. 31, 1871	28,769 65
Saint Joseph, Mo	Oct. 1, 1870	Mar. 31, 1872	473 66
Miami, Ohio	Mar. 31, 1871	Mar. 31, 1872	8,394 01
Sandusky, Ohio	Apr. 1, 1871	Mar. 31, 1872	4,548 47
Cuyahoga, Ohio	Dec. 16, 1868	June 30, 1871	7,482 63
Cincinnati, Ohio	July 1, 1871	Mar. 31, 1872	39,378 03
Evansville, Indiana	Jan. 1, 1871	Dec. 31, 1871	5,055 11
New Albany, Ind	Oct. 1, 1860	Mar. 31, 1871	1,348 64
Madison, Ind	....	....	....
Chicago, Ill	Apr. 1, 1871	Mar. 31, 1872	85,808 12
Alton, Ill	July 1, 1871	June 30, 1872	553 06
Galena, Ill	July 1, 1871	Mar. 31, 1872	654 20
Quincy, Ill	Apr. 1, 1871	June 30, 1872	2,726 53
Cairo, Ill	July 1, 1871	June 30, 1872	2,123 41
Detroit, Mich	Apr. 1, 1871	Mar. 31, 1872	38,616 88
Superior, Mich	Jan. 1, 1871	Dec. 31, 1871	11,388 10
Port Huron, Mich	Apr. 1, 1871	Mar. 31, 1872	37,394 19
Michigan, Mich	Apr. 1, 1871	Mar. 31, 1872	8,405 27
Milwaukee, Wis	Mar. 1, 1871	Mar. 31, 1872	13,365 67
Minnesota, Minn	Apr. 1, 1871	Dec. 31, 1871	13,001 42
Du Luth, Minn	Nov. 1, 1870	June 30, 1872	3,457 56
Burlington, Iowa	July 1, 1870	Mar. 31, 1871	318 24
Keokuk, Iowa	Jan. 1, 1871	June 30, 1871	284 84
Dubuque, Iowa	Mar. 23, 1871	Mar. 31, 1872	764 90
San Francisco, California	July 1, 1870	Dec. 31, 1871	523,413 25

Statement showing the amount of moneys expended for collecting the revenue, &c.—Continued.

District or port.	Period reported.		Amount.
	From—	To—	
Oregon, Oreg.	Mar. 6, 1871	June 30, 1872	$29,441 16
Willamette, Oreg.	Oct. 1, 1870	Mar. 31, 1872	39,404 17
Puget Sound, Wash	Jan. 1, 1871	Dec. 31, 1871	23,522 66
Montana and Idaho	Oct. 1, 1870	Dec. 31, 1871	2,007 44
Alaska, Alaska	July 1, 1870	Feb. 29, 1872	27,010 91
Omaha, Nebraska	Sept. 1, 1870	Oct. 31, 1871	479 02
Augusta, Ga.	July 1, 1861	Feb. 28, 1861	201 76

Statement of the receipts for the fiscal year ended June 30, 1872.

From customs	$216,370,286 77
From internal revenue	130,642,177 72
From sales of public lands	2,575,714 19
From consular fees	586,817 06
From steamboat fees	248,416 45
From emolument fees	447,171 62
From registers' and receivers' fees	740,857 05
From fees on letters-patent	708,005 36
From consular receipts	14,325 77
From fines, penalties, and forfeitures—customs	674,232 77
From fines, penalties, and forfeitures—judiciary	48,051 99
From labor, drayage, and storage	70,404 82
From services of United States officers	343,003 17
From weighing fees	48,001 13
From marine-hospital tax	319,823 16
From miscellaneous sources	4,217 46
From semi-annual tax on circulation of national banks	6,523,396 39
From internal and coastwise intercourse fees	675 00
From surveying service	98,823 90
From rent of public buildings, &c	26,073 18
From salaries of store-keepers, &c	458,400 70
From Sioux City and Pacific Railroad Company	423 72
From Union Pacific Railroad Company	441,474 40
From Kansas Pacific Railroad Company	116,573 76
From Central Pacific Railroad Company	183,758 49
From Western Pacific Railroad Company	1,069 00
From sales of old material	8,023 17
From Central Branch Union Pacific Railroad Company	6,562 50
From wages of seamen forfeited	1,104 22
From exemplification of papers	4,864 42
From re-imbursements to United States to meet defaulted interest, Florida State stock, (trust fund)	4,063 75
Interest and premium on stocks, (trust fund)	212,613 15
Interest on deferred payments, (trust fund)	29,710 82
Sales of Indian trust land	499,469 48
Proceeds Osage lands, 2d article, &c	156,939 51
Re-imbursements to United States, (trust-fund stocks)	7,975 00
Proceeds of Indian trust-fund bonds	4,875 00
Six months' interest, Richmond and Danville Railroad stock	3,000 00
Moneys due the State of Arkansas	4,879 17
Prize cases, United States share	804 56
Profits on coinage	144,113 58
Copyright fees	11,673 16
Premium on transfer drafts	14,966 00
Premium on sale of coin	9,412,637 65
Conscience fund	3,204 94
Sale of old custom-house, Alexandria	4,150 00
Deductions from bullion deposits	63,147 12
Proceeds of lands in Saint Helena	957 44
Rent of Government property	1,930 37
Sale of Fort Gratiot military reservation	58,433 91
Mileage of examiners	800 45

Rebate of interest, United States bonds		$4,469 95
Deaths on shipboard		290 00
Interest on debts due the United States		11,526 38
Sale of certain tracts of lands		109 38
Omaha Coal Mining Company		18 00
Sale of Chippewa, &c., lands		12,935 65
Sale of Cherokee neutral lands		8,966 63
Sale of Osage lands, act July 16, 1870		528,836 85
Sale of Osage lands, 1st article, &c		201 25
Coupons collected		2,160 00
Prize moneys to captors		121,560 55
Sale of pine logs		1,399 64
Vacant lands in Washington		20 00
Dividends on stocks of Detroit and Chicago Canal Company		43,875 00
Tax on seal-skins		322,863 38
Bribes offered United States officers		126 47
Re-imbursements to United States, (1st National Bank, New Orleans)		65,826 40
Transportation account, Navy-pension fund		2,859 05
1, 2, 3, and 5 cent pieces		13,925 33
Sale of waste paper		23,291 10
Sale of Government property, Treasury Department		2,756 97
Sale of Government property, War Department		571,996 44
Sale of Government property, Navy Department		3,601 58
Sale of Government property, miscellaneous		168 05
Confiscations		330 45
Forfeitures, act July 13, 1861, &c		4,850 00
Sale of Point Gammon light-house site		751 00
Captured and abandoned property		77 66
Donations to national debt		4,000 00
Total receipts exclusive of loans		374,106,867 56
Three per cent. certificates	$65,000 00	
Legal-tender notes	69,599,804 00	
Coin certificates	63,229,500 00	
Fractional currency	31,816,900 00	
Consuls of 1867	1,900 00	
Loan of July and August, 1861	3,100 00	
Funded loan of 1881	140,330,850 00	
		305,047,054 00
		679,153,921 56

Net expenditures of the United States for the fiscal year ended June 30, 1872.

	Expenses on account of unexpended balances.	Excess of repayments on account of unexpended balances.	Expenses on account of appropriations.	Net expenditures.	Total.
CIVIL LIST.					
Legislative:					
Senate, compensation			$414,897 41	$414,897 41	
Senate, miscellaneous and contingent	$16,288 17		259,402 27	275,690 44	
House of Representatives, compensation		$12 00	1,373,672 49	1,373,660 49	
House of Representatives, miscellaneous and contingent		1,974 85	577,565 58	575,590 73	
Library of Congress, compensation			26,000 00	26,000 00	
Library of Congress, miscellaneous and contingent	3,000 00		16,500 00	19,500 00	
Botanic Garden, compensation	1 98		12,146 00	12,147 98	
Botanic Garden, miscellaneous and contingent			20,840 00	20,840 00	
Printing office, compensation			12,514 00	12,514 00	
Printing office, miscellaneous and contingent	292 68		1,294 99	1,587 67	
Printing office, paper for public printing	45,556 11		390,298 78	435,854 89	
Printing office, public printing	13,227 68		651,000 00	664,227 68	
Printing office, public binding	62,754 49		466,000 00	528,754 49	
Printing office, lithographing and engraving	6,501 62		35,970 56	42,472 18	
Court of Claims, compensation			29,840 00	29,840 00	
Court of Claims, miscellaneous and contingent		369 99	4,000 00	3,630 01	
Court of Claims, payment of judgments	38,366 97		197,012 72	235,379 69	$4,672,597 66
Executive:					
President, Vice-President, &c., compensation	4,584 31		44,057 32	48,641 63	
President, Vice-President, &c., miscellaneous and contingent			4,000 00	4,000 00	
Department of State, compensation		370 40	76,000 00	75,629 60	
Department of State, miscellaneous and contingent		461 71	103,212 00	102,750 29	
Treasury Department, compensation		22,358 50	2,641,514 32	2,619,155 82	
Treasury Department, miscellaneous and contingent		2,005 56	240,088 44	238,082 88	
Navy Department, compensation		486 00	116,757 61	116,271 61	
Navy Department, miscellaneous and contingent		529 16	10,950 00	10,420 84	
War Department, compensation		343 35	550,203 31	549,859 96	
War Department, miscellaneous and contingent		4,475 58	76,124 32	71,648 74	
Interior Department, compensation		8,036 93	1,264,040 00	1,256,003 07	
Interior Department, miscellaneous and contingent		14 97	265,870 78	265,855 81	
Post-Office Department, compensation	99 02		397,000 00	397,099 02	
Post-Office Department, miscellaneous and contingent			70,310 26	70,310 26	
Agricultural Department, compensation	275 72		74,707 92	74,983 64	
Agricultural Department, miscellaneous and contingent	4,326 06		112,053 21	116,379 27	
Department of Justice, compensation	123 92		94,204 28	94,328 20	
Department of Justice, miscellaneous and contingent	4,715 64		133,213 56	137,929 20	
Southern claims commission, compensation and expenses of	1,747 25		29,744 56	31,491 81	
Promoting the efficiency of the civil service, expenses of			8,300 00	8,300 00	6,289,141 5

Judiciary:					
Expenses of United States courts	155, 853 99	....	3, 062, 535 43	3, 218, 389 42	
Compensation of judges, associate judges, marshals, district attorneys, &c	922 27	....	374, 765 83	375, 688 10	3, 594, 077 52
Territorial expenses:					
Compensation of governors, judges, &c	3, 271 57	....	121, 719 65	124, 991 22	
Miscellaneous and contingent expenses	15, 927 19	....	141, 934 30	157, 861 49	
Salaries and expenses of the District of Columbia	2, 725 15	....	28, 195 56	30, 920 71	313, 773 42
Assistant treasurers and their clerks, depositaries, &c.:					
Assistant treasurers and their clerks, compensation	603 12	....	298, 125 14	298, 728 26	
United States depositaries, compensation	3, 395 66	....	34, 580 00	37, 975 66	
Independent Treasury, compensation	....	....	6, 000 00	6, 000 00	
Independent Treasury, miscellaneous and contingent	....	....	88, 131 88	88, 131 88	430, 835 82
Surveyors-general:					
Compensation of surveyors-general and their clerks	30, 106 33	....	105, 256 52	135, 362 85	
Miscellaneous and contingent expenses	9, 064 20	....	25, 369 23	34, 433 43	169, 796 28
Registers and receivers:					
Compensation of	15, 613 09	....	332, 049 94	347, 663 03	
Miscellaneous and contingent expenses	1, 229 20	....	38, 670 84	39, 900 04	387, 563 07
Inspectors of steam-vessels:					
Compensation	1, 845 39	....	157, 868 21	159, 713 60	
Miscellaneous and contingent	10, 105 75	....	48, 864 98	58, 970 73	218, 684 33
MISCELLANEOUS.					
Post-Office Department:					
Deficiency in postal service	485, 000 00	....	3, 083, 750 00	3, 568, 750 00	
Pay for carrying free mail matter	....	....	700, 000 00	700, 000 00	
Telegraphing between Atlantic and Pacific States	9, 972 60	....	13, 479 45	23, 452 05	
Steam-ship service between the United States and Brazil	37, 500 00	....	150, 000 00	187, 500 00	
Steam-ship service between San Francisco, Japan, and China	125, 000 00	....	500, 000 00	625, 000 00	
Steam-ship service between San Francisco, and Sandwich Islands	18, 750 00	....	75, 000 00	93, 750 00	
Expenses, national loan	....	1, 094 90	2, 402, 007 16	2, 400, 912 26	
Refunding national debt	....	....	644, 169 12	644, 169 12	
Expenses, national currency	....	....	72, 653 72	72, 653 72	
Suppressing counterfeiting and frauds	1, 000 00	....	124, 028 70	125, 028 70	
Plates, paper, special dies, &c., office of the Comptroller of the Currency	158, 879 11	....	....	158, 879 11	
Contingent expenses, safe keeping the public revenue	59, 860 60	....	....	59, 860 60	
Mint establishment:					
Compensation	....	14, 126 15	124, 725 00	110, 598 85	
Miscellaneous and contingent	....	14, 058 48	612, 767 50	598, 709 02	
Building, &c	7, 832 53	....	177, 558 42	185, 390 95	
Court-house, post-office, &c:					
Portland, Maine	6, 248 74	....	11, 876 64	18, 125 38	
Boston, Massachusetts	285, 897 27	....	356, 483 75	642, 381 02	
New York, New York	999, 191 24	....	810, 614 62	1, 809, 805 86	
Omaha, Nebraska	....	....	50, 000 00	50, 000 00	
Columbia, South Carolina	....	....	52, 411 25	52, 411 25	
Miscellaneous	7, 241 00	....	....	7, 241 00	

Net expenditures of the United States for the fiscal year ended June 30, 1872—Continued.

	Expenses on account of unexpended balances.	Excess of repayments on account of unexpended balances.	Expenses on account of appropriations.	Net expenditures.	Total.
MISCELLANEOUS—Continued.					
Surveys of the coast			$729,000 00	$729,000 00	
Return of proceeds of captured and abandoned property			1,278,493 77	1,278,493 77	
Expenses of the Smithsonian Institution	$19,500 00		19,500 00	39,000 00	
Expenses of the ninth census			1,348,722 80	1,348,722 80	
Expenses of the eighth census	7,456 81			7,456 81	
Packing congressional documents			7,000 00	7,000 00	
Columbia Institution for the Deaf and Dumb and the Blind, current expenses			40,500 00	40,500 00	
Columbia Hospital for Women, current expenses			18,500 00	18,500 00	
Maryland Institute for the Blind, current expenses			1,200 00	1,200 00	
Government Hospital for the Insane, current expenses	21,111 78		90,000 00	111,111 78	
Metropolitan police, compensation		$1,900 64	207,870 00	205,969 36	
National Soldiers and Sailors' Home, (orphans,) current expenses			15,000 00	15,000 00	
Penitentiaries and libraries in the Territories	2,832 19		5,427 64	8,259 83	
Repayments for lands erroneously sold			22,084 83	22,084 83	
Deposits by individuals for expenses of surveys of public lands	2,452 86		37,715 40	40,168 26	
Five per cent. fund, &c.:					
Iowa			18,463 15	18,463 15	
Michigan			16,971 82	16,971 82	
Minnesota			13,009 58	13,009 58	
Nevada			3,313 55	3,313 55	
Oregon			6,568 76	6,568 76	
Wisconsin			37,121 75	37,121 75	
Florida			4,063 75	4,063 75	
Three per cent. fund, &c., Missouri			9,391 43	9,391 43	
Two per cent. fund, &c., Missouri			6,260 95	6,260 95	
Indemnity for swamp-lands purchased by individuals			8,364 97	8,364 97	
Surveys of public lands, &c	202,467 51		636,047 45	838,514 96	
Purchase of United States Statutes at Large	7,000 00			7,000 00	
Purchase of the building known as the Club House, Charleston, South Carolina	9,735 22			9,735 22	
Public buildings:					
State, War, and Navy Department buildings			700,000 00	700,000 00	
Treasury Department building, repairs, &c		769 08	15,000 00	14,230 92	
Interior Department building, repairs, &c	5,300 00		26,500 00	31,800 00	
Navy Department building, repairs, &c			12,290 00	12,290 00	
Columbia Institute building, repairs, improvement of grounds, &c			15,500 00	15,500 00	
Government Hospital for the Insane, repairs, improvement of grounds, &c	39,492 00		25,000 00	64,492 00	
Smithsonian Institution, completing hall and preservation of collections			20,000 00	20,000 00	
Capitol extension, new dome, repairs, &c			101,500 00	101,500 00	
Capitol, improving grounds		50	27,000 00	26,999 50	
Government Printing Office building, repairs, &c			25,000 00	25,000 00	

Dredging the Washington Canal	37, 029 89			37, 029 89	
Improvement of avenues, streets, &c., in Washington	5, 858 42		222, 541 25	228, 399 67	
Repairs, &c., of bridges in Washington		1 11	5, 000 00	4, 998 89	
Washington aqueduct	43, 499 70		114, 196 00	157, 695 70	
Repairs, &c., Executive Mansion			26, 345 00	26, 345 00	
Lighting the Capitol, Executive Mansion, &c			50, 000 00	50, 000 00	
Support and treatment of transient paupers	1, 000 00		11, 000 00	12, 000 00	
Miscellaneous accounts	700 66		6, 746 02	7, 446 68	
Reliefs			206, 969 68	206, 969 68	$18, 818, 554 15
INTERNAL REVENUE.					
Expenses of assessing and collecting internal revenue	626, 718 62		5, 070, 569 72	5, 697, 288 34	
Allowances or drawbacks on articles on which internal tax or duty has been paid			650, 414 80	650, 414 80	
Punishment for violating internal revenue laws	14, 673 58		20, 526 03	35, 199 61	
Stamps, paper, dies, &c	96, 882 89		328, 701 82	425, 584 71	
Refunding duties, &c			604, 297 70	604, 297 70	
Miscellaneous			5, 333 25	5, 333 25	7, 418, 118 41
CUSTOMS.					
Expenses, collecting the revenue from customs			6, 950, 189 81	6, 950, 189 81	
Repayment to importers of excess of deposits			2, 420, 555 13	2, 420, 555 13	
Debenture, drawbacks, bounties, or allowances			625, 188 23	625, 188 23	
Refunding duties			137, 215 70	137, 215 70	
Distributive shares, fines, penalties, and forfeitures			353, 427 42	353, 427 42	
Return of proceeds of captured and abandoned property	7, 420 64		27, 029 37	34, 450 01	
Expenses of the revenue-cutter service	23, 199 53		907, 050 28	930, 249 81	
Building, &c., vessels for revenue-cutter service	148, 262 27			148, 262 27	
Public buildings, repairs, preservation, furniture, fuel, &c	10, 904 77		633, 182 48	644, 087 25	
Light-house Establishment, supplies, incidental expenses, buoyage, wages, &c	86, 369 23		1, 541, 135 36	1, 627, 504 59	
Light-houses, building, &c.:					
Maine			110, 000 00	110, 000 00	
New Hampshire			37, 000 00	37, 000 00	
Vermont			11, 000 00	11, 000 00	
Massachusetts			25, 000 00	25, 000 00	
Rhode Island		40 98	57, 000 00	56, 959 02	
Connecticut		2 25	13, 131 96	13, 129 71	
New York	420 41		136, 792 83	137, 213 24	
Pennsylvania	389 84		2, 000 00	2, 389 84	
New Jersey			1, 000 00	1, 000 00	
Delaware			4, 000 00	4, 000 00	
Maryland	9, 976 37			9, 976 37	
Virginia		99 58	15, 000 00	14, 900 42	
North Carolina	29, 648 22		65, 000 00	94, 648 22	
South Carolina			9, 000 00	9, 000 00	
Florida	81, 811 53		161, 414 94	243, 226 47	
Alabama			59, 535 88	59, 535 88	
Louisiana	21, 598 57		127, 807 97	149, 406 54	
Texas	28, 812 49		35, 000 00	63, 812 49	
Ohio			49, 014 00	49, 014 00	
Illinois			8, 549 04	8, 549 04	

Net expenditures of the United States for the fiscal year ended June 30, 1872—Continued.

	Expenses on account of unexpended balances.	Excess of repayments on account of unexpended balances.	Expenses on account of appropriations.	Net expenditures.	Total.
CUSTOMS—Continued.					
Light-houses, building, &c.:					
Michigan	$42, 488 11		$155, 939 77	$198, 427 88	
Wisconsin			11, 000 00	11, 000 00	
Minnesota			5, 490 90	5, 490 90	
California	36, 424 94		112, 445 81	148, 870 75	
Oregon	1, 249 12		66, 371 44	67, 620 56	
Washington			10, 000 00	10, 000 00	
Preserving life and property from shipwrecked vessels			51, 246 17	51, 246 17	
Custom-houses:					
Maine	3, 709 16		37, 106 48	40, 815 64	
New York, (barge office)	10, 856 62			10, 856 62	
Pennsylvania, (appraiser's store)	39, 146 41		681 65	39, 828 06	
Maryland	9, 635 00		50, 000 00	59, 635 00	
South Carolina	19, 073 63		60, 000 00	79, 073 63	
Louisiana			148, 415 75	148, 415 75	
Tennessee	40, 939 50		89, 841 28	130, 780 78	
Ohio	4, 707 34			4, 707 34	
Michigan	513 30			513 30	
Illinois	40, 130 08		36, 220 53	76, 350 61	
Minnesota			105, 927 83	105, 927 83	
Oregon	37, 426 36		24, 217 94	61, 644 30	
California	49 35			49 35	
Marine hospital establishment	59, 311 80		362, 585 23	421, 897 03	
Marine hospital, Chicago, Illinois			153, 245 93	153, 245 93	
Miscellaneous accounts			2, 560 20	2, 560 20	
Reliefs			30, 126 28	30, 126 28	
					$16, 832, 255 37
FOREIGN INTERCOURSE.					
Salaries of ministers	10, 309 46		305, 024 81	315, 334 27	
Salaries of secretaries of legation	302 32		29, 816 67	30, 118 99	
Contingent expenses of foreign intercourse	7, 832 09		65, 204 50	73, 036 59	
Salary of interpreters to consulates	2, 423 14		6, 147 10	8, 570 24	
Salary of marshals for consular courts	2, 647 38		4, 511 30	7, 158 68	
Salary of consuls	181, 273 98		234, 312 51	415, 586 49	
Contingent expenses of United States consulates	18, 956 55		67, 821 86	86, 778 41	
Salaries and expenses of United States and Mexican claims commission	2, 239 04		26, 197 66	28, 436 70	
Salaries and expenses of commission between United States and Spain			12, 047 35	12, 047 35	
Expenses of interpreters, guards, &c., in Turkish dominion	905 49		2, 346 90	3, 252 39	
Prisons for American convicts	2, 053 60		6, 067 32	8, 120 92	

Bringing home criminals from foreign countries	595 81		1,584 67	2,180 48	
Relief and protection of American seamen	13,811 80		195,463 73	209,275 53	
Rescuing shipwrecked seamen	75 00		5,000 00	5,075 00	
Scheldt dues	1,000 00		60,584 00	61,584 00	
Claims of Hudson Bay and Puget Sound Agricultural Companies		$10,130 97	325,000 00	314,869 03	
Consular receipts			9,087 39	9,087 39	
Diplomatic and consular war expenses in Madrid, Paris, Berlin, and London			40,886 96	40,886 96	
Salaries and expenses of the commission between the United States and Great Britain			56,493 13	56,493 13	
Tribunal of arbitration at Geneva			117,566 59	117,566 59	
Expenses of the embassy from Japan			25,000 00	25,000 00	
Miscellaneous accounts	5,000 00		3,310 00	8,310 00	
					1,639,309 14
Total					60,984,757 42

Analysis of the foregoing statement.

CIVIL LIST.

Compensation:		
Legislature	$1,869,059 88	
Executive	5,263,464 36	
Judiciary	375,688 10	
Territorial expenses	155,911 93	
Assistant treasurers, depositaries, &c	342,703 94	
Surveyors-general	135,362 85	
Registers and receivers	347,663 63	
Inspectors of steam-vessels	159,713 60	
Total compensation		$8,649,568 29
Miscellaneous and contingent:		
Legislative	$896,838 85	
Executive	1,025,677 29	
Judiciary, (expenses of courts)	3,218,389 42	
Territorial expenses	157,861 49	
Assistant treasurers, depositaries, &c	88,131 88	
Surveyors-general	34,433 43	
Registers and receivers	39,900 04	
Inspectors of steam-vessels	58,970 73	
Expenses of Public Printing Office, (paper, binding, &c.)	1,671,309 24	
Payment of judgments Court of Claims	235,379 69	
Total miscellaneous and contingent		7,426,892 06
Total civil list		16,076,460 35

MISCELLANEOUS.

Post-Office Department, deficiencies, for mail-matter, and telegraphic communication	$4,292,202 05	
Post-Office Department, steamship-service	906,250 00	
National debt, expenses of refunding, &c	3,551,503 51	
Mint establishment	894,698 82	
Court-houses, post-offices, &c	2,579,964 51	
Surveys of the coast	729,000 00	
Return of proceeds of captured and abandoned property	1,278,493 77	
Expenses of the eighth and ninth censuses	1,356,179 61	
Metropolitan police	205,969 36	
Current expenses of benevolent institutions in Washington, D. C	198,311 78	
Repayments for lands erroneously sold	70,618 06	
Five per cent. fund of the net proceeds from the sales of public lands	115,164 74	
Surveys of the public lands	838,514 96	
Public buildings in Washington	1,077,147 42	
Improvement of streets, avenues, &c., in Washington, Washington aqueduct	478,124 15	
Miscellaneous accounts	39,441 73	
Reliefs	206,969 68	
Total miscellaneous		18,818,554 15

INTERNAL REVENUE.

Expenses of collecting, stamps, dies, &c	$6,163,405 91	
Allowances or drawbacks, refunding duties, &c	1,254,712 50	
Total internal revenue		$7,418,118 41

CUSTOMS.

Expenses of collecting revenue	6,950,189 81
Expenses of revenue-cutter service	1,078,512 08
Repayment to importers, debentures, refunding duties	3,182,969 06
Distributive shares, fines, penalties, and forfeitures	353,427 42

Return of proceeds of captured and abandoned property	$34,450 01	
Public buildings, repairs, &c	644,087 25	
Light-House Establishment	3,222,122 09	
Custom-houses	758,678 21	
Marine hospital establishment	575,142 96	
Miscellaneous accounts	2,560 20	
Reliefs	30,126 28	
Total customs		$16,832,255 37
Foreign intercourse:		
Salaries of ministers, consuls, &c	874,345 85	
Miscellaneous and contingent expenses	282,425 18	
Relief and protection of American seamen	209,275 53	
Claims of Hudson Bay and Puget Sound Agricultural Companies	314,869 03	
Diplomatic and consular war expenses	40,886 96	
Tribunal of arbitration at Geneva	117,566 59	
		1,839,369 14
Total civil, miscellaneous, foreign intercourse, &c., expenditures		60,984,757 42

The following accounts, refunding, &c., are not legitimate expenses, and ought properly to be deducted from the receipts instead of classed as expenditures, viz:

Return of proceeds of captured and abandoned property	$1,278,493 77	
Repayments for lands erroneously sold	70,618 06	
Five per cent. fund, net proceeds sales of lands	115,164 74	
Allowances, refunding, &c., internal revenue	1,254,712 50	
Repayment to importers, debentures, &c., customs	3,182,959 06	
Distributive shares, fines, penalties, and forfeitures	353,427 42	
Return of proceeds captured and abandoned property	34,450 01	
		6,289,825 56
Net expenditures, (deducting refunding, &c., as above)		54,694,931 86

The following are extraordinary and *not* current expenditures:

Payment of judgments Court of Claims	$235,379 69	
Building court-houses, post-offices, &c	2,579,964 51	
Expenses of the census	1,356,179 61	
Public buildings in Washington	1,077,147 42	
Reliefs	237,095 96	
Claims of Hudson Bay and Puget Sound Agricultural Companies	314,869 03	
Diplomatic and consular war expenses	40,886 96	
Tribunal of arbitration at Geneva	117,566 59	
		5,959,089 77
Total civil, miscellaneous, and foreign intercourse *current* expenses of the Government		48,735,842 09

MILITARY ESTABLISHMENT.

Pay Department		$10,408,246 90
Commissary Department		1,418,676 43
Quartermaster's Department		10,663,169 74
Ordnance		94,299 15
Forts and fortifications		1,540,747 65
Improvement of harbors:		
Maine	$32,000 00	
Vermont	35,000 00	
Massachusetts	104,800 00	
Connecticut	59,093 01	
New York	220,722 79	
Pennsylvania	38,200 00	
Delaware	8,500 00	
Maryland	15,000 00	
Ohio	123,425 34	
Michigan	205,220 76	

Improvement of harbors—Continued.		
Indiana	$20,177 12	
Illinois	169,999 89	
Wisconsin	323,394 66	
Alabama	52,378 13	
Texas	43,000 00	
Minnesota	60,000 00	
		$1,510,911 70
Improvement of rivers, &c.:		
Maine	73,975 00	
New Hampshire	5,000 00	
Massachusetts	28,000 00	
Rhode Island	56,991 82	
Rhode Island and Connecticut	9,000 00	
Connecticut	78,999 70	
New York	70,000 00	
Removing obstructions in East River and Hell-gate, New York	315,000 00	
New Jersey	25,000 00	
Pennsylvania	7,000 00	
Delaware	79,500 00	
Maryland	41,243 54	
District of Columbia	15,000 00	
Virginia	85,000 00	
North Carolina	95,000 00	
South Carolina	154 26	
Florida	27,000 00	
Arkansas	25,000 00	
Louisiana and Arkansas	41,000 00	
Louisiana	2,551 25	
Tennessee	30,000 00	
Ohio	2,784 26	
Illinois	29,000 00	
Michigan	137,781 21	
Wisconsin	33,000 00	
Minnesota	10,137 47	
Oregon	40,814 11	
California	145,000 00	
(General appropriations) improving the Ohio River	63,699 30	
(General appropriations) improving the falls and canals at Louisville	419,999 00	
(General appropriations) improving the Mississippi River	244,717 00	
(General appropriations) improving the Upper Mississippi River	77,000 00	
(General appropriations) improving the Mississippi, Missouri, and Arkansas	140,000 00	
(General appropriations) improving the Des Moines Rapids, Mississippi	400,000 00	
(General appropriations) improving the Rock Island Rapids, Mississippi	173,000 00	
(General appropriations) improving the Rock Island Bridge	453,000 00	
(General appropriations) snag-boats, &c., Western rivers	8,233 09	
(General appropriations) examinations and surveys	361,911 54	
(General appropriations) repairs, &c., of river and harbor works	40,089 37	
		3,890,581 92
Military Academy		85,865 00
Chief Signal-Officer		168,501 00
General of the Army		4,409 75
Surgeon General		486,539 83
Commissioner of Freedmen		173,882 15
Secretary of War		266,153 94
Bounty act of July 28, 1866		4,506,996 42
Payment to members of certain military organizations in Kansas		308,475 28
Claims of loyal citizens for supplies furnished during the rebellion		191,707 07

Refunding to States expenses incurred in raising volunteers by Vermont	$56,502 18	
Refunding to States expenses incurred in raising volunteers by Michigan	58,892 00	
Refunding to States expenses incurred in raising volunteers by Iowa	101,376 02	
Refunding to States expenses incurred in raising volunteers by Massachusetts	79,375 41	
		$296,145 61
Payment under relief acts		192,605 49
		36,207,915 03
From which deduct the following excess of repayments on appropriations where the repayments exceed the expenditures		835,757 83
Total net expenditures, War Department		35,372,157 20

NAVY DEPARTMENT.

Secretary's office	$7,632,036 43
Marine Corps	821,166 79
Bureau Yards and Docks	2,143,221 23
Bureau Equipment and Recruiting	1,566,809 34
Bureau Navigation	256,200 92
Bureau Ordnance	932,708 69
Bureau Construction and Repair	4,426,797 26
Bureau Steam-Engineering	1,062,584 48
Bureau Provisions and Clothing	2,018,994 68
Bureau Medicine and Surgery	297,905 99
Bureau Reliefs and Indefinite	90,784 13
Total net expenditures Navy Department	21,249,809 99

INTERIOR DEPARTMENT.

War pensions	$25,150,859 42	
War of 1812 pensions	2,906,812 26	
Navy pensions	475,731 08	
		$28,533,402 76
Indians		7,061,728 82
Total Interior Department		35,595,131 58

PUBLIC DEBT.

Appropriations, designating titles.	Redemption.	Interest.	Premium.
Temporary loan	$2,000 00	$101 03	
Certificates of indebtedness of 1870		27,330 00	
Coin certificates	51,029,500 00		
Three per cent. certificates	19,730,000 00	944,480 26	
Navy pension fund		420,000 00	
Treasury notes prior to 1846	100 00	5 00	
Treasury notes of 1861	50 00	6 00	
Seven-thirties of 1861	3,100 00	530 55	
Old demand notes	8,209 25		
Legal-tender notes	68,090,304 00		
Fractional currency	31,543,939 29		
One-year notes of 1863	21,250 00	1,062 50	
Two-year notes of 1863	9,800 00	933 85	
Compound interest notes	174,920 00	36,168 07	
Seven-thirties of 1864 and 1865	120,650 00	18,860 24	
Loan of 1842	6,000 00		
Loan of 1847	500 00	1,020 00	
Bounty-land scrip	75 00	2 53	
Loan of 1848	10,400 00		
Texan indemnity stock	7,000 00	800 00	
Loan of 1858		1,002,350 00	
Loan of 1860	29,000 00	875 00	
Loan of February, 1861, (1881's)		1,101,996 00	
Oregon war debt		57,501 00	
Loan of July and August, 1861, (1881's)		11,374,159 12	
Five-twenties of 1862	184,234,750 00	25,035,157 15	$2,072,577 40
Loan of 1863, (1881's)		4,492,501 50	
Ten-forties of 1864		9,758,043 08	
Five-twenties of March, 1864	270,100 00	150,223 23	21,508 93
Five-twenties of June, 1864	13,120,100 00	4,936,033 73	915,434 40
Five-twenties of 1865	8,151,150 00	9,868,375 72	640,725 51
Consols of 1865	20,905,850 00	14,589,939 66	2,371,750 09
Consols of 1867	7,949,500 00	19,675,292 66	925,280 44
Consols of 1868	160,500 00	2,364,494 77	10,989 99
Central Pacific stock		1,554,881 92	
Kansas Pacific stock, (U. P. E. D)		377,760 00	
Union Pacific stock		1,633,140 72	
Central branch Union Pacific stock, (A. and P. P)		95,970 00	
Western Pacific stock		118,205 18	
Sioux City and Pacific stock		97,429 20	
Funded loan of 1881		7,021,493 10	
Total	405,007,307 54	117,357,839 72	6,958,266 76

Redemption	$405,007,307 54
Interest	117,357,839 72
Premium	6,958,266 76
Total	529,323,414 02

RECAPITULATION.

Net expenditures:	
Civil list	$16,076,460 35
Miscellaneous	16,832,255 37
Internal revenue	7,418,118 41
Customs	18,818,554 15
War Department	35,372,157 20
Foreign intercourse	1,839,369 14
Navy Department	21,249,809 99
Interior Department	35,595,131 58
Interest on the public debt	117,357,839 72
Premiums	6,958,266 76
Total net expenditures exclusive of redemption of the public debt	277,517,962 67
Redemption of the public debt	405,007,307 54
Total net expenditures	682,525,270 21

Statement of judgments of the Court of Claims paid by the Treasury Department.

Date.	In whose favor.		To whom paid.	Amount.
Aug. 10, 1871	H. D. Norton		H. D. Norton	$489 71
Aug. 25, 1871	H. Eckford		J. D. McPherson	4,827 51
	E. Calahan*			
	M. C. Espy*			
	E. P. Wilcox*			
	H. L. Lee*		E. Calahan and others	275 00
Aug. 30, 1871	New York, Newfoundland and London Telegraph Company.		New York, Newfoundland and London Telegraph Company.	32,240 75
Sept. 27, 1871	J. W. Price		J. W. Price	234 00
Oct. 23, 1871	J. W. Seeberger		J. W. Seeberger	300 00
Dec. 1, 1871	William W. Burns		William W. Burns	113,100 35
Dec. 12, 1871	William W. Hubbell		William W. Hubbell	72,922 37
April 4, 1872	E. D. Wheeler		E. D. Wheeler	589 60
May 16, 1872	Wm. J. Patton		William J. Patton	1,000 00
May 22, 1872	C. H. Manning	$240 16	C. Manning and others	1,745 94
	T. A. Fitzpatrick	100 07		
	George W. Hall	144 10		
	John Bohn	172 92		
	T. E. Sytle	179 72		
	C. F. Holbrook	200 14		
	L. La Rien	216 15		
	J. G. Richards	179 72		
	William A. Newman	312 96		
May 24, 1872	M. Daily		M. Daily	350 00
June 11, 1872	A. Morrill		A. Morrill	4,816 46
June 13, 1872	S. H. Talbott			
	P. S. J. Talbott			
	J. R. Talbott			
	L. F. Talbott			
	A. Brown			
	George W. Simpson		S. H. Talbott and others	
	J. Small		Owners schooner Keokuk	2,128 00
	George H. Miller		George H. Miller	360 00
	Total			235,379 69

* Amount paid to each party not specified in account.

Statement of revenue collected from the beginning of the Government to June 30, 1872, from the following sources.

(By calendar years to 1843, and subsequently by fiscal years.)

Years.	Customs.	Internal revenue.	Direct taxes.	Postage.	Public lands.	Dividends & sales of bank stock and bonus.	Miscellaneous.	Net revenue.	Loans and Treasury notes, &c.	Total receipts.
From Mar. 4, 1789, to Dec. 31, 1791	$4,399,473 09	....	....	....	....	....	$19,440 10	$4,418,913 19	$5,791,112 56	$10,210,025 75
1792	3,443,070 85	$208,942 81	....	....	....	88,028 00	9,918 65	3,669,960 31	5,070,806 46	8,740,766 77
1793	4,255,306 56	337,705 70	....	$11,020 51	....	38,500 00	10,390 37	4,652,923 14	1,067,701 14	5,720,624 28
1794	4,801,065 28	274,089 62	....	29,478 49	....	303,472 00	23,799 48	5,431,904 87	4,609,196 78	10,041,101 65
1795	5,588,461 26	337,755 36	....	22,400 00	....	160,000 00	5,917 97	6,114,534 59	3,305,268 20	9,419,802 79
1796	6,567,987 94	475,289 60	....	72,909 84	$4,836 13	1,240,000 00	16,506 14	8,377,529 65	362,800 00	8,740,329 65
1797	7,549,649 65	575,491 45	....	64,500 00	83,540 60	385,220 00	30,379 29	8,688,780 99	70,135 41	8,758,916 40
1798	7,106,061 93	644,357 95	....	39,500 00	11,963 11	79,920 00	18,692 81	7,900,495 80	308,574 27	8,209,070 07
1799	6,610,449 31	779,136 44	....	41,000 00	....	71,040 00	45,187 56	7,546,813 31	5,074,646 53	12,621,459 84
1800	9,080,932 73	809,396 55	$734,223 97	78,000 00	443 75	71,040 00	74,712 10	10,848,749 10	1,602,435 04	12,451,184 14
1801	10,750,778 93	1,048,043 43	534,343 38	79,500 00	167,726 06	88,800 00	266,149 15	12,935,330 95	10,125 00	12,945,455 95
1802	12,438,235 74	621,898 89	206,565 44	35,000 00	188,628 02	1,327,560 00	177,905 86	14,995,793 95	5,597 36	15,001,391 31
1803	10,479,417 61	215,179 69	71,879 20	16,427 26	165,675 69	....	115,518 18	11,064,097 63	....	11,064,097 63
1804	11,098,565 33	50,941 29	50,198 44	26,500 00	487,526 00	....	112,575 53	11,826,307 38	9,532 64	11,835,840 02
1805	12,936,487 04	21,747 15	21,882 91	21,342 50	540,193 80	....	19,039 80	13,560,693 20	128,814 94	13,689,508 14
1806	14,667,698 17	20,101 45	55,763 86	41,117 67	765,245 73	....	10,004 19	15,559,931 07	48,897 71	15,608,828 78
1807	15,845,521 61	13,051 40	34,732 56	3,614 73	466,163 27	....	34,935 69	16,398,019 26	....	16,398,019 26
1808	16,363,550 58	8,210 73	19,159 21	....	647,939 06	....	21,802 35	17,060,661 93	1,882 16	17,062,544 09
1809	7,296,020 58	4,044 39	7,517 31	....	442,252 33	....	23,638 51	7,773,473 12	....	7,773,473 12
1810	8,583,309 31	7,430 63	12,448 68	....	696,548 82	....	84,476 84	9,384,214 28	2,759,992 25	12,144,206 53
1811	13,313,222 73	2,295 95	7,666 66	37 70	1,040,237 53	....	60,068 52	14,423,529 09	8,309 05	14,431,838 14
1812	8,958,777 53	4,903 06	859 22	85,039 70	710,427 78	....	41,125 47	9,801,132 76	12,837,900 00	22,639,032 76
1813	13,224,623 25	4,755 04	3,805 52	35,000 00	835,655 14	....	236,571 00	14,340,409 95	26,184,435 00	40,524,844 95
1814	5,998,772 08	1,662,984 82	2,219,497 36	45,000 00	1,135,971 09	....	119,399 81	11,181,625 16	23,377,911 79	34,559,536 95
1815	7,282,942 22	4,678,059 07	2,162,673 41	135,000 10	1,287,959 28	....	150,282 74	15,696,916 82	35,264,320 78	50,961,237 60
1816	36,306,874 88	5,124,708 31	4,253,635 09	149,787 74	1,717,985 03	....	123,994 61	47,676,985 66	9,494,436 16	57,171,421 82
1817	26,283,348 49	2,678,100 77	1,834,187 04	29,371 91	1,991,226 06	202,426 30	80,389 17	33,099,049 74	734,542 59	33,833,592 33
1818	17,176,385 00	955,270 20	264,333 36	20,070 00	2,606,564 77	525,000 00	87,547 71	21,585,171 04	8,765 62	21,593,936 66
1819	20,283,608 76	229,593 63	83,650 78	71 32	3,274,422 78	675,000 00	57,027 10	24,603,374 37	2,291 00	24,605,665 37
1820	15,005,612 15	106,260 53	31,586 82	6,465 95	1,635,871 61	1,000,000 00	54,872 49	17,840,669 55	3,040,824 13	20,881,493 68
1821	13,004,447 15	69,027 63	29,349 05	516 91	1,212,966 46	105,000 00	152,072 52	14,573,379 72	5,000,324 00	19,573,703 72
1822	17,589,761 94	67,665 71	20,961 56	602 04	1,803,581 54	297,500 00	452,355 15	20,232,427 94	....	20,232,427 94
1823	19,088,433 44	34,242 17	10,337 71	110 69	916,523 10	350,000 00	141,019 15	20,540,666 26	....	20,540,666 26
1824	17,878,325 71	34,663 37	6,201 96	....	984,418 15	350,000 00	127,603 60	19,381,212 79	5,000,000 00	24,381,212 79
1825	20,098,713 45	25,771 35	2,330 85	469 56	1,216,090 56	367,500 00	129,982 25	21,840,858 02	5,000,000 00	26,840,858 02
1826	23,341,331 77	21,589 93	6,638 76	300 14	1,393,785 09	402,500 00	94,288 52	25,260,434 21	....	25,260,434 21
1827	19,712,283 29	19,885 68	2,626 90	101 00	1,495,845 26	420,000 00	1,315,621 83	22,966,363 96	....	22,966,363 96
1828	23,205,523 64	17,451 54	1,218 81	20 15	1,018,308 75	455,000 00	65,106 34	24,763,629 23	....	24,763,629 23
1829	22,681,965 91	14,502 74	11,335 05	86 60	1,517,175 13	490,000 00	112,561 95	24,827,627 38	....	24,827,627 38
1830	21,922,391 39	12,160 62	16,980 59	55 13	2,329,356 14	490,000 00	73,172 64	24,844,116 51	....	24,844,116 51

1831	24,224,441 77	6,933 51	* 10,506 01	561 02	3,210,815 48	490,000 00	583,563 03	28,526,820 82		28,526,820 82
1832	28,465,237 24	11,030 65	6,791 13	244 95	2,623,381 03	659,000 00	99,276 16	31,865,561 16		31,865,561 16
1833	29,032,508 91	2,759 00	394 12		3,967,682 55	610,285 00	334,796 67	33,948,426 25		33,948,426 25
1834	16,214,957 15	4,196 09	19 80	100 00	4,857,600 69	586,649 50	128,412 32	21,791,935 55		21,791,935 55
1835	19,391,310 59	10,459 48	4,263 33	893 00	14,757,600 75	569,280 82	696,279 13	35,430,087 10		35,430,087 10
1836	23,409,940 53	370 00	728 79	10 91	24,877,179 86	328,674 67	2,209,891 32	50,826,796 08		50,826,796 08
1837	11,169,290 39	5,493 84	1,687 70		6,776,236 52	1,375,965 44	5,562,190 80	24,800,864 69	2,992,989 15	27,883,853 84
1838	16,158,800 36	2,467 27			3,081,930 47	4,512,102 22	2,517,252 42	26,302,561 74	12,716,820 86	39,019,382 60
1839	23,137,924 81	2,553 32	755 22		7,076,447 35		1,265,068 91	30,023,966 68	3,857,276 21	*33,881,242 89
1840	13,499,502 17	1,682 25			3,292,285 58	1,774,513 80	874,662 28	19,442,646 08	5,589,547 51	25,032,193 59
1841	14,487,216 74	3,261 36			1,365,627 42	672,769 38	331,285 37	16,860,160 27	13,659,317 38	30,519,477 65
1842	18,187,908 76	495 00			1,335,797 52	56,912 53	383,895 44	19,965,009 25	14,808,735 64	34,773,744 89
1843, (to June 30)	7,046,843 91	103 25			897,818 11		286,235 99	8,231,001 26	12,551,409 19	20,782,410 45
1843–'44	26,183,570 94	1,777 34			2,059,939 80		1,075,419 70	29,320,707 78	1,877,847 95	31,198,555 73
1844–'45	27,528,112 70	3,517 12			2,077,022 30	5,000 00	328,201 78	29,941,853 90		29,941,853 90
1845–'46	26,712,667 87	2,897 26			2,694,452 48		289,950 13	29,699,967 74		29,699,967 74
1846–'47	23,747,864 66	375 00			2,498,355 20	4,340 39	186,467 91	26,437,403 16	28,900,765 36	55,338,168 52
1847–'48	31,757,070 96	375 00			3,328,642 56	34,834 70	377,775 99	35,698,699 21	21,293,780 00	56,992,479 21
1848–'49	28,346,738 82				1,688,959 55	8,953 00	676,424 13	30,721,077 50	29,075,815 48	59,796,892 98
1849–'50	30,668,686 42				1,859,894 25		2,064,308 21	43,592,888 88	4,056,500 00	47,649,388 88
1850–'51	49,017,567 92				2,352,305 30	260,243 51	924,922 60	52,555,039 33	207,664 92	52,762,704 25
1851–'52	47,339,326 62				2,043,239 58	1,021 34	463,228 06	49,846,815 60	46,300 00	49,893,115 60
1852–'53	58,931,865 52				1,667,084 99	31,466 78	853,313 02	61,463,730 31	16,372 50	61,500,102 81
1853–'54	64,224,190 27				8,470,798 39		1,105,352 74	73,800,341 40	1,950 00	73,802,291 40
1854–'55	53,025,794 21				11,497,049 07		827,731 40	65,350,574 68	800 00	65,351,374 68
1855–'56	64,022,863 50				8,917,644 93		1,116,190 81	74,056,699 24	200 00	74,056,899 24
1856–'57	63,875,905 05				3,829,486 64		1,259,920 88	68,965,312 57	3,900 00	68,969,212 57
1857–'58	41,789,620 96				3,513,715 87		1,352,029 13	46,655,365 96	23,717,300 00	70,372,665 96
1858–'59	49,550,416 04				1,756,687 30		1,454,596 24	52,761,699 58	28,996,857 72	81,758,557 30
1859–'60	53,187,511 87				1,778,557 71		1,088,530 25	56,054,599 83	20,786,808 00	76,841,407 83
1860–'61	39,582,125 64				870,658 54		1,023,515 21	41,476,299 39	41,895,340 74	83,371,640 13
1861–'62	49,056,397 62		1,795,331 73		152,203 77		904,011 50	51,907,944 62	529,760,860 50	581,668,805 12
1862–'63	69,059,642 40	37,640,787 95	1,485,103 61		167,617 17		3,735,794 37	112,088,945 50	717,284,707 01	889,373,652 51
1863–'64	102,316,152 99	109,741,134 10	475,648 96		588,333 29		49,621,084 98	262,742,354 32	1,130,709,452 85	1,393,451,807 17
1864–'65	84,928,260 60	209,464,215 25	1,200,573 03		996,553 31		26,503,183 73	323,092,785 92	1,482,840,464 90	1,805,933,250 82
1865–'66	179,046,651 58	309,226,813 42	1,974,754 12		665,031 03		128,733,397 70	619,646,647 91	651,065,430 91	1,270,712,078 82
1866–'67	176,417,810 88	266,027,537 43	4,200,233 70		1,163,575 76		42,103,024 57	489,912,182 34	640,426,910 29	1,130,339,092 63
1867–'68	164,464,599 56	191,087,589 41	1,788,145 85		1,348,715 41		46,949,033 09	405,638,083 32	625,111,433 20	1,030,749,516 52
1868–'69	180,048,426 63	158,356,460 86	765,685 61		4,020,344 34		†27,754,900 50	370,945,817 94	238,678,081 06	609,623,899 00
1869–'70	194,538,374 44	184,899,756 49	229,102 88		3,350,481 76		28,237,762 06	411,255,477 63	285,474,496 00	696,729,973 63
1870–'71	206,270,408 05	143,098,153 63	580,355 37		2,388,646 68		30,986,381 16	383,323,944 89	268,768,523 47	652,092,468 36
1871–'72	216,370,286 77	130,642,177 72			2,375,714 19		24,518,688 88	374,106,867 56	305,047,054 00	679,153,921 56

* $1,458,782 93 deducted from the aggregate receipts, as per account of the Treasurer, No. 76922.
† $2,070 73 added, being net amount paid by depositaries previously deducted as unavailable.

Statement of expenditures from the beginning of the

[The year 1867, and subsequent, are from the account of warrants on the

Years.	Civil list.	Foreign intercourse.	Miscellaneous.	Military service.	Pensions.
From March 4, 1789, to December 31, 1791	$757,134 45	$14,733 33	$311,533 83	$632,804 03	$175,813 88
1792	380,917 58	78,766 67	194,572 32	1,100,702 09	109,243 15
1793	358,241 08	89,500 00	24,709 46	1,130,249 08	80,087 81
1794	440,946 58	146,403 51	118,248 30	2,639,097 59	81,399 24
1795	361,633 36	912,685 12	92,718 50	2,480,910 13	68,673 22
1796	447,139 05	184,859 64	150,476 14	1,260,263 84	100,843 71
1797	483,233 70	669,788 54	103,880 82	1,039,402 66	92,256 97
1798	504,605 17	457,428 74	149,004 15	2,009,522 30	104,845 33
1799	592,905 76	271,374 11	175,111 81	2,466,946 98	95,444 03
1800	748,688 45	395,288 18	193,636 59	2,560,878 77	64,130 73
1801	549,288 31	295,676 73	269,803 41	1,672,944 08	73,533 37
1802	596,981 11	550,925 93	315,022 36	2,179,148 25	85,440 39
1803	526,583 12	1,110,834 77	205,217 87	823,055 85	62,902 10
1804	624,795 63	1,186,655 57	379,558 23	875,423 93	80,092 80
1805	585,849 79	2,798,028 77	374,720 19	712,781 28	81,854 59
1806	684,230 53	1,760,421 30	445,485 18	1,224,355 38	81,875 53
1807	655,524 65	577,826 34	464,546 52	1,288,685 91	70,500 00
1808	691,167 80	304,992 83	427,124 98	2,900,834 40	82,576 04
1809	712,465 13	166,306 04	337,032 62	3,345,772 17	87,833 54
1810	703,994 03	81,367 48	315,783 47	2,294,323 94	83,744 16
1811	644,467 27	264,904 47	457,919 66	2,032,828 19	75,043 88
1812	826,271 55	347,703 29	509,113 37	11,817,798 24	91,402 10
1813	780,545 45	209,941 01	738,949 15	19,652,013 02	86,989 91
1814	927,424 23	177,179 97	1,103,425 50	20,350,806 86	90,164 36
1815	852,247 16	290,892 04	1,755,731 27	14,794,294 22	69,656 06
1816	1,208,125 77	364,620 40	1,416,995 00	16,012,096 80	188,804 15
1817	994,556 17	281,995 97	2,242,384 62	8,004,236 53	297,374 43
1818	1,109,559 79	420,429 90	2,305,849 82	5,622,715 10	890,719 90
1819	1,142,180 41	284,113 94	1,640,917 06	6,506,300 37	2,415,939 85
1820	1,248,310 05	253,370 04	1,090,341 85	2,630,392 31	3,208,376 31
1821	1,112,292 64	207,110 75	903,718 15	4,461,291 78	242,817 25
1822	1,158,131 58	164,879 51	644,985 15	3,111,981 48	1,948,199 40
1823	1,058,911 65	292,118 56	671,063 78	3,096,924 43	1,780,588 52
1824	1,336,266 24	5,140,099 83	676,942 74	3,340,939 85	1,499,326 59
1825	1,330,747 24	371,666 25	1,046,131 40	3,659,914 18	1,308,810 57
1826	1,256,745 48	232,719 08	1,110,713 23	3,943,194 37	1,556,593 83
1827	1,228,141 04	659,211 87	826,123 67	3,938,977 88	976,138 86
1828	1,455,490 58	1,001,193 66	1,219,368 40	4,145,544 56	850,573 57
1829	1,327,069 36	207,765 85	1,566,679 66	4,724,291 07	949,594 47
1830	1,579,724 64	294,067 27	1,363,624 13	4,767,128 88	1,363,297 31
1831	1,373,755 99	298,554 00	1,392,336 11	4,841,835 55	1,170,665 14
1832	1,800,757 74	325,181 07	2,451,202 64	5,446,034 88	1,184,422 40
1833	1,562,758 28	955,395 88	3,198,091 77	6,704,019 10	4,589,152 40
1834	2,080,601 60	741,562 35	2,082,565 00	5,696,189 38	3,364,285 30
1835	1,905,551 51	574,750 28	1,549,396 74	5,759,156 89	1,954,711 32
1836	2,110,175 47	933,382 65	2,749,721 60	12,169,226 64	2,882,797 96
1837	2,357,035 94	4,603,905 40	2,932,428 93	13,682,730 80	2,672,162 45
1838	2,688,708 56	1,215,095 52	3,256,860 68	12,897,224 16	2,156,057 29
1839	2,116,982 77	987,667 92	2,621,340 20	8,916,995 80	3,142,750 51
1840	2,736,769 31	683,278 15	2,575,351 50	7,095,267 23	2,603,562 17
1841	2,556,471 79	428,410 57	3,505,999 09	8,801,610 24	2,388,434 51
1842	2,905,041 65	563,191 41	3,307,391 55	6,610,438 02	1,378,931 33
1843, (to June 30)	1,222,422 48	400,566 04	1,579,724 48	2,908,671 95	839,041 12
1843–'44	2,454,958 15	636,079 66	2,554,146 05	5,218,183 66	2,032,008 99
1844–'45	2,369,652 79	702,637 22	2,839,470 97	5,746,291 28	2,400,788 11
1845–'46	2,532,232 92	409,292 55	3,769,758 42	10,413,370 58	1,811,097 56
1846–'47	2,570,338 44	405,079 10	3,910,190 81	35,840,030 33	1,744,883 63
1847–'48	2,647,802 87	448,593 01	2,554,455 37	27,687,334 21	1,228,496 48
1848–'49	2,865,196 91	6,908,996 72	3,111,140 61	14,558,473 26	1,328,867 64
1849–'50	3,027,454 39	5,990,858 81	7,025,450 16	9,687,024 58	1,866,886 02
1850–'51	3,481,219 51	6,256,427 16	8,146,577 33	12,161,965 11	2,293,377 22
1851–'52	3,439,923 22	4,196,321 59	9,867,926 64	8,521,506 19	2,401,858 78
1852–'53	4,265,861 68	950,871 30	12,246,335 03	9,910,498 49	1,756,306 20
1853–'54	4,621,492 24	7,763,812 31	13,461,450 13	11,722,282 87	1,232,665 00
1854–'55	6,350,875 88	997,007 26	16,738,442 29	14,648,074 07	1,477,612 33
1855–'56	6,452,256 35	3,642,615 39	15,200,475 94	16,963,160 51	1,296,229 65
1856–'57	7,611,547 27	999,177 65	18,946,189 91	19,159,150 87	1,309,115 81
1857–'58	7,116,339 04	1,396,508 72	17,847,851 19	25,679,121 63	1,219,768 30
1858–'59	5,913,281 50	981,946 87	16,873,771 68	23,154,720 53	1,222,222 71
1859–'60	6,077,008 95	1,146,143 79	20,708,233 43	16,472,202 72	1,100,802 32
1860–'61	6,074,041 83	1,147,786 91	16,026,524 79	23,001,530 67	1,034,599 73
1861–'62	5,886,615 07	1,339,226 66	14,160,020 86	389,173,562 29	852,170 47
1862–'63	6,204,605 97	1,241,325 03	15,602,451 37	603,314,411 82	1,078,513 36
1863–'64	7,909,083 50	1,239,893 66	18,332,639 71	690,391,048 66	4,985,473 90

Government to June 30, 1872, *under the following heads:*

Treasurer issued; all previous years are from the account of warrants paid.]

Indians.	Naval establishment.	Net ordinary expenditures.	Public debt, including principal and interest.	Total.	Balances in the Treasury at the end of each year.
$27,000 00	$570 00	$1,919,589 52	$5,287,949 50	$7,207,539 02	$973,905 75
13,648 85	53 02	1,877,903 68	7,263,665 99	9,141,569 67	783,444 51
27,282 83	......	1,710,070 26	5,819,505 29	7,529,575 55	753,661 69
13,042 46	61,408 97	3,500,546 65	5,801,578 09	9,302,124 74	1,151,924 17
23,475 68	410,562 03	4,350,658 04	6,084,411 61	10,435,069 65	516,442 61
113,563 98	274,784 04	2,531,930 40	5,835,846 44	8,367,776 84	888,995 42
62,396 38	382,631 89	2,833,590 96	5,792,421 82	8,626,012 78	1,021,899 04
16,470 09	1,381,347 76	4,623,223 54	3,990,294 14	8,613,517 68	617,451 43
20,302 19	2,858,081 84	6,480,166 72	4,596,876 78	11,077,043 50	2,161,867 77
31 22	3,448,716 03	7,411,369 97	4,578,369 95	11,989,739 92	2,623,311 99
9,000 00	2,111,424 00	4,981,669 90	7,291,707 04	12,273,376 94	3,295,391 00
94,000 00	915,561 87	3,737,079 91	9,539,004 76	13,276,084 67	5,020,697 64
60,000 00	1,215,230 53	4,002,824 24	7,256,159 43	11,258,983 67	4,825,811 60
116,500 00	1,189,832 75	4,452,858 91	8,171,787 45	12,624,646 36	4,037,005 26
196,500 00	1,597,500 00	6,357,234 62	7,369,889 79	13,727,124 41	3,999,388 99
234,200 00	1,649,641 44	6,080,209 36	8,989,884 61	15,070,093 97	4,538,123 80
205,425 00	1,722,064 47	4,984,572 89	6,307,720 10	11,292,292 99	9,643,850 07
213,575 00	1,884,067 80	6,504,338 85	10,260,245 35	16,764,584 20	9,941,809 96
337,503 84	2,427,758 80	7,414,672 14	6,452,554 16	13,867,226 30	3,848,056 78
177,625 00	1,654,244 20	5,311,082 28	8,008,904 46	13,319,986 74	2,672,276 57
151,875 00	1,965,566 39	5,592,604 86	8,009,204 05	13,601,808 91	3,502,305 80
277,845 00	3,959,365 15	17,829,498 70	4,449,622 45	22,279,121 15	3,862,217 41
167,358 28	6,446,600 10	28,082,396 92	11,108,123 44	39,190,520 36	5,196,542 00
167,394 86	7,311,290 60	30,127,686 38	7,900,543 94	38,028,230 32	1,727,848 63
530,750 00	8,660,000 25	26,953,571 00	12,628,922 35	39,582,493 35	13,106,592 88
274,512 16	3,908,278 30	23,373,432 58	24,871,062 93	48,244,495 51	22,033,519 19
319,463 71	3,314,598 49	15,454,609 92	25,423,036 12	40,877,646 04	14,989,465 48
505,704 27	2,953,695 00	13,808,673 78	21,296,201 62	35,104,875 40	1,478,526 74
463,181 39	3,847,640 42	16,300,273 44	7,703,926 29	24,004,199 73	2,079,992 38
315,750 01	4,387,990 00	13,134,530 57	8,628,494 28	21,763,024 85	1,198,461 21
477,005 44	3,319,243 06	10,723,479 07	8,367,093 62	19,090,572 69	1,681,592 24
575,007 41	2,224,458 98	9,827,643 51	7,848,949 12	17,676,592 63	4,237,427 55
380,781 82	2,503,765 83	9,784,154 59	5,530,016 41	15,314,171 00	9,463,922 81
429,987 90	2,904,581 56	15,330,144 71	16,568,393 76	31,898,538 47	1,946,597 13
724,106 44	3,049,083 86	11,490,459 94	12,095,344 78	23,585,804 72	5,201,650 43
743,447 83	4,218,902 45	13,062,316 27	11,041,082 19	24,103,398 46	6,358,686 18
760,624 88	4,263,877 45	12,653,095 65	10,003,668 39	22,656,764 04	6,668,286 10
705,084 24	3,918,786 44	13,296,041 45	12,163,438 07	25,459,479 52	5,972,435 81
576,344 74	3,308,745 47	12,660,490 62	12,883,867 78	25,044,358 40	5,755,704 79
622,262 47	3,239,428 63	13,229,533 33	11,355,748 22	24,585,281 55	6,014,539 75
930,738 04	3,856,183 07	13,864,067 90	16,174,378 22	30,038,446 12	4,502,914 45
1,352,419 75	3,956,370 29	16,516,388 77	17,840,309 29	34,356,698 06	2,011,777 55
1,802,980 93	3,901,356 75	22,713,755 11	1,543,543 38	24,257,298 49	11,702,905 31
1,003,953 20	3,956,260 42	18,425,417 25	6,176,565 19	24,601,982 44	8,892,858 42
1,706,444 48	3,864,939 06	17,514,950 28	58,191 00	17,573,141 56	26,749,803 96
4,615,141 49	5,807,718 23	30,868,164 04	......	30,868,164 04	46,708,436 00
4,348,036 19	6,646,914 53	37,243,214 24	21,822 91	37,265,037 15	37,327,252 69
5,504,191 34	6,131,580 53	33,849,718 08	5,605,720 27	39,455,438 35	36,891,196 94
2,528,917 28	6,182,294 25	26,496,948 73	11,117,987 42	37,614,936 15	33,157,503 68
2,331,794 86	6,113,896 89	24,139,920 11	4,086,613 70	28,226,533 81	29,963,163 46
2,514,837 12	6,001,076 97	26,196,840 29	5,600,689 74	31,797,530 03	28,685,111 08
1,199,099 68	6,397,242 95	24,361,336 59	8,575,539 94	32,936,876 53	30,521,979 44
578,371 00	3,727,711 53	11,256,508 60	861,596 55	12,118,105 15	39,186,284 74
1,256,532 39	6,498,199 11	20,650,108 01	12,991,902 84	33,642,010 85	36,742,829 62
1,539,351 35	6,297,177 89	21,895,369 61	8,595,039 10	30,490,408 71	36,194,274 81
1,027,693 64	6,455,013 92	26,418,459 59	1,213,823 31	27,632,282 90	38,261,959 65
1,430,411 30	7,900,635 76	53,801,569 37	6,719,282 37	60,520,851 74	33,079,276 43
1,252,296 81	9,408,476 02	45,227,454 77	15,427,688 42	60,655,143 19	29,416,612 45
1,374,161 55	9,786,705 92	39,933,542 61	16,452,880 13	56,386,422 74	32,827,082 69
1,663,591 47	7,904,724 66	37,165,990 09	7,438,728 17	44,604,718 26	35,871,753 31
2,829,801 77	8,880,581 38	44,049,949 48	4,426,154 83	48,476,104 31	40,158,353 25
3,043,576 04	8,918,842 10	40,389,954 56	6,322,654 27	46,712,608 83	43,338,860 02
3,880,494 12	11,067,789 53	44,078,156 35	10,498,905 39	54,577,061 74	50,261,901 09
1,550,339 55	10,790,096 32	51,142,138 42	24,330,980 66	75,473,119 08	48,591,073 41
2,772,990 78	13,327,095 11	56,312,097 72	9,852,678 24	66,164,775 96	47,777,672 13
2,644,263 97	14,074,834 64	60,333,836 45	12,392,505 12	72,726,341 57	49,108,229 80
4,355,683 64	12,651,694 61	65,032,559 76	6,242,027 61	71,274,587 37	46,802,855 00
4,978,266 18	14,053,264 64	72,291,119 70	9,771,067 04	82,062,186 74	35,113,334 22
3,490,534 53	14,690,927 90	66,327,405 72	17,351,237 20	83,678,642 92	33,193,248 60
2,991,121 54	11,514,649 83	60,010,062 58	17,045,013 07	77,055,075 65	32,979,530 78
2,865,481 17	12,387,156 52	62,537,221 62	22,850,141 46	85,387,363 08	30,963,857 83
2,327,948 37	42,640,353 09	456,379,896 81	109,287,461 27	565,667,358 08	46,965,304 87
3,152,032 70	63,261,235 31	604,004,575 56	205,811,335 09	809,815,911 25	36,523,046 13
2,629,975 97	85,704,963 74	811,283,679 14	484,257,435 72	1,295,541,114 86	134,433,738 44

Statement of expenditures from the beginning of the

Years.	Civil list.	Foreign intercourse.	Miscellaneous.	Military service.	Pensions.
1864-'65	$10, 584, 604 17	$1, 251, 120 10	$27, 798, 654 98	$1, 030, 690, 400 06	$16, 347, 621 34
1865-'66	11, 984, 773 97	1, 315, 749 04	27, 312, 591 16	283, 154, 676 06	15, 605, 549 88
1866-'67	15, 128, 830 90	1, 793, 307 98	33, 876, 120 13	98, 715, 832 12	20, 939, 789 69
1867-'68	13, 127, 783 70	1, 442, 632 00	38, 092, 091 55	123, 107, 147 96	23, 792, 276 87
1868-'69	*26, 171, 003 04	1, 091, 171, 05	29, 413, 497 12	78, 663, 649 23	28, 475, 855 67
1869-'70	15, 867, 336 32	1, 491, 214 53	36, 084, 808 87	57, 615, 801 87	28, 402, 241 20
1870-'71	†18, 760, 779 46	1, 604, 373 87	40, 116, 762 90	35, 799, 991 82	34, 443, 894 88
1871-'72	16, 076, 460 35	1, 839, 369 14	43, 068, 927 93	35, 372, 157 20	28, 533, 402 76

* This includes .... $7, 200, 000 00 paid for Alaska.
Also .... 5, 505, 451 79 paid for mail service, Post-Office Department.

12, 705, 451 79

Government to June 30, 1872, *&c.*—Continued.

Indians.	Naval establishment.	Net ordinary expenditures.	Public debt, including principal and interest.	Total.	Balances in the Treasury at the end of each year.
$5,059,360 71	$122,617,434 07	$1,214,349,195 43	$692,084,135 94	$1,906,433,331 37	$33,933,657 89
3,295,729 32	43,285,662 00	385,954,731 43	753,389,350 52	1,139,344,081 95	165,301,654 76
4,687,715 66	31,074,965 90	206,216,571 38	890,134,995 28	1,096,351,566 66	199,289,180 73
4,100,660 41	25,734,658 88	229,397,251 37	839,974,993 99	1,069,372,245 36	160,666,451 89
6,961,466 96	20,055,004 89	190,851,647 96	394,281,641 16	585,133,289 12	185,157,061 77
3,410,279 41	21,786,591 64	164,658,273 84	538,497,117 60	703,155,391 44	178,731,643 96
7,426,997 44	19,431,027 21	157,583,827 58	534,097,031 32	691,680,858 90	....
7,061,728 82	21,249,809 99	153,201,856 19	529,323,414 02	682,525,270 21	....

†For the years 1871 and 1872 this statement is from warrants *issued*; prior to 1871 for warrants *paid*.

Statement of outstanding principal of the public debt of the United States on the 1st of January of each year, from 1791 to 1842, inclusive; and on the 1st of July of each year, from 1843 to 1872, inclusive.

January 1, 1791	$75, 463, 476 52	January 1, 1832	$24, 322, 235 18
1792	77, 227, 924 66	1833	7, 001, 698 83
1793	80, 352, 634 04	1834	4, 760, 082 08
1794	78, 427, 404 77	1835	37, 513 05
1795	80, 747, 587 39	1836	336, 957 83
1796	83, 762, 172 07	1837	3, 308, 124 07
1797	82, 064, 479 33	1838	10, 434, 221 14
1798	79, 228, 529 12	1839	3, 573, 343 82
1799	78, 408, 669 77	1840	5, 250, 875 54
1800	82, 976, 294 35	1841	13, 594, 480 73
1801	83, 038, 050 80	1842	20, 601, 226 28
1802	80, 712, 632 25	July 1, 1843	32, 742, 922 00
1803	77, 054, 686 30	1844	23, 461, 652 50
1804	86, 427, 120 88	1845	15, 925, 303 01
1805	82, 312, 150 50	1846	15, 550, 202 97
1806	75, 723, 270 66	1847	38, 826, 534 77
1807	69, 218, 398 64	1848	47, 044, 862 23
1808	65, 196, 317 97	1849	63, 061, 858 69
1809	57, 023, 192 09	1850	63, 452, 773 55
1810	53, 173, 217 52	1851	68, 304, 796 02
1811	48, 005, 587 76	1852	66, 199, 341 71
1812	45, 209, 737 90	1853	59, 803, 117 70
1813	55, 962, 827 57	1854	42, 242, 222 42
1814	81, 487, 846 24	1855	35, 586, 958 56
1815	99, 833, 660 15	1856	31, 972, 537 90
1816	127, 334, 933 74	1857	28, 699, 831 85
1817	123, 491, 965 16	1858	44, 911, 881 03
1818	103, 466, 633 83	1859	58, 496, 837 88
1819	95, 529, 648 28	1860	64, 842, 287 88
1820	91, 015, 566 15	1861	90, 580, 873 72
1821	89, 987, 427 66	1862	524, 176, 412 13
1822	93, 546, 676 98	1863	1, 119, 772, 138 63
1823	90, 875, 877 28	1864	1, 815, 784, 370 57
1824	90, 269, 777 77	1865	2, 680, 647, 869 74
1825	83, 788, 432 71	1866	2, 773, 236, 173 69
1826	81, 054, 059 99	1867	2, 678, 126, 103 87
1827	73, 987, 357 20	1868	2, 611, 687, 851 19
1828	67, 475, 043 87	1869	2, 588, 452, 213 94
1829	58, 421, 413 67	1870	2, 480, 672, 427 81
1830	48, 565, 406 50	1871	2, 353, 211, 332 32
1831	39, 123, 191 68	1872	2, 253, 251, 078 78

REPORT OF THE SOLICITOR OF THE TREASURY.

REPORT

OF

THE SOLICITOR OF THE TREASURY.

DEPARTMENT OF JUSTICE,
OFFICE OF THE SOLICITOR OF THE TREASURY,
Washington, D. C., November 13, 1872.

SIR: I have the honor to transmit, herewith, seven tabular statements, exhibiting the amount, character, and results of the litigation, under the direction of this Office for the fiscal year ending June 30, 1872, so far as the same are shown by the reports received from the United States attorneys for the several districts. These tables embrace respectively:

1. Suits on custom-house bonds.
2. Suits on transcripts of accounts of defaulting public officers, excepting those of the Post-Office Department, adjusted by the accounting officers of the Treasury Department.
3. Post-office suits, embracing those against officers of the Post-Office Department, and cases of fines, penalties, and forfeitures, for violation of the postal laws.
4. Suits for the recovery of fines, penalties, and forfeitures under the customs revenue and navigation laws.
5. Suits in which the United States are interested, not embraced in the other classes.
6. Suits against collector of cutsoms, and other agents of the government, for refund of duties and acts done in the line of their official duty.
7. A general summary or abstract of all the other tables.

An examination of this summary will show that the whole number of suits commenced within the year was 1854, of which—

295 were of class 1, for the recovery of	$1,350,773 62
115 were of class 2, for the recovery of	2,767,857 36
207 were of class 3, for the recovery of	39,760 23
432 were of class 4, for the recovery of	3,189,421 71
596 were of class 5, for the recovery of	1,219,372 19
209 were of class 6	....
Making a total sued for, as reported, of	8,567,185 11

Of the whole number of suits brought, 593 were decided in favor of the United States; 23 were adversely decided; 258 were settled and dismissed; in 12 penalties were remitted by the Secretary of the Treasury; leaving 968 still pending.

Of those pending at the commencement of the year, 357 were decided for the United States; 75 were decided adversely; 858 were settled and dismissed; and in 8 penalties were remitted by the Secretary of the Treasury.

The entire number of suits decided, or otherwise disposed of during the year, was 2,184; the whole amount for which judgments were obtained, exclusive of decrees *in rem*, was $942,365.67, and the entire amount collected from all sources was $1,000,422.41.

The following tables exhibit a comparative view of the litigation of the last year, and the next preceding one:

Date.	In suits commenced during the fiscal years ending June 30, 1871, and June 30, 1872.								
	Aggregate sued for.	Aggregate in judgments for the United States.	Collected.	Decided for the United States.	Decided against the United States.	Settled and dismissed.	Remitted.	Pending.	Total number of suits brought.
June 30, 1871...	$12, 604, 601 01	$280, 410 97	$586, 271 76	493	24	387	9	1, 203	2, 116
June 30, 1872...	8, 567, 185 11	397, 949 82	478, 450 65	593	23	258	12	968	1, 854

Date.	In suits commenced prior to the fiscal years ending June 30, 1871, and June 30, 1872.					Proceedings in all suits.			
	Aggregate of judgments in old suits.	Decided for the United States.	Decided against the United States.	Settled and dismissed.	Collections in old suits.	Total number of suits disposed of.	Total number of judgments in favor of United States.	Whole amount of judgments.	Whole amount collected.
June 30, 1871..	$908, 058 20	566	183	1, 142	$703, 657 30	2, 804	1, 059	$1, 188, 469 17	$1, 289, 929 06
June 30, 1872..	544, 415 85	357	75	858	521, 971 76	2, 164	950	942, 365 67	1, 000, 422 41

I am, very respectfully

E. C. BANFIELD,
Solicitor of the Treasury.

Hon. GEORGE S. BOUTWELL,
Secretary of the Treasury.

No. 1.—*Report of suits on custom-house bonds instituted during the fiscal year ending June 30, 1872, in the several United States courts, and of proceedings had during said period in suits which were instituted prior thereto.*

SUMMARY.

Judicial districts.	In suits brought during the fiscal year.								In suits commenced prior to the fiscal year.					Whole number of suits disposed of.	Whole number of judgments for United States during the year.	Total judgments during the year.	Total collections during the year.
	Number of suits.	Aggregate sued for.	Aggregate in judgment.	Collections.	Decided for the United States.	Decided against United States.	Settled, dismissed, &c.	Pending.	Judgments in old suits.	For United States.	Against United States.	Settled, &c.	Collections in old suits.				
Massachusetts	14	$1,560 00					3	11						3			
New York, northern district	1						1							1			
New York, southern district	213	1,136,056 00					63	150	$3,514 87	5		140	$477 34	208	5	$3,514 87	$477 34
New York, eastern district									3,654 89	31		4		35	31	3,654 89	
Pennsylvania, eastern district	2		$523 00		2				406 66	2				4	4	929 66	
Maryland	8	1,772 30	599 08		5		1	2				6		12	5	599 08	
Virginia, eastern district	2	992 00	700 00		2									2	2	700 00	
Alabama, southern district	1	48 53	50 00		1									1	1	50 00	
Louisiana	43	195,306 76	4,296 38	$1,190 73	10		5	28	2,676 47	5	1	4	493 74	25	15	6,972 85	1,684 47
Texas, eastern district	3	3,058 90				1		2	3,600 00	2	5			8	2	3,600 00	
California	8	11,979 13					8					7		15			
Total	295	1,350,773 62	6,168 46	1,190 73	20	1	81	193	13,852 89	45	6	161	971 08	314	65	20,021 35	2,161 81

No. 2.—*Report of suits on Treasury transcripts other than post-office cases instituted during the fiscal year ending June 30, 1872, in the several United States courts, and of proceedings had during said period in suits which were instituted prior thereto.*

SUMMARY.

Judicial districts.	In suits brought during the fiscal year.									In suits brought prior to the fiscal year.					Whole number of suits disposed of	Whole number of judgments in favor of United States.	Total judgments.	Total collections.
	Number of suits.	Aggregate sued for	Aggregate in judgment.	Collections.	For the United States.	Against the United States.	Settled, dismissed, &c.	Remitted.	Pending.	Judgments in old suits.	For the United States.	Against the United States.	Settled, &c.	Collections.				
Maine																		
New Hampshire																		
Massachusetts																		
Rhode Island																		
Vermont																		
Connecticut	1	$639 84	$675 03	$675 03	1										1	1	$675 03	$675 03
New York, northern district	2	15,839 70		3,314 21			1		1	$25,450 48	1				2	1	25,450 48	3,314 21
New York, southern district	4	190,423 28		27,390 00			1		3				2	$8,768 52	3			36,158 52
New York, eastern district	2	22,355 37							2									
New Jersey	1	9,522 84							1				1	21,245 99	1			21,245 99
Pennsylvania, eastern district	6	415,307 44		1,962 73			2		4	7,311 30	2		3	40,563 00	7	2	7,311 30	42,525 73
Pennsylvania, western district	3	20,660 28							3	34,532 12	2		1	33,320 93	3	2	34,532 12	33,320 93
Delaware	1	4,632 70							1									
Maryland	4	51,838 69		792 00					4	2,190 15	3		1	11,943 94	4	3	2,190 15	12,735 94
Virginia, eastern district	5	69,884 10	34,164 49		1				4	12,904 60	2		2	32,109 02	5	3	47,069 09	32,109 02
Virginia, western district	1	697 46							1	7,975 39	2				2	2	7,975 39	

Mississippi, northern district	2	3,611 25							2									
Mississippi, southern district	6	158,482 58	9,811 25		2				4						2	2	9,811 25	
Louisiana	6	146,621 05							6				1	23,074 29	1			23,074 29
Texas, eastern district	1	55,110 05	51,573 76		1					21,542 69	3		1	1,000 00	5	4	73,116 45	1,000 00
Texas, western district	6	457,273 99							6									
Arkansas, eastern district	2	1,726 91		136 45			1		1						1			136 45
Arkansas, western district										351 00	1				1	1	351 00	
Tennessee, eastern district	1	3,254 25							1	5,027 57	4			383 24	4	4	5,027 57	383 24
Tennessee, middle district	1	10,000 00	11,344 05		1					1,186 37	2			144 31	3	3	12,530 42	144 31
Tennessee, western district	1	777 88							1	6,099 32	3				3	3	6,099 32	
Kentucky																		
Ohio, northern district													1	386 25	1			386 25
Ohio, southern district	3	27,787 06	7,258 66		2				1	149,893 59	3		1	4,984 89	6	5	157,152 25	4,984 89
Indiana	4	6,042 51	601 24	5,720 75	2		1		1	23,849 95	4			12,788 91	7	6	24,451 19	18,509 66
Illinois, northern district	1	3,405 15							1	22,052 42	3			16,342 33	3	3	22,052 42	16,342 33
Illinois, southern district	5	33,368 03	15,177 71	28,724 71	2		1		2	1,497 23	1				4	3	16,674 94	28,724 71
Michigan, eastern district	5	52,042 77		4,356 54			2		3						2			4,356 54
Michigan, western district	1	7,353 66		7,353 66			1								1			7,353 66
Wisconsin, eastern district	3	11,814 37							3									
Wisconsin, western district	2	6,709 57		6,709 57			2								2			6,709 57
Missouri, eastern district	1	179,025 25							1				1	6,363 63	1			6,363 63
Missouri, western district	4	44,880 95	2,698 18	2,442 86	3				1	19,381 07	1				4	4	22,079 25	2,442 86
Iowa																		
Minnesota																		
Kansas	1	127 25	145 30	145 30	1								1	1,153 90	2	1	145 30	1,299 20
California	3	446,995 17							3				2	1,775 83	2			1,775 83
Oregon													1	800 31	1			800 31
Nevada																		
Nebraska	1	2,948 21		2,948 21			1								1			2,948 21
New Mexico																		
Utah																		
Washington Territory												1			1			
Colorado	1	2,598 08							1									
Dakota																		
Arizona	1	9,480 84							1									
Idaho	2	16,573 83		5,500 00					2									5,500 00
Montana																		
Wyoming																		
Total	115	2,767,857 36	145,942 68	104,423 13	21	....	14	....	80	351,199 13	39	1	23	247,867 25	98	60	497,141 81	352,290 38

No. 3.—*Report of post-office suits instituted during the fiscal year ending June 30, 1872, in the several United States courts, and of proceedings had during said period in suits which were instituted prior thereto.*

SUMMARY.

Judicial districts.	In suits brought during the fiscal year.								In suits commenced prior to the fiscal year.					Whole number of suits disposed of.	Whole number of judgments in favor of United States.	Aggregate judgments.	Aggregate collections.
	Number of suits.	Aggregate sued for.	Aggregate in judgment.	Collections.	For the United States.	Against the United States.	Settled, &c.	Pending.	Judgment in old suits.	For the United States.	Against the United States.	Settled, &c.	Collections.				
Maine				$12 37									$7 16				$19 53
New Hampshire	3							3									
Massachusetts	2	$3,407 86		1,763 01			1	1						1			1,763 01
Connecticut	1							1									
New York, northern district	3	3,665 17	$4,147 37	4,147 37	2			1				1	253 71	3	2	$4,147 37	4,401 08
New York, eastern district													262 90				262 90
Pennsylvania, eastern district	1							1	$618 67	2			495 93	2	2	618 67	495 93
Pennsylvania, western district	15	52 00	1,800 00	100 00	4		1	10						5	4	1,890 00	100 00
Maryland	3	470 46	107 40	107 40	1			2						1	1	107 40	107 40
Virginia, eastern district	4	109 97						4	7,300 42	4			5,794 94	4	4	7,300 42	5,794 94
Virginia, western district	6	405 06	293 40	153 50	3		1	2						4	3	293 40	153 50
West Virginia	1	3,342 01						1									
North Carolina	7	1,152 93	212 12		1			6						1	1	212 12	
South Carolina	9	742 58	182 75		4	1	1	3	2,718 84	4			242 13	10	8	2,901 59	242 13
Georgia	4	2,234 63	1,757 20	1,238 94	1			3	1,514 67	2			1,571 70	3	3	3,271 87	2,810 64
Florida, northern district	5	1,417 76						5					444 19				444 19
Alabama, northern district	1	117 01						1									
Alabama, southern district	1	287 73	313 46		1								5,000 00	1	1	313 46	5,000 00
Alabama, middle district	4	118 01	169 62		2			2	601 76	2			608 17	4	4	771 38	608 17
Mississippi, northern district	10	1,107 69	870 39		2			8	1,808 10	4			2,330 12	6	6	2,768 49	2,330 12
Mississippi, southern district	9	3,090 79	910 70	755 54	3		1	5	940 71	4				8	7	1,860 41	755 54
Louisiana	5	895 12	141 07		1		1	3	626 76	3			522 64	5	4	767 83	522 64
Texas, eastern district	2							2	2,321 28	5	1		2,748 25	6	5	2,321 28	2,748 25
Texas, western district	11	4,367 76	1,037 66	251 07	6			5						6	6	1,037 66	251 07
Arkansas, eastern district	2				2				466 94	1			1,330 90	3	3	466 94	1,330 90
Arkansas, western district	3	150 00	210 00		1			2	167 31	1				2	2	377 31	
Tennessee, eastern district													279 69				270 69
Tennessee, middle district	3	328 64						3	1,088 06	1	1		31 09	2	1	1,088 06	31 09
Tennessee, western district									2,470 35	3			834 40	3	3	2,470 35	834 40
Kentucky	5				3			2					122 40	3	3		122 40
Ohio, northern district	10	503 44	2,308 61	1,808 61	10			0					920 59	10	10	2,308 61	2,720 20

Ohio, southern district	8	1,122 20	105 00	526 00	1		1	6					417 74	2	1	105 00	943 80
Indiana	5	429 23	289 00		2			3						2	2	289 00	
Illinois, northern district													1,263 33				1,263 33
Illinois, southern district	5	3,604 73						5					77 48				77 48
Michigan, eastern district	1	717 87	770 64	776 64	1				4,385 52	1			14,944 02	2	2	5,162 16	15,720 66
Michigan, western district	4	754 77		656 46			1	3						1			656 46
Wisconsin, eastern district	2	287 50					1	1						1			
Wisconsin, western district	1		5 00		1									1	1	5 00	
Missouri, eastern district	1	65 78						1									
Missouri, western district	15	607 67	976 46		4	1	4	6					1,277 54	9	4	976 46	1,277 54
Iowa													55 29				55 29
Minnesota	1	51 48						1									
Kansas	21	2,119 18	1,423 74	132 89	8		3	10					220 15	11	8	1,423 74	353 04
California	1	127 14	127 14		1									1	1	127 14	
Oregon	1		615 52	75 00	1									1	1	615 52	75 00
Nevada									1,094 23	1				1	1	1,094 23	
Nebraska													1,302 02				1,302 02
New Mexico	1		500 00		1									1	1	500 00	
Utah	2	47 57						2									
Montana									1,333 45	1			256 00	1	1	1,333 45	256 00
Wyoming	1	217 70						1									
Washington	1	1,630 89						1					756 00				756 00
Total	207	30,790 23	19,280 25	12,504 86	67	2	16	122	29,550 07	39	2	1	44,370 48	127	106	48,836 32	56,875 34

No. 4.—*Report of suits for fines, penalties, and forfeitures under the customs revenue laws, &c., instituted during the fiscal year ending June 30, 1872, in the several United States courts, and of proceedings had during said period in suits which were instituted prior thereto.*

SUMMARY.

Judicial districts.	In suits brought during the fiscal year.									In suits brought prior to the fiscal year.						Whole number of suits disposed of.	Whole number of judgments in favor of United States.	Aggregate judgments.	Aggregate collections.
	Number of suits.	Aggregate sued for.	Aggregate in judgments.	Collections.	For the United States.	Against the United States.	Settled, &c.	Remitted.	Pending.	Judgments in old suits.	For the United States.	Against the United States.	Settled, &c.	Remitted.	Collections.				
Maine	11		$1,095 00	$1,067 50	10				1		1		7	1	$11,526 99	19	11	$1,095 00	$12,594 49
New Hampshire																			
Massachusetts	30	$2,339,400 00	102,100 00	105,407 08	8		5		17	$21,850 00	5		1		31,296 43	19	13	123,950 00	136,703 51
Rhode Island	1								1										
Vermont	25						1		24	225 00	2		9	2	2,360 64	14	2	225 00	2,360 64
Connecticut	2						2				2				825 33	4	2		825 33
New York, northern district	22	500 00	750 00	3,011 11	14	1		1	6	23,710 54	6	3	2	1	5,951 23	28	20	24,460 54	8,962 34
New York, southern district	66	799,906 54		205,990 52	23	1	18	1	23		16	1	29		100,835 09	89	39		306,825 61
New York, eastern district	25	6,134 36	550 00	734 30	5		7	1	12		2	1	3		1,778 65	19	7	550 00	2,513 01
New Jersey	7	2,014 22	2,014 22	16,706 64	5				2						1,368 79	5	5	2,014 22	18,075 43
Pennsylvania, eastern district	3				1		1		1				1			3	1		
Pennsylvania, western district	1				1											1	1		
Delaware																			
Maryland	81	13,676 59	616 60	1,020 00	13	3	22	7	36	100 00	1		1		12,100 00	47	14	716 60	13,120 00
Virginia, eastern district	28	4,000 00					1		27							1			
Virginia, western district																			

Mississippi, southern district	15	2,960 00	460 00		5	2			8	1,800 00	6		87		150 00	100	11	2,260 00	150 00
Louisiana	20	12,180 00							20						215 48				215 48
Texas, eastern district	21	1,000 00	500 00	1,211 90	13	2	2		4	50 00	6	5	7	1	10,142 34	36	19	550 00	11,354 24
Texas, western district	2					1			1							1			
Arkansas, eastern district																			
Arkansas, western district											1					1	1		
Tennessee, eastern district																			
Tennessee, middle district													1			1			
Tennessee, western district													1			1			
Kentucky	2	500 00		710 00	1		1									2	1		710 00
Ohio, northern district	3		50 00		1		1		I							2	1	50 00	
Ohio, southern district	3	700 00	100 00	100 00	1		2					1	2			6	1	100 00	100 00
Indiana													3			3			
Illinois, northern district	1		50 00	50 00	1					6,220 00	1				6,220 00	2	2	6,270 00	6,270 00
Illinois, southern district	2	200 00						2								2			
Michigan, eastern district	37	50 00	5,228 00	7,68d 38	29		4		4	1,165 00	2		1		5,764 72	36	31	6,393 00	13,453 10
Michigan, western district														1		1			
Wisconsin, eastern district	1					1										1			
Wisconsin, western district																			
Missouri, eastern district	2								2		1					1	1		
Missouri, western district																			
Iowa																			
Minnesota																			
Kansas																			
California	11			7,014 21	6		3		2		2		2	1	15,105 48	14	8		22,119 69
Oregon	1	200 00	200 00		1					7,356 47	1					2	2	7,556 47	
Nevada																			
Nebraska																			
New Mexico																			
Utah																			
Washington										1,000 00	1					1	1	1,000 00	
Colorado																			
Dakota																			
Arizona																			
Idaho																			
Montana																			
Wyoming																			
Total	432	3,189,421 71	114,113 82	350,961 70	140	11	70	12	199	64,654 94	58	52	150	8	205,819 10	510	198	178,768 76	556,780 80

No. 5.—*Report of miscellaneous suits instituted during the fiscal year ended June 30, 1872, in the several United States courts, and of proceedings had during said period in suits which were instituted prior thereto.*

SUMMARY.

Judicial districts.	In suits brought during the fiscal year.								In suits brought prior to the fiscal year.					Whole number of suits disposed of.	Whole number of judgments in favor of United States.	Total judgments.	Total collections.
	Number of suits.	Aggregate sued for.	Aggregate in judgment.	Collections.	For the United States.	Against the United States.	Settled, &c.	Pending.	Judgment in old suits.	For the United States.	Against the United States.	Settled, &c.	Collections.				
Maine	5		$355 70	$235 45	3		2		$1,503 63	1			$1,503 63	6	4	$1,659 33	$1,730 08
New Hampshire	2	$594 53						2									
Massachusetts	29	500 00	740 00		24			5		1				25	25	740 00	
Rhode Island	2		1,000 00		2									2	2	1,000 00	
Vermont	1	5,000 00	5,000 00		1									1	1	5,000 00	
Connecticut	2		630 55	630 55	2									2	2	630 55	630 55
New York, northern district	44	31,626 28	4,223 00		14		10	20	4,462 92	5		5	2,519 37	34	19	8,685 92	2,519 37
New York, southern district	50	14,517 48		794 00			12	38	16,000 00	4	1	2		19	4	16,000 00	794 00
New York, eastern district	4	11,500 00						4	3,000 00	1				1	1	3,000 00	
New Jersey	2	721 48						2				1	3,000 00	1			3,000 00
Pennsylvania, eastern district	2	314 00				1		1			1			2			
Pennsylvania, western district	21	2,482 69	6,718 65	1,775 93	17			4	2,000 00	4			2,940 21	21	21	8,718 65	4,716 14
Delaware	1		1,000 00		1								1,028 20	1	1	1,000 00	1,028 20
Maryland	20	6,609 88	850 00	875 00	5	2	3	10	6,184 23	4	1	1	656 41	16	9	7,034 23	1,531 41
Virginia, eastern district	11	1,007,950 00	750 00	500 00	2			9						2	2	750 00	500 00
Virginia, western district	2	2,800 00						2									
West Virginia																	
District of Columbia																	
North Carolina	27	1,150 00	20,000 00		24		2	1	80 00	1				27	25	20,080 00	
South Carolina	47	3,400 00	11,595 00		46			1			1			47	46	11,595 00	
Georgia	5	590 45	590 45	251 44	5				21,133 88	22	1		105 92	28	27	21,724 33	357 36
Florida, northern district	1		500 00		1				515 00	2			764 00	3	3	1,015 00	764 00
Florida, southern district	5	750 00	100 00		1			4	50 00	2				3	3	150 00	
Alabama, northern district																	
Alabama, middle district																	
Alabama, southern district	1		250 00	250 00	1				750 00	1				2	2	1,000 00	250 00
Mississippi, northern district	1	1,500 00	1,500 00		1				700 00	3			1,018 20	4	4	2,200 00	1,018 20

Mississippi, southern district	3		550 00		2		1		9,727 36	4				7	6	10,277 36	
Louisiana	4	2,964 47	451 97		3			1	800 00	2	1			6	5	1,251 97	
Texas, eastern district	1	14,847 21						1	1,600 00	18	1	1		20	18	1,600 00	
Texas, western district																	
Arkansas, eastern district	10	4,530 00	2,000 00		3		1	6	200 00	2		3	276 00	9	5	2,200 00	276 00
Arkansas, western district	103		20,030 00		89	3	5	6	2,500 00	6			370 35	103	95	22,530 00	370 35
Tennessee, eastern district	3	197 45	343 81		2			1	1,000 00	1				3	3	1,343 81	
Tennessee, middle district	18		5,500 00		6		7	5				2		15	6	5,500 00	
Tennessee, western district	19	10,000 00						10	1,500 00	3		53		56	3	1,500 00	
Kentucky	14		500 00	1,310 38	9		5		1,085 00	7		1	931 04	22	16	1,645 00	2,241 42
Ohio, northern district	15	3,500 00	5,350 00		14			1						14	14	5,350 00	
Ohio, southern district	16	15,321 42	3,270 10	1,032 89	8		3	5	280 00	4		1	500 00	16	12	3,550 10	1,532 89
Indiana	10	3,177 81	1,950 58	239 28	6		2	2	1,000 00	1		6	1,020 00	15	7	2,950 58	1,259 28
Illinois, northern district	3			631 00			2	1						2			631 00
Illinois, southern district	6	2,656 19	2,474 39		5			1	364 00	1				6	6	2,838 39	
Michigan, eastern district	2		254 78		1		1		156 80	5				7	6	411 58	
Michigan, western district	1	172 40						1					425 00				425 00
Wisconsin, eastern district	8	160 60	591 60	291 60	8					1		2		11	9	591 60	291 60
Wisconsin, western district	2		105 00		2									2	2	105 00	
Missouri, eastern district	2	248 72	100 00		1			1			1	5		7	1	100 00	
Missouri, western district	20	3,560 00	2,270 00		6		8	6	7,600 00	4		2	423 00	20	10	9,870 00	423 00
Iowa	5	500 00	1,030 00		5									5	5	1,030 00	
Minnesota																	
Kansas	26	19,481 85	6,759 03	262 05	19		3	4	460 00	6			733 60	28	25	7,219 03	995 65
California	13	42,831 28						13					4,728 92				4,728 92
Oregon	2	1,800 00	1,850 00	290 66	2									2	2	1,850 00	290 66
Nevada																	
Nebraska																	
New Mexico												52		52			
Utah																	
Washington Territory	3	1,300 00	1,200 00		2			1						2	2	1,200 00	
Colorado																	
Dakota																	
Arizona																	
Idaho									500 00	1	1			2	1	500 00	
Montana										3				3	3		
Wyoming	2						2							2			
Total	596	1,219,372 19	112,444 61	9,370 23	343	6	69	178	85,152 82	120	9	137	22,943 85	684	463	197,597 43	32,314 08

No. 6.—*Report of suits against collectors of customs and other officers instituted during the fiscal year ended June 30, 1872, in the several United States courts, and of proceedings had during said period in suits which were instituted prior thereto.*

SUMMARY.

Judicial districts.	In suits brought during the fiscal year.					In suits bro't prior to the fiscal year.			Whole number of suits disposed of.	Whole number of judgments for United States during the year.
	Number of suits.	Decided for the United States.	Decided against the United States.	Settled, dismissed, &c.	Pending.	For the United States.	Against the United States.	Settled, &c.		
Maine	1				1					
Massachusetts	13			3	10				3	
New York, northern district	1		1			2			3	2
New York, southern district	185			3	182	54	1	375	433	54
New Jersey	4		2	2					4	
Pennsylvania, eastern district	1				1			1	1	
Louisiana	1		1					1	2	
Texas, eastern district	1		1						1	
Ohio, southern district							4		4	
Michigan, eastern district	2				2					
Total	209		5	8	196	56	5	377	451	56

No. 7.—*Statistical summary of business arising from suits, &c., in which the United States is a party, or has an interest, under charge of the Solicitor of the Treasury, during the fiscal year ending June* 30, 1872.

Judicial districts.	Suits brought during the fiscal year ending June 30, 1872.															
	Suits on Treasury transcripts.		Post-office suits.		Fines, penalties, and forfeitures, under the customs revenue laws.		Suits on custom-house bonds.		Suits against collectors of customs and ag'ts or officers of the United States.		Miscellan's suits.		Total amount reported sued for.	Total amount reported in judgment in favor of United States.	Total amount reported collected.
	No.	Amount.	No.	Amount.	No.	Amount.	No.	Amount.	No.	Amt.	No.	Amount.			
Maine					11				1		5			$1,450 70	$1,315 32
New Hampshire			3								2	$594 53	$594 53		
Massachusetts			2	$3,407 86	30	$2,339,400 00	14	$1,560 00	13		29	500 00	2,344,867 86	102,840 00	107,170 09
Rhode Island					1						2			1,000 00	
Vermont					25						1	5,000 00	5,000 00	5,000 00	
Connecticut	1	$639 84	1		2						2		639 84	1,305 58	1,305 58
New York, northern district	2	15,839 70	3	3,665 17	22	500 00	1		1		44	31,626 28	51,631 15	9,120 37	10,472 69
New York, southern district	4	100,423 28			66	799,906 54	213	1,136,056 00	185		50	14,517 48	2,140,903 30		234,174 52
New York, eastern district	2	22,355 37			25	6,134 36					4	11,500 00	39,989 73	550 00	734 36
New Jersey	1	9,522 84			7	2,014 22			4		2	721 48	12,258 54	2,014 22	16,706 64
Pennsylvania, eastern district	6	415,307 44	1		3		2		1		2	314 00	415,621 44	523 00	1,962 73
Pennsylvania, western district	3	20,660 28	15	52 00	1						21	2,482 69	23,194 97	8,518 65	1,875 93
Delaware	1	4,652 70									1		4,652 70	1,000 00	
Maryland	4	51,838 69	3	470 46	81	13,676 59	8	1,772 30			20	6,699 88	74,457 92	2,173 08	2,794 40
Virginia, eastern district	5	69,884 10	4	109 97	28	4,000 00	2	992 00			11	1,007,950 00	1,082,936 07	35,614 49	500 00
Virginia, western district	1	627 46	6	405 06							2	2,800 00	3,832 52	293 40	153 50
West Virginia	2	13,546 73	1	3,342 91									16,889 64		414 00
District of Columbia	3	2,903 23											2,903 23		
North Carolina	3	210,098 88	7	1,152 93							27	1,150 00	212,401 81	20,212 12	
South Carolina	2	947 00	9	742 58							47	3,400 00	5,089 58	11,777 75	
Georgia	4	16,449 51	4	2,234 63	2						5	590,45	19,274 59	9,757 45	2,025 64
Florida, northern district	4	11,094 52	5	1,417 76	3	6,000 00					1		18,512 28	5,833 21	
Florida, southern district					4						5	750 00	750 00	250 00	
Alabama, northern district			1	117 01									117 01		
Alabama, middle district	3	22,455 13	4	118 01									22,573 14	169 62	5,551 85
Alabama, southern district			1	287 73			1	48 53			1		336 26	613 46	250 00
Mississippi, northern district	2	3,611 25	10	1,107 69							1	1,500 00	6,218 94	2,370 39	
Mississippi, southern district	6	158,482 58	9	3,099 79	15	2,960 00					3		164,542 37	11,731 95	755 54
Louisiana	6	146,621 05	5	895 12	20	12,180 00	43	195,306 76	1		4	2,964 47	357,967 40	4,889 42	1,190 73
Texas, eastern district	1	55,110 05	2		21	1,000 00	3	3,058 90	1		1	14,847 21	74,016 16	52,073 76	1,211 90
Texas, western district	6	457,273 99	11	4,367 76	2								461,641 75	1,037 66	251 07
Arkansas, eastern district	2	1,720 91	2								10	4,550 00	6,276 91	2,000 00	136 45
Arkansas, western district			3	150 00							103		150 00	20,240 00	

Statistical summary of business arising from suits, &c.—Continued.

Judicial districts.	Suits brought during the fiscal year ending June 30, 1872.						In suits commenced prior thereto.						Whole number judgments returned in favor United States during the year.	Total of suits disposed of.	Whole amount judgments rendered in favor United States during the fiscal year ending June 30, 1872.	Whole amount collections from all sources during the fiscal year ending June 30, 1872.
	Decided for the United States.	Decided against the United States.	Settled, dismissed, &c.	Remitted.	Pending.	Total number suits commenced.	Amount judgments reported in all old suits this year.	Decided for the United States.	Decided against the United States.	Settled, dismissed, &c.	Remitted.	Amount reported collected in all old suits this year.				
Maine	13	......	2	......	2	17	$1,503 63	2	......	7	1	$13,037 78	15	25	$2,954 33	$14,353 10
New Hampshire	......	......	......	......	5	5	......	......	......	......	......	......	......	......	......	......
Massachusetts	32	......	12	......	44	88	21,850 00	6	......	1	......	31,296 43	38	51	124,690 00	138,466 52
Rhode Island	2	......	......	......	1	3	......	......	......	......	......	......	2	2	1,000 00	......
Vermont	1	......	1	......	24	26	225 00	2	......	9	2	2,360 64	3	15	5,225 00	2,360 64
Connecticut	3	......	2	......	1	6	......	2	......	......	......	825 33	5	7	1,305 58	2,130 91
New York, northern district	30	2	12	1	28	73	53,623 94	14	3	8	1	8,724 31	44	71	62,744 31	19,197 00
New York, southern district	23	1	97	1	396	518	19,514 87	70	3	548	......	110,080 95	102	752	19,514 87	344,255 47
New York, eastern district	5	......	7	1	18	31	6,654 89	34	1	7	......	2,041 55	39	55	7,204 89	2,775 91
New Jersey	5	2	2	......	5	14	......	......	......	2	......	25,614 78	5	11	2,014 22	42,321 42
Pennsylvania, eastern district	3	1	3	......	8	15	8,336 63	6	1	5	......	41,058 93	9	19	8,859 03	43,021 66
Pennsylvania, western district	22	......	1	......	17	40	36,532 12	6	......	1	......	36,261 14	28	30	45,050 77	38,137 07
Delaware	1	......	......	......	1	2	......	......	......	......	......	1,028 20	1	1	1,000 00	1,028 20
Maryland	24	5	26	7	54	116	8,474 38	8	1	9	......	24,700 35	32	80	10,647 46	27,494 75
Virginia, eastern district	5	......	1	......	44	50	20,205 02	6	......	2	......	37,903 96	11	14	55,819 51	38,403 96
Virginia, western district	3	......	1	......	5	9	7,975 39	2	......	......	......	......	5	6	8,268 79	153 50
West Virginia	......	......	......	......	3	3	......	......	......	1	......	2,247 47	......	1	......	2,061 47
District of Columbia	......	......	......	......	3	3	......	......	......	......	......	1,352 82	......	......	......	1,352 82
North Carolina	25	......	2	......	10	37	80 00	1	......	......	......	......	26	28	20,292 12	......
South Carolina	50	1	1	......	6	58	2,718 84	4	1	......	......	242 13	54	57	14,496 59	242 13
Georgia	10	......	......	......	5	15	32,602 43	26	41	1	......	18,795 29	36	78	42,359 88	20,820 93
Florida, northern district	3	......	......	......	10	13	1,515 00	3	1	2	1	1,208 19	6	10	7,348 21	1,208 19
Florida, southern district	2	......	......	......	7	9	227 93	3	......	......	......	177 93	5	5	477 93	177 93
Alabama, northern district	......	......	......	......	1	1	......	......	......	......	......	......	......	......	......	......
Alabama, middle district	2	......	1	......	4	7	601 76	2	......	......	......	608 17	4	5	771 38	6,160 02
Alabama, southern district	3	......	......	......	......	3	750 00	1	......	2	......	15,000 00	4	6	1,363 46	15,250 00
Mississippi, northern district	3	......	......	......	10	13	2,598 10	7	......	......	......	3,348 32	10	10	4,968 49	3,348 32
Mississippi, southern district	12	2	2	......	17	33	12,477 07	14	......	87	......	150 00	26	117	24,209 02	905 54
Louisiana	15	......	6	......	58	79	4,103 23	10	2	6	......	24,306 15	25	39	8,992 05	25,496 88
Texas, eastern district	15	3	2	......	9	29	29,113 97	34	12	9	1	13,690 59	49	76	81,187 73	15,102 49
Texas, western district	6	1	......	......	12	19	......	......	......	......	......	......	6	7	1,037 66	251 07
Arkansas, eastern district	5	......	2	......	7	14	666 94	3	......	3	......	1,606 90	8	13	2,666 94	1,743 35
Arkansas, western district	90	3	5	......	8	106	3,018 31	9	......	......	......	370 35	99	107	23,258 31	370 35

Statistical summary of business arising from suits, &c.—Continued.

Judicial districts.	Suits brought during the fiscal year ending June 30, 1872.														
	Suits on Treasury transcripts.		Post-office suits.		Fines, penalties, and forfeitures, under the customs revenue laws.		Suits on custom-house bonds.		Suits against collectors of customs and agents or officers of the United States.		Miscellaneous suits.		Total amount reported sued for.	Total amount reported in judgment in favor of United States.	Total amount reported collected.
	No.	Amount.	No.	Amount.	No.	Amount.	No.	Amount.	No.	Amt.	No.	Amount.			
Tennessee, eastern district	1	$3,254 25									3	$197 45	$3,451 70	$343 81	
Tennessee, middle district	1	10,000 00	3	$328 64							18		10,328 64	16,844 05	
Tennessee, western district	1	777 88									19	19,000 00	19,777 88		
Kentucky			5		2	$500 00					14		500 00	560 00	$2,020 38
Ohio, northern district			16	503 44	3						15	3,500 00	4,003 44	7,708 61	1,808 61
Ohio, southern district	3	27,787 06	8	1,122 20	3	700 00					16	15,321 42	44,930 68	10,733 76	1,658 95
Indiana	4	6,642 51	5	429 23							10	3,177 81	10,249 55	2,840 82	5,960 03
Illinois, northern district	1	3,405 15			1						3		3,405 15	50 00	681 00
Illinois, southern district	5	33,368 03	5	3,604 73	2	200 00					6	2,656 19	39,828 95	17,652 10	28,724 71
Michigan, eastern district	5	52,042 77	1	717 87	37	50 00			2		2		52,810 64	6,259 42	12,821 56
Michigan, western district	1	7,353 66	4	754 77							1	172 40	8,280 83		8,010 12
Wisconsin, eastern district	3	11,814 37	2	287 50	1						8	166 60	12,268 47	591 60	291 60
Wisconsin, western district	2	6,709 57	1								2		6,709 57	110 00	6,709 57
Missouri, eastern district	1	179,025 25	1	65 78	2						2	248 72	179,339 75	100 00	
Missouri, western district	4	44,880 95	15	607 67							20	3,560 00	49,048 62	5,944 64	2,442 86
Iowa											5	500 00	500 00	1,030 00	
Minnesota			1	51 48									51 48		
Kansas	1	127 25	21	2,119 18							26	10,481 85	12,728 28	8,328 07	540 24
California	3	446,995 17	1	127 14	11		8	$11,979 13			13	42,831 28	501,932 72	127 14	7,014 21
Oregon			1		1	200 00					2	1,800 00	2,000 00	2,065 52	365 66
Nevada															
Nebraska	1	2,948 21											2,948 21	500 00	2,948 21
New Mexico			1												
Utah			2	47 57									47 57		
Washington Territory			1	1,630 89							3	1,300 00	2,930 89	1,200 00	
Colorado	1	2,598 08											2,598 08		
Dakota															
Arizona	1	9,480 84											9,480 84		
Idaho	2	16,573 83											16,573 83		5,500 00
Montana															
Wyoming			1	217 70							2		217 70		
Total	115	2,767,857 38	207	39,760 23	432	3,189,421 71	295	1,350,772 62	209		596	1,219,372 19	8,567,185 11	397,949 82	478,450 65

Statistical summary of business arising from suits, &c.—Continued.

Judicial districts.	Suits brought during the fiscal year ending June 30, 1872.						In suits commenced prior thereto.						Whole number judgments returned in favor United States during the year.	Total of suits disposed of.	Whole amount judgments rendered in favor United States during the fiscal year ending June 30, 1872.	Whole amount collections from all sources during the fiscal year ending June 30, 1872.
	Decided for the United States.	Decided against the United States.	Settled, dismissed, &c.	Remitted.	Pending.	Total number suits commenced.	Amount judgments reported in all old suits this year.	Decided for the United States.	Decided against the United States.	Settled, dismissed, &c.	Remitted.	Amount reported collected in all old suits this year.				
Tennessee, eastern district	2				2	4	$6,027 57	5				$662 93	7	7	$6,371 38	$662 93
Tennessee, middle district	7		7		8	22	2,274 43	3	1	3		175 40	10	21	19,118 48	175 40
Tennessee, western district					20	20	10,069 67	9		54		834 40	9	63	10,069 67	834 40
Kentucky	13		6		2	21	1,085 00	7		1		1,053 44	20	27	1,645 00	3,073 82
Ohio, northern district	25		1		8	34				1		1,306 84	25	27	7,708 61	3,115 45
Ohio, southern district	12		6		12	30	150,173 50	7	5	4		5,902 63	19	34	160,907 35	7,561 58
Indiana	10		3		6	19	24,849 95	5		9		13,808 91	15	27	27,690 77	19,768 94
Illinois, northern district	1		2		2	5	28,272 42	4				23,825 66	5	7	28,322 42	24,506 66
Illinois, southern district	7		1	2	8	18	1,861 23	2				77 48	9	12	19,513 33	28,802 19
Michigan, eastern district	31		7		9	47	5,707 32	8		1		20,708 74	39	47	11,966 74	33,530 30
Michigan, western district			2		4	6					1	425 00		3		8,435 12
Wisconsin, eastern district	8	1	1		4	14		1		2			9	13	591 60	291 60
Wisconsin, western district	3		2			5							3	5	110 00	6,709 57
Missouri, eastern district	1				5	6		1	1	6		6,363 63	2	9	100 00	6,363 63
Missouri, western district	13	1	12		13	39	26,981 07	5		2		1,700 54	18	33	32,925 71	4,143 40
Iowa	5					5						55 29	5	5	1,030 00	55 29
Minnesota					1	1										
Kansas	28		6		14	48	460 00	6		1		2,107 65	34	41	8,788 07	2,647 89
California	7		11		18	36		2		11	1	21,610 23	9	32	127 14	28,624 44
Oregon	4					41	7,356 47	1		1		800 31	5	6	10,021 99	1,165 97
Nevada							1,094 23	1					1	1	1,094 23	
Nebraska			1			1						1,302 02		1	500 00	4,250 23
New Mexico	1					1				52			1	53		
Utah					2	2										
Washington Territory	2				2	4	1,000 00	1	1			756 00	3	4	2,200 00	756 00
Colorado					1	1										
Dakota																
Arizona					1	1										
Idaho					2	2	500 00	1	1				1	2	500 00	5,500 00
Montana							1,333 45	4				256 00	4	4	1,333 45	256 00
Wyoming			2		1	3								2		
Total	593	23	258	12	968	1,854	544,415 85	357	75	858	8	521,971 76	950	2,184	942,365 67	1,000,422 41

REPORT OF THE SUPERVISING ARCHITECT.

REPORT

OF

THE SUPERVISING ARCHITECT OF THE TREASURY.

TREASURY DEPARTMENT,
OFFICE OF SUPERVISING ARCHITECT,
October 18, 1872.

SIR: I have the honor to submit the following statement of the business transacted by this office since the date of my last report, and of the progress and condition of the public works under its charge.

Sites have been purchased for the custom-house, court-house, and post-office buildings, at Chicago, Illinois, Saint Louis, Missouri, and Trenton, New Jersey, and the custom-house at Rockland, Maine. A fine and valuable site has been presented by the city of Hartford, Connecticut, and accepted, subject to the approval of the title by the Attorney-General.

Proposals were invited for a site for the proposed new Government building at Cincinnati, but it has been found impossible to obtain proposals for a piece of property well located and of suitable size. The commissioners report that it will be necessary to postpone further action until authority can be obtained from the State to condemn the property required.

Proposals have also been invited for the purchase of sites for proposed Government buildings at Fall River, Massachusetts, Utica, New York, Philadelphia, Pennsylvania, Port Huron, Michigan, Little Rock, Arkansas, and Sacramento, California.

Plans have been prepared and work commenced upon the custom-house at Chicago, Illinois, and on the extension of the court-house and post-office at Indianapolis, Indiana. Plans have also been prepared for the court-house and post-office at Trenton, New Jersey, and work will be commenced as soon as the title is approved by the Attorney-General.

The custom-houses at Cairo, Illinois, and Machias, Maine, have been completed, and are now occupied. The custom-houses at Astoria, Oregon, and Saint Paul, Minnesota, and the Marine Hospital at Chicago, Illinois, are nearly completed, and will be ready for occupancy at an early day. The remodeling of the custom-house at Baltimore, Maryland, is also completed, together with the extension of the post-office toward Second street. The remaining wing is nearly completed, and will be finished at an early day.

The custom-houses and post-offices at New London, Connecticut, and Bristol and Newport, Rhode Island, have been remodeled and thoroughly repaired. Plans have been prepared for remodeling that portion of the custom-house in Philadelphia, Pennsylvania, assigned to the use of the Assisant Treasurer, and the work is now in a satisfactory state of progress.

Work has been continued on the post-office and sub-treasury Boston, Masssachusetts; court-houses and post-offices at New York City, New

York, Knoxville, Tennessee, and Columbia, South Carolina; on the custom-houses and post-offices at New Orleans, Louisiana, Portland, Oregon, Omaha, Nebraska; the custom-house at Charleston, South Carolina, and the United States Branch Mint at San Francisco, California.

Repairs, more or less extensive, have been made on the following buildings, viz: Custom-houses at Boston, Massachusetts, Dubuque, Iowa, Milwaukee, Wisconsin, New Haven, Connecticut, New York City, New York, Pittsburgh, Pennsylvania, Philadelphia, Pennsylvania, San Francisco, California, Saint Louis, Missouri, and Toledo, Ohio; court-houses at Boston, Massachusetts, and Philadelphia, Pennsylvania, and old post-office and sub-treasury, New York.

No action has been taken in regard to the court-house and post-office at Raleigh, North Carolina, the cost of the structure being limited to the sum of $100,000, which is an amount entirely inadequate for the construction of a suitable building. It should be borne in mind that the cost of building is greater in such locations than in the principal cities of the Eastern and Western States. I recommend that no action be taken until the limitation on the cost of the building be increased to a sum that will enable the Department to erect a suitable, satisfactory, and substantial building, which cannot, in my opinion, be accomplished for a less sum than $250,000.

I desire to renew the recommendations contained in my last annual report, to which I respectfully refer, in regard to the purchase of the Battery in New York, and the erection thereon of a suitable building for the customs department in that city, including a barge office, appraiser's stores, and custom-house, and to say that, in my opinion, no public buildings are more urgently needed at the present time.

I also desire to renew my recommendations for the purchase of the Merchants' Bank property in Baltimore, which joins and, in fact, forms a part of the custom-house building.

I also desire to renew my recommendations in regard to the iron building at New Orleans, intended for a marine hospital. The locality in which it is erected is, as I have previously stated, an unsuitable and unsatisfactory one. It would require to complete the building more than double the amount necessary to erect a suitable, convenient, and well-arranged hospital, of the pavilion plan, and would be inferior thereto. The building is rapidly falling into decay, and is, in its present condition, a disgrace to the Government. It should be completed, sold, or given to the city of New Orleans without delay.

I would also renew my recommendation that authority be obtained to sell the marine hospital at Pittsburgh, and to erect a pavilion hospital instead thereof. The building is in a dilapidated condition, and would require a very large sum to place it in repair, after which it would be of comparatively little value for hospital purposes, the defects in its plan being radical.

I desire most earnestly to recommend that an appropriation be obtained for re-building the east front and the center wing of the Treasury building, which would increase the capacity of those portions of the building nearly one-half, and would furnish very material relief to the overcrowded condition of the Treasury Department. In case this suggestion is approved, I would recommend that the entire granite work be cut, before the destruction of the old building is commenced, in which event the building could be rebuilt and ready for occupancy in a very short space of time, not exceeding two years. An examination of the building will show that the reconstruction is only a question of time, as the material of which the old building was constructed is entirely worthless, and is rapidly disintegrating. The rooms are also small, badly lighted, and without any proper means of ventilation, and are in every respect unsuitable for office purposes.

The business of the office has, as a rule, progressed during the past year in a very satisfactory manner. The principal obstacles have arisen from the difficulty of obtaining competent, industrious, and reliable superintendents, without which it is utterly impossible for this office to control the cost of work or to secure a vigorous prosecution of the same.

I also desire to say that the employés in this office have been harder worked and have performed a greater average amount of labor than any other bureau of the Department. Their duties are mostly of a technical nature, and their places are much more difficult to fill than ordinary clerkships. Many of the salaries paid are entirely inadequate to the duties required. In this connection I desire to call special attention to the salary of the assistant supervising architect, which is entirely disproportionate to the capacity required and the duties that devolve upon that office, and I most earnestly recommend that the salary be increased to an amount sufficient to make it an inducement for a competent gentleman to secure and retain the position.

In conclusion, I have to express my thanks for the kind consideration I have received from you during the past year, and remain,

With very great respect, your obedient servant,

A. B. MULLETT,
Supervising Architect.

HON. GEO. S. BOUTWELL,
Secretary of the Treasury.

Tabular statement of custom-houses, marine hospitals, court-houses, post-offices, branch mints, &c., under charge of this office, exhibiting the contract price of construction, actual cost of construction, cost of alterations and repairs, total cost of the work, including alterations and repairs to June 30, 1872, cost of site, and date of purchase.

Nature and location of work.	Contract price of construction.	Actual cost of construction.	Cost of alterations and repairs.	Total cost of work to June 30, 1872.	Cost of site.	Date of purchase.	Remarks.
CUSTOM-HOUSES.							
Alexandria, Va	$37, 149 37	$57, 913 64	$10, 562 53	$68, 476 17	$16, 000 00	May 3, 1856	
Astoria, Oreg					900 00	Mar. 27, 1856	Old site.
Do				41, 373 01	8, 000 00	May 7, 1868	In course of erection.
Bath, Me	47, 549 36	88, 831 53	3, 151 10	91, 982 63	15, 000 00	Feb. 7, 1852	
Bangor, Me	45, 5d4 39	103, 698 13	97, 901 15	201, 599 28	15, 000 00	June 5, 1851	
Barnstable, Mass	17, 250 00	34, 433 71	2, 706 22	37, 139 93	1, 500 00	April 24, 1855	
Baltimore, Md					*70, 000 00	July 16, 1817	Part of present building.
Do					*110, 000 00	Feb. 10, 1853	Do.
Do			262, 698 22	649, 698 22	*207, 000 00	May 28, 1857	Including both of above.
Belfast, Me	17, 500 00	30, 983 26	2, 607 48	33, 590 74	5, 600 00	Oct. 4, 1856	
Boston, Mass		884, 346 76	48, 483 70	932, 830 46	180, 000 00	Aug. 29, 1837	
Bristol, R. I	17, 522 00	22, 135 75	2, 005 13	24, 140 88	4, 400 00	Mar. 12, 1856	
Buffalo, N. Y	117, 769 05	191, 764 34	44, 941 86	236, 706 20	45, 000 00	Jan. 22, 1855	
Burlington, Vt	28, 238 40	44, 968 74	18, 491 22	63, 459 96	7, 750 00	Mar. 30, 1855	
Cairo, Ill				271, 042 94			Completed. Site donated.
Castine, Me			12, 020 50	13, 220 50	*1, 200 00	April 6, 1833	Total cost includes site.
Do					600 00	Jan. 16, 1872	Additional land.
Charleston, S. C			4, 493 94	2, 163, 692 40	130, 000 00	July 10, 1849	In course of erection.
Cleveland, Ohio	83, 500 00	138, 236 30	33, 847 41	172, 083 71	30, 000 00	April 9, 1856	
Cincinnati, Ohio		242, 107 23	74, 388 18	316, 585 41	50, 000 00	Sept. 1, 1851	
Chicago, Ill	276, 750 56	365, 694 18	77, 259 91	442, 954 09	26, 600 00	Jan. 10, 1855	Building destroyed by fire, Oct. 9, 1871.
Do					34, 200 00	July 31, 1857	Additional land.
Do					6, 400 00	Jan. 26, 1865	Do.
Chicago, Ill., (new)				3, 007 53	1, 250, 000 00	Aug. 26, 1872	New building commenced.
Detroit, Mich	103, 160 66	190, 933 00	18, 760 86	209, 693 86	24, 000 00	Nov. 13, 1855	
Dubuque, Iowa	87, 334 50	179, 095 96	3, 137 54	182, 233 50	20, 000 00	Feb. 17, 1857	
Eastport, Me						Feb. 17, 1830	Old building; acquired for debt.
Do	30, 500 00	32, 509 60	9, 946 47	42, 456 87	2, 780 00	July 3, 1847	
Ellsworth, Me	9, 200 00	22, 258 47	1, 387 95	23, 646 42	3, 000 00	April 11, 1855	
Erie, Pa			5, 648 44	34, 648 44	*29, 000 00	July 2, 1849	Total cost includes site.
Galena, Ill	43, 629 00	61, 372 44	4, 265 58	65, 638 02	16, 500 00	Mar. 24, 1857	
Galveston, Tex	94, 470 74	108, 359 62	20, 987 38	129, 347 00	6, 000 00	Sept. 1, 1855	
Georgetown, D. C	41, 582 00	55, 368 15	7, 252 79	62, 620 94	5, 000 00	Oct. 23, 1856	
Gloucester, Mass	26, 596 78	40, 765 11	989 71	41, 754 82	9, 000 00	June 6, 1855	
Kennebunk, Me				2, 343 42	*1, 575 00	Nov. 19, 1832	Total cost includes site.
Key West, Fla				9, 341 89	*4, 000 00	July 26, 1833	Do.
Knoxville, Tenn				191, 726 28	5, 000 00	Sept. 26, 1870	In course of erection.
Do					5, 300 00	Mar. 3, 1871	Additional land.

Louisville, Ky	148, 158 00	246, 640 75	72, 426 97	319, 067 72	16, 000 00	Oct. 7, 1851	
Machias, Me				21, 000 00	1, 000 00	May 7, 1870	Completed.
Middletown, Conn		12, 176 64	17, 219 95	29, 396 59	3, 500 00	Feb. 8, 1833	
Milwaukee, Wis	130, 064 03	161, 779 61	27, 768 47	189, 548 08	12, 200 00	Feb. 16, 1855	
Mobile, Ala		382, 159 93	25, 846 09	408, 006 02	12, 500 00	Oct. 13, 1851	
Nashville, Tenn					20, 000 00	Feb. 17, 1857	
Newark, N. J	81, 252 90	109, 873 00	22, 623 18	132, 496 18	50, 000 00	May 30, 1855	
New Bedford, Mass		24, 500 00	12, 375 86	36, 875 86	4, 900 00	April 9, 1833	
Newburyport, Mass		23, 188 50	7, 967 30	31, 155 80	3, 000 00	Aug. 9, 1833	
New Haven, Conn	88, 000 00	158, 256 00	21, 672 30	179, 928 39	25, 500 00	June 1, 1855	
New London, Conn		14, 600 00	3, 690 35	18, 290 35	3, 400 00	May 18, 1833	
New Orleans, La				3, 220, 201 89			In course of erection; site donated.
Newport, R. I		9, 100 00	5, 526 88	14, 626 88	1, 400 00	Sept. 16, 1829	
New York, N. Y			288, 444 24	1, 288, 444 64	*1, 000, 000 00	April 29, 1865	Total cost includes site.
Norfolk, Va		34, 552 33	3, 450 00	38, 002 33	9, 000 00	Dec. 6, 1817	Old building.
Do		203, 893 75	9, 223 34	213, 117 09	13, 500 00	Feb. 28, 1852	
Ogdensburgh, N. Y		216, 575 58	2, 782 25	218, 357 83	8, 000 00	Feb. 4, 1857	
Oswego, N. Y	77, 255 00	114, 012 03	10, 251 72	124, 263 75	12, 000 00	Dec. 15, 1854	
Plattsburgh, N. Y	51, 224 94	66, 425 17	2, 581 83	69, 006 00	5, 000 00	June 10, 1856	
Pensacola, Fla	27, 115 00	49, 177 43	5, 000 17	54, 177 60			Site acquired from Spain.
Petersburgh, Va	67, 619 88	84, 664 88	18, 057 70	102, 722 58	15, 000 00	Feb. 5, 1856	
Pittsburgh, Pa	39, 866 00	99, 747 00	-16, 948 82	116, 695 82	41, 000 00	May 8, 1851	
Philadelphia, Pa			69, 323 16	326, 323 16	*257, 000 00	Aug. 27, 1844	Total cost includes site.
Plymouth, N. C			426 70	2, 932 70	*2, 506 00	May 17, 1834	Do.
Portsmouth, N. H	82, 728 96	145, 046 91	15, 381 43	160, 428 34	19, 500 00	June 28, 1857	
Portland, Me		490, 189 82		490, 189 82	5, 500 00	Oct. 4, 1828	
Do					35, 000 00	Dec. 21, 1866	Additional land.
Providence, R. I		10, 504 00	2, 988 26	13, 492 26	3, 000 00	Nov. 26, 1817	Old building used as warehouse.
Do	151, 000 00	109, 841 71	29, 824 18	239, 665 89	40, 000 00	Oct. 9, 1854	
Portland, Oreg				120, 627 49	15, 000 00	Apr. 6, 1868	In course of erection.
Perth Amboy, N. J				1, 374 66	2, 000 00	July 30, 1857	
Richmond, Va	110, 000 00	194, 404 47	32, 899 99	227, 304 46	61, 000 00	June 22, 1853	
San Francisco, Cal	400, 000 00	628, 581 49	37, 612 07	666, 193 56	150, 000 00	Sept. 5, 1854	
Sandusky, Ohio	47, 560 00	64, 019 41	9, 663 52	73, 682 93	11, 000 00	Dec. 28, 1854	
Savannah, Ga		156, 434 35	17, 963 57	174, 397 92	20, 725 00	Dec. 16, 1845	
Salem, Mass		14, 271 77	16, 566 82	30, 838 59	5, 000 00	June 23, 1818	
Saint Louis, Mo		321, 987 08	25, 935 74	347, 922 82	37, 000 00	Oct. 31, 1851	
Saint Paul, Minn				378, 462 38	16, 000 00	Apr. 10, 1867	In course of erection.
Suspension Bridge, N. Y			19, 883 37	25, 883 37	*6, 000 00	May 25, 1867	Total cost includes site.
Toledo, Ohio	45, 530 11	83, 543 52	1, 664 79	85, 208 31	12, 000 00	Feb. 20, 1855	
Waldoborough, Me	15, 800 00	22, 824 68	308 25	23, 132 93	2, 000 00	Nov. 29, 1852	
Wheeling, W. Va	85, 070 82	96, 618 64	8, 384 38	105, 003 02	20, 500 00	Sept. 7, 1855	
Wilmington, N. C		42, 039 75	3, 762 45	45, 802 20	1, 000 00	May 17, 1845	
Wilmington, Del	29, 234 00	40, 146 34	11, 542 78	51, 689 12	3, 500 00	May 27, 1853	
Wiscasset, Me	17, 000 00	27, 007 25	53 03	27, 060 28	1, 800 00	June 20, 1868	
MARINE HOSPITALS.							
Chelsea, Mass	122, 185 39	233, 015 31	110, 437 27	343, 452 48	50, 000 00	July 12, 1858	
Cleveland, Ohio	20, 000 00	87, 703 66	19, 268 93	106, 972 59	12, 000 00	Oct. 11, 1837	

* Building and site.

Tabular statement of custom-houses, marine hospitals, court-houses, post-offices, branch mints, &c.—Continued.

Nature and location of work.	Contract price of construction.	Actual cost of construction.	Cost of alterations and repairs.	Total cost of work to June 30, 1872.	Cost of site.	Date of purchase.	Remarks.
MARINE HOSPITALS—Continued.							
Chicago, Ill.				$350, 674 09	$10, 000 00	Jan. 22, 1867	In course of erection.
Detroit, Mich	$54, 637 12	$78, 215 14	$7, 671 99	85, 887 13	23, 000 00	Nov. 19, 1855	
Key West, Fla			9, 174 87	33, 674 87	500 00	Nov. 30, 1844	Purchased.
Louisville, Ky		61, 378 97	31, 073 50	92, 452 47	6, 000 00	Nov. 3, 1842	
Mobile, Ala		41, 400 00	3, 140 00	44, 540 00	4, 000 00	June 20, 1838	
Do					6, 000 00	Aug. 25, 1856	Additional land
Natchez, Miss		59, 750 00		59, 750 00	7, 000 00	Aug. 9, 1837	
New Orleans, La		110, 388 97	6, 383 73	116, 772 70	6, 000 00	Aug. 4, 1837	Hospital, McDonough.
Do	360, 000 00	498, 118 55	19, 972 29	518, 090 84	12, 000 00	Aug. 7, 1855	
Ocracoke, N. C		7, 827 07	300 00	8, 127 07	1, 100 00	May 15, 1843	
Pittsburgh, Pa		55, 889 38	6, 302 73	62, 192 11	10, 253 00	Nov. 7, 1842	
Portland, Me	66, 200 00	84, 758 73	26, 832 15	111, 590 88	11, 000 00	Nov. 22, 1852	
San Francisco, Cal		223, 400 00	7, 871 10	231, 271 10	600 00	Nov. 13, 1852	
Saint Louis, Mo		86, 288 00	22, 892 52	109, 180 52		Mar. 7, 1850	Site ceded by War Department.
COURT-HOUSES, POST-OFFICES, ETC.							
Baltimore, Md., court-house	112, 808 04	205, 176 97	8, 115 45	213, 292 42	50, 000 00	June 6, 1859	
Boston, Mass., court-house			25, 074 68	125, 074 68	*105, 000 00	1859	Total cost includes site.
Boston, Mass., post-office, &c				1, 314, 990 75	458, 415 00	Mar. 25, 1868	In course of erection.
Do					68, 278 75	Apr. 29, 1871	Additional land
Charleston, S. C., court-house			30, 000 00	90, 000 00	*60, 000 00	Feb. 14, 1818	Total cost includes site.
Columbia, S. C., court-house, &c				54, 412 61			In course of erection; site donated.
Des Moines, Ia., court-house		221, 437 00	837 55	222, 274 55	15, 000 00	Oct. 16, 1866	
Indianapolis, Ind., court-house	98, 983 78	166, 240 00	21, 958 62	188, 198 62	17, 160 00	Nov. 5, 1856	
Key West, Fla., court-house					3, 000 00	Apr. 28, 1858	
Madison, Wis., court-house		329, 388 97		329, 388 97		Mar. 25, 1867	Site donated.
Memphis, Tenn., court-house					75, 000 00	June 6, 1860	
New York, N. Y., court-house					500, 000 00	Apr. 11, 1867	In course of erection
New York, N. Y., post-office			43, 033 26	243, 033 26	*200, 000 00	Oct. 29, 1860	Total cost includes site.
Omaha, Nebr., post-office, &c				98, 251 04		May 19, 1870	In course of erection; site donated.
Portland, Me., court-house, &c				388, 816 64		July 5, 1849	Built on site of old custom-house.
Philadelphia, Pa., court-house			107, 014 99	268, 014 99	*161, 000 00	Oct. 6, 1860	Total cost includes site.
Raleigh, N. C., court-house					7, 700 00	Aug. 7, 1860	
Rutland, Vt., court-house	55, 701 75	71, 324 43	10, 936 96	82, 261 39	1, 400 00	July 4, 1857	
Do					500 00	May 17, 1859	Additional land.
Saint Augustine, Fla., court-house			2, 000 00	2, 000 00			Acquired from Spain.
Springfield, Ill., court-house		285, 841 03	445 15	286, 286 18	6, 000 00	Mar. 2, 1857	
Do					3, 000 00	Oct. 1, 1872	Additional land.
Windsor, Vt., court-house	53, 258 84	71, 347 32	18, 766 45	90, 113 77	4, 700 00	Mar. 4, 1857	

MINTS, ASSAY-OFFICES, ETC.							
Boisé City, assay-office		76, 925 34		76, 925 34		July 8, 1869	Includes machinery; site donated.
Carson City, branch mint		352, 983 85		352, 983 85		May 3, 1865	Includes machinery; site donated.
Charlotte, N. C., branch mint		26, 000 00	9, 692 15	35, 693 15	1, 500 00	Nov. 2, 1835	
Dalles City, branch mint				103, 280 00		Feb. 28, 1862	Work suspended; site donated.
Denver City, branch mint			68, 377 69	93, 377 69	*25, 000 00	Nov. 25, 1862	
New Orleans, branch mint		327, 548 53	287, 277 33	614, 825 86		June 19, 1835	Use of site granted by New Orleans.
New York, assay-office			183, 358 75	713, 358 75	*530, 000 00	Aug. 21, 1854	
New York, sub-treasury		858, 846 76	193, 960 37	1, 052, 807 13	200, 000 00	Jan. 9, 1833	
Do					*70, 000 00	Dec. 16, 1816	Old custom-house; now part of sub-treasury.
Philadelphia, mint			193, 374 70	230, 508 03	*5, 466 66	July 18, 1792	
Do					*31, 666 67	Apr. 30, 1829	Total cost includes site.
San Francisco, branch mint			10, 070 90	300, 000 00	*283, 929 10	May 2, 1854	Old building; total cost includes site.
Do				936, 458 28	100, 000 00	Jan. 1, 1867	In course of erection.
MISCELLANEOUS.							
Baltimore, appraisers' stores		241, 672 61	11, 741 67	253, 414 28	30, 000 00	June 10, 1833	
New York, barge-office		214, 752 82		214, 752 82	10, 000 00	Mar. 30, 1867	Sea-wall built.
New York, 23 Pine street			3, 153 97	14, 291 57	*11, 137 60	1859	Total cost includes site.
New Orleans, quarantine building			39, 865 12	39, 865 12		Sept. 23, 1858	Building and site donated.
Pass á Loutre, boarding-station		12, 000 00	4, 361 70	16, 361 70		Feb. 1, 1856	Use of site granted by New Orleans.
Philadelphia, appraisers' stores		376, 669 41	3, 200 95	379, 870 36	*250, 000 00	Mar. 2, 1857	Built on site of Pennsylvania bank building.
Philadelphia, buildings and wharves, Lazaretto Point.				8, 832 00			
San Francisco, appraisers' stores	53, 000 00	93, 566 75	10, 594 85	104, 161 60		Feb. 1, 1856	
Santa Fé, penitentiary				20, 000 00			
Santa Fé, capitol				50, 000 00	5, 000 00	1854	
Santa Fé, adobe palace			14, 107 39	14, 107 39			Acquired by conquest.
South West Pass, boarding station			3, 835 70	7, 335 70	*3, 500 00	May 9, 1857	Total cost includes site.
Utah, public buildings				20, 000 00			
Utah, penitentiary		44, 998 90	8, 363 00	53, 361 90			
Washington Territory, public buildings				5, 000 00			
Washington Territory, capitol				10, 085 00			
Washington Territory, penitentiary				10, 060 00			
Washington, D. C., Treasury		6, 395, 307 65	277, 422 07	6, 935, 041 68			

* Building and site.

REPORT OF THE CHIEF OF THE BUREAU OF STATISTICS.

REPORT

OF THE

CHIEF OF THE BUREAU OF STATISTICS.

TREASURY DEPARTMENT,
Bureau of Statistics, November 4, 1872.

SIR: I have the honor to submit the following report of the operations of this Bureau during the fiscal year ended June 30, 1872:

CLERICAL FORCE.

The clerical force of the Bureau at the close of the year consisted of twenty-nine male and eight female clerks, who were employed as follows:

Division.	Name of chief.	Number of clerks.		
		Male.	Female.	Total.
Examination	J. N. Whitney	4	1	5
Compilation	Thomas Clear	14	2	16
Tonnage and immigration	L. F. Ward	3	1	4
Registry of merchant marine	J. B. Parker	3	1	4
Revision, translation, and miscellaneous	A. W. Angerer	2	1	3
Publication and miscellaneous	James Ryan	1	......	1
Library and files	E. T. Peters	1	1	2
Stationery, pay, property, and copying	J. D. O'Connell	1	1	2

In addition to the female clerks above designated, one has charge of the correspondence.

At the present time the clerical force consists of one chief clerk, thirty male and nine female clerks, one of the latter being assigned from another Bureau.

WORK OF THE BUREAU.

The peculiar and varied character of the work performed in the Bureau renders it impossible to furnish a tabular statement of its nature and extent.

Division of examination.—The following embraces a part of the work performed in this division:

Number of pages of letters written	5,314
Letters acknowledged	2,317
Acknowledgments of statements written	6,300
Statements examined	2,130
Statements called for	929
Statements corrected by correspondence	1,503

The above figures give, however, a very inadequate conception of the critical and elaborate examination of the various monthly and quarterly returns from the various custom-houses, or of the variety of work of a miscellaneous character performed in that division.

Compilation.—This division is divided into sections, embracing, respectively, statistics of home consumption, indirect and *in transitu* trade, and of merchandise warehoused and withdrawn from warehouse.

It is impossible to present any statement which will give an adequate idea of the amount of labor performed by the clerks employed in the compilation of statistics of commerce in this division.

Immigration and navigation.—The difficulties of obtaining accurate statistics of the nationality and occupation, as well as the sex, &c., of each immigrant to this country, have been increased by the larger volume of immigration and by the carelessness of those who originally record the *data.* Special efforts have been made to induce an improvement in this direction, which have only been partially successful. Exertions have been made to secure for publication accurate statistics of the departure of emigrants from this country, not entirely without success, but rendered difficult by the absence of compulsory legislation.

The compilation of statistics of navigation forms a considerable part of the work of this division, which has been increased by their publication monthly, instead of quarterly as formerly.

Numbering of vessels, tonnage, &c.—During the year official numbers were assigned to about 2,900 vessels, which involved a considerable amount of labor in carefully searching the previous records to avoid duplication, in filling up and forwarding notices to the owners, and entering the awards upon a manuscript list as well as upon the permanent records of the office. The compiling, copying, proof-reading, and distribution of the last annual list of merchant-vessels, and the usual compilations for the monthly and annual reports of the Bureau, with a variety of miscellaneous work, fully occupied the remaining time of the clerks of this division.

A statement showing the number of vessels and amount of tonnage belonging to the several custom-districts of the United States, on the 30th of June, 1872, geographically classified, is appended to this report. The aggregate tonnage of the country was 4,150,033, a net increase over that at the close of the preceding fiscal year of 38,621 tons and 521 vessels.

Revision and translation.—The large and increasing amount of statistics compiled for publication and in response to requests for information, renders the work of revision one of great magnitude. Receiving periodically, as this Bureau does, the statistical publications of various countries in continental Europe, which contain information of great value, the translation previous to publication, in addition to the translation of other information, adds very considerably to the work performed in this division.

Publication, library, and miscellaneous.—A detailed mention of the variety of work performed in these divisions would occupy too much space. It is sufficient to say that the duties of the clerks so employed are onerous and responsible.

PUBLICATIONS OF THE BUREAU.

Monthly reports of commerce and navigation.—The monthly reports of this Bureau have, as heretofore, been regularly published. Compiled at the earliest date possible after the receipt and correction of the returns, they have, no doubt, been printed as early as the arrangements of the Congressional Printing-Office would permit.

It is to be regretted that the returns cannot be obtained and published as early as is done in England; but this will be impossible while the area of our territory is so extensive, and our customs-districts so remote. Custom-house returns can be conveyed from the most distant part of the United Kingdom to London in a few hours, while for transmission from Alaska and Santa Fé to Washington, several weeks' time is usually required. A single district, like that of Texas for instance, covers an extent of territory equal to the area of England, including within its limits several remote out-ports from which reports must be received at the principal office at the port of entry of the district before monthly statements can be prepared and transmitted by the collector. If, however, the statements could be earlier received, their immediate publication prior to the correction of the numerous errors which they contain, would be deemed unwise, as tending to mislead. And while it is admitted that the monthly reports are not published so promptly as in some European countries, the undersigned is convinced from his personal observation, as well as by the admission of Government officials abroad, that in accuracy of statement the statistics of commerce and navigation, as prepared by this Bureau, are in a high degree satisfactory, and will favorably compare with most carefully prepared and trustworthy publications of other countries.

In addition to the usual statistics, miscellaneous information of great interest is published in each number, and every effort made to give the monthly increased value.

Annual report of commerce, immigration, and navigation.—The volume for the fiscal year 1871 was, in consequence of extra exertions, compiled and sent to the Congressional Printer sufficiently early to hope for its presentation to Congress in a printed form in December. But the pressure of other work upon the Congressional Printing-Office at that season, enhanced by the great amount of labor required in the composition and printing of over 800 pages of rule-and-figure work, caused some delay in its completion and distribution. The statements for the fiscal year 1872 have also been compiled and sent to the printer at the usual period; and every effort will be made to furnish the *data* to Congress early in the ensuing session.

List of merchant-vessels of the United States.—The fourth annual statement of "vessels registered, enrolled, and licensed, under the laws of the United States, designating the class, name, and place of registry," as well as the official number and signal letters awarded to each vessel, was prepared agreeably to the requirements of the act of July 28, 1866, and 2,500 copies published for distribution to the officers of customs, the commanders of United States war-vessels, and the largest merchant vessels engaged in the foreign trade, as well as to the principal ship-owners.

History of the customs-tariff legislation of the United States.—During the period under review, I had the honor to submit to you a special report on the above subject. The following extract from the introductory paragraph will partially explain the reasons why I charged myself with this extra duty:

> Regarding it as being within the legitimate province of this Bureau to furnish any statistics of public utility, especially such as may supply the *data* needed in national legislation, and aware of the absorbing interest which attaches to a discussion of questions affecting the customs tariff, I have deemed it my duty to anticipate and make provision for the calls for information which, no doubt, will soon be made.

Its reception, when published, by members of Congress and others, who stated that it supplied a want long felt, and the demand for its distribution, not only at home, but abroad, confirmed the views expressed in the above extract.

In view of the fact that urgent requests for copies of this report have been made beyond the ability of the Bureau to supply, it is to be regretted that the resolution of the House Printing Committee to print seven thousand extra copies for distribution was not reported at a period of the session sufficiently early to insure its passage.

Personal requests from our commercial representatives in Europe were made to the undersigned for copies of this document with its appended "statement of the rates of duties under the several tariff acts from 1789 to 1870," which they averred would prove of great value to the legations and consulates of the United States.

Special report on immigration.—Ten thousand copies of this report having been printed by order of Congress for gratuitous distribution in the United Kingdom of Great Britain and Ireland, a considerable part has been sent to the consuls of the United States and others for circulation; and the undersigned, while recently in that country, made such arrangements as will insure their distribution in those places where it is believed the information will be of most service. The value of this document, and its influence in affording such information as has led to the movement of a desirable class of emigrants to this country, have been felt and acknowledged. The only drawback is the absence of funds to pay for its transmission to intending emigrants, by mail or otherwise, from Liverpool or Glasgow, to which places steamship lines have, when requested, carried the books from New York free of charge. Congress also ordered the publication of the report in the German and French languages, and the distribution of ten thousand copies of each to the countries in Europe where those languages are spoken. A translation into the German language was made in this Bureau. When ready for delivery, the edition in French will be sent to Havre and Antwerp, and that in German to Bremen or Hamburg; and efforts have already been made, to some extent, by the undersigned, and will, in the future, be exerted to have them conveyed to the interior of France, Belgium, Switzerland, Germany, and Austria. But the benefits expected from such publication cannot be realized unless funds be provided for the transmission of these books into the remote districts of the countries named, more especially of Germany, from which country the emigration of its people is not encouraged. Many copies might be so circulated, during the exposition at Vienna, as to reach interior portions of German and French speaking countries. The appropriation of a few hundred or even a few thousand dollars for the purpose indicated would, no doubt, prove a profitable investment.

The total number of persons of foreign birth who, in the year ended June 30, 1872, decided to make the United States their future home is 404,806, an increase of 83,456 over the immigration of the fiscal year 1871, of which 49,442 were males. The largest increase from any country was 58,555 from Germany, while from England the excess over the previous year was 13,234, and from Ireland 11,293. The increase from France was nearly 200 per cent., being 3,137 in 1871, and 9,317 in 1872. If the average value of an immigrant, as stated by the undersigned in the report above referred to, be $800, the increment to our national wealth from this source in the past year amounts to $66,764,800, while the aggregate economical value of the total addition to our population reaches the sum of $323,844,800. Surely, so large an addition to our national wealth will justify the expenditure of a few hundred dollars for the diffusion of such information as will serve to increase the volume of this tide of immigration.

The recommendation to publish an edition of at least 5,000 copies in the Danish-Norwegian language, which was submitted last year, is again renewed, and the conviction more strongly entertained that the distribution of such an edition in Scandinavian countries would yield a rich return.

STATISTICS OF INDUSTRY AND OF TRANSPORTATION.

In two previous reports, to which attention is invited, the obstacles which prevented the obtaining the above statistics were mentioned and the fact deplored. In view of the fact that such statistics are obtained by many of the governments of Europe, it is humiliating to confess that the statistics of industry are here only obtained decennially, there being no legislation to compel annual returns to the Government of the United States.

It is especially desirable to obtain information regarding the movement of the crops toward the sea-board, and of merchandise into the interior; and from the data cheerfully furnished during the past year by officers of railroads, in response to circulars from this Bureau, it is believed that it will be able, before long, to publish valuable statistics of transportation.

INTERNATIONAL STATISTICAL CONGRESS.

Having been appointed by the President official delegate to the eighth session of the international statistical congress, the chief of this Bureau left New York for St. Petersburgh in June last to attend the sittings of that body. Although the official report of his action will be made to the Department of State, it will not be inappropriate to refer here briefly to his labors as a member of that congress, especially as he was chiefly engaged in the sections, respectively, of commerce and industry. In the former section he was a member of the committee charged with the preparation of a plan for the uniform nomenclature and classification, for international purposes, of mercantile commodities to be used in the published statements of external commerce, and in the movement of merchandise by railways and on navigable waters. The report of the committee on this subject was subsequently adopted by the congress. The want of a uniform classification and a uniform nomenclature in the various branches of statistics has long been felt and deplored, rendering extremely difficult a comparison of the statistical results obtained by different countries; and the supply of this deficiency is a subject which has long enlisted the earnest efforts of the leading statisticians of the world.

In the section on industry much time was also devoted to the preparation of a uniform classification, for international purposes, of the various elements which enter into industrial statistics.

STATISTICS OF LABOR.

During his visit to Europe, for the purpose above indicated, the undersigned employed his time, before and after the meeting of the congress, in investigating the cost and condition of labor in those branches which compete with similar industries in the United States. Although such an investigation formed no part of his duties, either as delegate to the international statistical congress, or as chief of the Bureau of Statistics, and although no funds were provided by the Treasury to defray the expenses necessarily incurred in obtaining the desired information, yet as such *data* were called for by a large number of members of Congress, and sought with avidity by the public, he charged himself with this task and personally visited the most important manufacturing localities in Great Britain, Belgium, and Germany. In England he visited Liverpool, Birkenhead, Birmingham, Wolverhampton, Sheffield, Manchester, Halifax, Bradford, Leeds, Nottingham, and other places in their vicinity, as well as the "black country," and other iron-producing regions. In Scotland the iron-ship building works on the Clyde, and the manufactories of Glasgow and Dundee, occupied his chief attention. On the continent he visited Antwerp, Brussels, Liege, Seraing, Huy, Namur, Charleroi, and Jumet, in Belgium; Aix-la-Chapelle, Cologne, Dusseldorf, Eberfield, Barmen, Crefeld, Essen, and the coal and iron districts in its vicinity, in Rhenish Prussia; Chemnitz, Dresden, and Leipsic, in Saxony, with Berlin, Frankfort, and other Prussian cities; also a number of smaller places in the several countries named. Among the most prominent industries examined on the continent may be mentioned the renowned steel-works of Mr. Krupp, at Essen; the iron and machine works of the John Cockerill Company, at Seraing; the paper-mills at Huy, and other places; the glass, iron, and coal productions of the Charleroi district; and the various manufactories in and near Chemnitz.

In France, owing to the unsettled state of the labor market, but few facts were obtained, and those chiefly in Paris, Lyons, and in those districts in the northern part of that country in which the textile fabrics and iron are chiefly produced.

In Russia the chief towns which he visited were St. Petersburg, Cronstadt, Moscow, Nijni-Novgorod, and Warsaw, none of which, except the first named, have important industries. Russia iron, the superior quality of which is universally known, being manufactured in a remote portion of Europe, the cost of production is not easily ascertained.

From some other parts of Continental Europe information was obtained through correspondence relative to the cost of labor and of subsistence.

The inquiries made in the places named embraced not only the rates of wages and the weekly earnings of male and female employés in the various industries pursued, but the cost of the chief articles of subsistence, the weekly expenditures for food, room-rent, &c., and the condition and habits of the working people as to health, comfort, education, and temperance.

Owing to the recent decided advance in the cost of labor in Europe, the published statistics on this subject were rendered comparatively valueless. If it were deemed important that the rates of wages which ruled during the past season, and which still prevail, be ascertained, extraordinary means must be resorted to; and it is manifest that the desirable result could only be accomplished through personal investigation and inquiry. The obtaining of such information was necessarily attended with difficulties, but these had to be met and surmounted. If the *data* thus personally obtained, at no small cost of labor and money, be not so full as may be desired, they are as a whole more accurate, and consequently more trustworthy than can be gathered from other sources.

The information already in the possession of the undersigned, supplemented by the facts which may yet be obtained from Europe and

America, will be compiled at as early a period as his official engagements will permit.

SALARIES OF OFFICERS.

In bearing testimony to the industry and efficiency of the clerks and other employés of this Bureau, the undersigned cannot close this report without again inviting your attention to the insufficient salaries paid to the officers. The responsible duties and exhaustive labors of the chiefs of division and other officers justly entitle them to a more adequate compensation than the salaries of clerks of the fourth class. It is respectfully urged, therefore, that several of these officers receive the salary of head of division, as provided by law for the Office of Internal Revenue.

Very respectfully, yours,

EDWARD YOUNG,
Chief of Bureau.

Hon. GEORGE S. BOUTWELL,
Secretary of the Treasury.

Table exhibiting the number of merchant-vessels and amount of tonnage belonging to the several customs-districts and ports of the United States, June 30, 1872, geographically classified.

Customs-districts.	Sailing-vessels.		Steam-vessels.		Unrigged vessels.		Total.	
	No.	Tons.	No.	Tons.	No.	Tons.	No.	Tons.
ATLANTIC AND GULF COASTS.								
Maine.								
Bangor	214	34, 351. 74	3	240. 82			217	34, 592. 56
Bath	236	117, 442. 84	13	3, 959. 71	1	151. 42	250	121, 553. 97
Belfast	341	70, 791. 60	1	103. 13			342	70, 894. 73
Castine	350	24, 230. 14					350	24, 230. 14
Frenchman's Bay	253	16, 944. 90	1	32. 18			254	16, 977. 08
Kennebunk	39	3, 567. 74					39	3, 567. 74
Machias	221	25, 618. 11	2	133. 91			223	25, 752. 02
Passamaquoddy	185	21, 860. 09	10	3, 771. 96			195	25, 632. 05
Portland and Falmouth	338	78, 774. 85	21	8, 522. 46			359	87, 297. 31
Saco	27	3, 715. 37	3	340. 02			30	4, 055. 39
Waldoborough	557	92, 694. 70	2	45. 25			559	92, 739. 95
Wiscasset	167	9, 582. 58	1	49. 64			168	9, 632. 22
York	16	735. 51	1	15. 47			17	750. 98
Total	2, 944	500, 310. 17	58	17, 214. 55	1	151. 42	3, 003	517, 676. 14
New Hampshire.								
Portsmouth	65	16, 734. 98	5	450. 92			70	17, 194. 90
Massachusetts.								
Barnstable	551	47, 051. 09	1	266. 64			552	47, 317. 73
Boston and Charlestown	854	284, 045. 12	61	17, 527. 18			915	301, 572. 30
Edgartown	17	1, 973. 86					17	1, 973. 86
Fall River	128	11, 481. 89	12	2, 137. 09			140	13, 618. 98
Gloucester	527	27, 691. 52	3	160. 19			530	27, 851. 71
Marblehead	61	2, 502. 75					61	2, 502. 75
Nantucket	8	755. 00	1	484. 00			9	1, 239. 00
New Bedford	259	51, 142. 33	7	2, 096. 09			266	53, 238. 42
Newburyport	71	10. 443. 47	3	57. 38	1	122. 99	75	10. 623. 84
Plymouth	98	4, 017. 03					98	4. 017. 03
Salem and Beverly	88	7, 743. 21	2	52. 07			90	7, 795. 28
Total	2, 662	468, 847. 27	90	22, 780. 64	1	122. 99	2, 753	471, 750. 90

Table exhibiting the number of merchant-vessels and amount of tonnage, &c.—Continued.

Customs-districts.	Sailing-vessels.		Steam-vessels.		Unrigged vessels.		Total.	
	No.	Tons.	No.	Tons.	No.	Tons.	No.	Tons.
ATLANTIC AND GULF COASTS—Continued.								
Rhode Island.								
Bristol and Warren	16	1,167.03	2	76.56	......	....	18	1,243.59
Newport	79	4,832.34	10	15,190.99	54	430.65	143	20,453.98
Providence	64	9,150.68	21	9,964.89	......	....	85	19,115.57
Total	159	15,150.05	33	25,232.44	54	430.66	246	40,813.14
Connecticut.								
Fairfield	151	8,612.51	8	1,963.03	6	746.82	165	11,322.36
Middletown	127	12,265.14	28	6,558.18	2	489.39	157	19,312.71
New Haven	142	13,782.41	12	3,204.41	7	1,383.43	161	18,370.25
New London	178	10,351.04	15	9,210.36	1	651.44	194	20,221.84
Stonington	106	12,504.48	3	6,354.29	......	....	114	18,858.77
Total	704	57,515.58	71	27,299.27	16	3,271.08	791	88,085.93
New York.								
New York	2,433	462,250.67	679	313,689.31	2,201	256,752.75	5,313	1,032,692.73
Sag Harbor	224	5,598.96	1	33.50	......	....	225	5,632.46
Total	2,657	467,849.63	680	313,722.81	2,201	256,752.75	5,538	1,038,325.19
New Jersey.								
Bridgetown	286	13,672.46	6	1,263.57	1	123.88	293	15,059.91
Burlington	39	3,119.65	14	2,754.77	77	7,237.86	130	13,112.28
Great Egg Harbor	132	16,454.76	......	....	......	....	132	16,454.76
Little Egg Harbor	53	5,331.99	......	....	......	....	53	5,331.99
Newark	61	2,600.61	25	3,160.55	48	5,248.68	134	11,009.84
Perth Amboy	221	10,420.43	41	14,256.44	52	7,679.88	314	32,356.68
Total	792	51,599.90	86	21,435.33	178	20,290.23	1,056	93,325.46
Pennsylvania.								
Philadelphia	779	100,199.59	258	52,334.50	1,749	164,946.27	2,786	317,480.36
Delaware.								
Delaware	163	10,722.98	15	3,961.64	11	1,202.76	189	15,887.38
Maryland.								
Annapolis	71	1,669.76	2	81.17	......	....	73	1,750.93
Baltimore	721	44,154.34	101	40,151.31	608	36,400.43	1,430	120,706.08
Eastern District	608	15,578.01	......	....	......	....	608	15,578.01
Total	1,400	61,402.11	103	40,232.48	608	36,400.43	2,111	138,035.02
District of Columbia.								
Georgetown	78	2,081.09	25	5,084.51	309	18,490.45	412	25,656.05
Virginia.								
Alexandria	81	1,911.69	12	473.80	89	5,824.54	182	8,210.03
Cherrystone	380	7,250.64	......	....	......	....	380	7,250.64
Norfolk and Portsmouth	295	4,840.30	37	3,410.49	12	818.08	344	9,077.87
Petersburgh	1	8.22	2	23.18	......	....	3	31.40
Richmond	6	248.95	15	1,833.21	58	3,308.00	79	5,390.16
Tappahannock	47	1,136.65	......	....	......	....	47	1,136.65
Yorktown	90	2,142.12	1	62.03	......	....	91	2,204.15
Total	900	17,538.57	67	5,811.71	159	9,950.62	1,126	33,300.90
North Carolina.								
Albemarle	48	871.86	4	369.00	7	151.64	59	1,392.50
Beaufort	68	1,000.23	......	....	......	....	68	1,000.23
Pamlico	89	1,703.15	3	376.81	......	....	92	2,079.96
Wilmington	23	573.57	18	1,755.25	......	....	41	2,328.82
Total	228	4,148.81	25	2,501.06	7	151.64	260	6,801.51

Table exhibiting the number of merchant-vessels and amount of tonnage, &c.—Continued.

Customs-districts.	Sailing-vessels.		Steam-vessels.		Unrigged vessels.		Total.	
	No.	Tons.	No.	Tons.	No.	Tons.	No.	Tons.
ATLANTIC AND GULF COASTS—Continued.								
South Carolina.								
Beaufort	4	49.04					4	49.04
Charleston	137	3,590.15	15	2,415.99			152	6,006.14
Georgetown	5	295.64	8	254.96			13	550.60
Total	146	3,934.83	23	2,670.95			169	6,605.78
Georgia.								
Brunswick	9	868.93	1	51.44			10	920.37
Saint Mary's			2	80.04			2	80.04
Savannah	26	1,105.63	16	5,173.53			42	6,279.16
Total	35	1,974.56	19	5,305.01			54	7,279.57
Florida.								
Apalachicola	9	275.83	10	1,786.68			19	2,062.51
Fernandina	3	49.22	1	183.16			4	232.38
Key West	81	1,930.62					81	1,930.62
Pensacola	59	1,662.41	12	1,431.36			71	3,093.77
Saint Augustine	2	22.64					2	22.64
Saint John's	4	141.24	17	1,806.98			21	1,948.22
Saint Mark's	10	298.68	2	258.25			12	556.93
Total	168	4,380.64	42	5,446.43			210	9,847.07
Alabama.								
Mobile	78	1,971.96	34	7,820.99	92	4,015.99	204	13,808.94
Mississippi.								
Pearl River	64	1,511.00	2	86.00			66	1,597.00
Louisiana.								
New Orleans	379	13,565.79	163	39,784.17	8	1,305.84	550	54,655.80
Teche	28	565.83	13	1,280.47	3	214.05	44	2,060.35
Total	407	14,131.62	176	41,064.64	11	1,519.89	594	56,716.15
Texas.								
Brazos de Santiago	6	98.03	6	1,528.13			12	1,626.16
Corpus Christi	26	407.93					26	407.93
Saluria	46	769.63					46	769.63
Texas	160	3,700.71	35	6,427.90	23	2,883.26	218	13,011.87
Total	238	4,976.30	41	7,956.03	23	2,883.26	302	15,815.59
WESTERN RIVERS.								
Alton, Ill			3	755.51	1	100.72	4	856.23
Burlington, Iowa			6	532.79			6	532.79
Cairo, Ill			11	1,490.40			11	1,490.40
Cincinnati, Ohio			127	42,431.97	138	30,567.33	265	72,999.30
Dubuque, Iowa			6	597.26			6	597.26
Evansville, Ind			56	9,046.30			56	9,046.30
Galena, Ill			36	9,303.97	75	9,098.99	111	18,402.96
Keokuk, Iowa			8	802.17			8	802.17
Louisville, Ky			42	10,489.33	11	3,310.80	53	13,800.13
Memphis, Tenn			42	9,214.51			42	9,214.51
Minnesota, Minn			67	9,380.21	80	9,019.32	147	18,399.53
Nashville, Tenn			20	3,485.53			20	3,485.53
Natchez, Miss			2	111.36			2	111.36
Paducah, Ky			11	2,772.77			11	2,772.77
Pittsburgh, Pa			153	39,583.79	180	36,859.79	333	76,443.58
Quincy, Ill			11	1,328.23	13	722.33	24	2,050.56
Saint Joseph, Mo			8	1,117.45			8	1,117.45
Saint Louis, Mo			138	64,842.73	81	33,185.41	219	98,028.14
Vicksburgh, Miss			14	1,918.93			14	1,918.93
Wheeling, W. Va			65	8,022.71	71	5,845.91	136	13,868.62
Total			826	217,227.92	650	128,710.60	1,476	345,938.52

Table exhibiting the number of merchant-vessels and amount of tonnage, &c.—Continued.

Customs-districts.	Sailing-vessels.		Steam-vessels.		Unrigged vessels.		Total.	
	No.	Tons.	No.	Tons.	No.	Tons.	No.	Tons.
NORTHERN LAKES.								
Buffalo Creek, N. Y	95	35,278.55	120	49,975.39	511	50,862.87	726	145,116.81
Cape Vincent, N. Y	30	3,984.30	1	17.63	......	......	31	4,001.93
Champlain, N. Y	90	5,787.52	11	925.22	655	42,427.85	756	49,140.59
Chicago, Ill	351	69,702.00	85	5,984.79	235	23,980.17	671	99,666.96
Cuyahoga, Ohio	155	35,873.10	56	14,835.12	208	10,577.14	419	61,285.36
Detroit, Mich	187	28,433.52	111	33,137.22	50	12,795.97	348	74,366.71
Dunkirk, N. Y	1	357.75	1	13.84	1	120.39	3	491.98
Erie, Pa	15	3,554.10	23	9,375.99	46	2,061.65	84	14,991.74
Genesee, N. Y	8	1,132.36	5	448.28	189	23,561.47	202	25,142.11
Huron, Mich	122	9,455.24	92	16,649.56	60	13,506.55	274	39,611.35
Miami, Ohio	25	4,694.09	17	1,104.60	157	9,564.70	199	15,363.90
Michigan, Mich	101	6,545.24	66	4,564.93	17	3,716.35	184	14,826.52
Milwaukee, Wis	217	29,965.53	51	15,497.02	......	......	268	45,462.55
Niagara, N. Y	6	1,057.63	2	281.44	16	1,939.76	24	3,278.83
Oswegatchie, N. Y	10	1,326.99	8	267.79	8	473.70	26	2,068.48
Oswego, N. Y	73	15,560.80	18	920.59	858	91,144.83	949	107,626.22
Sandusky, Ohio	72	10,202.99	22	3,510.14	1	175.00	95	13,978.13
Superior, Mich	14	1,418.98	36	2,053.44	......	......	50	3,472.42
Vermont, Vt	13	767.73	6	4,760.64	10	684.46	29	6,212.83
Total	1,585	265,189.02	731	164,323.63	3,022	296,592.86	5,338	726,105.51
PACIFIC COAST.								
Alaska	7	248.96	......	......	......	......	7	248.96
Oregon, Oregon	28	983.57	14	1,160.91	3	147.15	45	2,291.63
Puget Sound, W. T	64	17,858.40	24	3,032.11	8	167.33	96	21,057.84
San Francisco, Cal	690	74,450.27	141	44,972.70	63	8,246.65	894	127,669.62
Willamette, Oregon	8	873.26	36	9,047.78	8	798.41	52	10,719.45
Total	797	94,414.46	215	58,213.50	82	9,359.54	1,094	161,987.50

RECAPITULATION.

	No.	Tons.
Sailing-vessels	17,049	2,146,585.12
Steam-vessels	3,625	1,048,205.26
Unrigged vessels	9,174	955,242.73
Grand total	29,848	4,150,033.11

Summary by States and coasts.

States and coasts.	Vessels.	Tons.
Maine	3,003	517,676.14
New Hampshire	70	17,194.20
Massachusetts	2,753	471,750.90
Rhode Island	246	40,813.14
Connecticut	791	84,085.93
New York	5,538	1,038,325.19
New Jersey	1,056	93,325.46
Pennsylvania	2,786	317,480.36
Delaware	169	15,887.38
Maryland	2,111	138,033.02
District of Columbia	412	25,656.05
Virginia	1,126	33,300.90
North Carolina	260	6,801.51
South Carolina	169	8,605.78
Georgia	54	7,279.57
Florida	210	9,847.07
Alabama	204	13,808.24
Mississippi	66	1,597.00
Louisiana	504	56,716.15
Texas	302	15,815.59
Total on the Atlantic and Gulf coasts	21,940	2,916,001.58
Total on western rivers	1,476	345,938.52
Total on northern lakes	5,338	728,105.51
Total on Pacific coast	1,094	161,987.50
Grand total	29,848	4,150,033.11

REPORT OF THE DIRECTOR OF THE MINT.

REPORT

OF

THE DIRECTOR OF THE MINT.

MINT OF THE UNITED STATES,
Philadelphia, September 30, 1872.

SIR: I have the honor to submit the following report of the operations of the Mint and branches during the fiscal year ending June 30, 1872.

The deposits of bullion and the coinage of the past fiscal year compare very favorably with those of the previous year. The increase is satisfactory and encouraging.

The deposits of bullion at the Mint and branches during the fiscal year were as follows: Gold, $40,382,551.98; silver, $10,119,414.15; total deposits, $50,501,966.13. Deducting from this total the re-deposits or bars made at one branch of the Mint and deposited at another for coinage, the amount will be $46,417,453.84.

For the same period the coinage was as follows: Gold coin, number of pieces, 1,096,415—value, $20,376,495; unparted and fine gold bars, $15,816,692.73; silver coin, number of pieces, 9,591,362—value, $3,029,834.05; silver bars, $10,391,945.32; nickel, copper, and bronze, number of pieces, 3,635,500—value, $23,020. Total number of pieces struck, 14,323,277; total value, $49,737,987.10.

The distribution of the bullion received and coined at the Mint and branches was as follows:

Philadelphia.—At Philadelphia, gold deposited, $2,318,773.78; gold coined, $2,053,145; fine gold bars, $98,125.16; silver deposited and purchased, $2,000,623.86; silver coined, $1,979,327.55; silver bars, $72,976.95; nickel, copper, and bronze coinage, $123,020. Total deposits of gold and silver, $4,319,397.64; total coinage, $4,326,594.66; total number of pieces, 10,465,737.

San Francisco.—At the branch mint, San Francisco, California, the gold deposits were $25,351,270.74; gold coined, $25,344,840.22; silver deposited and purchased, $1,039,822.43; silver coined, $1,137,240.04. Total deposits and purchases, $26,391,093.17; total coinage, $26,482,080.26; total number of pieces, 3,593,200.

New York.—The assay office in New York received during the year, in gold bullion, $7,302,344.89; in silver bullion, including purchases, $2,868,986.71; total value received, $10,171,331.60. Number of fine gold bars stamped, 11,139—value, $7,110,853.76; number of fine silver bars stamped, 16,531—value, $2,267,940.80. Total value of gold and silver bars stamped, $9,378,794.56.

Denver.—At the assay office, (late branch mint,) Denver, Colorado, the deposits for unparted bars were: Gold, $985,228.27; silver, $16,336.54; total deposits, $1,001,564.81. As heretofore, this institution is engaged in melting, assaying, and stamping gold and silver bars bearing the Government stamp of their weight and fineness. This office fully meets all the demands of the mining interests of Colorado, and is efficiently and economically conducted.

Charlotte.—The deposits at the branch mint at Charlotte, North Carolina, have not increased during the past year. They are assayed and returned to depositors in the form of unparted bars. The superintendent is sanguine in the belief that the deposits for the present year will exhibit a decided increase. The deposits for bars during the fiscal year were: Gold, $16,277.94; silver parted from gold, $213.96; total deposits, $16,491.90.

Dahlonega and New Orleans.—The branch mints at these places have very properly been abandoned. Certainly no present necessity, local or national, requires their re-opening or re-establishment.

Carson City.—This branch mint has been most successful in its operations during the past year. The great increase of deposits during the past over the fiscal year ending June 30, 1871, is deserving of especial notice, and is evidence of the rapid development of the rich mineral resources of that region. The deposits during the year were: Gold, $4,371,573.55; gold coined, $533,350; silver deposits and purchases, $4,192,863.14; silver coined, $95,006.50; unparted and fine bars, $7,809,287.53. Total deposits and purchases, $8,564,436.69; total number of pieces, 264,340.

From this statement we have the gratifying fact that the deposits of gold and silver bullion, in value, during the fiscal year have exceeded those of the past $6,269,942.04, an increase nearly threefold. Full confidence in the future of this branch mint is felt and expressed by its energetic superintendent. The following extracts from the annual report of the superintendent speak for themselves, and his recommendations for an increase of clerical force and salaries are fully approved. He says that—

The business has steadily increased during the past year, and now exhibits an extent and promise of permanence which are highly gratifying, the last three months of the year having shown an average of over one million of dollars per month. * *

From these statements it will be seen that the value of the gold and silver deposits during the year 1871–'72 was $8,564,436.69; and during the year 1870–'71 was $2,294,494.45, and that the work executed during the two periods amounted for 1871 and 1872 to $8,497,644.03, and for the year 1870–'71 to $2,253,235.05, having nearly quadrupled during the past year. * * * * * *

I beg again to submit the necessity of increasing the clerical force by the appointment of an additional clerk in the treasurer's office, at a salary of $1,800 per year. During the past year it has frequently happened that the statements and accounts from the treasurer's office could not be made up and forwarded to the Department at Washington as promptly as they should have been, from the insufficient force in the treasurer's office. * * * * * * *

I have, also, to renew the recommendation made in my report for the fiscal year 1870–'71, of an increase in the salaries of the chief clerk and treasurer's clerk, whose compensation is quite inconsistent with the duties and responsibilities of their positions. These are as onerous as those of any department of this branch mint, and require, for their proper fulfillment, persons of good business qualifications. The efficient and satisfactory manner in which the duties of their positions have been discharged by the chief clerk and acting treasurer, entitles them, I feel, to an advance of their salaries to $2,500 per year, each. * * * * * *

In relation to the future productiveness of the mines in connection with the deeper workings, he says:

The past year's experience on the Comstock lode has established a point upon which there had hitherto been some uncertainty in the public mind, and some among experts in mining matters, viz, that in the deeper workings of the mines, deposits of ore are reached even more extensive and rich than are found nearer the surface. This has created great faith in the permanence of the lode, and greater confidence in exploring and working it. The developments in the lowest levels of some of the prominent mines at a depth of 1,500 feet, have given a fresh impetus to work upon the lode. Many partially-prospected claims upon which work had been for some time suspended have again been opened; new and extensive hoisting-machinery provided, and some are already showing veins of pay matter.

All the suggestions of this report are judicious, and worthy of consideration. The efficiency and economy exhibited in the management of this branch deserve commendation.

The early completion of the new branch-mint building at San Francisco is most desirable, as also important and necessary. Every effort should be made to complete it at the earliest day practicable. The work is progressing rapidly, and, with the energy already exhibited, the building will soon be ready for occupation

Boise City.—The assay office in Boise City, Idaho, is now in active operation. In March, 1872, the first deposits were received, and from that time to the close of the fiscal year ending June 30, 1872, the total amount was: Gold, $37,082.81; silver parted from gold, $567.51; total deposits, $37,650.32. These deposits were assayed, and returned in the form of stamped unparted bars to the depositor.

The superintendent in his report suggests that the general business of the office, including assaying, would be much increased "if that office were directed by the Secretary of the Treasury to issue drafts or certificates of deposit upon the Treasury or assistant treasurers of the United States in payment for deposits, as authorized by the 5th section of the act of Congress, of February 19, 1869, establishing that office." A favorable contract could be made with the express companies to transport the bullion to Philadelphia, and the cost thereof deducted from depositors.

The superintendent also refers to the fact that he has no bullion-fund out of which depositors can be paid, and that in returning the unparted bars he is compelled to give to the depositor the "assay chips," or to pay the value of such "chips" out of his private funds, to be reimbursed by the sale of the chips. This should be avoided, and he asks "that the Boise City assay office be placed on an equal footing with the others in this respect." Approving of his suggestions, I ask for them the favorable consideration of the Department and Congress. The salaries of the officers in that office are so undeniably inadequate, that I earnestly recommend their increase. The assayer (who is also superintendent) receives $1,800 currency; the assayer in a private office in the vicinity receives $3,000 in gold. Equal scientific knowledge and greater responsibility should command at least equal compensation. This new institution will, it is hoped, greatly aid in developing the mineral wealth of Idaho, and promote and encourage its general productive industries.

REDEMPTION OF COPPER, NICKEL, AND BRONZE COINS.

The redemption of the copper, nickel, and bronze coins by the Treasurer at the Mint, under the act of March 3, 1871, during the year ending June 30, 1872, was, in tale or nominal value, $475,352.31.

The following statement shows the different kinds of the small coins redeemed during the year:

Statement of the amount and kind of each denomination of base coins redeemed at the Mint of the United States during the fiscal year ending June 30, 1872, under the act of March 3, 1871.

Denominations and kinds.	Number of pieces.	Value.
Copper one-cent pieces	1, 706, 641	$17, 966 41
Nickel one-cent pieces	8, 343, 767	83, 437 07
Bronze one-cent pieces	7, 405, 794	74, 057 94
Bronze two-cent pieces	3, 125, 247	62, 504 94
Nickel three-cent pieces	673, 040	20, 191 20
Nickel five-cent pieces	4, 343, 883	217, 194 15
Total for the year	25, 648, 372	475, 352 31
Redeemed prior to June 30, 1871	10, 615, 899	178, 133 75
	36, 364, 271	653, 486 06

During the same period large orders were received for the bronze and copper-nickel coins, and the issue of the same on orders is constantly increasing. From present indications the issue of these coins will in the future exceed their redemption.

The alloy of the minor coinage has been duly assayed and regularly reported by the assayer of the Mint. The legal proportions of the constituent metals have been properly maintained.

ABRADED COINS AS A LEGAL TENDER.

The subject of the abrasion of coins, and at what limit abraded coins should cease to be a legal tender, has recently attracted much attention. The importance of the questions involved in the consideration of the subject will be at once recognized by all intelligent men.

In my last annual report I referred to this subject at length. To the views then expressed, and suggestions made, I now ask a careful attention.

TOKEN COINAGE.

Having heretofore stated my views on the convenience and necessity of a "silver token coinage," I would refer to what has been said on this subject in previous reports.

CHLORINE PROCESS.

By the authority of the Secretary of the Treasury, and with the consent of the proprietor of the chlorine process for refining and separating gold and silver, arrangements have been made for testing the same on a large scale. The necessary room has been secured in the Mint building, the apparatus provided, and when properly arranged the business of refining will commence. The experience of our Mint, and of other mints that have extensively used this process, leads to the belief, the almost irresistible conclusion that it will supersede all others within the scope of its adaptation. For a full explanation of the process, its economy and general adaptation to the required result, I respectfully refer to my remarks on this subject in my last report.

TABLE OF FOREIGN COINS.

The statement of the weight, fineness, and value of foreign coins, required by law to be made annually, will be found appended to this report. The additions will be found in this annual statement.

REVIEW OF FOREIGN COINS.

A regular part of every annual report of the Mint consists of a statement in regard to the denominations, weight, fineness, and value of foreign gold and silver coins. This is a requirement of law, and serves various useful purposes.

It will be proper, however, at this time, in addition to the statistical tables which give these details, to enlarge somewhat upon foreign systems and practice of coinage, especially as we have lately received a large accession of specimens of recent issue. These comprise not only the gold and silver but also the finishing out (*d'appoint*) of each series in copper or other cheap metal, which last, rarely departing from home, is more difficult for us to obtain than the costlier kinds. In a commercial sense, the lowest grade of foreign currency is of no importance to us, but it is quite important we should know what rules are observed abroad in regard to such issues, what kinds of metal are used, what sizes represent a given value, and to what degree of minuteness the sizes are carried, as also the general style of device and appearance. No collection of coins is complete without them. I will, therefore, offer some miscellaneous remarks, as may be called for in each series.

Austria.—As in other nations of Europe, the coinage of this empire has been, during the last few years, in a state of transition, we might say almost of confusion. There are three series of gold coins, of different bases, and as many of silver, without respect to the differences of device and inscription growing out of the severance of Hungary from Austria proper. They still coin the gold ducat and the quadruple ducat, but they have recently discontinued the souverain and introduced the four-florin or ten-franc piece, corresponding to the same coin issued in France and some other countries.

The fourfold ducat, (*vierpache ducaten*,) or quadruple, is a beautiful and remarkable coin, and I wish to notice it particularly, because it fulfills certain conditions which have heretofore been spoken of, by which coins can be protected from the most dangerous kind of tampering or fraud. It has a larger diameter than our double eagle, and is of finer metal, and yet has less than half the value of that coin. Of course it is proportionately thin, but this tenuity entirely sets at naught the cunning villainy of sawing out the interior and inserting a disk of inferior metal, by which a few of our coins have been turned into frauds. If it be said that a thin coin cannot well bring up the devices in a coining-press, these perfectly-struck pieces furnish a reply. On the other hand, it must be allowed that there are advantages in having a good body for the coin, and it is not intended to argue the question, but merely to present the point in passing.

The last annual statement of Austrian coinage shows considerable activity, though not what we might expect from a rich and populous empire. This falling off appears to be true at the present time of all the mints in Europe, except those of London and Berlin.

When Austrian rule extended over a part of Italy, there were five mints in the whole realm; now there are three, in Austria, Hungary, and Transylvania. The coins struck in Hungary, though similar in denominations and value to those of Austria, bear the language of the Magyars.

The new gold pieces, one marked eight florins, the other four florins, the latter alone having been struck so far, are intended as an offering to the scheme of international currency, being concurrent with the gold coins of France, Belgium, Italy, and Sweden. It will serve a commercial, but hardly a domestic use, in Austria, since it is not strictly on a par with four silver florins, but is to be rated by agreement of parties. The ducat series, also, is mainly for foreign trade.

It is surprising that Austria and other German powers still keep up the system of making *billon*-coins, base mixtures of silver and copper, which look very well with their whitened surface when they first leave the mint, but soon acquire a mongrel hue, by no means so agreeable as mere copper. By far the largest part of mint work in Austria, in 1870, was upon these pieces of twenty and ten kreutzers. There is a very large profit on them, as compared with the whole florin piece. The latter is coined at the rate of 90 florins to one kilogram of fine silver. The base pieces are at the rate of 150 florins to the kilogram. This new proportion was introduced in 1868.

It is a curious fact that the thaler or dollar of the Empress Maria Theresa, originally bearing date 1780, has always been a favorite at the eastern ports of the Mediterranean, and for that reason has continued to be coined for that trade ever since. We have a fine specimen coined in 1871, but dated 1780.

It is worth while to notice, for its bearing on an interesting controversy in mint legislation, in which strong minds have taken opposing sides, that in 1868 there was a coinage of some millions of this "Levant thaler," mainly to supply the needs of the English army going to the Abyssinian war, not, indeed, to be spent in that far-off country, but at places along the road. Now, if it were the law in Austria to coin *without charge*, it would be an exhibition of liberality hard to account for, to help the British government in that way, and not quite fair toward the opposite party in Africa. Yet we would be doing the same thing by making silver dollars to pass in China or India, and dimes for the West Indies and South America, and gold coin for any foreign use, without deducting something for the manufacture. England is doing this in sending her gold coin abroad simply as so much bullion, paying the cost of the coinage out of her treasury, whereby she has indeed the honor of seeing her sovereign's image and superscription in all lands, and of making a universal commercial currency. Still it is desirable and just to promote the coinage of gold and silver by making the charge as light as possible.

Germany.—The new gold coins of the German empire are the pieces of twenty marks and ten marks, at the rate of 125.55 pieces of ten marks to be coined out of one mint pound (half kilogram) of gold, nine-tenths fine; the larger piece in proportion. This makes the piece of twenty marks to weigh 7.965 grams, or 122.92 grains troy, and its value $4.76.2. (Ten marks, $2.38.1.) This does not harmonize with any system, English, French, Austrian, or American, and seems to be a declaration against international standards. A very large issue of this money has commenced, the material for which is in a great degree derived from the melting down of coins which lately bore the head of Napoleon. A change in the balance of trade, or the influx of Germans, may bring this coin to us in quantities. At present we must be limited to specimens.

It may seem a small matter, and yet it is significant, that this new money displays the effigy of the Emperor without the wreath of laurel on the brow. It was there recently, while he was King of Prussia, but the change of state seems to have brought with it an advance of popular ideas. Monarchs are not as far above their subjects as formerly. Indeed, it is stated that the new coining-die was engraved with this ancient mark of distinction on the one hand and subjection on the other, but the Emperor forbade its use, and insisted on appearing without crown or laurel.

It is plainly the intention that both gold and silver shall be legal tenders in all payments; yet the two do not fit neatly together. The piece of ten marks is to be equal to $3\frac{1}{3}$ silver thalers, or $5\frac{5}{6}$ florins of South Germany, or 8 marks $5\frac{1}{3}$ schillings of Hamburg. That rate makes the Prussian thaler equal to 71.46 cents (gold) of our money, which is just about what it would be worth in gold in the bullion-market of London. The proposed new coinage-charges on gold, when reduced to intelligible terms, are about $\frac{2}{7}$ of one per cent. for twenty-mark pieces, and $\frac{3}{7}$ for ten-mark pieces.

Of the lesser German states, Wurtemberg, Bavaria, Baden, Hanover, and others, we have recent specimens in silver and copper. They are chiefly interesting for two reasons: that this is the last of them, on account of being merged in the new empire; and that they are such perfect specimens of the minting art. In this latter respect they must claim the victory over the coins of much larger countries. Perhaps their mints have so little to do that they can afford to do it as if a prize awaited them. However, the German states, and some of the Italian, have long held this superiority.

Russia.—Very little is to be said of the coinage of this vast empire. Platinum is no longer used, and even gold is scarce, although this is largely a gold-producing country. The smaller silver coins show a notable reduction of weight, following the principle of making them tokens, and not of full value.

Sweden.—We have the novelty of a gold *carolin*, or piece of ten francs, according to the French standards. It bears no relation to the usual silver currency of the country.

France.—No gold coinage is executed here at present. The silver remains as before, with a return to the republican dies of 1848, and the vast female head which symbolizes liberty.

Spain.—The coins of this country show the changes of history and of monetary names and devices. The head of Isabella is followed by the full-length recumbent figure of republican Spain, stretched out from the Pyrenees to the straits of Gibraltar. This is displaced by the new series of King Amadeo I. Formerly the *escudo* was a gold money, intended to be equal to two dollars. In later times it has been the normal money of account, and represented both in gold and silver, being worth about half a dollar. But now, in 1869-'70, we have the *peseta*, or pistareen, parallel with the franc, and taking rank as the normal piece. It is divided centesimally, so that there are silver pieces of fifty centesimos, and copper down to one cent. The old Spanish dollar has been brought down to a level with the French piece of five francs. It is called five pesetas.

The coins of *Denmark* and *Belgium* require no special notice. Nickel has been used in the inferior Belgian currency for about twelve years.

Italy.—A change to the lira system was made in the papal coins in 1869; but now that coinage is entirely superseded, and the money of the kingdom substituted.

England continues to take the lead in the amount of coinage. Until recently no official annual report of minting operations was issued, but now there is such a document, containing much valuable information, not confined to the account of British moneys. The mint-officers are thoroughly imbued with the spirit of improvement.

The mints of Sydney and Melbourne, in Australia, contribute largely to swell the aggregate of gold coin. The last named, which is near the gold-fields, has recently gone into operation. Engraved views of the interior of this mint, which have lately reached us, evince perfection of art and completeness of arrangement. We are surprised, unreasonably, of course, at such results in what was regarded as the end of the earth only a few years since.

The Anglo-Indian mints of Calcutta and Bombay show, by their annual reports, much activity and a large amount of work, especially in silver. Great system is manifest, and the average fineness is identical with the legal standard, or as nearly so as can anywhere be shown.

Japan.—By one of those immense strides which have signalized this country of wonderful progress, a new mint and a new series of coin have been established, taking rank with the foremost. The former master of the Anglo-Chinese mint at Hong-Kong has taken charge of the mint of Japan. It is all the more honourable to the government of that empire that it is ready to make use of aid from abroad so long as it may be needed. The gold and silver series are almost coincident with our own in weight and fineness, except the lower class of silver. There are five denominations of gold coin, and as many of silver. They have been thoroughly examined and tested by the proper officers of this mint, and a detailed report upon them was made in May last. It will be seen by the annexed tables that the gold piece of twenty *yen* is nearly parallel with our piece of twenty dollars. Under this are the denominations of ten, five, two, and one *yen*. In silver there is the piece of one *yen*, or dollar, for commercial use, and not for home currency; below this the fifty, twenty, ten, and five *sen*, a word corresponding to *cents*. These four pieces are only 800 fine. The values are given in the tables.

We have new coins of other nations and provinces also, most of which are interesting to the numismatist rather than to the trader. Those of *Finland*, *Servia*, and *Roumania* are rarely seen here.

MEDAL DEPARTMENT.

This department has been in successful operation during the year. A large number of medals have been made and sold, and the demand is constantly increasing. This department does honor to the Government, and should be continued and encouraged.

THE MINT-CABINET.

The cabinet of coins and medals continues to attract large numbers of visitors. The full set of the new and improved coins of the Japanese empire was presented to the cabinet by the Emperor of Japan, through the recent embassy from that country. They have been placed in juxtaposition with the ancient coins of Japan, and mark at once the great improvement in their coinage, and the advancing civilization of that people.

The cabinet, in its collection of the new and the old, the present and the past, is a place of much interest to the antiquarian and numismatist. The centuries of the past speak to the present through their coins and medals. Valuable additions have been made to the collection of coins during the year. The annual appropriation for this cabinet should be increased.

STATISTICAL TABLES.

The statistics relating to the deposits of bullion and coinage at the

Mint of the United States and branches will be found in the tables hereto annexed. They are prepared with care, and are believed to be accurate.

I am, sir, very respectfully, your obedient servant,

JAS. POLLOCK,
Director.

Hon. GEORGE S. BOUTWELL,
Secretary of the Treasury, Washington, D. C.

LIST OF TABLES IN APPENDIX.

APPENDIX.

A.—Statement of deposits at the Mint of the United States; the branch mint, San Francisco; assay office, New York; and branch mint, Denver, during the fiscal year ending June 30, 1872.

Description of bullion.	Mint of United States, Philadelphia.	Branch mint, San Francisco.	Assay office, New York.	Branch mint, Denver.	Branch mint, Charlotte.	Branch mint, Carson City.	Boise City Assay office.	Total.
GOLD.								
Fine bars		$17, 810, 822 51						$17, 810, 822 51
Mint bars redeposited			$943, 236 79					943, 236 79
Bars	$1, 616, 694 28							1, 616, 694 28
United States bullion	329, 356 74	7, 445, 006 40	4, 895, 206 12	$985, 228 27	$16, 277 94	$4, 371, 573 55	$37, 082 81	18, 079, 731 83
United States coin	122, 007 62		261, 014, 28					383, 021 90
Jewelers' bars	200, 564 20		551, 188 06					751, 752 26
Foreign coin	5, 808 94	45, 768 69	200, 685 45					252, 263 08
Foreign bullion	44, 342 00	49, 673 14	451, 014 19					545, 029 33
Total gold	2, 318, 773 78	25, 351, 270 74	7, 302, 344 89	985, 228 27	16, 277 94	4, 371, 573 55	37, 082 81	40, 382, 551 98
SILVER.								
Fine bars		560, 154 09						560, 154 09
Mint bars redeposited			6, 410 73					6, 410 73
Bars	1, 507, 173 18							1, 507, 173 18
United States bullion	359, 545 23	137, 791 57	2, 404, 695 83	16, 336 54	213 96	4, 192, 863 14	567 51	7, 112, 013 78
United States coin	105, 638 56		47, 073 88					152, 712 44
Jewelers' bars	21, 571 84		155, 558 57					177, 130 41
Foreign coin	6, 562 55	327, 577 99	164, 306 03					498, 446 57
Foreign bullion	132 50	14, 298 78	90, 941 67					105, 372 95
Total silver	2, 000, 623 86	1, 039, 822 43	2, 868, 986 71	16, 336 54	213 96	4, 192, 863 14	567 51	10, 119, 414 15
Total gold and silver	4, 319, 397 64	26, 391, 093 17	10, 171, 331 60	1, 001, 564 81	16, 491 90	8, 564, 436 69	37, 650 32	50, 501, 966 13
Less redeposits at different institutions:								
Gold	1, 627, 691 59		943, 236 79					
Silver	1, 507, 173 18		6, 410 73					
Total redeposits								4, 084, 512 29
								46, 417, 453 84

B.—*Statement of gold and silver of domestic production deposited at the Mint of the United States; the branch mint, San Francisco; assay office, New York; branch mints, Denver, Charlotte, Carson City; and assay office, Boise City, during the fiscal year ending June 30, 1872.*

Description of bullion.	Mint of United States, Philadelphia.	Branch mint, San Francisco.	Assay office, New York.	Branch mint, Denver.	Branch mint, Charlotte.	Branch mint, Carson City.	Boise City Assay office.	Total.
GOLD.								
Alabama	$1,989 49							$1,989 49
Arizona	347 82	$218,859 24	$6,089 96	$642 95				225,939 97
California	12,709 79	6,496,349 28	383,318 61					6,802,377 68
Colorado	31,124 22		181,489 60	956,480 38				1,169,094 20
Branch mint, Colorado	7,423 89							7,423 89
Georgia	19,061 72		18,453 02					37,514 74
Idaho	25,896 69	214,239 61	721,557 08	906 28			$28,551 34	991,151 00
Montana	126,400 16	68,697 33	3,136,874 12	509 20			56 97	3,332,537 78
Maryland								
Nebraska	118 29		5,756 30					5,874 59
Nevada		4,062 54	63,885 40			$382,892 03		450,840 57
New Mexico	18,745 69		79,442 76	26,427 23				124,615 68
North Carolina	27,228 86		67,782 99		$16,277 94			111,289 79
Branch mint, North Carolina	3,573 42							3,573 42
Kansas	163 26							163 26
Oregon	4,580 81	398,951 96					8,474 50	412,007 27
South Carolina	2,506 74		518 27					3,025 01
Tennessee								
Utah	1,575 29	7,458 00	36,328 20					45,361 49
Virginia	6,395 78		165 99					6,561 77
Vermont			152 09					152 09
Wyoming	1,731 10		22,764 71	262 23				24,758 04
Washington	528 82	3,852 71						4,381 53
Parted from silver	6,654 64	*32,535 73	145,052 04			165,099 54		349,341 95
Source unknown	30,540 26		25,284 80					55,825 06
Bars						3,823,581 38		3,823,581 38
Congress medal			290 18					290 18
Total	329,356 74	7,445,006 40	4,895,206 12	985,228 27	16,277 94	4,371,573 55	37,082 81	18,079,731 83
SILVER.								
Arizona				4 60				4 60
California			75,462 37					75,462 37
Colorado	2,772 62		246,678 68	15,369 88				264,821 18
Branch mint, Colorado								
Idaho	1,078 93		278 85	14 34			466 69	1,838 81
Lake Superior	5,747 94		632,012 37					637,760 31

* Contained in silver.

B.—*Statement of gold and silver of domestic production deposited at the Mint of the United States, &c.*—Continued.

Description of bullion.	Mint of United States, Philadelphia.	Branch mint, San Francisco.	Assay office, New York.	Branch mint, Denver.	Branch mint, Charlotte.	Branch mint, Carson City.	Boise City Assay office.	Total.
SILVER—Continued.								
Montana	$246 22		$77,733 87	$2 79			$1 27	$77,984 15
New Mexico	9,422 10		30,564 29	939 76				40,926 15
Nevada	323,501 09	$80,694 71	823,284 27			$66,417 78		1,293,896 85
Nebraska			177,023 12					177,023 12
North Carolina	133 13				$213 96			347 09
Utah	2,876 61		254,548 24					257,424 85
Parted from gold	11,048 28	*57,096 86	87,110 77			16,442 89		171,698 80
Wyoming				5 08				5 08
Source unknown	2,718 31							2,718 31
Bars						4,110,002 47		4,110,002 47
Oregon							99 55	99 55
Total	359,545 23	137,791 57	2,404,695 83	16,336 54	213 96	4,192,863 14	567 51	7,112,013 78
Total gold and silver of domestic production	688,901 97	7,582,797 97	7,299,901 95	1,001,564 81	16,491 90	8,564,436 69	37,650 32	25,191,745 61

* Contained in gold.

C.—*Statement of the coinage at the Mint of the United States; branch mint, San Francisco; assay offices, New York and Boise City; and branch mints, Charlotte, Carson City, and Denver, during the fiscal year ended June 30, 1872.*

Denomination.	United States Mint, Philadelphia.		Branch mint, San Francisco.		Assay office, New York.	Branch mint, Denver.	Branch mint, Carson City.		Branch mint, Charlotte.	Boise City Assay office.	Total.	
	Pieces.	Value.	Pieces.	Value.	Value.	Value.	Pieces.	Value.	Value.	Value.	Pieces.	Value.
GOLD.												
Double eagles	100, 505	$2, 010, 000 00	870, 000	$17, 400, 000 00			19, 425	$388, 500 00			989, 930	$19, 798, 500 00
Eagles	1, 800	18, 000 00	19, 800	198, 000 00			3, 860	38, 600 00			25, 460	254, 600 00
Half eagles	2, 090	10, 450 00	25, 400	127, 000 00			21, 250	106, 250 00			48, 740	243, 700 00
Three dollars	2, 030	6, 090 00									2, 030	6, 090 00
Quarter eagles	3, 030	7, 575 00	26, 000	65, 000 00							29, 030	72, 575 00
Dollars	1, 030	1, 030 00									1, 030	1, 030 00
Fine bars	195	98, 125 16			$7, 110, 853 76						195	7, 208, 978 92
Unparted bars				7, 554, 840 22		$998, 731 37			$16, 491 90	$37, 650 32		8, 607, 713 81
Total gold	110, 680	2, 151, 270 16	941, 200	25, 344, 840 22	7, 110, 853 76	998, 731 37	44, 535	533, 350 00	16, 491 90	37, 650 32	1, 096, 415	36, 193, 187 73
SILVER.												
Dollars	1, 109, 435	1, 109, 435 00					3, 526	3, 526 00			1, 112, 961	1, 112, 961 00
Half dollars	1, 039, 635	510, 817 50	1, 766, 000	883, 000 00			167, 350	83, 675 00			2, 972, 985	1, 486, 492 50
Quarter dollars	148, 235	37, 058 75	51, 000	12, 750 00			21, 150	5, 287 50			220, 385	55, 096 25
Dimes	1, 839, 535	183, 953 50	360, 000	36, 000 00			25, 180	2, 518 00			2, 224, 715	222, 471 50
Half dimes	2, 580, 035	129, 001 75	475, 000	23, 750 00							3, 055, 035	152, 751 75
Three-cent pieces	2, 035	61 05									2, 035	61 05
Bars	647	72, 976 95			2, 267, 940 80		2	2, 295 62			649	2, 343, 213 37
Unparted bars				181, 740 04			2, 597	7, 866, 991 91			2, 597	8, 048, 731 95
Total silver	6, 719, 557	2, 052, 304 50	2, 652, 000	1, 137, 240 04	2, 267, 940 80	a	219, 805	7, 964, 294 03			9, 591, 362	13, 421, 779 37
COPPER.												
Five-cent pieces	1, 784, 000	89, 200 00									1, 784, 000	89, 200 00
Three-cent pieces	611, 000	18, 330 00									611, 000	13, 330 00
Two-cent pieces	308, 500	6, 170 00									308, 500	6, 170 00
One-cent pieces	932, 000	9, 320 00									932, 000	9, 320 00
Total copper	3, 635, 500	123, 020 00									3, 635, 500	123, 020 00
Total coinage	10, 465, 737	4, 326, 594 66	3, 503, 200	26, 482, 080 26	9, 378, 794 56	998, 731 37	264, 340	8, 497, 644 03	16, 491 90	37, 650 32	14, 323, 277	49, 737, 987 10

D.—*Coinage of the Mint and branches from their organization to the close of the fiscal year ended June* 30, 1872.

MINT OF THE UNITED STATES, PHILADELPHIA.

Period.	GOLD COINAGE.						
	Double eagles.	Eagles.	Half eagles.	Three dollars.	Quarter eagles.	Dollars.	Fine bars.
	Pieces.	*Pieces.*	*Pieces.*	*Pieces.*	*Pieces.*	*Pieces.*	*Value.*
1793 to 1817...	....	132, 592	845, 909	....	22, 197	....	....
1818 to 1837...	....	....	3, 087, 925	....	879, 903	....	....
1838 to 1847...	....	1, 227, 759	3, 269, 921	....	345, 526	....	....
1848 to 1857...	8, 122, 526	1, 970, 597	2, 260, 390	223, 015	5, 544, 900	15, 348, 608	$33, 612, 140 46
1858 to 1867...	5, 740, 871	179, 745	795, 075	66, 381	1, 609, 749	2, 360, 834	1, 078, 168 51
1868	188, 540	3, 050	5, 750	4, 900	3, 650	10, 550	98, 848 03
1869	152, 525	9, 485	1, 785	2, 525	4, 345	5, 925	130, 141 91
1870	137, 845	2, 535	4, 035	3, 535	4, 955	6, 335	171, 624 97
1871	157, 740	1, 640	2, 840	1, 340	5, 360	3, 940	129, 184 88
1872	100, 505	1, 800	2, 090	2, 030	3, 030	1, 030	98, 125 16
Total.....	14, 600, 552	3, 529, 203	10, 275, 720	303, 726	8, 423, 615	17, 737, 222	35, 318, 233 92

Period.	SILVER COINAGE.						
	Dollars.	Half dollars.	Quarter dollars.	Dimes.	Half dimes.	Three cents.	Bars.
	Pieces.	*Pieces.*	*Pieces.*	*Pieces.*	*Pieces.*	*Pieces.*	*Value.*
1793 to 1817...	1, 439, 517	13, 104, 433	650, 280	1, 007, 151	265, 543	....	....
1818 to 1837...	1, 000	74, 793, 560	5, 041, 749	11, 854, 949	14, 463, 700	....	....
1838 to 1847...	879, 873	20, 203, 333	4, 952, 073	11, 387, 995	11, 093, 235	....	....
1848 to 1857...	350, 250	10, 691, 088	41, 073, 080	35, 172, 010	34, 368, 520	37, 778, 900	$32, 355 55
1858 to 1867...	758, 700	12, 032, 630	22, 955, 730	6, 042, 330	12, 995, 330	4, 209, 330	73, 552 45
1868	54, 800	411, 500	29, 900	423, 150	85, 800	4, 000	6, 729 94
1869	231, 350	387, 350	16, 550	49, 050	10, 550	5, 050	92, 090 12
1870	576, 150	891, 450	87, 250	721, 830	734, 450	3, 850	195, 078 01
1871	657, 625	941, 125	82, 097	10, 675	126, 925	4, 325	143, 647 75
1872	1, 109, 435	1, 039, 635	148, 235	1, 839, 535	2, 580, 035	2, 035	72, 976 95
Total.....	6, 058, 700	135, 090, 304	75, 036, 944	68, 508, 695	76, 724, 088	42, 007, 490	616, 430 77

Period.	COPPER COINAGE.				
	Five cents.	Three cents.	Two cents.	One cents.	Half cents.
	Pieces.	*Pieces.*	*Pieces.*	*Pieces.*	*Pieces.*
1793 to 1817..........	....	....	....	29, 316, 272	5, 235, 513
1818 to 1837..........	....	....	....	46, 554, 830	2, 205, 200
1838 to 1847..........	....	....	....	34, 967, 663	....
1848 to 1857..........	....	....	....	51, 449, 979	544, 510
1858 to 1867..........	32, 574, 000	16, 987, 000	38, 245, 500	284, 909, 000	....
1868	28, 902, 000	3, 613, 000	3, 066, 500	9, 856, 500	....
1869	22, 025, 000	2, 146, 000	1, 730, 750	7, 881, 000	....
1870	9, 750, 000	1, 423, 000	1, 144, 500	5, 836, 500	....
1871	3, 439, 000	921, 000	1, 105, 250	6, 207, 500	....
1872	1, 784, 000	611, 000	308, 500	932, 000	....
Total............	98, 474, 000	25, 701, 000	45, 601, 000	477, 911, 244	7, 985, 223

Period.	TOTAL COINAGE.				
	No. of pieces.	Value of gold.	Value of silver.	Value of copper.	Total.
	Coined.	*Dollars.*	*Dollars.*	*Dollars.*	*Dollars.*
1793 to 1817..........	52, 019, 407	5, 610, 957 50	8, 268, 295 75	319, 340 28	14, 198, 593 53
1818 to 1837..........	158, 882, 816	17, 639, 382 50	40, 566, 897 15	476, 574 30	58, 682, 853 95
1838 to 1847..........	86, 327, 378	29, 491, 010 00	13, 913, 019 00	349, 676 63	43, 753, 705 63
1848 to 1857..........	244, 898, 373	256, 950, 474 46	22, 365, 413 55	517, 222 34	279, 833, 110 35
1858 to 1867..........	443, 062, 405	128, 252, 763 01	14, 267, 879 35	5, 752, 310 00	148, 272, 952 36
1868	46, 663, 590	3, 963, 273 03	321, 479 94	1, 713, 385 00	5, 998, 137 97
1869	34, 659, 240	3, 308, 779 41	526, 836 62	1, 279, 055 00	5, 114, 671 03
1870	21, 328, 740	2, 830, 752 50	1, 152, 960 50	611, 445 00	4, 595, 158 00
1871	13, 670, 015	3, 335, 944 88	1, 299, 903 00	283, 760 00	4, 919, 607 88
1872	10, 465, 737	2, 151, 370 16	2, 052, 304 50	123, 020 00	4, 326, 594 66
Total............	1, 113, 977, 701	453, 534, 707 45	104, 734, 980 36	11, 425, 788 55	569, 695, 385 36

E.—BRANCH MINT AT SAN FRANCISCO.

Period.	GOLD COINAGE.							
	Double eagles.	Eagles.	Half eagles.	Three dollars.	Quarter eagles.	Dollars.	Unparted bars.	Fine bars.
	Pieces.	*Pieces.*	*Pieces.*	*Pieces.*	*Pieces.*	*Pieces.*	*Value.*	*Value.*
1854	141, 468	123, 826	268	....	246	14, 632	$5, 641, 504 05	$5, 863 16
1855	859, 175	9, 000	61, 000	6, 600	....	....	3, 270, 594 93	88, 782 50
1856	1, 181, 750	73, 500	94, 100	34, 500	71, 120	24, 600	3, 047, 001 29	122, 136 55
1857	604, 500	10, 000	47, 000	5, 000	20, 000	....	....	....
1858	885, 940	27, 800	58, 600	9, 000	49, 200	20, 000	816, 295 65	....
1859	689, 140	2, 000	9, 720	....	8, 000	15, 000	....	19, 871 68
1860	579, 975	10, 000	16, 700	7, 000	28, 800	13, 000	....	....
1861	614, 300	6, 000	8, 000	....	14, 000	....	....	....
1862	760, 000	18, 000	18, 000	....	30, 000	....	....	....
1863	866, 423	9, 000	16, 500	....	4, 000	....	....	....
1864	947, 320	5, 000	10, 000	....	8, 800	....	....	....
1865	925, 160	8, 700	12, 000	....	8, 256	....	....	....
1866	876, 500	30, 500	53, 420	....	46, 080	....	....	....
1867	901, 000	2, 000	24, 000	....	26, 000	....	....	....
1868	696, 750	12, 500	25, 000	....	26, 000	....	....	....
1869	911, 000	11, 500	44, 000	....	38, 000	....	....	....
1870	959, 750	2, 930	13, 000	....	9, 500	3, 000	....	....
1871	983, 000	8, 000	17, 000	....	16, 000	....	6, 376, 006 23	....
1872	870, 000	19, 600	254, 000	....	26, 000	....	7, 554, 840 22	....
Total	15, 153, 151	390, 056	782, 308	62, 100	430, 002	90, 232	26, 706, 242 37	236, 653 89

Period.	SILVER COINAGE.					
	Dollars.	Half dollars.	Quarter dollars.	Dimes.	Half dimes.	Bars.
	Pieces.	*Pieces.*	*Pieces.*	*Pieces.*	*Pieces.*	*Value.*
1854	....	....	....	....	....	....
1855	....	121, 950	412, 400	....	....	....
1856	....	211, 000	286, 000	....	....	$23, 609 45
1857	....	86, 000	28, 000	....	....	....
1858	....	218, 000	63, 000	30, 000	....	19, 752 61
1859	15, 000	463, 000	172, 000	90, 000	....	29, 469 87
1860	5, 000	693, 000	24, 000	40, 000	....	211, 411 52
1861	....	350, 000	52, 000	100, 000	....	71, 485 61
1862	....	1, 179, 500	120, 000	219, 500	....	1, 278 65
1863	....	1, 542, 000	43, 000	291, 250	100, 000	224, 763 68
1864	....	648, 000	20, 000	140, 000	90, 000	120, 909 02
1865	....	613, 000	22, 000	150, 000	36, 000	145, 235 58
1866	....	490, 000	10, 000	210, 000	204, 000	442, 342 64
1867	....	1, 216, 000	52, 000	130, 000	....	146, 048 54
1868	....	1, 482, 000	120, 000	310, 000	400, 000	....
1869	....	736, 000	76, 000	190, 000	....	....
1870	....	1, 114, 000	....	200, 000	230, 000	....
1871	....	1, 444, 000	30, 900	90, 000	161, 000	161, 240 24
1872	....	1, 766, 000	51, 000	360, 000	475, 000	181, 740 04
Total	20, 000	14, 373, 450	1, 591, 300	2, 610, 750	1, 696, 000	1, 779, 287 45

Period.	TOTAL COINAGE.			
	No. of pieces.	Gold value.	Silver value.	Total value.
1854	280, 440	$9, 731, 574 21	....	$9, 731, 574 21
1855	1, 470, 125	20, 957, 677 43	$164, 075 00	21, 121, 752 43
1856	1, 076, 570	28, 315, 537 84	200, 609 45	28, 516, 147 29
1857	806, 500	12, 490, 000 00	50, 000 00	12, 540, 000 00
1858	1, 361, 540	19, 276, 095 65	147, 502 61	19, 423, 598 26
1859	1, 463, 800	13, 906, 271 68	327, 969 87	14, 234, 241 55
1860	1, 417, 475	11, 889, 000 00	572, 911 52	12, 461, 911 52
1861	1, 144, 300	12, 421, 000 00	269, 485 61	12, 690, 485 61
1862	2, 345, 000	15, 545, 000 00	642, 978 65	16, 187, 978 65
1863	2, 872, 173	17, 510, 960 00	1, 040, 638 68	18, 551, 598 68
1864	1, 869, 120	19, 068, 400 00	468, 409 02	19, 536, 809 02
1865	1, 775, 116	18, 670, 840 00	474, 035 58	19, 144, 875 58
1866	1, 929, 500	18, 217, 300 00	723, 292 64	18, 940, 592 64
1867	2, 351, 000	18, 225, 000 00	780, 048 54	19, 005, 048 54
1868	3, 072, 250	14, 250, 000 00	822, 000 00	15, 072, 000 00
1869	2, 006, 500	18, 650, 000 00	406, 000 00	19, 056, 000 00
1870	2, 592, 180	19, 316, 050 00	594, 500 00	19, [illegible]10, 550 00
1871	2, 649, 900	24, 241, 006 23	908, 015 27	25, 149, 021 50
1872	3, 593, 200	25, 344, 840 22	1, 137, 240 04	26, 482, 080 26
Total	36, 970, 749	338, 026, 553 26	9, 729, 712 46	347, 756, [illegible] 74

F.—BRANCH MINT, NEW ORLEANS.

Period.	GOLD COINAGE.					
	Double eagles.	Eagles.	Half eagles.	Three dollars.	Quarter eagles.	Dollars.
	Pieces.	*Pieces.*	*Pieces.*	*Pieces.*	*Pieces.*	*Pieces.*
1838 to 1847	....	1,026,342	709,925	....	550,528	....
1848 to 1857	730,500	534,250	108,100	24,000	540,100	1,004,000
1858	47,500	21,500	13,000	....	34,000	....
1859	24,500	4,000	....	....	....	....
1860	4,350	8,200	....	....	....	....
1861	9,600	5,200	....	....	....	....
Total	816,450	1,599,492	831,025	24,000	1,130,628	1,004,000

Period.	SILVER COINAGE.						
	Dollars.	Half dollars.	Quarter dollars.	Dimes.	Half dimes.	Three cents.	Bars.
	Pieces.	*Pieces.*	*Pieces.*	*Pieces.*	*Pieces.*	*Pieces.*	*Value.*
1838 to 1847	59,000	13,509,000	3,273,600	6,473,500	2,780,000	....	....
1848 to 1857	40,000	21,406,000	4,556,000	5,690,000	8,170,000	720,000	....
1858	....	4,614,000	1,416,000	1,540,000	2,540,000	....	$334,096 47
1859	200,000	4,912,000	544,000	440,000	1,060,000	....	25,422 33
1860	280,000	2,212,000	388,000	370,000	1,060,000	....	16,818 33
1861	395,000	828,000	....	....	....	....	....
Total	974,000	47,481,000	10,177,600	14,513,500	15,619,000	720,000	377,237 13

Period.	TOTAL COINAGE.			
	Number of pieces.	Value of gold.	Value of silver.	Total value coined.
1838 to 1847	28,390,895	$15,189,365 00	$8,418,700 00	$23,608,065 00
1848 to 1857	43,528,950	22,934,250 00	12,881,100 00	35,815,350 00
1858	10,226,000	1,315,000 00	2,942,000 00	4,257,000 00
1859	7,184,500	530,000 00	3,223,996 37	3,753,996 37
1860	4,322,550	169,000 00	1,598,422 33	1,767,423 33
1861	1,237,800	244,000 00	825,818 33	1,069,318 33
Total	94,890,695	40,381,615 00	29,890,037 03	70,271,652 03

G.—BRANCH MINT, DAHLONEGA, GEORGIA.

Period.	GOLD COINAGE.					
	Half eagles.	Three dollars.	Quarter eagles.	Dollars.	Total pieces.	Total value.
	Pieces.	*Pieces.*	*Pieces.*	*Pieces.*		
1838 to 1847	576,553	....	134,105	....	710,658	$3,218,017 50
1848 to 1857	478,392	1,120	60,605	60,897	601,014	2,607,729 50
1858	19,256	....	900	1,637	21,793	100,167 00
1859	11,404	....	642	6,957	19,003	65,582 00
1860	12,800	....	1,602	1,472	15,874	69,477 00
1861	11,876	....	....	1,566	13,442	60,946 00
Total	1,110,281	1,120	197,854	72,529	1,381,784	6,121,919 00

H.—BRANCH MINT, CHARLOTTE, NORTH CAROLINA.

Period.	GOLD COINAGE.				
	Half eagles.	Quarter eagles.	Dollars.	Total pieces.	Total value.
	Pieces.	*Pieces.*	*Pieces.*		
1838 to 1847	269, 424	123, 576		393, 000	$1, 656, 060 00
1848 to 1857	500, 872	79, 736	103, 899	684, 507	2, 807, 599 00
1858	31, 066	9, 056		40, 122	177, 970 00
1859	39, 500		5, 235	44, 735	202, 735 00
1860	23, 005	7, 469		30, 474	133, 697 50
1861, (March 31, 1861)	14, 116			14, 116	70, 580 00
Total	877, 983	219, 837	109, 134	1, 206, 954	5, 048, 641 50

I.—ASSAY OFFICE, NEW YORK.

Period.	Fine gold bars, value.	Fine silver bars, value.	Total value.
1854	$2, 888, 059 18		$2, 888, 059 18
1855	20, 441, 813 63		20, 441, 813 63
1856	19, 396, 046 89	$6, 792 63	19, 402, 839 52
1857	9, 335, 414 00	123, 317 00	9, 458, 731 00
1858	21, 798, 691 04	171, 961 79	21, 970, 652 83
1859	13, 044, 718 43	272, 424 05	13, 317, 142 48
1860	6, 831, 532 01	222, 226 11	7, 053, 758 12
1861	19, 948, 728 88	187, 078 63	20, 135, 807 51
1862	16, 094, 768 44	415, 603 57	16, 510, 372 01
1863	1, 793, 838 16	158, 542 91	1, 952, 381 07
1864	1, 539, 751 27	173, 308 64	1, 713, 059 91
1865	4, 947, 809 21	165, 003 45	5, 112, 812 66
1866	8, 862, 451 00	459, 594 00	9, 322, 045 00
1867	11, 411, 258 26	425, 155 26	11, 836, 413 52
1868	5, 567, 082 77	449, 506 54	6, 016, 589 31
1869	9, 221, 914 30	642, 100 55	9, 864, 014 85
1870	6, 656, 268 11	707, 400 04	7, 363, 668 15
1871	5, 461, 801 10	1, 269, 501 75	6, 731, 302 85
1872	7, 110, 853 76	2, 267, 940 80	9, 378, 794 56
Total	192, 325, 800 44	8, 117, 457 72	200, 470, 258 16

K.—BRANCH MINT, DENVER.

Period.	Gold bars, value.	Silver bars, value.	Total value.
1864	$486, 329 97		$486, 329 97
1865	545, 363 00		545, 363 00
1866	159, 917 76		159, 917 76
1867	130, 559 70		130, 559 70
1868	360, 879 26		360, 879 26
1869	847, 272 32		847, 272 32
1870	1, 001, 984 52		1, 001, 984 52
1871	1, 104, 147 10	$18, 561 63	1, 122, 708 73
1872	998, 731 37		998, 731 37
Total	5, 635, 185 00	18, 561 63	5, 653, 746 63

K.—BRANCH MINT, CARSON CITY.

Period.	GOLD COINAGE.			
	Double eagles.	Eagles.	Half eagles.	Fine bars.
	Pieces.	*Pieces.*	*Pieces.*	*Value.*
1870	3,329	3,488	1,890	$66 05
1871	5,222	6,085	11,885	....
1872	19,425	3,060	21,250	....
Total	27,976	14,633	35,020	66 05

Period.	SILVER COINAGE.				
	Dollars.	Half dollars.	Quarter dollars.	Dimes.	Bars.
	Pieces.	*Pieces.*	*Pieces.*	*Pieces.*	*Number.*
1870	12,158	12,800	4,940	....	....
1871	304	100,417	6,890	6,400	740
1872	3,526	167,350	21,150	25,180	2,509
Total	15,988	280,567	32,980	31,580	3,339

Period.	TOTAL COINAGE.			
	Number of pieces.	Value of gold.	Value of silver.	Total value coined.
1870	38,566	$110,576 05	$19,793 00	$130,369 05
1871	138,543	230,715 00	2,022,520 05	2,253,235 05
1872	264,340	533,350 00	7,964,294 03	8,497,644 03
Total	441,449	874,641 05	10,006,607 08	10,881,248 18

K.—ASSAY OFFICE, BOISE CITY.

Period.	Gold bars, value.	Total value.
872	$37,650 32	$37,650 32

L.—Summary exhibit of the coinage of the Mint and branches to the close of the year ending June 30, 1872.

Mints.	Commencement of coinage.	Gold coinage, value.	Silver coinage, value.	Copper coinage, value.	Entire coinage.	
					Pieces.	Value.
Philadelphia	1793	$453, 436, 482 29	$104, 662, 012 41	$11, 425, 788 55	1, 113, 976, 859	$569, 524, 283 25
San Francisco	1854	338, 026, 553 26	9, 729, 712 48	....	36, 970, 749	347, 756, 265 74
New Orleans, to January 31, 1861	1838	40, 381, 615 00	29, 890, 037 03	....	94, 890, 695	70, 271, 652 03
Charlotte, to March 31, 1861	1838	5, 048, 641 50	....	....	1, 206, 954	5, 048, 641 50
Dahlonega, to February 28, 1861	1838	6, 121, 919 00	....	....	1, 381, 784	6, 121, 919 00
New York	1854	192, 325, 800 44	8, 117, 457 72	....	....	200, 443, 258 16
Denver	1863	5, 635, 185 00	18, 561 63	....	....	5, 653, 746 63
Carson City	1870	874, 641 05	10, 006, 607 08	....	441, 449	10, 881, 248 13
Charlotte, re-opened	1869	50, 069 75	681 88	....	....	50, 751 63
Boise City	1872	37, 650 32	....	....	....	37, 650 32
Total	....	1, 041, 938, 557 61	162, 425, 070 23	11, 425, 788 55	1, 248, 868, 490	1, 215, 789, 416 39

M.—Statement of gold of domestic production deposited at the Mint of the United States and branches to the close of the year ending June 30, 1872.

MINT OF THE UNITED STATES, PHILADELPHIA.

Period.	Parted from silver.	Virginia.	North Carolina.	South Carolina.	Georgia.	Tennessee.	Alabama.	New Mexico.	California.	Nebraska.	Wyoming Territory.
1804 to 1827	....	....	$110, 000 00	....	....	....	....	....	....	....	....
1828 to 1837	....	$427, 000 00	2, 519, 500 00	$327, 500 00	$1, 763, 900 00	$12, 400 00	....	....	....	....	....
1838 to 1847	....	518, 294 00	1, 303, 636 00	152, 366 00	566, 316 00	16, 499 00	$45, 493 00	....	....	....	....
1848 to 1857	....	534, 491 50	469, 237 00	55, 626 00	44, 577 50	6, 669 00	9, 451 00	$48, 397 00	$226, 839, 521 62	....	....
1858 to 1867	$105, 070 16	77, 889 48	214, 453 74	6, 156 15	129, 940 00	635 88	530 06	9, 685 33	4, 098, 277 30	$3, 645 08	....
1868	8, 808 92	10, 235 21	51, 199 64	1, 019 11	36, 675 88	....	153 13	16, 001 14	25, 640 20	2, 231 00	....
1869	4, 672 44	10, 578 55	56, 618 34	466 10	31, 049 27	122 94	1, 146 18	46, 935 48	19, 205 51	8, 872 23	....
1870	7, 230 53	11, 357 32	60, 929 87	1, 797 19	22, 412 43	....	2, 354 23	53, 361 54	28, 423 37	....	$153 93
1871	6, 696 62	5, 974 24	61, 213 84	3, 043 08	14, 451 74	....	5, 720 60	15, 941 40	4, 865 44	965 02	2, 147 40
1872	6, 654 64	6, 395 78	30, 802 28	2, 566 74	19, 061 72	....	1, 989 49	18, 745 69	12, 709 79	118 29	1, 731 10
Total	139, 202 31	1, 602, 216 08	4, 877, 590 71	550, 540 46	2, 028, 984 54	36, 526 82	66, 837 69	209, 067 57	231, 026, 643 23	15, 831 62	4, 032 43

M.—*Statement of gold of domestic production, &c.*—Continued.

MINT OF THE UNITED STATES, PHILADELPHIA.

Period.	Montana.	Oregon.	Colorado.	Mary-land.	Arizona.	Washington Territory.	Kansas.	Idaho.	Utah.	Nevada.	Other sources.	Total.
1804 to 1827												$110,000 00
1828 to 1837											$13,200 00	5,063,500 00
1838 to 1847											21,037 00	2,623,641 00
1848 to 1857		$54,285 00									7,218 00	223,069,473 62
1858 to 1867	$3,990,940 52	123,238 80	$5,855,150 23		$7,768 28	$26,127 55		$2,799,559 81	$4,327 11	$2,522 67	5,108 85	17,459,227 00
1868	985,061 53	6,680 39	65,410 70		115 01			90,035 17		860 97	150 53	1,300,338 53
1869	935,003 94	4,500 70	26,896 36	$89 15			$846 36	50,047 24		511 70		1,198,162 58
1870	648,000 75	11,672 86	32,695 34		252 80	451 22		81,652 73	228 17		27,929 43	990,972 71
1871	374,108 19	2,357 10	20,944 38	18 85	4,039 31			42,599 42	1,384 02	227 22	27,515 39	603,393 26
1872	126,400 16	4,580 81	38,541 11		347 82	528 82	163, 26	25,896 69	1,575 29		30,540 26	329,356 74
Total	7,059,575 09	207,315 66	6,048,645 12	108 00	12,523 22	27,107 50	1,009 62	3,089,791 06	7,694 59	4,122 56	132,609 46	257,748,065 44

N.—BRANCH MINT, SAN FRANCISCO.

Period.	Parted from silver.	California.	Colorado.	Mexico.	Nevada.	Oregon.	Dakota.	Sitka.	Washington.	Idaho.	Arizona.	Montana.	Refined gold.	Utah.	Total.
1854		$10,842,281 23													$10,842,281 23
1855		20,860,437 20													20,860,437 20
1856		29,209,218 24													29,209,218 24
1857		12,526,826 93													12,526,826 93
1858		19,104,369 90													19,104,369 99
1859		14,098,564 14													14,098,564 14
1860		11,319,913 83													11,319,913 83
1861		12,206,382 04													12,206,382 04

O.—BRANCH MINT, NEW ORLEANS.

Period.	North Carolina.	South Carolina.	Georgia.	Tennessee.	Alabama.	California.	Colorado.	Other sources.	Total.
1838 to 1847	$741 00	$14, 306 00	$37, 364 00	$1, 772 00	$61, 903 00	....	....	$3, 613 00	$119, 699 00
1848 to 1857	....	1, 911 00	2, 317 00	947 00	15, 379 00	$21, 606, 461 54	....	3, 677 00	21, 630, 692 54
1858	....	....	1, 500 00	164 12	....	448, 439 84	....	....	450, 163 96
1859	....	....	....	....	....	93, 272 41	....	....	93, 272 41
1860	....	....	....	....	661 53	97, 135 00	$1, 770 39	....	99, 566 92
1861, (to January 31)	....	....	....	....	....	19, 932 10	1, 666 81	....	21, 598 91
Total	741 00	16, 217 00	41, 241 00	2, 883 12	77, 943 53	22, 265, 240 89	3, 437 20	7, 290 00	22, 414, 993 74

P.—BRANCH MINT, DAHLONEGA.

Period.	Utah.	North Carolina.	South Carolina.	Georgia.	Tennessee.	Alabama.	California.	Colorado.	Other sources.	Total.
1838 to 1847	....	$64, 351 00	$95, 427 00	$2, 978, 353 00	$32, 175 00	$47, 711 00	....	....	....	$3, 218, 017 00
1848 to 1857	....	28, 278 82	174, 811 91	1, 159, 420 98	9, 837 42	11, 918 92	$1, 124, 712 82	....	$951 00	2, 509, 931 87
1858	....	....	32, 322 28	57, 891 45	107 33	....	5, 293 52	....	....	95, 614 58
1859	....	2, 656 88	4, 610 35	57, 023 12	....	....	699 19	$82 70	....	65, 072 24
1860	....	3, 485 70	2, 004 36	35, 588 92	....	....	1, 097 37	2, 490 86	....	44, 667 21
1861, (February 28)	$145 14	812 79	2, 066 91	22, 182 14	....	....	4, 213 79	32, 772 28	....	62, 193 05
Total	145 14	99, 585 19	311, 242 81	4, 310, 459 61	42, 119 75	59, 629 92	1, 136, 016 69	35, 345 84	951 00	5, 995, 495 95

Q.—BRANCH MINT, CHARLOTTE, NORTH CAROLINA.

Period.	North Carolina.	South Carolina.	California.	Total.
1838 to 1847	$1, 529, 777 00	$143, 941 00	....	$1, 673, 718 00
1848 to 1857	2, 503, 412 68	222, 754 17	$87, 321 01	2, 813, 487 86
1858	170, 560 33	5, 507 16	....	176, 067 49
1859	182, 489 61	22, 762 71	....	205, 252 32
1860	134, 491 17	....	....	134, 491 17
1861, (to March 31)	....	65, 558 30	....	65, 558 30
1869	3, 160 40	....	....	3, 160 40
1870	16, 108 60	....	....	16, 108 60
1871	14, 522 81	....	....	14, 522 81
1872	16, 277 94	....	....	16, 277 94
Total	4, 570, 800 54	460, 523 34	87, 321 01	5, 121, 644 89

R.—ASSAY OFFICE, NEW YORK.

Period.	Parted from silver.	Virginia.	North Carolina.	South Carolina.	Georgia.	Alabama.	New Mexico.	California.	Montana.	Wyoming.
1854 to 1864	$282, 975 00	$20, 320 00	$52, 159 07	$24, 519 29	$121, 338 28	$5, 720 62	$13, 837 00	$140, 327, 002 42	....	....
1865	14, 003 00	....	....	....	3, 422 00	2, 269 00	3, 924 00	2, 177, 954 04	$1, 217, 518 00	....
1866	79, 304 00	1, 693 00	29, 536 00	....	11, 161 00	1, 135 00	....	4, 456, 392 00	3, 132, 370 00	....
1867	42, 935 50	700 74	27, 354 50	713 93	8, 084 31	....	9, 616 33	5, 103, 602 24	4, 246, 410 00	....
1868	12, 971 90	970 18	38, 706 38	567 81	15, 889 05	....	21, 299 10	2, 308, 861 39	2, 087, 756 32	....
1869	33, 089 23	1, 847 74	56, 893 86	5, 894 49	23, 151 24	112 41	59, 939 48	4, 199, 736 35	2, 670, 499 70	....
1870	40, 141 65	358 66	24, 071 95	6, 754 74	21, 017 99	102 49	79, 988 77	1, 559, 728 45	2, 231, 119 67	$83, 963 53
1871	105, 204 79	916 40	20, 030 78	1, 600 78	29, 144 92	....	61, 794 67	197, 680 72	2, 775, 930 82	22, 630 82
1872	145, 052 04	165 90	67, 782 89	518 27	18, 453 02	....	79, 442 76	383, 318 61	3, 136, 874 12	22, 764 71
Total	755, 677 11	26, 972 71	316, 535 53	40, 508 31	251, 661 81	9, 339 52	329, 842 11	160, 714, 276 22	21, 498, 478 83	129, 359 06

Period.	Nebraska.	Idaho.	Colorado.	Utah.	Arizona.	Oregon.	Nevada.	Vermont.	Other sources.	Total.
1854 to 1864	....	$201, 298 00	$4, 267, 237 00	$78, 414 00	$22, 618 00	$28, 296 00	$40, 920 00	$298 00	$150, 168 00	$145, 637, 110 68
1865	....	....	938, 593 00	....	707 00	9, 876 00	949 00	316 00	364, 857 00	4, 734, 388 04
1866	....	205, 844 00	496, 805 00	....	....	8, 705 00	5, 710 00	....	129, 100 00	8, 557, 755 00
1867	....	108, 467 43	657, 390 60	....	....	4, 377 32	....	....	....	10, 209, 652 99
1868	....	40, 656 38	657, 694 35	4, 783 30	293 25	5, 225 14	338 36	898 86	273 64	5, 197, 205 21
1869	....	145, 479 57	830, 029 47	5, 517 47	5, 123 33	750 87	8, 399 67	3, 508 09	8, 714 26	8, 058, 687 23
1870	....	512, 045 86	703, 468 44	5, 572 67	669 33	4, 644 80	9, 359 24	439 13	651 23	5, 284, 098 80
1871	$2, 793 65	532, 833 20	472, 378 58	4, 951 63	1, 657 24	8, 978 81	19, 420 47	....	102 85	4, 258, 120 13
1872	5, 756 30	721, 557 08	181, 460 00	36, 328 20	6, 089 96	....	63, 885 40	152 09	25, 574 98	4, 895, 206 12
Total	8, 549 95	2, 468, 171 52	9, 205, 086 13	135, 567 27	37, 158 11	70, 853 94	149, 042 14	5, 611 97	679, 441 96	196, 832, 224 20

S.—BRANCH MINT, DENVER.

Period.	Colorado.	Montana.	Idaho.	Wyoming.	Oregon.	New Mexico.	Arizona.	Total.
1864	$486, 329 97	....	....	....	....	....	....	$486, 329 97
1865	375, 065 90	$93, 613 01	$71, 310 49	....	$1, 230 16	....	$339 48	541, 559 04
1866	96, 521 38	44, 134 13	19, 549 89	....	777 54	....	....	160, 982 94
1867	110, 203 82	13, 758 92	531 61	....	6, 065 35	....	....	130, 559 70
1868	357, 935 11	....	....	....	....	....	....	357, 935 11
1869	795, 560 38	....	....	....	....	....	....	795, 560 38
1870	814, 939 03	10, 740 38	....	$4, 425 75	....	$159, 958 02	....	990, 063 18
1871	992, 712 70	8, 218 25	4, 348 75	798 65	....	97, 536 25	532 50	1, 104, 147 10
1872	956, 420 38	509 20	906 28	262 23	....	26, 427 23	642 95	985, 228 27
Total	4, 985, 754 67	170, 973 89	96, 647 02	5, 486 63	8, 073 05	283, 921 50	1, 514 93	5, 552, 371 69

S.—BRANCH MINT, CARSON CITY.

Period.	Parted from silver.	Nevada.	Other sources.	Total.
1870	$23, 858 20	$100, 296 24	....	$124, 154 44
1871	107, 600 04	164, 888 77	$731, 320 80	1, 003, 809 60
1872	165, 099 54	382, 892 63	3, 823, 581 38	4, 371, 573 55
Total	296, 557 78	648, 077 64	4, 554, 902 17	5, 499, 537 59

S.—ASSAY OFFICE, BOISE CITY.

Period.	Montana.	Idaho.	Oregon.	Total.
1872	$56 97	$28, 551 34	$8, 474 50	$37, 082 81

T.—*Summary exhibit of the entire deposits of domestic gold at the Mint of the United States and branches, to June 30, 1872.*

Mint.	Parted from silver.	Virginia.	North Carolina.	South Carolina.	Georgia.	Alabama.	Tennessee.	Utah.	Nebraska.	Colorado.	California.	Wyoming.	Kansas.
Philadelphia	$139, 202 31	$1, 602, 216 08	$4, 877, 590 71	$550, 540 46	$2, 628, 984 54	$66, 837 69	$36, 526 82	$7, 694 59	$15, 831 62	$6, 048, 645 12	$231, 026, 043 23	$4, 032 43	$1, 009 62
San Francisco	3, 498, 965 10	....	....	....	....	....	....	2, 740 18	....	60, 152 00	227, 735, 528 05	....	....
New Orleans	....	....	741 00	16, 217 00	41, 241 00	77, 943 53	2, 883 12	....	....	3, 437 20	22, 205, 240 80	....	....
Charlotte	....	....	4, 570, 800 54	460, 523 34	....	....	....	....	....	....	87, 321 01	....	....
Dahlonega	....	....	99, 585 19	311, 242 81	4, 310, 459 61	59, 629 92	42, 119 75	145 14	....	35, 345 84	1, 136, 016 69	....	....
N. York assay-office	755, 677 11	26, 972 71	316, 535 53	40, 598 31	251, 661 81	9, 339 52	....	135, 567 27	8, 549 95	9, 205, 086 13	160, 714, 276 22	129, 359 06	....
Denver	....	....	....	....	....	....	....	....	....	4, 985, 754 67	....	5, 486 63	....
Carson City	296, 557 78	....	....	....	....	....	....	....	....	....	....	....	....
Boise City	....	....	....	....	....	....	....	....	....	....	....	....	....
Total	4, 690, 402 30	1, 629, 188 79	9, 865, 252 97	1, 379, 121 92	7, 232, 346 96	213, 750 66	81, 529 69	146, 147 18	24, 381 57	20, 338, 420 96	642, 965, 026 00	138, 878 12	1, 009 62

Mint.	Sitka.	Maryland.	Montana.	Arizona.	New Mexico.	Oregon.	Nevada.	Washington.	Dakota.	Vermont.	Idaho.	From other sources.	Total.
Philadelphia	....	$108 00	$7, 059, 575 09	$12, 523 22	$209, 067 58	$207, 315 66	$4, 122 56	$27, 107 59	....	....	$3, 089, 791 06	$132, 609 46	$257, 748, 065 44
San Francisco	$397 64	....	1, 919, 180 46	924, 205 13	190 10	11, 300, 202 18	209, 037 83	40, 637 79	$5, 760 00	....	11, 458, 302 90	79, 851, 627 83	337, 007, 047 19
New Orleans	....	....	....	....	....	....	....	....	....	....	....	7, 200 00	22, 414, 993 74
Charlotte	....	....	....	....	....	....	....	....	....	....	....	....	5, 118, 644 89
Dahlonega	....	....	....	....	....	....	....	....	....	....	....	951 00	5, 995, 495 95
N. York assay-office	....	....	21, 498, 478 83	37, 158 11	329, 842 11	70, 853 94	149, 042 14	....	....	$5, 611 97	2, 468, 171 52	670, 441 96	196, 832, 224 20
Denver	....	....	170, 973 89	1, 514 93	283, 921 50	8, 073 05	....	....	....	....	96, 647 02	....	5, 552, 371 69
Carson City	....	....	....	....	....	....	648, 077 64	....	....	....	....	4, 554, 902 17	5, 499, 537 59
Boise City	....	....	56 97	....	....	8, 474 50	....	....	....	....	28, 551 34	....	37, 082 81
Total	397 64	108 00	30, 648, 265 24	975, 401 39	823, 021 29	11, 594, 979 33	1, 010, 280 17	67, 745 38	5, 760 00	5, 611 97	17, 141, 523 84	85, 226, 912 42	836, 205, 463 50

U.—*Statement of the silver coinage at the Mint of the United States, and branches at San Francisco and New Orleans, under the act of February 21, 1853.*

Year.	United States Mint, Philadelphia.	Branch mint, San Francisco.	Branch mint, New Orleans, to January 31, 1861.	Branch mint, Carson City.	Total.
1853	$7,806,461 00		$1,225,000 00		$9,031,461 00
1854	5,340,130 00		3,246,000 00		8,586,130 00
1855	1,393,170 00	$164,075 00	1,918,000 00		3,475,245 00
1856	3,150,740 00	177,000 00	1,744,000 00		5,071,740 00
1857	1,333,000 00	50,000 00			1,383,000 00
1858	4,970,980 00	127,750 00	2,942,000 00		8,040,730 00
1859	2,926,400 00	283,500 00	2,689,000 00		5,898,900 00
1860	519,890 00	356,500 00	1,293,000 00		2,169,390 00
1861	1,433,800 00	198,000 00	414,000 00		2,045,800 00
1862	2,168,951 50	641,700 00			2,810,651 50
1863	326,817 80	815,875 00			1,142,692 80
1864	177,544 10	347,500 00			525,044 10
1865	274,608 00	328,800 00			603,408 00
1866	340,764 50	280,950 00			621,714 50
1867	295,871 00	634,000 00			929,871 00
1868	259,950 00	822,000 00			1,081,950 00
1869	203,396 50	406,000 00			609,396 50
1870	1,152,960 50	594,500 00		$7,635 00	1,755,095 50
1871	498,630 25	746,775 00		52,571 00	1,297,976 25
1872	869,892 55	955,500 00		91,480 50	1,916,873 05
Total	35,443,957 70	7,930,425 00	15,471,000 00	151,686 50	58,997,069 20

V.—*Statement of the amount of silver of domestic production deposited at the Mint of United States and branches, from January, 1841, to June 30, 1872.*

Year.	Parted from gold.	Oregon.	Arizona.	Nevada.	Lake Superior.	Idaho.	Georgia.	Kansas.	California.	Montana.
1841 to 1857	$2,700,728 50									
1858	300,849 38				$15,623 00					
1859	219,647 34				30,122 13					
1860	138,561 70		$13,357 00	$102,540 57	25,880 58					
1861	364,724 73		12,260 00	213,420 84	13,372 71					
1862	245,122 47		105 00	737,446 60	21,366 38				$8,224 00	
1863	188,394 94			850,043 27	13 111 32					
1864	166,791 55			311,837 01	8,765 77					
1865	251,757 87			355,910 42	13,671 51				459 18	
1866	271,888 51	$1,580 51	139 63	340,345 87	22,913 96	$38,859 49	$403 83		453 00	
1867	263,869 59	183 68	3,212 26	579,931 76	18,555 35	160,269 24			310 26	$19,095 48
1868	147,358 87		6,711 29	290,415 51	26,595 72	37,602 56			9,196 94	23,547 73
1869	188,259 81		2,322 75	269,280 28	25,582 44	16,332 52		$468 00	13,973 30	16,568 77
1870	159,885 46			692,569 22	15,910 83	31,922 59			437 25	11,502 53
1871	99,299 33		1,760 46	2,476,209 84	173,308 80	4,856 38			47,906 73	28,139 91
1872	114,601 94	99 55	4 69	1,293,898 85	637,760 31	1,838 81			75,462 37	77,984 15
Total	5,821,721 97	1,863 74	39,873 08	8,539,868 04	1,062,540 81	291,681 59	403 83	468 00	156,423 03	176,838 57

Year.	New Mexico and Sonora.	North Carolina.	Colorado.	Bars.	Wyoming.	Nebraska.	Utah.	Source unknown.	Total.
1841 to 1857									$2,700,728 50
1858									316,472 30
1859		$33,398 00							273,167 47
1860	$1,200 00	12,257 00							293,796 85
1861		6,233 00							610,011 28
1862									1,032,264 45
1863									1,057,549 53
1864	45 00								487,439 33
1865	25 84								621,824 62
1866			$419 00	$16,278 22					893,282 02
1867			543 78	10,709 00					1,056,680 40
1868	473 56	73 75	46,881 13	397,478 40					986,335 46
1869	2,778 18	9 57	197,678 54	168,714 73					901,968 89
1870	1,671 35	1,792 54	236,689 49	174,267 31	$74 25				1,326,722 82
1871	4,533 23		367,510 31	421,039 89	7 15	$23,953 41	$3,779 26	$32 84	3,632,338 14
1872	40,926 15	347 09	264,821 18	4,110,802 47	5 08	177,023 12	257,424 85	2,718 31	7,054,916 92

W.—*Statement of domestic gold and silver deposited at the United States Mint and branches, for coinage, to June 30, 1872.*

From—	Gold.	Silver.	Gold and silver.
California	$642, 965, 026 09	$156, 423 03	$643, 121, 449 12
Montana	30, 648, 265 24	176, 838 57	30, 825, 103 81
Colorado	20, 338, 420 96	1, 114, 543 43	21, 452, 964 39
Idaho	17, 141, 523 84	291, 681 59	17, 433, 205 43
North Carolina	9, 865, 252 97	44, 110 95	9, 909, 363 92
Oregon	11, 594, 979 33	1, 863 74	11, 596, 843 07
Georgia	7, 232, 346 96	403 83	7, 232, 750 79
Virginia	1, 629, 188 79	....	1, 629, 188 79
South Carolina	1, 379, 121 92	....	1, 379, 121 92
Nevada	1, 010, 280 17	8, 539, 868 04	9, 550, 148 21
Alabama	213, 750 66	....	213, 750 66
Arizona	975, 401 39	39, 873 08	1, 015, 274 47
New Mexico	823, 021 29	....	823, 021 29
Utah	146, 147 18	261, 204 71	407, 351 89
Tennessee	81, 529 69	....	81, 529 69
Washington	67, 745 38	....	67, 745 38
Dakota	5, 760 00	....	5, 760 00
Nebraska	24, 381 57	200, 976 53	225, 358 10
Vermont	5, 611 97	....	5, 611 97
Other sources	85, 226, 912 42	2, 751 15	85, 229, 663 57
Parted from silver	4, 690, 402 30	....	4, 690, 402 30
Lake Superior	....	1, 062, 540 81	1, 062, 540 81
New Mexico and Sonora	....	51, 653 31	51, 653 31
Sitka	397 64	....	397 64
Wyoming	138, 878 12	86 48	138, 964 60
Maryland	108 00	....	108 00
Kansas	1, 009 62	468 00	1, 477 62
Fine bars	....	5, 298, 490 02	5, 298, 490 02
Parted from gold	....	5, 821, 721 97	5, 821, 721 97
Total	836, 205, 463 50	23, 065, 499 24	859, 270, 962 74

A statement of foreign gold, and silver coins, prepared by the Director of the Mint, to accompany his annual report, in pursuance of the act of February 21, 1857.

EXPLANATORY REMARKS.—The first column embraces the names of the countries where the coins are issued; the second contains the name of the coin, only the principal denominations being given. The other sizes are proportional; and when this is not the case the deviation is stated.

The third column expresses the weight of a single piece in fractions of the troy ounce, carried to the thousandth, and in a few cases to the ten thousandth of an ounce. The method is preferable to expressing the weight in grains for commercial purposes, and corresponds better with the terms of the Mint. It may be readily transferred to weight in grains by the following rules: Remove the decimal point; from one-half deduct four per cent. of that half, and the remainder will be grains.

The fourth column expresses the fineness in thousandths, *i. e.*, the number of parts of pure gold or silver in 1,000 parts of the coin.

The fifth and sixth columns of the first table express the valuation of gold. In the fifth is shown the value as compared with the legal contents or amount of fine gold in our coin. In the sixth is shown the value as paid in the Mint, after the uniform deduction of one-half of one per cent. The former is the value for any other purposes than recoinage, and especially for the purpose of comparison; the latter is the value in exchange for our coins at the Mint.

For the silver there is no fixed legal valuation, the law providing for shifting the price according to the condition of demand and supply. The present price of standard silver is 122¼ cents per ounce, at which rate the values in the fifth column of the second table are calculated. In a few cases, where the coins could not be procured, the data are *assumed* from the legal rates, and so stated.

X.—*Gold coins.*

Country.	Denominations.	Weight.	Fineness.	Value.	Value after deduction.
		Oz. Dec.	*Thous.*		
Austria	Ducat	0.112	986	$2 28.3	$2 27
Do	Souverain	0.363	900	6 75.4	6 72
Do	Four florins	0.104	900	1 93.5	1 91.5
Belgium	Twenty-five francs	0.254	899	4 72	4 69.9
Bolivia	Doubloon	0.867	870	15 59.3	15 51.5
Brazil	Twenty milreis	0.575	917.5	10 90.6	10 85.1
Central America	Two escudos	0.209	853.5	3 68.8	3 66.9
Do	Four reals	0.027	875	0 48.8	0 48.6
Chili	Old doubloon	0.867	870	15 59.3	15 51.5
Do	Ten pesos	0.492	900	9 15.4	9 10.8
Denmark	Ten thaler	0.427	895	7 90	7 86.1
Ecuador	Four escudos	0.433	844	7 55.5	7 51.7
England	Pound or sovereign, new	0.256.7	916.5	4 86.3	4 83.9
Do	Pound or sovereign, average	0.256.2	916	4 85.1	4 82.7
France	Twenty francs, new	0.207.5	899	3 85.8	3 83.9
Do	Twenty francs, average	0.207	899	3 84.7	3 82.8
Germany	Ten thaler, Prussian	0.427	903	7 97.1	7 93.1
Do	Twenty marks	0.256	900	4 76.2	4 73.8
Greece	Twenty drachms	0.185	900	3 44.2	3 42.5
Hindostan	Mohur	0.374	916	7 08.2	7 04.6
Italy	Twenty lire	0.207	898	3 84.3	3 82.3
Japan	Old cobang	0.362	568	4 44	4 41.8
Do	Old cobang	0.289	572	3 57.6	3 55.8
Do	Twenty yen	1.072	900	19 94.4	19 84.4
Mexico	Doubloon, average	0.867.5	866	15 53	15 45.2
Do	Doubloon, new	0.867.5	870.5	15 61.1	15 53.3
Do	Twenty pesos, (Max.)	0.086	875	19 64.3	19 54.5
Do	Twenty pesos, (Repub.)	1.081	873	19 51.5	19 41.6
Naples	Six ducati, new	0.245	996	5 04.4	5 01.9
Netherlands	Ten guilders	0.215	899	3 99.7	3 97.6
New Granada	Old doubloon Bogota	0.868	870	15 61.1	15 53.3
Do	Old doubloon Popayan	0.867	858	15 37.8	15 30.1
Do	Ten pesos	0.525	891.5	9 67.5	9 62.7
Peru	Old doubloon	0.867	868	15 55.7	15 47.9
Do	Twenty soles	1.055	898	19 21.3	19 11.7
Portugal	Gold crown	0.308	912	5 80.7	5 77.8
Russia	Five roubles	0.210	916	3 97.6	3 95.7
Spain	One hundred reals	0.268	896	4 96.4	4 93.9
Do	Eighty reals	0.215	869.5	3 86.4	3 84.5
Do	Ten escudos	0.270.8	896	5 01.5	4 99
Sweden	Ducat	0.111	875	2 23.7	2 22.6
Do	Carolin, 10 francs	0.104	900	1 93.5	1 91.5
Tunis	Twenty-five piasters	0.161	900	2 99.5	2 98.1
Turkey	One hundred piasters	0.231	915	4 36.9	4 34.8
Tuscany	Sequin	0.112	999	2 31.3	2 30.1

Y.—*Silver coins.*

Country.	Denominations.	Weight.	Fineness.	Value.
		Oz. Dec.	*Thous.*	
Austria	Old rix dollar	0. 902	833	$1 02. 3
Do	Old scudo	0. 836	902	1 02. 6
Do	Florin before 1858	0. 451	833	51. 1
Do	New florin	0. 397	900	48. 6
Do	New Union dollar	0. 596	900	73. 1
Do	Maria Theresa dollar, 1780	0. 895	838	1 02. 1
Belgium	Five francs	0. 803	897	98
Do	Two francs	0. 320	835	36. 4
Bolivia	New dollar	0. 801	900	98. 1
Brazil	Double milreis	0, 820	918. 5	1 02. 5
Canada	Twenty cents	0. 150	925	18. 9
Do	Twenty-five cents	0. 187. 5	925	23. 6
Central America	Dollar	0. 866	850	1 00. 2
Chili	Old dollar	0. 864	908	1 06. 8
Do	New dollar	0. 801	900. 5	98. 2
China	Dollar (English) assumed	0. 866	901	1 06. 2
Do	Ten cents	0. 087	901	10. 6
Denmark	Two rigsdaler	0. 927	877	1 10. 7
England	Shilling, new	0. 182. 5	924. 5	23
Do	Shilling, average	0. 178	925	22. 4
France	Five franc, average	0. 800	900	98
Do	Two franc	0. 320	835	36. 4
Germany, North	Thaler before 1857	0. 712	750	72. 7
Do	New thaler	0. 595	900	72. 9
Germany, South	Florin before 1857	0. 340	900	41. 7
Do	New florin	0. 340	900	41. 7
Greece	Five drachms	0. 719	900	88. 1
Hindostan	Rupee	0. 374	916. 5	46. 6
Italy	Five lire	0. 800	900	98
Do	Lira	0. 160	835	18. 2
Japan	Itzebu	0. 279	991	37. 6
Do	New itzebu	0. 279	890	33. 8
Do	One yen	0. 866. 7	900	1 06. 8
Do	Fifty sen	0. 402	800	44. 6
Mexico	Dollar, new	0. 867. 5	903	1 06. 6
Do	Dollar, average	0. 866	901	1 06. 2
Do	Peso of Maximilian	0. 861	902. 5	1 05. 5
Naples	Scudo	0. 844	830	95.
Netherlands	Two and one-half guilders	0. 804	944	1 03. 3
Norway	Specie daler	0. 927	877	1 10. 7
New Granada	Dollar of 1857	0. 803	896	98
Peru	Old dollar	0. 866	901	1 06. 2
Do	Dollar of 1858	0. 766	909	94. 8
Do	Half dollar 1835 and 1838	0. 433	650	38. 3
Do	Sol	0. 802	900	98. 2
Portugal	Five hundred reis	0. 400	912	49. 6
Rome	Scudo	0. 864	900	1 05. 8
Russia	Rouble	0. 667	875	79. 4
Spain	Five pesetas, (dollar)	0. 800	900	98
Do	Peseta, (pistareen)	0. 160	835	18. 2
Sweden	Rix dollar	1. 092	750	1 11. 5
Switzerland	Two francs	0. 320	835	36. 4
Tunis	Five piasters	0. 511	898. 5	62. 5
Turkey	Twenty piasters	0. 770	830	87

REPORT OF COMMISSIONER OF INDIAN AFFAIRS.

REPORT

OF

THE COMMISSIONER OF INDIAN AFFAIRS.

DEPARTMENT OF THE INTERIOR,
Washington, D. C., September 3, 1872.

SIR: Respectfully referring to your communication of August 8, 1872, asking to be furnished the usual annual statement of the liabilities of the United States to Indian tribes, I have the honor to state that the subject was referred to the Indian Office on the 10th ultimo, and herewith to inclose a copy of the Commissioner's report and the statement requested in your letter.

Very respectfully, yours,

W. H. SMITH,
Acting Secretary.

The Hon. SECRETARY OF THE TREASURY.

DEPARTMENT OF THE INTERIOR,
OFFICE INDIAN AFFAIRS,
Washington, D. C., September 2, 1872.

SIR: I have the honor to transmit herewith a statement showing the present liabilities of the United States to Indian tribes under stipulations of treaties, &c., to be forwarded to the Secretary of the Treasury, to accompany his report on the state of finances.

Very respectfully, your obedient servant,

F. A. WALKER,
Commissioner.

Hon. C. DELANO,
Secretary of the Interior.

Statement showing the present liabilities of the United States to Indian tribes under stipulations of treaties, &c.

Names of tribes.	Description of annuities, stipulations, &c.	Number of installments yet unappropriated; explanations, &c.	Reference to laws; Statutes at Large.	Annual amount necessary to meet stipulations indefinite as to time, now allowed, but liable to be discontinued.	Aggregate of future appropriations that will be required during a limited number of years to pay limited annuities incidentally necessary to effect the payment.	Amount of annual liabilities of a permanent character.	Amount held in trust by the United States on which five per cent. is annually paid, and amounts which, invested at five per cent., would produce permanent annuities.
Apaches, Kiowas, and Comanches.	Thirty installments, provided to be expended under 10th article treaty of Oct. 21, 1867.	Twenty-five installments unappropriated, at $30,000 each.	Vol. 15, pp. 581, 589.		$750,000 00		
Do	Purchase of clothing	10th article treaty Oct. 21, 1867	Vol. 15, pp. 581, 589, § 10.	$26,000 00			
Do	Pay of carpenter, farmer, blacksmith, miller, and engineer.	14th article treaty Oct. 21, 1867	Vol. 15, pp. 581, 589.	5,200 00			
Do	Pay of physician and teacher	......do	Vol. 15, pp. 581, 589, § 10.	2,500 00			
Do	Three installments, for seeds and agricultural implements.	Three installments, at $2,500 each, still due.			7,500 00		
Do	Pay of second blacksmith, iron and steel	8th article treaty Oct. 21, 1867	Vol. 15, p. 584	2,000 00			
Arickarees, Gros Ventres, and Mandans.	Amount to be expended in such goods, &c., as the President may from time to time determine.	7th article treaty July 27, 1866	Not published	75,000 00			
Assinaboines	Amount to be expended in such goods, &c., as the President may from time to time determine.	......do	......do	30,000 00			
Blackfeet, Bloods, and Piegans.	Amount to be expended in such goods, &c., as the President may from time to time determine.	8th article treaty Sept. 1, 1868	......do	50,000 00			
Calapooias, Molallas, and Clackamas of Willamette Valley.	Five installments, 4th series, of annuity for beneficial purposes.	Two installments, of $5,500 each, to be appropriated.	Vol. 10, p. 1114, § 2		11,000 00		
Cheyennes and Arapahoes.	Thirty installments, provided to be expended under 10th article treaty of Oct. 28, 1867.	Twenty-five installments unappropriated, at $20,000 each.	Vol. 15, p. 593		500,000 00		
Do	Purchase of clothing, same article			14,500 00			
Do	Pay of physician, carpenter, farmer, blacksmith, miller, engineer, and teacher.	13th article treaty Oct. 28, 1867	Vol. 15, p. 597	7,700 00			

Chickasaws	Permanent annuity in goods	Feb. 25, 1799	Vol. 1, p. 619			$3,000 00	
Chippewas — Boise Fort Band.	Twenty installments, for blacksmith and assistant, tools, iron, &c.	Thirteen installments, at $1,500	Vol. 14, p. 766		19,500 00		
Do	Twenty installments, for schools, instructing Indians in farming, and purchase of seeds, tools, &c.	Thirteen installments, at $1,600 each.	......do		20,800 00		
Do	Twenty installments of annuity, in money, goods, and other articles; in provisions, ammunition, and tobacco.	Annuity, $3,500; goods, &c., $6,500; provisions, &c., $1,000; thirteen installments unappropriated.			143,100 00		
Chippewas of Lake Superior.	Twenty installments, in coin, goods, implements, &c., and for education.	Two installments unappropriated	Vol. 10, p. 1111		38,000 00		
Do	Twenty installments, for six smiths and assistants, iron and steel.	Two installments unappropriated, at $6,360.	......do		12,720 00		
Do	Support of smith and shop, and pay of two farmers, during the pleasure of the President.	Estimated at	Vol. 11, p. 1112; vol. 14, p. 766.	1,800 00			
Do	Twenty installments, for the seventh smith, &c.	Four installments of $1,060 each	Vol. 10, p. 1111		4,240 00		
Chippewas of the Mississippi.	Money, goods, support of schools, provisions, and tobacco; 4th article treaty Oct. 4, 1842; 8th article treaty Sept. 30, 1854; and 3d article treaty May 7, 1864.	Four installments, 2d series, of $9,000.01.	Vol. 10, p. 111		36,000 04		
Do	Two farmers, two carpenters, two smiths and assistants, iron and steel; same article and treaty.	Ten installments, 2d series, at $1,400; four installments to be appropriated.	......do		5,600 00		
Do	Twenty installments, in money, at $20,000 each.	Two installments	Vol. 10, p. 1167		40,000 00		
Do	Ten installments, for support of schools, in promoting the progress of the people in agriculture, and assisting them in becoming self-sustaining; support of physician, and purchase of medicine.	Five installments, at $11,500			57,500 00		
Chippewas of the Mississippi, and Pillager and Lake Winnebagoshish bands of Chippewas.	Ten installments, of $1,500 each, to furnish said Indians with oxen, log-chains, &c.	One installment due	Vol. 13, p. 694		1,500 00		
Do	Pay of two carpenters, two blacksmiths, four farm-laborers, and one physician, ten years.	One installment of $7,700	......do		7,700 00		
Do	Pay for services and traveling expenses of a board of visitors, not more than five persons, to attend annuity payments.	Treaty of May 7, 1864	......do	480 00			
Do	To be applied for the support of a saw-mill as long as the President may deem necessary.	......do	Vol. 13, p. 694, § 6.	1,000 00			
Do	Pay of female teachers employed on the reservation.	......do	Vol. 13, p. 694, § 13.	1,000 00			
Chippewas — Pillager and Lake Winnebagoshish bands.	Thirty installments, in money, $10,666.66; goods, $8,000; and for purposes of utility, $4,000.	Twelve installments to be appropriated, at $22,666.66.	Vol. 10, p. 1168		271,999 92		

Statement showing the present liabilities of the United States to Indian tribes, &c.—Continued.

Names of tribes.	Description of annuities, stipulations, &c.	Number of installments yet unappropriated; explanations, &c.	Reference to laws: Statutes at Large.	Annual amount necessary to meet stipulations indefinite as to time, now allowed, but liable to be discontinued.	Aggregate of future appropriations that will be required during a limited number of years to pay limited annuities incidentally necessary to effect the payment.	Amount of annual liabilities of a permanent character.	Amount held in trust by the United States on which five per cent. is annually paid, and amounts which, invested at five per cent., would produce permanent annuities.
Chippewas—Pillager and Lake Winnebagoshish bands.	Twenty installments, for purposes of education; 3d article treaty Feb. 22, 1865.	Two installments, of $3,000, yet due.	Vol. 10, p. 1168, § 3	....	$6,000 00	....	....
Chippewas of Red Lake and Pembina tribe of Chippewas.	$10,000, as annuity, to be paid per capita to the Red Lake band, and $5,000 to the Pembina band, during the pleasure of the President.	3d article treaty Oct. 2, 1863, and 2d article supplementary treaty April 12, 1864.	Vol. 13, pp. 668, 689.	$15,000 00	....	....	....
Do	Fifteen installments, of $12,000 each, for the purpose of supplying them with gilling-twine, cotton maitre, linsey, blankets, &c.	Estimated, Red Lake band, $8,000; and Pembina band, $4,000; six installments to be appropriated.	Vol. 13, pp. 689, 690.	....	72,000 00	....	....
Do	Fifteen installments, for pay of one blacksmith, physician, &c., miller, farmer, $3,900; iron and steel, and other articles, $1,500; carpentering, &c., $1,000.	Six installments, at $6,400, yet due.	Vol. 13, p. 690	....	38,400 00	....	....
Do	Fifteen installments, to defray the expenses of a board of visitors, not more than three persons, to attend annuity payments.	Six installments to be appropriated, at $390 each.	Vol. 13, p. 668	....	2,340 00	....	....
Choctaws	Permanent annuities	2d article treaty Nov. 16, 1805, $3,000; 13th article treaty Oct. 18, 1820, $600; 2d article treaty Jan. 20, 1825, $6,000.	Vol. 7, pp. 99 and 614; vol. 11, pp. 213 and 236.	....	....	$9,600 00	....
Do	Provisions for smiths, &c	6th article, Oct. 18, 1820, and 9th article, Jan. 20, 1825.	Vol. 7, p. 212	....	....	920 00	....
Do	Interest on $390,257.92; articles 10 and 13 treaty January 22, 1855.	Five per centum for educational purposes.	Vol. 11, pp. 613 and 614.	....	....	19,512 89	$390,257 92
Confederated tribes and bands in Middle Oregon.	Five installments, for beneficial objects, at the discretion of the President; treaty June 25, 1855.	Two installments, of $4,000 each, yet due.	Vol. 12, p. 964, § 2.	....	8,000 00	....	....

Do	Fifteen installments, for pay and subsistence of one farmer, blacksmith, wagon and plow maker.	Two installments, of $3,500 each, yet due.	Vol. 12, p. 965		7,000 00		
Do	Twenty installments, for pay and subsistence of one physician, sawyer, miller, superintendent of farming, and school teacher.	Seven installments, of $5,600 each, yet due.			39,200 00		
Do	Twenty installments, for salary of head-chief.	Seven installments of $500 each			3,500 00		
Creeks	Permanent annuities	4th article treaty Aug. 7, 1790, $1,500; 2d article treaty of June 16, 1802, $3,000; 4th article treaty Jan. 24, 1826, $20,000.	Vol. 7, pp. 36 and 287; vol. 11, p. 700.			24,500 00	490,000 00
Do	Smiths, shops, &c	8th article treaty Jan. 24, 1826	Vol. 7, p. 287			1,110 00	22,200 00
Do	Wheelwright, permanent	8th article treaty Jan. 24, 1826; 5th article treaty Aug. 7, 1856.	Vol. 7, p. 287; vol. 11, p. 700.			600 00	12,000 00
Do	Allowance during the pleasure of the President.	5th article treaty Feb. 14, 1833; 8th article treaty Jan. 24, 1826.	ol. 7, pp. 287 and 419.	4,710 00			
Do	Interest on $200,000, held in trust; 6th article treaty August 7, 1856.	Five per centum for education	Vol. 11, p. 700			10,000 00	200 000 00
Do	Interest on $675,168, held in trust; 3d article treaty June 14, 1866.	Five per centum to be expended under the direction of the Secretary of the Interior.	Vol. 14, p. 786			33,758 43	675,168 00
Crows	For supplying male persons over fourteen years of age with a suit of good, substantial woolen clothing; females over twelve years of age, a flannel skirt or goods to make the same, a pair of woolen hose, calico and domestic; and boys and girls under the ages named, such flannel and cotton goods, &c.	Treaty May 7, 1868	Vol. 15, p. 652, § 9.	22,723 00			
Do	For the purchase of such articles from time to time as the conditions and necessities of the Indians may indicate to be proper.	do	do	10,000 00			
Do	Physician, carpenter, miller, engineer, farmer, and blacksmith.	do	Vol. 15, p. 652, §10	6,600 00			
Do	Twenty installments for pay of teacher, and for books, stationery, &c.	Seventeen installments, at $3,000, to be provided.	Vol. 15, p. 651, § 7.		51,000 00		
Do	Blacksmith, iron and steel, and for seeds and agricultural implements.	Estimated	Vol. 15, p. 651, § 8.	3,250 00			
Do	Purchase of such articles, from time to time, as the condition and necessities of the Indians may indicate to be proper.	do	Vol. 15, p. 652, § 9.	20,000 00			
Do	Four installments, to furnish Indians with flour and meat.	Treaty May 7, 1868; one installment to be provided.	Vol. 15, p. 652, § 11		131,400 00		
Delawares	Life annuity to chief	Private act to supplementary treaty Sept. 24, 1829, to treaty Oct. 3, 1818.	Vol. 5, p. 1040	100 00			
Do	Interest on $46,080 at five per centum, being the value of thirty-six sections of land, set apart by the treaty of 1829, for education.	Senate resolution Jan. 19, 1838	do			2,304 00	46,080 00
Dwamish and other allied tribes in Washington Territory.	$150,000 to be expended under the direction of the President.	Seven installments yet to be provided for.	Vol. 12, p. 928, § 6		31,000 00		

Statement showing the present liabilities of the United States to Indian tribes, &c.—Continued.

Names of tribes.	Description of annuities, stipulations, &c.	Number of installments yet unappropriated; explanations, &c.	Reference to laws: Statutes at Large.	Annual amount necessary to meet stipulations indefinite as to time, now allowed, but liable to be discontinued.	Aggregate of future appropriations that will be required during a limited number of years to pay limited annuities incidentally necessary to effect the payment.	Amount of annual liabilities of a permanent character.	Amount held in trust by the United States on which five per cent. is annually paid, and amounts which, invested at five per cent., would produce permanent annuities.
Dwamish and other allied tribes in Washington Territory.	Twenty installments, for agricultural school and teachers.	Treaty Jan. 22, 1855; seven, at $3,000 each, yet due.	Vol. 12, p. 929, § 14	....	$21,000 00	....	....
Do............	Twenty installments, for a smith and carpenter shop and tools.	Seven installments, at $500 each, yet due.	......do	....	3,500 00	....	....
Do............	Twenty installments, for blacksmith, carpenter, farmer, and physician.	Seven installments, at $4,000 each, yet due.	......do	....	32,200 00	....	....
Flatheads and other confederated tribes.	Twenty installments, for agricultural and industrial school, providing necessary furniture, books, stationery, &c., and employment of suitable instructors.	July 16, 1855, agricultural and industrial school, $300; pay of instructors, $1,800; seven installments of $2,100 yet to be appropriated.	Vol. 12, p. 977, § 5	....	14,700 00	....	....
Do............	Five installments, 3d series, for beneficial objects, under the direction of the President.	One installment yet due..........	Vol. 12, p. 976, § 4.	....	4,000 00	....	....
Do............	Twenty installments, for two farmers, two millers, blacksmith, gunsmith, tinsmith, carpenter and joiner, and wagon and plow maker, $7,400; and keeping in repair blacksmith, carpenter's, and wagon and plow maker's shops, and furnishing tools, $500.	Seven installments, of $7,900 each, to be provided.	Vol. 12, p. 976, § 5.	....	55,300 00	....	....
Do............	Twenty installments, for keeping in repair flour and saw mills, and supplying necessary fixtures.	Seven installments, of $500 each, to be provided.	......do	....	3,500 00	....	....
Do............	Twenty installments, for pay of physician, $1,400; keeping in repair hospital and for medicines, $300.	Seven installments, of $1,700 each, to be provided.	......do	....	11,900 00	....	....
Do............	Repairing buildings required for various employés, &c., for twenty years.	Seven installments, of $300 each, to be provided.	Vol. 12, p. 977, § 5	....	$2,100 00	....	....

Gros Ventres	Amount to be expended in such goods, provisions, &c., as the President may from time to time determine as necessary.	8th article treaty of July 13, 1868	Not published	$35,000 00			
Iowas	Interest on $57,500, being the balance on $157,500.	May 7, 1854	Vol. 10, p. 1071, § 9			$2,875 00	$57,500 00
Kansas	Interest on $200,000, at 5 per centum	January, 1846	Vol. 9, p. 842, § 2			10,000 00	200,000 00
Kickapoos	Interest on $100,000, at 5 per centum		Vol. 10, p. 1079, § 2			5,000 00	100,000 00
Do	Gradual payment on $200,000		do		10,000 00		
Klamaths and Modocs.	Five installments of $5,000, 2d series, to be applied under the direction of the President.	Three installments to be provided	Vol. 16, p. 707		15,000 00		
Do	Twenty installments, for repairing saw and flouring mill, and buildings for blacksmith, carpenter, wagon and plow maker, manual-labor school, and hospital.	Fourteen installments to be appropriated, at $1,000 each.	do		14,000 00		
Do	For tools and materials for saw and flour mills, carpenter's, blacksmith's, wagon and plow maker's shops, books and stationery for manual-labor school.	Thirteen installments to be appropriated.	do		19,500 00		
Do	Pay of superintendent farming, farmer, blacksmith, sawyer, carpenter, and wagon and plow maker.	Eight installments to be appropriated, at $6,000 each.	do		48,000 00		
Do	Pay of physician, miller, and two teachers, for twenty years.	Thirteen installments to be provided, at $3,600 each.	do		46,800 00		
Makahs	Ten installments, being 5th series, for beneficial objects, under the direction of the President.	Seven installments to be appropriated, of $1,000 each.	Vol. 12, p. 940		7,000 00		
Do	Twenty installments, for agricultural and industrial school and teacher, for smith and carpenter shops and tools, and for blacksmith, carpenter, farmer, and physician.	Seven installments to be provided for, at $7,600 each.	Vol. 12, p. 941		53,200 00		
Menomonees	Fifteen installments, to pay $242,686 for cession of land.	Eight installments, of $16,170.06, yet to be provided.	Vol. 10, p. 1065		129,360 48		
Miamies of Kansas.	Permanent provisions for smiths' shops, and miller, &c.	Say $940 for shop and $600 for miller.	Vol. 7, p. 191			1,540 00	30,800 00
Do	Twenty installments upon $200,000, 3d article treaty June 5, 1854.		Vol. 10, p. 1094		52,500 00		
Do	Interest on $50,000, at 5 per centum		do			2,500 00	50,000 00
Miamies of Indiana.	Interest on $221,257.86, in trust	Treaty June 5, 1854	Vol. 10, p. 1099			11,062 89	221,257 80
Miamies of Eel River.	Permanent annuities	4th article treaty 1795; 3d article treaty 1805; 3d article treaty 1809.	Vol. 7, p. 51, § 4; vol. 7, p. 91, § 3; vol. 7, p. 114, § 3.			1,100 00	22,000 00
Molels	Pay of teacher to manual-labor school, and subsistence of pupils, &c.	Treaty Dec. 21, 1855	Vol. 12, p. 982	3,000 00			
Mixed Shoshones, Bannocks, and Sheep-Eaters.	To be expended in such goods, provisions, &c., as the President may from time to time determine, &c.	Sept. 24, 1868		35,000 00			
Navajoes	For such articles of clothing, or raw materials in lieu thereof, for seeds, farming-implements, &c.	For clothing, or raw materials, $40,000; and for seeds, &c., $35,000.	Vol. 15, p. 669	75,000 00			

Statement showing the present liabilities of the United States to Indian tribes, &c.—Continued.

Names of tribes.	Description of annuities, stipulations, &c.	Number of installments yet unappropriated; explanations, &c.	Reference to laws: Statutes at Large.	Annual amount necessary to meet stipulations indefinite as to time, now allowed, but liable to be discontinued.	Aggregate of future appropriations that will be required during a limited number of years to pay limited annuities incidentally necessary to effect the payment.	Amount of annual liabilities of a permanent character.	Amount held in trust by the United States on which five per cent. is annually paid, and amounts which, invested at five per cent., would produce permanent annuities.
Navajoes	For the purchase of such articles as from time to time the condition and necessities of the Indians may indicate to be proper.	8th article, June 1, 1868	Vol. 15, p. 669	$14,000 00			
Do	For pay of two teachers	6th article, June 1, 1868	do	2,000 00			
Nez Perces	Five installments, 3d series, for beneficial objects, at the discretion of the President.	Two to be provided for, at $6,000	Vol. 12, p. 950		$12,000 00		
Do	Twenty installments, for two schools, &c., pay of superintendent of teaching and two teachers, superintendent of farming and two farmers, two millers, two blacksmiths, tinner, gunsmith, carpenter, wagon and plow maker, keeping in repair grist and saw mill, for necessary tools, pay of physician, repairing hospital and furnishing medicines, &c., repairing buildings for employés, and the shops for blacksmith, tinsmith, gunsmith, carpenter, wagon and plow maker, providing tools therefor, and pay of head chief.	Seven to be provided for, at $17,200	do		120,400 00		
Do	Sixteen installments, for boarding and clothing children who attend school, providing school, &c., with necessary furniture, purchase of wagons, teams, and tools, &c.	Nine to be provided for, at $3,000 each.	Vol. 14, p. 649		27,000 00		
Do	Salary of two subordinate chiefs	Treaty June 9, 1863	Vol. 14, p. 650	1,000 00			
Do	Fifteen installments, for repair of houses, mills, shops, &c., and providing furniture, tools, &c.	Nine to be appropriated, at $2,500 each.	do		22,500 00		
Do	Salary of two matrons, to take charge of the boarding-schools, two assistant teachers, farmer, carpenter, and two millers.	June 9, 1863	Vol. 14, p. 650, § 5.	7,600 00			

Nisqually, Puyallup, and other tribes and bands of Indians.	Payment of $32,500 in graduated payments..	Treaty Dec. 26, 1854, yet to be appropriated.	Vol. 10, p. 1133 ...	....	2,250 00	....	....
Do	Pay of instructor, smith, physician, carpenter, &c., for twenty years.	Two to be provided for, at $6,700 each.	Vol. 10, p. 1134 ...	....	13,400 00	....	....
Do	Support of agricultural and industrial school, smith and carpenter shops, and providing necessary tools therefor.	Two to be provided for, at $1,500 each.	......do	....	3,000 00	....	....
Northern Cheyennes and Arapahoes.	Purchase of clothing	Estimated	Vol. 15, p. 657	15,000 00	....	....	....
Do	To be expended by the Secretary of the Interior for Indians roaming, and in the purchase of such articles as may be deemed necessary.	......do	......do	18,000 00	....	....	....
Do	Four installments, to furnish flour and meat .	One installment yet to be appropriated.	....	....	66,576 00	....	....
Do	Pay of teacher, carpenter, miller, farmer, blacksmith, engineer, and physician.	Estimated	Vol. 15, p. 658	7,700 00	....	....	....
Omahas	Fifteen installments, 3d series, in money or otherwise.	Ten to be appropriated	Vol. 10, p. 1044 ...	....	200,000 00	....	....
Do	Ten installments, to pay engineer, miller, farmer, and blacksmith, keeping in repair grist and saw mill, support of blacksmith-shop, and furnishing tools.	Estimated, engineer, $1,200; miller, $900; farmer, $900; blacksmith, $900; repairs of mill and support of smith-shop, $600; three installments, of $4,500, to be appropriated.	Vol. 10, p. 1044; vol. 14, p. 668.	....	13,500 00	....	....
Osages	Interest on $69,120, at 5 per centum, for educational purposes.	Jan. 19, 1838, resolution of the Senate to treaty Jan. 2, 1825.	Vol. 7, p. 242	....	....	$3,456 00	$69,120 00
Do	Interest on $300,000, at 5 per centum, to be paid semi-annually, in money or such articles as the Secretary of the Interior may direct.	Treaty Sept., 29, 1865	Vol. 14, p. 687, § 1	....	....	15,000 00	300,000 00
Ottoes and Missourias.	Fifteen installments, 3d series, in money or otherwise.	Ten to be appropriated	Vol. 10, p. 1039 ...	....	90,000 00	....	....
Pawnees	Annuity goods and such articles as may be necessary.	Sept. 24, 1857	Vol. 11, p. 729, § 2	....	....	30,000 00	....
Do	Support of two manual-labor schools and pay of two teachers.	......do	Vol. 11, p. 730 ...	11,200 00	....	....	....
Do	For iron and steel and other necessaries for shops, and pay of two blacksmiths, one of whom to be tin and gunsmith, and compensation of two strikers and apprentices.	Sept. 24, 1857; for iron and steel, $500; two blacksmiths, $1,200; and two strikers, $480.	....	2,180 00	....	....	....
Do	Farming utensils and stock, pay of farmer, miller, and engineer, and compensation of apprentices to assist in working the mill, and keeping in repair grist and saw mill.	Estimated	....	4,400 00	....	....	....
Poncas	Ten installments, 2d series, to be paid to them or expended for their benefit.	March 12, 1868, one to be provided.	Vol. 12, p. 997, § 2	....	10,000 00	....	....
Do	Amount to be expended during the pleasure of the President, for aid in agricultural and mechanical pursuits.	....	......do	7,500 00	....	....	....

Statement showing the present liabilities of the United States to Indian tribes, &c.—Continued.

Names of tribes.	Description of annuities, stipulations, &c.	Number of installments yet unappropriated; explanations, &c.	Reference to laws: Statutes at Large.	Annual amount necessary to meet stipulations indefinite as to time, now allowed, but liable to be discontinued.	Aggregate of future appropriations that will be required during a limited number of years to pay limited annuities incidentally necessary to effect the payment.	Amount of annual liabilities of a permanent character.	Amount held in trust by the United States on which five per cent. is annually paid, and amounts which, invested at five per cent., would produce permanent annuities.
Pottawatomies	Permanent annuity in money		Vol. 7, p. 51, § 4; vol. 7, p. 114, § 3; vol. 7, p. 185, § 3; vol. 7, p. 317; vol. 7, p. 320; vol. 7, p. 855.			$8,449 65	$168,993 00
Do	For education, during the pleasure of the President.		Vol. 7, p. 855	$5,000 00			
Do	Permanent provision for three smiths		do			1,068 49	21,369 80
Do	Permanent provision for furnishing salt		do			165 77	3,315 40
Do	Interest on $243,632.11 at 5 per centum		Vol. 9, p. 854			12,181 61	243,632 11
Pottawatomies of Huron.	Permanent annuities		Vol. 7, p. 106, § 2			400 00	8,000 00
Quapaws	For education, smith, and farmer, and smith-shop, during the pleasure of the President.	Treaty May 13, 1833, $1,000 for education, and $1,660 for smith, farmer, &c.	Vol. 7, p. 423, § 3	2,660 00			
Quinaielts and Quillehutes.	$25,000, 5th series, to be expended for beneficial objects.	Two installments, of $1,000 each, to be provided.	Vol. 12, p. 972, § 4.		$2,000 00		
Do	Twenty installments for an agricultural and industrial school, employment of suitable instructors, support of smith and carpenter shop, and tools, pay of blacksmith, carpenter, farmer, and physician.	Seven installments of $7,600 each, to be provided.	do		53,200 00		
Rogue River	Five installments, in blankets, clothing, farming-utensils, and stock.	Two installments of $3,000 each, still due.	Vol. 10, p. 1019, § 4.		6,000 00		
River Crows	Amount to be expended in such goods, provisions, &c., as the President may from time to time determine, &c.	July 15, 1858	Laws not published.	35,000 00			
Sacs and Foxes of the Mississippi.	Permanent annuities	Treaty November 3, 1804	Vol. 7, p. 85, § 3			1,000 00	20,000 00
Do	Interest on $200,000 at 5 per centum	Treaty October 21, 1837	Vol. 7, p. 541, § 2			10,000 00	200,000 00

Do	Five installments, for support of physician, &c., and furnishing tobacco and salt.	For physician, $1,500; tobacco and salt, $350; one of $1,850 to be provided.	Vol. 15, p. 497		1,850 00		
Sacs and Foxes of the Missouri.	Interest on $157,400, at five per centum	Treaty Oct. 21, 1837	Vol. 7, p. 543, § 2			7,870 00	157,400 00
Do	Interest on $11,615.25, at five per centum	Treaty March 6, 1861	Vol. 12, p. 1170			2,030 49	11,615 25
Seminoles	Interest on $500,000, 8th article treaty Aug. 7, 1856.	$25,000, annuities	Vol. 11, p. 702, § 8			25,000 00	500,000 00
Do	Interest on $70,000, at five per centum	For support of schools	Vol. 14, p. 757, § 3			3,500 00	70,000 00
Senecas	Permanent annuities	Sept. 9 and 17, 1817	Vol. 7, pp. 161 and 179, § 4.			1,000 00	20,000 00
Do	Smith and smiths' shops, and miller	Feb. 28, 1831	Vol. 7, p. 349, § 4	1,660 00			
Senecas of New York.	Permanent annuities	Act Feb. 19, 1841	Vol. 4, p. 442			6,000 00	120,000 00
Do	Interest on $75,000, at five per centum	Act June 27, 1846	Vol. 9, p. 35			3,750 00	75,000 00
Do	Interest on $43,050, transferred from Ontario Bank to United States Treasury.	do	do			2,152 50	43,050 00
Senecas and Shawnees.	Permanent annuities	Treaty Sept. 17, 1818	Vol. 7, p. 119, § 4			1,000 00	20,000 00
Do	Support of smith and smiths' shops	July 20, 1831	Vol. 7, p. 352, § 4	1,060 00			
Senecas, Shawnees, Quapaws, Peorias, Ottawas, Wyandotts and others.	Five installments, for blacksmith and assistant, shop and tools, iron and steel for shop, for Shawnees.	do Feb. 23, 1867	do Vol. 15, p. 518, § 8.		500 00		
Do.	Six installments, for blacksmith and necessary iron, steel, and tools, for Peorias, Kaskaskias, &c.	Two installments, of $1,123.29 each, to be provided.	Vol. 15, p. 520, § 27		2,246 58		
Shawnees	Permanent annuities, for education	Aug. 3, 1795; May 10, 1854	Vol. 7, pp. 51 and 100, § 4.			3,000 00	60,000 00
Do	Interest on $40,000, at five per centum	do	Vol. 10, p. 1056, § 3			2,000 00	40,000 00
Shoshones — Western band.	Twenty installments, of $5,000 each, under direction of the President.	Eleven installments to be appropriated.			55,000 00		
Shoshones—Eastern band.	Twenty installments, of $10,000 each, under direction of the President.	do			110,000 00		
Shoshones—Northwestern band.	Twenty installments, of $5,000 each, under direction of the President.	do	Vol. 13, p. 663		55,000 00		
Shoshones—Goship band.	Twenty installments, of $1,000 each, under direction of the President.	do	Vol. 13, p. 682		11,000 00		
	For Shoshones:						
Shoshones and Bannocks.	Three installments, to purchase seeds and implements.	Treaty July 3, 1868. One installment to be provided for.	Vol. 15, p. 675, § 8		2,500 00		
Do	Purchase of clothing for men, women, and children.	Estimated	Vol. 15, p. 676, § 9	13,874 00			
Do	For the purchase of such articles as may be considered proper by the Secretary of the Interior, &c.	do	do	30,000 00			
Do	Pay of physician, carpenter, teacher, engineer, farmer, and blacksmith.	do	Vol. 15, p. 676, § 10	6,800 00			
Do	Three installments, for presents	One installment yet due	Vol. 15, p. 676, § 12		500 00		
Do	Blacksmiths, and for iron and steel, &c	Estimated	Vol. 15, p. 675	2,000 00			

Statement showing the present liabilities of the United States to Indian tribes, &c.—Continued.

Names of tribes.	Description of annuities, stipulations, &c.	Number of installments yet unappropriated; explanations, &c.	Reference to laws: Statutes at Large.	Annual amount necessary to meet stipulations indefinite as to time, now allowed, but liable to be discontinued.	Aggregate of future appropriations that will be required during a limited number of years to pay limited annuities incidentally necessary to effect the payment.	Amount of annual liabilities of a permanent character.	Amount held in trust by the United States on which five per cent. is annually paid, and amounts which, invested at five per cent., would produce permanent annuities.
	For Bannacks:						
Shoshones and Bannocks.	Purchase of clothing for men, women, and children.	Estimated	Vol. 15, p. 675, § 9	$6,937 00			
Do	Purchase of such articles as may be considered necessary by the Secretary of the Interior, for persons roaming, &c.	do	do	16,000 00			
Do	For seeds and agricultural implements	do	Vol. 15, p. 675, § 8	2,500 00			
Do	Pay of physician, carpenter, miller, teacher, engineer, farmer, and blacksmith.	do	do	6,800 00			
Six Nations of New York.	Permanent annuities in clothing, &c	Treaty November 11, 1794	Vol. 7, p. 46, § 6			$4,500 00	$90,000 00
Sisseton and Wahpeton of Lake Traverse and Devil's Lake.	Amount to be expended in such goods, provisions, and other articles as the President may from time to time determine, &c.	February 19, 1867	Vol. 15, p. 509	100,000 00			
Sioux of different tribes.	Purchase of seeds and agricultural implements.	April 29, 1868	Vol. 15, p. 638, § 10	15,000 00			
Do	Purchase of clothing for men, women, and children.	Twenty-seven to be appropriated, at $159,400 each.	do		$4,303,800 00		
Do	Blacksmith, and for iron and steel, &c	Estimated	Vol. 15, p. 638, § 8	2,000 00			
Do	For such articles as may be considered proper by the Secretary of the Interior, for persons roaming, &c.	Twenty-seven to be provided at $236,000 each.	Vol. 15, p. 638, § 10		6,372,000 00		
Do	For beef, flour, sugar, bacon, &c., in proportionate quantities.	One to be provided at $1,314,000	do	1,314,000 00			
Do	Physician, five teachers, carpenter, miller, engineer, farmer, and blacksmith.	Estimated	Vol. 15, p. 638, § 13	10,400 00			
S'Klallams	Five installments on $60,000, fifth series	Two to be provided at $2,400 each	Vol. 12, p. 934, § 5		4,800 00		
Do	Twenty installments for agricultural and industrial school, pay of teacher, blacksmith, carpenter, farmer, and physician.	Seven to be provided at $7,100 each	Vol. 12, pp. 934, 935, § 11.		49,700 00		
Do	Smith and carpenter shop and tools		do	500 00			

Tabequache band of Utahs.	Ten instalments of $20,000 each	Goods, $10,000; provisions, $10,000, one to be provided.	Vol. 13, p. 675, § 8	....	20,000 00	....	....
Do	Purchase of iron, steel, and tools for blacksmith shop, and pay of blacksmith and assistant.	Iron and steel, $220; blacksmith, and assistant, $1,100.	Vol. 13, p. 675 § 10	1,320 00	....	....	....
Tabequache, Muache, Capote, Weminuche, Yampa, Grand River, and Uintah band of Utes.	For iron and steel, and necessary tools for blacksmith shop.	Estimated	Vol. 15, p. 621, § 11	220 00	....	....	....
Do	Two carpenters, two millers, two farmers, one blacksmith, and two teachers.	......do	Vol. 15, p. 622, § 15	11,000 00	....	....	....
Do	Thirty installments of $30,000, to be expended under the direction of the Secretary of the Interior, for clothing, blankets, &c.	Twenty-six installments to be provided, at $30,000 each.	......do	....	780,000 00	....	....
Do	Annual amount to be expended under the direction of the Secretary of the Interior, in supplying said Indians with beef, mutton, wheat, flour, beans, &c.	....	......do	30,000 00	....	....	....
Umpquas and Calapooias of Umpqua Valley, Oregon.	Five installments, 4th series, of annuities for beneficial purposes.	Two installments to be provided for, at $1,000 each.	Vol. 10, p. 1126, § 3	....	2,000 00	....	....
Do	Support of teachers, &c., for twenty years	Two installments, of $1,450 each	Vol. 10, p. 1127, § 6	....	2,900 00	....	....
Umpquas, (Cow Creek band.)	Twenty installments of $550 each	One installment unappropriated	....	....	550 00	....	....
Walla-Walla, Cayuse and Umatilla tribes.	Five installments, 3d series, to be expended under the direction of the President.	Two installments to be provided, at $4,000 each.	Vol. 12, p. 946, § 2	....	8,000 00	....	....
Do	Twenty installments, pay of two millers, farmer, superintendent of farming operations, two school teachers, physician, blacksmith, wagon and plow maker, and carpenter and joiner.	Seven installments to be provided, at $11,200 each.	Vol. 12, p. 947, § 4	....	78,400 00	....	....
Do	Twenty installments for mill-fixtures, tools, medicines, books, stationery, furniture, &c.	Seven installments to be provided, at $3,000 each.	....	....	21,000 00	....	....
Do	Twenty installments of $1,500 each, for pay of head chiefs, three in number, at $500 per annum each.	Seven installments to be appropriated, at $1,500 each.	....	....	10,500 00	....	....
Winnebagoes	Interest on $886,909.17, at five per cent. per annum.	Nov. 1, 1837; Senate amendment July 17, 1862.	Vol. 7, p. 546, § 4	....	....	44,345 46	886 909 17
Do	Thirty installments of interest on $75,387.28, at five per cent. per annum.	Four installments to be provided, at $3,769.36.	Vol. 9, p. 879, § 4	....	15,077 44	....	....
Do	Interest on $78,340.41, at five per cent. per annum, to be expended under the direction of the Secretary of the Interior.	....	....	....	....	3,917 02	78,340 41
Wal-pah-pe tribe of Snake Indians.	Ten installments, 2d series, under the direction of the President.	Nine installments to be appropriated, at $1,200 each.	Vol. 14, p. 684, § 7	....	10,800 00	....	....
Yankton tribe of Sioux.	Ten installments of $40,000 each, 2d series, to be paid to them, or expended for their benefit.	Six installments to be appropriated, at $40,000 each.	Vol. 11, p. 744, § 4	....	240,000 00	....	....

Statement showing the present liabilities of the United States to Indian tribes, &c.—Continued.

Names of tribes.	Description of annuities, stipulations, &c.	Number of installments yet unappropriated; explanations, &c.	Reference to laws: Statutes at Large.	Annual amount necessary to meet stipulations indefinite as to time, now allowed, but liable to be discontinued.	Aggregate of future appropriations that will be required during a limited number of years to pay limited annuities incidentally necessary to effect the payment.	Amount of annual liabilities of a permanent character.	Amount held in trust by the United States, on which five per cent. is annually paid, and amounts which, invested at five per cent., would produce permanent annuities.
Yakamas	Five installments, 3d series, for beneficial objects, under the direction of the President.	Two installments to be appropriated, at $600 each.	Vol. 12, p. 953, § 4		$1,200 00		
Do	Twenty installments for two schools, one of which is to be an agricultural and industrial school, keeping the same in repair, and providing books, stationery, and furniture.	Seven installments to be provided, at $500 each.	......do		3,500 00		
Do	Twenty installments for superintendent of teaching, two teachers, superintendent of farming, two farmers, two millers, two blacksmiths, tinner, gunsmith, carpenter, and wagon and plow maker.	Seven installments to be provided, at $14,600 each.	Vol. 12, p. 953, § 5		102,200 00		
Do	Twenty installments for keeping in repair hospital, and furnishing medicines, &c., pay of physician, repairing grist and saw mill, and furnishing necessary tools.	Seven installments to be provided, at $2,000 each.			14,000 00		
Do	Twenty installments for keeping in repair buildings for employés.	Seven installments to be provided, at $300 each.	......do		2,100 00		
Do	Salary of head chief for twenty years	Seven installments to be provided, at $500 each.	......do		3,500 00		
Do	Twenty installments for keeping in repair blacksmith's, tinsmith's, gunsmith's, carpenter's, and wagon and plow maker's shops, and furnishing tools.	Seven installments due, at $500 each.			3,500 00		
	Total			$2,154,874 00	15,819,310 46	$371,776 20	$6,524,608 92

REPORT OF THE SUPERINTENDENT OF THE UNITED STATES COAST SURVEY.

REPORT

OF THE

SUPERINTENDENT OF THE UNITED STATES COAST SURVEY.

COAST SURVEY OFFICE,
Washington, D. C., September 30, 1872.

SIR: I have the honor to present an abstract showing the places at which the work of the survey has been in progress, within the year, on the Atlantic, Gulf, and Pacific coasts of the United States.

In all the northern sections parties are yet in the field, and will so continue until the approach of winter, when transfers will be made for resuming operation in the southern sections of the coast.

The details of the work done by each of the parties will be given, as heretofore, in my annual report, after the receipt of statements showing the results of the present season in the northern sections.

Surveying-parties are now engaged either in triangulation, topography, or hydrography on the coast of Maine, at Bass Harbor, Mount Desert Island; at Blue Hill Bay; on the islands between it and Isle au Haut Bay; and in the vicinity of Castine, for the survey of the east side of Penobscot Bay; on the west side of that bay above and below Belfast; and in Penobscot Bay north of Islesborough; on the western side of the Kennebec, in Maine, for the determination of geographical points, and for like service in New Hampshire. Special astronomical observations have been made at Cambridge, Massachusetts, to determine the precise relation in longitude between points in the United States and points in Europe; one of the parties in that service occupied a station on St. Pierre, Miquelon Island. The magnetic elements have been determined at stations on the coast of Massachusetts.

Special examinations have been made to verify the sailing-directions for harbor charts of the coast of New England. The tides have been recorded constantly during the year at North Haven, in Penobscot Bay, and at the Charlestown navy-yard. A hydrographic party is now at work near the Monomoy Shoals, and off-shore soundings have been continued along the northern sections of the coast. The plane-table survey of the coast of Rhode Island is in progress near Perrysville, west of Point Judith, and also the detailed survey of New Haven Harbor. Views have been drawn for the charts of several harbors between Portland and New York. Special hydrographic investigations are in progress in New York Harbor and in the adjacent waters; and the tides have been steadily recorded at Governor's Island. Field-parties are completing the shore-line survey at the south end of Lake Champlain, and others are sounding its northern branches.

Triangulation is in progress near Barnegat, and plane-table work and hydrography near Little Egg Harbor, on the coast of New Jersey. Points have been determined for the construction of a comparative chart of the Schuylkill River at Philadelphia, for which the soundings were made last winter, and the magnetic elements have been determined in that vicinity, and also at Washington City. The tides have been regularly recorded at Old Point Comfort, Virginia. Geodetic reconnaissance is in progress near Harper's Ferry. The detailed survey of the James River, Virginia, has been extended upward to Warwick River; that of Pamlico River, at Washington, North Carolina, has been completed, and also that of the lower part of Pungo River, and the vicinity of Cedar Island, in the lower part of Pamlico Sound. In that sound, the main triangulation has been extended and progress has been made in the soundings. Cape Hatteras has been included in a resurvey which revealed changes in contour; and recent soundings develop the dangers to navigation at the Hatteras Shoals. Plane-table work has been completed at Bear Inlet and Brown's Inlet, on the coast of North Carolina; and the several channels leading into Cape Fear River have been sounded. Little River entrance, near the boundary-line of South Carolina, has been examined, and much of the coast-line traced southward to connect with a detailed survey which now includes the shores of Winyah Bay. The survey of the Sea Islands and channels between Coosaw River and Broad River, South Carolina, has been well advanced toward completion; and the sea-water channels inside of Saint Simon's Island, on the coast of Georgia, and between Talbot Island and Saint John's River, have been sounded. Latitude, azimuth, and the magnetic elements were determined at a station on Saint Simon's Island. The measurement of a primary base-line near Atlanta, Georgia, and the determination of points in geodetic connection with the line, are now in progress.

Along the eastern coast of Florida the survey south of Matanzas Inlet, including the branches of Matanzas River, is well advanced toward Mosquito Inlet. Below Cape Canaveral, a shoal has been developed near Indian River Inlet. Soundings have been continued in the approaches to the Florida Reef and in the Gulf of Mexico; and the inshore hydrography has been completed at the eastern approach of Saint George's Sound, as also the survey of the Gulf coast between Saint Andrew's and Mobile entrance, including Choctawhatchee Bay. The hydrography has also developed the approaches from deep water to the Mississippi Delta, and the vicinity of Trinity Shoal off the coast of Louisiana. In the Mississippi River the survey has advanced from Magnolia upward to Jesuit Bend, including determinations for latitude and azimuth. On the coast of Texas the hydrography has been continued in San Antonio and the adjacent bays; and the longitude of Austin has been determined.

Sherman Station, in Wyoming Territory, and Verdi, on the Union Pacific Railroad, in Nevada, have been occupied as points in the geodetic connection between the Atlantic and Pacific coasts, and collateral observations of much interest have been recorded.

On the western coast of the United States the following sites have been, or will be occupied in prosecuting the field and hydrographic operations now in progress in accordance with the plan of work for the season. The parties are all in the field, and will, as heretofore, report their results at the end of October.

Progress has been made in the hydrographic reconnaissance between Panama and San Diego. The station near Cape San Lucas, at which the transit of Venus was observed in 1769, will be determined in latitude and longitude. At San Diego the tides have been constantly recorded. The survey of the coast of California will be resumed at San Pedro Bay; that of the Santa Barbara Islands has been continued; and the crest-line of the mountains which range along the Santa Barbara Channel has been traced. Reconnaissance has determined suitable points for the triangulation between Santa Barbara and Monterey; the survey of the coast is well advanced between Point Conception and Point Arguello; also south of San Luis Obispo, toward Point Sal, and south of San Simeon; and the latitude and azimuth will be determined, if practicable, at both stations before the close of the season. In the operations of the year are included the survey of the South Farallon Island, and the outline of sand-drift on the San Francisco peninsula; the contour of Table Mountain, north of the Golden Gate; comparative soundings at San Francisco entrance, and the tides of the year at that port. Cordell's Bank will be developed by soundings in the course of the season; at Mendocino Bay latitude and azimuth will be determined, and the survey in progress in that vicinity will be extended northward. Magnetic observations will be made generally at stations which may be occupied by the astronomical party. Soundings have been made to develop a bank off Cape Mendocino; the survey of the coast below Shelter Cove is in progress; latitude and azimuth will be determined there, and longitude at Eureka, when the telegraph reaches that place. Soundings are in progress along the coast of California between Shelter Cove and Rocky Point; the survey is extending south of the False Klamath River, California, and along the coast of Oregon north of Chetko River. At Astoria the tides of the year have been recorded, and longitude will be determined when telegraphic facilities reach that port. The survey of both shores of the Columbia River has been continued, and that of Shoalwater Bay, in Washington Territory. At False Dungeness the astronomical station has been connected with the triangulation of the Strait of Fuca, and Smith's Island has been occupied for completing the main triangulation which embraces the waters of Washington Sound. The plan for this season includes, also, determinations of latitude and azimuth at Steilacoom and Dwamish Bay; the selection of a site for a base-line on Whidbey Island, and triangulation for extending the survey in Puget Sound.

On the coast of Alaska good progress has been made in the hydrographic reconnaissance. Observations of much importance have been made on the tides and currents, and a number of geographical points have been determined.

The office operations in drawing and engraving have kept up with the results in field-work and hydrography. Twenty new charts have been published, and nine others, which show extensive additions in comparison with their first issue. Fifty charts, of which thirteen were commenced within the year, have been in hand in the drawing-division. Of the engraved charts 11,500 copies have been printed and distributed. Ninety of the manuscript maps on file in the archives have been copied within the year, to meet calls for information. As these usually pertain to places near the more important ports, a few of the topographical sheets, showing much variety in details, have been reproduced by lithography. The process is cheap, and its extension is under advisement, as affording means of special usefulness in the inception of local improvements, in which success must depend on accurate information in regard to the surface-contour.

Tide-tables for the ensuing year have been prepared, and will be published as heretofore.

Respectfully submitted.

BENJAMIN PEIRCE,
Superintendent United States Coast Survey.

HON. GEORGE S. BOUTWELL,
Secretary of the Treasury.

REPORT OF THE LIGHT-HOUSE BOARD.

LIGHT-HOUSE BOARD OF THE UNITED STATES.

(Organized in conformity to the act of Congress approved August 31, 1852.)

LIST OF MEMBERS.

Hon. GEORGE S. BOUTWELL, *Secretary of the Treasury, ex-officio President.*
Professor JOSEPH HENRY, LL.D., *Secretary Smithsonian Institution.*
Brevet Major-General A. A. HUMPHREYS, *Chief of Engineers, United States Army.*
Brevet Major-General J. G. BARNARD, *Colonel of Engineers, United States Army.*
Professor B. PEIRCE, LL.D., *Superintendent Coast Survey.*
Rear-Admiral T. BAILEY, *United States Navy.*
Rear-Admiral HENRY WALKE, *United States Navy.*
Rear-Admiral CHARLES S. BOGGS, *United States Navy.*
Major GEORGE H. ELLIOT, *Corps of Engineers, United States Army.*

CHAIRMEN OF COMMITTEES.

Finance—General HUMPHREYS.
Engineering—General BARNARD.
Experiments—Professor HENRY.
Lighting—Professor PEIRCE.
Floating Aids—Rear-Admiral BAILEY.

The Chairman and Secretaries are *ex-officio* members of all committees.

MEMBERS OF THE BOARD EMPLOYED IN THE OFFICE.

Professor JOSEPH HENRY, *Chairman.*
Rear-Admiral CHARLES S. BOGGS, *United States Navy, Naval Secretary.*
Major GEORGE H. ELLIOT, *Corps of Engineers, United States Army, Engineer Secretary.*

CLERKS.

ARNOLD B. JOHNSON, *Chief Clerk.*

WM. D. O'CONNOR.
BRUCE SMALL.
Mrs. E. J. BEARE.
FRANK BAKER.
ALBERT H. SAWYER.
SAMUEL STONE.

PAUL J. PELZ, *Chief Draughtsman.*

CLERKS TEMPORARILY DETAILED FROM OTHER OFFICES.

H. C. JOHANNES.
E. P. RANKIN.
Miss MAY E. COLE.
Z. B. BROOKE.
HENRY KALLUSSOWSKI.

REPORT

OF

THE UNITED STATES LIGHT-HOUSE BOARD.

TREASURY DEPARTMENT,
Office of the Light-House Board, August 31, 1872.

Hon. GEORGE S. BOUTWELL, *Secretary of the Treasury*:

SIR: The following report of the operations of this Board during the last year is respectfully submitted:

There are now in the Light-House Establishment of the United States:

ON THE ATLANTIC COAST.

Sea-coast lights	61
Harbor and river lights	262
Light-ships	21
Fog-signals, operated by steam or hot-air engines	17
Day or unlighted beacons	284
Buoys actually in position	2,262

ON THE COAST OF THE GULF OF MEXICO.

Sea-coast lights	18
Harbor and river lights	31
Light-ships	1
Fog-signals, operated by steam or hot-air engines	2
Day or unlighted beacons	68
Buoys actually in position	205

ON THE PACIFIC COAST.

Sea-coast lights	18
Harbor and river lights	7
Light-ships	none
Fog-signals, operated by steam or hot-air engines	7
Day or unlighted beacons	1
Buoys actually in position	81

ON THE NORTHERN AND NORTHWESTERN LAKES.

Lake-coast lights	82
Harbor and river lights	94
Light-ships	none
Fog-signals, operated by steam or hot-air engines	7
Day or unlighted beacons	1
Buoys actually in position	214

TOTALS FOR THE ENTIRE ESTABLISHMENT.

Sea and lake-coast lights	179
Harbor and river lights	394
Total light-houses	573
Light-ships	22
Fog-signals, operated by steam or hot-air engines	33
Day or unlighted beacons	354
Buoys actually in position	2,762

The number of light-keepers now in service is 809.

It has been the endeavor of the Board to conduct the administration of the establishment at all times with the most rigid regard to true economy and efficiency, holding officers and light-keepers to the strictest personal responsibility in the performance of duty; making frequent supervisory visits to, and examination of, works of construction and repair, and requiring inspections and reports, at short intervals of all existing light-houses, light-ships fog-signals, beacons, and buoys in position. The light-houses and light-ships (so far as the exhibition of efficient lights is concerned) are, it is believed, equal to any in the world, and those beacons and buoys actually in position are efficient day-marks to guide clear of the obstructions for which they were established.

The detailed statements under the heads of the twelve geographical districts into which the United States Light-House Establishment is divided, based mainly upon the annual reports of the engineers and inspectors, embrace the work which has been done since the last annual report, the works now in progress, those for which there are existing appropriations, (but which are not yet executed,) and those for which appropriations for their early erection are recommended to Congress.

It will be seen that while the lights and other aids are in a condition of efficiency, so far as they are required to meet the wants of the mariner, there are many stations at which reconstructions and renovations are greatly needed. The necessity for these arises from the natural decay of old buildings, some of them dating back into colonial days, and the erosion of sites, so greatly exposed to the action of storms, winds, and heavy seas, as are most of the light and beacon stations, during the equinoctial and winter seasons.

The new lights recommended for appropriations were, many of them, recommended in our last annual report and in the reports of preceding years; and it will be observed that of the eight new sea-coast lights recommended, four are north of Cape Hatteras, viz: two at Cape Elizabeth, coast of Maine, (reconstruction—built in 1828;) one at Monomoy Point, coast of Massachusetts, (a very important light for the immense commerce which passes through Vineyard Sound,) and one at a point midway between Cape Henry and Body's Island, coast of North Carolina. During the last year an important step has been taken in lighting the previously unlighted coast of eighty miles between Capes Charles and Hatteras, by the construction of the light-house at Body's Island, and there remains forty miles of this dangerous coast yet unlighted.

The necessity of a light-house at the third point mentioned will be manifest by referring to the remarks under the head of *Body's Island*, in the fifth district, where it will be seen that in the thirteen months during which that light-house has been under construction, the loss of property by wrecks in the vicinity has been more than $130,000, or more than the cost of the light-house. The great number of wrecks occurring along this dangerous part of our coast, owing to the peculiar currents which set against it, has for many years attracted attention, and there should be no delay in completing its illumination.

On the completion of the light-house recommended to be placed between Cape Henry and Body's Island, there will be no unlighted space on our Atlantic coast from the mouth of the river St. Croix, on our northern frontier, to Cape Hatteras.

South of this cape the board have estimated for four primary or sea-coast lights, viz: at Morris Island, coast of North Carolina; at Tybee Island, coast of Georgia; at Mosquito Inlet, coast of Florida, and on the "Fowey Rocks," one of the great reefs off the coast of Florida. Also for the completion of six others now under construction at the following points, viz: Hunting Island, coast of South Carolina; Alligator Reef, one of the Florida reefs; Saint Augustine, coast of Florida; Trinity Shoal and Timbalier, Gulf of Mexico, and Matagorda Island, coast of Texas.

The southern portions of our sea-coast are not so thickly inhabited as the northern, and the lights are not therefore of so much benefit for local commercial purposes; but it must be remembered that our great sea-coast lights everywhere, are for the benefit of the commerce of all sections and all countries. The commerce between the great commercial centers and the West Indies, South America, the Gulf of Mexico and California, passing along our southern coast is immense, and no part of our sea-coast is more dangerous to lives and treasure, on account of the great shoals and reefs which extend to long distances into the ocean. The other lights recommended in the report are for our harbors and for the northern and northwestern lakes, and are made necessary by the increasing wants of commerce.

You will observe that for several of our light-stations the board have recommended the erection of powerful fog-signals. The great loss of life and property through shipwrecks and collisions, caused by vessels getting out of their courses in foggy and thick weather, is attracting attention throughout the world, and the board is not only placing as many of these most useful aids to navigation as its appropriations will allow, but it is experimenting, with a view of obtaining more powerful machines, which can be heard with certainty above the noise of the surf and the storm. The problem is one of much more difficulty than the lighting of our coasts, and it is attracting the attention of light-house engineers abroad as well as in this country; but it is believed that our present signals—the trumpet, the whistle, and the syren—all operated by steam or hot-air engines, though not as powerful as are desired, are by far the best in the world.

There is a small estimate for a light and fog-signal at the mouth of the river Columbia, Oregon, which the board deems of importance, and to which it desires to call the attention of Congress. The trade into the River Columbia is rapidly increasing, and the entrance is unusually dangerous, on account of its very bad bar, and the dense fogs which envelope it at almost all seasons of the year.

The south channel, which is now almost exclusively used, has no aid to navigation whatever, except its buoys and the light at Cape Disappointment, which are of no assistance in foggy weather.

At the last session of Congress the following provisions of law were made, which have very greatly assisted the board in the construction of its works, viz:

* * * * * * *

Appropriations for light-house purposes shall be available for expenditure for two years after acts of legislatures ceding jurisdiction over sites: *Provided, however,* That this section shall not apply to any general appropriations for light-house purposes: *And provided further,* That in no case shall any special appropriation be available for more than two years without further provision of law; and the unexpended balances of appropriations for special works under the Light-House Board made by the act approved March third, eighteen hundred and seventy-one, entitled "An act making appropriations for sundry civil expenses of the Government for the fiscal year ending June thirtieth, eighteen hundred and seventy-two, and for other purposes," are hereby re-appropriated for the purposes therein specified:

* * * * * * *

Provided, That all appropriations for public buildings under the Treasury Department shall hereafter be available immediately upon the approval of the acts containing such appropriations.

Under the law which required appropriations to be limited to one year, and that all balances were then to revert to the surplus fund, it was found almost impossible to carry on our works satisfactorily and economically.

Light-house works of construction cannot be carried on safely and with economy north of Chesapeake Bay during the winter months, nor on the southern coast during the months when epidemics almost always prevail, more or less severely. Besides these drawbacks and difficulties, these works, from their greatly exposed positions on the sea or lake coast, require not only to be built of the best and most durable materials that can be procured, but those materials ought not to be put together too hurriedly; and hence, as a rule, the large and expensive structures require a much longer time than one year to commence and complete them properly, and with this view it is earnestly recommended that *all light-house appropriations for special works shall in future laws be made available for two years after acts of appropriation and cessions of jurisdiction by the States, provided that no appropriation shall be available for more than two years.*

In regard to the general estimates for repairs of light-houses, for supplies (including oil, &c.) for light-ships, and for buoys, the board has to say that it has always been the custom of this office, in preparing the annual estimates for supporting the existing and authorized aids to navigation, and the construction of new ones, to make as close a calculation of items, quantities, and prices as the information at hand would allow, and to endeavor to so manage the disbursements as at all times to have ample funds available to supply any losses and repair any damage, however serious, to which this service is so peculiarly liable during the winter months.

For *repairs and incidental expenses of light-houses* we have estimated the same amount ($225,000) as was estimated last year. Congress failed to appropriate the whole amount of this estimate by $25,000, and, in consequence, many of our old light-houses and sites were not repaired and protected as was required by economical considerations, and the cost this year for the same will be enhanced.

For *expenses of fog-signals* we have estimated the same amount as last year, viz, $50,000.

For the *salaries of light-keepers* the estimate is $535,800, and the increase is owing to the increase in the number of light-keepers authorized by the appropriations for new lights. There are in actual employment and required for new lights appropriated for, 893 light-keepers, and the average pay authorized by law is $600 per annum.

For *supplies of light-houses* the estimate is $360,837, and the increase is due, as above, to the increased number of lights authorized by law.

For the *expenses of light-ships* the estimate is $217,732 50; and the decrease is owing to the substitution during the last year of screw-pile light-houses for light-ships in two instances, and of shore range-lights for a light-ship in the remaining case.

For *expenses of buoyage* our estimate is $300,000, and the increase is due to the increased demand for these aids to navigation, the decay of those in use, and losses by ice and storm.

The application, by your direction, of the new rules of the civil service to the Light-House Establishment will greatly increase its efficiency.

The board is of the opinion that of all the branches of the civil service of the Government, there is none in which it is more important to have men of ability, integrity, and experience.

We have, as we have stated, about eight hundred principal and assistant light-keepers distributed among our five hundred and ninety-five light-houses and light-ships, and the number is increasing from year to year as new light-houses are constructed.

These keepers are scattered along our coasts, many of them in exposed positions, of which examples are our rock light-houses, such as Minot's Ledge, off the coast of Massachusetts, and the reef light-houses off the Florida coast. Many of them, especially those on the capes of our Pacific coast, are hundreds of miles away from civilization, and the supervising officers can inspect them only at long intervals. Their's is a life of exposure and hardship, and they should be strong and able-bodied. They should be honest, for they have charge of, in the aggregate, a large amount of Government property. They should have sufficient intelligence and skill to manage our delicate and costly lenses and the machinery connected therewith, as well as the steam machinery of our fog-signals. At many of our distant stations, if, through the carelessness or incapacity of a keeper, these are disarranged, the light may not be exhibited or the signal sounded for weeks before repairs can be made, and commerce can have that security which should be assured to it. On the intelligence, fidelity, and experience of the keepers depend the thousands of lives and millions of property which are nightly approaching, leaving, or sailing along our eight thousand miles of sea, gulf, and lake coasts.

In the light-house service of other countries which have the same excellent system of illumination as our own, (the Fresnel,) the keepers when appointed are young men who have been required to pass medical and intellectual examinations, and they remain in service during good behavior. In Great Britain their moral characters must be vouched for by the clergymen of their parishes. There is promotion for merit, and when superannuated they are pensioned.

Previous to your administration political considerations governed, in a great measure, the appointment and discharge of keepers, and even up to this time it has been found impossible to eradicate all the evils of this custom.

While it cannot be expected to introduce at once all the reforms which would place our light-house service, as far as the character of the keepers is concerned, in as high a condition as those of some other countries, it is to be hoped that, while the nomination (which is now a virtual appointment) is not removed from the collector of customs, to whom it is now confided, so much of reform may be continued as will require that every applicant shall pass a competitive examination before a board composed of experienced officers of the light-house service, before appointment, and that, when once in service, the commerce of the country may have the benefit of his experience and his ambition to do well, which will result when he finds that he has hope of promotion, and that he will be subject to discharge only for dereliction of duty.

During the last year the following changes have occurred in the board:

Rear-Admirals Shubrick and Stribling, both long connected with the board, (the former having been its chairman from its establishment in 1852, and the latter a member since 1866,) having retired, were succeeded by Rear-Admirals Bailey and Walke, and Professor Henry was elected chairman.

Rear-Admiral Jenkins, a member and naval secretary of the board since its establishment, (except for a few years during the war,) and to whom the present efficiency of the light-house service is in a very great degree due, retired from the board in February last, having been ordered to the command of the Asiatic fleet, and was succeeded by Rear-Admiral Boggs. The other members of the board (viz, Professor Henry, General Humphreys, General Barnard, Professor Peirce, and Major Elliot, engineer secretary,) remain as at the date of the last annual report.

Lieutenant-Colonel Williamson, of the Corps of Engineers of the Army, for many years light-house engineer on the coast of California, and one of the board's most zealous and efficient officers, was relieved from light-house duty in May last, on account of ill-health, having been granted leave of absence in Europe by the War Department.

The board has to deplore the loss by death of one of its officers during the last year, Commodore Macomb, inspector of lights in the fourth district, who died at Philadelphia on the 15th of the present month.

While the board recognizes the great value of most of the officers who have been detailed by the War and Navy Departments to report to you for duty under its direction, it is due to the memory of the late Commodore Macomb to bear witness to the ability which he always displayed in the discharge of his duties and in his intercourse with this office.

FIRST DISTRICT.

The first district extends from the northeastern boundary of the United States (Maine) to, and including, Hampton Harbor, New Hampshire, and includes all the aids to navigation on the coasts of Maine and New Hampshire.

Inspector.—Commander A. E. K. Benham, United States Navy, until December 17, 1871; Commander Thomas O. Selfridge, United States Navy, present inspector.

Engineer.—Lieutenant-Colonel J. C. Duane, Corps of Engineers, brevet brigadier-general, United States Army.

In this district there are:

Light-houses and lighted beacons	49
Light-ships	none
Fog-signals operated by steam or hot-air engines	8
Day or unlighted beacons	51
Buoys actually in position	351
Spare buoys, for relief and to supply losses	322
Tender (steam) Myrtle, for engineer's construction and repairs, (used also in second district;) launch Mary	2
Tender (steamer) Iris, buoy-tender	1
Tender (sail) repair-schooner Wave	1

The following numbers, which precede the names of stations, correspond with those of the Light-house List of the Atlantic, Gulf, and Pacific Coasts of the United States, issued January 1, 1872.

3. *Little River, west side of entrance to harbor of Little River, Maine.*—A fog-bell tower has been erected, and a fog-bell operated by Stevens's striking apparatus has been placed at this station.

6. *Nash's Island, off the mouth of Pleasant River, Maine.*—There is required at this station a new lantern, deck, and parapet, also repairs on tower.

——. *Burntcoat Harbor, Swan's Island, coast of Maine.*—Two range-lights have been erected at this important harbor of refuge during the year, and have been lighted.

25. *White Head, Penobscot Bay, Maine.*—Extensive repairs of the keeper's dwelling have been made, a fog signal-house 24 feet by 23 feet, of stone, has been erected, a pier or wharf of stone 45 feet by 25 feet by 23 feet high, with a wheeling stage connecting it with the coal-shed, have been built.

34. *Manheigan Island, Manheigan Island, Maine.*—A steam fog-whistle has been established at this station in place of a Daboll trumpet, which has been removed to Portland Head.

40. *Seguin, on Seguin Island, off the mouth of river Kennebec, Maine.*—The upper part of the tower at this station leaks badly. The stone parapet should be replaced by one of iron. There will be required an iron parapet, deck, and lantern-base.

41. *Half-Way Rock, near Portland, Maine.*—This station was lighted for the first time on the 15th of August, 1871. A boat-slip and masonry boat-house have been built.

42. *Cape Elizabeth, near Portland, Maine.*—These towers were built of rubble-stone in 1828, and are now in such condition that it has become necessary to rebuild them. An estimate is submitted for the erection of two new towers.

44. *Portland Head, near entrance to Portland Harbor, Maine.*—The Daboll trumpet, which was removed from Manheigan, has been established at this station.

49. *Whale's Back, near Portsmouth, New Hampshire.*—A new tower has been erected at this station, and the light is now exhibited from it.

50. *Portsmouth Harbor, New Hampshire.*—The old dwelling has been taken down and a new one erected on the same foundation.

REPAIRS.

At each of the following-named light-stations in the first district there have been repairs and renovations more or less extensive during the year:

1. *St. Croix*, on Dochet's Island, river St. Croix, Maine.
2. *West Quoddy Head*, west entrance to Passamaquoddy Bay, Maine.
3. *Little River*, west side of entrance to harbor of Little River, Maine.
4. *Libby Island*, entrance to Machias Bay, Maine.
5. *Moose Peak*, on Moose Peak Head, Maine.
6. *Nash's Island*, west end of Moose Peak Reach, Maine.
7. *Narraguagus*, entrance to Narraguagus Bay, Maine.
8. *Petit Menan*, on Petit Menan Island, Maine.
9. *Prospect Harbor*, east side of entrance to Prospect Harbor, Maine.
12. *Winter Harbor*, west side of Winter Harbor, Maine.
13. *Mount Desert*, on Mount Desert Rock, Maine.
14. *Baker's Island*, southwest side of entrance to Frenchman's Bay, Maine.
15. *Bear Island*, east side of entrance to Northeast Harbor, Maine.
16. *Bass Harbor Head*, east side of entrance to Bass Harbor, Maine.

17. *Eggemoggin*, near east end of Eggemoggin Reach, Maine.
18. *Saddleback Ledge*, in Isle-au-Haut Bay, Maine.
19. *Heron Neck*, west entrance to Carver's Harbor, Maine.
20. *Deer Island*, west entrance to Thoroughfare, Maine.
21. *Eagle Island Point*, west side of Isle-au-Haut Bay, Maine.
22. *Pumpkin Island*, west entrance to Eggemoggin Reach, Maine.
23. *Matinicus Rock*, off Penobscot Bay, Maine.
26. *Owl's Head*, west side of Muscle Ridge Channel, Penobscot Bay, Maine.
27. *Brown's Head*, south side of west entrance to Fox Island Thoroughfare, Maine.
28. *Negro Island*, south side of entrance to Camden Harbor, Maine.
29. *Grindel's Point*, north side of entrance to Gilkey's Harbor, Maine.
30. *Dice's Head*, north side of entrance to Castine Harbor, Maine.
31. *Fort Point*, west side of entrance to Penobscot Bay, Maine.
32. *Tenant's Harbor*, south side of entrance to Tenant's Harbor, Maine.
33. *Marshall's Point*, east entrance to Herring Gut Harbor, Maine.
34. *Manheigan Island*, off George's Islands, Maine.
35. *Franklin Island*, on east side of west entrance to George's River, Maine.
36. *Pemaquid Point*, on Pemaquid Point, Maine.
37. *Burnt Island*, west side of entrance to Townsend Harbor, Maine.
38. *Hendrick's Head*, east side of entrance to Sheepscot River, Maine.
39. *Pond Island*, west side of entrauce to River Kennebec, Maine.
40. *Seguin*, off River Kennebec, Maine.
42. *Cape Elizabeth*, on southwest side of Casco Bay, Maine.
44. *Portland Head*, on southwest side of entrance to Portland Harbor, Maine.
45. *Portland Breakwater*, on outer end of breakwater, Portland Harbor. Maine.
46. *Wood Island*, west side of entrance to River Saco, Maine.
47. *Goat Island*, east side of entrance to Cape Porpoise Harbor, Maine.
48. *Boone Island*, off York Harbor, Maine.
51. *Isle of Shoals*, on White Island, off Portsmouth, New Hampshire.

The following-named light-stations in the first district require repairs to be made during the current and ensuing year:

3. *Little River*, west side of entrance to Harbor of Little River, Maine.
6. *Nash's Island*, off the mouth of Pleasant River, Maine.
18. *Deer Island Thoroughfare*, on Mark Island, western entrance of Deer Island Thoroughfare, Maine.
33. *Franklin Island*, on east side of western entrance to George's River, Maine.
40. *Cape Elizabeth*, on southwest side of Casco Bay, Maine.

LIGHT-SHIPS.

There are no light-ships in this district.

FOG-SIGNALS OPERATED BY STEAM OR HOT-AIR ENGINES.

West Quoddy.—Ten-inch steam-whistle, in good condition.
Petit Menan.—Ten-inch steam-whisle, in good condition.
Matinicus.—Ten-inch steam-whistle, in good condition.
White Head.—Ten-inch steam-whistle, in good condition.
Manheigan.—Six-inch steam-whistle, in good condition.

Seguin.—Ten-inch steam-whistle, in good condition.
Cape Elizabeth.—Ten-inch steam-whistle, in good condition.
Portland Head.—Daboll air-trumpet, in good condition.

DAY, OR UNLIGHTED BEACONS.

Names and positions of the day, or unlighted beacons, in the first district:

Jerry's Point, Portsmouth Harbor, New Hampshire.

South Beacon, Portsmouth Harbor, New Hampshire.—Stone beacon, in good condition.

North Beacon, Portsmouth Harbor, New Hampshire.—Wooden mast, in good condition.

Willey's Ledge, Portsmouth Harbor, New Hampshire.—Iron spindle, in good condition.

York Ledge, off river York, Maine.—Iron spindle, in good condition.

Fishing Rocks, Kennebunkport, Maine.—Iron spindle, broken off, spar-buoy substituted.

Stage Island Monument, entrance to river Saco, Maine.—Stone tower, 40 feet high, in good condition.

Sharp's Rocks, entrance to river Saco, Maine.—Iron socket and wooden shaft, socket broken off, spar-buoy substituted.

Back Cove Beacon, Portland Harbor, Maine.—Pile-beacon, in good condition.

White Head Ledge, in White Head passage to Portland Harbor, Maine.—Iron spindle, slightly bent, in good condition otherwise.

Trott's Rock, in White Head passage, Maine.—Iron spindle, broken off within a few feet of the ledge.

Mark Island Monument, Casco Bay, Maine.—Stone tower, 50 feet high, in good condition.

Black-Jack Rock, river Kennebec, Maine.—Iron socket, wooden shaft, socket broken.

Seal Rock, river Kennebec, Maine.—Iron spindle, copper cylinder, in good condition.

Lee's Rock, river Kennebec, Maine.—Iron socket, wooden shaft, socket broken, spar-buoy substituted.

Ram Island Ledge, river Kennebec, Maine.—Iron socket, wooden shaft, in good condition.

Winslow's Rocks, river Kennebec, Maine.—Iron socket, wooden shaft, socket broken off, spar-buoy substituted.

Ames' Ledge, river Kennebec, Maine.—Iron socket, wooden shaft, in good condition.

Beef Rock, river Kennebec, Maine.—Iron socket, wooden shaft, in good condition.

Lime Rock, Back River, Maine.—Iron socket, wooden shaft, in good condition.

Carleton's Ledge, Back River, Maine.—Iron socket, wooden shaft, in good condition.

Clough's Rock, river Sheepscot, Maine.—Iron socket, wooden shaft, in good condition.

Merrill's Ledge, river Sheepscot, Maine.—Iron socket, wooden shaft, in good condition.

Yellow Ledges, Penobscot Bay, Maine.—Iron shaft, copper cylinder, in good condition.

Garden Island Ledge, Penobscot Bay, Maine.—Iron shaft, copper cylinder, and one ball. Shaft good, lower part of cylinder partially broken away, and ball gone.

Otter Island Ledge, Penobscot Bay, Maine.—Iron shaft, copper cylinder, and two balls. Shaft bent, lower part of cylinder partially broken away, and one ball gone.

Ash Island Point, Penobscot Bay, Maine.—Iron socket, wooden shaft, in good condition.

Dodge's Point Ledge, Penobscot Bay, Maine.—Wooden shaft attached to stump of iron spindle, in good condition.

Pottersfield Ledge, Penobscot Bay, Maine.—Stone beacon, in good condition.

Lowell's Rock, Penobscot Bay, Maine.—Iron spindle and cage, in good condition.

Seals' Ledge, Penobscot Bay, Maine.—Iron spindle and cage, in good condition.

Harbor Ledge, Penobsbot Bay, Maine.—Stone beacon, in good condition.

Shipyard Ledge, Penobscott Bay Maine.—Iron spindle, broken off, not necessary.

Fiddler's Ledge, Penobscot Bay, Maine.—Stone beacon. Two or three stones of the upper course are out of place; otherwise in good condition.

North Point of Northeast Ledge, Camden Harbor, Maine.—Iron spindle, in good condition.

Morse's Point Ledge, Camden Harbor, Maine.—Iron spindle, in good condition.

Hosmer's Ledge, Castine Harbor, Maine.—Stone monument, in good condition.

Steel's Ledge, Belfast Harbor, Maine.—Stone beacon, in good condition.

Fort Point Ledge, river Penobscot, Maine.—Stone beacon, in good condition.

Odom's Ledge, river Penobscot, Maine.—Stone beacon, in good condition.

Buck's Ledge, river Penobscot, Maine.—Iron beacon, in good condition.

Centre Harbor Ledge, Edgemoggin Reach, Maine.—Iron socket, wooden shaft, in good condition.

Ship and Barges, Blue Hill Bay, Maine.—Iron socket, wooden shaft, in good condition.

Bunker's Ledge, Mount Desert, Maine.—Stone beacon, in good condition.

Half-Tide Ledge, Narraguagus Harbor, Maine.—Iron socket, wooden shaft, in good condition.

Norton's Reef, Pleasant River, Maine.—Iron tripod, shaft, and ball, in good condition.

Snow's Rock, Moosepeak Reach, Maine.—Iron socket, wooden shaft, in good condition.

Gilchrist's Rock, Moosepeak Reach, Maine.—Iron shaft and ball, in good condition.

Moose Rock, Moosepeak Reach, Maine.—Iron tripod, in good condition.

Western Bar, Lubec Narrows, Maine.—Wooden crib filled with stone, in good condition.

The Ledge, river Saint Croix, Maine.—Wooden crib filled with stone, in good condition.

DEPOT.

A wharf at the light-house depot at House Island, Portland Harbor, Maine, has been built during the year. Experiments with, and tests of steam and air fog-signals have been made at this depot since the last annual report, and are now in progress. Two steam fog-signals have been sent to the eighth light-house district, and a duplicate machine has been sent to Boston light-station, second district.

SECOND DISTRICT.

The second district extends from Hampton Harbor, New Hampshire, to include Gooseberry Point, entrance to Buzzard's Bay, and embraces all the aids to navigation on the coast of Massachusetts.

Inspector.—John G. Walker, United States Navy, until May 1, 1872; Commander George H. Perkins, United States Navy, present inspector.

Engineer.—Lieutenant-Colonel J. C. Duane, Corps of Engineers, brevet brigadier-general, United States Army.

In this district there are:

Light-houses and lighted beacons	58
Light-ships, (in position)	8
Light-ships, (for relief)	2
Fog-signals operated by steam or hot-air engines	2
Day or unlighted beacons	49
Buoys actually in position	506
Spare buoys for relief and to supply losses	375
Tender (steam) Verbena	1
Tender (sail) Florida	1

The numbers preceding the names of stations correspond with those of the "Light-House List of the Atlantic, Gulf, and Pacific Coasts of the United States," issued January 1, 1872.

52. *Newburyport, Massachusetts.*—A frame dwelling for the keeper has been erected.

——. *Newburyport range-lights.*—Negotiations are in progress for obtaining titles to the range-light sites in this harbor, and as soon as obtained the work of erecting suitable buildings will be commenced.

58. *Cape Ann, Thatcher's Island, Massachusetts.*—As there are now five keepers for the two lights and steam fog-signals at this station and but two dwelling-houses, a new dwelling for the principal keeper is required.

64. *Hospital Point, Salem Harbor, Massachusetts.*—A wooden dwelling for the keeper and a brick tower have been erected. The light, which has been exhibited from a temporary building, has been removed to, and is now established on, the new tower.

65. *Fort Pickering, Salem Harbor, Massachusetts.*—A wooden dwelling for the keeper and a concrete and iron tower have been erected. The light, which has been exhibited from a temporary structure, has been removed to, and is now established on, the new tower.

66. *Derby Wharf, Salem Harbor, Massachusetts.*—A permanent building of brick has been erected, and the light, which was exhibited from an old building near by, has been removed to it.

70. *Boston, Massachusetts.*—A Daboll fog-trumpet has been established at this station, and a duplicate machine furnished.

75. *Duxbury Pier, Plymouth Harbor, Massachusetts.*—This light-house was completed last season, and the light first exhibited September 15, 1871.

——. *Wood End, Cape Cod, Massachusetts.*—Preparations are being made for the erection of a light-house at this place.

82. *Nanset Beach, Cape Cod, Massachusetts.*—The dwelling-house should be enlarged, or a small cottage built for the accommodation of the assistant keeper, as the building now occupied is entirely too small.

88. *Monomoy Point, Cape Cod, Massachusetts.*—The last annual report of the Light-House Board contains the following statement in relation to increasing the efficiency of this light:

Monomoy Point.—The light at this station, which is of the fourth order, on a tower about 40 feet high, was originally intended as a guide to *Old Stage Harbor*. The harbor has been filled with sand, and cannot now be entered, and the light is therefore of no further use for that purpose. But, inasmuch as nearly all vessels (both steamers and sailing) plying between New York and the eastern ports pass this point, and have now no other guide than the light-ships, which cannot be seen a sufficient distance, it is considered a matter of the greatest importance that this light should be replaced by one of sufficient power to guide vessels safely through this intricate passage. For this purpose, there is recommended a second-order fixed light, varied by red flashes, for which an estimate is submitted.

——. *Point Gammon, near Hyannis, Massachusetts.*—This old light-house site has been disposed of at public sale.

91. *Nantucket, Island of Nantucket, Massachusetts.*—The beacon has been removed to the new site, and a keeper's dwelling erected.

106. *Holmes's Hole, Inner Harbor, Massachusetts.*—The lantern has been taken off and stored at the Wood's Hole Depot, and the land and buildings disposed of at public sale.

——. *Holmes's Hole, (East Chop,) Massachusetts.*—A private light-station near Holmes's Hole, Vineyard Sound. Three 21-inch reflectors have been loaned to the keeper.

REPAIRS.

At each of the following-named stations, in the second district, there have been repairs more or less extensive during the last year:

54. *Ipswich*, entrance to Ipswich Harbor, Massachusetts.
56. *Annisquam*, entrance to Ipswich Harbor, Massachusetts.
57. *Straitsmouth*, Straitsmouth Island, Massachusetts.
58. *Cape Ann*, Massachusetts.
60. *Eastern Point*, Gloucester Harbor, Massachusetts.
61. *Ten-Pound Island*, Gloucester Harbor, Massachusetts.
62. *Baker's Island*, Salem Harbor, Massachusetts.
67. *Marblehead*, Marblehead Harbor, Massachusetts.
68. *Egg Rock*, off Nahant, Massachusetts.
69. *Minot's Ledge*, Boston Bay, Massachusetts.
71. *Narrows*, Boston Harbor, Massachusetts.
72. *Long Island Head*, Boston Harbor, Massachusetts.
73. *Plymouth*, Plymouth Harbor, Massachusetts.
76. *Race Point*, Cape Cod, Massachusetts.
77. *Long Point*, Cape Cod, Massachusetts.
78. *Mayo's Beach*, Wellfleet Bay, Massachusetts.
79. *Billingsgate*, Wellfleet Harbor, Massachusetts.
80. *Sandy Neck*, Barnstable Bay, Massachusetts.
81. *Cape Cod*, (Highlands Truro) Massachusetts.
82, 83, 84. *Nauset Beach*, (beacons,) Cape Cod, Massachusetts.
85, 86. *Chatham*, Cape Cod, Massachusetts.
87. *Pollock Rip*, light-ship, Massachusetts.
88. *Monomoy Point*, Cape Cod, Massachusetts.
89. *Shovelful Shoals*, light-ship, Massachusetts.
90. *Handkerchief*, light-ship, Massachusetts.
91. *Nantucket*, (Great Point,) Massachusetts.
92. *Sankaty Head*, Nantucket, Massachusetts.

93. *Nantucket*, South Shoal, light-ship, Massachusetts.
94. *Gay Head*, Martha's Vineyard, Massachusetts.
95. *Brant Point*, Nantucket Harbor, Massachusetts.
96. *Nantucket*, range-beacon, Massachusetts.
97. *Nantucket*, cliff, range beacon, (front,) Massachusetts.
98. *Nantucket*, range-beacon, (rear) Massachusetts.
99. *Bass River*, Vineyard Sound, Massachusetts.
100. *Bishop and Clerk's*, Vineyard Sound, Massachusetts.
101. *Hyannis*, Hyannis Harbor, Massachusetts.
102. *Cross Rip*, light-ship, Massachusetts.
103. *Cape Poge*, Martha's Vineyard, Massachusetts.
104. *Succonnessett*, light-ship, Massachusetts.
105. *Edgartown*, Edgartown Harbor, Massachusetts.
106. *Holmes' Hole*, (west chop,) Vineyard Haven Harbor, Massachusetts.
107. *Nobsque Point*, Wood's Hole Harbor, Massachusetts.
108. *Tarpaulin Cove*, Naushon Island, Massachusetts.
109. *Vineyard Sound*, light-ship, (Sow and Pigs,) Massachusetts.
110. *Hen and Chickens*, Light-ship, Massachusetts.
111. *Cuttyhunk*, Buzzard's Bay, Massachusetts.
112. *Dumpling Rock*, Buzzard's Bay, Massachusetts.
113. *Clark's Point*, New Bedford Harbor, Massachusetts.
114. *Palmer's Island*, New Bedford Harbor, Massachusetts.
115. *Ned's Point*, Mattapoisett Harbor, Massachusetts.
116. *Bird Island*, Sippican Harbor, Massachusetts.
117. *Wing's Neck*, Buzzard's Bay, Massachusetts.

The following-named light-stations in the second district require repairs to be made during the current and ensuing year:

57. *Straitsmouth*, Straitsmouth Island, Massachusetts.
77. *Long Point*, Cape Cod, Massachusetts.
116. *Bird Island*, Sippican Harbor, Massachusetts.
111. *Cuttyhunk*, Buzzard's Bay, Massachusetts.
91. *Nantucket*, (Great Point,) Massachusetts.
88. *Monomoy Point*, Cape Cod, Massachusetts.
99. *Bass River*, Vineyard Sound, Massachusetts.
82. *Nauset Beach*, (beacons,) Cape Cod, Massachusetts.
86. *Chatham*, Cape Cod, Massachusetts.
105. *Edgartown*, Edgartown Harbor, Massachusetts.
103. *Cape Poge*, Martha's Vineyard, Massachusetts.
——. *Wood End Bar*, Provincetown Harbor, Massachusetts.

LIGHT-SHIPS.

87. *"Pollock Rip," off Chatham, Massachusetts.*—This vessel was carried by the ice in March last among the breakers of Great Round Shoal, and was rescued with great difficulty by the tender Verbena, with the loss of her moorings. She was supplied with new moorings, and returned to her station within two days from the time she was carried away. The cost of repairs, new moorings, &c., was $1,765.38.

89. *"Shovelful," on Shovelful Shoal, off Chatham, Massachusetts.*—This vessel parted her moorings on account of the ice on the 7th March, and was towed into Vineyard Sound by United States revenue steam-cutter Mahoning. She was supplied with new moorings and returned to her station on the 12th of the same month. Cost of repairs and fittings, including new moorings, was $1,858.40.

90. "*Handkerchief,*" *on Handkerchief Shoal, in Vineyard Sound.*—This vessel was taken to New Bedford on the 22d of June, and is now being thoroughly repaired, at an estimated cost of $7,500.

93. "*Nantucket Shoals,*" *New South Shoal.*—This vessel broke adrift in a severe gale on the 5th March, experienced much heavy weather, and was driven far to the southward, arrived at Tarpaulin Cove on the 16th, then was towed to New Bedford, and all damages made good—supplied with new moorings, and returned to her station on the 25th of the same month. The cost of all the repairs, including the new moorings, amounted to $2,705.23.

102. "*Cross Rip,*" *off Cross Rip Shoal, in Nantucket Sound.*—This vessel will soon require extensive repairs, and will be brought in for the purpose as soon as a relief light-vessel is available. Cost of repairs and fittings amounted, during the past year, to $168.77.

104. "*Succonnessett,*" *between Succonnessett and Eldridge Shoals, Nantucket Sound.*—This vessel was taken into port in December last, and her station temporarily supplied by the York Spit light-ship No. 24. After a careful examination, it was thought expedient to repair her, as her services were absolutely necessary, Congress having failed to pass the appropriation asked for at the last session for a new light-ship. She is now being thoroughly repaired, at an estimated cost of $6,000.

109. "*Vineyard Sound,*" *(Sow and Pigs,) on Succonnessett Shoal, western entrance to Vineyard Sound.*—This vessel is in good order generally, but will require repairs during this fiscal year. Cost of repairs and fittings amounted, during the past year, to $607.81.

110. "*Hen and Chickens,*" *entrance to Buzzard's Bay.*—This vessel is in good condition, and will require a new foremast before the winter sets in. Cost of repairs and fittings during the past year was $337.12.

Relief No. 9.—This vessel has had her upper works recalked; is now in excellent order; at present she is on the Handkerchief Shoal. Expenses of repairs and outfits for the last year, $532.90.

Relief No. 29.—This vessel was repaired and put in good order last autumn, at cost of $2,658.57, and is now on the Succonnesett Shoal.

FOG-SIGNALS OPERATED BY STEAM OR HOT AIR ENGINES.

Cape Ann, Massachusetts.—A steam fog-whistle.

Boston, Massachusetts.—An air-trumpet.

DAY OR UNLIGHTED BEACONS.

Names and positions of the day or unlightened beacons in the second district:

No. 1. *Old Cock, Buzzard's Bay, Massachusetts.*—Iron spindle 36 feet high, with cage at top.

No. 2. *Egg Island, Buzzard's Bay, Massachusetts.*—Granite cone, with iron spindle and vane at top.

No. 3. *Range Beacon, Fairhaven, Fort Point, Massachusetts.*—Iron triangular pyramid 40 feet high.

No. 4. *Cormorant Rocks, south side of northeast entrance to Mattapoisett Harbor, Buzzard's Bay, Massachusetts.*—Iron spindle, cage at top.

No. 5. *Lone Rocks, northeast entrance to Wood's Hole, Massachusetts.*—Iron spindle, cage at top.

No. 6. *Collier's Lodge, entrance to Centreville Harbor, Vineyard Sound, Massachusetts.*—Granite base, iron spindle, ball, and vane.

No. 7. *Great Rock, west of Point Gammon, Vineyard Sound, Massachusetts.*—Iron spindle, cage at top.

No. 8. *Hyannis Breakwater, east end, Massachusetts.*—Wooden spindle, four arms, and cask at top.

No. 9. *Sunken Pier, northeast part of Bass River Bar, Massachusetts.*—Wooden spindle, cask at top.

No. 10. *Spindle Rock, entrance Edgartown Harbor, Massachusetts.*—Iron spindle, cask at top.

No. 11. *Billingsgate Shoal, Massachusetts.*—Old site, timber beacon, with masts and slats.

No. 12. *Egg-Island Rock, entrance Wellfleet Harbor, Massachusetts.*—Wooden spindle, cask at top.

No. 13. *Duxbury Beacon, Massachusetts.*—Square granite and granite post at top.

No. 14. *Breakwater Beacon, Massachusetts.*—Square granite, with wooden spindle and cage.

No. 15. *Hogshead Beacon, Massachusetts.*—Iron spindle, with arm, cask, and cage at top.

No. 16. *North Beacon, entrance Scituate Harbor, Massachusetts.*—Iron spindle, with two rounds.

No. 17. *South Beacon, entrance Scituate Harbor, Massachusetts.*—Iron spindle, with two lozenges.

No. 18. *Londoner, off Thatcher's Island, Cape Ann, Massachusetts.*—Iron spindle, with cage at top.

No. 19. *Point Alderton, Massachusetts.*—Square granite pyramid, with cone at top.

No. 20. *False Spit, Massachusetts.*—Granite base, with iron spindle and cage at top.

No. 21. *Spit Beacon, Massachusetts.*—Square granite pyramid.

No. 22. *Nix's Mate, Massachusetts.*—Square granite base, with octagonal pyramid.

No. 23. *Great Farm Bar, Massachusetts.*—Square granite base, and granite cone, with iron spindle and cage at top.

No. 24. *Deer Island Point, Massachusetts.*—Square granite pyramid.

No. 25. *Bird Island, southeast point of Bird Island, Massachusetts.*—Iron spindle, with cage at top.

No. 26. *Sunken Island, Massachusetts.*—Granite base, with wooden spindle and cage at top.

No. 27. *Pig Rock, Massachusetts.*—Granite pyramid, with wooden spindle and cage at top.

No. 28. *Half-tide Rock, Massachusetts.*—Wooden shaft, with cask at top.

No. 29. *Cat Island, Massachusetts.*—Wooden spindle.

No. 30. *Marblehead Rock, Massachusetts.*—Conical granite, with wooden spindle.

No. 31. *Little Aquavitæ, entrance to Salem Harbor, Massachusetts.*—Granite, with wooden spindle and cage at top.

No. 32. *Great Aquavitæ, entrance to Salem Harbor, Massachusetts.*—Granite, with wooden spindle and cage at top.

No. 33. *Hardy's Rock, Massachusetts.*—Wooden spindle, with two triangles at top.

No. 34. *Bowditch Beacon, Massachusetts.*—The angular pyramid of granite, with wooden spindle and cage at top. Fallen down; should be rebuilt.

No. 35. *Half-way Rock, Massachusetts.*—Granite beacon, in ruins.

No. 36. *Little Haste, Massachusetts.*—Wooden mast, cask at top.

No. 37. *Abbott's Monument, Massachusetts.*—Square granite, with wooden mast and cask at top.

No. 38. *Monument Bar, Massachusetts.*—Square wooden crib filled with stone, mast and cage at top.

No. 39. *Ram's Horn, Massachusetts.*—Square wooden crib filled with stone, wooden shaft at top.

No. 40. *Lobster Rocks, Beverly Harbor, Massachusetts.*—Stone, with wooden spindle.

No. 41. *Black Rock, Gloucester Harbor, Massachusetts.*—Iron spindle, with cage at top.

No. 42. *Harbor Rock, Gloucester Harbor, Massachusetts.*—Iron spindle, with ball and cage at top.

No. 43. *Five-Pound Island, Gloucester Harbor, Massachusetts.*—Granite base, with iron spindle and ball at top.

No. 44. *Lobster Rock, Annisquam, Massachusetts.* — Square granite beacon is being rebuilt.

No. 45. *Lane's Point, Massachusetts.*—Square wooden beacon.

No. 46. *Point Neck Rocks, Massachusetts.*—Iron spindle, with ball at top.

No. 47. *Black Rocks, Newburyport Harbor, Massachusetts.*—Iron spindle, with cask at top.

No. 48. *North Pier, Newburyport Harbor, Massachusetts.*—Wooden crib filled with stone.

No. 49. *South Pier, Newburyport Harbor, Massachusetts.*—Wooden crib filled with stone.

DEPOT.

At Wood's Hole depot some repairs required on the wharf have been made. An adjoining lot of land has been purchased, and a frame building which stands on this lot has been repaired, and is now occupied by the lampist.

TENDERS.

The Verbena (steam) proving insufficient for the buoy-service of the second district, the schooner Florida (captured during the war and turned over at New Orleans for light-house purposes) was sent to Boston. Very soon after her arrival she capsized in a heavy squall off Boston Bay and foundered, and, with her cargo of coal for the light-houses in the vicinity, was a total loss. The crew were saved.

THIRD DISTRICT.

The third district extends from Gooseberry Point, Massachusetts, to include Squam Inlet, New Jersey, and embraces all the aids to navigation on the sea and sound coasts of Rhode Island, Connecticut, and New York; Narragansett and New York Bays; rivers Providence and Hudson, Whitehall Narrows, and Lake Champlain.

Inspector.—Commodore James H. Strong, United States Navy.

Engineer.—Colonel I. C. Woodruff, Corps of Engineers, brevet brigadier-general, United States Army.

In this district there are:

Light-houses and lighted beacons	125
Light-ships, (in position)	6
Light-ships, (for relief)	3
Fog-signals, operated by steam or hot-air engines	7
Day or unlighted beacons	41
Buoys actually in position	436
Spare buoys, (for relief and to supply losses)	436
Buoy-tenders (steam) Putnam, Cactus	2

Tender (steam) for engineer's constructions and repairs, Mistletoe	1
Launch (steam) for engineer's constructions and repairs, Rose	1
Supply-vessels (schooners) for supplying the light-houses of the Atlantic and Gulf coasts, Pharos and Guthrie	2

The numbers preceding the names of stations correspond with the Light-house List of the Atlantic, Gulf, and Pacific Coasts, and the Northern and Northwestern Lakes of the United States, issued January 1, 1872.

——. *The Whale, Narragansett Bay, Rhode Island.*—This is a reef of rocks awash at all stages of tide, and a dangerous obstruction to navigation in the approach to the west channel of Narragansett Bay. This channel is habitually used by the daily line of Providence steamers which pass the locality during the night, carrying large numbers of passengers and valuable freights, and it is recommended that a light and fog-bell be erected on the ledge. The estimate of the engineer of the district for the structure is $35,000, which is embraced in the estimates of the board.

119. *Beaver Tail, Rhode Island.*—The annual report of last year stated that a steam fog-signal (syren) would be erected at this station during the season. The examination of the locality for water for the use of the steam-engine proved entirely unfavorable, and sufficient water could not be collected from the roofs of the buildings and from the surface of the ground into cisterns, except at great expense. It was, therefore, decided to retain the character of the present signal, an air-trumpet, operated by a hot-air engine, but to increase very materially the power, by duplicating the engine and attaching a third reservoir to the apparatus, which it is believed will render the signal fully effective.

The housing, as well as the apparatus, is well advanced, and will be erected and put in operation as early as the middle of September.

——. *Muscle Bed Beacon, Narragansett Bay, Rhode Island.*—In the annual report of last year it is stated as follows:

> The construction of a light-house on Hog Island Reef has been petitioned for during several years past, but hitherto Congress has not granted an appropriation therefor. The erection of a portable light and a fog-bell on the existing stone-tower on the Muscle Bed, one-half mile distant, on the opposite side of the channel, at a cost of $3,000, will, it is believed, obviate the necessity for this light-house, which would be a very expensive structure.

The steamboat company at Fall River keep a light and fog-signal at Hog Island Reef for their own benefit, and for that of others using the channel to Fall River, and it is deemed proper that the expense for the maintenance of a light and signal at this locality should devolve upon the Light-House Establishment. The recommendation for an appropriation is therefore renewed.

128. *Conimicut, River Providence, Rhode Island.*—In the annual report of last year, it was stated that—

> When the light on the shoal off Conimicut Point was lighted as a substitute for the light on the main-land, at Nayat Point, (distant about one mile,) the only available means of attending upon it was to allow the keeper to retain the dwelling at the old light-station, and to visit the new light by boat. The land constituting the site of the old light-station at Nayat Point is valuable, and would bring at public sale a good price. The old tower is not worth the cost of tearing down, and the dwelling not having been repaired, in anticipation of an appropriation for completing the building at Conimicut Point, to include a proper dwelling for the keeper, it now becomes necessary, either to make considerable expenditure upon the Nayat Point dwelling, or ask for a special appropriation for the necessary protection-pier against running ice, and for a dwelling at that light-station. The estimated cost of the work is $30,000.

The recommendation is renewed.

——. *Bullock's Point, River Providence, Rhode Island.*—The beacon, heretofore a day-mark, will be lighted by the 1st of October next, an appropriation of $1,000 having been made for the purpose at the last session of Congress, on the petition of persons interested in the navigation of the channel, and after favorable reports from the inspector and engineer of the district had been made, to whom the subject was referred for examination.

129. *Sabin's Point, River Providence, Rhode Island.*—The contractor for this structure has made good progress with the work. The foundation and pier are completed, and the dwelling is advanced as far as the second story. It is contemplated to exhibit the light at the station by the 1st of October next.

130. *Pumham Rock, River Providence, Rhode Island.*—The light was first exhibited at this station on the 1st of December last. A boat-house and landing are needed, the estimate of which is $1,200.

131. *Fuller's Rock, River Providence, Rhode Island.*—During the construction of this beacon it was lighted by a steamboat company for the benefit of the navigation of the channel to Providence. The failure of the contractor to comply with the terms of this contract has made it necessary to reject the work.

132. *Sassafras Point, River Providence, Rhode Island.*—During the construction of this beacon it was lighted by a steamboat company for the benefit of the navigation of the channel to Providence. In consequence of the failure of the contractor to comply with the terms of this contract, payment has not been made for the work.

133. *Point Judith, Rhode Island.*—In accordance with the recommendation in the last annual report an appropriation of $5,000 was made at the last session of Congress for a steam fog-signal. The construction of this signal is in progress. It will be of that class characterized a syren, and of the first order. The housing is nearly completed, and the signal will be in operation early in September. The present signal will be retained as a spare apparatus, to be sounded in case of accident to the new one.

134. *Block Island, (north end,) eastern entrance to Long Island Sound.*—The sand-drifts threatened serious damage to the dwelling by the encroachment of the chasm, caused by the high winds. Partial remedies have been made by grading and facing the surface of the site in the immediate vicinity of the dwelling, and upon the north or exposed side with paving-stone. The work is not yet finished, and with the view of completing it, an appropriation recommended in the last annual report was made at the last session of Congress.

——. *Block Island, (south end,) eastern entrance to Long Island Sound.*—An appropriation of $75,000 was made by the last Congress for a light-house and fog-signal at this locality, under a petition of persons interested in the navigation of this part of the coast. A preliminary survey of the southeast end of the island has been made, and a site favorable for the service of a steam fog-signal—a syren; a pond of fresh water being upon the site recommended, has been selected. Plans for the light-house and for fog-signal are in progress.

136. *Montauk Point, (New York,) eastern end of Long Island.*—The appropriation for the repairs of this station, and for the erection of a fog-signal as recommended in the last annual report, having been made, immediate measures will be taken for carrying into effect the object intended. It is proposed to erect a signal operated by a hot-air engine; in consequence of the difficulty of obtaining sufficient water for steam purposes, no other engine than that operated by hot air could be adopted at this locality.

141. *New London, Connecticut.*—The fog-signal having been in use fifteen years, needs renewing, and an estimate of $4,500 is submitted for the purpose.

143. *Race Rock, Long Island Sound, New York.*—The proposals for the construction of the foundation and pier of this structure were so excessive in rates, and so much above the amount of the appropriation on hand, that no more than the landing and the enrockment of the foundation, and two courses of the pier, could be contracted for. This embraces 8,000 tons of dimension-stone, weighing from eight to ten tons each, for the enrockment alone. The landing has been commenced, and good progress made upon it.

The riprap foundation, consisting of ten thousand tons of riprap stones, irregular in shape, and weighing from three to five tons on an average, was completed in November last, and remained without displacement during the storms of winter and spring, and no appearance of settling is manifest. An appropriation for continuing the construction of the pier and erecting the dwelling is required, and the sum of $75,000 is estimated, basing the estimate upon the proposal of the lowest bidder for the work now under contract.

144. *Little Gull Island, Long Island Sound, New York.*—This station needs an appropriation of $5,000 for completing the landing, reference to which was made in the last annual report. There is special need for the facilities of a landing for the reason that the shelter from the sea is so limited that the difficulty of landing supplies of the station, including a large quantity of coal for the steam fog-signal, is unusually great. The recommendation for the appropriation of $5,000 for completion of the landing is renewed.

147. *Long Beach Bar, Long Island, New York.*—The breakwater, for which an appropriation of $20,000 was made, is under contract, and the iron-pile light-house will be placed under its shelter from the floating ice-fields that threaten destruction to buildings of this class, without such protection, in northern climates. The past winter endangered the structure, and the alarm of the keeper and his assistant was so great as to cause its desertion for two nights, during which no light was exhibited nor fog-bell sounded. The above light-house was completed, and the light exhibited for the first time, on the 1st day of December, 1871. The station is provided with a fog-bell struck by machinery.

150. *Calves Island, River Connecticut.*

151. *Brockway's Reach, River Connecticut.*

152. *Devil's Wharf, River Connecticut.*

The foundations of these structures are liable to disturbance by the river-currents, and efforts have been made to prevent their being undermined by throwing at their base riprap stone. There is now required for protection of the last-named structure a large quantity of stone; for this purpose, and for the protection of all these foundations, the sum of $2,500 is recommended to be appropriated.

155. *Faulkner's Island, Long Island Sound, New York.*—The wasting away of the clay-bank continues slowly during the freezing and subsequent thawing of the soil. The beach requires to be protected at an estimated cost of $2,500, which is recommended to be appropriated.

156. *New Haven Harbor, Connecticut.*—In answer to a resolution of Congress relating to the transfer of the light-house to Southwest Ledge, under date of April 16, 1872, it is stated as follows:

Southwest Ledge lies in the middle of the main ship-channel into New Haven Harbor, and forms a great danger to navigation. There are but 7 feet 6 inches of water on the rock at mean low water, and the question is between the removal of the rock by the

Engineer Department of the Army, and the erection by the board of a light and fog-signal to keep vessels from running upon it and other dangerous rocks in the vicinity. The main light at the entrance is now at Five-mile Point, on the mainland, on the east side of the harbor, and distant one mile from, and inside of Southwest Ledge. It was established in 1805, and last refitted in 1856. There is no doubt but that a light in the channel on this ledge would serve the interests of navigation better than the present light, and that it and a fog-signal also placed on the rock would be of more benefit to commerce than the removal of the ledge, since vessels could always run for the light, and keep clear of all the many dangers to navigation, which it will be observed exist at the entrance to New Haven Harbor. A light-house at Southwest Ledge would involve a very large expense on account of its submarine foundation, and the strength which would be required to resist the large fields of ice by which it would be assailed. The expense is estimated at $117,800.

158. *Stratford Point, Connecticut*—The buildings of this station are very old and unfit for occupation. An estimate for a suitable dwelling over which the tower may be placed, was submitted in the last annual report. It is recommended that the amount then submitted be appropriated, viz, $15,000.

——. *Stratford Point Shoal, Long Island Sound, New York.*—A special report was called for from the engineer of the district, with estimate of cost for a structure to supersede the light-ship. After a preliminary survey of the Middle Ground, he proposed to erect a light-house thereupon, and to discontinue the light-ship. The character of the formation is deemed suitable for a structure, the foundation of which should be riprap of large irregular blocks of granite from three to five tons each in weight. The least depth of water found at low tide is 5 feet 5 inches. An area of 100 feet diameter gives an average depth of 8 feet of water. The Middle Ground is composed of large gravel, unyielding to the iron rod driven by hand. The estimated cost of the structure is $125,000.

160. *Bridgeport Harbor, Connecticut.*—The iron-pile light-house adopted for this locality has been completed and occupied by the keeper. The light has been exhibited in the new structure since November, 1871. A stone breakwater surrounding the light-house and protecting it from the floating ice-fields has recently been constructed. The light in the old structure has been discontinued.

161. *Penfield Reef, Connecticut.*—The foundation of riprap was laid during the previous season, and stood uninjured throughout the winter gales. The landing, wharf, and pier are in progress of construction under contract, and will be completed so far this season as to admit of the commencement of the dwelling, which is also under contract. The contractor for the pier, owing to his want of adequate means, has delayed the work, and the forbearance of the engineer toward him has alone prevented the annulling of his contract and the commencement of suit to recover the amount of the bonds.

162. *Old Field Point, Long Island, New York.*—Measures have been taken for the purchase of a right of way from the station to the public highway, there being two land-holders from whom the purchase must be made. Difficulties of removing claims have postponed the matter until next autumn, when it is believed satisfactory purchase may be concluded.

163. *Black Rock, Connecticut.*—The buoy-shed and wharf have been completed, coal-bins and derrick erected, and the station put in readiness for the storage of buoys, coal, and other articles to be used as an auxiliary depot for the district. The tower and keeper's dwelling (erected in 1808) are in an advanced state of decay, and need rebuilding. The new structure may be planned with the tower over the keeper's dwelling, and erected at a cost of $9,500.

165. *Lloyd's Harbor, Long Island, New York.*—The sea-wall built only the previous season has been damaged by the ice of last winter, but measures will be taken to repair the same with the means on hand, as it is believed that the cost will be small.

——. *Hart Island, Long Island Sound, New York.*—An appropriation having been made for a light-house at this station, the preliminary examination and survey have been made, and plans prepared for foundation, pier, and dwelling, preparatory to advertising for the construction.

169. *Sand's Point, Long Island, New York.*

173. *Great West Bay, Long Island, New York.*

174. *Fire Island, Long Island, New York.*

A special appropriation having been made for the repair of these stations measures will be speedily taken to place them in a good condition, and to repair the inclosures before the winter sets in.

176 *and* 177. *Highlands of Navesink, New Jersey.*—Application has been made to the Light-House Board to cause the substitution of a revolving light in one of the towers, and the question is now under consideration.

179. *East Beacon, Sandy Hook, New Jersey.*—The abrasion of the beach at this station is increasing; since the last annual report was submitted the abrasion has been about 80 feet. This increase was anticipated, as will be seen by the report referred to, and is due to the erection of the jettees for its protection near the fort, which cut off the supply of sand from the eastward. It is necessary that recourse be had to similar works to protect the light-house property, for which the estimate rendered last year of $20,000 is renewed.

185. *Elm Tree Beacon, New York Bay, New York.*—The abrasion of the beach at this station is caused by a long wharf on the northward, which is struck by the rolling seas from the southeast, which diverts their course to the beach, and creates a violent disturbance; at the same, on the cessation of the storm, the usual littoral accretion is cut off by the same wharf and retained to the northward. The small jettee constructed on the south line of the station had been damaged by the sea, and a breach made severing its connection with the shore. This breach is in progress of repairs as well as general repairs of the jettee. It is likely that recourse must finally be had to a riprap along the entire front of the station for its preservation.

187. *Princess Bay, New York Bay, New York.*—The progress of the protecting wall commenced last season has been slow. The contractor having lost a capacious barge on the occasion of a storm, considerable delay has ensued in the work, and less than 500 feet of the wall has been completed. The work is in progress, and so far as built has produced good results.

188. *Fort Tompkins, New York Bay, New York.*—The plans for the light-house appropriated for at the last session of Congress have been made, and the work will be put under contract for completion before the winter season. As the station lies within the inclosure of the defensive works, the space occupied will be reduced to the smallest limit, and the plans contemplate the placing of the tower over the keeper's dwelling. The old site will then be relinquished for the purposes of a battery.

195. *West Point, River Hudson, New York.*—The rebuilding of the beacon is progressing, and will be completed at an early day. The site of the beacon is connected with that of the former stake-light, and no change in the sailing directions is made.

196. *Esopus Meadow, River Hudson, New York.*—The new light-house,

with tower over the keeper's dwelling, is nearly completed, and the light will probably be exhibited during the month of August. The distance from the old light-house site is small, and no important change in sailing directions is made.

198. *Saugerties, river Hudson, New York.*—The old light-house dwelling at this place has been sold, and the proceeds of the sale deposited and carried to the surplus fund.

——. *Middle Ground, near Hudson, River Hudson, New York.*—The preliminary survey of the site has been made, and the plans have been prepared.

201. *Stuyvesant, River Hudson, New York.*—The old dwelling has been refitted, with the view of using it as a store-house for the river Hudson beacons during the winter season on the suspension of navigation. The roadway has been raised above the level of the freshets, and a small bridge built, with projection of piles against the bridge and its approaches.

202–213. *River Hudson Beacons, New York.*—Ten crib and stone piers for the portable beacons have been rebuilt during the past season, and the beacons reset on the opening of navigation. One of the sites, that of 209, *Cow Island*, has been encroached upon by the freshets, some 25 feet of the island having been washed away. A pile protection will be necessary to save the foundation from entire destruction. 211, *Van Wies Point* beacon, is also being undermined by the waves caused by the passing steamers. For its protection 100 tons of stone are needed.

——. *Whitehall Narrows, Lake Champlain, New York.*—Eight of the beacons were removed during the winter and replaced after the ice disappeared. The recommendation to replace two stake lights by portable beacons, in the last annual report, is renewed, the estimated cost of same being $1,600.

Two stake-lights, maintained at the expense of the commerce through the Narrows, should be assumed by the Light-House Establishment and portable beacons placed in their stead. The cost of the two will be $1,600.

446. *Crown Point, Lake Champlain, New York.*—The buildings authorized by the appropriation of the last session of Congress will be erected, and all the necessary repairs will be attended to during the present season.

447. *Barber's Point, Lake Champlain, New York.*—The contract for the erection of the dwelling and tower is being carried out, with a prospect of completing the work before the close of navigation; but it is questionable whether the light can be exhibited before next season.

448. *Split Rock, Lake Champlain, New York.*—The boat-house and ways, with capstan and rigging, authorized by the special appropriation of last year, have been constructed.

449. *Juniper Island, Lake Champlain, New York.*—The boat-house and wharf authorized by the appropriation of March 3, 1871, were completed during the past season.

450, 451. *Burlington Breakwater, Vermont.*—The extension of the breakwater by the Engineer Department of the Army northward has been postponed, and in consequence thereof that end of the work has been marked by a portable beacon instead of erecting the dwelling contemplated by the appropriation of March 3, 1871. This, however, answers every purpose that is needed, although it is not so convenient for the keeper to serve the beacon.

452. *Colchester Reef, Lake Champlain, Vermont.*—The past winter has subjected the structure, so recently built, to a severe test. The fields

of ice have caused some injury, and the foundation is said to have settled. The examination has not thus far been made by the engineer of the district, and the precise extent of the injury is not known.

453. *Bluff Point, Valcour Island, New York.*—The title to the site not having been declared valid by the proper authorities, no measures have been taken to commence the work, a contract for which was made in anticipation of such declaration.

456. *Cumberland Head, Lake Champlain, New York.*—Negotiations are yet pending for the purchase of the land on the lake shore for the purpose of removing trees that obstruct the light from the channel to the northward.

458. *Isle La Motte, Lake Champlain, New York.*—The recommendation for a dwelling at this station, at an estimated cost of $8,000, in the last annual report, is renewed.

REPAIRS.

At each of the following stations in the third district, repairs, more or less extensive, have been made during the year:

121. *Newport*, Rhode Island.
122. *Rose Island*, Rhode Island.
127. *Warwick Neck*, Rhode Island.
128. *Conimicut*, Rhode Island.
133. *Point Judith*, Rhode Island.
135. *Watch Hill*, Rhode Island.
136. *Montauk Point*, New York.
140. *North Dumpling*, Long Island Sound.
141. *New London*, Connecticut.
144. *Little Gull Island*, New York.
145. *Gardiner's Island*, New York.
154. *Horton's Point*, New York.
155. *Faulkner's Island*, New York.
162. *Old Field Point*, New York.
163. *Black Rock*, Connecticut.
165. *Lloyd's Harbor*, New York.
166. *Norwalk Island*, Connecticut.
168. *Execution Rocks*, New York.
169. *Sands' Point*, New York.
170. *Throgg's Neck*, New York.
171. *North Brother Island*, New York.
173. *Great West Bay*, New York.
174. *Fire Island*, New York.
176-177. *Highlands of Navesink*, New Jersey.
178. *Sandy Hook*, New Jersey.
181. *Conover Beacon*, New Jersey.
188. *Fort Tompkins*, New York.
189. *Robbins's Reef*, New York.
194. *Stony Point*, New York.
196. *Esopus Meadows*, New York.
197. *Rondout*, New York.
198. *Saugerties*, New York.
200. *Coxsackie*, New York.
201. *Stuyvesant*, New York.
430-445. *Whitehall Narrows*, New York.
446. *Crown Point*, New York.
449. *Juniper Island*, New York.

450, 451. *Burlington Beacons*, Vermont.
457. *Point au Roches*, New York.
459. *Windmill Point*, New York.

The following-named stations in the third district require repairs to be made during the current and ensuing year:

121. *Newport Harbor*, Rhode Island.
124. *Poplar Point*, Rhode Island.
125. *Prudence Island*, Rhode Island.
126. *Bristol Ferry*, Rhode Island.
127. *Warwick Neck*, Rhode Island.
134. *Block Island*, Rhode Island.
146. *Plum Island*, New York.
149. *Saybrook*, Connecticut.
150. *Calves Island*, Connecticut.
151. *Brockway's Reach*, Connecticut.
152. *Devil's Wharf*, Connecticut.
158. *Stratford Point*, Connecticut.
163. *Black Rock*, Connecticut.
169. *Sand's Point*, New York.
173. *Great West Bay*, New York.
174. *Fire Island*, New York.
178. *Sandy Hook*, New Jersey.
182. *Chapel Hill*, New Jersey.
184. *Waackaack*, New Jersey.
192. *Passaic*, New Jersey.
197. *Rondout*, New York.
198. *Saugerties*, New York.
199. *Four-Mile Point*, New York.
200. *Coxsackie*, New York.
201. *Stuyvesant*, New York.
209. *Cow Island*, New York.
211. *Van Weis Point*, New York.
249. *Juniper Island*, New York.

The following-named stations in the third district are not mentioned elsewhere:

120. *Lime Rock*, Newport Harbor, Rhode Island.
123. *Dutch Island*, Narragansett Bay.
137. *Stonington Harbor*, Connecticut.
139. *Morgan's Point*, Connecticut.
148. *Ceder Island*, New York.
157. *New Haven Long Wharf*, Connecticut.
167. *Great Captain Island*, Long Island Sound.
183. *Point Comfort Beacon*, New Jersey.
190. *Bergen Point*, New Jersey.
191. *Corner Stake*, New Jersey.
193. *Elbow Beacon*, New Jersey.

LIGHT-SHIPS.

118. *"Brenton's Reef," on Brenton's Reef, off entrance to Newport Harbor, Rhode Island.*—This vessel is now undergoing repairs at New London, and her place is supplied by Relief No. 19.

138. "*Eel Grass*," *on Eel-Grass Shoal, in Fisher's Island Sound, Connecticut.*—This is a third-class light-ship formerly stationed in Roanoke Sound, North Carolina. A screw-pile light-house having been erected there, her services were no longer necessary, and she was removed to this station, and will probably last for two or three years.

142. "*Bartlett's Reef*," *off New London, Connecticut.*—This vessel requires her upper deck to be calked; otherwise she is in good condition.

153. "*Cornfield Point*," *Long Island Sound, off mouth of Connecticut River.*—This vessel, which was removed from *Eel-Grass Shoal*, is in good condition, except damage amounting to $175, caused by being run into by the schooner J. G. Drew, of Belfast, Maine. This damage is now being repaired.

159. "*Stratford*," *on "Middle Ground," Long Island Sound, off Stratford Point.*—This vessel is in fair condition, but in a few years she will require rebuilding, as will be observed elsewhere in this report. It is recommended that a fourth-order light be erected on this shoal, as being more economical and far more durable than a light-ship.

175. "*Sandy Hook*," *off New York Bay.*—This vessel, stationed seven miles outside of Sandy Hook, has been repaired during the last year, at a cost of $17,159.60. A new mooring-chain, costing $1,158.80, has been supplied. She is now in excellent condition. A "Thiers automatic fog-signal, bilge-pump, and ship ventilator" has been placed on the vessel for experiment and test-trial. It has been found successful as a bilge-pump and ventilator, and will be retained. As a fog-signal it did not prove satisfactory.

Relief No. 19.—This vessel is in good condition, and is now on Brenton's Reef, off Newport, while the vessel belonging to that station is being repaired.

Relief No. 20.—This vessel, which is also in good order and ready for any emergency, is now at the light-house depot at Staten Island, New York Harbor.

Relief No. 25.—The condition of this vessel, owing to age and service, is found on a strict examination to be so bad as to render her unworthy of further repairs; she has been removed from Cornfield Point and taken to New London, Connecticut, and her sale is recommended.

FOG-SIGNALS OPERATED BY STEAM OR HOT-AIR ENGINES.

119. *Beaver Tail, Rhode Island.*—First-class Daboll trumpet.

133. *Point Judith, Rhode Island.*—Third-class Daboll trumpet.

141. *New London, Connecticut.*—Third-class Daboll trumpet.

144. *Little Gull Island, New York.*—Second-class syren, (in duplicate.)

164. *Eaton's Neck, New York.*—Second-class syren, (in duplicate.)

168. *Execution Rocks, New York.*—Second-class Daboll trumpet, (in duplicate.)

179. *Sandy Hook, entrance to New York Harbor.*—First-class syren, (in duplicate.)

DAY OR UNLIGHTED BEACONS.

All the beacons in the third district comprised in the following list are in good condition, unless otherwise stated:

1. *East Lime Rock, near Newport.*—A granite structure, surmounted by a spindle and cage.

2. *South Point, Rose Island, Narragansett Bay.*—Granite structure, surmounted by a spindle and cage.

3. *Half-way Rock, three-fourths of a mile southward of Prudence Island Point, Narragansett Bay.*—Spindle and square cage.

4. *Bullock's Point, Narragansett Bay.*—Stone beacon with iron spindle. This beacon will be lighted under an appropriation of the last session of Congress for the purpose.

5. *Pawtuxent Beacon, Narragansett Bay.*—Of stone, surmounted by a black ball.

6. *Pumham Beacon, River Providence.*—A stone beacon, with vane and black ball.

7. *Muscle Bed, east side of the channel, below Bristol Ferry, Rhode Island.*—A stone beacon, with iron spindle and day-mark.

8. *Borden's Flats, opposite Fall River.*—A stone beacon, with iron column and day-mark.

9. *Castle Island, near north end of Hog Island, Bristol Harbor.*—A stone beacon, surmounted by a red ball.

10. *Allen's Rock, River Warren.*—Stone beacon, one-eighth of a mile north of Adams's Point.

11. *Warwick or Spindle Rock, west channel of Narragansett Bay, and entrance to Greenwich Harbor, between Warwick Neck and Pojack Point.*—Iron spindle, with square wooden cage.

12. *White Rock Beacon, at the entrance of Wickford Harbor, Narragansett Bay.*—Stone beacon, with iron column and day-mark.

13. *Watch Hill Spindle, entrance to Fisher's Island Sound from light-house, southwest by south three-fourths of a mile.*—Stands on a rock which is bare at low water, and is surmounted by a cage.

14. *Sugar Reef Beacon, Fisher's Island Sound.*—Iron pile-beacon, with cage-work day-mark in the form of a cone.

15. *East or Catumb Reef Spindle, entrance to Fisher's Island Sound by Lord's Channel, one and one-fourth miles east of east point of Fisher's Island.*—An iron pile-beacon, with square cage-work.

16. *West or Wiccopesset Spindle Rock, entrance to Fisher's Island Sound by Lord's Channel, northwest of east spindle, two-thirds of a mile.*

17. *Latimer's Reef, Fisher's Island Sound, one mile northwest of east point of Fisher's Island, and three-fourths of a mile southeast of Eel Grass Shoal light-vessel.*—An iron spindle, bearing a square cage-work.

18. *Ellis's Reef, Fisher's Island Sound, three-fourths of a mile northwest of Eel Grass Shoal light-vessel.*—An iron spindle with a square cage-work.

19. *Ram Island Reef, Fisher's Island Sound, one-half of a mile southeast of Ram Island.*

20. *Spindle on The Whale, River Mystic.*—An appropriation of $5,000 has been made for substituting a stone-beacon for the iron spindle destroyed by ice. The structure is under contract, and will be completed before the season of fall gales.

21. *Crook's Spindle, River Mystic.*—Is an iron spindle, with keg on top.

22. *Groton Long Point, Fisher's Island Sound.*—An iron spindle, bearing a case-work in the form of an inverted cone.

23. *Sea Flower Beacon, Fisher's Island Sound, Connecticut.*—An appropriation of $4,200 has been made for rebuilding this beacon. It is under contract, and will be completed at an early day.

24. *Black Ledge, entrance to New London Harbor, Connecticut.*—The iron spindle on this ledge was carried off during the last season subsequent to submitting the annual report. It is recommended that a stone beacon of a substantial kind be substituted for the iron spindle, for which an estimate of $5,500 is submitted for the beacon and the renewal

of the iron shaft bearing a cage-work, formed by two cones connected at the vertices.

25. *Saybrook Beacon, River Connecticut.*—Stone beacon, with globe, on Saybrook Bar.

26. *Hen and Chickens, Long Island Sound.*—Iron spindle, bearing a square cage, painted black.

27. *Branford Reef Beacon, Long Island Sound.*—Granite beacon, surmounted by an iron shaft bearing a black day-mark.

28. *Quixe's Ledge, entrance to New Haven Harbor, Connecticut.*—An iron spindle, with a cask on top. Stands on a rock which is dry at half tide.

29. *Southwest Ledge Spindle, entrance to New Haven Harbor, Connecticut,* marked by a second-class buoy.

30. *Stratford River Beacon, entrance to River Stratford.*—Granite beacon, with iron column and mark.

31. *Inner Beacon, Bridgeport Harbor, Connecticut.*—A frustum of a square pyramid of wood, surmounted by a wooden mast, with a cask painted black.

32. *Outer Beacon, Bridgeport Harbor, Connecticut.*—The same as the inner beacon.

33. *Black Rock Beacon, Long Island Sound.*—An iron pile-beacon, with a cage on top.

34. *Southport Beacon.*—Granite beacon, with iron column and day-mark.

35. *Southport Breakwater Beacon.*—Granite beacon, with iron column and day-mark.

36. *Norwalk Beacon, southwest of Norwalk Island, Connecticut.*—A granite structure, supporting a shaft and day-mark of iron.

37. *Great Reef, off Norwalk Island; entrance to Norwalk Harbor.*—A wooden spindle, with cage day-mark.

38. *Sand's Spit Beacon, Sag Harbor, Long Island, New York.*—The contractor for building this beacon has not placed the same on the site designated, nor has he built it in accordance with agreement. Payment has therefore been withheld until he complies with the contract, or until an adjustment for the value of the work executed can be concluded between him and the engineer of the district that may be satisfactory to the Light-House Board. The contractor has been notified to this effect.

—— *Oyster Pond Point, Plum Gut, entrance to Gardiner's Bay.*—An appropriation of $5,000 has been made for a beacon of granite as a substitute for the iron spindle destroyed by ice. The structure has been put under contract, and will be completed before the season of autumn gales.

40. *Success Rock, Long Island Sound.*—An iron shaft, with conical cage-work.

41. *Romer Shoal Beacon, New York Bay.*—The riprap protection for this beacon, authorized by the appropriation of March 3, 1871, has been made, and consists of 950 tons of granite blocks of large irregular shape. The painting of the upper section of the tower remains to be done.

42. *Mill Reef Beacon, Kill van Kull, opposite New Brighton.*—This is a sheet-iron beacon, filled in with concrete, and secured to a granite base. It is conical in shape, and supports an iron shaft with an iron cage on top.

LIGHT-HOUSE GENERAL DEPOT, AT STATEN ISLAND, NEW YORK HARBOR.

This depot contains the manufacturing establishment, vaults for the storage, and apparatus for photometrical tests, of oil, and store-houses for the general supplies, &c., for the service of the lights in the Atlantic,

Pacific, Gulf and Lake coasts of the United States. The office building has been completed, and occupied by the engineer and inspector of the third district during the last fiscal year. The dwelling of the inspector has been repaired, and occupied by him. The other buildings have been repaired; also the fences and wharves, including additional piling for the convenience of the tenders in coaling, &c. One derrick of ten tons' lifting capacity has been erected on one of the wharves, and another of similar capacity is in readiness to be erected on the other wharf. The grounds have been partly graded and drained. The coal-bin has been enlarged to increase the capacity for 400 tons additional of coal. A new boiler has been supplied for the workshop, and the old one repaired and ready for resetting as a duplicate or reserve. The oil-vaults will soon undergo considerable repair, rendered necessary by defective drains, the capacity of which were found to be insufficient, and with so little declivity that the filling up by sediment has been rapid. Drains of 18 inches radius and semicircular in form have been authorized by the board, as also drains in the rear of the vault, and lateral drains to connect with the large 12 and 18-inch drains of the grounds. This will involve considerable expense. For this purpose and for the completion of the grading and drainage of the grounds, the construction of a large cistern for collecting the rain-fall from the buildings now mostly wasted, and which can be utilized for the use of the light-house tenders, the sum of $10,000 will be required, and is recommended to be appropriated.

The following is a statement of the number of boxes, barrels, packages, &c., containing articles of supply and outfit for light-stations, and received at and shipped from light-house general depot, Tompkinsville, Staten Island, from July 1, 1871, to July 31, 1872, inclusive:

	Boxes.	Barrels.	Packages, cases, &c.	Totals.
Received	3,136	2,918	5,542	11,596
Shipped	2,632	2,663	5,058	10,553
Total	5,968	5,581	10,600	22,149

Lenses received from France and delivered from light-house depot, Staten Island, from July 1, 1871, to June 30, 1872.

	1st order.	2d order.	3d order.	3½ order.	4th order.	5th order.	6th order.	Steamer lenses.	Pressed lenses.	Canal lenses.	Totals.
Received	4	3	2	1	20	12	25	3	11	3	84
Delivered	3	....	3	1	8	6	14	2	10	2	49
Total	7	3	5	2	28	18	39	5	21	5	133

Number of boxes containing illuminating apparatus received at and shipped from light-house depot, Staten Island, from July 1, 1871, to June 30, 1872.

	1st order.	2d order.	3d order.	3½ order.	4th order.	5th order.	6th order.	Steamer lenses.	Pressed lenses.	Canal lenses.	Total.
Received	145	70	25	10	61	29	60	7	12	10	......
Delivered	99	....	34	....	22	19	42	3	11	6	......
Total	244	70	59	10	83	48	102	10	23	16	665

List of articles manufactured and repaired in lamp-shop, light-house depot, Staten Island, from July 1, 1871, to June 30, 1872.

	Lenses.	Lamps.	Lamp burners.	Miscellaneous articles.	Totals.
Manufactured	.....	236	295	657	......
Repaired	9	90	11	1,135	......
Total	9	326	306	1,792	2,433

FOURTH DISTRICT.

The fourth light-house district extends from Squam Inlet, New Jersey, to and including Metomkin Inlet, Virginia. It includes the sea-coast of New Jersey below the Highlands of Navesink, the bay coasts of New Jersey and Delaware, the sea-coasts of Delaware and Maryland, and part of the sea-coast of Virginia.

Inspector.—Commodore William H. Macomb, United States Navy, till his death, August 12, 1872; Captain Reigart B. Lowry, United States Navy, present inspector.

Engineer.—Colonel I. C. Woodruff, Corps of Engineers, brevet brigadier-general, United States Army.

In this district there are:

Light-houses and lighted beacons	18
Light-ships, (in position)	2
Light-ships, (for relief)	1
Buoys actually in position	111
Spare buoys for relief and to supply losses	66
Tender (steam) Violet	1

The numbers preceding the names of stations correspond with those of the Light-House List of the Atlantic, Gulf, and Pacific Coasts of the United States, issued January 1, 1872.

214. *Barnegat, sea-coast of New Jersey.*—The semi-monthly measurements along the beach near the light-house have been continued throughout the year, and there have been no important changes in the water-lines along the light-house lot. Thus far the works of protection have proved a success.

215. *Tucker's Beach, sea-coast of New Jersey.*—In September last the color of the tower and keeper's dwelling were changed from gray to red, to serve better as a day-mark for passing vessels.

216. *Absecum, sea-coast of New Jersey.*—The semi-monthly measurements along the beach in the vicinity of the light-house have been continued throughout the year, and favorable changes in the beach have been found to have taken place along the entire front of Atlantic City. There has been a gradual widening of the beach on the ocean-front, and at the point of the inlet. The north-channel cut of the inlet has been buoyed, and is now used by the largest vessels entering the harbor, as it is a more direct course in and out of the inlet.

The time is not distant when the south channel will be closed; it is a crooked and narrow one, and the strength of the current in the ebb-tide is not so great as formerly. It is reported that most of the vessels, passing in and out of the inlet, go through the north channel, and recently a schooner of 260 tons, loaded with ice for Atlantic City, drawing 8½ feet water passed in through the north channel at about half-tide. It is a matter of regret that possession of the necessary land along the inlet front cannot be obtained for the works of protection of the beach. From careful examinations it is manifest that if small stone jettees were placed along the inlet, a much greater quantity of the ebb-tide water would be thrown through the north channel, and the time would not be long before the south channel would be closed. At the present time no fears need be apprehended for the safety of the light-house site. The color of the tower was changed in September last, to better serve as a day-mark for passing vessels, as follows: the lower section for 52 feet from the base, white; the middle section 52 feet, red; and the upper section, including the lantern, parapet, and gallery-railing, white. The authorities of Atlantic City have not yet furnished the deed from the property owners for the occupation of the land required for sites, &c., for works of protection. The mayor states that there is now but one person to sign the grant, to enable him to have the papers prepared giving possession to the Government for commencing the work.

——*Hereford Inlet, sea-coast of New Jersey, ten and three-quarters nautical miles north of Cape May's light-house.*—Congress at its last session having appropriated $25,000 for erecting a light-house at or near this point, measures will be taken without delay to locate its site, and make arrangements for the purchase of a suitable piece of ground, with the necessary steps for the cession of jurisdiction by the legislature of New Jersey to the Government of the United States.

219. *Cape Henlopen, sea-coast of Delaware, entrance to Delaware Bay.*—Trouble has been anticipated at this station by the encroachment of the "Big Sand Hills" near it. There are changes constantly going on, but no serious inconvenience has yet resulted from them, nor is it thought there will be as long as the space between the tower and dwelling is kept open by removing the sand as fast as it accumulates.

220. *Cape Henlopen Beacon, Delaware Bay.*—On the 28th of July last the building was struck by lightning, and it tore off the cornice of the building, but did no other damage.

221. *Delaware Breakwater, Delaware Bay.*—A new frame structure for the fog-bell and striking-machinery has been erected. The bell and machinery have been thoroughly cleaned, the machinery has been repaired, the motive weight has been reduced about 600 pounds, and the fog-signal is now in good condition.

——. *Mispillion, Delaware Bay.*—Congress, at its last session, appropriated $5,000 for re-establishing the small light-house at this point, and it will be commenced at an early day.

——. *Light-houses at Cross Ledge Shoal, Ship John Shoal, and Bulk-head Shoal, Delaware Bay and River.*—During the last session of Congress a petition was received for lights at Ship John Shoal and Bulk-head Shoal, in the river Delaware, of which the following is a copy:

PHILADELPHIA, *January*, 1872.

To the Hon. GEORGE S. BOUTWELL,
Secretary of the Treasury:

The aids to navigation in the Delaware River and Bay, which have long been insufficient, are now, when steamships are to a great extent superseding sail-vessels, altogether inadequate to the requirements there. These ships run at all seasons of the year, and at all hours, by night as well as by day, and the buoys which mark the shoals and serve, when they can be seen, as guides to the mariner in keeping the channel, are useless in dark nights always, and in winter they are deceptive and dangerous; for at that season the drift-ice which covers these waters changes the location of some of these buoys and sweeps others entirely away. Experienced mariners, conversant with the navigation here, are, therefore, clearly of opinion that permanent light-houses are the most efficient guides to navigation in the long and intricate channels of the Delaware, and the only ones that are available at all times and all seasons of the year. The last annual report of the Light-House Board (pages 27 and 28) recognizes this fact by its recommendation of a light-house in place of the light-ship on the Cross Ledge, which is often displaced by drifting ice, and also recommends the erection of a light-house on Tinicum Island, above Chester. These recommendations, if carried into effect, will be great and permanent benefits to the commerce of this port; but there is also urgent need of light-houses at other points, viz, at the Ship John Shoals, at Reedy Point, and at the upper end of the Bulk-head Shoals.

The undersigned corporations and citizens of Philadelphia, interested in its commerce, respectfully ask your attention to the foregoing statements, and earnestly request you to institute such measures as will supply the requisite aids to the navigation of our river and bay as herein set forth.

JOEL PARKER,
Governor of New Jersey.
JAMES PONDER,
Governor of Delaware, and others.

The question as to the necessity of these lights, and their cost, was submitted to the district officers, and in their replies it was stated that there was great necessity for the lights at the points named, and more so now than formerly, on account of the greater number of steamers navigating the river and bay at all hours of night and day; and when there is floating ice, the buoys being either cut off or drifted from proper positions, and during darkness invisible, the soundings cannot be taken, the lead frequently lighting on the cakes of ice, while the vessel in motion is liable to run on shore before getting another cast of the lead; whereas, were lights in their positions they could steer their courses.

The necessity for a light on Ship John Shoals is to guide vessels up the channel and prevent them from getting ashore on Ship John Shoals and the one opposite, the tide being such as to drift them at times on either shoal. This drifting is frequently experienced in this part of the channel.

On the north end of Bulk-head Shoals, a light is necessary to further show the channels past Bulk-head Shoals, and in order that vessels may shape their course past Deep-Water Point.

In view of the fact that neither the light-house at Ship John Shoals nor Bulk-head Shoals can be constructed in a single fiscal year, and the impossibility of leaving either structure in an unfinished condition over winter without a probability of the loss of the whole of it by the ice, making it necessary to use one entire season, including spring, summer, and fall, (parts of two fiscal years,) for its erection at the site, after the preparation of the material during the previous season, it is earnestly recommended that the appropriation for Ship John Shoals and Bulk-head Shoals, if Congress should deem it proper to make them, in view of the facts presented in the accompanying reports, shall be available during two entire fiscal years.

It was further stated that the cost of each light-house would be $125,000.

The want of a light-house at Cross Ledge Shoals, in Delaware Bay, is very great, for the reasons, 1st, that the light-ship now stationed there is often driven from her moorings by fields of ice, endangering her own safety and (by absence from her station) the safety of commerce. 2d. The erection of a light-house to take the place of the light-ship, would save the very considerable expense of her crew, and the repairs which from year to year are necessary, and involve much expense. The policy of the board is to replace, in all cases where it is possible, our light-ships by light-houses on the shoals which the former are intended to mark, being more certain in their service and involving much less expense for maintenance. The board recommends appropriations for the erection of lights at Cross Ledge, Ship John, and Bulk-head Shoals, the estimated cost of which is $125,000 each.

226. *Mahon's River, Delaware Bay.*—As was stated in the last annual report, the abrasion of the marsh in which this light-house stands is so great as to compel a change of site. There is a good location about a quarter of a mile north of the present site, which will serve equally well the purposes of navigation. If all the material can be prepared ready to commence the work of erection of the structure at the site by the 1st of July next, the whole can be completed ready for lighting by the following November. If a site and right of way can be purchased, at a moderate cost, the amount asked for by the board, viz, $15,000, will be sufficient to erect a building.

Proposed light-house, Reedy Point, Delaware Bay.—An appropriation of $3,000 for a beacon-light on this point was approved on the 3d August, 1854. The price asked by the owners for the necessary site, with the right of way, was $3,000, being the whole amount appropriated, which was allowed to revert to the Treasury, as the demands of the owners were considered unreasonable. During the last year petitions for this light have been received; but it is believed that a sixth-order lens light placed on the south end of Pea Patch Island (Fort Delaware) would serve the purpose of navigation as well. To construct a suitable structure, including the lens, will cost about $8,000, and an estimate therefor is presented.

REPAIRS.

At each of the following-named light-stations in the fourth district there have been repairs and renovations more or less extensive since the last annual report.

214. *Barnegat*, sea-coast of New Jersey, Barnegat Inlet.
215. *Tucker's Beach*, sea-coast of New Jersey, Little Egg Harbor Inlet.
216. *Absecum*, sea-coast of New Jersey, Absecum Inlet.
218. *Cape May*, sea-coast of New Jersey, entrance to Delaware Bay.
219. *Cape Henlopen*, sea-coast of Delaware, entrance to Delaware Bay.
220. *Cape Henlopen Beacon*, entrance to Delaware Bay.
221. *Delaware Breakwater*, Delaware, entrance to Delaware Bay.
223. *Maurice River*, New Jersey, mouth of River Maurice, entrance to Delaware Bay.
229. *Reedy Island*, Delaware, Delaware Bay.
230. *Christiana*, Delaware, mouth of River Christiana, Delaware Bay.
231. *Fort Mifflin*, Pennsylvania, River Delaware.
233. *Fenwick Island*, sea-coast of Delaware.

The following named light-stations in the fourth district require repairs during the ensuing year:

218. *Cape May*, sea-coast of New Jersey.
222. *Brandywine Shoal*, Delaware Bay.
223. *Maurice River*, New Jersey, Delaware Bay.
224. *Egg Island*, New Jersey, Delaware Bay.
226. *Mahon's River*, Delaware, Delaware Bay.
227. *Cohansey*, New Jersey, Delaware Bay.
228. *Bombay Hook*, Delaware, Delaware Bay.
231. *Fort Mifflin*, Pennsylvania, Delaware Bay.

The following are names of light-stations in the fourth district not mentioned elsewhere in this report:

234. *Assateague*, about two miles from the southwest point of Assateague Island, Virginia.

LIGHT-SHIPS.

217. "*Five-Fathom Bank*," *on Five-Fathom Bank, off the capes of the Delaware.*—This vessel is in excellent condition, and well adapted for the position. During the month of March she parted her moorings and drifted from her anchorage. The United States revenue steamer Colfax, while on a cruise, took her in tow and replaced her on her station. A new chain (made at the Washington navy-yard and purchased from the Navy Department) and a mushroom anchor of 4,000 pounds have been supplied, and will make her moorings more secure than before.

225. "*Cross Ledge*," *on Cross Ledge Shoal, in Delaware Bay.*—No repairs have been made on this vessel since the last annual report, and she is in good condition. She was driven from her station by the ice during the month of December, 1871, and took refuge under the Delaware Breakwater, where she remained until February 28, 1872, when she was replaced on her station. March 6th she was driven again from her anchorage and took refuge in Maurice River Cove, and was replaced on her station a few days after. The erection of a light-house, to replace the light-ship on this dangerous shoal, is strongly recommended, as will be observed elsewhere in this report.

Relief light-ship, No. —, is in good condition, and ready for service at the depot at Christiana.

FOG-SIGNALS OPERATED BY STEAM OR HOT-AIR ENGINES.

There are no fog-signals operated by steam or hot-air engines in this district.

DAY OR UNLIGHTED BEACONS.

There are no day or unlighted beacons in this district.

DEPOT.

Christiana, Delaware.—The construction of the wharves and buildings for fitting this station for a buoy-depot and a winter harbor for light-vessels, reported in operation in the last annual report, was continued until the 1st of last November. The depot consists of two wharves on Christiana River, and a large store-house for one of the wharves. This wharf extends from the front of the store-house into the river a distance of 164 feet (to 8 feet of water at ordinary low tide) by a width of 32 feet. The store-house is 50 feet by 140 feet, on plan, and two stories of 8 feet in height to the eaves of the roof. The first or lower floor is divided into two parts. The front room is 50 by 63 feet, designed for storing miscellaneous articles. The balance, 50 by 77 feet, is fitted with a coal-bin, skids for second and third class iron buoys, and space for storing spar-buoys, ballast, balls, chains, &c. This apartment has a well-constructed brick water-cistern of 5,000 gallons capacity, and is supplied by rain-water from the roof. The second story is in one room, with suitable stairway leading from first story. A railroad track from the outer end of the wharf, and two cars for transporting supplies into the building, have been supplied. The other wharf is completed, and extends from the proposed front of the building in its rear into the river a distance of 140 feet (to 8 feet water at ordinary low tide) by a width of 32 feet. The piles for the foundation of the store-house in rear of this wharf are all driven and girdage logs placed. The design for this building is in plan 50 by 150 feet, and one story of 10 feet in height to take in first-class buoys. It is recommended that an appropriation be made for its completion. To erect the building the cost is estimated at $10,000. This will provide room for storage of first-class iron buoys, which the other store-house is not designed for.

FIFTH DISTRICT.

The fifth district extends from Metomkin Inlet, Virginia, to include New River Inlet, North Carolina, and embraces part of the sea-coasts of Virginia and North Carolina, the sounds of North Carolina, Chesapeake Bay, and the Rivers James and Potomac.

Inspector.—Commodore Fabius Stanley, United States Navy.

Engineer.—Major Peter C. Hains, Corps of Engineers, brevet lieutenant-colonel, United States Army.

In this district there are—

Light-houses and lighted beacons	69
Light-ships, (in position)	1
Light-ships, (for relief)	0
Fog-signals operated by steam or hot-air engines	0
Day or unlighted beacons	100
Buoys actually in position	634
Spare buoys for relief and to supply losses	264
Tender (steam) Heliotrope, (buoy-tender)	1
Tender (steam) Tulip, for engineer's construction and repairs	1
Tender (sail) Maggie, (buoy-tender)	1
Tender (sail) Spray, engineer-tender for construction and repairs	1

The numbers preceding the names of stations correspond with the Light-House List of the Atlantic, Gulf, and Pacific Coasts of the United States, issued January 1, 1872.

237. *Cape Henry on south side of main entrance to Chesapeake Bay, Virginia.*—Under instructions from the Light-House Board, the engineer of the district visited this station and made a personal examination of the tower and keeper's dwelling, with the view of determining what repairs or alterations are necessary at the station. The tower is a frustum of an octagonal pyramid, built on a raised foundation of loose stone some 30 feet above the level of the sea. The masonry of the outside is a soft sandstone, with an inside brick cylinder, the latter having been built in 1857, at which time the station was last refitted. Of the eight faces of the tower, six of them show on the outside large cracks or openings, extending from the base upward. Four of them are apparently less dangerous than the other two, and alone would not warrant any great apprehensions of danger, but the latter, viz, those on the north and south faces, where the strength of the masonry is lessened by openings for windows, are very bad, extending from the base almost to the top of the tower. These cracks cannot be seen on the inside, on account of the brick cylinder, (which is of more recent construction than the outside masonry,) and doubtless terminate at the air-space between the outer and inner walls. At present the tower is in an unsafe condition, and there is no way of repairing the damage satisfactorily, and a new one must be built. This old tower has done good service, having been built in 1791, and is now the oldest tower on the coast south of Cape Henlopen; but it has seen its best days, and now, from age and per-

haps defective workmanship, it is in danger of being thrown down by some heavy gale.

The light is of the second order, and cannot be seen as far at sea as its importance in respect to location demands. It is undoubtedly one of the first lights, in point of importance, on the coast. A new tower should be built at this station without delay, and the light made of the first order. A good site can be had near the present location, on Government land, and materials for building purposes can be landed without difficulty. It also should be noted that the keeper's dwelling is in a dilapidated condition, and at too great a distance from the tower to insure proper attendance. It is a frame building, and is now more than thirty years old. It is too small for the number of keepers at this station, and should be enlarged. At present it affords very poor protection to the keepers from inclemency of the weather in winter. A new dwelling is an absolute necessity for this station.

It is estimated that the cost of a first-order tower, with lens, keeper's dwelling, &c., complete, will be, at this place, $85,000, and an appropriation of $50,000 is asked to commence the work.

238. "*The Thimble,*" *entrance to Hampton Roads, Virginia.*—This light-house is designated to take the place of the Willoughby Spit light-ship, which is in need of extensive repairs. It is located on the shoalest point of Horseshoe Bar, at the entrance to Hampton Roads, called "The Thimble," which is the source of great danger to vessels navigating the bay, and others coming in from sea, this being particularly the case at night, when the buoy which has heretofore marked this shoal could not be seen.

After duly advertising for bids, a contract was made August 31, 1871, with the lowest bidder to furnish the iron-work to be used in the foundation at this new light-house, but the impracticability of having it ready in time to plant the piles during the working season of that year, necessitated a delay until May of the present, the exposed locality rendering it necessary to secure a season of calm weather in order to build the platform from which the work of screwing the piles into the shoal is carried on. While the iron-work was in process of construction, the frame of the superstructure was prepared at the depot at Lazaretto Point, Maryland. The material was shipped to its destination the latter part of May, and on the 10th of June the platform completed. As was anticipated, the shoal proved to be very hard, consisting of fine compact sand, which rendered the process of screwing in the piles very slow. Further delay was experienced by the breaking of a cast-iron column used as a follower on the pile, when the top of the latter reaches nearly the level of the platform and prevents the working of the levers; and also by the breaking of one of the screws, owing to a defective casting. The damage in each case was repaired with the least loss of time practicable, and the work resumed. The last pile was planted on the 1st of August, and it is expected that this structure will be finished by October 1, 1872. This will enable the light-ship to be withdrawn, and there will then be no light-ship in service in this district. The light will be of the fourth order.

241. *Lambert's Point, on the shoal off Lambert's Point, River Elizabeth, Virginia.*—The screw-pile light-house, for which an appropriation was made by act of Congress approved March 3, 1871, was finished in May last. The original plan of a light-house on six piles was modified, in order to make use of some iron piles that were on hand. It is now a square house on five piles, and shows a red light of the fifth order. The

station is provided with a fog-bell which strikes by machinery in foggy weather every ten seconds.

245. *Deep Water Shoals, River James, Virginia.*—This light-house was painted throughout, and had other repairs made to it. The piles of the old light-house, which was destroyed by ice in 1866, were taken out and sent to the depot at Lazaretto Point, where they will be available for other works in the district or for dumb-beacons.

——. *Solomon's Lump, in Kedges Strait, between Tangier Sound and Chesapeake Bay.*—In compliance with a resolution of the House of Representatives, an examination and report to Congress was made, during the last session, upon the necessity and expediency of establishing a light to mark the shoal known as Solomon's Lump, in Kedges Strait, between Tangier Sound and Chesapeake Bay. Solomon's Lump is a point of land on the north end of Evans Island. There is a shoal that extends out a considerable distance from this point in a northerly direction, and is a source of danger to vessels navigating Kedges Strait at night. Near its extreme point is the regular channel. The shoal itself has not more than about 5 feet water on it to a point near the red buoy, which marks its extreme northerly end. At night this buoy cannot be seen a sufficient distance to be of any use. The only light in this vicinity is that on Fog Point, about one and one-fourth miles in a west-southwest direction, but, on account of its distance and location, it affords no security to vessels from going ashore on the reef off Solomon's Lump. The light at Fog Point was established in 1827, before the introduction of the screw-pile system of light-houses, and though it has served to mark the entrance to Kedges Strait for a long time, it is of little valué as compared with other positions that could have been selected for a screw-pile structure, which would not only have marked the entrance to the strait, but would have been a guide all the way through. A light established on the shoal off Solomon's Lump, near its extreme point, and in 5 feet water, or on the shoal on the opposite side of the channel would accomplish both these objects, and render navigation through Kedges Strait safe at all times. As the sailing course in either direction would be a straight line passing just north of the light-house at Solomon's Lump, in case a light was established there, that at Fog Point would be no longer of use, and could be discontinued. It would, therefore, not increase the number of lights, nor add anything to the annual cost of maintenance. An appropriation of $15,000 is, therefore, asked to establish a light-house off Solomon's Lump to take the place of that at Fog Point.

260. *Point Lookout, on the north side of the entrance to River Potomac, Maryland.*—Under instructions from the Light-House Board, the engineer of the district has commenced the work of establishing a large fog-bell on the north side of the mouth of the river Potomac, under the general appropriation for fog-signals. This is a very desirable aid to navigation, and will be equally valuable to vessels navigating the bay and river.

264. *River Choptank, opposite the entrance to the Rivers Choptank and Treadhaven, Maryland.*—A contract was made in March, 1871, for the construction of this light-house, which was not completed until the 23d of December, partly owing to the character of the foundation, which was very hard, and to the want of experience on the part of the contractor in this kind of work. The light-house stands on ten wooden piles encased in cast-iron. Six of the piles form the foundation for the light-house proper, the other four being fender-piles, serving as ice breakers. The superstructure is an hexagonal frame building, with a lantern on the top, and shows a light of the sixth order. The light-

house stands in 11 feet water, mean tide, on a shoal about one and one-half miles from Benonis Point. As soon as the light-house was completed, the light-vessel, which was formerly stationed in this vicinity, was permanently withdrawn. This station is provided with a fog-bell, struck by machinery, at intervals of ten seconds.

265. *Thomas's Point, north side of mouth of South River, Maryland.*—It will be observed by reference to the Coast Survey chart of the Chesapeake Bay that the light-house at Thomas's Point, on the north side of South River, from four miles south of entrance to Annapolis Harbor, Maryland, can serve but poorly its purpose as a warning of the dangerous shoal that makes out from it a distance of one and one-quarter miles into the bay. This light-house was built in 1825, before the introduction of the system of light-houses in the water on iron piles. Its present location is such that little use can be made of it at night, and in times of foggy or thick weather it is utterly useless. Under no circumstances can vessels drawing more than 8 feet water pass within one and a quarter miles of it, as the shoal is continuous, and has on it only that depth at the outer extremity, and less between this point and the shore. The outer extremity of the shoal is only marked by a buoy, and it is a matter of frequent occurrence to see vessels ashore here. The ineligibility of its present location is frequently a source of complaint by mariners. This is particularly the case when coming up the bay, as the course is changed twice after passing Sharp's Island, and approaching Thomas's Point.

A light-house on the point of the shoal, in 8 feet water, which will be distant from the shore about one and a quarter miles, is recommended for this place. The new light-house should be provided with a fog-bell, the want of which is another defect at the old station, as the distance from the track of vessels going up or down the bay is so great that it would be useless if put there, as it could not be heard. This station is also in a bad state of repair. The rain, in windy weather, beats through the old masonry of the tower, flooding the inside of the structure, and frequently damaging the material in charge of the keeper.

If a light-house were built at the place referred to, viz, near the outer extremity of the shoal, and provided with a fog-bell, it would supply a defect long felt by the commerce of Chesapeake Bay, and render the maintenance of an almost useless light unnecessary. It is recommended, therefore, that an appropriation be made to build a light-house on Thomas's Point Shoal, supplied with a fog-bell, to take the place of a light-house on Thomas's Point. The estimated cost is $20,000.

268. *Love Point Shoal, mouth of River Chester, Maryland.*—An appropriation of $15,000 was made last year by Congress for a light-house on the shoal at the mouth of river Chester, near the north end of Kent Island, the exact location of which was fixed at a point on the shoal in 10 feet water, mean tide, distant from the north end of Love Point about one and a quarter miles in a northeasterly direction. The light-house is a duplicate of that erected in the river Choptank. A contract was made for the construction of this work, (after public advertisement for bids,) and it was expected that the work would have been completed the fall of last year. Unforeseen delays, however, were experienced by the contractor, in consequence of which it was found necessary to defer work till the spring of the present year. The lateness of the season, and several severe gales, however, caused further delay, so that it was not finished till August 1. The light was exhibited August 15. A fog-bell, struck by machinery, at intervals of five seconds, is provided.

——. *Craighill Channel Range Beacons, Chesapeake Bay, Maryland.*—

An appropriation was made by Congress at its last session for two beacon-lights to mark the range of the channel just below the mouth of the river Patapsco, which is being widened and deepened, under appropriations by Congress. The plans are now being prepared, after which the work of building will be commenced without unnecessary delay. The range will mark a channel which is perfectly straight, has deep water, and will shorten the distance to the port of Baltimore, for large vessels, by several miles.

—— *Shipping Point, River Potomac, Virginia.*—Plans and specifications are being prepared for the small light, for which an appropriation was made, to mark the entrance to the anchorage of Shipping Point, river Potomac, Virginia. Some delay will doubtless be experienced, however, owing to the fact that an act of the State legislature will be required, ceding jurisdiction over this site before any work can be done. Steps will be taken at an early day to secure the necessary legislation in the case.

—— *A first-order light-house at or near Poyner's Hill, a point about midway between Cape Henry and Body's Island light-house, sea-coast of North Carolina.*—The attention of Congress was drawn in the last annual report to the importance of speedily establishing a light-house to illumine the dark space of forty miles on the coast of Virginia and North Carolina between Body's Island and Cape Henry.

The recommendations contained in that report are again referred to, and the earnest attention of Congress called to the importance of establishing this needful light-house. The distance from Body's Island to Cape Henry is eighty miles, of which there is an unlighted space of forty miles. The land along the coast in this vicinity is low and in many places without trees, so that even in day-time there is danger of vessels getting into unsafe proximity to the coast before becoming aware of it. This danger is enhanced by the fact that vessels bound around Cape Hatteras from the northern and eastern ports keep well to the westward, in order to avoid the strong current of the Gulf Stream, and for the additional reason they have a favorable current of about a mile an hour, nearly as far as Hatteras, and a smoother sea in bad weather; but in the absence of powerful sea-coast lights sufficiently near each other to give warning of approach to danger, many vessels ladened with valuable lives and cargoes are in danger of being lost between these points. It is now believed that the construction of this tower should be no longer delayed. A glance at the chart of the coast will show its importance. An appropriation therefor of $50,000 is accordingly submitted to commence the work.

An appropriation was made about ten years ago for this light, but the money reverted to the Treasury. The light-house should be similar to that building at Body's Island, with a focal plane 150 feet above the sea, and visible at a distance of eighteen nautical miles. It is estimated that the total cost of a first-order light-house at this place will be $95,000.

288. *Body's Island, sea-coast of North Carolina.*—After having contracted with the lowest bidders for furnishing material to be used in this structure, a working party was dispatched to build the necessary temporary quarters, store-house, roadway, &c., for landing and taking care of material. This having been done, work on the tower was commenced the latter part of November, 1871, and has steadily progressed since that time. The prevalence of storms in this vicinity has, however, retarded its progress to some extent, as was anticipated. The tower and keeper's dwelling are now well advanced toward completion. The

lantern was set in August, and the light will be exhibited for the benefit of commerce October 1, 1872.

The difficulty of landing material at this station necessitated the erection of a derrick in Roanoke Sound, in 6 feet water, at which vessels could lie and be discharged of the stone used in the foundation. This was successfully accomplished at little expense, though some delay was experienced owing to the want of promptness on the part of contractors for some of the material used in the structure. This work is built of the most substantial and durable material. It is 150 feet high, and will show a light of the first order, which can be seen about eighteen nautical miles. The base of the tower is a frustum of an octagonal pyramid, built of granite, surmounted by a brick shaft of the form of a frustum of a cone. The establishment of this light will supply a want long felt by the commerce of the country, as may be readily seen from the number of wrecks that have been strewn along the beach, from time to time, for twenty miles to the south, and the same distance north of the light-house. Efforts have been made to secure a correct list of the vessels that have gone ashore near this station, and the damage sustained by each, but up to the present time a full authentic list has not been obtained.

The following is a list of vessels that have gone ashore in this vicinity since the work of building the light-house was commenced, with such particulars as to tonnage, damage, &c., as could be ascertained:

List of vessels that have gone ashore at Body's Island, North Carolina, since the new light-house was commenced in July, 1871, as near as can be ascertained.

Name.	Class.	Tonnage.	Cargo.	Where bound.	When wrecked.
Muscovado	Brig	160	Sugar	Baltimore	July 23, 1871.
Marion	Schooner	350	Iron	Savannah, Ga	August 20, 1871.
Sarah Peters	Brig	180	Furniture, &c.	Savannah, Ga	December 13, 1871.
Baltic	Bark	360	Ballast	Saint Mary's, Fla.	February 7, 1872.
Willie	Schooner	104	Sugar	Baltimore	February 14, 1872.
	Schooner		Coal	South	March —, 1872.

The Marion escaped with a loss of $8,000; the rest were total wrecks. If $15,000 is allowed as the average value of each vessel, and $10,000 the average value of cargo, we have in less than one year, viz, from June, 1871, to March, 1872, a loss to the commerce of the country of $133,000, without taking into consideration the probable loss of life. Here is a loss of more than enough to build the light-house. Further comments on the importance of this structure, and the one (for which an appropriation is asked) between it and Cape Henry, are deemed unnecessary.

A complete record of all vessels that have gone ashore near Body's Island since the old light-house was destroyed by the confederates has been sought, but there seems to have been no authentic record kept by any of the inhabitants in the vicinity, and the information to be obtained is only vague, and to an extent unreliable, but it is well known that many valuable vessels, cargoes, and lives have been lost there every year.

299. *Roanoake Marshes, North Carolina, on the east side, and about in the middle of the narrow channel connecting Pamlico and Croatan Sounds, North Carolina.*—It was built in 1860, on what was at that time a marsh, which was dry or nearly so at low water. The foundation consists of seven wood piles covered with cast iron, the latter, when the structure

was first built, being screwed into the ground several feet. Since then the marsh has been washed away so that there are now 10 feet water at the light-house. The piles being of wood, as soon as they were exposed, by the washing away of the shoal below the depth covered by the cast-iron sleeve, were attacked by worms. In order to save the light-house from falling, three coppered piles were driven at each angle of the structure, capped by heavy squared timbers. A short time ago a raft drifted against the light-house and carried away three of the coppered piles above referred to. The house has settled some inches on the west side, and though the damage sustained by the striking of the raft has been repaired, it is not considered in a safe condition, nor can it be made so except at great expense, for which an appropriation would be necessary. It will be cheaper in the end to build a new structure, and an appropriation for this purpose is recommended. The estimated cost of a light-house near the present site, but in about 6 feet water, is $15,000.

304. *Cape Lookout, near the extremity of the Cape, North Carolina.*—The repairs and renovations authorized by act of Congress will be taken in hand without delay. They are much needed, the keeper's dwelling being in a very dilapidated condition.

REPAIRS.

During the year repairs and renovations, more or less extensive, have been made at each of the following-named light-stations in the fifth district:

235. *Hog Island*, Virginia, west point of Hog Island, Great Matchepungo Inlet.

236. *Cape Charles*, Virginia, entrance to Hampton Roads.

237. *Cape Henry*, Virginia, entrance to Hampton Roads.

240. *Craney Island*, screw-pile light-house, Virginia, mouth of river Elizabeth.

242. *Naval Hospital light*, Virginia, on wharf at Naval Hospital, river Elizabeth.

246. *Jordan's Point*, Virginia, river James.

247. *Cherrystone*, Virginia, mouth of Cherrystone Inlet, Chesapeake Bay.

248. *Back River*, Virginia, entrance to Back River.

249. *York Spit*, screw-pile light-house, Virginia, easterly end of York Spit, entrance to river York.

250. *New Point Comfort*, Virginia, entrance to Mobjack Bay, Chesapeake Bay.

251. *Wolf Trap*, screw-pile light-house, Virginia, Wolf Trap Shoal, Chesapeake Bay.

252. *Stingray Point*, Virginia, mouth of River Rappahannock, Chesapeake Bay.

253. *Windmill Point*, screw-pile light-house, Virginia, Windmill Point Shoals, Chesapeake Bay.

254. *Watt's Island*, Virginia, Tangier Sound, Chesapeake Bay.

255. *Jane's Island*, screw-pile light-house, Maryland, Tangier Sound, Chesapeake Bay.

256. *Somer's Cove*, screw-pile light-house, Maryland, Tangier Sound, Chesapeake Bay.

257. *Smith's Point*, screw-pile light-house, Virginia, mouth of River Potomac, Chesapeake Bay.

258. *Fog Point*, Maryland, Smith's Island, Chesapeake Bay.

259. *Clay Island*, Maryland, Tangier Sound, Chesapeake Bay.
260. *Point Lookout*, Maryland, entrance to River Potomac, Chesapeake Bay.
261. *Hooper's Straits*, screw-pile light-house, Maryland, off mouth of River Honga, Chesapeake Bay.
262. *Cove Point*, Maryland, mouth of River Patuxent, Chesapeake Bay.
263. *Sharp's Island*, screw-pile light-house, Maryland, mouth of River Choptank, Chesapeake Bay.
265. *Thomas's Point*, Maryland, north side of mouth of South River, Chesapeake Bay.
266. *Greenbury Point*, Maryland, mouth of River Severn, Chesapeake Bay.
267. *Sandy Point*, Maryland, Chesapeake Bay.
269. *Seven Foot Knoll*, screw-pile light-house, Maryland, mouth River Patapsco, Chesapeake Bay.
272. *Fort Carroll*, Maryland, River Patapsco.
273. *Hawkins's Point*, Maryland, River Patapsco.
275. *Leading Point*, screw-pile light-house, Maryland, River Patapsco.
276. *Lazaretto Point*, Maryland, River Patapsco.
277. *Pool's Island*, Maryland, off mouth of River Gunpowder, Chesapeake Bay.
278. *Turkey Point*, Maryland, mouth of the River Elk, head of Chesapeake Bay.
279. *Fishing Battery*, Maryland, mouth of River Susquehanna, Chesapeake Bay.
280. *Havre de Grace*, Maryland, Concord Point, mouth of River Susquehanna, Chesapeake Bay.
281. *Piney Point*, Maryland, River Potomac.
282. *Blackistone's Island*, Maryland, entrance Clement's Bay, River Potomac.
283. *Lower Cedar Point*, screw-pile light-house, Virginia, Yates's Shoal, River Potomac.
284. *Upper Cedar Point*, screw-pile light-house, Maryland, off mouth Tobacco River.
285. *Fort Washington*, Maryland, River Potomac.
286. *Jones Point*, Virginia, River Potomac, near Alexandria.
289. *Cape Hatteras*, North Carolina, Cape Hatteras.
296. *Neuse River*, North Carolina, west side of entrance to River Neuse.
297. *Pamlico Point*, North Carolina, south side of entrance to River Pamlico, Pamlico Sound.
299. *Roanoke Marshes*, screw-pile light-house, North Carolina, east side of channel connecting Pamlico and Croatan Sounds.
301. *North River*, screw-pile light-house, North Carolina, on bar at entrance to North River. A fog-bell has been placed at this station.
302. *Wade's Point*, screw-pile light-house, North Carolina, west side of River Pasquotank, Albemarle Sound.

The following are the names of the light-stations in the fifth district not mentioned elsewhere:

239. *Old Point Comfort*, Virginia, entrance to Hampton Roads.
243. *White Shoals*, Virginia, River James.
244. *Point of Shoals*, Virginia, River James.
270. *North Point*, (lower,) Maryland, entrance to River Patapsco, Chesapeake Bay.

271. *North Point*, (upper,) Maryland, River Patapsco, Chesapeake Bay.

287. *Bowler's Rock*, screw-pile light-house, Virginia, River Rappahannock.

290. *Cape Hatteras Beacon*, North Carolina, Cape Hatteras.

291. *Ocracoke*, North Carolina, entrance to Ocracoke Inlet.

292. *Southwest Point Royal Shoal*, screw-pile light-house, North Carolina, Pamlico Sound.

293. *Northwest Point Royal Shoal*, screw-pile light-house, North Carolina, Pamlico Sound.

294. *Harbor Island*, screw-pile light-house, North Carolina, between Pamlico and Core Sounds.

295. *Brant Island Shoal*, screw-pile light-house, North Carolina, Pamlico Sound.

298. *Long Shoal*, screw-pile light-house, North Carolina, east end of Long Shoal, Pamlico Sound.

300. *Croatan*, screw-pile light-house, North Carolina, Pamlico Sound.

303. *River Roanoke*, screw-pile light-house, North Carolina, near mouth of River Roanoke.

LIGHT-SHIPS.

238. "*Willoughby Spit*," entrance to Hampton Roads, Virginia.

The completion of the screw-pile light-house on "*The Thimble*" shoal will enable the board to remove this light-ship on the 1st of October next. This is the only light-ship in the fifth district.

FOG-SIGNALS OPERATED BY STEAM OR HOT-AIR ENGINES.

There are no fog-signals operated by steam or hot-air engines in this district.

DAY OR UNLIGHTED BEACONS.

Names and positions of the day or unlighted beacons in the fifth district:

Smith's Point, port side of mouth of River Potomac, old tower.

Bodkin's Point, south side of mouth of River Patapsco, old tower.

Day's Point, half a mile from Day's Point, River James, iron shaft with cage on top.

Woodstock, entrance into Bell's Bay, &c., North Carolina.

Hunting Quarter, Core Sound, mid-channel, spar with barrel.

Wilson's Bay, Core Sound, mid-channel, spar with barrel.

Piney Point, Core Sound, mid-channel, two spars with barrels.

Yellow Shoal, Core Sound, mid-channel, spar with barrel.

There are, besides the above-named beacons, forty stake-beacons planted to mark channels in Core Sound and other places.

DEPOTS.

Lazaretto Point, River Patapsco, Maryland.—A large number of spar-buoys were manufactured to supply the places of those lost or rendered unserviceable in the northern part of the district. The stone sea-wall was repaired, and the place put in good condition. During the winter the frame-work of the screw-pile light-houses was prepared here.

Portsmouth, Virginia.—The buoy depot at Portsmouth, Virginia, was finished about seven months ago, and it is now in full working order.

It is in good condition, well kept, and admirably adapted to its purposes; a great saving to the Government not only in rents, but in protection to public property.

SIXTH DISTRICT.

The sixth district extends from New River Inlet, North Carolina, to and including Cape Canaveral light-house, Florida, and embraces part of the coast of North Carolina, the coasts of South Carolina and Georgia, and part of the coast of Florida.

Inspector.—Captain Richard T. Renshaw, United States Navy, until January 18, 1872; Commander Charles S. Norton, United States Navy, present inspector.

Engineer.—Major Peter C. Hains, United States Engineers, brevet lieutenant-colonel, United States Army.

In this district there are:

Light-houses and lighted beacons, (including those in process of construction,)	36
Light-ships	4
Fog-signals operated by steam or hot-air engines	0
Day or unlighted beacons	43
Buoys actually in position	224
Spar-buoys, (for relief and to supply losses)	22
Tenders (steam) Alanthus (buoy-tender) and Dandelion, (used in engineer's constructions and repairs)	2
Tender (sail) Mignonette, (used in engineer's constructions and repairs)	1

The numbers preceding the names of the stations correspond with those given in the "List of Light-Houses, Lighted Beacons, and Floating Lights of the Atlantic, Gulf, and Pacific Coasts of the United States," published January 1, 1872.

307. *Oak Island beacons, at the south entrance to River Cape Fear, North Carolina.*—These beacons mark the range over the bar at the Oak Island entrance to river Cape Fear. They are, however, badly located, being so near each other that considerable deviation from the true course is necessary to make them appear to separate. The front beacon is an open-frame frustum of a square pyramid resting on a rail tramway, which allows of its being moved to the right or left, to suit the changes in the channel. The rear light is placed on a wooden tower, immediately over the center of the keeper's dwelling. The shore-line at this place, as at many others on the southern coast, is not permanent, being washed away by the abrasive action of the sea. The latter has gradually encroached upon the land, till at present the high-water mark is only a few feet from the front beacon, which renders it in imminent danger of being destroyed in any southeasterly gale. The two beacons being already so close together as to have their usefulness seriously impaired, the front beacon cannot be moved back any farther. To move both would be an expensive undertaking at this place, and would necessitate the discontinuance, for a time, of the lights; besides, there is no appropriation available. It would be more satisfactory, and doubtless cheaper in the end, to build two new frame beacons detached from the keeper's dwelling. The present ones could then remain as they now are until the new ones are established. By this means the change would cause no inconvenience to commerce, and such locations and relative elevation could be given them as would make them much more useful than they now are.

It is very important that this range be well maintained, as the channel which it marks is the most reliable, permanent, and the deepest of the several entrances to River Cape Fear. An appropriation of $4,000 is therefore asked to re-establish the range.

314. *Morris Island range-beacon, (rear,) south end of Morris Island, South Carolina.*—There are two beacons on Morris Island, both of which are very low. They answer their purpose very well, however, so far as marking the line of range for crossing the bar of the main ship or "Pumpkin Hill Channel" into Charleston Harbor; but it is highly important, also, that one of these beacons should be made to answer the purpose, in addition, of a sea-coast light. This cannot be done by using either of the present towers. The front beacon has on it a light which can be seen from any direction at sea; the rear one has only a small angle of visibility, being intended only to mark a range-line. The former can only be seen at the level of the sea at a distance of five miles, or, estimated from the deck of a vessel 15 feet above the level of the sea, a distance of nine and a half miles; and the light being only of the fifth order, and red, is not visible at this distance, except on very clear nights.

Previous to the war, there was a sea-coast tower and light at this station, and the same reasons that existed for establishing it then, exist still. It will be observed, by reference to the chart, that along the coast, from Cape Romain to the River Saint John continuous shoals extend out from the main-land to a considerable distance, in many places reaching out as far as six and seven miles. Timely warning of their proximity is necessary for the safety of the lives and cargoes of the large number of vessels that pass them. This can only be given by the establishment of sea-coast lights, or by placing light-ships outside of them. The latter is by far the most expensive plan, besides being open to serious objections. The present light, owing to want of sufficient range, leaves a dark space on the South Carolina coast, between it and Hunting Island, which should be lighted. This can and should be done by making a new rear tower on Morris Island, 150 feet above the sea, and establishing on it a first-order sea-coast light. It is estimated that the cost of making this change would be $85,000, for which an appropriation is asked.

316. *Sullivan's Island range-beacons, Charleston Harbor, South Carolina.*—An appropriation was made by act of Congress approved March 3, 1871, for range-beacons to guide into Charleston Harbor, after passing the bar of the main ship-channel. At the date of last report plans and specifications were prepared, but, owing to certain laws of the State of South Carolina, a satisfactory title to a site on Sullivan's Island could not be obtained without further legislation on the part of the State. As this would have caused considerable delay, and might not have been obtained after all, and as, under the act approved July 12, 1870, the appropriation would revert to the Treasury at the end of the fiscal year, application was made to the War Department for permission to establish the beacons on the land held by the Government at Fort Moultrie. This permission was given, but the location was hardly as good as might have been obtained elsewhere, under more favorable circumstances. So far, however, as its value to commerce is concerned, the range is a good one. The front beacon is a frame structure resting on the parapet of the fort. The rear one is an open-frame square pyramid. The keeper's dwelling is detached. The beacons and dwelling were finished in June, and the lights exhibited July 15. On the same night the light of the Weehawken light-ship was discontinued, and, a few days after, the vessel was withdrawn.

The "Weehawken," light-ship marked the wreck of the monitor of that name; this obstruction has been partially removed, and the remainder, it is reported, has sunk deeply into the sand. The lights of the Sullivan's Island range are red. Besides marking the range from Pumpkin Hill Bar, they mark a good range over the Southwest Bar, so that vessels coming up from southerly ports can enter Charleston Harbor at night, without the necessity of going up to the main ship-channel, thereby saving a run of several miles.

317. *Fort Sumter Beacon, Charleston Harbor, South Carolina.*—This beacon formerly stood on the east face of Fort Sumter, but on account of the meliorations that are being made in the fort it became necessary to remove it to the center of the southwest face. The beacon was also in need of considerable repairs. The change of position and repairs were made from the general appropriation for repairs and incidental expenses of light-houses.

——. *Light-house on or near Hunting Island, entrance to Saint Helena Sound, South Carolina.*—An appropriation was made by act of Congress for a second-order light-house at or near Hunting Island. Under the law governing this appropriation, the light-house site must be selected from lands now owned by the Government. A personal examination was recently made of the locality by the district engineer. There are only two positions that give suitable sites for this light-house, one on the north side of Saint Helena Sound, on Edisto Island, near the southern extremity, and the other at a point some distance south of the site of the former light-house on Hunting Island. It is understood, however, that the Government does not own any land on Edisto Island. In this case it will be necessary to place the light on Hunting Island, where it is known the Government does own land. The objection to this side of Saint Helena Sound lies in the fact that the island is being washed away by the abrasive action of the sea upon its low banks. A survey was made, under the direction of the district engineer, of the north end of the island, from which it appears that about one hundred and fifty acres of this portion of the island have been washed away, the present shore-line having receded about half a mile from its position as given by the Coast-Survey chart of 1869. There is deep water now where at that time there was dry land. The Government formerly owned a tract of fifty acres of that portion of the island which has been washed away. Owing to the danger to which a light-house site on the north end of Hunting Island will be subjected, and the provisions of the act which make it necessary to select a site on land owned by the Government, it will perhaps be necessary to erect such a structure as could be removed in case of necessity to some other place. An iron light-house would answer this purpose, but an additional appropriation will be necessary to complete the work. An appropriation of $50,000 is accordingly asked, and the light should be of the first instead of the second order, as named in the last appropriation bill.

321. *Tybee light-station, Tybee Island, entrance to River Savannah, Georgia.*—The recommendation contained in the last annual report is again made. As then stated, the tower is not in a safe condition, owing to the damage it sustained in the cyclone of 1871. This tower is very old, having been built in 1793. It is a frustum of an octagonal pyramid, built of Savannah brick. Five of its faces show dangerous cracks. As stated in a previous report, its great age, and neglect during the war, render it impracticable to properly repair it. An appropriation of $50,000 is therefore asked to commence the building of a new structure. This can be done without delay on Government land near the site of the present tower.

323. *Tybee Knoll, River Savannah, Georgia.*—A light-ship is now stationed off Tybee Knoll, in the River Savannah, which could readily be dispensed with in case a screw-pile light-house was built at this place. An appropriation was made by Congress for this purpose, but reverted to the Treasury under the operation of the act approved July 12, 1870.

A screw-pile light-house will serve the purposes of navigation quite as well as the light-ship, and the expense of maintenance will be considerably lessened. Borings were made more than a year ago, to determine the character of the foundation; it was found to be soft mud to a depth of 19 feet. A light-house on five or six hollow cast-iron piles, with large flanges to give bearing, could be built at very little more than the usual cost of such structures. Its erection would insure the permanent removal of the light-ship, which is now in need of extensive repairs. It is estimated that the cost of this light-house will be $18,000, and an appropriation of this amount is recommended.

——. *Daufuskie Island range-beacons, Calibogue Sound, South Carolina.*—As stated in the last annual report, plans and specifications were prepared, and the securing of proper sites was only necessary in order to commence the work. The sites were selected on the northeastern end of Daufuskie Island; in the aggregate, they amount to five acres. The investigation of the title was intrusted to the United States district attorney for the district in which the land lies, but, owing to the difficulty of procuring information bearing on this subject, and to the loss of records during the war, considerable delay was experienced. It was not until June 13 that the district attorney reported on its validity, which report was approved by the Attorney-General of the United States on the 3d of August. No further delay is now apprehended, and it is proposed to let out the work by contract without delay. The front beacon is to be an open-frame structure; the rear one, a small tower built on the keeper's dwelling. The lights will be of the fifth order, both white.

——. *Day-beacons in the River Savannah, Georgia.*—The four day-beacons on Jones's and Long Islands, which were built entirely of wood, were destroyed by the burning of the high marsh-grass. They were rebuilt without delay, and the precaution was taken to have the grass cut in the vicinity. It would be more economical, however, to use iron beacons, which would not be subject to this danger. The estimated cost of four such beacons to replace the frame ones is $2,500, and an appropriation for this purpose is asked.

——. *Light on the obstructions in River Savannah, Georgia.*—It is proposed to extinguish this light as soon as the obstructions are removed by the Engineer Department of the Army. It is expected that this work will be accomplished during the present season.

326. *Fig Island, on the east end of Fig Island, River Savannah, Georgia.*—A new landing was built at this station, as the old one had rotted away. The house had other repairs made, and was painted throughout.

331. *Saint Simon's light-station, north side of the entrance to Saint Simon's Sound, Georgia.*—This light-house, which was contracted for in the fall of 1869, was delayed from various causes, the death of the contractor and one of his bondsmen (each while successively superintending the work) being the main cause. At date of last report the tower was 51 feet high. It was then taken in hand by the surviving bondsman, and by him the work has been completed. The tower is built of brick, of the form of a frustum of a cone, focal plane 108 feet above the sea-level, and will show a fixed light of the third order, varied by flashes alternately red and white, the interval between the

flashes being one minute. The light was exhibited for the first time on the night of September 1, 1872.

333, 334. *Amelia Island north range-beacons, at entrance to Fernandina Harbor, Florida.*—The work on this range was commenced in December, 1871, and finished in May, 1872. The rear light is mounted on the keeper's dwelling, and the front one on an open-frame square pyramid, which rests on a tramway, and can be moved to the right or left, to conform to the changes in the bar which are generally effected after a severe northeasterly or southeasterly gale. The lights at this station were exhibited June 1, 1872.

338. *Dame's Point screw-pile light-house, off Dame's Point, River Saint John, Florida.*—This structure was framed at the workshops at Lazaretto Point, Maryland, during the winter, and the iron-work prepared under contract. In March, 1872, a working party was dispatched to erect the structure, which was completed in June. The light-house stands on a shoal in 8 feet of water. It is built on six wood piles, with cast-iron sleeves, and has two fender-piles, one up and the other down stream. The light, which is fixed white, was exhibited July 15, 1872.

339. *Saint Augustine light-house, north end of Anastasia Island, Florida.*—A site for this light-house, for which an appropriation was made by Congress, was selected about half a mile from the old tower. The lot consists of five acres.

Considerable difficulty and delay were experienced in procuring a valid title and complying with the necessary legal forms incident to the purchase of land by the Government, in consequence of which, work on the tower was not commenced until late in the spring. Borings were made to test the character of the foundation, which was found to be fine sand with some loam, to a depth of about 15 feet, where loose coquina shell was encountered, underlying which is a stratum of compact coquina, called, in this section of the country, *coquina rock*, but of such character as to be totally unfit to enter into the construction of a light-house.

Previous to commencing work on the tower it was necessary to build a wharf and store-sheds, and temporary quarters for the men; also a tramway for moving with facility the material from the landing to the site. Contracts were made, after public advertisement, with the lowest bidders for furnishing the iron and brick. The latter have all been delivered, and there are now at the site sufficient brick to complete the work. All the iron-work is on the way. Unfortunately, the last appropriation was so small that operations may have to be suspended by December for want of funds. The foundation of the tower was finished July 29, 1872, and the tower is now several feet above the ground. The base is to be an octagonal pyramid, on which will rest a frustum of a cone. It will be 150 feet high, and show a light of the first order. There is no good building-sand in this locality, and it has to be procured at a distance and transported to the site. This is a source of additional expense, but one absolutely necessary to insure good work.

Observations show that the water has again commenced washing away the shore. At date of last report, high-water mark was 48 feet from the corner of the old tower; it is now about 35 feet distant. It is desirable, therefore, as the old tower may be destroyed at an early day, that this work be finished with as little delay as practicable, and an appropriation of $25,000 is asked for this purpose. This amount is necessary to complete the work.

——. *Mosquito Inlet, east coast of Florida.*—In common with all the inlets and harbors on the east coast of Florida, this bar shifts constantly, so that no soundings can be relied on. The general effect of westerly winds is to reduce the depth of water, and that of northeasterly gales to increase it; thus the inlet may be opened or closed one or more times each year. The wrecks lying on or near the bar give a practical illustration of the uncertainty of the channel. For all practical purposes of construction of a light-house, it may, however, be safely assumed that the material can be delivered without any very serious difficulty or delay, although additional expense would be incurred by reason of the remoteness of the station, and the small-sized vessels that would be required for transportation. As regards the necessity of a light at this point, it is manifest that the commerce passing through the inlet would not justify an expenditure by the United States for a light for merely local purposes, or at least that there are other points that may justly take precedence of it. But a light-house between Saint Augustine and Cape Canaveral lights is necessary, as one of a system of coast lights, and Mosquito Inlet is undoubtedly the proper site, as, in the first place, the light there would answer the double purpose of a harbor and coast guide, and in the second, for a landing-place, both for the original construction and subsequent supply and inspection, which could be made with more safety and certainty there than at any other point along the open-sea beach. A tower 150 feet high, lighted by a first-order Fresnel lens, is recommended for this position, and for the commencement of its construction an estimate of $60,000 is submitted.

REPAIRS.

At each of the following-named light-stations in the sixth district there have been repairs and renovations, more or less extensive, during the last year, viz:

310. *Cape Romain.*—Raccoon Key, South Carolina.

313, 314. *Morris Island range-lights*, entrance to Charleston Harbor, South Carolina.

317. *Fort Sumter*, Charleston Harbor, South Carolina.

318. *Castle Pinckney*, Charleston Harbor, South Carolina.

319. *Combahee Bank*, entrance to Saint Helena Sound, South Carolina.

321, 322. *Tybee light and beacon*, Tybee Island, Georgia.

324. *Cockspur*, River Savannah, Georgia.

325. *Oyster-Beds Beacons*, River Savannah, Georgia.

326. *Fig Island*, River Savannah, Georgia.

327, 328, *Sapelo light and beacon*, entrance to Doboy Sound, Georgia.

329, 330, *Wolf Island*, entrance to Doboy Sound, Georgia.

332. *Little Cumberland Island*, entrance to Saint Andrew's Sound, Georgia.

335, 336. *Amelia Island light and beacon*, Saint Mary's Bar, Fernandina, Florida.

337. *River Saint John*, south side of entrance to Jacksonville, Florida.

The following are the names of light-stations in the sixth district not mentioned elsewhere:

305. *Federal Point*, New Inlet, River Cape Fear, North Carolina.

309. *Georgetown*, entrance to Winyaw Bay, South Carolina.

311. *Bull's Bay*, Bull's Island, South Carolina.

340. *Cape Canaveral*, on northeast pitch of cape, east coast of Florida.

LIGHT-SHIPS.

"Frying-Pan Shoals," off Cape Fear, North Carolina.—This vessel was taken from her station on the 2d of June, 1872, and sent to Wilmington, North Carolina, where she is undergoing extensive repairs. Her place is supplied temporarily by Relief No. 32.

"Rattlesnake Shoal," off Charleston Harbor, South Carolina.—The present vessel on this station was placed on this station September 11, 1871. She has received no repairs and requires none; is a new vessel, and is in very good condition.

"Weehawken," entrance to Charleston Harbor, South Carolina.—The vessel lately on this station was placed in position over the wreck of the Monitor Weehawken June 23, 1865. Her general condition is good. The wreck having been removed by the Engineer Department of the Army, and range-lights having been established on Sullivan's Island to mark the main ship-channel, the light-ship was removed July 15, 1872.

"Martin's Industry," off Port Royal, South Carolina.—The vessel now on this station was placed on her present station September 1, 1871, having been thoroughly repaired at Charleston, South Carolina, in August, 1871. She is in good condition.

"Tybee," on Tybee Island Knoll, mouth of River Savannah, Georgia.—This vessel has been on the station for over three years, or since June, 1869. No repairs have been made since, except new standing rigging. Her general condition is very bad, and she is not worth repairs. A small screw-pile light-house should take the place of this light-ship, being more economical in maintenance, and to save the very considerable expense of her necessary repairs.

Relief No. 30.—This vessel was taken from Rattlesnake Shoal and condemned as unfit for service, in August, 1871. By authority of the Secretary of the Treasury, after removing everything from her of value to the light-house establishment, she was sold at public auction for $916, and the amount was turned into the Treasury.

Relief No. 32.—This vessel was stationed at Charleston, South Carolina, as a relief light-ship, until June, 1872, when she was placed on Frying-Pan Shoals, till the proper light-ship for that station can be repaired. She will require a new gang of rigging before winter; otherwise, her condition is good.

FOG-SIGNALS OPERATED BY STEAM OR HOT-AIR ENGINES.

There are no fog-signals operated by steam or hot-air engines, in this district.

DAY OR UNLIGHTED BEACONS.

The following is a list of the unlighted beacons in the sixth district:

Bald Head, mouth of the river Cape Fear, old tower, discontinued on the establishment of Frying-Pan Shoal light-vessel.

Price's Creek, River Cape Fear, discontinued during the rebellion, not relighted.

Campbell's Island, River Cape Fear, discontinued during the rebellion, brick house, with iron lantern.

Orton's Point, River Cape Fear, discontinued during the rebellion, open frame beacon.

Fort Point, Georgetown, South Carolina, discontinued during the rebellion.

Battery Light, (White Point Garden,) iron spindle, light discontinued during the rebellion.

Cape Romain, old tower, near present light-house.

Savannah City Beacon, iron spindle, light discontinued during the rebellion.

River Saint John, Florida, old tower.

Dumb-Beacons at Oyster Rocks, River Savannah, near Cockspur Island, iron-pile beacons.

River Savannah day-marks.

River Saint John, Florida, wooden piles.

DEPOT.

Fort Johnston, Charleston Harbor, South Carolina.—The wharf at this depot is in a very dilapidated state. Many of the piles have been eaten away by the worms. Repairs of a temporary nature have been made, but it will be necessary to secure another site, as the present one is too much exposed to northerly winds, which render it frequently impossible, for days at a time, for vessels to lie there; and even in calm weather there is danger in getting to and from it, on account of the eddies in the current, and the proximity of the stone jettces thrown out to protect the shore from the abrasive action of the sea.

SEVENTH DISTRICT.

The seventh district extends from (but does not include) Cape Canaveral to, and including, Cedar Keys, Florida.

Inspector.—Commander C. A. Babcock, United States Navy, to April 13, 1872; Commander Albert Kautz, United States Navy, present inspector.

Engineer.—Lieutenant-Colonel C. E. Blunt, Corps of Engineers, brevet colonel, United States Army.

In this district there are:

Light-houses	11
Light-ships	0
Fog-signals, operated by steam or hot-air engines	0
Day or unlighted beacons	53
Buoys actually in position	99
Spare buoys for relief and to supply losses	60
Tender (steam) Arbutus, (employed by the engineer in construction and repairs)	1
Tender (sailing-schooner, buoy-tender) Florida	1

The numbers preceding the names of stations correspond with those of the Light-House List of the Atlantic, Gulf and Pacific Coasts of the United States, issued January 1, 1872.

344. *Alligator Reef, Florida Reefs.*—The preparations for the erection of the new iron-pile light-house, of the first order, on this reef, have been continued and completed. These preparations consist in the construction at Indian Key, the selected depot, (being four miles from the reef and the nearest land,) of a building for quarters for mechanics and laborers, with a capacious cistern, and ample storage-room in the cellar, a smithery and a large shed for the iron-work and other material for the light-house, whence it can be transported as wanted to the reef. A fuel-wharf has also been built, adjoining which the coal for the tender and other purposes is stored. The temporary platform on the site of the light-house has also been finished.

The piles, foundation-disks, and first section of the light-house were delivered at Indian Key by the contractor, in January, 1872, and the remainder of the work at the close of the year. The steam-engine for hoisting pile-driver hammers, and other purposes, the pile-driver shears, forges, &c., &c., were also received in January.

The site selected is at the northeast end of the reef, about 30 yards from the site of the day-beacon "C;" the position is an excellent one, and the foundation found, by boring and driving test-rods into the coral, to be very good. The work of erection of the light-house has now been fairly commenced, and will be prosecuted as rapidly as possible until the available funds are exhausted.

Three foundation-disks have been accurately placed, and the center and northwest piles have been driven. The average penetration of these piles into the coral, the 2,000-pound hammer falling 18 feet average, was 1 inch per blow.

The funds will not be sufficient to complete the structure, and an additional appropriation of $25,000 is asked for.

347. *Key West.*—A new lantern has been made and shipped to this station, and will be erected at an early day.

REPAIRS.

At each of the following-named light-stations in the seventh district there have been repairs, more or less extensive, during the last year.

342. *Cape Florida*, coast of Florida.

243. *Cary's Fort Reef*, Florida Reefs.

351. *Egmont Key*, Tampa Bay, Florida.

352. *Seahorse Key*, Cedar Keys, Florida.

The following are the names of lights in the seventh district not otherwise mentioned:

341. *Jupiter Inlet*, between Jupiter Inlet and Gilbert's Bar, Florida.

344. *Alligator Reef*, Florida Reefs, Florida.

345. *Dry Bank*, off Dry Bank, near Coffin's Patches and Sombrero Key, Florida Reefs, Florida.

346. *Sand Key*, Florida Reefs, Florida.

347. *Key West Harbor-light*, on Key West Island, Florida.

348. *Northwest Passage*, Key West, Florida.

349. *Dry Tortugas*, on Loggerhead Key, Florida.

350. *Dry Tortugas Harbor*, on Fort Jefferson, on Garden Key, one of the Tortugas group, Florida.

LIGHT-SHIPS.

There are no light-ships in this district.

FOG-SIGNALS OPERATED BY STEAM OR HOT-AIR ENGINES.

There are no fog-signals operated by steam or hot-air engines in this district.

DAY OR UNLIGHTED BEACONS.

Florida Reef beacons.—Four new iron day-beacons, marking the line of the Florida Reefs, have been erected, viz: "E" on Coach Reef, "F" on Pickle's Reef, "C" on French Reef, and "P" on Fowey Rocks, the latter a very important one. During the next year the erection of these important aids to navigation will be continued as rapidly as the other necessary works in the district will permit.

DEPOT.

Egmont Key, Tampa Bay, Florida.—This depot is situated in the seventh district, was built by the engineer of the eighth district, having been commenced and finished during the year. The building is of wood, stands on thirty-three piles, and is 30 feet by 60 feet on the outside. A tramway provided with a car, on a platform 208 feet long and 6 feet wide, which is supported by palmetto piles, connects it with the wharf. The wharf, 20 by 60 feet, built on palmetto piles, was constructed in 16 feet of water on the outer edge. These piles were procured on the key. The depot stands on the east side of the key, a small island two and a half miles long by a quarter of a mile broad. It is provided with twenty-eight wooden rollers, each two feet long and one foot in diameter, which materially assist in the handling of the buoys. The building is of the most substantial character, and was put up entirely by hired labor.

EIGHTH DISTRICT.

The eighth light-house district extends from Cedar Keys, Florida, to the Rio Grande, Texas, and embraces a part of the Gulf coast of Florida, and the coasts of Alabama, Mississippi, Louisiana, and Texas.

Inspector.—Commander William P. McCann, United States Navy, until September 5, 1871; Commander Robert Boyd, United States Navy, present inspector.

Engineer.—J. H. Simpson, Colonel, Corps of Engineers, brevet brigadier-general, United States Army.

Assistant Engineer.—Captain A. N. Damrell, Corps of Engineers, brevet major, United States Army.

In this district there are:

Lights and lighted beacons	48
Light-ships, (in position)	1
Light-ships, (for relief)	0
Fog-signals operated by steam or hot-air engines	2
Day or unlighted beacons	15
Buoys actually in position	106
Spare buoys for relief and to supply losses	147
Tenders (steam) Geranium, (buoy-tender) Ivy, (used in engineer's constructions and repairs)	2
Tender (sail) Magnolia, (used in engineer's constructions and repairs)	1

The numbers preceding the names of stations correspond with those of the List of Light-Houses, Lighted Beacons, and Floating Lights of the Atlantic, Gulf, and Pacific Coasts of the United States, issued January, 1872.

353. *Saint Marks, Florida.*—The light-house is in very good condition generally, but the engineer reports the land in front of the house as washing away, and though the building is in no imminent danger, it is threatened with peril from very heavy storms.

354. *Dog Island, Saint George's Sound, Florida.*—The brick tower is in a very precarious situation from wearing of the beach. It has been expected for several years that the first heavy gale from the southeast would undermine and overturn it. Some time ago the precaution was taken of driving a triple row of piles about six feet long in a circle around the foundation, at a distance from its outside of about ten feet,

en the piling and the tower to the depth of about :ete, with a smooth cement surface on top. A storm o washed away the sand on the south side nearly to les, tore some of them out, and broke up the con· ıs undermined on this side and settled, so that now south, about one foot out of the perpendicular. It 'or some time by correcting the fault of inclination, the base and concreting as before, only carrying both o a greater depth. But as it would eventually be encroachments of the sea, it is considered better to and lens from the tower and place them on the hich is on screw-piles and farther from the beach s will be done, and it will be necessary to strengthen al iron braces, of which this building is destitute. will require $2,500, and the arrangement ought to ı number of years, except in case of some extraor-

's Bay, Florida.—Between Cape San Blas and Pensa· xtent of one hundred and twenty miles of unlighted erefore recommended that there be established a the entrance of Saint Andrew's Bay, thirty miles an Blas. It would not only be useful as a coast to the entrance of Saint Andrew's Bay, a very fine The light-house would probably be of the ordinary though a critical examination of the ground might ı of a small brick or iron tower as more preferable. ; plan might finally be selected, the cost would be an appropriation of $22,000 is asked for.

' Pensacola Bay, Florida.—Preparations are in pro· establishment of six day beacons, consisting simply to piles, bound together by three iron bolts to each with sheet-zinc on their tops, the center pile pro- ıers and surmounted by a barrel. They are to serve ı in Santa Maria de Galvaez and Blackwater Bays, ola Bay, the Board having authorized their con· of these six beacons is estimated at $606. The trict has recommended the establishment of two rs; one to be a fifth-order screw-pile structure, in White's Point, near the mouth of Santa Maria de econd to be a fifth-order light placed on the keeper's the point of land opposite Pierce's Point, at the Bay, and a little over eleven nautical miles from the

off Mobile Harbor, Alabama.—A temporary frame der lens, erected to replace a brick tower destroyed ts at this station, but is in danger of destruction by f the sea, making it highly desirable that the new speedily completed. Indeed, it is on this account been twice removed back from the water. The 's south of the mouth of Mobile Bay and is merely ıt four hundred acres in extent, constantly changing w tower has been located in what is, apparently, of the island. During the previous fiscal year the d by the construction of a wharf and pier over 1,000 ued early in the present fiscal year by the erection orkmen and store-rooms, but the work was checked by illness of employés from malarial complaints. The foundation, consisting of a double course of sill timbers resting on one hundred and seventy-one piles and overlaid with a depth of 12 feet of concrete, was put down. At the close of the present year, the tower had reached a height of 9 feet 6 inches above the grade line, and is progressing rapidly. It is to be a conical brick shaft, the well containing the iron stairway being also of conical form, with a height of focal plane of 125 feet above the grade line, to be provided with a lens of the second order. The granite-work about the entrance and windows is taken from the ruins of the old tower. Plans and estimates have been made for a double frame dwelling of two stories. Sand Island beacons, Nos. 1 and 2, were entirely destroyed during the war. A previous report recommended their re-establishment as soon as the new light would be in operation. The object of the first, taken in connection with the main light, is to range vessels over the outer bar, and if the second, taken in connection with beacon No. 1, to form a range which shall prevent vessels from getting on the west bank to the northward of Sand Island. The shipping interests of Mobile strongly urge the re-establishment of these minor lights. Inasmuch as the present appropriation is inadequate to complete even the tower, not counting the cost of keeper's dwelling, and the two beacons, an appropriation of $20,000 is asked for.

360. *Mobile Point, entrance to Mobile Harbor, Alabama.*—A temporary light-house, standing on the southwest bastion of Fort Morgan, now marks the entrance to Mobile Bay, but is about to be replaced by a fourth-order iron tower 30 feet in height from base to focal plane, and, like the temporary frame, will stand on the same bastion, giving the light an elevation of 45 feet above the sea level. During the past fiscal year a neat and substantial frame dwelling of four rooms was added to the old one-room house of the keeper. The wharf at the fort was extended and repaired in conjunction with the Engineer Department of the Army, nine iron screw-piles from abandoned light-houses of another district and masses of brick for riprapping from the ruins of the old Sand Island tower being used for the purpose. The extinguished beacons Nos. 3 and 4 are recommended to be re-established. The two together will range the east bank in the same manner that Sand Island beacons will range the west bank. In addition, No. 4, in connection with the main light, will range the channel northwest one-half north, and guide vessels to clear the Middle Ground. Both these beacons, like those at Sand Island, are highly important to the commercial interests of Mobile. It is believed that on the completion of the tower funds sufficient for the erection of the beacons will remain on hand.

——. *Mobile Bay range-lights, Alabama.*—Six temporary beacons to mark the channel over Dog River and Choctaw Pass Bars were authorized and put up during the year. Two are on shore, being elevated on poles, and those in the water on wooden piles, and all lighted by ordinary lanterns. The General Government and the State are both now engaged in increasing the depth and extending the length of the channel, so that it will ultimately be about 45,000 feet long. On its completion a different arrangement of the beacons will be necessary, and when the change is required, it would be highly advisable to alter at the same time the present style of temporary beacons to a more durable form of structure when the time for making the alteration draws near. The lighting of the beacons is now cared for by a party under contract, but it is intended to place it in charge of the keeper of Battery Gladden light-house, using one of the launches belonging to the Light-House Establishment, and the additional assistance of two sailors. By this system a considerable sum can be saved yearly.

361. *Battery Gladden, Mobile Bay, Alabama.*—The light-house marking the entrance to Mobile Harbor was undertaken and finished during the year. The light replaces an extinguished one that stood on Choctaw Point, at the west side of the mouth of river Mobile, and is a frame dwelling on five wrought-iron screw-piles, surmounted by a fourth-order lantern, of the general design for screw-pile light-houses. The site is an artificial island made by the confederates during the civil war as a defensive work for the city of Mobile, and lies at the head of Mobile Bay, five-eighths of a mile east of Choctaw Point. The iron and wood work, prepared by contract at the North, and the building, was put up by hired labor; the work commencing in December, 1871, by erecting a temporary wharf and workmen's quarters, was furnished March 11, 1872, and lighted for the first time the 8th of April following.

——. *Horn Island, Mississippi Sound, Mississippi.*—The establishment of a light at the eastern end of Horn Island is recommended as being necessary toward the completion of aids to navigation in Mississippi Sound. It is much needed both in the navigation of the sound and in the use of Horn Island Pass from the Gulf to the sound. The light-house should be of the ordinary screw-pile character, and would require an appropriation of $22,000.

366. *Cat Island, Mississippi Sound, Mississippi.*—All material for the screw-pile light-house at this station was shipped from the North and delivered to Cat Island July, 1871. Malarial illness prostrated many of the laborers, and seriously retarded the work. The building is of the ordinary form of screw-pile light-houses, square in plan, and supported on five piles. It was lighted for the first time December 15, 1871. The illuminating apparatus is a fifth-order Fresnel lens, showing a fixed white light, varied by flashes, and has its focal plane 45 feet above the mean level of Mississippi Sound.

369. *Saint Joseph's Island, Mississippi Sound, Mississippi.*—The light-house, a substantial wooden structure, resting on five wooden piles, situated 300 feet north of the most southerly point of the island, a low, marshy plat of land, about half a mile long, and not 400 feet wide in the broadest part, about eight acres in extent, elevated only 3 feet above low water, is in danger of destruction from the abrasion of the eastern shore of the island by the action of the waves. It had been previously attempted to preserve the light-house by a riprapping of 120 tons of brick from the old Cat-Island tower, and spreading thereon 54 cubic yards of concrete, but this proving insufficient, it is now proposed to build a breakwater around from the north to the south sides, about 275 feet in length, as the only economical means of protecting it. The breakwater will be of palmetto piles, (the only kind of wood which resists the attack of the sea-worm in this latitude,) bound on its inner and outer faces with string-pieces, and securely braced at intervals of 12 feet with palmetto logs, abutting against piles of the same. A contract to build the breakwater at the rate of $13 per foot has been submitted and approved by the board, and the work is to be completed not later than the 1st of February next.

373. *Point aux Herbes, Lake Pontchartrain, Louisiana.*—A fifth-order light has been authorized, but the site for the purpose has not yet been secured. Plans and estimates have been prepared, preparatory to commencing work as soon as the purchase of the site shall have been effected. The light-house will be a wooden building 28 feet square, surmounted by a lantern, with lens of fifth order, and in design the

same with all screw-pile light-houses built in this district. The substructure, however, instead of being of iron, will be five brick pyramidal piers, 4 feet square at the base, and a little over 8 feet in height, resting on a bed of concrete 18 inches in depth at the center, which will overlay a grillage of two courses of timber, each 6 inches in thickness, the sub-soil of the site being considered too soft and yielding to permit the use of screw-piles. An appropriation of $15,000 is available.

378. *Pass Manchac, Lake Pontchartrain, Louisiana.*—A breakwater 200 feet long was built at a cost of $7.50 per linear foot at the east side of the light-house, to protect it from the destructive action of the waves. The work has two faces, meeting at an angle of 120°, is built of sawed 12-inch by 12-inch yellow pine piles, connected by two courses of 10-inch by 10-inch stringers, faced with sheet-piling of 3-inch plank, and capped with the same. All the piling has a penetration of 8 feet, and the breakwater projects above the surface of the land, on which it is principally located, 7 feet.

—— *Errol Island, Gulf of Mexico, Louisiana.*—A light-house has been recommended to be established at this locality as necessary, to fill the gap of fifty-two miles in sea-coast lights existing between Chandeleur Island and Pass à l'outre, but no exact survey has yet been made on which to base an estimate for an appropriation.

380. *Pass à l'outre, river Mississippi, Louisiana.*—A 12-inch steam fog-whistle has been put up, and is now in operation at this light-house.

382. *Head of the Passes, river Mississippi, Louisiana.*—The light-house being in danger of destruction from the washing of the river bank, it has been removed 200 feet farther inland to a place of greater security, and the building is now being repaired and strengthened. A breakwater formerly protected the site, but a large portion of it was carried away in a gale, last October.

383. *Southwest Pass, River Mississippi, Louisiana.*—It has already been reported that the foundation for a new light-house at the station was completed. A first-order iron tower is under contract in the North, and will be erected on its site during the coming year. The old light-house and dwelling are not in very good condition, but will answer all purposes until the completion of the new tower. By the act of Congress approved June 10, 1872, an appropriation of $25,000 has been granted for completing the erection of this tower. A 12-inch steam fog-whistle has been set up, and is now in operation at this light-house.

385. *Timbalier, Timbalier Bay, Louisiana.*—A first-order iron tower, to be elevated on screw-piles, is under contract in the North. Its design is a skeleton frame-work with a spiral stairway inclosed by sheet-iron, giving access to the lantern, and provided with keeper's dwelling in the lower part of the tower. It will be placed in the water, under the lee of West Timbalier Island. As the available funds are insufficient to finish the erection of the building, it is deemed advisable to store the iron until an additional appropriation of $44,000 can be granted by Congress for its completion.

387. *Southwest Reef, Atchafalaya Bay, Louisiana.*—The iron screw-pile tower has already once been seriously damaged in a storm by the waves breaking the cast-iron floor of the lower story, and is in danger of being carried away altogether by any hurricane which may visit this vicinity. The lower story, now used as a part of the keeper's quarters, will be replaced by an open iron frame-work. An appropriation of $5,000 is asked to make the change.

——. *Grand Lake, Louisiana.*—Application has been made by parties interested for the establishment of a light or lights in Grand Lake to accommodate the commerce seeking an outlet to the Gulf by way of the river Atchafalaya. The subject has not yet been fully examined, but there seems to be little doubt that a light-house at the northern end of the lake near Chicot Pass, would be of great benefit. The land in most places is high, with soil suitable for foundation, and could be purchased at from $5 to $10 per acre, and a light-house can be constructed, without doubt, at a small expense, but the board are not prepared to recommend an appropriation therefor.

388. *Trinity Shoal, Gulf of Mexico.*—This is an extent of fifteen miles of hard sand, on over 6 miles of which there is less than 12 feet of water, lying 20 miles south of the Louisiana coast. A skeleton iron tower, exactly similar to that for Timbalier, is in course of preparation, under contract in the North. It will probably be located in 14 feet water, and the light, which will be of the first order, will have an elevation of about 131 feet above the sea. A survey of the shoal has just been completed by the Coast Survey. The iron-work will be ready for delivery at an early date, but, for lack of funds adequate to complete the erection, will have to be stored until an additional appropriation is granted, and $44,000 is asked for it.

389. *Calcasieu, mouth of River Calcasieu, Louisiana.*—A site for a new light-house has been surveyed and steps have been taken toward the purchase of the land, the matter having been placed in the hands of the United States district attorney, who has not yet been heard from. The structure is to be a fourth-order iron tower, similar to that at Southwest Reef, with focal plane of about 50 feet, supported on hollow cast-iron screw-piles, four in number, and strengthened by braces abutting against four exterior piles. The tower will be sheathed with plate-iron. It is already contracted for in the North, and will be erected on its site during the coming year.

392. *Bolivar Point, entrance to Galveston Bay, Texas.*—The foundation of this light-house was completed previous to the last annual report. It is to be a conical sheet-iron tower inclosing a wall of brick; the focal plane of the light (third order) to be 110 feet above the base. When the tower had reached a height of 40 feet the past April, work was suspended by order of the board for want of funds. A new appropriation of $10,000 having been granted, the construction party will very shortly recommence and the tower be completed at an early date. The lens and all the iron-work are on the ground.

396. *Matagorda, entrance to Matagorda Bay, Texas.*—An appropriation of $20,000 having been made, a new site for an iron tower similar to that at Bolivar Point, to be provided with a third-order light, has been selected nearly two miles from the old destroyed tower, from which nearly all the iron will be serviceable for the new one. At the close of the year the foundation was under way, and it is proposed to continue the work until the present appropriation is exhausted, when it must be suspended until an additional appropriation of $12,000 is granted to complete it, which is included in the estimates.

397 and 398. *West Shoal and East Shoal, entrance to Matagorda Bay, Texas.*—The screw-pile light-houses were prepared, and a party organized at Baltimore, in the fifth district, for their erection. They were built simultaneously, and finished in the month of March last. Both lights are on screw-piles. The West Shoal light-house being nearest the Gulf, exhibits a *white* light, and the East Shoal, about one-half mile distant, shows a *red* light.

401. *Brazos Island Beacon, Texas.*—This is the last light but one that exists on the Texas coast before reaching the Mexican boundary. The

present wooden tower is decayed, and is subject to destruction in heavy gales. The vibration of the building in storms causes the breaking of the glass in the lantern, and it is highly important that something be done at this station at an early day. A new light-house of the ordinary screw-pile character of iron foundation is recommended. The distance of the station and the high prices ruling there would enhance the cost of the building above the ordinary rates for such structures even in this district, and an appropriation of $25,000 is asked.

REPAIRS.

At each of the following-named stations in the eighth district there have been repairs, more or less extensive, during the past year:

——. *Buoy and coal depot*, Fort Pickens, Florida.

369. *Saint Joseph's Island*, Mississippi Sound, Mississippi.

380. *Pass à l'Outre*, River Mississippi, Louisiana.

386. *Ship Shoal*, Gulf of Mexico, Louisiana. The entire building had the rust scraped off, cleansed with acid and coal-tarred, and a new iron cistern furnished. The fog-bell, which had been only temporarily hung, was permanently fitted in an iron frame.

It is proposed to make repairs at the following-named stations in the eighth district during the coming year:

353. *Saint Mark's*, Florida.
355. *Cape Saint George*, Florida.
356. *Cape San Blas*, Florida.
363. *East Pascagoula River*, Mississippi.
364. *Ship Island*, Mississippi Sound, Mississippi.
368. *Morrill's Shell Bank*, Mississippi Sound, Mississippi.
369. *Saint Joseph's Island*, Mississippi Sound, Mississippi.
372. *West Rigolets*, entrance to Lake Pontchartrain, Louisiana.
374. *Port Pontchartrain*, Lake Pontchartrain, Louisiana.
377. *Tchefuncti River*, Lake Pontchartrain, Louisiana.
379. *Chandeleau*, Gulf of Mexico, Louisiana.
381. *South Pass*, River Mississippi, Louisiana.
384. *Barrataria Bay*, Louisiana.
386. *Ship Shoal*, Gulf of Mexico, Louisiana.
399. *Half-Moon Reef*, Matagorda Bay, Texas.

The following are the names of the light-stations in the eighth district not mentioned elsewhere:

357. *Pensacola*, south side Pensacola Bay, near Barrancas, Florida.
362. *Round Island*, off Pascagoula, Mississippi.
365. *Biloxi*, entrance Biloxi Bay, Mississippi.
367. *Pass Christian*, six and one-half miles northwest of Cat Island.
370. *Rigolets*, (Pleasanton's Island,) mouth River Pearl.
371. *Proctorville Beacon*, near fort at Proctorville, Lake Borgne.
375. *Bayou Saint John*, five miles north of New Orleans.
376. *New Canal*, entrance New Canal, Louisiana.
390. *Sabine Pass*, on Brant Point, east side entrance river Sabine.
391. *Galveston light-vessel*, inside Galveston Bar, Texas.
393. *Half-Moon Shoal*, in Galveston Bay, between Pellican Island and Dollar Point, Texas.
394. *Red-Fish Bar*, to mark channel across Red-Fish Bar, Galveston Bay, Texas.

395. *Clopper's Bar*, to mark channel across Clopper's Bar, Galveston Bay, Texas.
400. *Aransas Pass*, on Low Island, inside Aransas Pass, Texas.
402. *Point Isabel*, at Point Isabel, Brazos Santiago, Texas.

LIGHT-SHIPS.

"*Galveston*," *inside of Galveston Bar, Texas.*—This vessel is very much in want of repair, and she leaks so much that she cannot be kept afloat. She will be removed at once, and a chartered vessel will be procured as a temporary substitute and until the Galveston can be repaired.

There are no other light-ships in this district.

FOG-SIGNALS OPERATED BY STEAM OR HOT-AIR ENGINES.

Pass à L'outre.—A 12-inch steam-whistle, in good condition.
Southwest Pass.—A 12-inch steam-whistle, in good condition.

DAY OR UNLIGHTED BEACONS.

The day-beacons of the eighth district are all in good condition as far as known, except the one at Stake Island, Southwest Pass, which requires a very trifling strengthening of the bracing to make it more secure.

Day-beacons in Mississippi Sound have been authorized by the board to be established at Horn Island, Round Island, Biloxi, and Pass Christian, and it is proposed to erect them during the coming year. There are five old wrought-iron screw-piles in store, which will answer the purpose, and will be used.

An iron day-beacon about 20 feet in height, and of the form of a tripod surmounted by a hoop-iron globe, has been erected to take the place of the wooden one destroyed in the heavy gales of last fall at Pass à L'outre. It rests on three hollow cast-iron piles filled with concrete.

A day-beacon of the same design as that at Pass à L'outre, but of a height of 50 feet, has been put up in place of a wooden one that was damaged at Stake Island, mouth of river Mississippi, in the same storms that destroyed the Pass à L'outre Beacon.

DEPOTS.

Depot at Head of the Passes, River Mississippi.—This building is in fair condition, but threatened by the wearing away of the river-bank. The cost of protective works to insure the safety of the building, makes it a question as to whether it would not be advisable to remove the depot back from the river, as in the case of the light-house, or to abandon the site for some other eligible location in the western portion of the district.

The cost of everything that enters into light-house construction on the Mexican Gulf coast is exceedingly high compared with other parts of the Union; the small number of cities where supplies necessary can be obtained at any price, in a district extending over one thousand miles of coast, measured on the shortest line, not taking into consideration the bays, sounds, and estuaries; the delays experienced from illness among working-parties from malarial fevers; the soft and yielding nature of the land and shoals in the greater part of the district, making the operation of putting down foundations difficult and expensive; the unreliable means of communication with distant field-parties, by reason of the deficiency of railroads and packet-lines, have prevented the board from completing many of the works in the eighth district.

TENTH DISTRICT.

The tenth district extends from the mouth of River Saint Regis, New York, to include Grassy Island light-house, River Detroit, Michigan, and embraces all the aids to navigation on the American shores of Lake Erie, Lake Ontario, and River Saint Lawrence.

Inspector.—Commodore Gustavus H. Scott, United States Navy, until 18th September, 1871; Commodore Napoleon Collins, United States Navy, present inspector.

Engineer.—Major George L. Gillespie, Corps of Engineers, brevet lieutenant-colonel, United States Army.

In this district there are:

Light-houses and lighted beacons	56
Light-ships	0
Fog-signals operated by steam or hot-air engines	0
Day or unlighted beacons	1
Buoys actually in position	76
Spare buoys for relief to supply losses	84
Tenders	0

The numbers preceding the names of stations correspond with those of "Light-House List of the Northern Lakes and River Coasts of the United States," issued January 1, 1872.

461. *Cross-Over Island, River Saint Lawrence, New York.*—The tower and dwelling are both in very bad condition, and are not worth repair. The tower is of wood, and rises from the roof of the brick dwelling; the timber is so decayed, and the interior framing so badly arranged, that water finds its way into the interior at all points of the connection with the roof. The brick of which the old dwelling is built were originally very inferior, and have been so injured by frosts that the walls are now unserviceable, and cannot be used for supporting any new work. They were sheathed on the outside with boards, in 1869, but this was a temporary expedient, serving only to relieve the cold and dampness of the dwelling, until the whole could be renewed. An appropriation of $11,000 is required for a new tower and dwelling.

470. *Oswego, Lake Ontario, New York.*—A small frame beacon, with a focal plane 23 feet above the lake-level, was established at the end of the pier, and a communication with the main light formed by a strong elevated wall. The apparatus used is a lens of the sixth order, showing a fixed white light.

471. *Fair Haven, Little Sodus Bay, Lake Ontario, New York.*—An appropriation was made, March 3, 1871, for the erection of a pier, light-house, and dwelling at this station. In May, 1871, a lot of four acres, the smallest which could be obtained, was purchased on the west bank, as the site for the keeper's dwelling. No work was done during the working season on account of the delay of the seller in presenting warrantee deed for the light-house lot for examination. Finally, in May, 1872, the title-papers were presented, but not proving acceptable to the United States district attorney they were returned. Having determined early in the spring to build the frame beacon, irrespective of the dwelling, sealed proposals were publicly invited for the necessary materials. No bids were offered. The materials were accordingly purchased in open

market at Oswego, New York, and framing done there by days' labor. The beacon was shipped from Oswego in May, 1872, erected on the west pier, and the light exhibited June 10, 1872. The apparatus is a Fresnel lens of the fourth order, arc 270°, showing a fixed white light. The height of focal-plane above the lake-level is 34 feet. Should the Board not be able to obtain title to the lot selected, another will be purchased on the opposite side of the bay upon which to erect the keeper's dwelling.

——. *Thirty-mile Point, Lake Ontario.*—It is recommended that a lake-coast light be established near the point where the boundary line between Niagara and Orleans Counties intersects the south shore of Lake Ontario. The point is designated on some maps as Thirty-mile Point, being just thirty miles from the mouth of Niagara River. The necessity for this light will be apparent when it is considered that the first light to the eastward of the mouth of the Niagara River is at Oak Orchard, New York, a fourth-order light on a pier, and which, from its re-entrant position, can be of but little service to shipping making the Welland Canal. The light proposed is of the third order. An appropriation therefor is required of $30,000.

478. *Fort Niagara, mouth of Niagara River, New York.*—An appropriation was made, March 3, 1871, for rebuilding the light-house at this station. Immediately after the passage of the act plans were prepared for the new buildings, sealed proposals were publicly invited for the delivery of the necessary building-materials, and contracts made. The former light was placed on one of the old military buildings of the fort, and unsuccessful efforts were made to locate the new tower within the walls, being near the point which the light is intended to mark, the main object, however, being to serve as a lake-coast light, but it was found that the only place practicable was the lot on which stands the light-keeper's dwelling; this, although further from the point than is desirable, serves very well for both of the above purposes. Work was commenced in July, 1871, and pushed rapidly, but cold weather coming on unusually early, masonry was suspended November 30, 1871. Work was resumed April 15, 1872, and the light exhibited June 10, 1872. The tower and oil-room were completely finished June 27, 1872. When it was decided to place the tower upon the light-house lot, a careful inspection of the bank of the river showed that some protection should be made to arrest the abrasion constantly in operation by the currents and the ice of the river. A thick, low, rubble-stone wall was run along the greater part of the shore, near the water edge, and behind this the bank was terraced and sodded. Six heavy timber jettees, 14 feet to 30 feet in length, filled with stones, were run out from the wall perpendicular to the shore. These have caused the water to shoal, and, it is believed, now perfectly protect the lot. The station is now in fine order.

480. *Buffalo breakwater, (north end,) Lake Erie, New York.*—The work in progress at the date of last report was suspended again September 9, 1871, on account of the continued and irregular setting of the pier of protection, and was not resumed during the working season further than to throw in some heavy stone around northwest corner, to prevent the undermining of the crib, and to protect the angles of the crib with a sheathing of boiler-iron against injury from ice. Work was resumed as early in the spring as the ice would permit, and has been continued, with a few interruptions, to date. The interior finish of the house was completed on the 10th July. The fog-bell is suspended on the exterior, and the striking-apparatus, occupying one of the rooms of the dwelling, has been properly adjusted to strike three times in quick succession, at

intervals of thirty seconds, during foggy weather. The lens is of the fourth order, arc 360°, and the light shown is a fixed red.

485. *Erie Harbor, Pennsylvania.*—An appropriation was made, March 3, 1871, for renovating this station. It was expended in raising the roof, renewing the brick-work around windows, renewing floors, replastering the house, renewing the barn, and building a fence partially around the buildings. The station is in good order.

488. *Presqu'ile beacon-range No. 3, Erie Harbor, Lake Erie.*—A small octagonal frame tower has been erected upon the east end of the north pier, to mark the extremity of the new extension. The height of focal plane above lake-level is 12 feet. The apparatus is a sixth-order lens, showing a fixed white light.

——. *Presqu'ile, Lake Erie, Erie, Pennsylvania.*—An appropriation was made, June 10, 1872, for building a light-house on the north shore of peninsula covering the harbor of Erie. Plans have been prepared, and proposals will be publicly invited at an early day for the delivery of the necessary building-materials. The buildings will consist of a tower and keeper's dwelling attached, and will be built of limestone. The apparatus will be a Fresnel lens of the fourth order, revolving, showing a white light. The height of focal-plane above lake level will be 45 feet.

491. *Conneaut, Lake Erie, Ohio.*—An appropriation was made, March 3, 1871, for building a light-keeper's dwelling at this station. Proposals were publicly invited for its construction, and a contract was made. The contract has been satisfactorily executed excepting a part of the interior finish. The dwelling is a one-story and attic frame structure, with an oil-room, and is situated on the left bank of the stream, a short distance from the piers.

492. *Ashtabula, Lake Erie, Ohio.*—An appropriation was made, March 3, 1871, for building a light-keeper's dwelling at this station. Proposals were publicly invited for its construction, and a contract was made. The contract has been satisfactorily executed, and the building has been accepted. It is a building of the same character as that at Conneaut, Ohio, and is situated on the left bank of the stream, within the township of Ashtabula. The beacon on the east pier is very old and dilapidated, and by the irregular setting of its crib has been much thrown out of verticality. It should be removed, and a pier-head beacon should be established in its stead. The appropriation required is $3,400.

493. *Grand River, Lake Erie, Fairport, Ohio.*—Work in progress at date of last report was so far completed as to exhibit the light from the new tower on the 11th of August, 1871. The new building and oil-room were completed 20th of October, 1871. The order of the original light was not changed. The east pier of entrance to the harbor at this station is being extended 400 feet, and as the frame beacon is very old and needs renewing, it should be taken down and a new frame beacon should be erected at the pier-head of the new extension. An appropriation is required of $3,400.

495. *Cleveland, Lake Erie, Ohio.*—The work of building the stone wall in closing the lot, in progress at date of last report, was completed in July. Proposals were publicly invited for the necessary building-materials for the new tower and dwelling, and a contract was made for the stone. One bid was offered for the brick, but as the sample presented was of a very inferior kind, it was rejected. No bid was offered for lumber. The stone were delivered in November, and the winter was consumed in dressing them, and in preparing all the necessary carpentry. On account of the great fire in Chicago, it was found impossible to buy in

Cleveland, at anything like a reasonable price, brick at all suitable for exterior work. The engineer, therefore, was compelled to make a contract with a firm at La Salle, New York, for the supply of the brick needed. This season has been most unfavorable for their manufacture, and the contractors have not supplied them at the time nor in the quantities expected. A small lot has been delivered, and the work of construction has advanced to 5 feet above the water-table. On the 15th of July it was expected that the full amount ordered would have been delivered, and that after that date the construction would advance without interruption.

498. *Black River, Lake Erie, Ohio.*—This station has no keeper's dwelling. An appropriation of $4,000 is required for the construction of a frame dwelling similar to the one at Ashtabula, Ohio.

499. *Vermillion, Lake Erie, Ohio.*—The house and lot purchased in this village for the use of the light-keeper were transferred to the United States in April. A few alterations have been made to the house to furnish accommodations for oil, and a cellar, a neat inclosure, and a stone sidewalk have been added. The station is in fine order.

500. *Huron, Lake Erie, Ohio.*—An appropriation was made March 3, 1871, for building a light-keeper's dwelling at this station, and a lot has been purchased for it. There was great delay in making the title-papers satisfactory to the district attorney, but they have been perfected at last, and have been forwarded to the Attorney-General of the United States for examination and approval. The construction of the dwelling is under contract, and work will commence immediately after the acceptance of the title-papers by the Attorney-General.

508. *Maumee outer range, (rear,) Toledo, Ohio.*—Work in progress at date of last report was satisfactorily completed in October. The dwelling was accepted, and the keeper immediately installed. There are two points in the southwest channel through Maumee Bay, Ohio, which require to be marked by day-beacons. The one is in the position now occupied by red can-buoy No. 2, and the other is that occupied by black can-buoy No. 1. Vessels making the harbor frequently strike these buoys and either break their moorings or drag them out of the place, to the great embarrassment of shipping. Vessels are continually grounding in the bay from this cause. The foundation and superstructure of the beacons should be made of 12-inch pine timber, framed and bolted like ordinary crib-work for harbor-piers, and filled with heavy stone; the foundation to be 30 feet square, sunk in 10 feet water, and its exposed angles protected by piling. The superstructure will be sheathed on the outside with heavy oak timber. The whole will be surmounted by an iron cage. One beacon will be painted red and the other black. An appropriation of $12,000 is required for these beacons.

511. *Maumee inner range, (front,) Toledo, Ohio.*—A frame buoy-house has been built on the water-front of the light-house property. It is established about 200 feet from shore upon a crib of protection 25 feet square, sunk in 6 feet of water.

514. *Gibraltar, mouth of River Detroit, Lake Erie, Michigan.*—An appropriation was made June 10, 1872, for rebuilding tower and keeper's dwelling at this station. It is proposed to remove the old tower, relinquish the site, and to erect the new buildings upon the light-house lot. Sealed proposals will be publicly invited at an early day for the supply of the necessary building-materials. The plans contemplate a tower, and dwelling attached, constructed of brick. It is expected to complete the work before the close of the working season.

REPAIRS.

At each of the following-named stations in the tenth district there have been repairs and renovations more or less during the year:

461. *Cross-Over Island*, New York, River Saint Lawrence.
462. *Sister Islands*, New York, River Saint Lawrence.
464. *Rock Island*, New York, River Saint Lawrence.
469. *Oswego*, New York, Lake Ontario.
470. *Oswego pier-head light*, New York, Lake Ontario.
473. *Big Sodus beacon, (rear,)* New York, Lake Ontario.
474. *Big Sodus*, New York, Lake Ontario.
475. *Genesee*, New York, Lake Ontario.
476. *Genesee beacon*, Lake Ontario, moved to end of pier.
477. *Oak Orchard beacon*, Lake Ontario, moved to end of pier.
479. *Horseshoe Reef*, Buffalo, New York, lantern changed.
482. *Buffalo*, New York.
483. *Dunkirk*, New York, Lake Erie.
489. *Peninsula range No.* 1, Lake Erie.
490. *Peninsula range No.* 2, Lake Erie.
494. *Grand River*, Fairport, Ohio, Lake Erie.
504. *Green Island*, Lake Erie, Ohio.
505. *West Sister*, Lake Erie, Ohio.
506. *Turtle Island*, Maumee Bay, Ohio.
508, 510, 511, 512. *Maumee ranges*, Toledo, Ohio.
513. *Monroe*, Lake Erie, Michigan.
515. *Mamajuda*, River Detroit, Michigan.
516. *Grassy Island*, Detroit River, Michigan.

Stations at which repairs in the tenth district will be made during the next year:

462. *Sister Islands*, River Saint Lawrence, New York.
464. *Rock Island*, River Saint Lawrence, New York.
465. *Tibbets's Point*, Lake Ontario, New York.
479. *Horseshoe Reef*, Buffalo, New York.
483. *Dunkirk*, Lake Erie, New York.
491. *Conneaut*, Lake Erie, Ohio.
500. *Huron*, Lake Erie, Ohio.

The following are the names of the light-stations in the tenth district not mentioned elsewhere:

460. *Ogdensburgh*, River Saint Lawrence, New York.
463. *Sunken Rock*, River Saint Lawrence, New York.
466. *Galloo Island*, Lake Ontario, New York.
467. *Sackett's Harbor*, Lake Ontario, New York.
468. *Stony Point*, Lake Ontario, New York.
472. *Big Sodus*, Lake Ontario, New York.
481. *Buffalo breakwater*, (south end,) Buffalo, New York.
482. *Buffalo*, Lake Erie, New York.
484. *Dunkirk beacon*, Lake Erie, New York.
486. *Presqu'isle range, No.* 1, Pennsylvania.
487. *Presqu'isle range, No.* 2, Pennsylvania.
496. *Cleveland, No.* 1, Ohio.
497. *Cleveland, No.* 2, Ohio.

501. *Cedar Point*, Sandusky Bay, Ohio.
502. *Cedar Point Beacon range*, Sandusky Bay, Ohio.
503. *Marblehead*, Sandusky Bay, Ohio.
507. *Maumee outer range*, (front,) Ohio.
509. *Maumee middle range*, Ohio.

LIGHT SHIPS.

There are no light-ships in this district.

FOG-SIGNALS OPERATED BY STEAM OR HOT-AIR ENGINES.

There are no fog-signals operated by steam or hot air in this district.

DAY OR UNLIGHTED BEACONS.

There are no day-beacons in this district.

DEPOT.

The construction of a wharf for the use of the light-house depot at Buffalo, New York, in progress at the date of last report, was prosecuted satisfactorily during the summer, and completed September 30, 1871. This wharf is 264 feet long, by 12½ feet wide, and is sunk 6 feet below low-water mark. At a distance of 3 feet in front of the wharf a row of protecting piles has been driven, 4 feet from center to center, and confined at top with walling pieces bolted through and through to each pile with seven bolts. During the winter it was found that snow penetrated the roof of the store-house and damaged articles in store there. The slate were removed in June, new boards and felting put on, and the slating renewed. The foundation of the exterior stairs being cracked and sunken, was removed and rebuilt; the decayed sleepers of the second floor were replaced by sound ones, and additional supporting-timbers placed underneath. All the buildings of the station have been painted, a new fence built in front, with spikes on top to exclude trespassers, and the grounds planted with shade-trees and grass. A commodious boat-house for two boats has been built at the east end of the wharf. The station is now in fine condition.

TENDER.

There is now no tender in the tenth district; and the Haze, belonging to the eleventh district, is used for supplying the lights in the tenth district, and for buoy service. The great distances between the extremes of the tenth and eleventh districts make it necessary to have another tender, to be used in the former for inspector's and engineer's purposes, and an estimate is submitted therefor.

ELEVENTH DISTRICT.

The eleventh district embraces all aids to navigation on the northern and northwestern lakes above Grassy Island light-house, River Detroit, and includes Lakes Saint Clair, Huron, Michigan, and Superior.

Inspector.—Commodore Alexander Murray, United States Navy.

Engineer.—Major O. M. Poe, Corps of Engineers, brevet brigadier-general, United States Army.

There are in this district:

Light-houses and lighted beacons	91
Light-ships	none
Fog-signals operated by steam or hot-air engines	7
Day or unlighted beacons	1
Buoys actually in position	138
Spare buoys for relief and to supply losses	99
Tender (steam) Haze, buoy-tender and supply-vessel, (common to tenth and eleventh districts)	1
Tender (steam) Warrington, (used in engineer's constructions and repairs)	1
Tender (sail) Belle, (used in engineer's constructions and repairs)	1

The numbers preceding the names of stations correspond with the "Light-House List of the Northern and Northwestern Lakes of the United States," issued January 1, 1872.

520, 521. *Saint Clair Flats Canal.*—These two light-houses were completed as proposed in the last annual report, and were lighted for the first time on the night of November 15, 1871. Simultaneously the temporary lights were discontinued. It was found that the foundations were liable to injury from the impact of rafts in tow of steam-tugs, as well as from other causes not connected with the construction. They were protected by special constructions, which thus far have proven perfectly satisfactory.

522. *Fort Gratiot, Lake Huron, Michigan.*—The steam fog-whistle under construction was completed in good time last season, and was in operation during all the thick and smoky weather consequent upon the great fires in the Northwest of last fall. Its use was most opportune, and the signal gives great satisfaction.

——. *A light-house between Fort Gratiot and Point aux Barques, Lake Huron, Michigan.*—The recommendation contained in the last annual report is renewed, together with the estimate of the cost of a suitable structure. This light-house is one of the coast-lights of the general system, and is not intended to serve any local interest. Its value to the general commerce will be great, as it will divide the long distance of seventy-five miles between Point aux Barques and Fort Gratiot.

528. *Thunder Bay Island, Lake Huron, Michigan.*—The steam fog-whistle under construction at this station at the date of the last annual report was duly completed, and has rendered excellent service.

532. *Spectacle Reef, Lake Huron, Michigan.*—At the date of the last annual report (July 1, 1871,) the crib, 92 feet square, with a central opening of 48 feet square to receive the coffer-dam which was to form the pier of protection, as well as a landing-place for materials during the building of the light-house, was in course of construction at Scammon's Harbor. The original intention was to put the crib in position in four sections, but upon further consideration it was decided to attempt placing it as a whole upon the reef, which was successfully accomplished, as is detailed hereafter.

In order to get accurate soundings to guide in shaping the bottom of the crib, and to fix with a degree of certainty the position of these soundings and that to be occupied by the crib, the following method was pursued: Four temporary cribs, each 15 feet by 25 feet, of round timber, were placed in from 8 to 10 feet of water, in a line corresponding with the proposed eastern face of the pier of protection, and filled to the level of the water with ballast-stone. These four cribs were then decked over and connected together. Upon the pier thus formed about seventy cords of ballast-stone were placed, ready at the proper time to be thrown into the crib forming the pier of protection. The lower two complete courses of the pier of protection, having been fastened together by screw-bolts, forming a raft, constituting a ground-plan of the pier of protection, were then towed from the harbor where framed to the reef, and moored directly over the position to be occupied by the finished pier. Its position was marked upon the temporary pier referred to above, and soundings taken at intervals of two feet along each timber in the raft, thus obtaining accurate contours of the surface of the reef within the limits of these timbers. The raft was then towed back to the harbor, hauled out upon ways, and by means of wedges of timber the bottom was made to conform to the surface of the reef. The raft, now become the bottom of the pier of protection, was then launched, and additional courses of timber built upon it, until its draught of water was just sufficient to permit its being floated into position on the reef, at which time it was estimated that the top of the pier would be one foot out of water.

The depth of water on the reef at the points to be occupied by the four corners of the pier of protection was found to be as follows: At northeast corner, 10 feet 6 inches; at northwest corner, 13 feet; at southwest corner, 14 feet 6 inches; and at southeast corner, 9 feet 6 inches; the position to be occupied by the pier of protection having been so chosen that the sides would correspond to the cardinal points of the compass. Meanwhile five barges at the harbor had been loaded with ballast-stone, making, together with those on the temporary pier at the reef, 290 cords (about 1,800 tons) at command, with which to load the pier of protection and secure it to the reef as soon as it should be placed in position.

On the evening of the 18th of July, 1871, everything being in readiness, and the wind, which had been blowing freshly from the northwest for three days previously, having somewhat moderated, at 8 p. m. the tugs Champion (screw-propeller) and Magnet (side-wheel) took hold of the immense crib and started to tow it to the reef, fifteen miles distant, followed by the Warrington (screw-propeller) having in tow the schooner Belle, (the two having on board a working force of 140 men,) the tug Stranger (screw-propeller) with barges Ritchie and Emerald, and the tug Hand with two scows of the Light-House Establishment. The barge Table Rock, with fifty cords of stone on board, was left in reserve at the harbor. The construction-scow, with tools, &c., on board, was towed with the crib. At 2 a. m. next morning, six hours after starting, the fleet hove to off the reef awaiting daylight and the abatement of the wind, which had again freshened up. At 6½ a. m., it having moderated, the pier, with considerable difficulty, was placed in position, and after being secured to the temporary pier and the moorings previously set for the purpose, all hands went to work throwing the ballast-stone into the compartments, and by 4 p. m. succeeded in getting into it about 200 cords (1,200 tons.) By this time the wind was blowing freshly and the sea running so high as to make it necessary to stop work for the time, but early next morning all the reserve stone were put into the compartments.

The tugs Magnet and Stranger were discharged as soon as the pier was in position, but for fear of accident the Champion (a steamer of great power) was retained until all the stone were in place, when she was discharged, and started for Detroit with the barges Ritchie and Emerald in tow. The Table Rock was retained in service until the 30th July, when she was dispensed with. After the pier was in position the schooner Belle was moored on the reef to serve as quarters for the working force, which proceeded to build up the pier to the required height above water, (12 feet.) The Warrington having gone to Detroit to receive a new boiler, the tug Hand was retained to tow the scows carrying the ballast-stone used in completing the filling of the compartments, until the return of the Warrington on the 12th of September, when she, too, was discharged. By this time the pier had been built up to its full height, and by the 20th of September quarters for the workmen had been completed upon it, which were at once occupied, and the Belle returned to the harbor. By means of a submarine diver the bed-rock within the opening of the pier was then cleared off, and the work of constructing the coffer-dam was taken in hand. The coffer-dam itself consisted of a hollow cylinder, 41 feet in diameter, composed of wooden staves, each 4 inches by 6, and 15 feet long. The cylinder was braced and trussed internally, and hooped with iron externally, so as to give it the requisite strength. It was put together at the surface of the water, and when complete was lowered into position on the bed-rock by means of iron screws. As soon as it rested on the rock, (which was quite irregular in contour,) each stave was driven down so as to fit as closely as it would admit and a diver filled all openings between its lower end and the rock with Portland cement. A loosely-twisted rope of oakum was then pressed close down into the exterior angle between the coffer-dam and rock, and outside of this a larger rope made of hay. The pumping-machinery having meanwhile been placed in readiness, the coffer-dam was pumped dry, and on the same day (14th October) a force of stone-cutters descended to the bottom and commenced the work of leveling off the bed-rock, and preparing it to receive the first course of masonry. The bed-rock was found to consist of dolomitic limestone, (confirming the previous examinations,) highest on the western side, (toward the deepest water,) and sloping gradually toward the eastern. In order to make a level bed for the first course of masonry, it was necessary to cut down about two feet on the highest side, involving a large amount of hard labor, rendered more difficult by the water forcing its way up through seams in the rock. But the work was finally accomplished, the bed being as carefully cut and leveled as any of the courses of masonry. The first course of masonry was then set, completing it on the 27th of October. While setting this course much trouble was caused by the water, already referred to as forcing its way up through seams in the rock, which attacked the mortar bed. For this reason water was let into the dam every evening (and pumped out next morning) to give the mortar time to harden during the night. This mortar was composed of equal parts of Portland cement and screened siliceous sand. Specimens of it obtained the following spring, after being in place under water for seven months, were quite as hard or harder than either the bed-rock or the stone used in building the tower.

The weather having now become very boisterous, with frequent snow-squalls, often interrupting the work, and the setting of any additional stone requiring the removal of a portion of the most important of the interior braces of the coffer-dam, it was deemed prudent to close the work for the season. This, too, would give ample time for the hardening of the mortar used in bedding the stone, and in the concrete used for filling cavities in the bed-rock, as well as the space between the outside of the first course and the coffer-dam, (which was solidly filled with concrete to the top of the first course.) Therefore the coffer-dam was allowed to fill with water, the process being hastened by boring holes through it to admit the water, and it was secured to prevent its being lifted by the ice during the winter. The machinery was laid up, and on the last of October all the working force, except two men, were removed. These two men were left to attend to the fourth-order light, which had been established on top of the men's quarters, and the fog-signal, consisting of a whistle attached to one of the steam-boilers. At the close of navigation they were taken off the pier by the light-house tender Haze.

The degree of success of this novel coffer-dam may be inferred from the fact that although prepared with pumps of an aggregate capacity of five thousand gallons per minute, not more than a capacity of seven hundred gallons was used, except when emptying the coffer-dam, and then only to expedite the work. Once emptied, a small proportion of this capacity was ample to keep the coffer-dam free from water; and this at a depth of 12 feet of water, on rock, at a distance of nearly eleven miles from the nearest land. Every person connected with the work may well feel a just pride in its success. All the stone which had been delivered at the harbor, consisting of the first five courses, (each course 2 feet thick,) having been cut by this time, the work there was also closed.

The season opened a month later in 1872 than in 1871, consequently work was not resumed at the harbor until the 3d of May, and upon the reef on the 20th of the same month. On the 13th of May the ice in the coffer-dam was still a compact mass, of some feet in thickness. Masses of ice still lay on top of the pier itself. As soon as anything could be done, the ice still remaining was cleared out of the coffer-dam, the machinery put in order, the braces removed from the interior of the coffer-dam, and the work of setting additional courses begun. This has continued without interruption to the present time, when the masonry is well above the water, and going on at such a rate that one entire course is set, drilled, and bolted complete every three days. If this continues, the tower will have reached a height of at least 40 feet above the lake-level before the close of the season.

It is greatly to be regretted that in a work of such difficulty and importance it was not found practicable to use granite. The first contractor to furnish stone agreed to supply granite from a quarry at Duluth, Minnesota. After a trifling effort to quarry the stone, he utterly failed, and he abandoned the contract. It was then so late in the season that the engineer was compelled either to stop operations or to go into the open market and purchase such stone as he could get. The best available was the Marblehead limestone from the vicinity of Sandusky, Ohio, and this was used. In February, 1872, proposals for the remaining stone were received, and of these the granite offered was at such a price as to exclude it, and no other suitable stone except the Marblehead limestone being offered, he was again driven to use it.

It is hoped that the work will be entirely completed by the close of the season of 1873. It seems now as though the appropriations available would be sufficient to complete the work, but for fear they may not, it is deemed advisable that $20,000 be appropriated for the important work, in addition to the balance of appropriations on account of this work, which have heretofore reverted to the Treasury, or which may do so under existing laws, previous to the time at which it is possible to complete it.

536. *Detour, Lake Huron, Michigan.*—A steam fog-whistle has been established at this station, greatly to the benefit of navigation.

——. *Saint Helena Island, Straits of Mackinac.*—An appropriation for this work is available, and it will be taken in hand as soon as practicable.

——. *Little Traverse, Lake Michigan, Michigan.*—Attention was directed to the necessity of a light-house to make this fine harbor of refuge available at all times, by an inquiry from the Senate Committee on

Commerce, which inquiry was referred to the engineer officer of the district, and he reported under date of April 11, 1871, in a communication of which the following is a copy:

Referring to a letter from the Light-House Board, dated March 28, 1871, inclosing a copy of a communication from the chairman of the Senate Committee on Commerce, covering a resolution of the legislature of Michigan, relative to establishing a light-house, &c., at the mouth of Little Traverse Bay, Michigan, and directing me to report as to the utility and cost of the constructions asked for, I have the honor to submit the following:

By reference to the tracing of the lake-survey detail chart of Little Traverse, inclosed herewith, and the engraved lake-survey chart of the northeast end of Lake Michigan, including Big and Little Traverse Bays and the Fox and Manitou Islands, a copy of which is supposed to be in the office of the board, or can be readily obtained at the office of the Chief of Engineers, the relation of the harbor of Little Traverse to the navigation of Lake Michigan can be readily seen and appreciated. The harbor itself is excellent in every respect, easy of access, affording good anchorage, and a complete shelter from all winds.

A light-house of the fifth order, together with a fog-bell of 600 pounds, with Stevens's striking-apparatus will make the harbor available.

In addition to its relation to the general commerce of Lake Michigan, the harbor has some local importance. This is increasing and doubtless will continue to do so.

The proposed aids to navigation should be placed at the extreme end of the point, on the south side of the harbor, as indicated on the accompanying tracing, and would cost about $12,000, which sum, for the purpose indicated, I respectfully recommend be included in the next annual estimates.

544. *South Manitou Island, Lake Michigan.*—The work of improving this station, which was in progress at the date of the last annual report, was duly completed.

546. *Manistee, Lake Michigan, Michigan.*—This light-station was destroyed during the great fire of the night of the 8th of October, 1871. The keeper, with commendable energy, established a temporary light within a few days afterward, and under the act of Congress approved May 18, 1872, making an appropriation for rebuilding the station, a working party was dispatched some time since from Detroit for the work.

548. *Pere Marquette, Lake Michigan, Michigan.*—This station is as yet without a keeper's dwelling, and an appropriation of $4,000 is required for the purpose in question.

——. *Little Point au Sable, Lake Michigan, Michigan.*—The site required for the proposed coast-light at this point has been reserved, and as soon as practicable the erection of the station, under the act of Congress approved June 10, 1872, will be undertaken.

——. *White River, Lake Michigan, Michigan.*—A pier-head light has been established at this point, but a dwelling for the keeper is much needed, there being none at the station, and an appropriation of $4,000 is required for the purpose.

550. *Muskegon pier-light, east shore of Lake Michigan, Michigan.*—This light, in course of construction at the date of the last annual report, was duly completed, and has been in operation since.

552. *Grand Haven pier-light, Lake Michigan, Michigan.*—This light has also been established since the date of the last annual report. It is one of the general system of pier-head lights.

553. *Holland, Michigan, at the mouth of Black Lake, east side Lake Michigan, Michigan.*—The construction of a dwelling for the keeper at this station will be undertaken as soon as a title to the requisite site can be obtained. The necessary funds were appropriated by act of Congress approved June 10, 1872.

555. *South Haven, Lake Michigan, Michigan.*—The necessary buildings have been erected at this station and the light established.

559. *Michigan City pier-light, Lake Michigan, Indiana.*—As proposed at the date of the last annual report, this light was erected and in full operation before the close of last season.

——. *Calumet, Lake Michigan, Illinois.*—The re-establishment of this light has been delayed by the failure of the present owners to make to the United States the requisite title to the proposed site. Efforts to obtain title are still being made.

562. *Grosse Point, Lake Michigan, Illinois.*—The plans and specifications for the proposed buildings at this station have been made, and proposals for their construction will be invited within a few days.

——. *Racine Point, Lake Michigan, Wisconsin.*—The following are the remarks concerning the establishment of a coast-light at this point, contained in the last two annual reports:

This is a prominent point on the west coast of Lake Michigan, about three and a half miles north of Racine, and eighteen miles south of the North Cut beacon, at Milwaukee. The point shuts out to the northward the Racine light, which lies in a bay, and is not seen by vessels coming from the north, and keeping the shore well aboard, as they mostly do, until nearly abreast of it.

Frequent shipwrecks have occurred at this point for the want of a light. For vessels coming from the south it would also be a good guide for steering clear of Racine Reef.

A fog-signal should also be provided. For these two objects there is required an appropriation of $40,000.

——. *Racine pier-light, Lake Michigan, Wisconsin.*—A working party is now engaged in erecting a pier-head light and elevated walk at this place. It will be completed about the 1st of September of this year.

——. *Milwaukee pier-head light, Lake Michigan, Wisconsin.*—Upon completion of the pier-head light at Racine, the working party will be transferred to Milwaukee for the purpose of erecting a pier-head light at the outer end of the north pier, which has been extended during the present season. An elevated walk will be built to connect the light with the shore.

——. *Twin River Point, Lake Michigan, Wisconsin.*—This point is seven miles north of Manitowoc, and occupies a position on the west coast of Lake Michigan, similar to Grand Point au Sable on the east. It is the prominent landmark for vessels navigating Lake Michigan, and should be marked by a tower 100 feet high, with an apparatus of the third order. There is an old discontinued station at the village of Twin River, but the site is too far south of the point to answer the purpose of a coast-light. There is required for a proper light at this station an appropriation of $40,000.

——. *North Bay, Lake Michigan, Wisconsin.*—By act of Congress approved July 15, 1870, an appropriation of $7,500 was made for the purpose of establishing a light or lights to enable vessels to enter this harbor, and a price for the land required was agreed upon. But the owner found it impracticable to clear the title before the 30th June, when the appropriation reverted to the Treasury. It is recommended that the amount be re-appropriated and another attempt be made to obtain title.

——. *Poverty Island, Lake Michigan.*—The remarks contained in the last annual report, and those for the two preceding years, respecting the necessity for a light at this point, with estimate of cost of same, are repeated, as follows:

The already large and rapidly increasing commerce to and from the northern end of Green Bay, and the lower lake ports, now takes, in daylight, the northern passage from Lake Michigan into Green Bay, because of its being much shorter and more direct. To enable vessels to use the same passage in the night, a light-house on Poverty Island is necessary.

There is recommended an appropriation of $18,000 for the object stated.

——. *Big Sable, Lake Superior, Michigan.*—An appropriation for a light-house at this point was made at the last session of Congress, under the title of "*a light between White Fish Point and Grand Island Harbor.*" Steps have been taken to select the exact site; when this is done, the title will be secured as soon as possible, and the erection of the necessary buildings undertaken.

——. *Stannard's Rock, Lake Superior.*—The remarks and estimate contained in the last annual report, relating to a light-house at this point, are renewed as follows:

The rapid increase of the commerce between Du Luth, the eastern terminus of the Northern Pacific Railroad, and the lower lakes, will demand at no distant day the erection of a light-house on this danger so much dreaded by all vessels bound to or from ports above Keweenaw Point, and ports below. The case will be similar to that of Spectacle Reef, and all the costly apparatus and machinery purchased for the latter can be made available for the former, thereby greatly reducing the cost of construction. It is not proposed, however, to do anything further at this time than to make the preliminary examinations, and mature plans for the work, for which purpose it is recommended that the sum of $10,000 be appropriated.

——. *L'Anse, Lake Superior, Michigan.*—The last annual report contained the following remarks and estimate relating to the necessity of establishing a light at this place, which are repeated:

The railroad from Escanaba and Marquette, to Ontonagon, passes the head of L'Anse Bay, and will for the present terminate there. Efforts which will probably prove successful are now being made to complete the road to L'Anse before the close of this season, when the place will at once become an important point for the shipment of iron-ore. A good harbor is found at the head of the bay, and it should be lighted. A joint report upon this subject was made by the inspector and engineer. To establish such a light as is needed will require an appropriation of $12,000, which amount, for the purpose indicated, is recommended.

——. *Outer Island, Lake Superior.*—Concerning the necessity for a light at this point the following, contained in the report for the last year, is repeated:

The through commerce to and from the western end of Lake Superior increasing so rapidly, as the railroads having their terminus at Du Luth are extended to the westward, all passes outside of the Apostle Islands, and is greatly in need of a light-house on the northern end of Outer Island. This should be a light of the third order, and will cost $40,000, which sum is recommended for appropriation.

——. *Sand Island, Lake Superior.*—The remarks and estimate of last year are renewed as follows:

For reasons given in the preceding case, (Outer Island,) a light (of a lower order, however) is demanded on the northern end of Sand Island, the most westerly of the group, for which purpose an appropriation of $18,000 is recommended.

608. *Duluth, Lake Superior, Minnesota.*—A contract for the erection of this station has been made, and the work is now in progress.

——. *Passage Islands, Lake Superior.*—Respecting the importance of establishing a light at this place, the remarks contained in the last annual report are repeated with the estimate of cost, as follows:

The discovery of the silver mines on Lake Superior, and consequent sudden and remarkable increase of travel and traffic to that region, render it desirable that a light house should be built on Passage Island, to mark the channel between it and Isle Royale. The island is difficult of access, and therefore any structure put there will cost more than if erected at some more accessible point. There is recommended an appropriation of $18,000 for the purpose indicated.

PIER-HEAD LIGHTS.

These are being erected as rapidly as piers are reported by the Engineer Department of the Army ready to receive them, and apparatus can be supplied. The extension of this system of pier-lights must depend upon that of harbor improvements, which renders it somewhat difficult to estimate in detail until it is known just where these improvements are to be made.

REPAIRS.

Repairs, more or less extensive, were made or are in progress at the following stations in the eleventh district, viz:

518. *Saint Clair Flats*, Lake Saint Clair.
520. *Saint Clair Flats Canal*, (lower light.)
521. *Saint Clair Flats Canal*, (upper light.)
523. *Point aux Barques*, Michigan, Lake Huron.
524. *Tawas*, (Ottawa,) Michigan, Lake Huron.
526. *Saginaw Bay*, Michigan, Lake Huron.
534. *Cheboygan*, Michigan, Lake Huron.
538. *Skilligallee*, Michigan, Lake Michigan.
549. *Muskegon*, Michigan, Lake Michigan.
556. *Saint Joseph*, Michigan, Lake Michigan.
567. *Milwaukee*, Wisconsin, Lake Michigan.
568. *Milwaukee pier-light*, Wisconsin, Lake Michigan.
569. *Port Washington*, Wisconsin, Lake Michigan.
570. *Sheboygan*, Wisconsin, Lake Michigan.
575. *Port du Mort*, Wisconsin, Lake Michigan.
576. *Pottawatomie*, Wisconsin, Lake Michigan.
577. *Point Peninsula*, Michigan, Green Bay.
580. *Chambers Island*, Wisconsin, Green Bay.
582. *Tail Point*, Wisconsin, Green Bay.
585. *White Fish Point*, Wisconsin, Green Bay.
587. *Grand Island Harbor*, Wisconsin, Green Bay.
588. *Grand Island Harbor range*, (front light,) Wisconsin, Green Bay.
589. *Grand Island Harbor range*, (rear light,) Wisconsin, Green Bay.
592. *Huron Island*, *Michigan*, Lake Superior.
594. *Portage range*, (front light,) Michigan, Lake Superior.
595. *Portage range*, (rear light,) Michigan, Lake Superior.
596. *Manitou*, Michigan, Lake Superior.
597. *Gull Rock*, Michigan, Lake Superior.
598. *Copper Harbor*, Michigan, Lake Superior.
599. *Copper Harbor range*, (front light,) Michigan, Lake Superior.
600. *Copper Harbor range*, (rear light,) Michigan, Lake Superior.
605. *La Poinet*, Wisconsin, Lake Superior.
607. *Minnesota Point*, Wisconsin, Lake Superior.

The following are the names of the light-stations in the eleventh district, not mentioned elsewhere:

517. *Windmill Point*, River Detroit, entrance to Lake Saint Clair, Michigan.
525. *Charity Island*, mouth of Saginaw Bay, Michigan.
527. *Sturgeon Point*, Lake Huron, Michigan.
529, 530. *Presque Isle Harbor*, Lake Huron, Michigan.
531. *Presque Isle range-light*, Lake Huron, Michigan.
533. *Bois Blanc*, Bois Blanc Island, entrance to Straits of Mackinac, Lake Huron.
535. *McGulpin's Point*, Straits of Mackinac, Michigan.
537. *Waugoshance*, entrance to Straits of Mackinac, Lake Michigan.

539. *Beaver Island*, south end, Lake Michigan.
540. *Beaver Island*, north end, Lake Michigan.
541. *South Fox Island*, Lake Michigan.
542. *Grand Traverse*, entrance to Grand Traverse Bay, Michigan.
543. *Mission Point*, Grand Traverse Bay, Michigan.
545. *Point Betsey*, (Aux Becs Scies,) Lake Michigan, Michigan.
547. *Grand Point au Sable*, Lake Michigan, Michigan.
551. *Grand Haven*, Lake Michigan, mouth of Grand River, Michigan.
554. *Kalamazoo*, Lake Michigan, mouth of Kalamazoo River, Michigan.
558. *Michigan City*, Lake Michigan, Indiana.
560. *Chicago*, Lake Michigan, Illinois.
563. *Waukegan*, Lake Michigan, Illinois.
564. *Kenosha*, Lake Michigan, Wisconsin.
566. *Racine*, Lake Michigan, Wisconsin.
571. *Manitowoc*, Lake Michigan, Wisconsin.
572, 573. *Bailey's Harbor*, Lake Michigan, Wisconsin.
574. *Canu Island*, Lake Michigan, Wisconsin.
578. *Escanaba*, Green Bay, Wisconsin.
579. *Eagle Bluff*, Green Bay, Wisconsin.
581. *Green Island*, Green Bay, Wisconsin.
583. *Round Island*, White Fish Bay, Lake Superior, Michigan.
584. *Point Iroquois*, White Fish Bay, Lake Superior, Michigan.
586. *Grand Island*, Lake Superior, Michigan.
590. *Marquette*, Lake Superior, Michigan.
591. *Granite Island*, Lake Superior, Michigan.
593. *Portage River*, Keewenaw Bay, Lake Superior, Michigan.
602. *Eagle River*, Lake Superior, Michigan.
603. *Ontonagon*, Lake Superior, Michigan.
604. *Michigan Island*, Lake Superior, Wisconsin.
606. *Raspberry Island*, Lake Superior, Wisconsin.

LIGHT-SHIPS.

There are no light-ships in this district.

FOG-SIGNALS OPERATED BY STEAM OR HOT-AIR ENGINES.

White Fish Point, Lake Superior.—A steam fog-whistle.
Port du Mort, (Pilot Island,) Lake Michigan.—An air-trumpet.
Grand Haven, Lake Michigan.—A fog-bell, rung by hot-air engine.
Detour, Lake Huron.—A steam fog-whistle.
Spectacle Reef, Lake Huron.—A steam fog-whistle.
Thunder Bay Island, Lake Huron.—A steam fog-whistle.
Fort Gratiot, Lake Huron.—A steam fog-whistle.

DEPOT.

The fire-proof store-house of the light-house depot at Detroit was carried up two stories above the basement, and then covered with a temporary roof during last season. A line of sheet-piling was driven along the western line of the lot between the basin and the adjoining glue-factory. By act of Congress approved June 10, 1872, the sum of $25,000 was appropriated for this work, and will, it is thought, be sufficient to complete it.

The first work undertaken under this appropriation will be the erection of a suitable dwelling for the store-keeper and a close board fence along the top of the sheet-piling referred to. As soon as practicable it is also proposed to finish the store-house. This depot is already of great value, and its advantages will increase from year to year.

SURVEYS OF LIGHT-HOUSE SITES.

These surveys have been carried on as rapidly as possible. Those completed are Windmill Point and River Clinton, Lake Saint Clair; Fort Gratiot and Point aux Barques, on Lake Huron; Saginaw Bay and Tawas, on Saginaw Bay; Grand Haven, South Haven, Grosse Point, Beaver Island, and Beaver Island Harbor, on Lake Michigan; and Eagle River, on Lake Superior. The work will be continued in accordance with the plans of the board.

TENDERS.

The steam-barge Warrington has been almost exclusively used as a tender upon the work at Spectacle Reef. Last fall she was supplied with a new boiler and heater, both of the very best class, and her machinery for handling freight put into the best possible condition, and she has contributed greatly to the success of the work on Spectacle Reef.

The schooner Belle was used as quarters for the workmen on Spectacle Reef until the completion of the barracks on the pier of protection, when she was withdrawn from that duty and used for the general purposes of the work. During the latter part of the winter repairs of considerable extent were put upon her, which will enable her to perform good service for at least four years. Since the opening of this season she has been used principally in carrying coal and other heavy supplies to Spectacle Reef and the several steam fog-signals.

TWELFTH DISTRICT.

This district embraces all aids to navigation on the Pacific coast of the United States between the Mexican frontier and the southern boundary of Oregon, and includes the coast of California.

Inspector.—Commodore Alfred Taylor, United States Navy, until February 27, 1872; Commander Charles J. McDougal, United States Navy, present inspector.

Engineer.—Lieutenant-Colonel Robert S. Williamson, Corps of Engineers, United States Army, until May 1, 1872; Major N. Michler, Corps of Engineers, brevet brigadier-general, United States Army, present engineer.

There are in this district:

Light-houses	16
Light-ships	none.
Fog-signals, operated by steam or hot-air engines	6
Day or unlighted beacons	1
Buoys actually in position	35
Spare buoys for relief and to supply losses	26
Tenders Fern (ordered to the East to serve as supply-vessel for Atlantic and Gulf coast) and Shubrick, (common to twelfth and thirteenth districts,) used for inspector's and engineer's purposes	2

The following numbers, which precede the names of stations, correspond to those of the "Light-House List of the Atlantic, Gulf, and Pacific Coasts of the United States," issued January 1, 1872.

——. *Point Fermin, entrance to San Pedro Harbor, California.*—An appropriation of $20,000 was made June 10, 1872, for establishment of a light and fog-signal at this point. The site has been selected and a survey of the locality made. As there are several proprietors to the land, resort must be had to the California law of condemnation, in order to acquire title to the site, so that the construction will very probably be delayed beyond the fiscal year. A report, accompanied by a map of the site, has already been forwarded to the board. The structure can be rapidly built, as the material can be hauled over a very good road from New San Pedro, a distance of about five miles. The landing is safe and the anchorage-ground secure and well protected. A large well has been sunk near the settlement. It can furnish water during the construction, and, if necessary, can be purchased for the subsequent use of the keepers and for supplying the fog-signal.

——. *Point Hueneme, Santa Barbara Channel, California.*—An appropriation of $10,000, approved June 10, 1872, has been made for the establishment of a first-class fog-signal at this point. By direction of the board the site was selected in the month of June and surveys were made of the locality. Negotiations are in progress for its purchase.

405. *Point Conception, sea-coast of California.*—An appropriation was made March 3, 1871, for the establishment of a first-class steam fog-signal. A thorough examination and survey of the point were made with a view to ascertain the best location for the signal, and the supply of water. The structure has been completed, and the marchinery placed in position. Owing to ignorance on the part of the light-house keeper, the latter soon needed repairs. The pipes connecting the hydraulic ram with the cistern were not laid according to directions from the district engineer, and will have to be relaid. The cistern and water-shed, said to have been damaged by the recent earthquakes, will require an additional coat of cement. An abundant supply of water from an adjoining spring furnishes all that is required for the light-house and fog-signal. Many minor repairs to the light-house are needed.

——. *Piedras Blancas, sea-coast of California.* — This point is about midway between Point Conception and Point Pinos light-houses, distant one hundred and fifty miles from each. An appropriation of $75,000 was approved June 10, 1872, for a first-order light and fog-signal at this point. By direction of the Board, an examination of the locality was made, a site selected for the light, and necessary surveys made to connect it with previous ones, by the county surveyor, for the purpose of defining the limits of the reservation set aside by direction of the President for light-house purposes. A report, accompanied by a sketch of the locality, has been submitted for the information of the board. The site belongs to the United States, and as soon as certain details in regard to it can be obtained, the plans will be made and the work commenced.

406. *Point Pinos, sea-coast of California, entrance to Monterey Bay.*—The suit for condemnation of land for right of way to this light-house has not yet been decided, the owners having appealed the case from the district court to the supreme court of California.

408. *Año Nuevo Island, sea-coast of California.*—A steam fog-whistle and keeper's dwelling have been constructed on this island, and it has been in operation since the 29th of May of this year.

409. *Pigeon Point, sea-coast of California.* — An appropriation was approved March 3, 1871, for continuing and completing the light-house and fog-signal at this point. The work was commenced June 9, 1871, and the tower and keeper's dwelling are already completed. The para-

pet, lantern, and lens are still to be placed in position. It is expected to have the light in full operation by the end of August of this year. A steam fog-whistle has been erected on this point, and has been in operation since September 10, 1871.

——. *Pillar Point, sea-coast of California.*—Two and a half nautical miles north of this point a light-house and steam-fog signal are required, and an appropriation of $50,000 is recommended for their establishment. This point is approximately midway between Pigeon Point and Point Bonita, and within a few miles of Point San Pedro, from which extends a dangerous reef of rocks.

411. *Point Bonita, entrance to San Francisco Harbor, California.*—An appropriation for the establishment of a first-class steam fog-signal at this point was made March 3, 1871. The structure was completed, the machinery placed in position, and the signal, a syren, was put in operation May 29, 1872.

——. *Point San Pablo, between San Francisco and San Pablo Bays, California.*—An appropriation of $20,000, approved March 3, 1871, was made for a light-house and steam fog-signal on this point. On the 13th of July, 1871, a special proceeding was instituted in the district court of the fifteenth judicial district of the State of California to obtain condemnation of the necessary land for light-house purposes on this point. An award of $4,000 was given by the jury to the owners of the land, from which they appealed, and the case comes before the court for final hearing in October next.

——. *Entrance to the Straits of Karquines, California.*—An appropriation of $20,000, approved June 10, 1872, was made for the erection of a light-house and fog-signal to mark the entrance to the Straits of Karquines. A site on the southern shore, opposite Mare Island, having been recommended by the local officers and others, surveys were made there, but none suitable was found, and the engineer of the district has been ordered to locate the light on the southern end of Mare Island.

414. *Point Reyes, sea-coast of California.*—An appropriation of $10,000 was made by Congress, approved June 10, 1872, for rebuilding and re-establishing the steam fog-signal station at this point, which was destroyed by fire April 28, 1872, and the district engineer has received orders from the board for its reconstruction.

415. *Point Arena, sea-coast of California.*—Since the last annual report a steam fog-whistle has been constructed, and was put in operation November 25, 1871.

416. *Cape Mendocino, sea-coast of California.*—During the month of November, 1871, the keeper's dwelling and cistern, referred to in the last annual report, were completed.

418. *Trinidad Head, sea-coast of California.*—On the night of December 1, 1871, a fourth-order light of the system of Fresnel was exhibited for the first time from the tower built on the southern slope of Trinidad Head. The structures built consist of a pyramidal tower on a square base, 18 feet high from the ground-line to focal plane; a dwelling for the keeper, and a cistern.

REPAIRS.

At each of the following-named stations in the twelfth district there have been repairs, more or less extensive, during the last year:

406. *Point Pinos*, sea-coast of California, south side of entrance to Monterey Harbor.

412. *Fort Point*, entrance to San Francisco Harbor, California.

415. *Point Arena*, sea-coast of California.
417. *Humboldt*, entrance to Humboldt Bay, California.

The following are the names of light-stations in the twelfth district not mentioned elsewhere:

403. *Point Loma*, sea-coast of California, entrance to San Diego Bay.
404. *Santa Barbara*, sea-coast of California.
407. *Santa Cruz*, entrance to Santa Cruz Harbor.

LIGHT-SHIPS.

There are no light-ships in this district.

FOG-SIGNALS OPERATED BY STEAM OR HOT-AIR ENGINES.

Point Conception.—A 12-inch steam-whistle.
Año Nuevo Island.—A 12-inch steam-whistle.
Pigeon Point.—A 12-inch steam-whistle.
Point Bonita.—A first-order steam-syren.
Point Reyes.—A 12-inch steam-whistle.
Point Arena.—A 12-inch steam-whistle.

DAY OR UNLIGHTED BEACONS.

Fauntleroy Rock, Crescent City Harbor, California.—An appropriation for erecting a day-beacon on this rock was made March 3, 1871. It is now in course of construction under contract, and is expected to be completed at an early day.

BELL-BOAT OFF HUMBOLDT BAR, CALIFORNIA.

A bell-boat has been moored off this dangerous bar, in 16 fathoms of water, to aid in crossing it in foggy weather.

DEPOTS.

San Diego, California.

Yerba Buena Island, Harbor of San Francisco, California.—A selection of a site for a buoy depot, to serve instead of the present inconvenient depot at Mare Island, has been made on the eastern side of the island of Yerba Buena. A sketch showing the site selected, the depth of water, and proposed plan of building, is being prepared, and will be forwarded to the board at an early day.

Eureka, Humboldt Bay, California.—This depot is on rented ground, and it is proposed to remove it to the Humboldt light-house, and place it under charge of the keeper.

THIRTEENTH DISTRICT.

This district embraces all aids to navigation on the Pacific coast of the United States north of the southern boundary of Oregon. It extends from the forty-first parallel of latitude to British Columbia, and includes the coasts of Oregon and the Territory of Washington.

Inspector.—Commodore Alfred Taylor, United States Navy, until February 27, 1872; Commander Charles J. McDougal, United States Navy, present inspector.

Engineers.—H. M. Robert, major of engineers, United States Army.

There are in this district:

Light-houses and lighted beacons	11
Light-ships	0
Fog-signals, operated by steam or hot-air engines	1
Unlighted or day beacons	0
Buoys actually in position	46
Spare buoys for relief and to supply losses	26
Tender (steam) Shubrick, common to the twelfth and thirteenth districts	1

The following numbers which precede the names of stations correspond with those of the "Light-House List of the Atlantic, Gulf, and Pacific Coasts of the United States," issued January 1, 1872.

422. *Yaquina Bay, Oregon.*—The light-house at this point was commenced May 1, 1871. It was completed the following October, and lighted November 3, 1871.

——. *Cape Foulweather, sea-coast of Oregon.*—Work has been seriously hindered by the difficulties connected with the transportation of materials. Since the commencement of work in the autumn of 1871 the lighters have been destroyed twice, and the schooner engaged in bringing materials from San Francisco has been obliged to discharge most of her freight at Newport, to be reshipped in milder weather, besides twice getting on the bar at the mouth of Yaquina Bay, and being once partially wrecked. Part of the materials have been hauled from Newport, six miles over an almost impassable road to the light-house site. The metal-work was completed at Portland, Oregon, June 1, 1872. After the failure of persistent efforts to charter a vessel for carrying iron and brick from Portland to the cape, the metal-work was shipped via San Francisco. About one-half the time since the work began has been lost on account of the difficulties of transportation. The foundation of the tower has been laid, and work commenced on the keeper's dwelling, a double frame house. Both will probably be completed this season.

——. *Sand Island, mouth of river Columbia.*—The daily growing home and foreign commerce of the Columbia and Willamette Valleys demands that additional aids to navigation be judiciously disposed about this important outlet to the commerce of the Northwest. The chief difficulty in navigating the Columbia is the prevalence of fogs, and the fog-bell at Cape Disappointment cannot be heard in the south channel, through which the major part of the commerce of the Columbia is carried on.

A small light, to serve as a beacon leading into the south channel, and a powerful steam fog-signal, should be erected on Sand Island. As this island is shifting, a small dwelling, (surmounted by the light,) which can be moved from time to time, is designed for this place. The drift-wood on the island will furnish an inexhaustible supply of fuel for the fog-signal, and it, like the light-house, will be so erected that it can be moved from time to time as the position of the island is changed by the currents. An appropriation of $30,000 is recommended.

423. *Cape Disappointment, mouth of river Columbia, Territory of Washington.*—There was commenced in August and completed in December, 1871, a new double frame dwelling for the keepers. The old fog-bell frame having been shattered by a blast from a gun of a neighboring battery, in July, a new fog-bell house was built in August, 1871. A new oil-house is needed at this station, and will be built during the present fiscal year.

425. *Cape Flattery, Tatoosh Island, entrance to the Straits of Fuca, Terri-*

tory of Washington.—A first-class steam fog-whistle, with large fuel-house, a cistern holding 33,000 gallons, and a water-shed of 3,000 square feet, were completed June 6, 1872. The machinery and materials for this work were ready for shipment from Portland six weeks before transportation could be secured to any point in the Straits of Fuca or Puget Sound, and as, in the end, delivery at Tatoosh Island could not be obtained, they were shipped to Port Townsend, Territory of Washington. Although efforts were made to secure transportation in Puget Sound, the only vessel that could be had was one with mail and other contracts which could not be interfered with. One cargo was delivered safely on the island early in October, 1871, but the time consumed by the steamer in other work made the second trip so late that only part of the cargo could with great risk be discharged at Tatoosh Island, and the balance was landed at Neah Bay, on the main-land, November 1. This necessitated suspension of work on the island, then well under way, until the next season. In order, if possible, to complete the cistern in time to make sure of a sufficient supply of water for the summer of 1872, work was carried on at intervals during February, March, and April, but great difficulties were experienced in carrying freight by Indian canoes from Neah Bay. A party was sent May 1 from Portland which completed the work June 6. As no supply of water can be had until the next rainy season, the fog-whistle cannot be operated before that time, (about November.) Much as this delay of twelve months is to be regretted, it could not have been avoided, in the dearth of vessels in the North Pacific and Straits of Fuca.

——. *New Dungenness, Straits of Fuca, Territory of Washington.*—This station is exposed to heavy surfs, and the fact that in the North Pacific and Straits of Fuca fogs prevail to a considerable extent during storms, makes the fog-bell now at this station almost if not quite useless. An appropriation of $8,000 is required for a steam fog-whistle to replace the fog-bell at this point.

——. *Point No Point, Puget Sound, Territory of Washington.*—This point is about twenty miles from Port Townsend on the route to Seattle, Territory of Washington. The rapidly increasing importance of the commerce of Puget Sound, which will be still more augmented by the Northern Pacific Railroad, requires the construction of such aids to navigation as will more effectually open these waters to foreign as well as to home trade. An appropriation of $25,000 is required for a light-house.

——. *West Point, Puget Sound, Territory of Washington.*—This point marks the entrance to Dwamish Bay, the harbor of Seattle. The reasons given for the preceding apply with equal force to this case and also the following, (Point Defiance.) An appropriation of $25,000 is required for a light.

——. *Point Defiance, entrance to the Narrows, Puget Sound, Territory of Washington, nine miles north of Steilacoom.*—This is a most difficult point to avoid in fogs and cloudy nights. A light at this important point would greatly aid in navigating the upper sound, for which an appropriation of $25,000 is required.

REPAIRS.

Repairs have been made at the following stations in the thirteenth district during the year:

423. *Cape Disappointment,* Territory of Washington.

Repairs and renovations are needed at each of the following-named stations during the next year:

422. *Yaquina Bay*, Oregon.
423. *Cape Disappointment*, mouth of river Columbia, Washington Territory.
425. *Cape Flattery*, entrance Straits of Fuca, Territory of Washington.
426. *Ediz Hook*, Straits of Fuca, Territory of Washington.
427. *New Dungenness*, Straits of Fuca, Territory of Washington.
429. *Admiralty Head*, Admiralty Inlet, Territory of Washington.

The following are the names of light-stations in the thirteenth district not mentioned elsewhere:

420. *Cape Blanco*, sea-coast of Oregon.
421. *Cape Arago*, sea-coast of Oregon.
424. *Shoalwater Bay*, Territory of Washington.
428. *Smith's (or Blunt's) Island*, Washington Sound.

LIGHT-SHIPS.

There are no light-ships in this district.

FOG-SIGNALS OPERATED BY STEAM OR HOT-AIR ENGINES.

Cape Flattery.—A 12-inch steam-whistle.

DEPOT.

The depot for the buoys of the thirteenth district is now at Astoria, at the mouth of the river Columbia, but it is proposed to remove it to Cape Disappointment, and place it under charge of the light-house keeper.

Respectfully submitted.

JOSEPH HENRY,
Chairman.
CHAS. S. BOGGS,
Rear-Admiral, U. S. N., Naval Secretary.
GEORGE H. ELLIOT,
Major of Engineers, U. S. A., Engineer Secretary.

INDEX TO SECRETARY'S REPORT.

I. REPORT OF THE SECRETARY OF THE TREASURY.

Tables accompanying the report.

II. REPORTS OF TREASURY OFFICERS.

COMMISSIONER OF INTERNAL REVENUE:

LIST OF TABLES IN APPENDIX.

www.ingramcontent.com/pod-product-compliance
Lightning Source LLC
Chambersburg PA
CBHW022125020426
42334CB00015B/761
* 9 7 8 3 7 4 1 1 3 5 7 4 3 *